OXFORD STUDIES IN
MEDIEVAL EUROPEAN HISTORY

General Editors
JOHN H. ARNOLD   PATRICK J.
and
JOHN WATTS

David Crouch is a Fellow of the British Academy and former professor of medieval history in the University of Hull.

ALSO PUBLISHED IN THIS SERIES

The Chivalric Turn

Conduct and Hegemony in Europe before 1300

DAVID CROUCH

OXFORD
UNIVERSITY PRESS

OXFORD

UNIVERSITY PRESS

Great Clarendon Street, Oxford, OX2 6DP,
United Kingdom

Oxford University Press is a department of the University of Oxford.
It furthers the University's objective of excellence in research, scholarship,
and education by publishing worldwide. Oxford is a registered trade mark of
Oxford University Press in the UK and in certain other countries

First published 2019
First published in paperback 2020

Published in the United States of America by Oxford University Press
198 Madison Avenue, New York, NY 10016, United States of America

British Library Cataloguing in Publication Data
Data available

Library of Congress Cataloging in Publication Data
Data available

ISBN 978–0–19–878294–0 (Hbk.)
ISBN 978–0–19–883034–4 (Pbk.)

Preface

This is a book about the medieval obsession with defining and practising superior conduct and the consequences that followed from it. It is also a book about how historians since the seventeenth century have understood medieval conduct, because in many ways we still see it through the eyes of the writers of the Enlightenment. This is nowhere more so in its defining of superior conduct on the figure of the knight, and categorizing it as Chivalry. There will be several nouns in this book—such as Chivalry—which will begin with capitals in a quite eighteenth-century way; others are Nobility and Courtliness. When I do this, it is not to annoy you, the reader, but to signal the word is being used in its classic socio-historical sense.

Now, what follows will not suggest the Enlightenment scholars got it wrong, in fact far from it. As a pan-European intellectual society, the Enlightenment was just as fixated on defining its elites through superior conduct as had been the Middle Ages, though in less military and more cultural ways. Indeed, in the inter-change between the French aristocratic scholars Jean-Baptiste de la Curne de Sainte-Palaye and Anne-Claude de Tubières, Count of Caylus, the ancient dichotomy between virtue and blood in Nobility was still being debated, as between representatives of the *noblesse de robe* and *noblesse d'épée*.[1] Many scholars, both clerical and lay, had struggled and argued in the Middle Ages to define the precious quality of Nobility principally as a property of mind and morality, though they were never able to persuade the generality of society, which persisted in defining it genetically, on blood.

Charles II of England is credited with the observation that sums up the failure of this medieval project to define Nobility and moral superiority on the knight: that as king he could make a knight, but could not make a gentleman. The Enlightenment mind largely succeeded where the Middle Ages failed, and its development of the 'gentleman' (rather than the knight) as the representative superior male is some evidence of this.[2] The Enlightenment scholars I will be citing here therefore had an innate sensitivity to the sort of society they were examining, in ways that we of the twenty-first century do not. Like medieval scholars they also looked at things on a European and not a local scale, though of course within the continuing cultural predominance of the French language and on the basis of a universal classical Latin education, which is something the twentieth century lost.

The Enlightenment writers on Chivalry had their differences but they all were convinced that it was principally a moral, not a military, code. Some of them,

---

[1] A. C. Montoya, 'Bourgeois versus Aristocratic Models of Scholarship: Medieval Studies at the Académie des Inscriptions, 1701-1751', in *The Making of the Humanities 2, From Early Modern to Modern Disciplines*, ed. R. Bod, J. Maat, and T. Weststeijn (Amsterdam, 2012), 303–20.

[2] L. R. N. Ashley, 'Spenser and the Ideal of the Gentleman,' *Bibliothèque d'Humanisme et Renaissance*, 27 (1965), 108–32.

notably the influential figure of La Curne de Sainte-Palaye, thought that Chivalry may have had a long history but that it reached its full bloom in a particular part of what we call the Middle Ages, partly defined by the rise of the courtly romance in the time of Chrétien de Troyes and his imitators, and La Curne called this the '*âge d'or*' of Chivalry. This book will not be differing much from him on the subject of chronology. What it will be doing is to examine Chivalry jointly with another vexed subject, that of Nobility, and it will find that the two are by no means unrelated. The eighteenth century had its blinkers too. This book benefits from being written in an era where the complications of gender and the significance of women in society have long been accommodated within social history, a perspective to which the Middle Ages was largely blind, and the Enlightenment only marginally less so. It turns out to have been important, as we will see, for in the end this is a book about social hegemony and (in Hegel's notorious dialectic) what can masters be without slaves, and slaves without masters?

In my treatment of the subject of conduct I have taken advantage, as a social historian, of social theory—curiously, much less used by historians of medieval society than it is by scholars who deal with medieval literature, at least in the anglophone sphere. In the field of conduct the theories of Pierre Bourdieu have much to offer this study and, in my view, they are applicable to past societies even as remote as the Middle Ages. Medieval historians firmly of the British empirical tradition would therefore be advised to skip Chapter 1, as indeed should future scholars who encounter this book, no doubt at a time when the social thought incorporated in this book becomes dated, as it inevitably will.

The research and writing of this book were only possible through the magnificent boon of a Leverhulme Trust Major Research Fellowship held between 2013 and 2016 at the University of Hull, and the additional benefit of a term's membership at the Institute for Advanced Study, Princeton, in 2015, assisted by an Elizabeth and J. Richardson Dilworth fellowship. For these substantial gifts and the interchange with scholars it enabled there and at the Pirenne Institute in the University of Ghent I am deeply grateful. I wish to particularly acknowledge by name the interest, friendship and tolerance of Martin Aurell, Xavier Baecke, Dominique Barthélemy, Keith Busby, Frederik Buylaert, Martha Carlin, Christopher Davies, Jeroen Deploige, Patrick J. Geary, Stephen Jaeger, Richard W. Kaeuper, Sara McDougall, Jean-François Nieus, Nicholas Paul, Jörg Peltzer, Liesbeth van Houts, Colin Veach, Louise Wilkinson and Claudia Wittig. Particular thanks to Martin, Keith, Martha, Patrick and Colin, who were kind enough to read and comment upon drafts. I am also more than happy to acknowledge the positive and helpful comments of Oxford University Press's anonymous reader. And finally I should thank Patrick Geary in particular for his interest in the project and his offer to give it a home in this series, and the officers of the Press itself for accepting and publishing it. Neil Morris as manuscript editor was in the best tradition of the thoughtful questioning of wayward authors.

Contents

PART IV. HEGEMONY

List of Abbreviations

Abril issia	Raimon Vidal, *Abril issi' e Mays intrava*, in *Nouvelles occitanes du moyen age*, ed. J-Ch. Huchet (Paris, 1992).
Acts and Letters	*The Acts and Letters of the Marshal Family, Marshals of England and Earls of Pembroke, 1145–1248*, ed. D. Crouch (Camden Society, 5th ser., 47, 2015).
Aragon, *De Nobilitate*	William of Aragon, *De Nobilitate Animi*, ed. and trans. W. D. Paden Jr and M. Trovato (Harvard Studies in Medieval Latin, 2, Cambridge MA, 2012).
Armëure	Guiot de Provins, *Armëure de Chevalier*, in *Les Oeuvres de Guiot de Provins*, ed. J. Orr (Manchester, 1915).
Aspremont	*La Chanson d'Aspremont*, ed. L. Brandin (2 vols, Paris, 1923–4).
Aurell, *Lettered Knight*	M. Aurell, *Le chevalier lettré: savoir et conduite de l'aristocratie aux xiie et xiiie siècles* (Paris, 2006), trans. as *The Lettered Knight: Knowledge and aristocratic behaviour in the twelfth and thirteenth centuries*, trans. J. C. Khalifa and J. Price (Budapest, 2017).
Baldwin, *Aristocratic Life*	J. W. Baldwin, *Aristocratic Life in Medieval France. The Romances of Jean Renart and Gerbert de Montreuil, 1190–1230* (Baltimore, 2000).
Banquets et manières	*Banquets et manières de table au moyen âge*, ed. M. Bertrand and C. Hory (Provence, 1996).
Barthélemy, *Chevalerie*	D. Barthélemy, *La chevalerie: de la Germanie antique à la France du xiie siècle* (Paris, 2007).
Bertran	*The Poems of the Troubadour Bertran de Born*, ed. and trans. W. D. Paden Jr, T. Sankovich, and P. H. Stäblein (Berkeley, 1986).
La Bible	Guiot de Provins, *La Bible*, in *Les Oeuvres de Guiot de Provins*, ed. J. Orr (Manchester, 1915).
BL	British Library.
Bloch, *Feudal Society*	M. Bloch, *La Société Féodale* (2 vols, Paris, 1949), trans. as *Feudal Society*, trans. L. Manyon (2nd edn, 2 vols, London, 1962).
Bloch, *Medieval Misogyny*	R. H. Bloch, *Medieval Misogyny and the Invention of Western Romantic Love* (Chicago, 1991).
BnF	Bibliothèque nationale de France
Brut	*Brut y Tywysogyon: the Red Book of Hergest Version*, ed. T. Jones (Cardiff, 1955).
Bumke, *Courtly Culture*	J. Bumke, *Höfische Kultur: Literatur und Gesellschaft im hohen Mittelalter* (Munich, 1986), trans. as *Courtly Culture: Literature and Society in the High Middle Ages*, trans. T. Dunlap (Berkeley, CA, 1991); refs are to the trans.

CCM	*Cahiers de Civilization Médiévale*
Chastoiement des dames	J. H. Fox, *Robert de Blois, son oeuvre didactique et narrative. Étude linguistique et littéraire suivie d'une édition critique avec commentaire et glossaire de l'"Enseignement des princes" et du "Chastoiement des dames"* (Paris, 1950).
Chastoiement d'un père	*Le Chastoiement d'un père à son fils*, ed. E. D. Montgomery Jr (Chapel Hill, 2017).
Chevalerie et Grivoiserie	*Chevalerie et Grivoiserie: Fabliaux de Chevalerie*, ed. and trans. J-L. Leclanche (Paris, 2003).
Chronica	*Chronica magistri Rogeri de Houedene*, ed. W. Stubbs (4 vols, Rolls Series, 1868–71).
Condé	*Dits et contes de Baudouin de Condé et de son fils Jean de Condé*, ed. A. Scheler (3 vols, Brussels, 1866–7).
Conte de Graal	Chrétien de Troyes, *Le Conte de Graal*, ed. F. Lecoy (Paris, 1984).
Courtiers' Trifles	*De Nugis Curialium or Courtiers' Trifles*, ed. and trans. M. R. James, rev. C. N. L. Brooke and R. A. B. Mynors (Oxford, 1983).
Coutumes de Beauvaisis	*Coutumes de Beauvaisis*, ed. A. Salmon (2 vols, Paris, 1899–1900), trans. as *The Coutumes de Beauvaisis of Philippe de Beaumanoir*, trans. F. R. P. Akehurst (Philadelphia, 1992).
Crouch, *Aristocracy*	D. Crouch, *The English Aristocracy, 1070–1272. A Social Transformation* (New Haven, 2011).
Crouch, *Image*	D. Crouch, *The Image of Aristocracy in Britain, 1000–1300* (London, 1992).
Crouch, *Marshal*	D. Crouch, *William Marshal* (3rd edn, London, 2016).
Crouch, *Nobility*	D. Crouch, *The Birth of Nobility: Constructing Aristocracy in England and France, 900–1300* (Harlow, 2005).
De Amore	*Andreas Capellanus on Love*, ed. and trans. P. G. Walsh (London, 1982).
De Nugis Curialium	Walter Map, *De Nugis Curialium or Courtiers' Trifles*, ed. C. N. L. Brooke and R. A. B. Mynors, trans. M. R. James (Oxford, 1983).
De Re Militari	*De re militari et triplici via peregrinationis Ierosolomitane*, ed. L. Schmugge (Beiträge zur Geschichte und Quellenkunde des Mittelalters, 6, Berlin, 1977).
Disciplina Clericalis	*The Disciplina clericalis of Petrus Alfonsi*, ed. E. Hermes and trans. P. R. Quarrie (Berkeley, CA, 1977).
Doctrinal	*Doctrinal Sauvage: publié d'après tous les manuscrits*, ed. A. Sakari (Jyväskylä, 1967).
Doctrine	Ramon Llull, *Doctrine d'Enfant*, ed. A. Llinares (Paris, 1969).
EHR	*English Historical Review*
E·l termini d'estiu	Garin lo Brun, *E·l termini d'estiu*, pub. as *Ensegnamen alla Dama*, ed. and trans. (It.) L. R. Bruno (Filologia Occitanica Studi e Testi, 1, Rome, 1996).
Enseignement des Princes	J. H. Fox, *Robert de Blois, son oeuvre didactique et narrative. Étude linguistique et littéraire suivie d'une édition critique*

	avec commentaire et glossaire de l'"Enseignement des princes" et du "Chastoiement des dames" (Paris, 1950).
Enseignements Trebor	*Les Enseignements de Robert de Ho: dits Enseignements Trebor*, ed. M. V. Young (Paris, 1901).
Essenhamen de la Donzela	Amanieu de Sescás, *Essenhamen de la Donzela*, ed, and trans. M. D. Johnston, in 'The Occitan *Enssenhamen de l'Escudier* and *Essenhamen de la Donzela*', in *Medieval Conduct Literature: an Anthology of Vernacular Guides to Behaviour for Youths*, ed. M. D. Johnston (Toronto, 2009).
Ensenhamens d'Onor	Sordello da Goito, *Le Poesie. Nuova edizione critica*, ed. and trans (It.) M. Boni (Bologna, 1954).
Estoire	Geoffrey Gaimar, *Estoire des Engleis*, ed. and trans. I. Short (Oxford, 2009).
Établissements	*Les Établissements de Saint Louis*, ed. P. Viollet (4 vols, Paris, 1881–6).
Facetus	L. Zatočil, *Cato a Facetus*. (Spisy Masarykovy University v Brně, Filosofická Fakulta/Opera Universitatis Masarykianae Brunensis, Facultas Philosophica, 48, 1952).
Feudal Society	M. Bloch, *La Société Féodale* (2 vols, Paris, 1949), trans. L. A. Manyon as *Feudal Society* (2 vols, 2nd edn, London, 1962). Refs are to the French edn.
Frauenbuch	Ulrich von Liechtenstein, *Das Frauenbuch* ,ed. and trans. (Ger.) C. Young (Stuttgart, 2003).
Freedman, *Images*	P. Freedman, *Images of the Medieval Peasant* (Stanford, CA, 1999).
Garin le Loherenc	*Garin le Loherenc*, ed. A. Iker-Gittleman (3 vols, Paris, 1996–7).
GCO	*Giraldi Cambrensis Opera*, ed. J. S. Brewer, J. F. Dimock, and G. F. Warner (8 vols, Rolls Series, 1861–91).
Gille de Chyn	Walter de Tournai, *L'Histoire de Gille de Chyn*, ed. E. B. Place (New York, 1941).
Gui de Warewic	*Gui de Warewic: roman du xiiiᵉ siècle*, ed. A. Ewert (2 vols, Paris, 1933).
Histoire	*L'Histoire des ducs de Normandie et des rois d'Angleterre*, ed. F. Michel (Paris, 1840).
History of William Marshal	*History of William Marshal*, ed. A. J. Holden and D. Crouch, trans. S. Gregory (3 vols, Anglo-Norman Text Society, Occasional Publications Series, 4–6, 2002–7).
Hofzucht	*Der Dichter Tannhäuser*, ed. J. Siebert (Halle, 1834), 195–203.
Ille et Galeron	*Ille et Galeron*, ed. and trans. P. Eley (King's College London, Medieval Studies, 13, 1996).
Jaeger, *Courtliness*	C. S. Jaeger, *The Origins of Courtliness: Civilising Trends and the Formation of Courtly Ideals, 939–1210* (Philadelphia, 1985).

Jaeger, *Ennobling Love* C. S. Jaeger, *Ennobling Love: In Search of a Lost Sensibility* (Philadelphia, 1999).

Jaeger, *Envy of Angels* C. S. Jaeger, *The Envy of Angels: Cathedral Schools and Social Ideals in Medieval Europe, 950–1200* (Philadelphia, 1994).

Kaeuper, *Chivalry* R. W. Kaeuper, *Medieval Chivalry* (Cambridge, 2016).

Kaeuper, *Holy Warriors* R. W. Kaeuper, *Holy Warriors: the Religious Ideology of Chivalry* (Philadelphia, 2009).

Karras, *Boys to Men* R. M. Karras, *From Boys to Men: Formations of Masculinity in Late Medieval Europe* (Philadelphia, 2003).

Karras, *Sexuality* R. M. Karras, *Sexuality in Medieval Europe: Doing unto Others* (London, 2005).

Keen, *Chivalry* M. Keen, *Chivalry* (New Haven, 1984).

Lambert of Ardres *Lamberti Ardensis historia comitum Ghisnensium*, ed. J. Heller, in *MGH Scriptores*, xxiv, trans. as *The History of the Counts of Guines and Lords of Ardres*, trans. L. Shopkow (Philadelphia, 2001). Refs are to the Latin text unless otherwise stated.

Lancelot *Lancelot: roman en prose du xiiiᵉ siècle*, ed. A. Micha (9 vols, Geneva, 1978–83).

Lancelot do Lac *Lancelot do Lac: the Non-Cyclic Old French Prose Romance*, ed. E. Kennedy (2 vols, Oxford, 1980).

Lett, *Hommes et femmes* D. Lett, *Hommes et femmes au moyen âge: histoire du genre, xiiᵉ–xvᵉ siècle* (Paris, 2013).

Liber Urbani *Urbanus Magnus Danielis Becclesiensis*, ed. J. G. Smyly (Dublin, 1939).

Livre des manières Stephen de Fougères, *Le Livre des Manières*, ed. and trans. (Fr.) J. T. E. Thomas (Leuven, 2013).

Llibre de l'Orde *Llibre de l'Orde de Cavalleria*, ed. A. Soler i Llopart (Barcelona, 1988), trans. as *The Book of the Order of Chivalry*, trans. N. Fallows (Woodbridge, 2013).

Llibre dels Fets King James I of Aragon, *Llibre dels Fets*, ed. J. M. Pujol (Barcelona, 1991), trans. as *The Book of Deeds of James I of Aragon*, trans. D. J. Smith and H. Buffery (Farnham, 2003).

Lorris, *Rose* *Roman de la Rose*, ed. and trans.(Fr.) A. Strubel (Paris, 1992).

Lost Letters *Lost Letters of Medieval Life: English Society, 1200–1250*, ed. and trans. M. Carlin and D. Crouch (Philadelphia, 2013).

Malmesbury, *GRA* William of Malmesbury, *Gesta Regum Anglorum*, ed. R. A. B. Mynors, R. M. Thomson, and M. Winterbottom (2 vols, Oxford, 1998–9).

Malmesbury, *HN* William of Malmesbury, *Historia Novella*, ed. E. King and trans. K. R. Potter (Oxford, 1998).

Marcabru *Marcabru: a critical edition*, ed. S. Gaunt, R. Harvey, and L. Paterson (Cambridge, 2000).

Materials *Materials for the History of Thomas Becket, Archbishop of Canterbury*, ed. J. C. Robertson and J. B. Sheppard (8 vols, Rolls Series, 1875–85).

Meung, *Rose*	*Roman de la Rose*, ed. and trans. (Fr.) A. Strubel (Paris, 1992).
MGH	Monumenta Germaniae Historica.
MHG	Middle High German.
Mons, *Chronique*	*La Chronique de Gislebert de Mons*, ed. L. Vanderkindere (Recueil de textes pour servir à l'étude de l'histoire de Belgique, 1904).
Morale Scolarium	*Morale Scolarium of John of Garland*, ed. and trans. L. J. Paetow (Memoirs of the University of California, 1, no. 2, Berkeley, 1927).
Moribus et Vita	A. Morel-Fatio, 'Mélanges de littérature catalane', *Romania*, 15 (1886), 224–35.
ODNB	*Oxford Dictionary of National Biography.*
Ordene	*Raoul de Hodenc, Le Roman des Eles. The Anonymous Ordene de Chevalerie*, ed. and trans. K. Busby (Utrecht Publications in General and Comparative Literature, Amsterdam, 17, 1983).
Orderic	Orderic Vitalis, *The Ecclesiastical History*, ed. M. Chibnall (6 vols, Oxford, 1969–81).
Paterson, *Occitan Society*	L. M. Paterson, *The World of the Troubadours: Medieval Occitan Society, c.1100–c.1300* (Cambridge, 1993).
Peire	*The Songs of Peire Vidal*, ed. and trans. V. M. Fraser (New York, 2006).
Phagifacetus	*M. Reineri Alemanici Phagifacetus*, ed. F. Jacob (Lübeck, 1838).
PL	*Patrologiae cursus completus: series Latina*, ed. J-P. Migne (221 vols, Paris, 1847–67).
Poeti del Duecento	*Poeti del Duecento*, ed. G. Contini (2 vols, Milan, 1960).
Proverbe au Vilain	*Li Proverbe au Vilain: die Sprichwörter des gemeinen Mannes: altfranzösische Dichtung*, ed. A. Tobler (Leipzig, 1895).
Proverbes français	*Proverbes français antérieurs au xve siècle*, ed. J. Morawski (Paris, 1925).
Quatre Tenz	*Les quatre âges de l'homme, traité moral de Philippe de Navarre publié pour la première fois d'après les manuscrits de Paris, de Londres et de Metz*, ed. M. de Fréville (Paris, Société des anciens textes français, 1888).
Qui comte vol apendre	J. De Cauna, *L'Ensenhamen ou code du parfait chevalier* (Mounenh en Biarn, 2007), 64–95.
Raimbaut	*The Poems of the Troubadour Raimbaut de Vaqueiras*, ed. J. Linskill (The Hague, 1964).
Rasos es e Mesura	M. Eusebi, 'L'ensenhamen di Arnaut de Mareuil', *Romania*, 90 (1969), 14–30 (with Italian trans.).
RHF	*Recueil des historiens des Gaules et de la France*, ed. M. Bouquet et al. (24 vols, Paris, 1864–1904).
Roman des Eles	*Le Roman des Eles*, ed. and trans. K. Busby (Utrecht Publications in General and Comparative Literature, Amsterdam, 17, 1983).

Roman des Franceis	D. Crouch, 'The *Roman des Franceis* of Andrew de Coutances: Significance, Text and Translation', in *Normandy and its Neighbours, c.900–1250: Essays for David Bates*, ed. D. Crouch and K. Thompson (Turnhout, 2011).
Rules	*The Rules of Robert Grosseste*, in *Walter of Henley and other Treatises on Estate Management and Accounting*, ed. and trans. D. Oschinsky (Oxford, 1971), 388–406.
Ruodlieb	*The Ruodlieb*, ed. and trans. C. W. Grocock (Warminster, 1985).
Schulze-Busacker, *Didactique*	E. Schulze-Busacker, *La didactique profane au moyen âge* (Paris, 2012).
Siete Partidas	*Las Siete Partidas del Rey Don Alfonso el Sabio*, ed. anon. (3 vols, Madrid, 1807), trans. as *Las Siete Partidas ii, Medieval Government*, trans. S. P. Scott and ed. R. I. Burns (Philadelphia, 1996).
Song	*Song of Roland: An Analytical Edition: Introduction and Commentary*, ed. and trans. G. J. Brault (2 vols, University Park, PA, 1978).
Speculum Duorum	Gerald of Wales, *Speculum Duorum*, ed. Y. Lefèvre and R. B. C. Huygens, and trans. B. Dawson (Cardiff, 1974),
Tesoretto	Brunetto Latini, *Il Tesoretto*, in *Poeti del Duocento*, 2: 175–277, trans. as *Le Petit Trésor*, ed. and trans. (Fr). B. Levergois (Aubenas, 1997).
TNA: PRO	The National Archives (Public Record Office).
Urbain le Courtois	H. Rosamond Parsons, 'Anglo-Norman books of courtesy and nurture', *PMLA*, 44 (1929), 383–455.
Usatges	*The Usatges of Barcelona: Fundamental Law of Catalonia*, trans. D. J. Kagay (Philadelphia, 1994).
Welsche Gast	Thomasin of Zirclaria, *Der Wälsche Gast*, ed. H. Rückert (Quedlingen, 1852), trans. as *Der Welsche Gast*, trans. M. Gibbs and W. McConnell (Kalamazoo, 2009).
Whelan, *Making of Manners*	F. Whelan, *The Making of Manners and Morals in Twelfth-Century England: The Book of the Civilised Man* (Abingdon, 2017).
Winsbecke	*Der Winsbecke*, ed. and trans. A. M. Rasmussen and O. Trokhimenko, in *Medieval Conduct Literature: An Anthology of Vernacular Guides to Behaviour for Youths*, ed. M. D. Johnston (Toronto, 2009).
Winsbeckin	*Winsbeckin*, ed. and trans. A. M. Rasmussen and O. Trokhimenko, in *Medieval Conduct Literature: An Anthology of Vernacular Guides to Behaviour for Youths*, ed. M. D. Johnston (Toronto, 2009).

PART I

INTRODUCTION

1

Conduct, Habitus and Practice

Individual humans acquire from the societies in which they are born ideas of social conduct appropriate to their time and place. Having acquired these, some people feel moved to explain them to—and sometimes impose them on—others, as desirable norms. The lay elite of the European High Middle Ages generated its own norms of conduct, as would any human society, and since it was a predominantly literate one (as is argued below), it did not just impose them on its members, it also left writings as evidence of them which we can examine. As a result historians have a chance to discover what sort of conduct the medieval mind thought acceptable and superior, how it changed and even why it changed over several centuries. It may also be said that medieval European conduct is not entirely disengaged from present Western society, the way medieval Japanese society would be. The society of the European High Middle Ages has left a social legacy which is still current in present attitudes centuries later, sometimes in quite surprising ways. So the medieval thought-world has a connection with present Western society in ways that other former societies do not. Medieval social norms have some relevance to explaining current attitudes, or at least attitudes which were current until relatively recently. So if it is possible to conduct an exercise in palaeo-sociology such as I am suggesting here, we can learn something about our own attitudes and society as well as reconstruct theirs.

So how can we do this? One of the great sociological advances of the twentieth century was to recognize that much (though not all) 'conduct' (a word rooted in the process of guidance and education) is simply absorbed by the observing mind rather than acquired through conscious teaching.[1] This sort of learning is conveyed through the 'habitus', a Latin word with Aristotelian resonances, and a long history in Western moral philosophy going back to the Middle Ages and indeed in use in a technical sense at the time of Abelard.[2] It was a word recruited by the French

[1] Bourdieu himself attributed his ambition to find universals in social structures ultimately to Jean-Paul Sartre, but it was prefigured in the work of Durkheim and Max Weber. His key observation was: 'L'habitus est une sorte de sens pratique de ce qui est à faire dans une situation donnée.' P. Bourdieu, *Raisons pratiques: sur la théorie de l'action* (Paris, 1994), 45.

[2] According to the understanding of the later thirteenth-century Aristotelian William of Aragon, the 'habitus' was what the soul acquired by pursuing its potential, which then informed its conduct. To William, Nobility was therefore a habitus, a state which had to be striven for and was manifested in good and decent public acts; Aragon, *De Nobilitate*, 20 and n. (cf. '*[N]obilitas est habitus qui movet ad talia opera faciendum que in bonitate communiter cognoscuntur, secundum quod pertinet ad eorum naturam*', ibid. 60). For the use of 'habitus' and the indirect penetration of Aristotelian ideas into the early twelfth-century schools, see, C. J. Nederman, 'Nature, Ethics, and the Doctrine of "Habitus": Aristotelian Moral Psychology in the Twelfth Century', *Traditio*, 45 (1989–90), 87–110.

sociologist Pierre Bourdieu (1930–2002) for the purpose of describing this social environment of behavioural norms, the difference between Bourdieu and an Aristotelian being that for him the habitus was not necessarily formed by conscious rational choice. His ideas arose out of his ethnographical work on the powerful habitus he found and described in the post-war Berber villages of the Maghreb in what was then French Algeria. Compelling though his explanation and exploration of life in the Maghreb in the 1950s were—and it is a stunning read—it was the fact that he could draw out of the exploration general rules on conduct within human society that was the truly remarkable departure in his work. It will be one of the arguments of this book that such a functioning habitus can be detected at work in one section of medieval society, one of the best documented parts: the lay elite. I will suggest it can also help account for one of the major documented changes in medieval society, the chivalric turn of the late twelfth century.

As Bourdieu's work was elaborated and debated, the habitus became an even more fascinating concept. It has been argued that there is a *primary* habitus of behavioural norms, the one small children are programmed to absorb from their family and the little society which surrounds them. The *secondary* habitus is the one that continues to form the choices of the maturing mind as a person finds a space in wider society. If he or she is in tune with their social context, which Bourdieu called the 'field', it becomes for them a social comfort zone where they know how things work and feel secure. They are fishes swimming happily in waters they know. The comfort may turn out to be illusory, however, for the habitus is not static and can shift, which can cause confusion, angst or (at worst) anger in the minds it has left behind it.

As far as individuals are concerned, their relationship with their habitus revolves around their choices and actions. They pick up the predominant views within their field, and knowing what they are informs their choices in any situation. An accomplished and sensitive mind finds security in this; it is indeed a fish in water. The impact choices make on others around them is registered by the sensitive and observant, and approval affirms the habitus as much as does disapproval. Disapproval has consequences for any offending person, so in this way an individual's behaviour is structured by the society around him. To that extent the effect of the habitus can be a largely unconscious internal process. It is recognizable only by the social anxiety that may accompany any choice or the inexplicable irritation when an observer perceives a trespass against what he understands the habitus to be, or when people move outside the field where they are comfortable and become fishes out of water, in Bourdieu's own phrase.[3] This book is not to be taken, however, as an exercise in 'Bourdieuian' thought (I believe that is the inelegant adjective). It is primarily an empirical reconstruction of medieval ideas of conduct. I will use the

---

[3] K. Maton, 'Habitus', in *Pierre Bourdieu: Key Concepts*, ed. M. Grenfell (2nd edn, Abingdon, 2012), 48–64. The concept is not without its critics, principally for the mystical force it appears to create behind human agency and its sub-Marxian social determinism, for example, M. de Certeau, *The Practice of Everyday Life*, trans. S. Rendall (Berkeley, CA, 1984), esp. 58–9.

terms 'field', 'habitus' and 'hysteresis' only in a general sense of established and observed social phenomena, as tools, not as the end of the study in itself.

Approval and disapproval are very much part of the way the habitus operates. This may be external (in the way words and deeds are received by people who witness them) or it may be internal (the way acts a person is contemplating might affect the internal sense of worth of their perpetrator). The idea was not in fact alien to the medieval people we are studying here. The Provençal knight, poet and courtier Sordello da Goito was well enough aware of the way he monitored his own behaviour in the 1230s:

> Shame is the lamp of reputation, so everyone should carry it in his heart should he want to act well. I tell you in all truth that a good man cannot really be discredited if he fears shame in his heart, where a very real anguish will afflict him more painful than the condemnation of his own people and the sneering of his accusers.[4]

Some of the most common words in conduct literature are associated with approval or disapproval: the binary concepts of honour (Lat. *honor*, MFr. *honeur*, MHG *Ere*, MEng. *worðschepe*) or dishonour (Lat. *pudor*, MFr. *deshonor*, *vergogne*, *honi*, MHG *Schande*, MEng. *scheome*). It is not difficult to find statements coupling these binary sentiments in medieval writings. Bertran de Born observed grandly in 1182: 'I prefer to hold a little piece of land in *onor* than a great empire with *desonor!*'[5]

This mechanism of social self-monitoring was obvious to early sociologists, to the extent that the honour–shame nexus was itself once taken to be the key to the analysis of behaviour in early societies and even the basis of class and status itself, as Max Weber believed.[6] Honour was a concept that was close to the hearts of early historians of Chivalry, and some of them mistook it for an aristocratic moral quality rather than a social monitoring exercise. But Weber failed to appreciate that the dialectic between honour and shame can apply as much to lower-status as high-status people; it worked more broadly in medieval society than in the elite conduct with which military historians have customarily associated it. Stephen de Fougères and other writers of the Salomonic sermon tradition apply it to women, merchants and peasants as much as to kings, magnates and knights. The recognition of honour as being no more than part of a sliding scale of social approval within the overarching concept of habitus has much improved the analysis of chivalric culture, though of course this is not to deny that it was a mechanism whose workings had serious consequences for those who played their social hand poorly (see Chapter 10).[7] It also had particular consequences in the courtly society of the High Middle Ages,

---

[4] *Ensenhamens d'Onor*, 226–7 (ll. 986–94) *Car vergoigna es de pretz la lutz/Per q'usquecs portar la deuria/En son cor, pos be far volria./E dic vos be que nulz om bos/No pot esser fort vergoignos/S'atretan non tem la vergoigna/De son cor que·l blasmes no·il poigna/Com fai los blasmes de las genz/Ni·l reprendre dels reprendenz.*

[5] Bertran, 181 (ll. 15–16).

[6] *Economy and Society: An Outline of Interpretive Sociology*, ed. G. Roth and C. Wittich, (2 vols, Berkeley, 1978) 2: 932–7.

[7] C. Taylor, *Chivalry and the Ideals of Knighthood in France during the Hundred Years War* (Cambridge, 2013), 54–61, presents an up-to-date contextualization of honour in analysing medieval noble society.

which learned to fear the social danger of the *losenger*, the secret and flattering enemy who subverted one's reputation and honour at court behind one's back (see Chapter 7).

A FRENCH SOCIOLOGIST IN KING ARTHUR'S COURT

Bourdieu studied human societies of his own day, and though his mind occasionally ventured back into the past, even as far back as the Middle Ages, his work and theory were not designed to explain any past society.[8] His explanation of habitus was that it was a phenomenon formed by history, an internalized, second-nature, influencing practice which arose from an accumulation of past decisions to which an individual was reacting, but that then those decisions were 'forgotten as history'.[9] So there is an obvious problem in applying his insights and theories to the past, in that historians are not investigative sociologists who can make observations in the field, return to accumulate further evidence, and choose where to direct their study accordingly.[10] A social historian's record is as random and scattered as a palaeontologist's fossil field, though, just like such a field, it has a context. It is this context which I would suggest can be studied by a historian and is where evidence for a former habitus may be found. Since habitus is universal in human societies, we can at least suggest that traces of it must be there to be found, if the evidence is deep enough.

If the human social mind is geared nowadays to tune into the dominant habitus in the field in which it finds itself, it always has been in the historical past. Medieval society itself did not know it had a habitus, but intelligent medieval people were nonetheless aware that their choices were made under some sort of influence, not least the actions and reactions of those around them. As basic a twelfth-century educational text as Facetus reflects, for the benefit of children: 'Everyone should live by the custom of the house in which he lives; he should take heed of when to be silent and when to speak.' Cato's distichs had been telling children since the fourth century that 'Another's life is a teacher', which was glossed by Robert of Ho in our period in more specific terms thus: 'Take any man as a lesson in humanity and keep those lessons in mind, for the sort of life each man leads can teach you about others.'[11]

---

[8] He regarded medieval scholastic thought as 'a habitus-forming force' within the medieval elite; P. Bourdieu, 'Systems of Education and Systems of Thought', in *Knowledge and Control: New Directions for the Sociology of Education*, ed. M. F. D. Young (London, 1971), 184.

[9] P. Bourdieu, *The Logic of Practice* (Stanford, CA, 1990), 53–4.

[10] A point neatly made by P. Buc, *The Dangers of Ritual: Between Early Medieval Texts and Social Scientific Theory* (Princeton, 2001), 248 and n., a study which principally deals with Carolingian texts. The texts which are our sources here are, however, much more varied and numerous, and to give them a social context is not in my view impossible, though it certainly has its difficulties.

[11] *Enseignements Trebor*, 50 (ll. 399–402): *D'aucun home essample prenez/E en memoire retenez/Ker [si] la vie de chascun/Est per l'enseignement d'aucun.*

There were times when the operation of a medieval habitus on their choices became evident to its more reflective occupants, even apart from those times when its perceived violation caused them to bristle. This was what brought the Occitan castellan and baron Garin lo Brun to observe that everyone could be courtly (*cortes*) if only people saw in themselves the conduct they condemned in others.[12] Others also observed the way that their social environment was informing their behaviour, not least the poet Arnaut de Mareuil, who mused: 'I do not pretend to know more than I have acquired by questioning and listening, by hearing and seeing: because no one has any learning without another's teaching.'[13] Commonplace though such observations may have been, they tangentially remark the restless alertness of the social mind in observing the way others are behaving, and registering the degree to which actions, their own and others, are finding approval or disapproval. If such norms changed within a field and the habitus became less comfortable, medieval people noticed. When Thomasin of Zirclaria wanted to express discontent with the changing and troubled world of 1216 he lived in, it was by declaring that accepted and time-honoured social norms were being turned on their heads: the views of the foolish were drowning out the wise, the young were pushing aside the old, servants now expected the lord to show them honour, and the riff-raff were up on horse-back while knights were walking. This is an example of what Bourdieu called *hysteresis*, where the inhabitants of a habitus find themselves in a position where their social context (the field) has changed around them faster than their under-standing of the habitus can mutate to catch up and bring about the match where people feel at home in their social world.[14]

In one sense this book is about a period of general hysteresis, when the estab-lished habitus of the later twelfth century was challenged by shifts within it, spe-cifically the move to concede social hegemony to a tiny male elite, which disturbed and disorientated the field we call courtly society, and made more exclusive the understanding of the quality of Nobility, limiting it to a much smaller elite. The movement was accompanied by widespread social debate and even caused resist-ance, not least in that group within medieval society which was most disadvan-taged by the shift: elite women, who found themselves even assailed by arguments that they were not in fact qualified to be called noble. Looked at in this way the chivalric turn takes on a new and more explicable guise. The concept of habitus suggests to us the mechanics of what it was that was transforming society at that point. It does not, of course, explain *why* the habitus shifted in that generation or suggest to us the forces that produced the shift. Those are entirely different questions,

---

[12] *E·l termini d'estiu*, 58 (ll. 157–60).

[13] *Rasos es e Mesura*, 17 (ll. 21–6): *De saber nom fenh ges/mas de so qu'ay apres/demanden et auzen,/ escotan e vezen:/car nuhls non a doctrina/ses autruy dessiplina.*

[14] *Welsche Gast*, 175–6 (ll. 6443–54). For background, C. Hardy, 'Hysteresis', in *Pierre Bourdieu: Key Concepts*, 126–45, and for Bourdieu's own statement, *The State Nobility: Elite Schools in the Field of Power*, trans. R. Nice (Cambridge, 1996), esp. p. 219. In historical studies, 'hysteresis' is a term mostly to be found in the analysis of twentieth-century financial panics. Amongst historians them-selves it is most commonly experienced when the accepted views they had acquired at graduate school are challenged by innovative studies, the stress and disorientation they feel having then to be exorcised through hostile journal reviews.

which need to be addressed empirically and will be the concern of Part Four of this book. But even so habitus explains how the minds of those twelfth-century people were working and why they were making the choices they did. It is the habitus that produced the defining social figures of the Middle Ages: the *preudefemme* and *preudomme*, the leaders of the earlier courtly world (see Chapters 4 and 5), whose long reign was overthrown by the usurping figure of the noble knight.

I would be the first to admit that there are dangers in using a sociological model to account for social change eight centuries ago, one being the caution Bourdieu himself gave. Such models have limits even when dealing with present societies, where the investigator is an outsider and does not live within the habitus he studies. The danger there is that the investigator produces an intellectual model and constructs a world of rules and causes that the people he studies would not recognize as their own.[15] How much more so is this likely to happen when the people offering the evidence have been dust for the best part of a millennium? Bourdieu's answer was that the observer has to be aware of the intellectual baggage he carries, which manifests itself in the questions he asks and the direction he gives to his curiosity, which are internal to him and the field in which he works. His analysis of the society he studies is a 'partial' representation, in more than one sense of the word. So the observer has to observe himself and his presuppositions as much as his field. I could also add that in a way the distance in time in this particular project assists a study in palaeo-sociology and offsets the danger Bourdieu himself identified. I may well project my intellectual concerns on the way I prioritize questions about the evidence, but I could never mistake my own world for that of the twelfth century and unthinkingly carry suppositions across. Its difference from my own perspective is profound.

The question of the nature of the evidence is another concern. I doubt that it would be possible to reconstruct an eleventh-century habitus for any part of medieval Europe other than (perhaps) the very small field of the monastic enclosure. Lay society does not begin to generate substantial records of its own views of itself and proper behaviour within it until the middle third of the twelfth century. But we are lucky in the volume and variety of what was then produced, and the fact that most of the observers were not clerics (who were to some extent outsiders) but lay people themselves, male and female. It would be tempting to see this sudden flood of tracts as itself symptomatic of trouble within the habitus, though it might equally well be claimed that there were other causes: the coincidental growth in vernacular literature or expanding literacy within the courtly world, for instance. Since the flood of social commentary begins in the generations before the formulations of chivalric hegemony, the two latter objections may well be valid. As I said earlier, the result is a bone dump of fossilized social commentary whose usefulness for the task I have set myself has to be interrogated. The reply to this anxiety is to be found in the analysis within the chapters that follow, but there is a considerable

---

[15] P. Bourdieu, *Outline of a Theory of Practice*, trans. R. Nice (Cambridge, 1977), 1–2, an objection dealt with critically in A. King, 'Thinking with Bourdieu against Bourdieu: a "practical" critique of the habitus', *Sociological Theory*, 18 (2000), 419–22.

volume of data available, and the more extensive and varied is the data, the more confident we can be in the reconstructions it enables.

FIRST IN THE FIELD

The 'field' of superior medieval conduct has been cultivated by very many scholars since the original generation of Enlightenment scholars found it and called it Chivalry. Perhaps the pioneer must be reckoned to have been the prolific Jesuit antiquary, Claude-François Menestrier (1631–1705), whose *Chevalerie ancienne et moderne* was published in 1683. Some of the basic ideas on Chivalry were his and were formulated in the age of Louis XIV, in whose father's lifetime the last courtly jousts had been staged in France (festivities which Menestrier himself elsewhere chronicled). Menestrier modestly contended in his work that no previous writer had ever truly understood Chivalry the way he did, and so had confused the word's several meanings, which he would clarify for his readers. But he had good reason to assert the importance of his analysis. *Chevalerie*, he was the first to say, was a complicated phenomenon to analyse because it comprehended numerous senses in French: the profession of the horseback warrior; an estate of lesser nobility; the holders of fiefs and membership of chivalric and religious associations.[16] In all its senses and in his discussion, however, Menestrier related Chivalry to Nobility, and to superiority in society. As far as he was concerned, the idea of *chevalerie* was a constant in society wherever there were aristocratic warriors, and he harked back as far as the order of Equites in Republican and Imperial Rome.

Menestrier thus brought together the profession of arms, social status and commitment to moral excellence under the heading of *chevalerie* and argued that as a phenomenon it was timeless. Under the heading of moral excellence, he was keen to emphasize the value of the benediction of arms and the ceremony of inauguration of a medieval knight at the altar as it developed in the later Middle Ages, a ritual on which there is still much to say, as Dominique Barthélemy has recently demonstrated (see below, pp. 267–70). Menestrier was not a man much enamoured of fiction, and he despised the Arthurian romances as sources for his reconstruction of Chivalry; he preferred legal and institutional evidence. His Chivalry naturally therefore gravitated to grants of Nobility and the rules of the curial and ecclesiastical orders of knights, of which he regarded the Order of the Hospitallers as the most noble and superior, so to that extent he acknowledged some link between Chivalry and crusading endeavour, as many others have done since.

The inadequacies of Menestrier's reasoning were systematically dissected soon after his death by the Carmelite friar, Blaise Vauzelle (1651–1729), otherwise

---

[16] The polysemous nature of the word *chevalerie* in French is still an obstacle to understanding and has caused confusion for Anglophones and Francophones alike, see for an example, F-L. Ganshof, 'Qu'est que c'est la chevalerie', *Revue Générale Belge* (Nov. 1947), 78. In English the sense of a code has long predominated, see comparative observations in, J. D. Adams, 'Modern Views of Medieval Chivalry, 1884–1984' in, *The Study of Chivalry: Resources and Approaches*, ed. H. Chickering and T.H. Seiler (Kalamazoo MI, 1988), 43–6.

known as the Père Honoré de Sainte-Marie, who published in 1718 his *Dissertations historiques et critiques sur la chevalerie*, in which he took apart many of Menestrier's proofs and categories. But, as often happens with controversialists, a fierce and austere desire to point out the inadequacies in the reasoning of someone else's theories was not coupled with the imagination to find adequate new ones. If anything, the good father took Menestrier's approaches further than he had. On the matter of Chivalry's origins, he took it for granted that wherever there had been noble warriors there had always been *chevalerie*, of which 'Christian Chivalry' was but the latest episode. In the universalizing manner of Enlightenment scholarship, he even found reason to believe the Aztec empire had possessed a knighting ceremony.[17] He did not quibble with Menestrier's linking of Chivalry with Nobility. For him, as also for Menestrier, Christian Chivalry owed something to crusading fervour. He even pursued and expanded upon Menestrier's eccentric argument (for which he had found material in De la Roque's *Traité de la Noblesse*) that *chevalerie* extended to women who embraced the crusading orders, and that there was a corresponding degree of 'chevaleresse' to the 'chevaler'.[18]

Father Honoré signalled, however, a turn in the study of chivalry, for he deployed a mass of medieval chronicles and romances in his support, and as a result his portrayal of the later stages of Christian Chivalry in Europe, as he would have looked at it, are much more vivid and evocative than that of his predecessor. This was the approach which was employed rather more rigorously and thoroughly by Jean-Baptiste de La Curne de Sainte-Palaye in the next generation, to produce a more familiar analysis of Chivalry, one that was located in the European (or rather, French) Middle Ages, and was reconstructed laboriously and self-consciously from the analysis of literary remains as much as legal texts. La Curne was a pioneering student of medieval French literature, and his edition of Froissart was to be the standard for over a century. So he was well equipped to reconstruct from his reading the training and ideals of the young medieval knight and the course of a typical career, a historical reconstruction which was the subject of his preliminary essays of the 1740s before he republished them in *Mémoires de l'ancienne chevalerie*. La Curne located the full definition of Chivalry entirely in the French Middle Ages, and since he saw the ceremony of the reception of arms as an indicator of *chevalerie* (in the sense of knighthood), he was happy to believe that it was a reality in the times of Charlemagne. Indeed, he was ready to accept that it might have been a characteristic of the Germanic warbands described by Tacitus, who reported that they practised delivery of arms. But the 'Golden Age of Chivalry', as he called it, was for him in the later middle ages when there were romances and tracts to describe and exalt the virtues of the true *chevaler*.

So it is in the 1740s that we find the first fully articulated historical model of Chivalry as we expect it to be: a pattern of exalted moral conduct which was

---

[17] Père Honoré de Sainte-Marie, *Dissertations historiques et critiques sur la chevalerie, ancienne et moderne seculière et regulière* (Paris, 1718), 337.

[18] See recently, S. Cassagnes-Brouquet, *Chevaleresses: une chevalerie au féminin* (Paris, 2013), esp. ch. 3 for the female houses of the crusading orders, where the gendered term *militissa* is mainly to be found.

expected of the (sometimes degenerate) military nobility of Europe in the centuries following the twelfth. La Curne's model rapidly passed into the European intellectual mainstream, and had already been absorbed in England by the 1760s, where it filtered into minds of the early thinkers of the Romantic movement.[19] La Curne's was a work widely read and respected across Europe, and as a result it encouraged for a while a consensus on the meaning and chronology of Chivalry across national historical traditions. The otherwise rebarbative Scottish controversialist Gilbert Stuart (1743–86), for instance, largely accepted La Curne's view of the origins and meaning of Chivalry without demur in his *View of Society in Europe* (1778).[20] Charles Nodier's introduction to the 1826 edition of the *Mémoires* took some space to assess the work's long-term significance and influence, concluding broadly (as had also Charles Mills in England the previous year) that La Curne had established Chivalry by his great work as being an essentially moral and improving phenomenon in an otherwise primitive age: 'il est certain qu'on y retrouve la peinture exacte et fidèle des moeurs et des usages des siècles simples et grossiers où le chevalerie étoit une institution importante.'[21] For Mills, Chivalry evolved into 'the most beautiful form of manners...that has ever adorned the history of man'.[22] Much the same verdict on La Curne's work was to be found in contemporary Germany, where in the 1780s Johann Gottfried von Herder (1744–1803) simply summarized his work (without acknowledgement) for his study of *Rittergeist in Europa*.[23] In 1823 Johann Gustav Gottlieb Büsching (1783–1829) repeated the Frenchman's model of Chivalry for the benefit of a German readership interested in its own national knighthood, merely adding his own rather florid and rambling observations drawn from medieval German literature.[24] Büsching's ideas were to be influential too: his work was to provide the intellectual scenery for Richard Wagner's medieval Teutonic fantasy, *Parsifal*. This was how the idea of Chivalry entered nineteenth-century social discourse in which—astonishingly in retrospect—it was to be weaponized by social liberals and conservatives alike in their programmes

[19] P. Burke, 'Origins of Cultural History', in *Varieties of Cultural History* (Ithaca, NY, 1998), 15–16.

[20] *A View of Society in Europe, in its progress from rudeness to refinement: or, Inquiries concerning the history of law, government, and manners* (Edinburgh, 1778), 56–68, 313–33. Stuart's chapter on the subject insensibly reproduces La Curne's *cursus vitae* of the knight, and for his polemical purposes adopted La Curne's broad chronology of its origins. His other principal source of inspiration was John Selden's *Titles of Honor*. See D. Allan, '"An Institution Quite Misunderstood": Chivalry and Sentimentalism in the Late Scottish Enlightenment', in *Chivalry and the Medieval Past*, ed. K. Stevenson and B. Gribling (Woodbridge, 2016), 15–34.

[21] *Mémoires de l'ancienne chevalerie considérée comme un établissement politique et militaire* (2 vols, 2nd edn, Paris, 1826), 1: 2.

[22] C. Mills, *The History of Chivalry or Knighthood and its Times* (2 vols, London, 1825), 1: 11. He may have been quoting Montesquieu's positive verdict on 'le système merveilleux de la chevalerie', which the great man believed had no match in any earlier society; *De l'esprit des lois* (5 vols, Paris, 1824), 3: 205.

[23] *Ideen zur Philosophie der Geschichte der Menschheit* (Leipzig, 1785): Teil 4, 20: 2. For which see L. Gossman, *Medievalism and the Ideologies of the Enlightenment: the World and Work of La Curne de Sainte-Palaye* (Baltimore, 1968), 331–2.

[24] *Ritterzeit und Ritterwesen* (2 vols, Leipzig, 1823). A translation of the *Mémoires* into German had long been available as *Das Ritterwesen des Mittelalters: nach seiner politischen und militärischen Verfassung*, trans. J. L. Klüber (3 vols, Nuremberg, 1786–91).

for radical social reform, to the extent that it quite left the sphere of academic debate until the later twentieth century, where we will begin to pick it up in the chapters that follow.[25]

THE MEDIEVAL LAY ELITE AND EDUCATION

To understand the nature of habitus and how it was communicated at the time of the chivalric turn, we need to consider also the topic of conscious education in conduct and the question of lay literacy. Many of our medieval princes, magnates and knights were far from unacquainted with the written word, which helps account for the fact that a large number of the tracts on which this book is based were authored by them. We meet some very learned lay characters, and not just the well-known late thirteenth-century intellectuals like Ramon Llull and Jean de Meung, who lived on the intellectual borderland between the lay and clerical worlds. Take, for instance, the 21-year-old Henry de Montfort who on 1 January 1259, probably in lodgings in Paris, put the final flourishes in his precise and practical book hand to the will his father, Earl Simon de Montfort of Leicester, had dictated to him. It was dictated and written in French, though young Henry would have been as capable of managing a Latin document, for he was a well-educated young man. This was not because he was intended for the Church. Henry's writing of his father's will was simply a manifestation of what might happen in an aristocracy where literacy was regarded as part of the essential social armoury of a nobleman. Henry and his younger brother Amaury had been schooled in the household of the academic bishop, Robert Grosseteste, where both Latin and Greek were taught.[26] Amaury de Montfort went on indeed to become something of an intellectual, schooled in advanced mathematics, a student at Padua, and the author of tracts on alchemy and theology. He followed a clerical career in minor orders between 1260 and 1287, but resigned his livings by taking up knighthood at the age of 45.

    These two brothers indicate that in the thirteenth century, literate noble fathers wanted literate sons—not just one son, with the skills of literacy with the option of palming him off on the Church—in preference to their being a drain on limited family resources, as Georges Duby once suggested. Henry and Amaury de Montfort were brought up in the circles and in the generation for which the learned Dominican, Vincent of Beauvais, wrote under Capetian patronage his *De eruditione filiorum nobilium*, where Ecclesiasticus, the classics, the Fathers, and the great masters of the twelfth century were marshalled into a diachronic chorus to urge that every (male) child of a family of consequence or aspiration should be taught both to read and form his letters and to pursue a course of the liberal arts, with a

---

[25] See survey in Crouch, *Nobility*, 8–16.
[26] For the will, C. Bémont, *Simon de Montfort, earl of Leicester*, trans. E. F. Jacob (Oxford, 1930), 276–8, including facsimile. For its context and the education of Henry and Amaury, J. R. Maddicott, *Simon de Montfort* (Cambridge, 1994), 94–7, 173–7, and see further, Aurell, *Lettered Knight*, 87–8.

particular emphasis on law and theology. Fra Vincent's priority in proposing his exhaustive syllabus was—it has to be said—the moral formation of wayward youth, not educational utility. But he did urge this requirement not just on the children of princes, but on the offspring of every one of the king's vassals (*fideles*) because, as he saw it, erudition erased their rough edges.[27] Education instilled superior conduct in those to whom the common people must look up, and gave a reason why their betters should be respected. For Vincent, then, though he would not perhaps have expressed it in this way, literacy was a mark of social distinction and a source of social capital. It also encouraged the laity in an education which reinforced moral norms, a view which still flourished happily in the nineteenth century, before mass literacy became perceived as the graphite in the engine of social change which was to enable the modern industrial nation state.

There are historians who still take the view that later medieval literacy was the province of the Church, despite medieval clerical writers themselves telling us that this was not so.[28] If any twelfth- and thirteenth-century lay aristocracy is perceived as distinctively literate, the Italians are usually allowed to be exceptional in that regard, but this underplays the evidence available from northern France.[29] No better contemporary exponent of the lay literacy in that sphere can be found than the layman and lawyer Giles of Paris, who in 1200, in the generation before Vincent of Beauvais, addressed thus the young son of Philip Augustus, Louis—then 14 years of age—in the dedication to his extended poem, the *Karolinus*, which is worth quoting at length:

> It was a good decision of your father to have you well-educated, as it will be conveni-
> ent in due course for a boy who will be the head of affairs and the centre of an entire
> kingdom to know what he needs of business, and, if he has to, to be able to read secret
> communications of great weight without the assistance of anyone else and without
> sharing their sensitive contents. It is proper for a king worthy of the title that his
> speech, judgement, intelligence and cleverness be superior to any lesser person's. So he
> should have a sound education. In reading books he will be able to adopt the behav-
> iour of the best people of the past, to detect treachery, to tell people how to do their
> jobs properly, to be a good man pleasing to God, to know the mysteries of the Church,
> to improve on his virtues, and be able to express himself far better than any other
> layman. He will be superior even to his own counsellors. He will know even the job
> his bishops do, and will have the capacity to rein in the excesses of the people over
> whom he rules. He will be able to instruct his own judges in law. When you, Louis,
> have been educated in the arts to the standard your father requires, you will be able to
> pursue the virtues.[30]

Though this comment is addressed to a future king, and a king is not a representative layman, Giles's younger contemporary, Vincent of Beauvais, tells us, despite all that,

---

[27] Vincent of Beauvais, *De eruditione filiorum nobilium*, ed. A. Steiner (MAA Publication, 32, 1938), p. 5: *Est autem erudire extra ruditatem ponere.*

[28] See, for instance, the author of *Facetus*, who urged young laymen with an aptitude for letters to acquire learning when young and learn to love books; *Facetus*, 225, ll. 63–7.

[29] Aurell, *Lettered Knight*, 77–82.

[30] M. L. Colker, 'The "Karolinus" of Egidius Parisiensis', *Traditio*, 29 (1973), 303.

what applied to the ideal king applied also to the ideal nobleman.[31] From Giles we find a range of arguments in favour of lay literacy, and they are rather more pragmatic than the ones marshalled by Fra Vincent. They are in fact striking in their cogency: the king needs to be the equal of his own advisers, or presumably they might be in a position to put one over on him. The king needs to be able to read confidential correspondence unaided so that secrets are contained—and Giles expected confidential intelligence reports to be confided to ink and parchment. The king needs education to be able to express himself with effect. The moral arguments also resonate with those Vincent would one day marshal: the educated layman will be instructed in the best conduct through the study of historical characters; he will acquire a knowledge of the scriptures; and through the acquisition of the arts he will acquire also virtue. The greater man's speech, judgement, intelligence and cleverness should be superior to any lesser person's, and only education could provide that. With Giles of Paris we have a medieval author who saw the primary purpose of education as the cultivation of superior social conduct in the laity.

Literacy and learning may have become specialized in the Church in the early Middle Ages, but it was not ever closed to lay people with leisure and aspirations.[32] In the thirteenth century we find a society which undeniably believed literacy was the province of both laymen and clergy, and put the belief into practice. It had a range of arguments why any layman of consequence should be educated—arguments pragmatic, moralistic and idealistic. To illustrate this further we need only refer to the dictaminal handbook or formulary. Formularies are important as they provide some data as to the extent of penetration of society by literate forms, which is otherwise lacking for much of the Middle Ages before 1250. The existence of formularies is evident enough in early thirteenth-century England, more so indeed than any part of Europe other than Italy. Three major English formularies predate 1250; there are several partial or lesser ones too. The earliest full example is a booklet now in the Walters Art Museum in Baltimore, which dates between 1202 and 1209 and contains an *epistolarium* of sixty-one sample letters. It is a fair assumption that these three are survivors of what was a more widespread early thirteenth-century genre, which copied and recopied exemplars in various combinations.[33]

It is the range and variety of the sample letters these formularies contain that is perhaps most significant and revealing of the extent of use of literate forms by the laity in or soon after 1200. Their dictaminal ancestor, Bernard of Meung's mid-twelfth-century French formulary, appends at most a dozen sample documents in the concluding *epistolarium* section, but these English formularies present hundreds of exemplars. The social range of the lay society they embrace includes not just earls, knights and barons, but freeholders (*liberi tenentes*) and peasants

---

[31] It might be noted that an eyewitness account of the consecration of the 7-year-old King Philip I of France in 1059 tells us that the boy *read* out his coronation oath in Latin; *Ordines Coronationis Franciae*, ed. R. A. Jackson (Philadelphia, 1995), 230–2.

[32] On schools and education, and the schooling of laymen, D. Luscombe, 'Thought and Learning', in *The New Cambridge Medieval History*, vol. 4, pt 1, *c.1024–c.1198*, ed. D. Luscombe and J. Riley-Smith (Cambridge, 2004), 461–82.

[33] *Lost Letters*, 3–9.

(*rustici*). The non-ecclesiastical situations they describe touch on a wide range of everyday circumstance. For the magnate, they concern the raising of credit, purchases of luxury goods by mail from London vintners, drapers and skinners, and instructions to bailiffs and seneschals. They include invitations to sponsor or join tournaments; instructions to knights to join their lord on expeditions, and on the stocking of parks and fishponds. For lesser people they concern loans of stock, money or agricultural implements, and the need to hire legal attorneys; they lament the oppressions of the king's local officers, and there is an interesting series of seven letters concerning the contract for the building of a windmill. There is also social correspondence. A knight absent on campaign writes to his wife and the rest of his family thanking her for linen sheets he had asked for and which she had subsequently sent. Several letters are from students to their parents, generally asking for money.

How far the embrace of literate forms penetrated the lower orders of the laity in 1200 is not so easy to say. However, the English formularies by no means ignore the world of the free tenant and bondsman. Nor do they stigmatize free or bonded peasants, as we will see in Chapter 6, as degenerate and devoid of any of the higher feelings literacy supposedly encouraged. Far from it in fact. They portray them as businessmen, men concerned with the duty of neighbourhood and with public rectitude. Whether many peasants could themselves write is an unanswerable question, though the necessity for a peasant reeve to cast accounts for his lord in the early thirteenth century is a pretty firm argument that some did. That peasant literacy troubled the Church is another argument. That particular aspiration was after all an indicator of noble status, which may be why several later twelfth-century writers believed education should be denied to the children of peasants, because, as Walter Map said, they were *ignobilis*, and the 'liberal arts' were reserved for free men (*liberi*).[34] He may have been mounting a rearguard action. Certainly the formulary letters despatched by and to people called *rustici* evoke a world where peasants needed to communicate at a distance to meet their agricultural needs, and somehow deployed written instruments to do so.

This is the literate world as we find it in the early Angevin period, in England and France. Literate forms at that point penetrated widely, and aspiration to education was widespread within it for both pragmatic and social reasons. In the 1170s we find the vernacular writer Walter of Arras advocating that noble children should be put to learn their letters at the age of 5.[35] Rather like Giles of Paris, Philip of Harvengt states in one of his letters that knightliness (*militia*) does not preclude learning (*scientia*) and that it was knowledge which 'ennobled' (*nobilaverat*) the mind of a magnate. He also observed in another work that in his day and province the knights were better educated in letters than the clergy, being their superior in both reading and the composition of Latin verse.[36] Gerald of Wales, across the Channel, echoed Philip in his handbook for princes: the greater the learning, he

[34] *De Nugis Curialium*, 12.
[35] *Eracle*, ed. G. Raynaud de Lage (Classiques français du moyen âge, 1976), ll. 252–8.
[36] Philip of Harvengt, *Epistolae*, in *PL* 203, col. 149; *De institutione clericorum* in ibid., col. 816.

said, the greater the warrior, recalling the historical examples of the Julio-Claudians and Carolingians.[37] Now it may be—as Martin Aurell says in a work which strongly argues the maximalist view of twelfth-century literacy—that the literary achievements of the twelfth-century nobility were not in fact colossal but, as he says, they lived in an educationally aspirational lay world.[38] They acquired an outlook that encouraged them towards education and literate communication which in turn formed ideas of superior conduct.

Intriguingly for our purposes here, literacy had intruded into the martial world of knighthood by a time as early as 1100. Amongst the sample letters of one formulary is a letter of Earl Ranulf III of Chester, whose original must have been sent in Richard's reign, quite possibly in 1196. It is of a genre that does not now otherwise survive, though one to which there is allusion in both the literary and charter record. It is a summons to military service, not from the king (of which the earliest surviving example I know is datable to 1188), but from the next level of mobilization down. Earl Ranulf had received a summons from the king to join a campaign, and he now sends a general letter on to his knights appointing a day and place to assemble in his retinue. Not only is this writ given, but there follow a number of letters of excuses that a knight might send back to his lord as to why he cannot answer the summons: he has no cash to meet his expenses, or his father has inconveniently died.[39] Such letters were indeed exchanged, and had been exchanged for many decades before 1200. It is a topos of early romance epic—and there are several instances in the Orange cycle going back to the 1130s—that when a count goes on campaign, he sends his *chartres* or *briés* (letters) to summon his knights.[40] A charter of Robert fitz Hamo, lord of Gloucester, which certainly dates before 1106 and may go back to the 1090s, talks of the written summons (*littere*) he will send to one of his enfeoffed serjeants when he wanted him to perform the service he owes him.[41]

This is for once a solid indication about the sort of written ephemera that a literate Anglo-French lay society was generating not just in the first quarter of the thirteenth century but in the century previous to the compilation of the formularies. Another known but ephemeral genre relating to the lay nobility is the letter of defiance. As early as the 1130s we hear of defiance being formally delivered by an aggrieved follower to his lord, and when it is, it is done by letter carried by an emissary. This was the case when the learned Earl Robert of Gloucester relinquished his allegiance to King Stephen of England in the autumn of 1138.[42] It was still the case a century later when the aggrieved Earl Richard Marshal of Pembroke—of whom Roger of Wendover remarks that he was 'well instructed in his letters' and

---

[37] *De principis instructione*, in *GCO* 8: 7.
[38] Aurell, *Lettered Knight*, 90.   [39] *Lost Letters*, nos 24–6.
[40] *Le Couronnement de Louis: chanson de geste du xiiᵉ siècle*, ed. E. Langlois (Paris, 1984), 9 (ll. 264–7), 62–3 (ll. 1996–8), 71 (ll. 2269–70). Wace of Bayeux (*c*.1155) refers to a summons by *bref* which is replied with *contre brief* by the recipient; *Le Roman de Brut*, ed. I. Arnold (2 vols, Paris, 1938–40), 1: ll. 3889–94.
[41] *The Langley Cartulary*, ed. P. R. Coss (Dugdale Society, 32, 199), 10.
[42] Malmesbury, *HN*, 40.

John of Waverley that he was 'singularly accomplished in the liberal arts'—sent letters to Henry III returning his allegiance and defying the king.[43] It is hardly surprising then that Richard Marshal and his brothers had less than a decade earlier commissioned the writing and publication of a vernacular life of their father, one of whose purposes was to proclaim that great man, the Regent of England, to be the very summit of lay conduct, *un preudomme de grand affaire*, from whose example all youth could learn superior conduct.

Ironically, there is reason to suspect that William Marshal the elder, the one medieval *preudomme* in our period to inspire a full and detailed biography, was not himself literate, at least in Latin, for all his concern that his children be educated to the highest standards of his day. However, in any gathering it would have been borne in on Marshal that his lords and many of his knightly colleagues alike were men whose upbringing had included learning their letters and an exposure to the liberal arts. As we will see in Chapter 9, at the very least it gave them some advantage as poets, musicians and raconteurs in the competitive culture of the hall, where performance was everything, on several levels.[44] These people have left us a legacy in their varied reflections on proper conduct which this book exploits. In fact it is educated laypeople who provide most of the evidence on which it is based: whether aristocrats such as Garin lo Brun of Veillac, Arnaut-Guilhem de Marsan, Marie de France, Huon d'Oisy, Raoul de Houdenc, Sordello da Goito, Huon de Méry, Brunetto Latini, Ulrich von Liechtenstein and the writer called Tanhäusser, or professional poets like Marcabru, Arnaut de Mareuil, Hartmann von Aue, Ramon Vidal de Besalú, Guiot de Provins, Peire Vidal, Baldwin de Condé, Raimbaut de Vaqueiras, or Robert de Blois, and quite a few more besides, such as the *fableors* and moralists whose names are not added to their work but whose perspective is decidedly not clerical. Then there are the writers who lived between the clerical and lay worlds as educators, men such as Daniel of Beccles, Elias of Thriplow, Robert of Ho and Buonvicino della Riva, who may have been in orders but whose principal concern was pedagogy. Daniel at least tells us that he was, as the father of two sons, a man who lived a secular life. The arguments of this book are therefore formed principally out of the evidence and views of the lettered layman of the twelfth and thirteenth centuries not the more constricted Salomonic rhetoric of the clergyman.

---

[43] *Calendar of Patent Rolls preserved in the Public Record Office* (6 vols, HMSO, 1901–13), 3: 35. For Richard's educational attainments, *Acts and Letters*, 22.

[44] One might reference here the Catalan viscount and poet Guerau de Cabrera, whose sarcastic twelfth-century composition (*Cabra juglar, no puesc mudar qu'eu non chan*) ridiculing the incompetence of his own household poet, Cabra, lists the skills and range of literature a performer must master to be respected in the hall; M. de Riquer, *Història de la literatura catalana: part antigua* (Barcelona, 1964), 56–61. His identity is contested between Guerau (III) (d. *c.*1161) and his grandson Guerau (IV), and a date for the poem in the 1190s is now argued; S. Cingolani, 'The *sirventes-ensenhamen* of Guerau de Cabrera: a proposal for a new interpretation', *Journal of Hispanic Research*, 1 (1992/3), 191–200.

2

The Field of Study

A basic assumption behind this book is that medieval Europe forms a coherent area of study in social history. It contends that the writers in Latin and the many vernaculars who produced the tracts and poems which are its sources occupied a thought-world which shared and debated ideas, from Spain to Scotland across to Austria and as far as Latin Greece and Cyprus. More than that, the elites of that world, in defiance of their multiplicity of vernaculars, shared a common culture, which meant that a knight or a merchant could venture from Cumberland to Montpellier (the proverbial end of the world for an Anglo-Norman) and still be in a social environment where they shared assumptions with their hosts. There were many reasons why this should have been so. The most obvious was that much of this huge subcontinental area had long been underpinned by a common Latin culture, the cultural inheritance from the days when most of it had been ruled from Imperial Rome, a foundation reinforced by the extravagant cultural ambitions of the revivalist Frankish empire of the eighth and ninth centuries, whose ruler was on several occasions praised as the 'Father of Europe'.[1] By the eleventh century, much of this inheritance from the Roman past had faded as the political superstructure of western Europe fractured into kingdoms, duchies and even counties, whose rulers all wanted to be a Caesar to their people.[2] But the pillars of Latin Europe represented by its common literate culture and religion were not just unshaken, they were being massively reinforced and ornamented in the emerging schools of France and Italy.

By 1050 the inhabitants of Latin Europe were again looking towards Rome, where the papal curia was ambitious to assume greater direction over the theology and discipline of the Church. The literate people of that century, not all of whom were by any means clergy, were literate in Latin, learned the language from common textbooks and word lists, and read the same universal chronicles and classics.[3]

---

[1] E. Fernie, 'The Origins of Europe,' *Journal of the Warburg and Courtauld Institutes*, 71 (2008), 45–7. J. Le Goff, *L'Europe, est-elle né au moyen age?* (Paris, 2003), 47–71, argues the tenth-century Ottonian period as a better candidate for the resurgence of a pan-European Romanism.

[2] C. Wickham, *The Inheritance of Rome: a History of Europe from 400 to 1000* (London, 2009), 552–64, places the point of discontinuity in European identity when political structures lost the Roman idea of public authority.

[3] The transnational commonalty of twelfth-century scholars is implicit in the recent work on 'communities of learning', the idea that scholarship and learning could take place amongst widespread networks of scattered scholars rather than in institutional schools; see C. Mews and J. Crossley 'Introduction', in *Communities of Learning. Networks and the Shaping of Intellectual Identity in Europe, 1100–1500*, ed. iidem (Turnhout, 2011).

The vital commonalty that a humanistic Latin education once gave the intelligentsia across the various national cultures of Europe lasted a long time. Edmund Burke could still write in 1796 that 'no citizen of Europe could be altogether an exile in any part of it'.[4] Such a feeling of cultural identity has only faded to nothing in the past three generations. In this culture a compendium of moral observations from the classics like the *Moralium Dogma Philosophorum*, which was compiled by William of Conches probably in the middle of the twelfth century, could spread its gleanings in a decade or two from France across Britain and the Empire, to be exploited by any number of scholars.[5] A German translation by the name of *Tugendspiegel* was made in Thuringia in the 1170s by a cleric called Wernher von Elmendorf.[6] The Latin work still exists in eighty-six medieval manuscripts, while fifty manuscripts survive of its thirteenth-century French translation, called by its translator *Li Romans de Moralitez*.

Such authors travelled as far in their world as their ideas, and in some numbers.[7] The poet, teacher, rhetorician and grammarian Serlo of Wilton (died 1181) left his native Wiltshire as a youth to study in Paris early in the 1130s and returned to England to serve as a clerk in Queen Adeliza's household. At some point after 1147 he took himself off to Occitan Provence, where in a poem appreciative of his place of exile near Nice and the protection of the local count he reported he found the city so full of other expatriates that it was almost another England. From the Mediterranean south he returned north after 1154 to teach for a while in the schools of Oxford and then perhaps also Paris, before succumbing to the lure of the cloister (in France) in the late 1150s.[8] The loss of its lands north of the Loire by the Angevin royal house in 1204 did not necessarily close off such careers to Englishmen. The aristocratic Kentish scholar Odo of Cheriton (died *c.*1246) studied and taught at Paris through the years of Angevin and Capetian warfare, and travelled widely. He was in Occitania and Spain for appreciable periods of time where he resided, wrote and preached. He was known and respected in the Empire as much as in France and England. Eventually in 1232 he returned to Kent on his father's death to take control of his ancestral honor.[9]

[4] 'First Letter on a Regicide Peace', in E. Burke, *The Writings and Speeches*, ed. P. Langford and others (12 vols, Oxford, 1981–2015), 9: 249, cited in M. D'Auria and J. Vermeiren, 'Narrating Europe', *History*, 103 (2018), 385.

[5] M. Lapidge, 'The Stoic Inheritance', in *A History of Twelfth-Century Western Philosophy*, ed. P. Dronke (Cambridge, 1998), 95–6.

[6] J. Bumke, 'Tugendspiegel', in *Die Deutsche Literatur des Mittelalters: Verfasserlexikon*, ed. W. Stammler and K. Langosch (2nd edn, 14 vols, Berlin, 1977–2008) 10: 925–7.

[7] For some observations on wandering intellectuals and clerks, I. Wei, 'Scholars and Travel in the Twelfth and Thirteenth Centuries', in *Freedom of Movement in the Middle Ages*, ed. P. Horden (Harlaxton Medieval Studies, 15, Donington, 2007), 73–85.

[8] A. C. Friend, 'The Proverbs of Serlo of Wilton', *Mediaeval Studies*, 16 (1954), 179 and n.; for Serlo and Provence, BnF, ms latin 6765, fo. 62v, esp.: *Nam gens Angligene locus hic est Anglia pene*, published in E. Faral, 'Le ms latin 3718 de la Bibliothèque Nationale,' *Romania*, 46 (1920), 267–9. On Serlo's life (on which there is still some contestation), A. G. Rigg, 'Serlo of Wilton: biographical notes,' *Medium Aevum*, 65 (1996), 96–101; R. M. Thomson, 'Serlo of Wilton and the Schools of Oxford,' *Medium Aevum*, 68 (1999), 1–12, and see cautions in R. Sharpe, *A Handlist of Latin Writers of Great Britain and Ireland before 1540* (Turnhout, 2001), 606–7.

[9] A. C. Friend, 'Master Odo of Cheriton', *Speculum*, 23 (1948), 641–58; B. J. Levy 'Cheriton, Odo of', *ODNB*.

But there was also a corresponding interlinked, vernacular world which grew up within Latin Europe, whether its language was Romance, Germanic or even Celtic. Illiterate people (meaning those who knew no Latin) travelled widely, and somehow or other they communicated with those they met. In part this was enabled by the spread of French aristocratic culture in the eleventh century beyond its heartland into southern Italy in the 1020s and the British archipelago in 1066. The formation of an aristocratic culture focused on the tournament, which evolved before 1100 in Picardy, Flanders and the Western Empire, was propagated by the crusading ventures which that same area espoused. It sponsored expeditions to the East and to Spain, and wherever it went it took its distinctive culture with it, charming the aristocracies of other language groups: Germans, Italians and even Gaelic Scots. French could form the basis of a European lingua franca by 1100, and it certainly assisted in communication across the polylingual British Isles.[10] Occitan in its various dialects encompassed its own huge cultural area from Aragon to Lombardy in the twelfth century, and Francien speakers of the north could get by in it at need.[11] A case has been made that a sort of pidgin Latin-French was a shared basic mode of communication across much of twelfth-century Europe for travellers of all levels and conditions, even though it may be barely recorded.[12]

So western and central Europe was a vast area geared to cultural interchange, and wherever its colonizing and travelling aristocrats went, whether to Ireland, Pomerania or Palestine, their assumptions about how society should be organized went with them into new contexts, as we will see in such diverse areas as table culture and formal declarations of animosity.[13] The dominant vernacular element in it was French: whether the Francien dialects of northern France, the western Empire and Britain, or the Occitan of the south, whose cultural empire included Catalonia, Provence and northern Italy. The scintillating poetry and epics of the French-speaking world had a homogenizing and increasing impact on other neighbouring vernacular cultures by the middle of the twelfth century, not just the Spanish and Italian but the non-Romance cultures of the Germans, English, Bretons and Welsh, so that its literary heroes—Arthur, Tristan, Lancelot and Charlemagne (three of them in fact hijacked from Atlantic Celtic cultures)—were as well known in Oxfordshire as in Braunschweig or Trentino.

We can see this Occidental Latin and vernacular interchange in action in the output of those of its writers we can get to know. A fine example is the female aristocratic writer of the later twelfth century known as Marie de France. She has

[10] I. Short, 'On Bilingualism in Anglo-Norman England', *Revue Philologique*, 33 (1979–80), 467–79.
[11] M. Pfister, 'La langue de Guilhem IX comte de Poitiers', *CCM*, 19 (1976), 112–13; Paterson, *Occitan Society*, 1–7.
[12] R. Harvey, 'Languages, Lyrics and the Knightly Classes', in *Medieval Knighthood*, 5, ed. S. Church and R. Harvey (Woodbridge, 1995), 197–220. For a thirteenth-century satire founded on such macaronic miscommunication, by two Englishmen stranded in France, K. Busby, 'Plus ça change...A case of medieval interlanguage', *Interlanguage Studies Bulletin*, 3 (1978), 118–26.
[13] As explored in R. Bartlett, *The Making of Europe: Conquest, Colonization and Cultural Change, 950–1350* (London, 1993), who defines this area of commonalty as 'Latin Europe', though Outremer does not help make geographical sense of this as a cultural area.

been credibly identified as a daughter of Count Waleran II of Meulan (1104–66), a distinguished nobleman of the Île-de-France with great possessions also in Normandy and England, and in his day a crusading leader. Marie's father was literate, a Latin poet and a highly educated man, and it is no surprise that he took care his children were too.[14] Marie was tutored in Latin and the classics (she knew her Ovid) and off her own bat she mastered Old English for good measure, as she tells us in the colophon to her French-language collection of fables, for she says she had consulted an English translation of the Latin Aesop (attributed to King Alfred the Great) when she was writing her own *Ysopet*. She had also read Old English and Latin lives of the saints and vernacular histories of Normandy and Britain. She was charmed by the Arthurian empire of the imagination, where one of her *Lais* ('Lanval') was set. Her intellectual curiosity even reached Wales, where her first cousin Richard fitz Gilbert (died 1176) was a marcher earl, for her *lai* 'Yonec' indicates that she had a personal familiarity with the topography of the southern March in Gwent, where Earl Richard was a dominant and aggressive lord.[15] She may even have had a knowledge of Welsh, since she discusses Brittonic words. Marie was a great lady of the Angevin court, a cousin indeed of the king of France, as well as a kinswoman of many of the great houses of northern France, the western Empire and England. But it was to the Île-de-France of her birth that she proudly gave her cultural allegiance. Perhaps most telling for our purpose is her consciousness of the structure of her own society and the conflicts and stresses within it. Her fables carry glosses which reveal she had firm views about conduct within her class, specifically the conduct of lords towards their dependants, and dependants to their lords, as well as an unsurprisingly low opinion of villeins, whom she thought credulous, immoral and comical, though she also had her class's redeeming belief that it had obligations to the poor. She wrote very much within that school of conduct which emphasized the constant danger that a courtier risks from his two-faced rivals (the *losengiers*), their deceits and plots (see below, pp. 208-11).[16]

Another such transnational character in the cultural world of western Europe was the Jewish convert and physician Peter Alfonsi. He practised at the court of King Alfonso I of Aragon (whose name he took on baptism in 1106), but it is clear

---

[14] Her identification with Mary of Meulan is not by any means undisputed, but in my opinion fits best the many cultural and geographical connections she reveals in her works. For the Meulan family and its intellectual milieu, D. Crouch, *The Beaumont Twins: the Roots and Branches of Power in the Twelfth Century* (Cambridge, 1986), esp. 196–212. The identity was championed by R. D. Whichard, 'A Note on the Identity of Marie de France', in *Romance Studies presented to William Morton Dey*, ed. U. T. Holmes, A. G. Engstrom, and S. E. Leavitt (Chapel Hill, 1950), 177–81, and compellingly argued in Y. de Pontfarcy, 'Si Marie de France était Marie de Meulan', *CCM*, 38 (1995), 353–61. The unapologetic secularity of her *Lais* and *Fables* would tend to rule out rival identifications as an Abbess Mary: Shaftesbury, Barking or Romsey have been suggested, but none of the abbatial candidates proposed originated in the Île-de-France.

[15] She refers in 'Yonec' to the stream of the Dowlais in Gwent, which in fact is a real stream that runs into the Afon Lwyd north of Caerleon; a detail not found elsewhere in the Arthurian canon.

[16] For the social commentary of her *Fables*, which is not found in Latin versions of the 'Ysopet', see *Les Fables*, ed. and trans. (Fr.) C. Brucker (Paris, 1998), 17–18; for her 'resolutely secular' outlook on society, S. Kinoshita and P. McCracken, *Marie de France: a Critical Companion* (Cambridge, 2012), ch. 3.

from his use of sources that he had travelled and practised widely before then in Muslim Iberia. At some time he moved north to England, where a thirteenth-century tradition says that he became a physician to King Henry I (reigned 1100–35). In fact all that can be said on the subject is that Peter was resident in England before 1120, when the Benedictine prior of Malvern referred to him as his master, but that he had been teaching in England for some time is clear by his familiarity with the works of Gilbert Crispin and St Anselm.[17] His miscellany of fables and sermon exempla, called the *Disciplina Clericalis*, contains amongst much other advice a chapter headed *de modo comedendi*, in which he discourses on polite dining to a youth concerned about the impression he might make in a hall. Peter's experience at that point might well have included the halls of Lleida, Rouen and Westminster, where dinners were apparently arranged on much the same criteria. *De modo comedendi* became a basic occidental tract on how to behave at table, circulating widely in schools across Europe. It was much copied and quoted, and was translated into vernacular French.[18]

The later twelfth century produced many such lay characters whose biographies and autobiographies detail their extensive travels and cultural adventures across the Latin Occident and even beyond, and sometimes too their travels crossed social boundaries. A representative example would be the attractive Occitan poet, Raimbaut de Vaqueiras (*c.*1155–1207), born in humble circumstances in the county of Orange. His fortunes were made when his talents earned him around 1180 a place in the household of the young Boniface of Montferrat as his retained poet and body squire. It was a time when Occitan verse and culture was highly prized in the courts of northern Italy, and Raimbaut was not alone in his day in reaping the benefit in social mobility. The intimacy between Raimbaut and his lord was to parallel the equally famous and contemporary one of William Marshal and the Young King Henry of England. Raimbaut travelled widely both on his own account and with his lord; at various times he was in Provence, Galicia, Aragon and Sicily, where he was knighted by Boniface in 1196 during the course of a military campaign. He participated in the Fourth Crusade, as a result of which his lord Boniface was created King of Thessalonika. Raimbaut likely died at his master's side when he was ambushed and assassinated by his Bulgarian enemies in 1207. Raimbaut's experience and career encompassed the entire northern Mediterranean littoral, and the courts not just of Occitan and Italian princes, but noble crusaders from the north and far west of Europe. To prove it, one of his surviving poems, *Eras quan vey verdeyar*, shows off his linguistic versatility by presenting successive verses in Provençal, Italian, Francien, Gascon and Galician Portuguese.[19]

We occasionally encounter other cultural travellers, who did not become authors but went out into the wider occidental world seeking a courtly education. One was an unnamed Italian boy sent from the papal *curia* to that of Henry II of England in the late 1150s to be taught civility and the management of the hall, which he

---

[17] For a recent critical reassessment of his life, J. Tolan, 'Afterword', in *Petrus Alfonsi and his Dialogus: Background, Context, Reception*, ed. C. Cardelle de Hartmann and P. Roelli (Florence, 2014), 371–7.
[18] *Chastoiement d'un père*, 39–219.   [19] Raimbaut, 4–37, 191–8.

achieved to his credit, according to Bishop Arnulf of Lisieux.[20] Hermann, margrave of Thuringia, was a youth at the court of King Louis VII of France, and there was an idea at the time that there ought to be traffic going the other way. Duke Henry the Lion of Saxony in the 1160s deliberately fostered a similar sort of cultural interchange—rather like a medieval Erasmus programme—when he wrote to Louis inviting him to send French noble squires to the Saxon court to get acquainted with the Empire and its German culture and language.[21] This was in fact not all that precocious. It was a natural development of the widespread and universal occidental social practice of fostering adolescent youths which is only rarely visible to the historian.[22] But when it can be observed, we find male children could travel quite some distance for their courtly education, thus helping form a cultural network at the highest level of medieval society that had no reference to the frontiers of its realms. Occasionally fosterage was perceived as such by a medieval writer, as Geoffrey of Monmouth appreciated in 1136 when meditating on what made the imaginary court of Arthur so very influential.[23]

Great and celebrated courts naturally attracted youths from neighbouring and sometimes distant lands. Ramon, the younger son of Duke William IX of Aquitaine, who became prince of Antioch (1136–49), was at the court of Henry I of England in 1129 and according to William of Tyre was fostered there.[24] English boys went in the other direction. So a son of William d'Aubigny (I) earl of Arundel and Queen Adeliza, who came to be known as 'Godfrey the Englishman', was sent to the Empire in the 1160s to be brought up at the court of Brabant, whose duke was Adeliza's great-nephew.[25] William de Mandeville, younger son and eventual heir of Earl Geoffrey (I) of Essex (and a possible dedicatee of Marie de France's *Fables*) was fostered in the 1160s into the glamorous and powerful court of Count Philip of Flanders and Vermandois, the social leader of the Western aristocracy of his day.[26] The young Arnold (II) of Guines was admirably schooled in manners and military skills at the same court in the 1170s. Most particularly, the boy Arnold was cele-brated in his time there as a youth 'outstanding in every civility of the court'.[27] It went without saying that Arnold and William and their like would mix in Count Philip's halls with the gilded youth of northern Europe's elite families, acquiring a

---

[20] *The Letters of Arnulf of Lisieux*, ed. F. Barlow (Camden Society, 3rd ser., 61, 1939), 18–21.

[21] Bumke, *Courtly Culture*, 84. L. Fenske, 'Der Knappe: Erziehung und Funktion', in *Curialitas. Studien zu Grundfragen der höfisch-ritterlichen Kultur*, ed. J. Fleckenstein (Göttingen, 1990), 83–4, observes the lack of corresponding sources for the German royal court, though discusses the fostering of the adolescent Sven, son of King Eric of Denmark, at the court of Conrad III in the 1130s.

[22] For studies of fosterage and its many suggested motivations across European cultures, Ll. Beverley Smith, 'Fosterage, Adoption and God-Parenthood: Ritual and Fictive Kinship in Medieval Wales', *Welsh History Review*, 16 (1992), 1–35; C. Dette, 'Kinder und Jugendliche in der Adelsgesellschaft des frühen Mittelalters', *Archiv für Kulturgeschichte*, 76 (1994), 1–34.

[23] *The Historia Regum Britannie of Geoffrey of Monmouth*, ed. and trans. N. Wright (Cambridge, 1991), 190–1.

[24] J. P. Phillips, 'A Note on the Origins of Raymond of Poitiers', *EHR*, 106 (1991), 66–7.

[25] Crouch, *Aristocracy*, 34, where other exotic fosterings of English youth are noted.

[26] *The Book of the Foundation of Walden Monastery*, ed. and trans. D. Greenway and L. Watkiss (Oxford, 1999), 44.

[27] Lambert of Ardres, 603, *in omni curiali facecia preclarus*.

common culture of manners and amusements, making friends, and no doubt also striking up rivalries which would form their later political lives. Mandeville was knighted by the count, and was in his household when he heard of his brother's death and his inheritance of the earldom of Essex in 1166. He returned to the court of Flanders on several occasions after he came into his inheritance and earldom, accompanying Count Philip on his 1177 pilgrimage to Jerusalem.[28] Such interchange also embraced the fringe cultures of Europe. The practice of diplomatic hostage-taking meant that boys (and increasingly girls) were sent for long periods of their childhood and youth into foreign courts.[29] This was the case in the eleventh and twelfth centuries in Britain. The itinerant courts of the Norman and Angevin kings of England were host to the children of Welsh, Norse, Gaelic and Galwegian royal houses, and we can sometimes document the powerful impact that mainstream occidental culture had on these outsiders, which it is all too tempting to see as an early manifestation of 'Stockholm syndrome'.

The Gaelic princes Donnchad (Duncan) and Dauvit (David), sons of King Máel Coluim III Ceann Mór of Alba, were at different times resident as youths at the courts of the Conqueror and his sons. Both were put through the rite of the delivery of arms at the king's hands, which made them knights, whose military culture they embraced. Donnchad was briefly king in 1094 and proved a cultural Francophile, maintaining a friendship with William II Rufus and a presence at his court. It also led to a nativist reaction against his rule that eventually ended with his death at the hands of his Gaelic aristocracy. Donnchad took a seal on which he was depicted as a knight, while Dauvit was to become a fixture on the tourneying circuit of northern France in the 1120s, participating in that definitively occidental elite cultural exercise, which the Scottish aristocracy was to embrace under his leadership.[30] The Anglo-Scottish dynasty of Máel Coluim III and Margaret which presided over the north of Britain was notoriously one where the common Latin European culture was appreciated and cultivated. King Alexander I of Scotland (died 1124), was celebrated by Ailred of Rievaulx in Bedan terms as 'a man learned in Latin (*litteratus*) very concerned with the building of churches, acquiring holy relics and the production of books of theology'.[31] William of Malmesbury also remarked on the intellectual pretensions of King Alexander's brother David, enthusing: 'It is without doubt a characteristic of your family to love the study of letters for, to say nothing of other members...your sister [viz. Queen Mathilda II of England] among her other virtues never ceased to support good literature and advance those who were devoted to it.'[32]

[28] *De Oorkonden der Graven van Vlaanderen*, ed. T. de Hemptinne, A. Verhulst, and L. De Mey, (3 vols, Koninklijke Academie van Belgie and Koninklijke Commissie voor Geschiedenis, Verzameling van der Akten der Belgische Vorsten, Brussels, 2009) 2: 142–3, 3: 338–9; *The Book of Walden*, 52–8.
[29] A.J. Kosto, *Hostages in the Middle Ages* (Oxford, 2012), 68–77.
[30] For Donnchad's knighting in 1087, *The Chronicle of John of Worcester* 3, ed. P. McGurk (Oxford, 1998), 48, and for career and his seal, A.A.M. Duncan, 'Yes, the earliest Scottish charters', *Scottish Historical Review*, 78 (1999), 2–13. For David's tourneying and the subsequent spread of the sport to Scotland, D. Crouch, *Tournament* (London, 2005), 20, 40–1.
[31] *Genealogia regum Anglorum* in, *PL*, 195, col. 736.   [32] Malmesbury, *GRA*, 1: 4.

We can occasionally glimpse the same cross-cultural exchange in later decades, though its result was not always a happy one. The court of Hugh de Lacy, lord of Meath in Ireland, was host to a noble Gaelic youth, one Gilla gan-nathair Ua Miadaigh, who regrettably took it into his head in 1186 to decapitate his host, which he accomplished with some finesse and even escaped with his life.[33] An apparently happier guest in a foreign culture was the Anglo-Scottish boy Patrick, younger son of the *mormair* Gospatric (II) of Dunbar, who is found in Yorkshire in the early 1160s in the entourage of the widowed Countess Isabel de Warenne (who was herself a first cousin of the then Scottish king, Máel Coluim IV).[34] The young Welsh aristocrat Owain ap Cadwgan of Powys, enticed into an alliance with King Henry I, was another alien favoured by a grant of arms; he subsequently enlisted in the Anglo-Norman armies in France, where he found himself quite at home.[35] A later Welsh hostage at Henry II's court, Hywel ap Rhys ap Gruffudd of Deheubarth, spent thirteen years there man and boy, and his acculturation is testified both by his Welsh soubriquet 'Sais' (the Saxon) and his well-attested subsequent loyalty to the Angevin kings of England, in whose armies he fought.[36] We can imagine, though not so easily document, the similar reaction that Scandinavian and Slavic youths might experience as hostages in the principalities of the Empire, or even Moorish ones in Spain.[37]

THE PROBLEM OF LATIN SOURCES

The principal sources used in the following study are what you might call 'conduct tracts', though that is a wide umbrella of a designation. Occidental Europe from around 1100 onwards has left us with a rich and expanding legacy of such works, richer and more extensive than is often appreciated and by no means all in Latin. To make this all the more concrete to medievalists as a genre, there have been projects to list and categorize such works for the medieval centuries, the most comprehensive offered by Claude Roussel in 1994.[38] As a genre conduct literature can

---

[33] C. Veach, *Lordship in Four Realms, the Lacy Family, 1166–1241* (Manchester, 2014), 66–7.

[34] Leeds University, Brotherton Library, Yorkshire Archaeological Society Collection, DD5/3/1. For Patrick son of Gospatric, lord of Hirsel and Greenlaw, E. Hamilton, *Mighty Subjects: the Dunbar Earls in Scotland, c.1072–1289* (Edinburgh, 2010), 79–82.

[35] *Brut*, 80–2.

[36] For comment on such Welsh–English interchange, see F. Suppe, 'Interpreter Families and Anglo-Welsh Relations in the Shropshire-Powys Marches in the Twelfth Century', in *Anglo-Norman Studies*, 30 (2007), ed. C. P. Lewis (Woodbridge, 2008), 196–212.

[37] The placing of noble Slavic youths in the households of tenth- and eleventh-century emperors is certainly known, as with Mieszko prince of the Poles; see Bruno of Querfurt, *Epistola ad Henricum regem*, ed. J. Karwasinska, in *Monumenta Poloniae Historica* (new series, 4: 3, Warsaw 1973), 97–106.

[38] The primary catalogue of medieval conduct literature is A. A. Hentsch, *La littérature didactique du moyen âge* (Cahors, 1903), though it is not analytic in its approach. For that see J. W. Nicholls, *The Matter of Courtesy: Medieval Courtesy Books and the Gawain-Poet* (Woodbridge, 1985), App. B; C. Roussel, 'Le Legs de la Rose: Modèles et préceptes de la sociabilité médiévale', in *Pour une histoire des traités de savoir-vivre en Europe*, ed. A. Montandon (Clermont-Ferrand, 1994), 1–90; and see also R. L. Krueger, 'Introduction', in *Medieval Conduct Literature*, ed. M. D. Johnston (Medieval Academy Books, no. 111, Toronto, 2009), pp. ix–xxxiii.

have many motivations, but what basically defines it is a concern to instil youth with an appreciation of the social norms which define superior behaviour.[39] In such works the youth (male or female) it addresses is being educated for the public world of the hall, which housed the theatre of the court. So in medieval parlance superior conduct was *cortoisie, curialitas or hofzuht*: conduct fit for the court.[40]

Broad though it is, some works associated with the genre do not quite fit into it under closer examination. Latin literature can be particularly problematical. There is no doubting the great resource that medieval clerical writers on conduct found in Cicero's *De Officiis* or Ovid's *De Amore*, and we can readily find traces of Ciceronian vocabulary and ideas penetrating the unambitious school exercises of Daniel of Beccles.[41] And since Daniel evidently designed his teaching for youngsters destined for lay occupations, it may well therefore be that some tinge of Ciceronian ideals reached the lay mind in the twelfth century. Another such conductor was Wernher von Elmersdorf's vernacular *Tugendspiel*, which was intended to present a compendium of Stoic moral observations to his German readers, who need not necessarily have been clerics.[42] William of Conches, the tutor of the future King Henry II of England in the 1140s, lavishly excerpted *De Officiis* in his works for the benefit of his students. Sometimes classical influence went as far as emulation. The northern French writer Andrew the Chaplain produced a provocative tract on conduct in sexual relations between social groups in a mischievous imitation of Ovid's style. John of Salisbury's moral tract *Entheticus de Dogmate Philosophorum* might also be taken as just such a work. He does after all proclaim that 'the Latin world held nothing greater than Cicero', though he meant the compliment to reflect on Cicero's Latin prose rather than the great man's personal conduct.[43] But though John certainly aimed to describe behaviour which is moral and pleasing to God, his book is not addressed to youth but to the author's peers, and makes no pretence to be courtly by educating in conduct in the hall, quite the reverse in fact. John portrayed the English court under its new king, William of Conches's pupil, as a sink of heedless immorality. His work condemns the court and does not prepare the reader to enter it. Apart from one brief paragraph on the behaviour of a guest in someone else's hall (*hospitium*), the work offers little that could be characterized as practical guidance at all.[44]

Another way that supposed Latin conduct literature can be problematical is in its intentions towards its audience. This would be particularly true of works written in the Catonian (or pedagogic) tradition. Their ultimate inspiration was that

---

[39] On genre in history source criticism, an evocative survey is R. Cohen 'Introduction: Theorizing Genres', *New Literary History*, 34 (2003), pp. v–xv. A study of hypotextual change in history-writing by the same author, relating it to changes in the parallel field of literary criticism, is 'Genre Theory and Historical Change', in *Theoretical Essays of Ralph Cohen*, ed. J. L. Rowlett (Charlottesville, VA, 2017), 145–69.

[40] Bumke, *Courtly Culture*, 57–60.

[41] Jaeger, *Courtliness*, 115–19; Whelan, *Making of Manners*, 40–1.

[42] D. Rocher, 'Tradition latine et morale chevaleresque (à propos du *Ritterliches Tugendsystem*)', *Études germaniques*, 19 (1964), 127–41.

[43] John of Salisbury, *Entheticus Maior and Minor*, ed. and trans. J. van Laarhoven (Studien und Texte zur Geistesgeschichte des Mittelalters, 17, 1987), 185 (l. 1215).

[44] Ibid., 200 (ll. 1463–74), 207 (ll. 1597–1618).

compendium of commonplace moral reflections called the *Disticha Catonis*, a work actually of the late third century, but Christianized and revised in a standard form known as the *Cato Novus* by around 1000.[45] Its importance was not so much in the depth of its moral reflections ('you came naked into the world, so bear poverty with patience') but in its developing use in the schools as a primary reader for the instruction of younger children in Latin.[46] Cato's distichs feature already as one of the four standard texts for Latin beginners by 1000, so we can be sure that most youths schooled in their letters—whether intended for the clergy or not—came into contact with them. The fact that most of the distichs contained moral reflection means that twelfth-century writers who wanted to create supplementary teaching texts for more advanced pupils would also write them within the same concern: conduct.[47] And so a rather strange but widespread paremiological subgenre of conduct literature formed whose home was in the schoolroom and which propagated a low-level *cultus virtutum* amongst Europe's literate youth. The problem with such works for the social historian is quite how far they can be taken as any reliable guide to medieval expectations of behaviour.

A case in point is one of the two twelfth-century Facetus poems, the one known as *Moribus et Vita*. The manuscript tradition indicates a German provenance, though it certainly circulated also in France and Spain.[48] Most of it is organized in unrhymed distichs, but the longer version expresses itself in more extended reflections. It was designed for older adolescents; for instance, it offers useful career advice. It fits best the students to be found in the *magna schola*, the high school, those between 10 and 15 years of age. Its themes do not just deal with moral conduct and public decorum; it also has rather a lot to say about sexual satisfaction. *Moribus et Vita* is full of good advice about not attempting the virtue of nuns or married women, or seeking satisfaction in brothels, but fixing on the young widow or virgin girl as the most satisfactory target for a teenager's sexual ambition. It considerately offered a step-by-step guide to the seduction of a girl, with the advice that if she tried to back out when the pair were down to skin on skin she should be taken by force, as that's what she really wants, and of course it must be true, because smirking Ovid said it was.[49]

---

[45] R. Hazelton, 'The Christianisation of "Cato": the *Disticha Catonis* in the light of late medieval commentaries', *Mediaeval Studies*, 19 (1957), 157–73; T. Hunt, 'The *Auctores* and the "Liber Catonianus"', in *Teaching and Learning Latin in Thirteenth-Century England* (3 vols, Cambridge, 1991), 1: 59–79; Roussel, 'Les legs de la Rose', 3–4.

[46] As a twelfth-century author of a list of required reading for the young puts it, 'After the child has learned his alphabet and is instructed in other basic grammar suitable for his age, he should be given and should learn from that useful little moral compendium which is generally called Cato's'; Latin text in Hunt, 'The *Auctores* and the "Liber Catonianus"', 79, from Cambridge, Gonville and Caius College MS 385, discussed in C. H. Haskins, 'A List of Text-Books from the close of the Twelfth Century', in *Studies in the History of Medieval Science* (Cambridge, Mass., 1924), 356–76.

[47] For the relationship between grammar and ethics in the teaching of the *parva schola*, P. Delhaye, *Enseignement et morale au xiiᵉ siècle* (Paris, 1988), 83–134.

[48] *Moribus et Vita* is often dated to the early thirteenth century, but its matter and the nature of its reflections do not justify so late a date.

[49] For Ovid in the twelfth-century schoolroom, R. J. Hexter, *Ovid and Medieval Schooling* (Münchener Beiträge zur Mediävistik- und Renaissance-Forschung, 38, Munich, 1986). For the Ovidian aspirations

One might get the idea from *Moribus et Vita* that the theory and practice of rape was on the school syllabus for a medieval adolescent boy and that sexual violence was acceptable in medieval conduct. But that would be to take the poem as more than it was. Such misogynistic and sexual passages in the classroom, which outrage modern sensibilities, were not regarded all that kindly in the twelfth century either. Consider the context: a medieval schoolroom on a warm afternoon with the master confronted by a class of dozy and distracted hormonal teenagers. How better for a lazy teacher to acquire and maintain their attention than to set them passages to paraphrase in Latin or render into the vernacular which are, to say the least, risqué and louche, and reflect male erotic fantasies? This medieval instructional mode has acquired a typology, erotodidacticism—instruction assisted by sexual titillation. A teacher who employed it in a modern high school would quite rightly be subject to immediate discharge and investigation of the hard drive of his computer. Nor was such a method regarded highly in the Middle Ages. It must be of such clerical masters that Stephen de Fougères says around 1160:

> Pure he should be in body and in speech
> so, be it far from one whose task's to preach,
> to foster idle talk in silly schools
> cracking jokes to brainless fools.[50]

So the genre of *Moribus et Vita* is not strictly conduct literature, though its subject matter is conduct; its genre lies within a recognizable line of pedagogical texts, and any deduction about expectations of medieval conduct drawn from its verses needs to be crafted with some caution. On the other hand, later generations might well take such works at face value and use them as moral handbooks. This can best be seen when they cross linguistic boundaries out of the schoolroom and into the vernacular. Cato's *Distichs* were circulating by 1200 in at least three Anglo-Norman versions known collectively as the *Livre Catun*, which are not simply translation aids but posture as moral literature.[51] It is also true that Cato gained a reputation wider than the schoolroom in the twelfth century. In the *Tristan*, for instance, Béroul puts the (translated) words of the pseudo-Cato into the mouths of King Mark's barons when they implored their lord not to go unescorted into solitary places.[52] And before the end of the twelfth century an English master called Robert of Ho had constructed a large moral compendium in Anglo-Norman (known as the *Enseignements Trebor*) framed largely around Cato, discoursing on and developing at length many of his moral maxims for—one assumes—more general edification than the schoolroom, though precisely what audience he had in mind is not an easy question to answer. But Robert of Ho does seem to have believed that the wisdom of Cato would be to the benefit of the conduct of any reader, clerical or lay.

---

of *Moribus et Vita*, F. Ziino, 'Alcune osservazioni sul *Facet* catalano,' in *La narrativa in Proenza e Catalogna nel XIII e XIV secolo* (Rome, 1994), 185–215.

[50] *Livre des Manières*, 42, c. 87.

[51] For the vernacular diffusion of the *Disticha*, Krueger, 'Introduction', in *Medieval Conduct Literature*, p. xiii; Schulze-Busacker, *Didactique*,104–6.

[52] Roussel, 'Les legs de la Rose,' 4.

Particularly problematical in this context is the text that I and others have called 'the earliest English conduct book', a verdict which it turns out is not really sustainable. This is the work called the *Urbanus Major* by its sole editor to date, but called by others the *Liber Urbani*, which is neatly translated by Robert Bartlett as the 'Book of the Civilised Man'. Of its author we know little other than his name, Daniel of Beccles, that he can be identified as a married clerk of that Suffolk town, and that he made his living principally as a schoolmaster.[53] The date of the compilation of the work, as we presently have it, seems locatable in the years between 1177 and 1183.[54] Although it is of English provenance, copies appear in French libraries already in the early thirteenth century. It evidently circulated widely by 1200 and by 1250 was a fixture in the libraries of Augustinian houses, including those of the order's provincial chapter abbeys of St Victor of Paris, St Thomas of Dublin and St Mary de Pratis in Leicester.

The *Liber Urbani* is a large and miscellaneous work of 2,840 hexameters, which makes it one of the more substantial conduct works of the Middle Ages. It has many things to say about proper conduct, some of them quite surprising if taken as straightforward conduct literature. But it is all too evidently intended as another advanced supplement to the school texts of the *Auctores*, not least because several of its passages develop themes from the *Disticha Catonis*. The work's organization and, in particular, the use of process marks or 'paraphs' in the four earliest surviving manuscript texts tell us the lost autograph texts were subdivided by the author into thematic exercises and distichons for the convenience of the masters who used them. It is not by any means the first such work to survive. The fourth book of the remarkable early compilation, the *Liber Jacobi*, contains just such a schoolbook, originally designed perhaps in Navarre in the early twelfth century to interest children in grammar by asking them to correct and paraphrase Latin adventure stories, with the aid of pictures. It circulated very widely across western Europe and was copied in Paris within a generation.[55] *Liber Jacobi* and the didactic works of the French master John of Garlande, just like the *Liber Urbani*, contain testing exercises in specialized vocabulary, such as Daniel's listing of the provisions necessary for a castle garrison; items needed for a well-stocked hall; and qualities that make wives repulsive to their husbands.[56] The *Liber Urbani* was, furthermore, written by a master who was also perhaps a little too fond of the erotodidactic method and knew male adolescent compulsions all too well, as we find amongst other things in his explanation of what not to do with the erect penis.[57]

The problem with using this text as a source for analysing medieval conduct is therefore the same we find with *Moribus et Vita*, but on a much larger scale. What makes the *Liber Urbani* particularly irritating to the social historian in this context is that its reflections have an undeniable value for the study of the medieval *habitus*.

---

[53] F. Lachaud, 'L'Enseignement des bonnes manières en milieu de cour en Angleterre d'après l'Urbanus magnus attribué à Daniel de Beccles', in *Erziehung und Bildung bei Hofe*, ed. W. Paravicini and J. Wettlaufer (Stuttgart, 2002), 53; Whelan, *Making of Manners*, 16–18.

[54] For dating see Appendix, p. 310.

[55] C. Hohler, 'A Note on Jacobus', *Journal of the Warburg and Courtauld Institutes*, 35 (1972), 33–48.

[56] *Liber Urbani*, ll. 1862–75, 2014–24, 2218–31.   [57] *Liber Urbani*, ll. 1991–6.

It might be added that contemporaries were themselves aware of the deficiencies of the *Liber Urbani* as a text through which to acquire moral conduct. There exists in the Bodleian Library a later thirteenth-century florilegium which abstracts 445 lines from the *Liber Urbani*.[58] The florilegist rubricated his abstracted distichs as 'Prouerbia Urbani', selecting each distichon for its moral content and deliberately omitting those he found less than moral. In effect he edited, bowdlerized and improved the *Liber* so as to convert it from a Latin exercise book into the book of conduct historians have taken it to be. The problem for social historians in dealing with such sources is this: many of the numerous twelfth-century Latin texts which have been understood to teach conduct turn out to have quite another purpose, one which limits them as sources for social history. But on the other side of the coin, the Catonian tradition did pervade the twelfth-century clerical and secular elite. The rhetoric of moral conduct informed its world view, and it was an outlook that then readily pollinated vernacular literature, where the true and full flowering of medieval conduct literature occurred.

THE PROBLEM OF VERNACULAR SOURCES

When we turn to vernacular conduct literature, we also find certain texts whose intention is not as straightforward as might appear at first sight. There was, however, a group of twelfth-century works which did have the frank purpose of teaching superior conduct to the socially aspiring and which fully meet the criteria of the genre. These are the works called in Occitan *ensenhamens*. The Occitan examples are by lay authors and address a lay audience in the vernacular specifically on social conduct which is acceptable and praiseworthy and which will get favourable notice; they give a broad range of advice on a variety of social situations. They have been recognized since the 1980s as a distinct subgenre particularly evident in the south of France and Catalonia, when Don Monson's pioneering generic study listed nine of them between the mid twelfth and fourteenth century meeting the criteria he set out.[59] Three of these date from before 1180: those of Garin lo Brun, Arnaut-Guilhem de Marsan and Arnaut de Mareuil. However, it seems now that the *ensenhamens* of the south were not quite so regional a genre as was once thought, though the Occitan examples may well have developed them in new ways. Northern French parallels can be found as early as the 1180s, and something that looks quite like one is embedded in the Latin *Ruodlieb*, a work originating in late eleventh-century Bavaria. Historians of the Carolingian world would rightly point out that the principal features and even the sentiments of the ninth-century Latin tract addressed by Dhuoda of Septimania to her son are exactly what one would expect from a twelfth-century *ensenhamen*. Literary historians might also point out generally that the *ensenhamen* fits broadly into a much older form of literature where a wise man explains the way of the world to a youth, as Jesus son

[58] Oxford, Bodleian Library MS Rawlinson C 552, esp. fo. 19v.
[59] A. Monson, *Les ensenhamens occitans: essai de définition et délimitation du genre* (Paris, 1981).

of Sirach did in Ecclesiasticus or the pseudo-Aristotle did for Alexander of Macedonia in the *Secretum Secretorum*.

The three Occitan works listed above, however, are rather more prescriptive than such general works. They provided a twelfth-century insider's view of a lay society which did not then believe that superior conduct lay at all in the Christianized ethical conduct that came to be assigned to knighthood. This is evident already in the earliest of them. Garin lo Brun's *E·l termini d'estiu* was the work of a castellan-poet of the Auvergne directed principally (though not solely) at the conduct of women, and hence doubly important as a conduct work. It might very well date to deep within the first half of the twelfth century, as Garin was dead by 1162. It opens by pondering gloomily on the way men can get to the point of derangement by their search for love and sexual satisfaction, before the author gets on to the subject in hand: what sensible conduct is for a woman. He does not tell us or otherwise indicate that the advice and analysis he presents is derived from any source outside his own head.[60] Garin's work might very well have had precursors, not least earlier Occitan poetry on the subject of the madness that females inspire in men, but otherwise I tend to believe most of its reflections are Garin's alone, generated out of the social habitus in which he lived. This can be best seen in his resort to paremiological turns of phrase such as 'a man of few words is thought more of than someone who spouts drivel',[61] for which you can find easy parallels in both Cato's distichs and Ecclesiasticus, though the saying need not have been drawn from either.

When Garin addressed his *amia*, his 'dear lady friend', it was for the most part to give her gendered and pragmatic advice on her hygiene and dress; the selection of her maidservants; the way she should walk or ride her palfrey to church; her hospitality to her guests, however objectionable they may be; and how to gauge precisely the degree of effusiveness with which to treat men in her hall. Restraint in speech is one theme he broached that spans gender. It featured in almost all conduct literature down the ages, for Solomon, Cicero, Seneca, Cato, Hincmar and Dhuoda of Septimania all tell us this in one way or another. Garin urged it when he warned that too much attention by a woman to the wrong sort of man might well encourage him and spark gossip. Garin is all too well aware of the male capacity for self-delusion in dealing with women, and saw that as the danger in intersexual relations, not women's sexual voracity, which is the hackneyed assumption found in the contemporary work of clerics such as Stephen de Fougères in his *Livre des Manières*. Also (unlike Stephen) Garin urged women that, for all the dangers it might pose, they should make the most of their natural high spirits and playfulness, which is what clearly fascinated Garin personally about women.

But most significantly for this book, Garin at one point altogether abandoned gendered concerns and broached the great theme of *cortesia* or, as we might say, 'Courtliness', in what is the earliest vernacular analysis of it as a conscious mode of superior conduct: 'for', as he says, 'the one who pursues it is respected by everyone so long as he demonstrates it'. Courtliness was for Garin literally *savoir vivre*: a

<hr/>

[60] *E·l termini d'estiu*, ll. 165–70.   [61] *E·l termini d'estiu*, ll. 341–2.

courtly person was one who knew what to say or do in any circumstance, which tallies nicely with what Bourdieu would say about a person in tune with their habitus and comfortable in how to make his social choices.[62] Garin went so far as to examine why it was that honest and upstanding folk of low birth could be credited as being courtly, becoming thus the earliest medieval writer to speculate as to why it is that natural aptitude rather than birth can produce superior conduct at all levels of society.[63] This is what makes his *E·l termini d'estiu* such an important text. It is an intelligent and independent insider's view of conduct amongst the twelfth-century aristocracy, which Garin regarded as a body of skills which could be taught to the receptive. Garin lo Brun was a 'conductor', a confident and comfortable resident within his habitus who consciously formulated for his fellows what he thought their conduct and social choices should be. And he calls that conduct 'Courtliness'.

However, for all the potential of vernacular conduct literature, those vernacular works produced by clerics before 1200 pose problems for the reconstruction of contemporary mores which the lay *ensenhamens* and *enseignements* do not. Clerical tracts generally had the same ethicizing mission as is found in the contemporary teaching of the liberal arts, and the same overtly moralizing intent as found in the Latin schoolbooks.[64] This tends to compromise, or at least devalue, clerical precepts as being genuinely educative in the superior conduct that would be encountered in the context of the hall. There is also the problem that it is never entirely certain precisely what audience clerical literature in the vernacular was intended for. Two twelfth-century examples illustrate this problem. Stephen de Fougères's *Livre des Manières* was a work by a Breton cleric working in England, probably dating to around 1160, and it broadcast its reactionary message to almost every condition of man and woman in his society on every available frequency.[65] Its most extensive passages excoriate women and their moral failings in the misogynistic vein of the more austere pastoral theology of the day, with barely a nod towards the idea of the Good Woman. The conclusion follows that the work is not so much conduct literature as vernacular notes for those sermons categorized as *ad status*: homilies on the different conditions of Christian as to his or her duty.[66] It is 'Salomonic' in inspiration; it looks back to biblical Wisdom literature as its ultimate inspiration, as its opening invocation of Solomon tells us. The *Livre des Manières* is not by any means worthless for our purposes here, as its dialectic between ideal and reality in kings, knights, bishops, priests, peasants and merchants has a contemporary reference for the 1150s and 1160s. But its intent and audience put it at one remove from common expectations of general and superior conduct in twelfth-century society.

---

[62] *E·l termini d'estiu*, ll. 421–9.   [63] *E·l termini d'estiu*, ll. 437–66.
[64] Jaeger, *The Envy of Angels*, 118–79.
[65] The latest edition mistakenly dates the work to Stephen's tenure of the see of Rennes (1168–78); see *Le Livre des Manières*, ed. and trans. (Fr.) J. T. E. Thomas (Louvain, 2013), 9–10. For dating see below, Appendix, p. 311.
[66] M. Zier, 'Sermons of the Twelfth-Century Schoolmasters and Canons', in *The Sermon*, ed. B. M. Kienzle (Typologie des sources du moyen âge occidental, fasc. 81–3, 2000), 325–51.

The *Livre des Manières* is a curious as well as revealing work. It combines serious theology, including perhaps a direct reference to John of Salisbury's thinking, as found in his *Policraticus*, with a lively vernacular engagement with social types. A natural assumption is that for a clerical author a resort to the vernacular, particularly in verse, was an extension of his pastoral duty to preach the gospel, and for that reason the *Livre* can be counted as a work of and for the court. It seeks to instruct in duty as much as warn about the consequences of immorality. It has been taken as an early example of a genre of 'estates satire', but for all its fierceness the *Livre* lacks the negativity and deep irony (*inversio*) that we find self-consciously deployed in the widespread and often-copied later twelfth-century Latin poem *Frequenter cogitans*, which is decidedly satirical and entirely negative about the human condition. *Frequenter cogitans* details the various conditions of humanity, only to condemn each utterly and offer warnings of damnation, not ways to make amends, as Stephen does.[67] The satirical use of the theme of the social estates would seem to derive rather from the harsh intellectual environment of the schools than the environs of the court.

The resort of an author to the vernacular might also be a leisure pursuit, to amuse himself and his friends. It was a less serious endeavour than writing in Latin, so the intention of a cleric like Robert of Ho in penning a vernacular tract on conduct needs careful pondering. He was not writing for the school, clearly. His *Enseignements Trebor* is not easy to date conclusively, but there are clear indicators that it belongs to the late 1180s or 1190s. The poem refers (lines 1741ff) to the need to recover the Latin kingdom of Jerusalem and a hope to restore it, which would indicate the aftermath of the events of 1187. It references the *History of the Kings of Britain,* but since it talks of Brutus as conqueror and lord not of Britain but of England, it places it at a time when the legend had been assimilated and nationalized by the Angevin English court. Its identifiable preoccupations correspond best with the last decade of the twelfth century and place it in the same generation as the work of Daniel of Beccles. But unlike the *Liber Urbani* it is not a pedagogic text. Its Catonian reflections would best fit an attempt to take schoolroom morality and turn it into moral literature intended for a more general edification.

A work with a social application which is not immediately to be expected of a proverb collection is *Li Proverbe au Vilain*, a source which Robert of Ho in fact considers. The most socially useful such collection was a courtly anthology, collected and glossed by a member of the cultured household of the great Philip of Flanders and published probably in the year 1176.[68] It was in effect a moral compendium in 280–300 chapters (depending on the reconstructions of the original MS).

---

[67] Since the work of Anthony Lodge there has been a tendency to categorize the *Livre* as an 'estates satire' (A. Lodge, 'The Literary Interest of the "Livre des Manières"', *Romania*, 93 (1972), 479), despite its predicatory hermeneutic between good and bad characters. Tony Hunt treats it as such in considering a rather later product, the *Deyputeysun entre Marcolf e Salomon*, an Anglo-Norman dialogue poem of the thirteenth century; 'Solomon and Marcolf', in *'Por le soie amisté'. Essays in Honor of Norris J. Lacy*, ed. K. Busby and C. M. Jones (Amsterdam, 2000), 203. For *Frequenter cogitans*, the earliest witness is Bibliothèque municipale de Douai, MS 751, fos 1v-2r, where it was copied soon after 1173.

[68] See Appendix, p. 312.

It was known in England before 1190 and inspired imitators, not least the rather shorter *Proverbe au comte de Bretagne*, a work of 54 sayings and glosses generated before 1221 at the Capetian court, and attached to the name of the duke of Brittany, Peter Mauclerc, cousin of King Philip Augustus.[69] Paremiological works such as these are diachronic: they include sayings from a range of historical periods and cultures and are not the product of one mind, only of one compiler. The universality of the message and application of proverbs has in fact been acknowledged since the rhetoricians of the late Roman period.[70] Though used in contemporary contexts, proverbs were obviously in many cases generated in much earlier times, nor did they answer contemporary preoccupations of the time of compilation. Many proverbs certainly long predate the later twelfth century in which they were first compiled in the vernacular.[71] The collection of Latin proverbs and sentences published by Odilo of St-Emmeram in 1054 totalled well over a thousand, of which he had found around a third in the Bible and Fathers, while another hundred were drawn from classical writers. Odilo, moreover, tells us he expected his collection to be used in the schoolroom, as being more wholesome than Cato's distichs for the young mind.[72]

But for the social historian, the chronological rootlessness, or anachronism, of the unadorned proverb is compensated for by the glosses on the meaning of each that the compiler occasionally added in later twelfth-century vernacular collections. These offer a distinctly contemporary social hermeneutic of the compiler's devising. Proverb collections of this sort in the twelfth and thirteenth centuries are not schoolroom products, but a courtly manifestation of literature. For instance, Sanson de Nanteuil's *Proverbes de Salemon* is not in fact a collection of common proverbs, but a vernacular translation of the biblical book of that name commissioned perhaps in the 1140s. However, just like several later proverb collections, it offered moral reflection on its material intended for the domestic edification of an aristocratic family.[73] There is good evidence some such collections were performed in the hall, as we learn in the case of the *Proverbe au Vilain* from its flattering and solicitous opening address to the author's patron, the count of Flanders, a flattery that also surfaces in several later sections. Its arch poetic glosses on common proverbs were certainly meant to amuse an audience which included the author's patron: 'If I leave the lord count's service he'll hear no more of me, and soon I'll be forgotten' (Out of sight, out of mind), and 'I don't worry about poverty, I'll not suffer any loss from which the lord count won't bail me out; so long as I don't bore him I'll always have enough, if he gives me a share of his wealth' (Drink up, if your

[69] J. Martin, *'Die Proverbes au Conte de Bretaigne': nebst Belegen aus germanischen und romanischen Sprachen* (Erlangen, 1892), and see E. Rattunde, *Li Proverbes au vilain. Untersuchungen zur romanischen Spruchdichtung des Mittelalters* (Heidelberg, 1966), 124–9.

[70] Schulze-Busacker, *Didactique*, 16–17.

[71] F. Fery-Hue, 'Proverbes en français', in *Dictionnaire des lettres françaises: le Moyen Âge*, ed. G. Hasenohr and M. Zink (Paris, 1992), 1206–7.

[72] Schulze-Busacker, *Didactique*, 53–4.

[73] *Proverbes de Salemon*, ed. C. C. Isoz (3 vols, Anglo-Norman Text Society, 44, 45, 50, 1988–94) 3: 11–18.

bed's made).[74] Proverbs are often quoted in twelfth- and thirteenth-century romances, and some writers make them a major feature of their work, pausing to comment upon their meaning. None was keener on them than Walter of Arras, one of the key vernacular writers in the framing of the chivalric turn, and the author of accomplished courtly romances.

THE CHIVALRIC TURN

In the final generation of the twelfth century, by which I mean the quarter-century before 1200, there is a shift in the intention and scope of moral literature addressed to the lay elite, which will be the business of the rest of this book to explain. If there is a point at which such an explanation can begin, it is with a particular work of the Paris-educated intellectual Ralph Niger, to which he gave the title *De re militari*. It is a miscellany of a book written in 1187 or 1188. It has been generally received as a work criticizing the crusading movement, though it has a lot more to say than that. It was not an influential work by any means; only one medieval copy survives, and its circulation was limited and local. Its views on knights and knightliness are, however, very significant for the courtly habitus of his day, not least from the fact that till 1183 Ralph was a cleric attached to the household of the Young King Henry, the tourneying paragon of the 1170s. After the king's death, Ralph seems to have found patronage, as did other of the Young King's followers, with his youngest brother, Count John of Mortain. Whatever his origins, which remain stubbornly obscure, Ralph Niger undeniably spent many years in contact with the courts of the younger royal Angevins, in whose very noble households knightly pursuits, festivals and amusements attained a height they previously never had, nor ever were to again according to writers of the next generation.

Ralph wrote his *De re militari* several years after the death of the Young King, in the aftermath of the traumatic collapse of the Latin kingdom of Jerusalem in 1187. So the prologue to his work reflects on the spiritual crisis this posed to the idea of pilgrimage as much as crusade, and even knighthood itself. The book that follows the prologue addressed just this crisis and did it through a moral commentary on knightly insignia and arms, symbols of an order that had now clearly failed Christendom. Ralph's tract is remarkable for the meticulous detail of the knightly equipment of the day which he cites, as much as for the elaborate theological explanation he attaches to each item. He is by no means the first writer to employ this device as a way of lecturing and chastising the errant and fallible Christian. He followed in a literary lineage begun by St Paul. But in this case the *miles Christi* Ralph describes is not simply a representative layman fighting his way through temptation towards salvation; he is intended also to be an idealized *miles* whose

---

[74] *Proverbe au Vilain*, nos 1, 40, 56; see also nos 84, 153. Schulze-Busacker, by contrast, sees the collection as a more formal, bookish product, consciously responding to the literary influence of Serlo of Wilton and French translations of the *Disticha Catonis*; see Schulze-Busacker, *Didactique*, 128–34.

material arms and armaments become sermon points designed to correct the moral failings of the all-too-human knight, for it was incumbent on the knight to be fitted out for the moral leadership of his failing society, a leadership which was beginning to be claimed for him.

This was the product of a time of all-too-rapid social change at the top of Western society, which I call 'the chivalric turn' because one of its symptoms was the emergence of a new and hybrid conduct genre, the chivalric tract. It was also a time of intense debate in schools and halls across Europe on the meaning of the concept of Nobility within society, which was intended to explain why it was that there were men who believed they were entitled to ask the unquestioning deference of their self-defined inferiors. And since these men were almost invariably inaugurated into the condition of knight, it was the knight who was offered as the pattern of what was superior and noble in a human being (women of course being deliberately excluded from the process). By 1210 the turn had been made, and a knight simply by receiving his order was regarded as morally superior and entitled to the deference of anyone who did not share his condition. By the 1270s the word *'chevalerie'*, which had long had in Romance cultures the dominant sense of 'deeds of arms', was used by the Catalan lay intellectual, Ramon Llull, explicitly to mean the hypermoral quality which a true nobleman must possess, which was the sense of Chivalry that Enlightenment scholars found in Llull and other later writers, most of whom drew their ideas from the French translation of his work. This book maps the field in which this took place, the anxieties with which it was afflicted, and the moment of hysteresis itself. I won't say that it is easily explained how it was that the concept of social hegemony shifted radically in Western society at the end of the twelfth century, but I will in the final chapter offer some suggestions as to why it may have done.

PART II
THE SOCIAL FIELD

3

The Origins of *Cortesia*

THE SOCIAL VIEWS OF GARIN LO BRUN

Garin lo Brun, castellan of Veillac in the Auvergne (*fl.* 1130–60), whom we have just met in the previous chapter, was a thoughtful man of affairs and, being an accomplished vernacular poet, was able to express his thoughts in becoming style. His was a generation and region where aristocratic circles valued such skills and celebrated them; indeed, literary accomplishment was very much thought a proper pursuit for a southern French aristocrat of his day. In his father's time the leader of that society, Duke William IX of Aquitaine (died 1126), was also its finest exponent of Occitan verse. Duke William's favoured subject of choice was love and its sexual expression, but that was not Garin's principal interest in his surviving verse; it was words and human interaction which fascinated him. He wrote *tensos* (debate poems) exploring contrasting concepts, of which one, *Nueyt e iorn suy en pessamen*, has survived. It weighs up the merits of self-restraint and light-heartedness in social interaction. It is a sophisticated and cultured work. But Garin had greater literary ambitions than *tensos*, and a much longer work of his has survived. It is of a type of composition which literary historians call an *ensenhamen* (or in northern French, an *enseignement*), an instructional tract concerning social conduct. Garin's is in fact the earliest of the genre to survive. Garin's prologue claims that he wrote it for the instruction of a young lady friend who had asked how she might behave in public so as to avoid social awkwardness. So he addressed himself seriously to the way that women should comport themselves and in particular how they should interact with men who might not necessarily have their best interests at heart.

In the course of his *ensenhamen* Garin makes an aside. Between passages on female vivacity (*gaieza*) and female adornment, he hops out of concerns associated with gender and into a different area, one he calls *cortesia*. Indeed, the change of subject is so abrupt, he might well have inserted a separate and earlier composition of his into the bigger project at this point, for this passage is by no means addressed to women alone. I give it here in its entirety:

> Dear lady, if you ever desire to acquire a greater reputation I urge you towards courtliness (*cortesia*), for the one who pursues it is respected by everyone so long as he demonstrates it. Courtliness consists of this – should you wish to know – in being one who knows exactly what to say or do. One ought to love by means of courtliness and keep oneself from bad manners. Someone who knows how to detect foolishness and to avoid unseemly behaviour and to behave agreeably to others can be held to be courteous (*cortes*). Courtliness makes a man to be held in esteem. Not everyone that people call courtly

is in fact of good birth, thus there are respectable people of low origins (*vilan proat*) who are credited as being courteous. The word is generally applied but is often used wrongly; it is applied in a way that does not fit the circumstances. It is easy enough to talk about courtliness but more difficult to attain it, because it is diverse in its expressions and in its forms. It diverges into many branches though it is rooted in but a few places, as a result of which there is nobody who can be definitively said to be courtly. One man may be richly endowed in it and another have barely any of it. Not all are equal, but those who have most are regarded more warmly. Courtliness resides in rich display and in being a gracious host; it lies in doing honour to others and in elevated speech; it lies in offering amusements – the aspect of it which pleases me most! When the time should come, for all the responsibility laid on me I would be unable to describe it in the way I ought to.[1]

Garin writes with becoming diffidence. He quotes no authorities for his views and there is every reason to believe his reflection arose out of his own experience of his aristocratic society and his conversations with friends. It is the view of an aristocrat of the first half of the twelfth century as to what superior social conduct is in his society, and he gives it a name, *cortesia*, which in English we translate as 'Courtliness' or 'courtesy'. Garin thought about *cortesia* a lot, apparently. Elsewhere in his *ensenhamen* he makes other incidental reflections on the subject. He lists *cortesia* as one of a number of desirable and admirable qualities any aristocrat should possess—along with good looks, reputation, family connections, ability and martial accomplishment (*chaballaria*).[2] It was not *cortesia*, Garin says, for a woman to hurry along the road at too fast a pace, or to stumble as she went, so he also thought it comprehended elegant gait.[3] Perhaps most significantly of all, in another passage he produces one of those opposing concepts he liked to explore in his *tensos*. He tells the lady who was to receive his tract that if her conduct (*contenemen*) is in conformity with *cortesia*, she will be kept from 'low behaviour' (*vilania*).[4] There was behaviour which gave you credit in his world, and behaviour which brought you down in people's estimation; indeed he comments that everyone could be courtly (*cortes*) if only people saw in themselves the conduct they condemned in others.[5]

Garin was not writing in intellectual isolation in his tower at Veillac, for there is evidence that he was touching on a wider concern in his early twelfth-century southern French society. This is in the work of the more celebrated professional Gascon poet, Marcabru, Garin's contemporary, a man who was by his own account not an aristocrat. But he too feels qualified to reflect on *cortezia* in his *sirventes* ('opinion piece') *Cortesamen vuoill comenssar*.[6] Though it is a more lightweight composition of only seven stanzas, Marcabru was plainly dealing like Garin with a commonly understood concept of superior social conduct, which both men are attempting to define, teach and pin down, for Marcabru claims he can instruct

---

[1] *E·l termini d'estiu*, 86–8 (ll. 421–66).   [2] *E·l termini d'estiu*, 73 (ll. 57–60).
[3] *E·l termini d'estiu*, 80 (ll. 249–52).   [4] *E·l termini d'estiu*, 75 (ll. 114–22).
[5] *E·l termini d'estiu*, 76 (ll. 157–60).
[6] *Marcabru: a critical edition*, ed. S. Gaunt, R. Harvey, and L. Paterson (Cambridge, 2000), 202–4. See the comments on Marcabru's *cortesia* in D. Nelson, 'Marcabru, Prophet of *Fin'amors*', *Studies in Philology*, 79 (1982), 229–30.

(*enseignar*) even the learned on the subject. Like Garin, he thinks sober and restrained behaviour (*mesura*) is a large part of it, and that anyone who falls from that standard has strayed into low behaviour, *vilania*, which for him is defined by wild speech and absurdity. For Marcabru, however, it is the social benefit of *cortesia* which is perhaps most important, and in particular in dealing with the opposite sex, for '*cortesia* is about loving'.

For these two very different contemporary Occitan writers—and therefore we must assume for their wider society—*cortesia* was a body of social skills which was not necessarily innate to a man or woman, for it could be acquired from a teacher. Although aristocrats would ideally have it, not all of them did, because some of them exhibited *vilania*. And as Garin pointed out, in something of surprise as to where his meditations had led him, even a low-born person (*vilan*) might be *cortes* if he were *proat* ('respectable' or 'upright'). Although Garin's *enseignement* was written for a lady of good birth with her own household, servants and hall to manage, *cortesia* was a set of skills not just for her sort. People of no consequence who interacted with the aristocratic world or stood in a public assembly might be admitted to have them, either through a natural social facility or through a determined effort to acquire them. Nor was Garin alone in thinking this; Marcabru in his *L'autrier jost' una sebissa* pictured himself attempting to seduce a peasant girl, flattering her by suggesting that her quick wit and sense came from her being the offspring of a knight who had taken advantage of a *corteza vilana*.[7] If these imaginary low-borns had *cortesia*, it was because of human aptitude, not birth. For that reason early twelfth-century lay *cortesia* cannot be said to constitute a noble code, for its possession was not thought to be exclusive to the higher orders. It was superior conduct that superior people ought to possess, so as to assist them in their interaction with their peers, their betters, and indeed in securing the object of their desires.

Garin's description of what he took Courtliness to be brings to the fore its utility. Those thought to be courteous got respect (*prez*) in company when they behaved according to its precepts, however understood. Understanding precisely what that might be was not easy, as it was a moving target, shifting with people's appreciation of what it meant to be courtly (which seems to be what the passage about its being generally applied but often used wrongly signifies). People in company observed and internally or openly debated conduct and what was acceptable and unacceptable in it. By debating it they established and sometimes modified it. Social respect and approval were the aim of the courtly because they made other things possible, and that aim energized the debate. The courtly had to have a capacity to sense, say and do the right thing in any situation, to have what we would call 'address', '*savoir vivre*' or 'self-confidence'. Bourdieu would recognize them as those fish happily besporting themselves in the warm waters of a habitus in which they were entirely at home. Such courtly folk must be sensitive to the impact of their remarks, especially to avoid those which might be taken by company as boorish, crude, foolish

---

[7] *Marcabru*, 378–82. It is worth noting here Bertran de Born's comment a generation later that warfare made even the low-born man *cortes*; Bertran, 461: *Gerra fai de vilan cortes*. Though his phrase may be interpreted as referring to a *vilan* as a man of low morals as much as of low birth.

or wild. When Garin said, 'it is easy enough to talk of courtliness but more difficult to attain it, because it is diverse in its expressions and in its forms', he was registering that there can be no hard and fast rule as to what is the courtly choice of thing to do in any situation, as social situations were unpredictable and gaffes inevitable. Even the most courtly person can put a foot wrong; but those 'richly endowed in it' carry off the misstep, presumably because they have the social confidence to retrieve the situation, as Bourdieu's 'conductor' was supposed to do. From Garin's last remarks he found the easiest aspect of it to define was the Courtliness implicit in hosting social events with style, grace and generosity; the Courtliness of a lord such as he was. A host always had the social advantage over his guests.

THE COURTLINESS OF GILBERT OF SURREY AND GEOFFREY GAIMAR

It is no accident that such behaviour as Garin and Marcabru described is called by them *cortesia*. It takes its name from the domestic compound (*curtis*) in which a great person held his court (*curia*) and had his hall (*aula*).[8] *Cortesia* was therefore conduct appropriate to and expected in the public eye; it was also what people had to possess who wished to thrive in such an environment. *Cortesia* was conduct well understood in the lay milieu of Garin lo Brun and Marcabru and, we must assume, throughout their Occitan society in the 1130s and before. So much is unarguable. But establishing this leads to further questions. We cannot assume that Courtliness was confined just to southern France, for all the claims made by some past writers for its sophistication and style over those of other parts of western Europe at the time. The reason Occitania may appear more socially developed is only that its aristocracy cultivated, composed and valued vernacular poetry and offered patronage to professional poets, many of whose works have been fortunately preserved in thirteenth-century compendia. Not that the composition of poetry by lay aristocrats was by itself a claim to social sophistication. Some contemporary Welsh aristocrats did it too in their own vernacular, but their society gets no consequent credit for its sophistication, which may have something to do with the less pleasant, indeed murderous, side to Welsh aristocratic culture, which had a very different view of what was appropriate to its courts.

It may well be that not all medieval courts were 'courtly' in their culture as we would interpret the word. The Welsh example tells us as much. But *cortesia* as a mode of behaviour cannot in fact have been unique to the south of France in the first half of the twelfth century, and there are many ways of proving this. The adjective *curtois* appears in the *Song of Roland*, a northern French work of around 1100, and is significantly applied to the wise *preudomme*, Oliver.[9] In the north of France, we

---

[8] Jaeger, *Courtliness*, 160. Middle High German's words for courtly behaviour (*hoveliche* and *husschliche*) are derived from the *hof* or *hus* in a parallel so perfect, it must be a deliberate translation of the concept from Latin or French.

[9] *Song*, 2: 36 (l. 576), 228 (l. 3755) *Oliver li proz e li curteis*. When characters in the *Song* speak *curteisement*, they do so in deferential attempts to persuade their fellow barons or the emperor himself; *Song*, 2: 74 (l. 1164), 233 (l. 3823).

find *courtoisie* and *vilonie* being written of as opposing forms of conduct in Picardy around 1170.[10] We can find instances beyond the francophone lands too. In Germany soon after 1149 we find that Mark, an Irish-born monk of Regensburg, could write of an accomplished young warrior (*miles*) from Cashel in Munster called Tnúthgal, an admirable youth of good birth with ease of manners (*habilis, affabilis atque jocundis*) who was, Mark says, 'raised in a courtly fashion' (*curialiter nutritus*). His comment perhaps relates more to German society than Irish.[11]

England was another case, and two English writers of the 1130s prove that what we see in the behaviour of the Occitan public person was not an isolated social phenomenon of premature sophistication. Gilbert 'the Knight', sheriff of Surrey, Cambridge and Huntingdon (died 1125), belonged to the generation before Garin lo Brun and Marcabru. He was a member of a curial family in the service of the Norman kings of England. His father, Roger, a man of the Conquest generation (died *c*.1107), had been sheriff of Cambridge and Huntingdon before his son. Gilbert had apparently been a royal household knight before his move into administration, hence his cognomen, Gilbert *miles*, and he had seen action in warfare in Normandy, presumably in the wars between Duke Robert II and his younger brothers in the 1090s and early 1100s. He was the founder of the Augustinian priory of Merton, and not long after his death a canon of the house memorialized his exemplary secular career in a biographical Latin tract. It naturally emphasized his godliness, charity and confessional piety, but it also reflected on the skills that made Gilbert such an outstanding courtier, particularly in securing the affection of the wife of Henry I, Queen Matilda II of England (died 1118), who seems to have been his especial patron at court:

> Counts and barons held him in the highest regard and they recognised his nobility of mind with great gifts. He also had the respect of the lesser attendants of the royal household to the extent that he was treated by them all as if they were his own servants. He was served by them all as well as if he were the king. You might frequently see many bishops and other people of the highest distinction hanging round the door of the royal chamber for long periods, begging to go in, but quite unable to get a hearing. But if Gilbert happened to appear the doors were flung open to admit him, as soon as the ushers knew who it was. He was admitted to the royal presence as often as he wanted. When the sheriffs of England assembled at the exchequer and were all agitated and apprehensive, Gilbert was the only man who turned up unperturbed and cheerful. As soon as he was summoned by the receivers of money, he sent the cash in and he promptly sat among them, quite at his ease, as if he were one of them himself. As everyone who knew him would confirm, it is impossible to underestimate the respect in which he was held, so much was he loved esteemed and praised.[12]

[10] *Ille et Galeron*, 54 (ll. 1617–20).

[11] *Visio Tnugaldi Lateinisch und Altdeutsch*, ed. A. Wagner (Erlangen, 1882), 6. A reference I owe to Keith Busby. That the young should embrace courtly (*hoveliche*) behaviour was a maxim in German literature, as Winsbecke explains; *Winsbecke*, 85, c. 38.

[12] Translated from M. L. Colker, 'Latin Texts concerning Gilbert, founder of Merton Priory', *Studia Monastica*, 12 (1970), 259–60; and see also for this Crouch, *Nobility*, 42–3.

The words appropriated by the canon of Merton to describe his patron are significant. He was *virorum probissimus*,[13] which must be a translation into Latin of the
vernacular term 'preudomme' (for which concept see Chapter 4), but for our purposes here his lifestyle is also characterized by the adjective *curialis*, 'courtly'. The
author of the biographical tract throughout his work acknowledges that Gilbert
operated in the sphere of the royal court with ease and distinction, and if so it was
because he exerted the self-control and projected the imperturbable affability
which our other writers on *cortesia* and *curialitas* commend. Gilbert was to the
author's mind practising self-conscious Courtliness.

We are told that in his own household Gilbert was open-handed to the point of
profligacy, unlikely though that might seem in an official whose primary job was
to collect taxes and dues owed the king in his shires for a set fee, and then reward
himself by creaming off a profit. But his biographer is out to portray his subject as
being a man who was courtly and upright beyond the norm for his sort. So he
notes that Gilbert employed no officers to deny the door of his hall to those seeking his hospitality, but welcomed all and entertained them to the extent he believed
they merited. He could not abide that the quality of the food, horses and clothing
available in his household should be anything less worthy (*honorabilis*), tasteful
(*elegans*), or 'courtly' (*curialis*) than in those of his peers or even his betters. His
biographer turns his outstanding hospitality and largesse into a theological virtue, for
he says Gilbert was thus obeying the injunction of Christ in the Sermon on the
Mount—'Ask and it will be given unto you' (Matt. 7:7)—though the biographer
modifies 'Ask' to 'Give'. Gilbert's heedless generosity demonstrated therefore his faith
and trust in the Lord, and when his household queried its extent he would paraphrase
the evangelist with a shrug: 'Each day brings its own sustenance with it' (*Venit dies,
uenit et cibus eius*).[14] He was particularly devoted to the poor within his areas of jurisdiction, supporting them lavishly in time of famine, a form of devotion he acquired
from his patron, Queen Matilda.[15] The Merton biographer thus provides one of the
earliest moral and theological justifications for the largesse that was so important a
part of lay Courtliness and in due course a recognized component of Chivalry.[16]

The Merton writer's description of his priory's founder as a man at the apex of lay
Courtliness is more than matched in the Courtliness described by his contemporary,
the English historian Geoffrey Gaimar. Gaimar's *Estoire des Engleis* was written most
probably around 1137 in the Anglo-Norman dialect of French. It originally dealt
with the entire history of Britain, but what survives of it now is largely a translation
and elaboration of the Anglo-Saxon Chronicle; though as John Gillingham has
pointed out, its elaborations are both intriguing and highly significant.[17] Gaimar
gave the old English annals a courtly facelift and added passages of his own reflecting
on court life in the reign of King William II Rufus (reigned 1087–1100). Though

---

[13] 'Latin Texts concerning Gilbert', 254.   [14] A likely reference to Matt. 6:34.
[15] 'Latin Texts concerning Gilbert', 260–1.
[16] D. Boutet, 'Sur l'origine et le sens de la largesse arthurienne', *Le Moyen Age*, 89 (1983), 397–411,
and see pp. 76–8 below.
[17] J. Gillingham, 'Kingship, Chivalry and Love. Political and Cultural Values in the Earliest
History Written in French: Geoffrey Gaimar's *Estoire des Engleis*', in *Anglo-Norman Political Culture
and the 12th-Century Renaissance*, ed. C. W. Hollister (Woodbridge, 1997), 33–58.

not to be trusted as history, Gaimar's work is important in two respects: he wrote it to suit the courtly tastes of his patron, a Lincolnshire lady of good family, and to put a contemporary courtly gloss on pre-Conquest English society. He also alluded to his connections with the more exalted circles of his own day, not least Queen Adeliza, widow of King Henry I, herself known as a patron of vernacular literature.[18]

The adjective *curteis* is to be found several times in Gaimar's work, applied to great and small folk alike, and when it is, it is associated with *prodom*. The combination is applied both to King William Rufus and to a humble but loyal fisherman.[19] Gaimar uses the word *curtesie* too on one occasion: when Rufus deflected with finesse a protest among his courtiers, he is said to have 'turned it to *curteisie*',[20] by which he seems to mean Rufus had accomplished a feat of courtly cleverness in deflecting tension, the sort of adroit social manoeuvre Garin lo Brun praised in his *ensenhamen*. Gaimar chose to dwell particularly on Hugh (I) earl of Chester (died 1101) as an example of a distinguished baron of the previous generation, and the description he offers has parallels with the Merton author's description of Gilbert of Surrey:

> Not even the emperor of Lombardy had a larger company than Hugh had in his personal retinue. The door of his house was never closed to any free-born or noble man; the food and drink that he dispensed was less likely to run dry than water in a fishpond or lake. His munificence knew no bounds: however much he might have given away one day, he would remember it on the following day, and then distribute just as much again.[21]

In another passage the same earl got in a tussle over precedence on the occasion of a ceremonial crown-wearing, unhappy at carrying a ceremonial sword before the king of England as being a task beneath his dignity and as reducing him to the status of a servant (*sergant*). When Earl Hugh protested at the indignity, the king gave him as another courtly gesture the golden sceptre to carry, the chief ensign of royalty, for it reflected honour both on him and the earl. Gaimar then took the opportunity to muse (as writers on conduct often do) on the backbiters who rejoice in *Schadenfreude* when a great man at court falls low, but themselves are in danger of just such a fall because they lack largesse, and are instead greedy misers.[22] These meditations from England in the 1130s are all very familiar themes, and taking the Merton material alongside Gaimar, we see facets of a courtly whole behind them.

THE PREHISTORY OF COURTLINESS: DHUODA OF SEPTIMANIA AND BRUN OF COLOGNE

Another question that arises out of the early twelfth-century Occitan sources relates to the antiquity of the lay *cortesia* we find described there. It cannot be true that self-conscious lay *cortesia* suddenly appears out of the blue in the 1130s.

---

[18] *Estoire*, for an analysis of the work, pp. ix–xvi.
[19] *Estoire*, 298 (l. 5505); 316 (l. 5850). As noted in Gillingham, 'Kingship, Chivalry and Love', 42.
[20] *Estoire*, 330 (l. 6096), my translation.   [21] *Estoire*, 316–18 (ll. 5860–72).
[22] *Estoire*, 328 (ll. 6055–76).

Numerous indications tell us otherwise, and though nothing is as explicit as the *ensenhamen* of Garin lo Brun, nonetheless the cumulative evidence is that courts and public assemblies had been modifying the behaviour of their more aspirational inhabitants for well over two centuries before the twelfth century began. I am not talking here about the generalized idea of 'courtly culture'—a diffuse idea embracing the patronage of intellectuals and craftsmen by princes, the construction of halls and palaces, festivities, music, ceremony, and the fostering of youth within the households, all developments which come under the wide umbrella of 'courtly culture'.[23] Courtliness is a more limited concept, the set of social skills and modified behaviour appropriate to the inhabitants of a princely court and household.

With one possible exception, we have no texts of *ensenhamens* such as Garin's before his day: self-conscious vernacular teaching aids for the socially aspirational in a courtly society. That does not mean that there were not analogous texts nor an intellectual interest in cultivating and practising courtly skills before 1100. It is worth noting that the most ancient Occitan text (surviving from around 1000) is no less than a vernacular retelling of the life of Boethius (died *c.*526), author of that ethical work the *Consolatio Philosophiae*, which became a subject of fascination and copious commentary in the Carolingian West after its discovery by Alcuin in the 780s. To study Boethius was to study the life and reflections of an undeservedly wronged courtier, hounded by his enemies, the 'dogs of the court' as he called them.[24] We need to exercise a little caution here on the matter of genre, which is one of the principal concerns of this book. At first sight the ancient genre of 'mirrors for princes' (Ger. *Fürstenspiegel*) might be taken for a species of conduct literature. The *speculum principis* has a generic pedigree going back before the eighth century and an intellectual inspiration going back even further, to St Augustine's *De civitate Dei*. But such 'mirrors' are texts written to urge moral restraint and religious feeling on kings, and are dialogues *with* power, not instruction on ways to facilitate a courtier's demeanour *towards* power. There is, however, an early medieval text which at one point approaches what an *ensenhamen* should be. This is the *Liber Manualis*, a handbook written in the year 841 by Dhuoda, an Aquitanian woman, wife of Duke Bernard of Septimania (that is, the

---

[23] As most broadly examined in the work of Bumke, *Courtly Culture*. Such a broad view of the court and its influence allows the term to be applied to an even earlier period, as in the collected essays, *Court Culture in the Early Middle Ages. The Proceedings of the first Alcuin Conference*, ed. C. Cubitt (Turnhout, 2003).

[24] *Der altprovenzalische 'Boeci'*, ed. C. Schwarze ('Forschungen zur romanischen Philologie', 12, Münster, 1963). For his abiding vernacular influence in France, G. M. Cropp, 'The Medieval French Tradition', in *Boethius in the Middle Ages*, ed. M. J. F. M. Hoenen and L. Nauta (Leiden, 1997), 243–65. For an overview of the author, the text and its reception, H. Chadwick, *Boethius* (Oxford, 1981). Medieval English kings were acquainted with it: Alfred the Great of Wessex famously translated it into his own vernacular around the end of the ninth century as part of his programme for the moral and educational reform of his battered realm—*The Old English 'Boethius': an Edition of the Old English Versions of Boethius's 'De Consolatione Philosophiae'*, ed. and trans. M. Godden and S. Irvine (2 vols, Oxford, 2009)—while William of Conches, King Henry II's tutor, had written an admired gloss on the *Consolatio* before he took up the post; L. Nauta, 'The "Glosa" as Instrument for the Development of Natural Philosophy, William of Conches' Commentary on Boethius', in *Boethius in the Middle Ages*, 9 and n.

Mediterranean coastlands between Barcelona and the River Rhône). It is addressed to her elder son, William, who had just reached 15 years of age, and who was at the time a hostage for his father's behaviour at the court of Charles the Bald, king of West Francia.[25]

Dhuoda's *Liber Manualis* tends to be classified by historians (though not without reservation) as an example of a *speculum principis*. She herself tells her son it is 'a little book of moral teaching' written just for him. It does not in many ways resemble the later *ensenhamen* genre, but it does in a few: to begin with, it was addressed by a concerned elder figure, a mother, to a younger, her teenage son. It was not by any means unusual in later centuries for such a teaching text to be put in the mouth of a woman (as Perceval's mother in the *Conte de Graal*; the Lady of the Lake to the boy Galaaz in the *Prose Lancelot*; or Love, personified as a female, to her suppliant William de Lorris in the *Roman de la Rose*). The *Liber Manualis* was written in Latin by a woman who was an avid reader and a Latin poet, a devotee of word and number games, with access to a useful library when she wrote it at Uzès in the Narbonnais. Dhuoda may perhaps have hoped that her son might have brought her work to the attention of the learned King Charles, and thus earn the family some indirect favour. Hers was not principally a handbook for survival and prosperity at court, it was a substantial miscellany of moral and theological reflection drawn from Scripture and the Fathers, and marshalled for the benefit of her son, himself apparently a keen reader. 'Reflection' is a good word for her writings, as Dhuoda offered her work to her son as a 'mirror' (*speculum*) in which to view his own conduct and indeed a mirror in which he might see her own image across the distance which separated them.[26]

The resemblance of the *Liber Manualis* to a later *ensenhamen* is closest where Dhuoda offered pragmatic advice to her distant boy on how to conduct himself in the dangerous place where he was, the Carolingian court, which she did in Books 3 and 4 of her work. Aided by copious reference to Scripture, she urged William to be loyal to King Charles and apt in his service: he should include the royal kindred in his good service; offer considered counsel if ever asked; choose his friends at court with care; try to look behind the appearance that his fellows put up to the world; not trust those who may not be what they seem; and he must particularly avoid prostitutes. A striking passage urged William to emulate the conduct of the most distinguished members of the court (*optimates*) about him; to acquire the habitus on the job, so to speak.[27] Dhuoda warned her son to be on good terms with everyone in hope of a return, but particularly those by whom he wanted to be acknowledged (*agnosci*), presumably because it was to his advantage to be.[28]

---

[25] Dhuoda, *Handbook for her Warrior Son: Liber Manualis*, ed. and trans. M. Thiebaux (Cambridge Medieval Classics, 8, 1998). For studies of Dhuoda and her views, P. Dronke, *Women Writers of the Middle Ages: A Critical Study of Texts from Perpetua to Marguerite Porete* (Cambridge, 1984), 36–54; M. A. Claussen, 'Fathers of Power and Women of Authority, Dhuoda and the *Liber Manualis*', *French Historical Studies*, 19 (1996), 785–809; V. L. Garver, *Women and Aristocratic Culture in the Carolingian World* (Ithaca, NY, 2009), especially 151–9. For the family, Bouchard, *Blood*, 181–91.

[26] Dhuoda, 27–8.   [27] Dhuoda, 106–8.   [28] Dhuoda, 112.

In theologically coloured terms, Dhuoda urged William to avoid secular quarrels, to eschew pride and adopt humility amongst his fellows.[29]

All of these injunctions of Dhuoda on her son's conduct at the court—cherry-picked here out of a much larger text—are to be found in conduct literature over the next half-millennium written in many realms by many authors in several languages. If this is so, it isn't because the later authors are quoting Dhuoda, which would be impossible. Her written injunctions to her son as regards his behaviour at court were drawn from a pragmatic pool of wisdom and experience that refilled itself in each generation, an environment of which twelfth-century vernacular *cortesia* was to be just one more iteration. We know about *cortesia* because a few writers actually tried to analyse Courtliness for the benefit of readers and gave it a name, as no one had directly done before then. Dhuoda's work certainly survived, in at least two copies in Catalonia and one at Nîmes (near Uzès, where she wrote it). Her genetic inheritance likewise survived through her younger son, Bernard, who gave rise to the line of the poet-prince Duke William IX of Aquitaine, but there can have been no transfer of her ideas and teaching into vernacular consciousness either through family tradition or scholarly reference.

What then can we do to recover the pragmatic wisdom that lurked in the environment of the court before the twelfth century, other than reading between the lines of the text Dhuoda constructed for her son? One answer was provided by Stephen Jaeger in 1985, in his celebrated work *The Origins of Courtliness*. Jaeger proposed to mine the genre of episcopal biographies from tenth- and eleventh-century imperial Germany as a conscious test bed for the sociological insight of Norbert Elias (first published in 1939): that the environment of the court modified the behaviour of its inhabitants who wanted to prosper and gain the favour of the prince. Elias's work on the court is not above criticism, not least because of its poor use of historical evidence and its overriding teleology, tracing the 'process of civilization' by steps from the brutish Iron Age past to the mannered civilization of late nineteenth-century western Europe into which Elias was born.[30] But in one respect it remains a sociological classic: it was the earliest demonstration of how a social habitus (the princely court) can consciously and unconsciously modify the behaviour

---

[29] The self-restraint in behaviour urged on the members of ninth-century Carolingian courts has been noted by several writers; see M. Innes, '"A Place of Discipline": Carolingian Courts and Aristocratic Youth', in *Court Culture in the Early Middle Ages*, ed. Cubitt, 59–60, 69–72, citing particularly Hincmar's *De Ordine Palatii*. It was a theme in Odo of Cluny's mid-tenth-century hagiographical treatment of the ninth-century Auvergnat aristocrat, Gerald of Aurillac (died *c*.909). Though not a source to be trusted on lay expectations, Odo offered circumstantial accounts of the mildness and tolerance of Gerald in company at table and amongst his dependants, also his restraint (though not austerity) in conversation, drinking and dress; *Vita sancti Geraldi Auriliacensis comitis* in, *PL*, 133, cols 639–704, trans. G. Sitwell, in *Soldiers of Christ: Saints and Saints' Lives from Late Antiquity and the Early Middle Ages*, ed. T. F. X. Noble and T. Head (University Park, PA, 1995), 293–362. See esp. *Vita sancti Geraldi*, cols 651–4.
[30] N. Elias, *Über den Prozess der Zivilisation* (2 vols, Basel, 1939), translated as *The Civilizing Process*, trans. E. Jephcott (2 vols, Oxford, 1994). His ideas in relation to early modern courts were more extensively developed in *Die höfische Gesellschaft: Untersuchungen zur Soziologie des Königtums und der höfischen Aristokratie* (Soziologische Texte, 54, Berlin, 1969), translated as *The Court Society*, trans. E. Jephcott (Oxford, 1983).

and choices of its habitués. Elias sketched the consequences of living in such a world: the need to please and entertain the prince; the necessity of stifling impulsive words and emotions which cause offence and earn disfavour and enmity; the fear of conspiracy by rivals competing for the same princely favour. In such an environment self-restraint, affability and self-possession were survival skills. To Elias this was a process of civilizing the savage and uncontained ego of the warrior aristocrat through fear of greater power. In the light of the reading of the documents we have already looked at here, Courtliness was nothing so dramatic: it was an ancient, natural and advantageous mode of human behaviour in the context of a court, where it brought rewards.

Stephen Jaeger's work is based on the biographies of Ottonian and Salian prelates in tenth- and eleventh-century Germany, taking as principal exemplar the career of the curial cleric Brun, archbishop of Cologne (953–65), brother of Emperor Otto I. Drawing on his biography and those of others from his curial milieu, Jaeger constructed what he called 'the type of the courtier-cleric', the imperial bishop or court-chaplain. These men, we are told, generally possessed (or acquired) certain qualities which fit them for success as *curiales* (courtiers): qualities denoted in Latin as superior manners (*nobilitas morum*), poise (*elegantia*), and a range of virtues other than the religious ones we would expect in a cleric, and other than those associated with an efficient business manager. Jaeger identifies these social virtues as mild and deferential good humour (*mansuetudo*); modesty about—and affected indifference to—one's very real talents; general amiability (*affabilitas*); moderation and balance (*mensura*). Jaeger's sources also consider the negative features of tenth- and eleventh-century court life in Germany: the corrosive nature of ambition to succeed; the stress of living behind a mask; the envy and backbiting; and the plotters who were constantly trying to bring others down.[31]

Jaeger's reconstructed clerical world of the court in pre-1100 Germany bears many points of comparison with the lay world of the Carolingian court into which Dhuoda saw her son William disappear in the year 839. Dhuoda recognized the same dangers and praised some of the same virtues a century before Brun became archbishop. This antedating of the courtly ethos is not by any means an idea Jaeger finds problematical; he is quite willing to accept that the courtly skills he described were in use long before Ottonian times. Indeed, he saw Ottonian Courtliness as directly influenced by the ancient world, in a revival of Ciceronian ideals of moral, statesmanlike conduct.[32] Jaeger's clerical ideal type also practised something resembling the much later *cortesia* of Garin lo Brun, not least in the appeal to *mensura*—Garin's much-praised *mesura*, on which he wrote a separate work— which he as much as tenth-century bishops believed a key quality in success at court. But the similarity in outlook is not that one source influenced the other.

[31] Jaeger, *Courtliness*, 32–81.
[32] This was in fact amply demonstrated by R. Schnell, 'Die höfische Kultur des Mittelalters zwischen Ekel und Ästhetik', *Frühmittelalterliche Studien*, 39 (2005), 1–100, but misunderstanding Jaeger's argument, he then attacked him for arguing what he did not, that Courtliness began in Ottonian Germany; see for this C. S. Jaeger, 'The Origins of Courtliness after 25 Years', in *Haskins Society Journal*, 11 (2009), 194–6.

Far from it. Dhuoda, the Ottonian and Salian careerist cleric, and Garin lo Brun were all simply reacting in similar ways to the same environment, the difference being that Garin in the first half of the twelfth century gives a name to his toolkit for dealing with social interaction at the court: he calls it *cortesia*. In his *Envy of Angels* Jaeger further remarked on the way clerical education developed in the Ottonian period as a pedagogy centred on personal ethics, a *cultus virtutum*, which indeed cuts to the heart of the origins of a literature of manners, as we will see when we deal with the appearance of Chivalry as a behavioural code. But it is at this point that I part company with him, for he sees the Courtliness of the twelfth century as something in which the clergy educated the laity, and the courtly romance as the point of collision between what he treats as two divorced intellectual worlds.[33] Garin lo Brun, Marcabru, Gaimar and the biographer of Gilbert of Surrey tell us something very different, I think.

We do not encounter the vernacular word *cortesia* before Garin and Marcabru describe the phenomenon for us, but Jaeger discusses a Latin cognate term, *curialitas*. It is a word that pops up not infrequently in twelfth-century sources, but Jaeger found it earlier, in a chronicle of the foundation of the church of Hildesheim by one Bishop Azelinus. The text dates from 1080, and it uses *curialitas* in a pejorative way. Bishop Azelinus, quite a successful court-cleric in his own way, had founded the monastery at Hildesheim, but his diocese and indeed the community of Hildesheim was said to have been infected by him with *ambitiosa curialitas*, which we are told put too much emphasis on fine clothing and dining and elegance of lifestyle—the lifestyle in effect which one might encounter at the court, causing proper monastic discipline to lapse.[34] So did Jaeger's German *curialitas* relate to and precede Occitan *cortesia*? Are they the same thing?[35] In one sense, plainly yes; two human generations separate their first occurrences, but *cortesia* and *curialitas* describe a similar phenomenon. The Hildesheim chronicler means *curialitas* to be taken negatively as a lifestyle tainted with the dissolute behaviour of the court, while Garin sees *cortesia* as very much the commendable behaviour of the respectable member of a court. We could then take *curialitas* as the Latinization of a vernacular term for the courtly life current by the 1080s across the eleventh-century Franco-Germanic world. By the evidence of the biography of Gilbert of Surrey we can suggest it had spread wider still, into the British Isles; in which case Courtliness cannot have been transmitted from the Empire westward into France, as Jaeger suggested. The deduction must be that people, lay and clerical, who had received a courtly education in the hall and chambers of a seigneurial residence and inhabited princely courts and travelled between them had become aware of 'Courtliness' as a conscious, admired, and discussed mode of behaviour across western Europe well before 1100, maybe even before 1000.

---

[33] Jaeger, *Envy of Angels*, 311.   [34] Jaeger, *Courtliness*,153–61.
[35] Jaeger notes as an argument against the identification, the derivation of OFr/Occ. *curteis/cortesia* from the late Latin *curtem* rather than *curia* (*Courtliness*, 160), but plainly Garin lo Brun relates *cortesia* to the behaviour expected of courtiers, so he had made the equation. To a twelfth-century writer *curtis* was in any case a synonym for *curia*, in the sense of a domestic enclosure.

THE LITERARY COURTLINESS
OF WALTHER AND RUODLIEB

Two literary productions can help test this assumption that elements of courtly behaviour permeated lay life as far back as the Carolingian period. Two Latin epics deriving from German authors survive, one from the tenth century and the other from the mid eleventh. The first is *Walther* (or *Waltharius*). It was evidently a widespread vernacular story already in the eighth century, which was most likely rendered from an East Frankish original into Latin verse at some point in the mid tenth century.[36] It was written as a historical epic set far back in the fifth century in the time of Attila and the Hunnish incursions into Eastern Europe. The hero is an Aquitanian prince, Walther, despatched to the court of King Attila in Pannonia as a hostage by his father. There he was brought up kindly by Attila and his discon- certingly civilized Huns, being instructed in the liberal arts as much as in weaponry.[37] He was appointed treasurer to the court and proved so useful a warrior that the king was led by his wife to suspect that Walther might try to leave, so he offered him any bride in Pannonia he might choose to wed. It is at this point, when he replied to Attila, that Walther revealed the mature skills of a courtier, for he had other ideas about his future which he was not going to share. He praised the king for his generosity in taking notice of 'a mere servant' (*modicus famulatus*) whose small services did not deserve his attention. If Walther were married, he would be distracted from giving his full attention to the more important business of tending to the king's affairs: 'nothing is as sweet to me as to be always in my lord's service!' he protested. Without the constraints of a young wife and children he would be ready for the king's commands at any time of day or night, and he pleaded with 'the best of fathers' to drop the scheme. Such modesty, flattery and dutifulness duly overcame the king, who withdrew his suggestion.[38]

Within this short passage are revealed the controlled speech and demeanour, the flattery and self-deprecation which will be urged on the ambitious by self-conscious writers on Courtliness for the next half-millennium and more. Walther masked his true feelings and skilfully deflected his lord's intentions towards him and so gained his true ends. It has to be said that the remainder of the epic is devoted more to the flight of the hero with his true love, and the many feats of arms in combat that he is obliged to undergo at the hands of the king of the Franks, his enemy, too many and rapid for him to reveal much in the way of other courtly behaviour; and indeed, uncontrolled battle rage is the predominant emotion of the rest of the text. After the final combat the hero did, however, exchange polite compliments with his final adversary, his old friend Hagen, who returned them with interest. *Walther*

[36] The Latin version has been attributed to a clerical author, but on the circular reasoning that since it was written in Latin it must have been written by a clerk.

[37] For the cultural absorption of Attila by Eastern European monarchies, E. Bozoky, 'L'épée d'Attila', in *Armes et jeux militaires dans l'imaginaire, xiiᵉ-xvᵉ siècles*, ed. C. Girbea (Bibliothèque d'histoire médiévale, 15, Paris, 2016), 357–68.

[38] *La Chanson de Walther: Waltharii Poesis*, ed. and trans (Fr) S. Albert, S. Menegaldo, and F. Mora (Grenoble, 2008), for the passage pp. 58–60 (ll. 142–69).

is no tenth-century courtly epic, but it is an epic where courtly modes of behaviour can be found.

The mid-eleventh-century work *Ruodlieb* is more revealing. Its origin in the monastic community of Tegernsee (Bavaria) is often assumed, as it survived in the bindings of a book from the Tegernsee library. However, its principal theme is the use of steadfast virtue in overcoming career disappointment in the lay world, which seems an unlikely theme for an author to address who had been principally a choir monk. Though it is a fragmentary and probably unfinished poem, the surviving passages tell the story of Ruodlieb, a young and unsuccessful knight who decided to travel to try to better his fortunes after a number of bad experiences with ungrateful local lords and hostile courts.[39] He came into the orbit of a great and moral king, who truly appreciated his qualities and rewarded him fittingly. *Ruodlieb* is therefore a genuine courtly epic, in the way *Walther* is not, as much of its focus is on the interrelationship between Ruodlieb and his employer, a king of almost messianic virtue. The royal court to which Ruodlieb became attached was a place of serene wisdom, justice and mercy, as well as a source of great and luxurious gifts to its servants. The author thus prefigured by nearly a century Geoffrey of Monmouth's depiction of the idealized royal court of Arthur at Caerleon and Geoffrey Gaimar's corresponding and contemporary description of the historical court of William Rufus. Ruodlieb rose high in his new master's court, most notably through the feat of negotiating a peace settlement with a neighbouring aggressor king. For this he took no reward from his master other than his food and clothing. He then had the satisfaction of his virtue being recognized by the very lords who mistreated him and drove him into exile, but who realized his worth once he had gone and who now asked him to return.

> For in giving advice there is no one equal to you, who can say what is right so justly or so nobly, and who defends as you do the widow and orphan when they are hurt by cruel greed, and who weep bitterly whenever they are oppressed.[40]

So Ruodlieb returned to his native land carrying the regrets of his fellow courtiers (and a great quantity of treasure the generous king concealed in his baggage). But most significantly on his departure, Ruodlieb asked the king for the benefit of his wisdom and so was taken aside and offered no less than an *enseignement*, a tract on the necessary conduct to assist his safe return home and his future prosperity. The king discoursed on the necessity for a wise man to avoid casual sexual relationships with low-born servants, and situations where he might be suspected of illicit sex. He was advised to find a proper relationship with a higher-status woman his mother approved of, a wife to be treated gently but still kept firmly in her place. He was to avoid resentments and keep his temper under control. He was advised of the futility of picking quarrels with his lord, who would be bound to best him in one way or another. A lord was also a bad person to lend things to, as he would

---

[39] K. Hauck, 'Heinrich III und der Ruodlieb', *Beiträge zur Geschichte der deutschen Sprache und Literatur*, 70 (1948), 372–419.
[40] *Ruodlieb*, 78.

never get them back and never get any gratitude for the act. He must be assiduous in attendance at church and never pass one without making a prayer. He must also take care how he cultivates his crops, so that the fields don't get trampled. He was particularly urged to avoid the company of redheads, who might be said to stand for the archetypically treacherous, lecherous and selfish companions a courtier always encounters, and who will bring him to grief if he ever trusts their advice.[41]

With *Ruodlieb* we find an idealized practitioner of Courtliness making his way in the eleventh-century world: a young man of talents but little in the way of resources. It is in fact a commentary on how to get on the world and weather its inevitable adversities, which is one reason why commentators on the text have seen it as prefiguring the themes of the *roman d'aventure* of the later twelfth century.[42] The hero struggled to make his way in a variety of situations, ever honest and hardworking, but treated badly by his ungrateful lords. But eventually friendship and fortune brought him where he could flourish and practise his talents under a good lord. He amassed respect and would have had vast wealth had he ever been a greedy fellow, but all he wanted was his lord's thanks and a fair wage. His virtue in the end brought even the veneration of the lords who had mistreated him, and the vast wealth he had not sought. And, of course, he made his mother proud. To bring the point home, the author then gives us the first surviving example of a tract on aspirational lay conduct, an *enseignement*, where we find the familiar warnings that sexual incontinence and lack of self-control in speech and action can bring disaster on the public man, as can trusting in the wrong sort of companion, universal courtly themes broached indeed by Dhuoda two centuries earlier.

THE COURTLY CENTURY

I am arguing, then, that by the time of Garin lo Brun the controlled courtly conduct he called *cortesia* was already long established as the way the lay elite conducted itself across western and central Europe. It was behaviour appropriate to the environment in which the elite lived, in the households in which they were fostered and educated for the hall, in their gatherings before the thrones of the great, or around the tables where lords entertained. *Cortesia* was informed and reinforced by widespread, and indeed proverbial, precepts common to many societies across western and central Europe by the eleventh century, from the Pyrenees to the Elbe. It was possible to learn and discourse upon it amongst fellow spirits caught in the same situation of dependence. What we see in the *Ruodlieb* and the *ensenhamen* of

---

[41] *Ruodlieb*, 90–6.

[42] P. Dronke, 'Ruodlieb: The Emergence of Romance', in *Poetic Individuality in the Middle Ages* (Oxford, 1970), 33–65; E. Archibald, 'Ruodlieb and Romance in Latin: Audience and Authorship', in *Telling the Story in the Middle Ages: Essays in Honour of Evelyn Birge Vitz* (Cambridge, 2015), 171–86. Cf. Jaeger, *Courtliness*, 269, who prefers to see it as a didactic exercise in courtly behaviour, as I do here, reflecting the older theme in scholarship of *Ruodlieb* being a composition on the ideal knight, as found in 1943 in *Verfasserlexikon des deutschen Mittelalters*, ed. W. Stammler and K. Langosch (15 vols, Berlin and Leipzig, 1931–55), 3: cols 1141–2.

Garin lo Brun are (in written form) the sort of musings and useful precepts that any young aspirant to public life would encounter in the eleventh and early twelfth century, whether he was destined for clerical or lay life. How it was taught and acquired became clearer in the period after Garin lo Brun wrote, and I will be returning to it in Chapter 7. It was not for nothing, however, that it had acquired the name *cortesia*, which by 1170 had several vernacular equivalents, including the German *hövescheit*.[43] It arose out of the *cort* or the *hof*, the high-status residence, whose central building was the hall. It was within the hall that the young served and observed correct behaviour under the chastisement and instruction of stewards and the eye of their lord, to graduate in due course into the equally demanding environment of an employer's household or the forum of the public assembly.

Norbert Elias, as we have seen, presented a theory that the courts of great persons inevitably and invariably generated a habitus which forced a modification of the behaviour of their more intelligent occupants if they had ambitions to survive and prosper.[44] It has been pointed out in Elias's support that courts have acted in much the same way in societies far away from medieval Europe in both space and time, such as imperial China and fourth-century Gupta India.[45] The twelfth-century evidence looked at here indicates that the *cortesia* of Latin Europe was a product of just such an environment. It arose out of a habitus that structured people's behaviours and choices, and indeed was an attempt at codifying the correct ones for the benefit of the socially ambitious. Approaching the subject of Courtliness through conduct tracts, as we do here, leads to very different conclusions from approaching it through twelfth-century romance literature in the way Gaston Paris did. He has left us with the distracting concept of *amour courtois*, which foregrounds what is only one element of the courtly whole, the way ideal knights supposedly interacted with their ladies. The sense of the word this encourages is what modern English calls 'courtesy', meaning no more than generalized civility and politeness in social interaction.[46] It is an English sense that the Renaissance poet Spenser burdened 'courtesy' with:

> And well beseemeth that in princes hall
> That vertue should be plentifully found,
> Which of all good manners is the ground
> And roote of civill conversation.   (*The Faerie Queen*, Book 6, canto 1)

[43] For the appearance of the German noun *hövescheit* see Bumke, *Courtly Culture*, 308.

[44] For Elias's prefiguring of Bourdieu's habitus as a tool for understanding social choice, B. Paulle, B. van Heerikhuizen, and M. Emirbayer, 'Elias and Bourdieu', in *The Legacy of Pierre Bourdieu*, ed. S. Susen and B. S. Turner (London, 2011), 147–68.

[45] For a summary of Elias's reception amongst social historians, A. Linklater and S. Mennell, 'Norbert Elias, the Civilizing Process: the Sociogenetic and Psychogenetic Investigations – an overview and assessment', *History and Theory*, 49 (2010), 384–411, esp. 389–400. For an example of such universalization, D. Ali, 'Violence, Courtly Manners and Lineage Formation in Early Medieval India', *Social Scientist*, 35 (2007), 3–21.

[46] See the definition offered by J. Frappier: 'Vues sur les conceptions courtoises dans les littératures d'oc et d'oïl du xiiᵉ siècle', *CCM*, 2 (1959), 136: 'En réalité les termes de *courtois* et de *courtoisie* tantôt désignent, dans un sens large, la générosité chevaleresque, les élégances de la politesse mondaine, une certaine manière de vivre, et tantôt, dans un sens plus restreint, un art d'aimer inaccessible au commun des mortels, cet embellissement du désir érotique, cette discipline de la passion et même cette religion de l'amour qui constituent l'*amour Courtois*.'

But 'courtesy' does not accurately translate the medieval French term *courtoisie*. What modern English means by 'courtesy' a medieval Frenchman would call being *plaisant* or *agréable*.

Cortezia/courtoisie in the twelfth century was a more structured and heavyweight concept than mere *politesse*, and for many it was a survival aid that had to be mastered, as the conduct tracts themselves make perfectly clear. To explain the pressing need to get by in their insecure world, a number of graduates and denizens of the hall took up their pens and attempted to codify correct behaviour out of their common wisdom for their fellows, and themselves attempted to structure their own habitus. So we find that Courtliness had formed as a social code well before the later twelfth century, and many of its demands and strategies had long been self-evident and self-conscious to those who lived under the rafters of the high-status hall. The aim of those who described and analysed it was to urge the need for Courtliness so as to survive and prosper. They catalogued its helpful qualities, which were to be summarized elegantly by the poet-knight William de Lorris in his *Roman de la Rose*.[47] William personified *Cortoisie* as a refined spirit rich in the defining qualities of wisdom and judgement, a good angel measured in speech and self-controlled in her behaviour, whose disciples were worthy to stand amongst the great in any assembly, idealized courtly humans who were called *preudommes* and *preudefemmes*, who will be addressed individually in the following Chapters 4 and 5.

[47] Lorris, *Rose*, 108 (ll. 1226–41).

4

The *Preudomme*

Every intelligent and ambitious medieval boy's aim was to grow to be respected and looked up to in the public assembly, and as he grew and acquired experience and reputation in his world he would hope to be recognized amongst his neighbours and peers as a 'worthy fellow', which ultimately is what the Middle French *preudomme* means.[1] The concept and its Latin and Middle High German equivalents (*probus homo, biderbe* or *zuhtic man*) are found across medieval Europe from the eleventh century onwards and in a wide variety of sources, not least those devoted to describing superior conduct amongst men. It has been suggested that its universality is such that it may draw on deep legal and cultural roots in the Stoic concept of the representative *vir bonus*.[2] Such a man had status: 'A *prodon* has every right to be respected', as a twelfth-century Champenois writer tells us.[3] The thirteenth-century translator of Peter Alfonsi's *Disciplina Clericalis* chose to interpret Peter's Latin idea of a *magna persona* ('great personage') as *preudon de grant affaire*.[4] We find the *prozdom* also as a social leader in the foundational work of French literature, the eleventh-century *Song of Roland*, which has been interpreted as an exploration of the tragic dilemma of a *prozdom*, in the way the *mesure* and intelligence of Count Oliver was subverted by the arrogant and reckless bravery of his friend Roland, with catastrophic results for France.[5] The term was therefore not only a social honorific; the *preudomme* was an ideal type of male on whom positive male qualities were projected. It was a rather more broadly gendered term than 'knight', as it could apply to superior males in all areas of medieval life: layman and cleric, aristocrat, townsman and peasant farmer. As a result, its modern French descendant, the *prud'homme*, is a term broadly used of adults in a legal capacity.

Many writers of the twelfth and thirteenth centuries use the idea and apply it to males in a wide variety of social and historical contexts, by no means all of them aristocratic or even secular. The early thirteenth-century Prose Lancelot cycle calls many of its leading male characters *preudomme*, not least the wise hermits who

---

[1] For a definition, Crouch, *Nobility*, 31. The *justus* (righteous man) in the early thirteenth-century Latin fables of Odo of Cheriton became *prodom* in the contemporary French translation; *Les Fables d'Eude de Cheriton*, ed. P. Ruelle (Recueil Général des Isopets, 4, Paris, 1999), pp. lviii, 36.

[2] M. Welti, '*Vir Bonus, Homo Bonus, Preudome*: Kleine Geschichte dreier nahe verwandter Begriffe', *Archiv für Begriffsgeschichte*, 38 (1998), 61–4. There is certainly evidence that Robert of Ho directly translated Seneca's *vir bonus* as *prodome*, *Enseignements Trebor*, 126, and see further below, p. 62 n.26.

[3] *La Bible*, 38 (l. 900), *molt devroit estre chiers prodon*.   [4] *Chastoiement d'un père*, 163.

[5] J. Subrenart, 'e Oliver est proz', in *Études de philologie romane et d'histoire littéraire à Jules Hovrent*, ed. J-M. d'Heur and N. Cherubini (Liège, 1980), 461–7; Crouch, *Nobility*, 32–3; *Song*, 1: ll. 1288, 1528, 3264.

offer confession and counsel to kings and knights.[6] Commerce carried no stain for a *preudomme*. At the beginning of the twelfth century Philip de Thaon discoursed in his *Comput* on the names of the days of the week: Tuesday (*marsdi*) was, he said, named after the god of war and in honour of knights, whereas Wednesday (*mecresdi*) was named after Mercury, who, he says, was *pruz hom* and a merchant.[7] An efficient and honest farmer might also be a *prodon*, as Guiot de Provins and Marie de France both observe, while the Butcher of Abbeville of Eustace d'Amiens's *fabliau* was *sages, cortois, vaillanz and loiaus*, the defining virtues indeed of the *preudomme*, though in his case the adjectives were being ironically applied (see pp. 67–78).[8] Thomas of Kent in the 1190s did not confine the use of the term to his own day and age. He discoursed on the height of civilization attained by Athens in ancient times and reflected that *cortoisie* first flowered there, so naturally its males were a most distinguished fellowship (*bachelerie*): *pruz hommes et sages et de grant chevalerie*.[9] The poet and *bailli* of Louis IX's reign, Philip de Remy, often used the word. He too transcended in its use his own day and age and applied the term to biblical patriarchs and kings: Adam, Abraham and David. Philip used it of all sorts and conditions of men: he had one of his characters, the astute squire Robin, assessing for his master the dependability of a ship's captain with whom they must make a voyage, finding him *preudome*, and therefore full of goodness of heart. Philip also regarded poor fishermen trying to be generous and helpful to the shipwrecked as *preudomme*.[10] Guiot de Provins for his part stated that all senior clergy should be regarded as *prodome*, though unlike Philip, since he was arguing for Nobility as a qualification for high church office, Guiot declined to believe that clerics of low birth could be reckoned as *prodomes*. He was not alone in that, but it was only a small minority of writers who wanted to appropriate the word to the aristocracy alone.[11]

The *preudomme* was a social signifier promiscuously spread around twelfth- and thirteenth-century literature, imaginative and educational alike. But the term was not used indiscriminately. All *preudommes*, whatever their occupation and status, and indeed whether they lived in Britain, France, the Empire or Spain, were assumed to respect high moral ideals and qualities. The Swabian poet Hartmann von Aue, in his *Die Klage* (c.1190), gives a poetic recipe for a potion to produce a

---

[6] *Lancelot* 1: 157–9. The clerical *preudomme* did, of course, have different demands on him: Walter de Coinci warned such men at length to flee any engagement with the temptations posed by women; *Les miracles de la Sainte Vierge*, ed. l'Abbé Pocquet (repr. Geneva, 1972), cols 644–6.

[7] *Comput*, ed. I. Short (London, 1984), 10 (ll. 447–62). Robert of Ho talks of the good sense in buying from a *prodom*; *Enseignements Trebor*, 95 (ll. 1485–8).

[8] *La Bible*, 19 (l. 311); *The Life of Saint Audrey*, ed. and trans. J. H. McCash and J. C. Barban (Jefferson, NC, 2006), 218 (ll. 4051–2), *a Grettone un prodom manoit ke de son labur droit vivoit*; *Cuckolds, Clerics and Countrymen: Medieval French Fabliaux*, ed. R. Eichmann and trans. J. Duval (Fayetteville, AR, 1982), 16 (ll. 7–14).

[9] *Le Roman de Toute Chevalerie*, ed. B. Foster (2 vols, London, 1976–7) 1: ll. 2346–54.

[10] *La Manekine*, ed. H. Suchier (Paris, 1884), ll. 1105–10, 4917–19; *Jehan et Blonde*, ed. S. Lécuyer (Paris, 1984), ll. 3699–701.

[11] *La Bible*, 44 (ll. 995–1110). Robert de Blois was vociferous against the idea of an unfree, bonded serf ever being found to be a *preudomme*, but also conceded that a free man of an otherwise humble peasant family might very well prove to be a fine *proudome*; *Enseignement des princes*, 115 (ll. 787–94).

supremely virtuous and loving man. The ingredients he lists are familiar qualities: generosity (*milte*), propriety (*zuht*), humility (*diemuot*), loyalty (*triuwe*), constancy (*stæte*), chastity (*kiuscheit*), modesty (*schame*) and outstanding manliness (*manheit*). It cannot be other than significant that Hartmann says he had found the recipe in France (Kärlingen).[12] As a result, the *preudomme* brings us closer to understanding medieval pan-European ideas of masculinity than any other sort of male identity. This has been fitfully recognized by historians, though usually in the context of explorations of the 'chivalric' male.[13] The aim of this chapter is to place him more centrally in the understanding and criticism of medieval masculinity; he was a lord of the courtly habitus and as a lord he was to be admired and imitated by its inhabitants. The standing that went with the name was valued and as such to be *preudomme* was a coveted honorific. In the words of the English moral tract of the early thirteenth century, the *Petit Plet*: 'It's a great shame to a *produme*, and his reputation is lessened, if he fails to get his due ration of praise.'[14]

THE LIFE OF THE *PREUDOMME*

Biographical studies of laymen are rare in the twelfth and thirteenth centuries, though there are a few, even putting aside the ones (such as the *vita* of the eleventh-century magnate Count Simon of the Vexin) which have an open, hagiographical intention. Such as they are, they deal with eminent men of affairs and are obviously written to portray them as *preudommes*, the summit of lay virtue. All were written after the death of their heroes. The career of the English administrator and sheriff Gilbert of Surrey (died 1126) is the subject of a biographical Latin essay by a grateful canon of Gilbert's foundation of Merton priory, who had sources who had known the man, but who was not arguing for Gilbert's sanctity. What we are invited to see him as is *probissimus virorum* (a great *preudomme*) and *curialius* (most courtly).[15] William Marshal, earl of Pembroke (died 1219), famously was the subject of a full vernacular treatment commissioned by his eldest son and the executors of his last testament in the mid 1220s, the most extensive and most skilful biography of a layman surviving from any period of the Middle Ages. It brings to the fore in its

---

[12] *Die Klage*, ed. C. Kiening (Altdeutsche Textbibliothek, no. 123, Berlin, 2015), 54–5 (ll. 1280, 1301–17).

[13] Recognition of the importance of the 'prud'homme' as a medieval social ideal is to be found in Bloch, *Feudal Society* 2: 305–6, who associated the idea with the practice of *courtoisie*, and see also Keen, *Chivalry*, 8, though he associates the word with the substantive *proesce*, rather than the less explicit adjectival *prou* or *preu* (deriving from the Latin *probus*). For the concept's literary manifestations, see E. Köhler, *L'aventure chevaleresque: idéal et réalité dans le roman courtois*, trans. E. Kaufholz (Paris, 1974), 149–59, who talks of a quality of *prodomie* and argues against its being a term confined to the nobility, though in thrall to his sources he saw it as a symptom of the emergence of a knightly *Tugendsystem* within society (p. 151). For my own exploratory essay on the subject, Crouch, *Nobility*, 29–37.

[14] *Le Petit Plet*, ed. B. S. Merrilees (Oxford, 1970), 26–7 (ll. 782–4).

[15] Crouch, *Nobility*, 42–3; Crouch, *Aristocracy*, 196–7.

discussion of its subject's character many of the key qualities of the *preudomme*.[16] It was also openly intended to instruct others how to become one, if they followed the career path and aspired to the virtues of the late Marshal.

Less well known and closely contemporary with the Marshal biography (though a somewhat more complicated work) is Walter de Tournai's earlier thirteenth-century verse account of the life of the twelfth-century Flemish knight and crusader Gilles de Chin (died 1137), most probably composed around 1230. It drew on and expanded an earlier, now lost, biography of Gilles by one Walter le Cordier—probably a Latin *vita*—which was written in the mid 1160s, just as William Marshal's career was beginning. Walter de Tournai's work, written four or five years after the Marshal biography, though fanciful, nonetheless drew on a real life and preserves at second hand some memory of a man who had died a century before it was composed. For our purposes it is useful as a depiction of the career and virtues of an idealized *preudomme* of Walter's day and age rather than as an example of a true biography.[17] But it is a useful comparison with the rather more factual life of William Marshal, because the portrayal of Gilles can be used as a colourful back-projection to the social ideal which Marshal aspired to and indeed matched. In the poem, Gilles ('who had been *prodon* all his days') is frequently called such, and in terms that locate him at the apex of male virtue; indeed, the count of Hainaut, his master, rejoiced to say: 'I am a greater lord than the emperor, since my land has such a *preudome* and the emperor has no one comparable at Rome.'[18] William Marshal—from the story of whose life, according to his biographer, all *prodome* should draw inspiration—likewise attracted eulogies from the leading characters of his own day and age. Public recognition was a necessary and natural part of being a *preudomme*, as was said above. On hearing of Marshal's death from a shocked King Philip of France, Count William des Barres of Rochefort, Marshal's old sparring partner (and indeed his doppelgänger at the Capetian court), gave his testimonial to the old man's son, Richard Marshal, that 'in our time there was never a better knight to be found anywhere'.[19]

But of course, it had not always been so in a *preudomme*'s life. His social eminence was made all the more cloud-capped when his humble and poorly appreciated origins were placed at the beginning of his story. Gilles de Chin was despised by his relatives as a youth, was unkempt and dressed shabbily as a boy, and no one had any expectation he would end up a landowner or come to any good. But his talents were recognized by a famous magnate he encountered, the castellan of Cambrai, who took him into his household and gave him the knightly equipment his own

---

[16] For some reflection on the Marshal as *preudomme*, D. Crouch, 'The Violence of the *Preudomme*', in *Prowess, Piety, and Public Order in Medieval Society: Studies in Honor of Richard W. Kaeuper*, ed. C. M. Nakashian and D. P. Franke (Turnhout, 2017), 87–101.

[17] N. L. Paul. 'In Search of the Marshal's Lost Crusade: the persistence of memory, the problems of history and the painful birth of crusading romance', *Journal of Medieval History*, 40 (2014), 306n.

[18] *Gille de Chyn*, 121 (ll. 4662–3), 135 (ll. 5254–6). For the evolution and sources of the work, *Gille de Chyn*, 5–11, and see also C. C. Willard, 'Gilles de Chin in History, Literature and Folklore', in *The Medieval Opus: Imitation, Rewriting and Transmission in the French Tradition* (Amsterdam, 1999), 357–66.

[19] *History of William Marshal*, 2: ll. 19138–9, 19159–64.

parents had failed to provide. As soon as Gilles was let loose by his lord on the tournament field, he proved his worth and attained almost instant celebrity, at last gaining his father's approval. William Marshal for his part was the fourth son of a moderately prosperous court official with no expectation of the inheritance of any land from his father. His biographer tells us that he was an unremarkable youth, and apparently Marshal himself used to say that sleeping and eating were all he was noted for as a squire. Yet as soon as he was launched on the tournament circuit in 1166 by his Norman cousin William de Tancarville, who had taken responsibility for his education and training, he is said to have found instant success, with the knights observing his performance clamouring to know who the new fellow was. So also with Gilles de Chin. As he rode his first field, everyone wanted to know 'Who is he?', and at the end of it he was awarded the prize as best knight of the day, a distinction Marshal was later to enjoy occasionally, though not on his first excursion.

This quick ascent of the hero to celebrity was a literary topos of its day, though nonetheless a true evocation of the optimistic daydreams with which a testosterone-charged young knight might launch himself on public life.[20] In reality it took three years before William Marshal finally secured a future by being retained into the Angevin royal household, after he fell out with his master, Tancarville, and took to the life of an itinerant tourneyer, earning a living by ransoms. It was not till 1175 that his great days as a tourneying champion and team captain began. Gilles, on the other hand, found a comfortable berth instantly in the tourneying-mad household of his lord, Gossuin d'Oisy, and fame wherever he travelled. Soon Gilles was being described as outstandingly *cortois et sage*, 'even though he was barely twenty years of age'.[21] In such a work as Chin's *Histore*, the young hero was fast-forwarded into the role of a mature *preudomme*. Little time was devoted to his necessary acquisition of experience, money and contacts, not to mention his inevitable setbacks, all of which necessities the Marshal biography does, by contrast, acknowledge at length. We see the same steep trajectory in the purely fictional romance *Gui de Warewic*, a work composed around 1199, where the eponymous English hero after his knighting launched himself on to the Continental tournament circuit as the place where a knight established international renown in the twelfth century. He too won instant celebrity and the tournament prize on his first outing, where everyone asked his name, and he then embarked on an illustrious tourneying career that took him across France into the Empire and even Lombardy before he crossed back home to England.[22]

The Marshal biography departs radically from the expectations of vernacular romance literature when it depicts its hero's relations with women and his eventual

[20] For the competitive establishment of masculine prowess, Karras, *Boys to Men*, 37–9, though working from medieval sources mostly after 1300.
[21] *Gille de Chyn*, 37 (ll. 1057–9).
[22] *Gille de Chyn*, 18–23; *Gui de Warewic* 1: 23–31. For a reconstruction of Marshal's early career, Crouch, *Marshal*, 25–41. There is little possibility that these three sources were in any way interlinked in their composition, though it might be argued that the Marshal biography was in part his family's answer to the purely fictional hero Guy, placed at the head of the genealogy of the earls of Warwick.

winning of a wife. Gilles de Chin, not to mention Guy of Warwick and any number of romance heroes, were energized in their pursuit of fame by the inspiration of true love, sometimes an unattainable one. Women were naturally important to Marshal, as patrons and judges of tournaments and (in the case of Eleanor of Aquitaine) as an employer. Despite the silence of his biographer, we know he was by no means immune to heterosexual impulses. He found ways in the 1170s to get a woman pregnant at a time well before he married, producing one known illegitimate child, a boy to whom he gave his family name. But his attitude towards securing his eventual bride was nothing other than pragmatic. He was given the custody of one young heiress in 1186 and held on to her as a possible wife-in-waiting while he kept his eyes open for better bargains. In 1188 King Henry II of England indeed offered just that possibility, trailing marriage to the heiress of Châteauroux and lady of Berry as an inducement for Marshal's continued support. But in 1189, when that match did not transpire, the stakes were raised further for him with the offer of Countess Isabel of Striguil, heiress of the great Irish honor of Leinster, whom he did eventually marry at around the age of 43 and with whom he went on to have ten children who grew to adulthood.[23]

Marshal sought and could offer love. He may well have been deeply attached to his first sexual partner, who herself eventually made a respectable marriage, and he took good care of their child's future welfare. His marriage to Isabel was to be very successful and the family they made together was obviously affective. The real-life *preudomme* approached marriage as a transaction, however, not as a romantic obsessive. As the case of Ulrich von Liechtenstein proves, and indeed also the case of William Marshal's elder brother John, aristocratic males might well pursue different women simultaneously for both pragmatic and erotic purposes and openly take a mistress as well as a wife, but such men imperilled their standing as *preudommes*. John Marshal is regarded with scant respect in his brother's biography, and the reckless dangers as well as temptations of open adultery are obsessively explored in thirteenth-century literature (for which see Chapter 8).

Career reverses were no condemnation of the *preudomme*; it was how such a man dealt with them that marked out his quality. Even the literary *preudomme* had to experience crisis and challenge to grow as a human being. William Marshal had several crises in his career. One was in 1182 when he fell out with his early patron, the Young King of England, and the other in 1205 when he finally lost his footing on the tightrope of favour he walked at the court of King John. In each case he clawed his way back painfully and with no apparent loss of credit to him. Spiritual crises were to be expected. Indeed, a time of darkness of the soul was a necessity. In the case of Guy of Warwick, disgust at his own violent life led first to crusade and then to an absolute renunciation of the world which had been so good to him, to end his life in a hermit's cell. William Marshal, in deep depression at his master's sudden and squalid death, quit his chosen world of royal courts and tournament spectacle in 1183 to travel to Jerusalem to fulfil as a proxy his dead master's oath to go on crusade. There he made some sort of commitment to the Templar order, in whose habit he was to be buried many years later. Gilles de Chin likewise experienced (after only three years to the Marshal's sixteen) a revulsion at the glamour of the tourneying world and was inspired, in the form of a miraculous letter of summons from Christ, to seek the Holy Land, where (unlike Marshal) we are told of any number of his spectacular deeds.[24] But just as Marshal returned from Outremer to enter a new life which resulted in a conventional marriage, the acquisition of land, and a new life as a royal captain, so too did Gilles. On his return from the Holy Land, the countess of Duras, his unattainable love, was recently dead and so (after a proper degree of mourning and the offering of commemorative rites) he was clear to resume his tourneying career, return in great triumph to his ancestral lordship, make a fortune from his prowess in arms, and arrange a conventional marriage with a young heiress who had rather been a nun until she met a man of his surpassing virtue. He became a trusted confidant and commander of the count of Hainaut and—according to Walter de Tournai—ended his career heroically at the Battle of Roucourt. Other and earlier sources say, however, that the real-life Gilles came to grief on a tourney field.[25]

ESSAYS ON *PREUDOMMIE*

Medieval occidental society was perfectly conscious of the *preudomme* as the ideal of male conduct and his life as being a teaching aid for youth, an idea in fact with already some lineage behind it in the world of education. Writing in the 1180s (and quoting Seneca), Robert of Ho tells us that any aspirant young male needed to search out a *preudomme* and take him as his exemplar in all he does and says:

> My son, listen to what I tell you: you must search out a *prodome* and when you've made a good choice I advise you in your interest whatever you may wish to do as a result in word or action, you must consider doing it in such a way as if the man were watching over your shoulder and is always standing there with you and is before your eyes to give his opinion on whatever he observes with which he may take issue with you. If you do as I say you'll make few mistakes, you can be sure.[26]

Baldwin de Condé puts it alliteratively: 'The *preudons* is the standard which is made to measure all those who are measured against him.'[27] The basic assumption

---

[24] For the crusading motif in twelfth-century ancestral tracts, N. L. Paul, *To Follow in their Footsteps: the Crusades and Family Memory in the High Middle Ages* (Ithaca, NY, 2012), 83–9. Like El Cid and other epic heroes, Gilles also had to master a lion.

[25] Willard, 'Gilles de Chin', 360.

[26] *Enseignements Trebor*, 126 (ll. 2251–64): *Fiz, escoute que te vuil dire:/Tu deiz un boen prodome eslire/E quant tu l'avras bien eslit/Ce te comant por tun profit/E[n] quanque tu voudras ovrer/En dit, en fet, si deiz penser/De fere le[i] en tel maniere/Cum s'il fut sor tei ton jugiere/E devant tei toz dis estasce/E te esguart en mi la face/Por jugier en quanq[ue] il verreit/Dont il reprendre te porreit./Se tu le fez si cum je di/ Meins mesferas, saches de fi.* The sentiment is Seneca's view of pedagogy, *Ad Lucilium Epistulae Morales*, Ep. 11: 8. Robert is likely quoting Seneca at first hand but possibly at second hand through William of Conches, translating Seneca's *vir bonus* as *prodome*; see on this Senecan passage Jaeger, *Ennobling Love*, 77–9.

[27] *Condé* 1: 98: *C'est mesure qui mesurer/Fait tous ceus en cui mesure a.*

that lies behind the comments of both these writers (and indeed many others) is that there was a generic *preudomme*, about whose qualities there was a medieval consensus, or at least an ongoing debate. As a result the *preudomme* became the subject of analytical treatises on conduct. The earliest of them occur in the second half of the twelfth century, just before the cultural turn which produced chivalric literature, so they are particularly important in establishing the characterization of the medieval public man of affairs before he was overlaid with the hypermoral expectations of the later medieval knight.

The twelfth- and thirteenth-century tracts on the ideal *preudomme* do not owe much to the Stoic ideals of the public man presented by Cicero and so admired amongst the Carolingian and Ottonian clerks studied by Stephen Jaeger.[28] Their prissy concern with enacting virtue through the mannered gait and gesture of the body is not to be found in the *ensenhamen*. Quite the opposite in some cases. The *ensenhamen* called *Qui comte vol apendre*, offered to a confused aristocratic youth in the 1170s by the Gascon baron Arnaut-Guilhem de Marsan, is particularly striking in its full-blooded secularity, so much at odds with the stilted Latin moral literature of the schoolroom. It is, however, by no means divorced from the contemporary aristocratic Occitan literature of love, even though *Qui comte vol apendre* is essentially (and occasionally seriously) about superior male conduct, not male sexuality. The literary context of his *ensenhamen* was in Marsan's mind as he wrote. He joked as he began that he was not going to talk of deep matters or of business, which may be interpreted as his mocking of the earnestly Catonian Latin conduct literature of his day, to which aristocrats were exposed as children as they learned their letters.[29] Marsan instead took on the voice of the troubadour and advocated the wealthy man of leisure ought to pursue women, though he should exercise caution in the matter of angry husbands. He was particularly energized about personal hygiene, fine clothing, military equipment and fashion accessories, and all his advice here was focused on securing female attention.

Eventually, however, the matter of conduct asserted itself and Marsan's attention shifted from seduction to education. He offered pragmatic advice about deportment and bodily self-control in company. As with literature destined for the instruction of women, he emphasized to his young male friend the importance of intelligent household attendants; they should be *cortes et ensenhatz* (civil and educated). He stressed the importance for any aristocrat's reputation of the well-managed and generous dining of guests and (consciously echoing a Latin Facetus text) the necessity of remembering the plight of the poor and needy when entertaining (see Chapter 10). He defined courtly behaviour as largesse (*larcx*) and keeping an open house. It meant a rejection of socially objectionable *lauzengers* (deceitful flatterers) and ill-natured doormen who (literally) stood in the way of generous entertaining. The temptation to seek privacy, and make oneself unavailable to guests and dependants,

---

[28] Jaeger, *Envy of Angels*, 111–16.
[29] A generation or two later Sordello likewise deliberately distanced his *ensenhamen* from the concerns of the school and academic theology and law, *Ensenhamens d'Onor*, 200 (ll. 23–31), appealing to his own 'native wit'.

was to be resisted. Arnaut found free-handed gambling a creditable occupation for
the rich aristocrat, presumably as it demonstrated noble largesse which cared
nothing for hoarding possessions. When he came to his conclusion, Marsan was a
little torn as to the core of his advice, his head at issue perhaps with the poetic
tradition in which he was writing. He had till then implied the successful pursuit
of women to be the ultimate aim of the behaviour of the superior male, but at the
end came out with the view that his ideal youth should 'Love the military life
(*cavalaria*) more than any riches and fix your heart there'. He ended his advice with
a long and lively paean of praise to war and the tournament, before signing off with
a list of women he claimed to have seduced.[30] Marsan was not an eccentric voice
in his day. The third 'epic letter' by which the Provençal household knight Raimbaut
de Vacqueiras solicited favour from his lord, the marquis of Montferrat, which
dates to 1205, affirmed Marquis Boniface as a lord in just Marsan's pattern: generous,
gallant to the ladies, disdainful of *lauzengiers*, rejoicing in fine clothes and armour,
generous and cultivated in his hall, but also sensible to the needs of the poor and
disadvantaged.[31]

But another Occitan *ensenhamen* of the same generation tells us that some found
Marsan's views frivolous and lacking in true Courtliness and indeed took issue with
them so as to correct them. This is Arnaut de Mareuil's *Rasos es e Mesura* (composed
for the court of the young Alfonso II of Aragon perhaps as early as the 1160s
but more likely the 1170s), which asserted in evident contradiction to Marsan
and his like:

> There are cultivated people who say that the pursuit of diversion is the main business
> of a court and pleasure is indeed always enjoyable as also is the game of flirtation, the
> dancing and merry-making and being among well-dressed folk.[32]

But this was not Mareuil's view. For him *cortezia* was the education that can be
acquired through superior company at court, and its accomplished male practitioner was the *pros honz*. His ideal male was a man who respected God and avoided
disreputable behaviour, *vilana* (the antithesis of *cortezia*). He was a good judge of
men and respected those of sense and intelligence: indeed, judgement (*sens*) was
one of his principal qualities, and triviality (*folor*) was alien to him. Such a man was
not against fun, but it had its proper time and place. The serious business of his life
was summarized as protecting his dependants and defending his honour by appropriately repaying offences against it. He must in doing so employ the biblical ethic
of respecting humble and decent folk and overbearing the proud. Arnaut made it
clear that in discussing the *pros honz* he was not just addressing the limited category
of the knight, but all superior males. He talked of *proeza* as a quality which can be
demonstrated in both spiritual and secular spheres. He made a point of stating that
urban males can share all the aspirations and virtues of aristocratic ones and achieve
reputation (*pretz*) without the advantage of good birth. A clerk too could earn
reputation by his *cortezia* as well as his literacy. Arnaut affirmed that every *pros honz*

---

[30] *Qui comte vol apendre*, esp. 82–6 (ll. 371–478).   [31] Raimbaut, 308 (ll. 91–106).
[32] *Rasos es e Mesura*, 22.

must work to earn his reputation, because unlike land it could not be inherited from a father; though, thinking no doubt of his audience, he followed up with the opinion that it was more likely to be found in eminent families. Arnaut was not here offering a tract on the chivalrous noble male, but the *preudomme*. And his early analysis of the qualifications of such a male is a key one for this chapter, for his *preudomme*'s virtues can be learned by anyone.

> In these five things, I assure you, prowess resides and flourishes. Knowledge and generosity are the keys to prowess while ability is the lock which nobody can unfasten without education and without which it can scarcely endure. So it is only appropriate in this metaphor that Intelligence keeps the keys. Education is a courtly and amiable messenger whose words are nothing but pleasant wherever they fall. I don't see that the reputation of any emperor, king, duke, count or baron or indeed any *home pro* can endure without those five virtues unless they can make a reasonable claim to them.[33]

Baldwin de Condé, a French poet of the lands of the western Empire, offered perhaps a natural summation of the views of these works and others in an essay explicitly on the subject of the *preudomme*. He wrote at some time in the second half of the thirteenth century with the intention of offering a definition of the concept, so widespread in his society. Baldwin's work quoted no earlier authorities on the subject, but it can be taken as a thoughtful digest of the mass of literature he had encountered on the subject of the ideal male. Baldwin, like Arnaut de Mareuil, wrote from the perspective of an itinerant poet existing on fees and commissions, so it is hardly surprising that in his poem the virtues of the *preudomme* he isolated are those of an ideal patron and lord. Such a man, he said, was welcoming and generous and did not patronize and demean his inferiors. His quality of *mesure* meant that he was predictable and could always be counted upon, which gave stability to his household and all who depended on him. *Preudommie* looked at from Baldwin's perspective was the very anchor of society.

Baldwin approached his task systematically, with typical medieval didactic dualism. The *preudomme*'s negative image was the same character who was also the antithesis of the courtly man, the villain (*li mauvais*).[34] Such was a widespread belief. We find this opposition in an anonymous Lombard *sirventes* of the early thirteenth century: 'a *prod'om* should be confident and have no anxiety about *vilana gente*.'[35] Middle High German literature has the same moral opposition between the *biderbe man* and the *bœse man*, whom Ulrich von Liechtenstein called 'opposites' (*ungelich*) in lifestyle and disposition.[36] In the 300 or so lines of his verse essay, Baldwin singled out the following defining qualities of his superior male. A *preudomme* kept his word, a virtue which gave him reputation (lines 25–30). He was generous and

---

[33] *Rasos es e Mesura*, 20–1 (ll. 177–96).

[34] The opposition of *preudomme* to *li malvais* is also found in the works of Walter of Arras, *Ille et Galeron*, 76 (ll. 2246–7), and see for the same dualism *Enseignement des princes*, 118 (l. 873); *Enseignements Trebor*, 36 (ll. 93–100).

[35] 'Prod'om sia securo qu'eo no curo vilana gente', in L. Spitzer, 'Remarks on the "Sirventese Lombardo"', in *Italica*, 28 (1951), 8.

[36] For a list of moral contrasts between the decent *biderbe man* and villainous *bœse man*, *Frauenbuch*, 102 (ll. 890–905; for the quotation, ll. 899–900).

charitable, unlike *li mauvais*, who would rather die than be caught in an act of generosity (lines 35–42). He was an honest and upright governor and administrator (lines 56–60). In the management of his affairs he was a devotee of reason, and in particular possessed the associated virtue of rational self-control (*mesure*) in judgement and action (lines 62–8). *Mesure* indeed was the cardinal virtue of the *preudomme*, according to Baldwin; it was the guideline (*ligne*) to his life. He was well spoken and spent his days profitably (lines 105–9). He was righteous in everything, which of course was pleasing to God, to whose worship and commands he was devoted (lines 110–15). He was a generous and affable host, the affability being the main thing: 'it is better seated at his table with only two courses than in the hall of a gloomy fellow who is offering five or six' (lines 116–25). It was the Courtliness in such a man that Baldwin appreciated. Such a man was *de cour courtois et larges*, and so, cheered Baldwin with some enthusiasm, 'God bless every *preudomme!*'[37]

Baldwin's contemporary, the jurist and *bailli* Philip de Beaumanoir (younger son of Philip de Remy, the poet), also offered an *enseignement* designed to define the *preudomme*, though he did not use the word as such.[38] In Philip's tract (*Les Diz Vertus*) we see the *preudomme* by contrast not as lord but as loyal servant, for Philip's task was to detail the positive qualities that were to be expected of any honest and honourable office holder of his day, the 1270s. As with many such medieval tracts, he enumerated the qualities for his readers. There were an unsurprising biblical ten of them. The first and most important to him was wisdom (*sapience*) which governed all the others. The second was a true love of God. The third was a good disposition, without any harshness and cruelty: a good judge should be kind and civil (*debonaires*) as he goes about his job. The fourth was patience in dealing with others (*soufrans*) and the avoidance of impatience and anger in his relations with those he had to deal with. The fifth virtue was vigour (*hardis*) in his activities and an avoidance of laziness, which brings him into disrepute. The sixth was a more general nest of virtues all linked to generosity (*largece*), from which Philip says flowed *courtoisie* and blamelessness (*netées*) and which countered the sin of avarice. In fact, as he portrayed it, this quality is the one most central to virtuous male conduct, and the least specific to the excellence of a professional *bailli*. The seventh virtue was obedience, obviously very necessary in a useful dependant. The eighth was also more generally applicable, and this was knowledgeability (*bien connoissans*), which Philip framed broadly as knowledge of self, of human nature, and possessing good intelligence of the minds of his lord and of his own subordinates. The ninth was managerial competence. And the tenth—which Philip himself regards as, alongside wisdom, the most important in a *bailli*—was loyalty.[39]

---

[37] *Condé* 1: 95–105.
[38] See on the social application of this source, M. Aurell, 'La noblesse au xiiie siècle: paraître, pouvoir et savoir', in *Discurso, Memoria y Representación: La nobleza peninsular en la Baja Edad Media* (Actas de la XLII Semana de Estudios Medievales de Estella-Lizarra, Pamplona, 2016), 7–8.
[39] *Coutumes de Beauvaisis*, 1: 10–27.

Our final witness is the German *enseignement* called *Winsbecke*, which is of particular importance in demonstrating how these developing ideals crossed cultures in medieval Europe. As it stands it is a mid-thirteenth-century revision and expansion of an earlier Franconian poem which, though undated, shows much in common with French and Occitan works of the first decades of the century.[40] *Winsbecke* was designed to educate a young man hoping one day to be a mature and worthy man of affairs, so that he should become *wolgezogen* (educated) and *hoveliche* (courtly). The work was intended for a youth who would be a knight, and there is a strong hint of the influence of early Latin or French chivalric tracts (such as the early thirteenth-century *Armëure de Chevalier* of Guiot de Provins and the *Ordene de Chevalerie*), which define male virtue by reflecting on items of military equipment, in *Winsbecke*'s case emphasizing the shield, which was also in Middle High German a metaphor for a knight and his service. *Winsbecke* indeed has many points of comparison with the French texts of its day. Like Beaumanoir the author placed the love and service of God first in his list of virtues. He went on to say that the clergy and one's wife should also be highly honoured. With an aplomb worthy of an Occitan, he saw no contradiction in urging a married man who had a mistress to be discreet about his relationship, and went on to set down at length a programme of intersexual relations by which a worthy male should ideally conduct himself towards females, which was a particular concern of this German author. But like his French counterparts he gives concentrated advice on the dangers of speech and the need for a public man to manage and bridle his tongue. French influence is also very evident in *Winsbecke*'s statements that generosity is important in the conduct of a superior male, but he must also exercise moderation (*mazze*) in the disposal of worldly goods and in the framing of his ambitions: the quality of *mesure* so important to French *enseignements*. The author echoed French warnings about unsuitable company, especially that his aspirant should avoid *die ungetriwen* (the treacherous), whom we can relate to the *lozengiers* the French tracts warn about (see pp. 142–5). He followed this with varied advice to a youth on the social dangers in several situations he might encounter: in the council chamber, at entertainments, and within his own household. He ended by summing up the three principal strategies the youth must adopt to be *zuhtic* (displaying propriety). He emphasized once more the love of God, living truthfully and acting with courtesy, from which he said flowed all the other public virtues.

DEFINING *PREUDOMMIE*

Constructing an analysis of the virtues of the *preudomme* over two centuries has its dangers, especially since there was a marked cultural shift within the same period

---

[40] For the stages of composition of the work, A. M. Rasmussen and O. Trokhimenko, 'Introduction', in *Medieval Conduct Literature: An Anthology of Vernacular Guides to Behaviour for Youths*, ed. M. D. Johnston (Toronto, 2009), 62–4. The name *Winsbecke* has been suggested to derive from the author of the original 'old poem' who advertised himself by the pseudonym 'the man from Winsbach' in a parallel with the Bavarian poet Tannhaüser.

which raised the standing of the knight as an ideal male above that of the *preudomme*. No male could aspire to the absolute plenitude and pinnacle of virtue after the beginning of the thirteenth century unless he were a knight, or at least so said the new generation of chivalric writers. This was a movement already under way in the last quarter of the twelfth century. It can be no coincidence that when Alan of Lille wrote his theological allegory on the creation of the godly and perfected New Man in the early 1180s, the hero was not portrayed as priest or monk, but very much as a young and beautiful knight. Alan was not writing his *Anticlaudianus* as a polemic against secular and worldly knighthood but to portray the evolution of a Christlike ideal male, yet he did not think it inappropriate that such a male should be portrayed in hauberk and helm. There is, then, an unavoidable overlap between knightly virtues and the virtues of the *preudomme*. Indeed, the argument of this book is that the model knight of the thirteenth-century tracts mounted a hostile takeover of the moral territory the *preudomme* had previously had to himself. So *Largesce* (Liberality, Generosity) is the subject of analysis both in this chapter and later on in the treatment of Chivalry, for it will be argued that the 'Queen of the Virtues' (as Robert de Blois called her) was interpreted differently in the context of a *preudomme* and in that of chivalric literature. The following analysis then favours twelfth-century sources over those of the thirteenth, though it uses thirteenth-century non-chivalric tracts which reflect on the ideal male without any restriction of social category.

I Sound Judgement (*Sens*) and Dependability (*Leauté*)

'Whoever has consulted with a *preudomme* can set his mind at ease,' says the *Proverbe au Vilain* in the 1170s, and explains that anyone heading off on a long journey should go with a *preudomme*, for he would get 'good counsel' from him.[41] Other proverbial vignettes give much the same message about his dependable judgement: 'You have to trust a *preudomme*'s counsel'; 'a *preudomme* puts things to right'; and 'the *preudomme*'s ideas are sensible and his conversation is sound'.[42] Robert de Blois preserved another proverb that tells us 'One *preudome* prefers the company of another', which argues they were a self-selecting elite of wise males.[43] It follows from this that maturity and experience are a large part of what made a *preudomme*, despite the literary topos of romance heroes being catapulted into the role almost as soon as they enter public life. A *preudomme* has to have had time to develop a reputation for giving sensible and sound advice, which has proved itself in the issue: another proverb had it that 'the end result demonstrates who's the *preudomme*'.[44] Medieval proverbial literature (the most basic surviving expression of a past habitus) in fact singles out more or less exclusively the dependability and good sense of the *preudomme* as his principal characteristic, and barely mentions any other, opposing him in this context naturally to the rash and reckless man (*fol*) who lacks a preudomme's *mesure*.

---

[41] *Proverbe au Vilain*, no. 249.   [42] *Proverbes français*, nos 414, 546, 1610.
[43] *Enseignement des princes*, 113 (l. 717): *Li proudons aimme le preudome*.
[44] *Proverbes français*, no. 47.

Sources other than proverbs have a rather more varied idea of what defined a *preudomme*, but they too always focus on good sense and judgement. Ramon Vidal pronounces: 'It's as true today as it always has been that all *prozoms* acquire influence from their intelligence (*sen*), their experience (*saber*) and from their good reputation.'[45] The argument of Robert de Blois is that it is from such men, not from the wicked (*les malvais*), that a prince should recruit his officers and advisers, as their judgement can obviously further his affairs. He launches into a paean exalting the service such select retainers can offer:

> *Proudomes* know at need to weather the hard knocks and dangerous setbacks in their affairs, the heat and the cold, and who can be counted on always to be prompt in the pressing affairs of their lord and devote their body and their honour to their lord's service; nor do they care either for their well-being or their own prosperity in doing their duty to their lord. These are the people the prince should retain around him and make much of; serving, respecting and enjoying himself with them, valuing them above all else. He may thus earn in one day that which would still have value in twenty years' time. No one can estimate or appreciate the value of a single *proudons* in one's affairs. His worth would not be overvalued were it assessed at the gold of fifteen cities.[46]

This definitive proverbial quality tallies with the eighth and ninth of Philip de Beaumanoir's virtues in his *enseignement* on the qualities of a good *bailli*. We are told by the anonymous author of the earliest cycle of the Prose Lancelot, writing around 1215, that such virtuous dispositions (*richece de cuer*) are nothing to do with inherited position and blood. The *preudomme*-hermit who advised King Arthur (at whose court every man was reputed to be *preudomme*) on how to bring his realm into order told him to seek talent actively amongst the humbler and poorer knights of his realm, and promote and favour those he found worthy.[47] Studies of the structure of the Norman, Angevin and Capetian courts alike tell us that capable kings had in fact long done precisely that, promoting intelligent and capable 'new men' from the lower end of their aristocracies to manage their affairs.[48]

Dependability was part of this, the vernacular quality of *leauté*. The moral quality of Bernier in *Raoul de Cambrai* was highlighted to the point of caricature by the fact that he long adhered to Raoul despite the man's repeated insults, open vicious-ness, and his part in the death of Bernier's mother. It was only an unprovoked physical assault on him that finally caused him to return his faith to Raoul.[49] This was an extreme case, of course, but it was a drama intended to test out and explore

---

[45] *Abril issia*, 72 (ll. 600–3).   [46] *Enseignement des princes*, 118 (ll. 885–904).

[47] *Lancelot do Lac* 1: 141, 287.

[48] It was not necessarily a strategy that everyone approved. A *contemptus mundi* poem of the mid twelfth century remarked sarcastically on the sort of officers they might turn out to be: 'Behold what miracle Mammon has accomplished; raising the proud and overbearing the humble!'; *Poésies inédites du moyen âge*, ed. M. Édélestand du Méril (Paris, 1854), 315 (ll. 49–58). Likewise, Robert de Blois clearly did not think a bonded serf was capable of the virtues demanded of a *preudomme*; *Enseignement des Princes*, 112–13 (ll. 675–703).

[49] *Raoul de Cambrai*, ed. and trans. (Fr.) W. W. Kibler (Paris, 1996), 132 (ll. 1618–19).

one of the foundations of public life. Dependability really was fundamental, and a mainstay of the social teaching offered the young. In the 1180s Robert of Ho observed that you could count on a *prodom* to remember and return favours. His *enseignement* offered a little homily on the pragmatic necessity of a lord being a dependable master to his servants:

> My son, if you have men under your charge you must care for and respect them more indeed than all your possessions, for there is one thing you must know and that's if you stand by them they will love you for it and work all the harder for you and will be behind you in all your ventures.[50]

Baldwin de Condé would in his day single out the same quality: a *preudomme* always kept his promises, or if not he lost his reputation.[51] Dependable loyalty was so much part of the daily currency of public life that it could be joked about. One of Philip of Flanders's courtiers could sing ironically in his lord's own hall that: 'When I hear all is lost and the lord count is utterly ruined, I'll make my way to Hainaut instead.'[52]

It was William Marshal's particular virtue, extolled by his biographer, that he was *leiaus*. He was consistent in his actions and fixed in his loyalty to his lord, even when his lord was the notorious tyrant-king, John of England, who was himself loyal to no one. His biographer conveys in his account of William's rallying to John in the troubled year of 1213 the astonishment of Marshal's followers at his consistent loyalty to John, despite the graceless and grudging treatment he had received from the court. Instead he answered the king's summons 'as a *preusdom* should', despite the king's open malice (*cruelté*) towards him, 'for he was ever a man to espouse the cause of *lealté*'.[53] We don't have Marshal's own words on this, but his younger contemporary, the Provençal courtier Sordello da Goito, gives us a career knight's take on the subject. It was his opinion that loyalty was the fundamental male virtue on which any public reputation (*pretz*) was built:

> Loyalty earns a man honour, it brings him wealth, it lengthens his life, it safeguards him from deceit and it is his true guide to salvation if he is indeed a loyal man. Every good quality that is in the world could not work without Loyalty.[54]

It should be no surprise, then, that when a *preudomme* felt he was obliged to renounce his allegiance to a lord, Western lay society surrounded such a momentous social event with ritual. This was the formal rupture called *defiance* or *diffidatio* ('unfaithing'), examples of which (such as Bernier's defiance of Raoul) are to be found in both vernacular literature and in the historical record. The loyal and dependable William Marshal himself went through it on one occasion. When in 1173 he had fled the Angevin court to Paris with the party of the Young King, he

---

[50] *Enseignements Trebor*, 86 (ll. 1267–74). Cf. *Enseignements Trebor*, 96 (ll. 1511–14).
[51] *Condé* 1: 96 (ll. 25–30).   [52] *Proverbe au Vilain*, no. 84.
[53] *History of William Marshal* 2: ll. 14853–90.
[54] *Ensenhamens d'Onor*, 210–11 (ll. 395–418), quotation ll. 409–16: *Lialtatz ten ome onrat;/ Lialtatz li dona rictat;/Lialtatz l'alonga sa via;/Lialtatz garda·l de bauzia;/Lialtatz l'aduz veramen/S'es be lials, a salvamen./Tug li bon aib, qu'el segle sion.*

and the rest of those who had previously sworn faith to King Henry II sealed a letter of defiance that was sent back to Normandy formally renouncing their allegiance to the elder king, and thus asserting that their subsequent violence towards him could not be characterized as treason.[55]

II Rationality (*Raison*)

Medieval scholastic thought believed rationality to be a characteristic male quality, a product of the hot and dry nature of the dominant male humours. This idea might very possibly have percolated into the medieval lay mind. However, the conduct tracts which deal with the *preudomme* are clearly tapping into a far wider pool of social attitudes when they also fix on rationality as one of the principal qualities of the ideal male. It is easy to see why this should be. Rationality in a lord allowed his followers to understand and respect his leadership and also to predict and appreciate his policy and actions, if they were themselves *preudommes*. This is what Philip de Beaumanoir says in a little essay on worthy and unworthy lords and their officers, the unworthy sort being incapable of behaving steadily (*loiaument*).[56] Wilfulness in a king or prince usually lay at the heart of their subjects' critiques of him as a ruler, and was indeed the root of tyranny. Significantly, even a renowned tyrant like John of England could see the point. In 1203, while on campaign in Normandy, he took time to dictate a letter rebuking the authorities in London who were failing to protect the Jewish minority in their city, and concluded: 'We know well enough that it's the idiots of your city not the respectable people that do this sort of thing, but sensible people must rein in the stupidity of fools.'[57]

On the other side of the divide of lordship, rationality in a household officer, bailiff or seneschal ensured sensible and defensible decisions, and a respect for proper process and justice. Its absence caused only confusion and incompetence. Thomasin of Zirclaria in 1216 reflected on this in similar terms to those Philip de Beaumanoir would one day use:

> Throughout each day you lords must provide us with an example of how we are to behave. If you act well then we shall gladly follow your good example but if you behave irregularly (*unrechte*) then we have no idea whom we should follow and we shall wander around lost at night until the morning. If you behave badly then you are like the night that takes the power of light away from us.[58]

The necessity for anyone, lord or not, to resort to mature and experienced advisers who could give rational counsel is pressed on their readers by many writers. The proverb had it that: 'What you do with *mesure* prospers and endures; what's done

---

[55] Crouch, *Marshal*, 51; Crouch, *Aristocracy*, 130–1.   [56] *Coutumes de Beauvaisis* 1: 24.

[57] *Rotuli Litterarum Patentium in Turri Londinensi asservati*, ed. T. Duffus Hardy (Record Commission, 1835), 33: *scimus enim bene quod per fatuos ville et non per discretos huiusmodi eveniunt, et debent discreti fatuorum stultitiam compescere.*

[58] *Welsche Gast*, 48 (ll. 1752–60).

without *raison* is destined to fall.'[59] An example of this is Daniel of Beccles's caution, expressed in proverbial distichons as if the wisdom of ages:

> When you need advice, take it from mature men seasoned in mind who are at heart to be trusted in what they say, and when you have asked them, you should stick to what they say. You should consider good advice more valuable than gold; complete ruin follows on from bad counsel.[60]

As a result, a man aspiring to be considered a *preudomme* was in danger every time he opened his mouth, for his words must enhance his air of deliberation, rationality, and wisdom, or the reputation he desired would be undermined. Ramon Vidal urges his readers to make sure their speech distanced them from being considered ill-natured, trivial and stupid:

> Whether among fools and villains or among worthy *prodomes* [see] that your words are [well chosen] and what you do is full of sense, and, above all, pleasant, well-bred and guided by good judgement.[61]

Baldwin de Condé therefore provides a rationale for the importance of reason in the conduct of the *preudomme*. Reason is the mother of restraint (*mesure*), he says, which to him is the central virtue of the *preudomme*. Reason allows the *preudomme* to lead an ordered and rational life pleasing to God, who is, of course, the source of all reason.[62] It was on the basis of his refusal to attend to wholesome advice and intelligent discourse in the hall that Gerald of Wales attacked his detested nephew and namesake. He grew to be a young man of entirely unfixed mind: distracted by trivia, attention-seeking, idle, facile and improvident. The younger Gerald in fact showed no interest in acquiring the rationality of a mature male and would even play games with children, 'though you were not now a small boy'. Without rationality he was infantile.[63]

III Restraint and Self-Control (*Mesure*)

One of the earliest identifiable aspects of the sort of behaviour appropriate to the court is what was called in Latin *disciplina*, a concept within secular conduct which Stephen Jaeger finds evident from the eleventh century onwards in German Latin sources. It was a characteristic of the behaviour of the exemplary courtier Ruodlieb, in the Latin courtly epic named after him. Ruodlieb was always in control of himself. In Jaeger's analysis of the quality, *disciplina* is neatly docketed as 'reason as the master of impulse', and he relates it to a desirable quality later prominent in German conduct literature—*zuht*, 'propriety'. He saw no French or Occitan word which could rate as an equivalent, but, as we will see, the Romance quality of

[59] *Proverbes français*, no. 1730.   [60] *Liber Urbani*, 28 (ll. 794–8).
[61] *Abril issia*, 102 (ll. 1123–8).   [62] *Condé* i, 99.
[63] *Speculum Duorum*, ed. Y. Lefèvre and R. B. C. Huygens, trans. B. Dawson (Cardiff, 1974), 132. Elsewhere Gerald also attacks his nephew as an 'undomesticated animal', the antithesis of reason and control; *Speculum Duorum*, 148.

mesure/meysura fits the bill more or less exactly.[64] It was being discussed as a desirable quality in a mature male well before 1150 by no less a person than Garin lo Brun, in a poem he wrote playfully mocking *Mesure*'s sober virtues as he was preparing to indulge himself and go off to enjoy a tournament. In *Nueyt e iorn suy en pessamen*, he contrasted it with Fun, or Levity (Occ. *leujairiai*, Fr. *legerie*). *Mesure* was the tiresome spoilsport who wanted to force Garin to be sober and businesslike, to be a man who was *pros*. It restrained his liberality and checked his light words; perhaps most significantly, it distanced him from the self-indulgent immaturity of youth.[65]

There were other twelfth-century voices raised in favour of *mesure* as the prince of virtues in a mature male.[66] Unsurprisingly in view of the German tradition identified by Jaeger, Hartmann von Aue in the 1180s continually recurred to *mazze* (restraint) as the principal virtue of the accomplished knight, lord or prelate: God-given self-control in conduct and ambition.[67] At much the same time Guiot de Provins, in his *Armëure de Chevalier*, hailed *Mesure* as the truest of virtues, a God-given weapon against Pride and Presumption, which stood behind all that was admirable in human art and all that was constant in human behaviour.[68] In 1196 the Provençal household knight Raimbaut de Vaqueiras debated which was the finest quality of a lord in a *jeu-parti* with the count of Valentinois, who voted for *mezura*. In 1205 we find out what Raimbaut meant by it when he listed for his lord these qualities amongst his own solid virtues when soliciting further favour and reward: 'in your court I have known how to behave myself in seemly fashion, to give and serve and to be patient and discreet, and never have I given any man cause to grieve.'[69] A heavily controlled *mezura* was in Thomasin of Zirclaria's Italian mind when he composed this passage in favour of restraint for a German audience.

> Anyone who submits to his anger says and does things he regrets afterwards. For this reason one should be careful not to let one's anger get the better of one. One should fasten it with bonds of good sense to the wall of correct behaviour. If a person maintains his composure when he is angry, a decent propriety (*guotiu zuht*) will accompany him.[70]

So for this reason Baldwin de Condé, like Garin lo Brun over a century earlier, singled out *mesure* as the defining quality of the *preudomme*, and he was not alone in his generation in doing so. In the *enseignement* incorporated within the romance of Biaudouz, the hero's solicitous mother pressed this view on her son: 'Restraint

[64] Jaeger, *Courtliness*, 130–3.
[65] '*Nueyt e iorn suy en pessamen*', ed. and trans. (It.) F. Carapezzo, in *Lectura Tropatorum*, 1 (2008), 15–18.
[66] It was, for instance, the central characteristic of the conduct of Wace's Arthur; see Aurell, *Lettered Knight*, 281–2.
[67] *Gregorius*, ed. H. Paul (Tübingen, 1966), 40 (ll. 1531–3): *Ritterschaft daz ist ein leben der im die mâze kan gegeben, so enmac nieman baz genesen*, and cf. ibid. 59 (ll. 2270–2), 98 (ll. 3793–5), 99 (ll. 3823–6).
[68] *Armëure*, 106–8. [69] Raimbaut, 139 (ll. 9–16); 308 (ll. 108–10).
[70] *Welsche Gast*, 19 (ll. 673–80).

(*Mesure*) surpasses all other virtues; because of this people say: "Moderation has its own rewards" (*mesure dure*).'[71] This common proverb is given more than one contemporary gloss. In the twelfth century it was explained as a warning against rash and impulsive actions that lose the wealthy their fortunes, and it was a quality frequently associated in twelfth-century sources with the wise (*sage*) man, who was invariably *amesuré*, 'restrained' or 'balanced'. A lengthy commentary on the same proverb was offered rather later by Philip de Novare, who took it as a quality desirable in all admirable men, not just in a rich lord:

> A man should work hard to be restrained, for it has long been said: 'Moderation has its own rewards (*mesure dure*).' Powerful magnates are much respected for their moderation. And if the powerless endure what they must with equanimity, they are said to be men of great goodness and humility. *Mesure* is a virtue that both God and men approve of, and people who are restrained benefit from it when in conflict with greater men; it can happen in two ways: one is that the great men will let them off more easily from their conflict; the other is that if there is a matter which requires the swearing of vengeance, lesser men can achieve vengeance and find a place to take it with more calculation. Poor men have no choice but to be circumspect, for rashness can disgrace and destroy them, and everyone will say that it would be justified. Their *mesure* can allow them to avoid harm and disgrace, and through their pains and service they might yet attain wealth.[72]

Restraint is not by any means to be taken as a virtue to be courted only by the male, for women too had to exercise moderation in all they did and said (see pp. 88–9 below). But in the female it was urged in the context of the charged relationships between men and women, which the *preudefemme* must control so as not to compromise her personal reputation. The male was to exercise *mesure* in the public sphere, in council and assembly, so as to enhance his standing as a wise and rational actor, and so be a man worthy of trust, recognition, promotion and patronage.

Speech here was a danger: a *preudomme* must weigh his words. Thomasin of Zirclaria urged young people going out in the world to adopt a sober air, since immoderate laughter was the characteristic of a fool. He advised a man to listen a lot and say little, as listening did no harm but talking often led to trouble. For him the quality of self-discipline (*vorhte*) was absolutely essential for a youth to acquire and display in any public context.[73] Robert de Blois made such discipline central to being a *preudomme*. He warned clerics and laymen alike who wanted to be considered among the ranks of the *preudommes* to avoid indulging in the malicious and scurrilous mockery of rivals and neighbours. It would bring a man among the ranks of the despised *lozengiers*—the lice (*verins*) in the body social, as Robert colourfully called them elsewhere in his work.

> Be wary of crude speech and jokes; very little store is placed on clerics and lay people of all conditions whose habit is to slander others. Is slander therefore so very wicked a

---

[71] *Biaudouz*, ed. J-Ch. Lemaire (Liège, 2008), 42, a proverb which occurs as early as the 1170s. She may have also been quoting another proverb: *De tout et par tout est mesure*; *Proverbes français*, no. 567.

[72] *Proverbe au Vilain*, no. 8; *Quatre Tenz*, 76–77 (c. 138).

[73] *Welsche Gast*, 15 (ll. 527–32), 16–17 (ll. 581–604).

mouthful? It most certainly is. It would not be a pleasant or attractive feature in a *proudome*. This one imperfection should shame any man who is prey to envy and it cancels out even great civility (*cortoisie*).[74]

The passage makes play with the contrast between unrestrained words, which are *vilains*, and the Courtliness to which a *preudomme* should aspire. Robert went on to say that unless he was one of the great of the world, to whom judgement properly belonged, a *preudomme* should not run down a man who deserved the world's contempt, even if such a man might be moved to examine and amend his behaviour when he heard the criticism repeated. That might be one good result of slander, he says, but a man who indulged in it had already lost the ability to restrain himself and was demonstrating a deep moral fault, 'a vein of pure villainy'.[75]

IV Fortitude (*Hardiesce*)

Earl Robert de Mowbray of Northumbria, according to Geoffrey Gaimar, lived a life characterized by ambition, violence, and, in 1096, rebellion. But after his capture and because of the trials of a long imprisonment, Earl Robert ended his days as *prodom*, 'who would never have refused to give away anything he had'.[76] The life of a *preudomme* might, then, not necessarily be a triumphal procession but be one of setbacks, distinguished because of the moral struggle which went with overcoming adversity, as we have seen above in the biography of William Marshal and as the tale of Ruodlieb attested a century and more earlier. This would be one reason why hermits appear so often as *preudommes* in vernacular sources. From thinking only of his own advancement, Robert de Mowbray became selfless under Fortune's chastisement. Their ability to take hard knocks (*durs essauz*) and overcome difficulties is what distinguishes *proudomes* to Robert de Blois, and he believed it was what made them profitable servants to a discriminating lord: 'They do not care either for body or for wealth in doing their duty for their lord. These are the people the prince should retain around him and make much of; serving, respecting and entertaining them, and holding them dear above all else.'[77]

This quality in a *preudomme* included enduring the hard grind of necessary but burdensome labour. It was *hardis*, the fifth virtue listed by Philip de Beaumanoir amongst the qualities desirable in a man of affairs: vigour in his activities and an avoidance of laziness. Two generations earlier Robert of Ho had recommended the same quality in these terms:

> My son, anyone who wants to become a *prodome* without doing a stroke of work won't make it. Anyone who wants to strive for honour needs must strive against laziness so as to achieve something that is not in the least pleasant for him to do.[78]

This sort of hardihood was, of course, a fine military virtue, as much as a civic one. As a result it was one of the qualities of a *preudomme* which was to be seized on by

---

[74] *Enseignement des Princes*, 101 (ll. 301–10).
[75] *Enseignement des Princes*, 102 (l. 340).   [76] *Estoire*, 334 (ll. 6176–9).
[77] *Enseignement des princes*, 118 (ll. 885–98).   [78] *Enseignements Trebor*, 131 (ll. 2384–9).

chivalric texts. Good and useful knights needs must be *hardiz* in their endeavours, and if one sees the pursuit of prowess as the energizing core of masculine knighthood, then the hardier a man was, the better a knight he was too, to the point where egregious suffering, and even wilful self-sacrifice, were welcomed as a way of demonstrating fortitude in the most devoted (and indeed devout) warriors.[79] But chivalric hardihood was easier to demonstrate than the moral fortitude of *preudommie*: the wise *prodom* Count Oliver may have been *hardiz* but so also was his friend, the suicidally ill-judging Roland.[80] The *hardement* of the *Song of Roland* was physical endurance, admirable for being fearless not for being judicious.

V Generosity (*Largesce*)

In discoursing on the life of Gilbert of Surrey, the canon of Merton makes much of his generosity, which may seem an unusual quality in a sheriff and justice at the court of that predatory king, Henry I of England (reigned 1100–35), whose demands weighed heavily on the consciences of his servants.[81] But if Gilbert was to be portrayed as a superior male, he must also be generous. So his charitable nature was depicted as so outstanding as to verge on the ridiculous; his young household servants used to masquerade as beggars as he rode past to benefit from the pennies he would freely distribute to those he passed, and then dash along the back lanes to encounter him further along the road and so get more undeserved alms from him.[82] Generosity to the poor was, of course, a virtue in an exemplary Christian like Gilbert, but he might very well have encountered in his eleventh-century education—as he was both numerate and literate—the commonplace reflection in the *Cato Novus* that generosity was expected in a man towards his friends and companions. *Facetus* in turn would reflect that 'Generosity will bring you credit in your personal affairs, though you will deserve nothing but contempt in being generous with another man's property.'[83]

The unapologetically secular writer Arnaut-Guilhem de Marsan was acquainted with Cato's distichs, and made much of generosity as a virtue of the ideal courtly twelfth-century aristocrat. The pragmatic necessity of generous hospitality in a lord is clear in his advice to an aspirant: 'Be generous in your expenses and keep an open house with neither closed door nor key.' But generosity became for Marsan a studied diffidence towards material possessions and almost evidence of aristocratic grandeur as he meditated on the necessity to play hard when gambling (and in this instance, to throw *mesure* to the winds):

Always pay up freely when you have debts. If money is running short play on willingly; go for the high game for the greater the risk, the greater the honour. Games of chance are not for a miserly fellow who throws the dice on the table a hundred times just to

---

[79] As explored in Kaeuper, *Holy Warriors*, 57–65.   [80] *Song*, 1: l. 2027.
[81] D. Crouch, 'The Troubled Deathbeds of Henry I's Servants: Death, Confession and Secular Conduct in the Twelfth Century', *Albion*, 34 (2002), 24–36.
[82] M. L. Colker, 'Latin Texts concerning Gilbert, Founder of Merton Priory', *Studia Monastica*, 12 (1970), 269.
[83] *Facetus*, 288.

gain a penny. A man who takes up the dice and then drops out is asking to lose his reputation: this is why I tell you to stick with the high game.[84]

Our thirteenth-century lay writers on superior conduct are unanimous in regarding generosity as central to what it was to be a virtuous man: it was after all a quality close to the mainspring of their society. Should then generosity be expected of every *preudomme*, or only of the rich lord who supported a household and maintained rule over provinces? The decided view of Count Robert le Dauphin of the Auvergne, as reported by Ramon Vidal, was that it was a quality principally demanded of the great of the earth, if they were to demonstrate Nobility in their lives.

> Truly, generosity (*adutz*) is for many reasons the source of reputation, of light and brilliance; from largesse comes a man's lands, rivers, lordship and demesne. All trickery aside, a noble spirit achieves through its endeavour more than is asked of it, generosity derives from it and it supports and distinguishes everything; largesse makes its possessor worthy. It is a fact that generous men, upright and distinguished in all they do possess a worthiness common people do not, and to a degree above all other barons.[85]

Robert de Blois, on the other hand, believed that the poor man who maintained *largesce* was one of the three types of men most beloved by God.[86] For Sordello da Goito largesse was indeed the finest thing there was in a man of means, but was folly unless it was done with discrimination and purpose, and could harm as much as exalt him.[87] Baldwin de Condé thought it a general and necessary characteristic of any worthy male: 'the *preudomme* is generous, but the wicked fellow despises any meaningful gift for he is so pained by his aversion to the idea of giving that he would prefer death to an act of generosity.'[88] Brunetto Latini went further still and reckoned *Larghezza* to be the principal of his four courtly virtues, to whom the allegorical figure of *Cortezia* deferred as her mentor, and indeed said that they were one and the same, though they carried different names.[89]

Philip de Beaumanoir summed up the view that passed into the chivalric thought-world. He regarded largesse as the exemplary characteristic of every *preudomme* and located it as a central virtue in his ideal male. Without generosity, he said, no man could be considered courtly and beyond reproach, and those two qualities allowed him to advance his career and achieve the love and respect of the world and God alike.[90] So, for Beaumanoir, generosity was demanded of both the lord and his dependant within the means of each. He brought forward a mix of pragmatic and moral justifications for why generosity was to be demanded of the *preudomme*. The moral message explicit in generosity explains why it was to become a male quality that was particularly favoured by chivalric writers, into whose hypermoral realm it was to be recruited and exalted to a Christlike virtue (see p. 145).

---

[84] *Qui comte vol apendre*, 84 (ll. 436–8), 86 (ll. 455–68).
[85] *Abril issia*, 68 (ll. 533–44).   [86] *Enseignement des princes*, 129 (l. 1270).
[87] *Ensenhamens d'Onor*, 719 (ll. 711–16).   [88] *Condé* 1: 97 (ll. 35–8).
[89] *Tesoretto*, 223 (ll. 1335–44), 231 (ll. 1583–98).
[90] *Coutumes de Beauvaisis* 1: 20. The quality of *netteté* which he mentions translates variously as 'purity' and 'cleanliness'; from the context, Philip means it to be taken as a moral/theological virtue, so I translate it as 'beyond reproach'.

Nonetheless, even after the chivalric turn, writers on conduct continued to take a pragmatic line on largesse in society, rather than an exclusively theological one. Philip de Novare, like Philip de Beaumanoir, sees it as demanded of all conditions of worthy males, not just the knight. He gives a mixed moral and pragmatic justification for its importance, and echoes Sordello in his robust caution that generosity should always be restrained by reason.

> Everyone should be as generous as his ability and circumstances permit, firstly for the sake of his soul and then for his honour in this world. But no one should be so generous as that generosity which is praised by fools, for profligacy is not generosity. A man should give sensibly, and if he has not the means to be liberal then no one is going to lose by the sort of gifts he can afford. But nonetheless no one should abandon the idea of generosity. Avarice is a very sordid vice, and Envy is even worse. The miser and the cheat cannot bear to pay or give anything; so they live in torment and the things they have mean nothing to them, for they cannot bear to take comfort in or do anything which would be to the benefit and honour of their souls and bodies.[91]

MASCULINITY AND THE *PREUDOMME*

The *preudomme* as analysed here becomes the ideal type of a male of the central Middle Ages, whose proverbial qualities defined what contemporaries thought was admirable in a man of any condition within society. He is therefore the closest that we can come to a self-conscious contemporary definition of masculinity in the twelfth and thirteenth centuries. From proverbs, conduct tracts and a wide range of literary references we find that the medieval occidental mind idealized a pattern of male behaviour which was anything but uncontrolled, competitive and violent; quite the opposite in fact. Nor was it necessarily founded on the sexual function of the male, though the medieval mind was certainly frank in the way it might express the importance of a man's sexual potency to his maleness, not least in the flaunting of phallic objects and imagery in daily life.[92] But *li mauvais* as much as *li preudomme* could be virile. Both were sexually potent; it was the morality of their sexual lives that differed. The sexuality of a wicked man was likely to be *lecherie*: it was debauched and perverted, and such a villain was the sort of man who resorted to rape. Advice to the young male from Dhuoda through to Facetus warned him against sinking so far in his need for sexual gratification as to compulsively seek out prostitutes.

The medieval idealizations of masculinity we have looked at in this chapter were not, then, defined by sexual function, but rather in demonstrating control of a man's worst impulses (sexual and otherwise) and in uncomplaining fortitude in his daily life. In this regard, it has been observed in studies of the thousands of English defamation cases in church courts that when later medieval men insulted other

---

[91] *Quatre Tenz*, 73–4 (c. 132).
[92] R. Gilchrist, *Medieval Life: Archaeology and the Life Course* (Woodbridge, 2012), 99–103.

men it was usually by impugning their honesty and reputation, not their virility.[93] There is evidence the same could be said of the thirteenth century in the examples of what constitutes defamation in a French custumary, where the choice insults were that a man was dishonest (*faus*), a thief (*larron*), a murderer (*murtrier*), or stinking (*pugnais*), while a woman might be called a whore (*putain*).[94] The ideal of masculinity represented by the *preudomme* was a man who could be relied on, who guarded his tongue, took what life threw at him, avoided confrontation, and tried to keep his (non-phallic) sword in its sheath if possible, though he should be doughty if combat was unavoidable. In all such a man said and did, he must show the sort of rationality and common sense that gained respect for his judgement and raised him in the public assembly. German, Occitan and Francien writers also observe that this pattern of behaviour would do him no harm in the eyes of the sort of women worth having. Contemporaries also pragmatically added that in demonstrating such qualities there was a career pay-off: respect and a good reputation were fine things in themselves, but they could be converted into the enhanced value of such a man to a potential lord and employer, for sensible lords wanted honest officers who acknowledged moral boundaries.[95] Restraint and control, however, did not apply to a tight grip on a man's purse strings, which would be characterized as miserliness, a most uncourtly quality. If a *preudomme* hoped to attract patronage of greater people in society by the self-control and dependability of his public behaviour, he must as a lord or employer be willing to be free-handed where he was able.

From the studied exaltation of these gendered male qualities, the *preudomme* can naturally be interpreted as also to some extent a critique of contemporary masculinity. His negative image would be a male who was violent, grossly lecherous, underhanded, reckless, irrational, quarrelsome, envious and grasping. We may assume—indeed we know—these were common accusations against males at the time. In fact we find in medieval sources a (non-gendered) archetype, the 'villain', who displayed all these faults and more besides. The villain directly confronted medieval men (but also women) with the worst features of their gender within society. To be '*vilain*' was to be outside the garden of *courtoisie* where *preudommes* and *preudefemmes* resided, and to be called such was taken as a grievous insult at all levels of society, even that of the 'villein' (see Chapter 6). This bears interesting comparison with the findings of a recent study of late medieval masculinity, which finds that the point of definition of maleness in the fifteenth century was also a moral one, between a 'true' and 'false' man: it was the man you could count on who was the ideal pattern of the male.[96] The fifteenth-century English 'true man' was in fact a translated *preudomme*, and thus his moral descendant.

---

[93] L. R. Poos, 'Sex, Lies, and the Church Courts of Pre-Reformation England', *Journal of Interdisciplinary History*, 25 (1995), 585–607, esp. 605–6 for the gender differential.

[94] *Établissements*, 2: 288–9 (c. 154).

[95] For the embrace of an ethic of public service founded on the same sources, F. Lachaud, 'Ethics and Office in England in the Thirteenth Century', in *Thirteenth-Century England*, 11 (2005), 16–30.

[96] D. Neal, *The Masculine Self in Late Medieval England* (Chicago, 2008), 42–7.

The *preudomme* was an ideal of masculinity that spanned medieval society; he might be rich or poor, cleric, warrior or merchant, but much the same characteristics were expected of him in whatever field he was. Writing in the early years of the reign of Louis IX of France, Robert de Blois makes it perfectly clear that the *preudomme* he described embraced ideals which applied across the board to '*clers et lais de touz mestiers*'.[97] So the stance I take here is at odds with the idea that there were medieval *masculinities*. This is a theory that depends on the exclusively biological definition of masculinity, which is more appropriate to a study of sexuality than to one of gender: by this reductionist approach a male was male because he used his penis for the purpose for which God gave it him. If a man was rendered celibate by choice or by castration, then he was no longer fully male. If a man was homosexually inclined, then he too was at odds with his own masculinity, especially in the case of a man who received another anally. This standpoint—developed by ecclesiastical historians with an uncritical approach to body theory—has led to an unwarranted conclusion that there was a crisis point in medieval ideas of gender when the papacy began around 1050 its long campaign to forbid clergy from entering into sexual relationships with women. The idea is that this threatened the clergy with forced feminization, or at least a lesser masculinity than the layman, who was still able to fulfil his biological role.[98] At its extreme this approach has produced a conclusion that the masculinity of a cleric was 'radically different' or 'contradictory' to that of a knight, and even to ideas that male clergy formed a third gender.[99]

It would be safe to assume that the celibacy demanded of the later medieval cleric might well have challenged him in all sorts of ways. But if so, this would not apply to the western Europe of most of the period studied here but to the later Middle Ages when ecclesiastical disciplinary machinery began to be more effective in hunting out offenders. The students and clergy who appear in the thirteenth-century French *fabliaux* may be hypocritical and greedy, but they are not attacked for double standards in their sex lives, which they are assumed to be enjoying, sometimes with more enthusiasm than was good for them.[100] Following the

---

[97] *Enseignement des Princes*, 101 (l. 303).

[98] This was first proposed in J. A. McNamara, 'The *Herrenfrage*: the restructuring of the Gender System, 1050–1150', in *Medieval Masculinities: Regarding Men in the Middle Ages*, ed. C. A. Lees (Minneapolis, 1994), 3–29. It is a view which has been discussed in French studies of masculinity; see Lett, *Hommes et femmes*, 48–9, where, however, the pursuit of celibacy is taken as a form of masculine endeavour, rather than a compromised masculinity. Karras, *From Boys to Men*, 8, finds crises in masculinity or femininity unhelpful models in gender studies. Ecclesiastical historians still offer a version of this theory, if subtler and less stark; P. H. Cullum and K. J. Lewis, 'Introduction', in *Religious Men and Masculine Identity in the Middle Ages*, ed. ead. (Woodbridge, 2013), 4–11.

[99] As in J. L. Nelson, 'Monks, Secular Men and Masculinity, *c*.900', in *Masculinity in Medieval Europe*, ed. D. M. Hadley (Harlow, 1999), 121–42, quotation from p. 131, who goes even beyond the *Herrenfrage* theory of a point of crisis, and applies the approach as far back as Carolingian times. Her study relies too much on tenth-century literature of monastic conversion, where extremes of alienation from secular life and norms are to be expected.

[100] Cf. *Estormi*, in *The French Fabliau, B.N. MS 837*, ed. and trans. R. Eichmann and J. DuVal (2 vols, London, 1984) pp. i, 24, a *fabliau* whose moral was not that its three lecherous priests, killed by an outraged husband, paid the price for trespassing against their vocation, but that 'it is folly to covet somebody else's wife'.

implications of the theory of a 'crisis of masculinity', later medieval historians have concluded that the clerical male was in their period so handicapped and challenged by a denial of his sexuality that his masculinity was defined as less than that of the layman, to the point that the cleric troubled by it was driven to ignore his vows and assert his sexual potency.[101] However, the sources we have looked at here make no such distinction for our earlier period, when celibacy was in practice optional for a secular clerk.[102] The extreme position adopted by writers who define masculinity by the monocausal function of the penis and its emissions is that medieval clergy were regarded in their day as neither male nor female.[103] This is not an idea I would entertain, not least because it argues an unacceptably limited medieval conception of what made a male and ignores a large corpus of medieval views on the subject. There is also the general point that medieval people did not incorporate anywhere near the degree of sexual imagery and discourse in their daily life that modern Western society does. In such a society its own definitions of gender naturally veered towards the moral rather than the biological.[104]

There were clear moral congruences across the variety of male characters within society: a hermit was *preudomme* because his life of self-imposed austerity and prayerful reflection demonstrated his moral excellence, as much as did the honesty, judgement and restraint of the *preudomme* who was a loyal seneschal to his lord, and also as did the lord who had fallen on hard times and who displayed fortitude under the lash of fate. Self-control, good judgement, loyalty, honesty and forbearance were appreciated in males of whatever condition. It has been observed in other studies that there were further commonalities in male behaviour and ideals across society, lay and clerical. The one principally fixed on is hormone-driven male competitiveness, found alike in university lecture halls, guilds merchant and on tournament fields. But the argument of this chapter is that as early as the eleventh century there were also shared moral and ethical, as much as behavioural, traits in the contemporary understanding of masculinity.

The construction of medieval masculinity can be approached in a number of ways. Medieval masculinity, as has been suggested, can be profitably explored by opposing it to femininity, or more directly and less crudely by opposing it to ideas of immaturity: the boy from whom the man develops into a mature male. But the ideal of the *preudomme* challenges assumptions that have so far been made about medieval masculinity, whose study at present is as yet in its early days. A man could

---

[101] P. H. Cullum, 'Clergy, Masculinity and Transgression in Late Medieval England', in *Masculinity in Medieval Europe*, 178–96, though this idea was contested in Neal, *The Masculine Self,* 118–22. J. D. Thibodeaux, *The Manly Priest: Clerical Celibacy, Masculinity and Reform in England and Normandy, 1066–1300* (Philadelphia, 2015) presents an argument that varying masculinities can be encountered in ecclesiastical rhetoric before 1200, where monks are presented as manlier than secular clergy. Though this may be so, to accept it as an argument for multiple masculinities one would have to define gender only by sexual function, which medieval people were far from doing.

[102] For a detailed study of the widespread resistance to celibacy amongst clergy well into the thirteenth century, H. M. Thomas, *The Secular Clergy in England, 1066–1216* (Oxford, 2014), 164–77.

[103] D. L. d'Avray, *Medieval Marriage: Symbolism and Society* (Oxford, 2005), 89–90, where the author tells us that the concept is very much 'in the air', an image I would adjust somewhat.

[104] Karras, *Sexuality*, 150–6.

be *preudomme* and yet also not be a lord or patriarch and thus personally powerful, the subjugating male of feminist scholarship. The *preudomme* was not a male who had to succeed by being endlessly (and sometimes pointlessly) competitive, as both physiological and literary interpretations of masculinity tend to assume he should be. The moral-ethical definition of masculinity offered by the *preudomme* presents a different image of the medieval male to that of writers who approach it through body theory, as is especially the case amongst historians of the clerical male, where frustrated sexuality is the principal and sometimes only point at issue. The twelfth-century sources we have looked at here which directly address the subject of masculinity are considered and analytical in the way they self-consciously define the gender. They see masculinity as a struggle, certainly, but not always with other males or their own sexuality. To be a worthy male and respected above others, the struggle can be a moral one waged against a man's own destructive impulses, and the winning male is the more rational, accomplished, good-humoured and intelligent man, the man fit for the court.

5

The *Preudefemme*

The need for an avatar of male excellence to reign over the courtly habitus made it inevitable that, as Adam needed an Eve to rule over Creation, the *preudomme* needed a *preudefemme* to preside beside him over the courtly world. It was a matter of grammatical necessity that if there was a discreet and mature *prodomme* acting in the world as the idealized male, then there had also to be a corresponding *prodefemme*, as Robert de Boron casually and unconsciously assumed in his *Merlin*.[1] An occasional French synonym for her was as a *preudame*, a form which made the understanding of her as a female counterpart to the *preudomme* all the more obvious.[2] The necessity of the concept meant it crossed vernaculars. The mind of Thomasin of Zirclaria translated the Romance term as Middle High German *biderbe wip* for his readers north of the Alps, and he talked of female models (*bilde*) of outstanding conduct in history and Scripture whom any woman should emulate. The author of *Winsbeckin* talked of the idealized 'honourable woman' (*erbær wip*) who was available to provide a model of good conduct for all females.[3]

What made a *preudefemme* was not, however, necessarily what made a *preudomme* or *biderbe man*. To begin with, there is the question of her profile. The *preudomme*, as we have seen, was a didactic object within the habitus: what a *preudomme* did and how he behaved was what other males should aspire to be and do. As a result he was a universal and idealized creature of proverb and tract. The same could not be said of a *preudefemme*, or at least not to the degree of her male counterpart. There are few proverbial notices of her conduct, and what does appear betrays limited expectations, such as the thirteenth-century caution that 'No *prodefemme* calls her maid a whore'.[4] Modest language appears elsewhere as a desirable trait in such a woman, as in Jean de Meung's amused dialogue between the prim male Lover and a rather too frank Lady Reason. He rebukes her for her language: 'I don't

---

[1] *Merlin: roman du xiiiᵉ siècle*, ed. A. Micha (Geneva, 2000), 100–1, and for Chrétien's use of it, E. Köhler, *L'aventure chevaleresque: idéal et réalité dans le roman courtois*, trans. E. Kaufholz (Paris, 1974), 158. Ulrich von Liechtenstein has *ein guot wip* matched to *ein biderber man* as the God-given summit of human happiness; *Frauenbuch*, 74 (l. 389).

[2] G. W. Carl, '"Tu cuides que nos seions taus come autres femes comunaus": the sexually confident woman in the *Roman de Troie*', in *Gender Transgressions: Crossing the Normative Barrier in Old French Literature*, ed. K. J. Taylor (New York, 1998), 119–20. It has been argued by at least one author that the Middle Ages had no concept of femininity, the untenability of which stance should be obvious from the title of this chapter; see T. Laqueur, *Making Sex: Body and Gender from the Greeks to Freud* (Cambridge, Mass., 1990), 8.

[3] *Welsche Gast*, 22 (ll. 788–90), 23 (l. 815); *Winsbeckin*, 118.

[4] *Proverbes français*, no. 1724.

consider you to be courtly when you refer by name to "testicles", a word which is out of place in the mouth of a well-brought up girl. I have no idea how you, so wise and fair, have the nerve to talk about them, or at least not to do so by some allusion, by which such polite evasion a *preudefame* would refer to them.'[5] Jean's comment, however whimsical, does at least impose the same obligation on a *preudefemme* to maintain courtly norms as is expected of her male counterpart.

TRACTS ON THE IDEAL WOMAN

Since medieval women went out into the world and were judged on the way they conducted themselves there, there was no shortage of advice and no lack of moral exemplars as to how they should behave under the world's gaze. But though both *preudomme* and *preudefemme* must be (for instance) sensible and respectable, the expectations on how a woman should fulfil her role were written far smaller. Late in the thirteenth century the philosopher and physician William of Aragon rationalized that men acted on a public stage and their deeds made greater demands in internal resources and effort. Women's lives were lived in the private and domestic sphere and concerned the family, so he therefore entertained the notion that a woman could not be expected to be as noble as a man, since he defined Nobility in moral terms. On the other hand, his syllogism included the observation that some women were more effective in their activities than men were. His resolution in the end accepted that for all that women might excel, in practical terms men had at least a greater capacity to demonstrate noble behaviour.[6]

We have no difficulty in finding out what the expectations were on women. There are a number of important works devoted to (male) expectations of female conduct before 1300. The earliest is very early: Garin lo Brun's Occitan *E·l termini del estiu*, which has to date to the first half of the twelfth century, is particularly valuable as being independent of any scholastic or theological Latin impulse towards defining the superior woman. Robert de Blois offered his *Chastoiement* (Cautions) to women in the 1230s, and his tract is important for our purposes here as the work deliberately sets out to define the *preudefemme*, and so we will return to it later in some detail. The same generation produced two other notable *enseignements* for women. An anonymous Picard writer offered a commentary on the female condition in the *Lai de Conseil*, which is framed as a discourse on how to manage relations between the sexes, given by a wise man of the world to a young and wealthy married woman looking for a lover. A very different discourse is an anonymous Middle High German dialogue on proper conduct between a mother and her daughter, known as the *Winsbeckin* (the proverbial lady from Windsbach, a place in Franconia). Later in the century, the inimitable Ulrich von Liechtenstein offered a full and frank discussion of women's place in the world in a dialogue between the sexes which goes by the name of *Das Frauenbuch* (*c*.1257). The last

---

[5] Meung, *Rose*, 424 (ll. 6924–32).   [6] Aragon, *De Nobilitate*, 88–90.

quarter of the thirteenth century produced more tracts: Amanieu de Sescás's Occitan *Essenhamen de la Donzela* (written very much in imitation of Garin lo Brun), and Philip de Novare's *Quatre Tenz* (which like *Das Frauenbuch* has parallel discussions of the male and female condition). A final thirteenth-century work on women is *Le Miroir des Bonnes Femmes*, which (unlike the others) is not so obviously directed at aristocratic women and was written by a cleric, a Franciscan friar. It has the virtue of indicating the extent to which these precepts penetrated broader society, or at least that section of it which had aspirations, in that copies of the *Miroir* were to be found in French bourgeois households.[7]

Quite a number of writers other than these felt the impulse to categorize female good qualities. Their efforts are incorporated within longer essays on conduct. Long excursions on the vices of bad women and the virtues of good ones were indulged in before 1216 by Stephen de Fougères, Daniel of Beccles and Thomasin of Zirclaria. Arnaut de Mareuil in the 1170s was another one of these, and his *Rasos es e Mesura* is notable in being one of the first compositions not just to set expectations of female conduct down in a concise and lapidary way but to look for a central defining principle of acceptable femininity. Though he was well aware that each woman had different gifts, he put together a succinct reflection as to how their best qualities might be categorized, which might be taken as the first explicit definition of the *preudefemme*.

> It is…true that ladies have a number of claims to be considered distinguished: some for their beauty, others for their virtue; some for their fine manner of speech, and others again for their dignity. Some are pleasant to be with and others are knowledgeable. You can't be unaware that good looks are much appreciated in ladies; but a woman is above all honoured for her easy manners, her wit and her knowledge, depending on how well she employs them.[8]

This was the sort of behaviour women were invited by Arnaut to see as praiseworthy (*lauzors*). Earning public approbation was the incentive that was offered them by him and their other male instructors, and it was certainly possible that a woman of those days might do so. As a writer of the same generation wrote in a passage in praise of female judgement in public affairs, 'a man should particularly prize his *prode feme*, value, love and rejoice in her; but he who has a bad woman (*malvaise*) should rather get rid of her.'[9] Arnaut pinned down the central concern in female conduct as *pretz* (reputation). This was important for men too, but modern writers on medieval masculinity tend to locate the core of male distinction not so much in general praise for being courtly as in the active reward for it—*proesce* (merit, achievement). Arnaut contrasted what got males approval with the way women got

---

[7] K. Ashley, 'The *Miroir des Bonnes Femmes*: Not for Women only?', in *Medieval Conduct*, ed. K. Ashley and R. L. A. Clark (Minneapolis, 2001), 86–105.

[8] *Rasos es e Mesura*, 22 (ll. 247–60): *Las donas eyssamens/an pretz diversamens:/las unas de beleza,/las autras de proeza;/las unas ben parlans,/las autras benestans;/las unas son plazens,/las autras conoissens./A domna, so sapchatz,/esta mot gent beutatz;/mas sobre tot l'agensa/sabers e conoissensa/quel fa cascun onrar/segon ques tanh a far.*

[9] *Aspremont*, 1: ll. 1452–4: *Sa prode feme doit on forment cierir/Et chier tenir et amer et joïr;/qui l'a malvaise, si s'en doit astenir.*

it in just such a gendered way: men have to marshal troops, fight bravely, excel as horsemen, and offer public service, and what defines their virtue is their *proeza*.[10] Women's concern in conduct was defending the reputation they had, not actively seeking out new sources of merit. Everything was to lose for a woman, therefore, and little was to gain.[11]

DEFINING THE *PREUDEFEMME*

All the authors of dedicated essays on female conduct wrote independently of each other (with the exception of Amanieu de Sescás), though of course they wrote within the same constraints and concerns of the established *enseignement* tradition (apart from the *Miroir*, which owed more to the sermon). But the fact that each was surveying the subject from his own watchtower has some advantages when we follow the route of constructing an epistemology of expectations out of them. They were surveying much the same social landscape from their different perspectives. Though the exercise was undertaken from the high ground of their male dominance, before we get too dismissive of the views these writers offered it is as well to remember that Garin lo Brun and Philip de Novare, at least, were sensitive and observant laymen who did not write within any scholastic straitjacket. It is also worth remembering that when at the turn of the fourteenth century we finally encounter a medieval female writer on female conduct, Christine de Pizan (died 1430), she did not offer in her work more than an expansion of the Franciscan *Miroir* (*Livre de la Cité des Dames*). She did not embark on a critique of it. She was principally writing to counter the unthinking misogyny of her day (see Chapter 8).[12] She took particular exception to the vernacular literature of misogyny spawned by Matthew of Boulogne's *Lamentations of Matheolulus*, a tract which appeared around 1290, at the end of the period of this book. Its principal purpose was to decry the deceits, perversity and immorality of women, as demonstrated through Matthew's own life experience, and scriptural, mythological and historical examples.[13] When a medieval woman got to write about female conduct she did not offer, then, anything more in the way of a feminist counterblast than the theologically sound and unarguable view that men were as morally frail and culpable as women.

---

[10] *Rasos es e Mesura*, 19, (ll. 119–28), 21 (ll. 227–38).

[11] This is a point also made (through reverse logic) by Philip de Novare around 1260, who stated that her reputation was the only thing that need concern a woman: 'Women have this advantage: they are able to defend their honour with ease, for, providing they wish it, in one thing only are they regarded as good. Men, on the other hand, have to contend on many fronts to be held to be good men. They need to be courtly, generous, tough and wise. Providing the woman keep her virtue whatever other faults she has are irrelevant, and she can go about with head held high.' *Quatre Tenz*, 20 (c. 31).

[12] R. Blumenfeld-Kozinski, 'Christine de Pizan and the Misogynistic Tradition', *Romantic Review*, 81 (1990), 279–92; J. M. Ferrante, *To the Glory of Her Sex: Women's Roles in the Composition of Medieval Texts* (Bloomington, IN., 1997), 204–5.

[13] *Lamentationes Matheoluli*, ed. T. Klein ('Quellen und Untersuchungen zur lateinischen Philologie des Mittelalters', 17, Stuttgart, 2014); N. McLoughlin, *Jean Gerson and Gender: Rhetoric and Politics in Fifteenth-century France* (Basingstoke, 2015), 96–127.

Since women of any significance were inhabitants of the same courtly world as their brothers, husbands, fathers, suitors and would-be seducers, there was much in their recommended conduct which was irrelevant to their gender. The obligations on a woman in her behaviour at mass or in conducting herself towards a great personage were much the same as those of a man, which was to avoid acts which could be characterized as *vilonie* (debased).[14] Courtliness crossed boundaries of sex and social levels, as we have seen. Indeed, women were so much a part of superior society that they were understood, whether as mothers or patrons, to be perfectly acceptable as instructors in what society required its model inhabitants to be. This comes out in both literature and history. When Chrétien de Troyes pictured his eager Welsh hero Perceval going out into the world from his secluded home, it was his mother who had brought him up in ignorance of the world who had to take responsibility for instructing him in what he would meet, and she did so by offering him a miniature *enseignement*. Her advice was that he should respect but be wary of women and not get sexually involved with casual acquaintances; travel the roads cautiously and beware of those he may meet on the way; and be dutiful in his religious observance. All are common themes of such lectures since *Ruodlieb* or indeed since the time of that solicitous, real-life ninth-century mother, Dhuoda of Septimania.[15] The Empress Matilda (died 1164) was another such concerned mother, to whom her son, Henry II of England (reigned 1154–89), certainly resorted for advice on a whole range of issues. It was the view of Henry's leading clerical courtier, Walter Map (died 1210), that Matilda took responsibility for instructing him in his public conduct as a youth, though the advice Map asserted she gave her son was actually counter to what *enseignements* usually recommended, as for instance that Henry should seclude himself away from his dependants and ration his appearances amongst them. But then, Walter disapproved of the grim old empress and her supposed influence, so her advice would be necessarily bad as far as he was concerned.[16] Matilda was not, however, unique in her family in the role of counsellor and guide to her sons: her aunt, Adela of Blois, and her great granddaughter, Blanche of Castile, are known to have been equally directive to their boys in their day.[17]

The following study will consider the area of medieval female conduct which was most obviously constructed with reference to gender, and offer a construct of expectations on the *preudefemme*. As much as men, they inhabited a social environment rank with anxiety, though in women's case the insecurity was more personal to them than in the case of men. For a man, the basic stakes were career, lordship and the defence of his masculinity. For a woman the focus was more firmly and

---

[14]   *Chastoiement des dames*, 144–6.

[15]   *Conte de Graal*, 21–2 (ll. 525–92). One should also note the more extensive maternal *enseignement* (some 250 lines) offered by his mother to the young hero Biaudous as he entered into the life of a knight, which dates to the 1250s; *Biaudouz*, ed. J-Ch. Lemaire (Liège, 2008), 40–54.

[16]   M. Chibnall, *The Empress Matilda* (Oxford, 1991), 62–3, 163–4; *De Nugis Curialium*, 479.

[17]   For Adela and her sons, K. A. LoPrete, *Adela of Blois, Countess and Lord* (Dublin, 2007), 149–56; for Blanche's attitude to her son Louis IX see L. Grant, *Blanche of Castile Queen of France* (New Haven, 2016), 107–9.

intimately on her personal appearance and reputation. The following section takes as its basis Robert de Blois's typology of social dangers to the woman, which is particularly useful as he was consciously seeking to define the behaviour of an ideal type. Robert probably wrote his *Chastoiement des dames* in the Capetian France of the later 1230s when it was emerging from the tutelage of the formidable queen regent, Blanche of Castile, a woman who was to Louis IX of France what the Empress Matilda had been to Henry II of England. The *Chastoiement* forms a lengthy work of 757 octosyllabic rhyming couplets organized in several chapters. Robert describes his work as a 'general guide' (*commun ensoignemant*), but it is clearly intended only for the elite of women, the inhabitants of the court. As such it deals more with public interaction than with the cultivation of virtues we find in clerical advice to women, and is all the more interesting for that. The women Robert described and advised were expected to be deeply concerned with what was owed both to them and to others in any social situation, as in this passage about how to socialize with other ladies after the end of mass:

> Approach the most important characters present individually, and bow to each as you do. If you are with a group of ladies give them every attention. Honour each and every one with distinction, the greater ones as well as the lesser folk. You should be more civil and at ease the more distinguished you yourself are: when the ladies are leaving the church and you are going out with them, this is how such folk behave who desire honour and despise all low-born behaviour.[18]

I Reticence

Speech and its dangers were among the most profoundly vexed and ancient areas of concern in human interaction, and speech was not in itself a gendered concern (see Chapter 10). The theme of the fatal consequences of indiscretion in intersexual relations permeates medieval literature to such an extent that it can only be tapping into deep roots of social anxiety.[19] The poet-knight Sordello da Goito offered the advice that a woman in society should only see what was of advantage for her to see, and be 'blind, deaf and mute' otherwise so far as she could. If she could not, then she must say as little as possible to avoid being compromised: reserve, or reticence (*retenenza*), should be her guiding principle.[20] Moralists such as Philip de Novare focused on unguarded social interchange between men and women as inherently dangerous, even if conducted in a public assembly. Unguarded conversation was a problem for both sexes. Sources as weighty as those of Scripture earnestly warned all the faithful against it, but women had to be cautious for different reasons than men. The danger lay as much in the self-deception of the male as in the foolishness of the female, as Garin lo Brun pointed out at the beginning of the twelfth century. He was not alone in that. In the 1230s Robert de Blois repeatedly highlighted the narrow line a sensible woman had to walk in how she

---

[18] *Chastoiement des dames*, 146 (ll. 441–52).   [19] Bloch, *Medieval Misogyny*, 114–42.
[20] *Ensenhamens d'Onor*, 232 (ll. 1173–92). See here J. Rudin, 'Between Concealment and Eloquence: the Idea of the Ideal Woman in Medieval Provençal Literature', in *The Inner Life of Women in Medieval Romance Literature*, ed. J. Rider and J. Friedman (Basingstoke, 2011), 146–58, esp. 152.

expressed herself and what she said. Assertiveness in particular was frowned on. The common proverb had it that a woman who talked like a man was as unnatural as a hen that crowed like a cockerel.[21] To claim a male voice was to claim male prerogatives, in the medieval view, and was an act of insurgency (for which see Chapter 8).

Every mature woman, like every *preudomme*, should be restrained (*amesurée*) in her speech, according to Robert, but she should not be mute (as clerical misogynists urged). Robert sketched out the problems. At one extreme, a woman who amused herself by indulging in deliberate sexually charged repartee was asking for trouble and was a public danger.[22] Should any woman chatter away heedlessly, she would attract condemnation as being ill-bred, but on the other hand if she said little, she would be ignored and gain no social credit. All men should get a degree of notice from her, but if she went over the top in her praise of a particular man who had attracted her approval, 'people may well say it is because of her love for him and she won't be worth a button'.[23] So a woman could become an innocent victim of her own *cortoisie*, even though she meant nothing by it.

But on the other hand there were considerable social penalties for a woman of means and standing who gave up the game and simply avoided company. Robert believed that (like it or not) it was the duty of such a woman to enter the public theatre of hall and court and conduct herself with credit, as her reputation demanded no less. To that extent she was being advised to adopt the same *mesure* in speech as the *preudomme*. But having less ability to defend herself, vigilance and politic reticence were more important to her than to the man. She had no choice but to entertain others, so she must gauge very carefully how it was to be done. If she entered too enthusiastically into the life of the hall there were people who would turn it to her discredit and insinuate that she was sexually forward and that once a man could get her on her own, she would be up for intercourse.[24] The *Lai de Conseil* goes to the extreme, purveying a view of society as intrinsically hostile, where no woman could be at ease with her own sex, let alone the male, so shot through is society with rumour and slander. Its author advised a woman in society to behave with apparent frankness amongst others but store up confidences and give away nothing of herself unless she really must to gain an advantage, and even then to confide it behind closed doors. In such a febrile society every woman was a *losengier*.[25]

II Personal Space and Poise

A woman had to assert control over her immediate space and her body, and she should not tolerate any interference with either.[26] Robert de Blois deplored a woman who would allow herself to be handled by a man other than her husband,

[21] *Proverbes français*, no. 737.   [22] *Chastoiement des dames*, 141 (ll. 295–300).
[23] *Chastoiement des dames*, 133 (ll. 36–7): *Si dient que c'est par amor/Et ele nes prise un bouton.*
[24] *Chastoiement des dames*, 134 (ll. 46–60).
[25] *Le Lai de Conseil*, ed. and trans. B. E. Grigoriu, C. Peersman and J. Rider (Liverpool Online Series, Critical Editions of French Texts, 18, 2013), 87–8 (ll. 372–98).
[26] I. Bennewitz, 'Der Körper der Dame. Zur Konstruktion von "Weiblichkeit" in der deutschen Literatur des Mittelalters', in *'Aufführung' und 'Schrift' in Mittelalter und Früher Neuzeit*, ed. J-D. Müller (Stuttgart, 1996), 222–38.

while acknowledging that groping by males was a social problem (the word he used was *tançon*). No *proudefemme* would allow such a physical trespass, he said. Social kissing, he believed, could be taken as an invitation by the obsessive male as an excuse to go further. Since a woman was inherently lustful, it was his belief that her baser nature could easily be ignited and all self-control lost in the passion of the here and now, which no consideration of family and loyalty could prevent.[27] Philip de Novare, too, was insistent that a proper sense of distance was very necessary in the education of a young woman:

> It is better if girls are a little diffident and superior in their manner than that they are accommodating, especially towards boys and girls who they meet frequently but who are below their station. It is rightly said that 'to know lords is to lose respect for them' and there is more to fear in familiarity with ladies than there is with lords.[28]

Ulrich von Liechtenstein fixated as a very young man on a lady who was adroit enough to know how to defend her personal space from nuisances such as he turned out to be. Ulrich's painful account of his first meeting as a callow youth around 1222 with this unnamed lady is particularly instructive as to interaction between the sexes at the time. She would not address him directly, hindered any approach to her by deploying officious servants and attendants, and firmly discouraged his attempts to get her to talk to him on a public street by a flash of anger and a bitter rebuke.[29]

Eye contact as a sign of challenge or sexual interest is a basic human social signifier, whether it is involuntary or deliberate. This was something well enough known to the ancient world and the Middle Ages where it was held to be the origin of desire.[30] The German *Winsbeckin* lectures the young woman about controlling her gaze so that she should not be seen to be searching around for an object of lust. The direction of her interest would be observed by ill-wishers and her reputation be compromised.[31] Amanieu de Sescás thought the danger of doing it most acute to a woman in church, where her attention ought to be properly fixed on the altar.[32] It was a danger that the *Miroir des Bonnes Femmes* recognized. Its Franciscan author warned against the consequences of an infatuated gaze, repeating the court gossip of a great woman of his own day dishonoured because she could not stop herself looking at an attractive young man while at a dance so that the whole hall noticed.[33] Therefore Robert de Blois said that women should not stare about them as it opened them to temptation when the gaze was fully met by the male object. His view of women's weakness led him to assume that a woman could then easily be led

---

[27] Ibid., 140 (ll. 255–59).

[28] *Quatre Tenz*, 18 (c. 28): *Et mieus vaut il qu'eles soient un po desdaigneuses en meniers et orguilleuses, que trop souples, especiaumant e ceus et celes qui repairent antor eles et font acoison de servir eles. Car l'an dit, et voirs est, que privez sires fait fole mainie; et plus granz perilz gist en privée dame que en privé seignor.*

[29] *The Service of Ladies*, trans. J. W. Thomas (Woodbridge, 2004), 21–6.

[30] Bloch, *Medieval Misogyny*, 112; M. Foucault, *The History of Sexuality*, trans. R. Hurley (3 vols, London, 1990) 2: 40–1. A gaze *en mi le vis* is taken as a direct and insolent challenge in *Lancelot*, 5: 117.

[31] *Winsbeckin*, 108–9.   [32] *Essenhamen de la Donzela*, 46.

[33] University of Pennsylvania Library, Special Collections, ms 659, fo. 81r '... *ses eulz sus vn iuen home trop aficheement*'.

to believe that male interest in her was through sincere love and more than just the heat of lust.[34]

III Modesty and Grooming

The importance of cleanliness and grooming was registered as much for women as for men, and was thought to advertise self-respect in both sexes. But the nature and arrangement of her physical covering and adornment were more of a particular theme for women in the literature of conduct than for men. Garin lo Brun, Robert de Blois, and Amanieu de Sescás all devote space to advising women on the scrupulous care of their fingernails, teeth and skin. As early as the time of Garin lo Brun, a woman was urged to pay close attention to the arrangement of her gown, with the explicit caution that a man's gaze was drawn to the areas of the breasts and hips, which sexually excited him. A sensible woman must therefore arrange her dress with care, to minimize the danger. Robert de Blois believed that a glimpse of stocking (let alone skin) was enough to set a man off. His censorious belief clearly was that for the men and women of his own day and age anything goes. In an unconscious metonymy he urged that women pay particular care to the tying of laces, which if loose might not just expose white flesh to the world's appreciative and salacious gaze, but the shape of a leg, and he repeated the proverb, 'What the eye can't see, the heart can't regret'. A woman who was not strait-laced and was careless how she exposed face, neck or even hands, was asking for trouble. Flaunting her body could be taken as a sign of promiscuity (*puitage*), and her all-important public reputation would sink as a result.[35]

Yet Robert de Blois, like Jacques de Vitry, goes on to express revulsion at the idea that women should therefore hide themselves away from the world, or choose to swathe head with wimple and veil, as nuns did (for more on this, see pp. 170–3). There had to be an acceptable mean, especially as women had a choice in this. Robert de Blois's advice was that if a woman had to veil her face, she should limit it to the road, but she should drop it at the church door if she were attending Mass or before entering any public assembly (though she might cover her mouth with her hand if she laughed). If she was ugly or in some way deformed, she could cover herself up for all he cared, indeed he thought it wise that a woman should conceal an egregious physical defect. But otherwise she should be open to admiration by both men and her fellow women, and take advantage of the social edge that her beauty gave her. A woman's natural social advantage was in her facial beauty, so society must see it openly. Male writers note with approval good-looking female characters who refuse to enclose their hair and face, an increasing fashion from the end of the twelfth century.[36] Ulrich von Liechtenstein—who was very much against veils and wimples—says as much in his *Frauenbuch*. He chided women

---

[34] *Chastoiement des dames*, 137–8 (ll. 145–68).
[35] *Chastoiement des dames*, 138–9 (ll. 189–212). For a similar caution to women about fastening clothing, *Essenhamen de la Donzela*, 47.
[36] *Gille de Chyn*, 24 (ll. 483–7): on the young countess of Duras, *deffublee estoit et sans ghimple*.

who bundled up their heads like nuns, women whose eyes were all a man could see. Amanieu de Sescás advised women: 'what one sees most you should make most pleasing'. A beautiful mouth, regular teeth, a clear complexion and a cute nose were given so as to be admired, not concealed.[37]

Bertran de Born had the opportunity to be charmed by the grace and facial beauty of any number of women, and his poetry is testimony to the excess of libido it inspired, as it also is to the female ability subsequently to deflect his interest and send him on his way. His contemporary, Hywel ab Owain Gwynedd (died 1170), a northern Welsh aristocrat, was also an accomplished and renowned poet. His verses likewise ache with longing for the slim beauty of young women he had met—their shy grace, laughter and fair complexions. Like the noble poets of the Midi, Hywel lets us know that he had the means and opportunity to have his way with quite a number of them and like his Occitan colleagues is reticent about giving their names, other than by coded *senhals* (or perhaps in his case, *ffugenwau*). But what energized his poetry were the women who had evaded his attentions and made their halls unwelcoming to him. What really hurt were those who snubbed his verses. The ability of women to cause pain to the male mind and ego was not just a romance theme.[38]

IV Gift-Giving

The social interchange represented by gift-giving was as much a danger as speech. This was because the acceptance of a gift could be taken as an emotional commitment. The unmarried Constance of Brittany herself wrote in 1160 of the many tokens she had been offered by men, but said she had kept her options open by refusing them.[39] Robert de Blois would not have been convinced. He believed that women were unable to turn down items of jewellery, as being less able than men to resist the desire for possessions (*covoitisie*). Not that he thought men had much innate merit in that area either. If a woman accepted an expensive gift from a male, his temptation would be to run off at the mouth about it, not just about the expense of the item but as to who it was who had accepted it. Modest gifts such as fine leather belts, pretty little knives, a nice purse, brooch or ring might be accepted from relatives with propriety as long as there was no other intention in giving and accepting than family affection.[40] But any item of real expense should not be accepted because it led to suspicion of both the giver and the recipient.

---

[37] *Gille de Chyn*, 143–4 (ll. 343–72); *Frauenbuch*, 64 (ll. 230–38); *Essenhamen de la Donzela*, 44.

[38] *Medieval Welsh Poems*, trans. J. P. Clancy (Dublin, 2003), 134–8.

[39] For text, *RHF* 16: 23. For the date, authenticity and context, U. Peters and R. Köhn, 'Höfisches Liebeswerben oder politisches Heiratsangebot? Zum Brief der Konstanze von Bretagne an Ludwig VII von Frankreich', *Beiträge zur Geschichte der deutschen Sprache und Literatur*, 111 (1989), 179–95; and for the emotional significance, Jaeger, *Ennobling Love*, 104–5.

[40] Just such a gift and the complicated personal interrelations that surrounded it were the subject of a letter of Countess Margaret de Lacy, *Acts and Letters*, no. 270. Andrew the Chaplain lists the many items males might offer to the women of their desires, all of which carry the expectation of a sexual return, and urges caution in their display; *De Amore*, 268–70 (XXI).

To Ulrich von Liechtenstein jewels given to women had to be only tokens; costly gifts led to suspicion that the woman was selling herself for sex—'Jewels should be mere trifles, so they can be accepted without conditions: they shouldn't be a precondition for love.'[41] Even accepting such things covertly was dangerous. Unloading them as soon as they were given was no defence either. Taking valuable gifts was an act of arrant folly as far as Robert de Blois was concerned in view of the suspicions it could arouse.[42] Philip de Novare tells a little fable where he relates the giving of the gift of an expensive knife by men as a present to a particularly promiscuous lady. The gift thus became in itself symbolic of sexual intercourse.[43] For him and others gift-giving between the sexes was darkened and compromised by suspicion and subtext.

V Social Address

Vernacular writers on ideal female conduct are less specific about certain character-istics which are nonetheless implicit in their definition of a *preudefemme*: her judgement (MFr. *sens*, MHG. *sinne*) and knowledgeability (MFr. *saver*, MHG. *lere*). As we have seen, their unanimous view is that a woman could only succeed in the world if she could read men's intentions and character, and deflect the obses-sive and the bore. The author of *Winsbeckin* was adamant that a woman had to be her own guide through the social minefield, that chaperoning would do little more than contain a silly woman and was in fact insulting to women of principle.[44] Bertran de Born, who complained often of the female ability to send him packing, had himself enough judgement not to make a play for Matilda, duchess of Saxony, whom he encountered heavily pregnant at the Plantagenet court in 1182. But it was not just her beauty that intimidated him and kept him awake at night, it was also her social address: her *cortesia*, her wit and *savoir faire*.[45]

As well as judgement, a woman needed a base of knowledge. No woman could make her mark in the social world of the hall unless she was instructed in the events and cultural currency of her day. So Garin lo Brun made a point of urging that his lady should be acquainted with and memorize *novas*, the lively Occitan genre of poetry which focused on political issues of the day. She could quote them as a conversational aid when she wanted to impress.[46] No writer, however, goes so far as to say that women should be formally educated to the standard of the male, and indeed the misogynistic, proverbial view repeated (disapprovingly) in *Winsbeckin* was that 'women have little wit, but lots of hair'. Men liked to be flattered by an assumption of feminine naivety and ignorance. Thomasin of Zirclaria, a cleric, therefore temporizes in his *Welsche Gast* (1216)

---

[41] *Frauenbuch*, 84 (ll. 587–9). Andrew the Chaplain likewise registers the danger of gifts being interpreted by men as creating an emotional bond, whatever a woman might think; *De Amore*, 266–8 (XIX).
[42] *Chastoiement des dames*, 139–40 (ll. 213–54).   [43] *Quatre Tenz*, 89–91 (cc. 162–4).
[44] *Winsbeckin*, 118–19.   [45] *Casutz sui de mal en pena*, in Bertran, 167.
[46] *E·l termini d'estiu*, 90–1 (ll. 525–34).

when talking of his own view of a truly superior woman (of whom he believed there were not that many):

> If…she has good sense then let her have the courtesy and wisdom not to show what good sense she has. No one is asking her to be a magistrate. A man should possess many skills. The training of the noble lady requires that a lady who is excellent and noble should not be too clever. Simplicity is a fine thing in a lady. However it is right that a lady should have the knowledge and the good sense to avoid animosity.[47]

Philip de Novare had markedly more negative views of female education, which he thought a waste of time, even for a nun. He saw female literacy as a danger: 'Such women may well dare to hand over, or to send letters, or even to secrete them where they may be found, which are full of folly and trifling,' and so they would come to a bad end.[48] This was a rather extreme position even for the Middle Ages. Vincent of Beauvais, a Dominican inhabitant of the court of that great lady, Blanche of Castile, believed that literacy was an advantage in a well-brought-up woman. Wholesome reading could at least keep women's unfixed minds from wandering into lustful and trivial pathways.[49] Needlework was recommended for much the same reasons.

THE PIETY OF THE *PREUDEFEMME*

A final requirement of the *preudefemme* was that in addition to her secular and social virtues she should be outstanding in her religious observance, without being a candidate for sanctity. Male writers on female conduct acknowledge this, though in two cases they write dismissively of female piety, as something they put on like jewellery. The wearing of rosaries as ornaments particularly irritated two of them, opening women in general to charges of insincerity in their piety. Ramon Vidal grumbled about the fashion, which was new to him in Occitania in the first years of the thirteenth century. He observed that several great ladies of his day in both Spain and southern France who were pious, good and noble, and who generously patronized the Church without any wish on their part to take religious vows, did not wear them.[50] At a more basic level, Ulrich von Liechtenstein affected to abhor the practice, not perhaps so much from the sin of vainglory which it implied, but because the heterosexual male eye automatically sought a woman's breasts, only to be brought up short by a reminder of pious renunciation of the flesh, rather than a pretty piece of jewellery (see p. 173).[51]

What few memorials of this time survive for leading lay women who died outside the cloister (other than queens) all emphasize their relationship with God, the Church, the clergy and the saints. The great Matilda of Canossa, Margravine

---

[47] *Welsche Gast*, 23–4 (ll. 841–52).   [48] *Quatre Tenz*, 16 (c. 25).
[49] *De eruditione filiorum nobilium*, ed. A. Steiner (MAA Publication, 32, 1938), 176. Alfonso the Wise of Castile recommended Latin tuition to young noblewomen, so they could read the office and psalter; *Siete Partidas* ii, tit. 7, ley 11.
[50] *Abril issia*, 88–90 (ll. 907–23).   [51] *Frauenbuch*, 65–6 (ll. 239–52).

and Duchess of Tuscany (died 1115), who dominated northern Italy during the Investiture Contest, and died as the Vicar of the Empire south of the Alps, was renowned for her military leadership, political astuteness, and indeed ruthlessness. Yet her biographer Donizo, a monk, memorialized her principally as a loyal daughter of St Peter, devoted to the building and ornamentation of churches, devout in following the divine office, protector and friend of the clergy and the poor. He provided a lavish, contemporary and detailed account of her final illness and godly death. Her gender was more or less irrelevant to his memoir: the dimension of her life that he dealt with was as a pious ruler and Christian; her specifically feminine virtues were entirely ignored.[52]

The long poem composed by Baudry de Bourgeuil in praise of Countess Adela of Blois (died 1137) at much the same time as Donizo was writing in Canossa likewise has little to say of her feminine virtues. Nor for that matter does he acknowledge her renowned political gifts, which preserved her children's futures after her husband's failures on crusade and premature death.[53] Baudry lauded her lineage and said she was not much inferior in her virtues to her father, William the Conqueror of England, except in the exercise of arms and her liking for books, which he did not share. He wrote to solicit a processional cope which she had promised him, and observed in passing that she was a great enricher of ecclesiastical treasuries.[54] This was the same virtue ascribed by Baudry's fellow Breton, Stephen de Fougères, to his patron Countess Cecilia of Hereford; in fact, this and her generosity to the poor are the only virtues of hers he praises, other than that she loved her husband.

> She has built chapels, endowed altars, fed the poor and housed them, she washes and gives them a bed regularly with a good heart, and not with distaste. She meets people of dignity, bishop, abbot, prior or monk, Hospitaller or black canon, and she honours and helps them promptly. She gives them amices and albs and chasubles made of cloth from the Trentino, which she trims and cuts with great patience, and buys out of her income.[55]

The symbolic image of the female as featured on their twelfth- and thirteenth-century seals across Europe is remarkably standard, and they project a similar message about the *preudefemme* they represent, particularly in the emphasis on passive piety. The image appears in wax from the 1120s onwards, originating amongst the aristocracies of the north-west of France and England, but rapidly spreading south and east. It takes its ultimate inspiration from the seals of queens, such as that of Queen Matilda II of England (died 1118), whose matrix would have been sculpted for her in 1100 and which apparently copied those of earlier queens. In the aristocratic version, the lady stands full or half face, garbed in a long dress, with a cloak (sometimes depicted as fur-lined) draped over her shoulders. The shape of the

[52] Donizo, *Vita Mathildis*, in *MGH Scriptores* 12: 405–9. It might be noted that it was precisely her exercise of lay power that led Bonizo of Sutri, by contrast, to condemn her as unnatural; D. J. Hay, *The Military Leadership of Matilda of Canossa, 1046–1115* (Manchester, 2008), 199.

[53] For an assessment of her career, LoPrete, *Adela of Blois*, 419–38.

[54] *Carmina Historica*, in *PL* 166, cols 1201–3.   [55] *Livre des manières*, 96.

matrix is almost always a vesica, like that of a cleric. The female figure may hold one of three items, a fleur-de-lis, a book (probably intended to be a psalter) or a falcon, and sometimes more than one of them. Occasionally a purse or aumoniere can be seen attached to her belt. The image has obvious parallels in secular and religious art: she could be modelled on that of April—the month of fertility—in depictions of the Labours. She quite evidently alludes (in lily and psalter) to the Virgin Mary, whose symbol was the fleur-de-lis, and evokes chastity. The cumulative message is one of femininity, domesticity and, above all, aspiration to pious conduct in the seals' obvious evocation of the Annunciation, the central theological expression of obedience to God's will. The only long-term change in these seals is the appearance of family heraldry in the later twelfth century, which is intended to symbolize the lineage and connections that the woman brings her husband and children.[56]

FEMININITY AND THE *PREUDEFEMME*

The construct of a *preudomme* offers us a way to study medieval ideas of masculinity, and the same is true for the *preudefemme* in exploring the idea of femininity. Modern constructs of medieval femininity to date have not explored her implications, which I think makes necessary some modification of our understanding of the expectations laid on medieval women, for she was constructed within the habitus to define those expectations. These were, of course, low. The basic assumption of the unfixed and wayward nature of women by the male writers we have looked at is inescapable, and is a feature which has already been well explored in scholarship. It was justified by the theory of humours, women being moist and cold, and therefore lacking the control and fixed nature of men. A woman was consequently expected to have less emotional stability and that lack of control extended to her sexuality, which was supposedly more voracious than that of a man and so could easily lead her into *putage*, sexual misbehaviour, or, to use a superannuated noun, harlotry. Female weakness equated to moral fragility, and it was assumed that her deficiency could be compensated for by male guidance, and at its extreme by an oppressive degree of chaperoning.[57] The academic lady Heloise, in corresponding

---

[56] For a descriptive list of Anglo-Norman female seals up to the mid thirteenth century, S. M. Johns, *Noblewomen, Aristocracy and Power in the Twelfth-Century Anglo-Norman Realm* (Manchester, 2003), 203–30, and for comments on style, 122–34. For origins, see particularly J-F. Nieus, 'Early Aristocratic Seals: an Anglo-Norman Success Story', in *Anglo-Norman Studies*, 38, ed. E. van Houts (Woodbridge, 2016), 119–20. See also, generally, B. Bedos Rezak, 'Women, seals and power in medieval France, 1150–1350', in *Women and Power in the Middle Ages*, ed. M. Erler and M. Kowaleski (Athens, GA, 1999), 1–36; Lett, *Hommes et femmes*, 59–63.

[57] The nineteenth-century approach to women's history by studying representative female lives survived well into the second half of the twentieth century, cf. A. Lehmann, *Le rôle de la femme dans l'histoire de France au moyen âge* (Paris, 1952); E. Power, *Medieval Women*, ed. M.M. Postan (Cambridge, 1973). The earliest original academic work on femininity in history is in French, and we find some basic parameters of the discussion laid down as early as the legal collection *La Femme* (3 vols, Receuil de la Société Jean Bodin, 11–13, Brussels, 1959–62). See historiographical critiques in S. Mosher Stuard, 'Fashion's Captives: Medieval Women in French Historiography', in *Women in*

with Abelard, is an example of a twelfth-century woman who digested and herself paid intellectual homage to this essentially ecclesiastical view of female weakness and inferiority.[58]

The overarching theme in the historiography of medieval women (and in women of other periods too) is that of female powerlessness, as opposed to male power. Medieval literature certainly provides material for this. Ramon Llull's summative study of Chivalry in the 1270s came out with the view that men had more sense, capacity and understanding than women, and this made them potentially superior in both goodness and Nobility, though on the other side of the coin it made men's moral failings all the worse.[59] The discourse of power and powerlessness in the historiography of medieval gender is in large part a legacy of the feudal under-standing of medieval society, where military tenure was understood to be its single operating principle and so civic and military power was the exclusive province of the male. The more recent historiography has been more subtle in feeling out the boundaries of female agency within medieval society, and has found that aristo-cratic women as both wives and widows might indeed have rather more ways to exert themselves within their families and world than was once conceded.[60] Body theory, drawing on medieval medical texts, has also added to the discussion of the social female, though it generally reinforces a negative outlook on the medieval condition. At its extreme, this approach leads to 'utero-centric' explanations of the female, where the reproductive function assigned her by Scripture is all that matters in a woman to medieval people, and her life and character is defined by her stages of fecundity. Giles of Rome could thus come out with the observation that a fool-ish woman was as likely as not a barren one.[61]

How does an analysis of the *preudefemme* from the twelfth- and thirteenth-century texts challenge the historiography? To begin with, the vernacular works that construct and criticize her were not written by scholastics, and rely more on personal observation of what women were than academic theories of what women should be. Arnaut de Mareuil's cheerful, later twelfth-century sketch of the better females of his day, which we began this chapter with (above, p. 85), is a text which conveys a positive picture of the morality and standing of a woman which is at variance with much of the Latin literature of the schools. His woman could be distinguished in a variety of ways: by her physical appearance, her high moral repu-tation, her verbal facility and her social address. She might be admirable in the way she could convey her knowledge, her wit, or simply in her steady kindness. All of these feminine virtues are at odds with ideas of lack of constraint and moral weak-ness as defining femininity, and they also presume a woman is a social actor who

---

Medieval History and Historiography (Philadelphia, 1987), 62–8; K. F. Werner, 'Les femmes, le pouvoir et la transmission du pouvoir', in *La femme au moyen âge* (Maubeuge, 1990), 365–79; E. Santenelli, *Des femmes éplorées? Les veuves dans la société aristocratiques du haut moyen âge* (Lille, 2003). See also below, Chapter 8.

[58] *The Letter Collection of Peter Abelard and Heloise*, ed. D. Luscombe and trans. B. Radice (Oxford, 2013), c. 9.

[59] *Llibre de l'Orde*, 168 (c. 7).   [60] Crouch, *Nobility*, 303–22.

[61] Cited in Lett, *Hommes et femmes*, 34.

has opportunities to display them. The dialogue between the sexes composed by the ageing Ulrich von Liechtenstein is in one of its aspects an extended and devastating satire on the falsity and hypocrisy of men in a society where social rhetoric was about containing the irresponsibility and immorality of women, but where incontinence and moral laxity were most frequently and despicably displayed by men. This sort of dualistic medieval thinking could work in women's favour: a good wife was a walking condemnation of a bad husband who sometimes had no choice but to defer to her, as in the moral authority the virtuous and self-controlled *prodefeme* Duchess Emmeline of Burgundy exercised over her oafish and erratic husband in the later twelfth-century *Chanson d'Aspremont*. The duke had the grace to admit her wisdom surpassed any he might have had, and it was through her advice (*ensegnement*) that he had so far maintained his rule of his principality.[62]

The *preudefemme* was therefore not only a didactic aid in the education of a girl into a mature female. She was an argument as to why a man should on occasion listen to and defer to a woman who was cleverer than he was. The wise, knowledgeable and mature wife was established in vernacular conduct literature as a superior type of femininity who must be listened to in any social assembly, and her advice heeded. The *History of William Marshal* is not in general a work which gives much attention to women; however, it cannot disguise that the countess, his wife, was routinely consulted in Marshal's council, of which she was a member, and her opinion was the one that was followed in more than one instance. From the *History* and other sources we know that Isabel governed her patrimony (the great Irish province of Leinster) for two extended periods in her husband's absences, on the first occasion, between 1200 and 1203, because she had the qualifications of blood and personality to stabilize it under Marshal rule.[63] She was in fact one of many great ladies to assume the governance of a duchy, county or other great lordship in the absence of a husband or during the minority of an heir.[64] The flip side of the *preudefemme* occupying a position of lay power with becoming modesty and quiet wisdom was the ill-judging virago, who usurped it either domestically or in the sphere of public authority. We will be looking at this representative figure later (in Chapter 8) but she needs to be registered here as a means of drawing a line for women's aspirations. The shrew or virago was a woman who made the mistake of being open about her desire for power over others and showed a relish for its exercise. She had stepped over the limits of gender expectations, and medieval literature is merciless on the men who allow her to get away with it, and the women who attempt it.[65]

---

[62] *Aspremont*, 1: ll. 1439–505, 2: ll. 11,119–23. The ability of a woman to influence her husband to the good is admitted in a few contemporary theological tracts; S. Farmer, 'Persuasive Voices: Clerical Images of Medieval Wives', *Speculum* 61 (1986), 526–34.

[63] Crouch, *Marshal*, 102–5, 122–32.

[64] For Flanders as an example, T. de Hemptinne, 'Les épouses des croisés et pèlerins flamands aux xie et xiie siècles: l'exemple des comtesses de Flandre Clémence et Sibylle', in *Autour de la Première Croisade: actes du colloque de la 'Society for the Study of the Crusades and the Latin East'*, ed. M. Balard (Paris, 1996), 89–92; K. S. Nicholas, 'Countesses as Rulers in Flanders', in *Aristocratic Women in Medieval France*, ed. T. Evergates (Philadelphia, 1999), 111–37.

[65] Lett, *Hommes et femmes*, 197–9; Karras, *Sexuality in Medieval Europe*, 64–5. For gendered attacks on the Empress Matilda (died 1164), who was open about her search for dominion, Chibnall, *Empress Matilda*, 96–7.

6

Villeins, Villains and *Vilonie*

Opposition was very much a medieval way of visualizing the world, and was embedded in its thought processes. The medieval writer knew on scriptural authority that 'all things go in pairs, one the counterpart of the other'.[1] So it is a sign of how much the Middle Ages valued superior conduct that it gave so much attention to its opposite, boorishness. Literary characters were frequently paired with the intention of highlighting a virtue by contrasting it with its opposite: so Oliver's prudence was explored through his friend Roland's rashness. The Courtliness and controlled speech of Gawain was all the more distinguished because he was always paired at court with the seneschal Kay, whose cross-grained nature and abusive tongue were legendary. Neither Roland nor Kay was a bad man, but both exhibited dangerous flaws of character. Sometimes, however, characters were deliberately drawn as representatives of good and evil. So Peire Vidal contrasted William of Orange with the anti-hero Doon of Nanteuil, while everything that was honourable and good in King Arthur had its negative image in King Claudas.[2] Virtue was the more starkly lit when set before the dark hangings of vice.

VILONIE AS CONDUCT

From the beginning of the twelfth century we find an established idea that there were already norms and expectations of superior lay conduct called Courtliness (Occ. *cortesia*, Fr. *corteisie*, Lat. *curialitas*) which could be taught and learned. Naturally, then, there had to be a contrasting idea of inferior conduct, which was called Villainy (Occ. *vilania*, Fr. *vilonie*, *vileinie*, Lat. *vilitas*). The two were mutually exclusive. In the words of an Italian saying of the thirteenth century, 'Courtliness will not go where Villainy is king'.[3] Some writers played mischievously with the idea that it too was a code of behaviour, taught to its disciples, who were called *vilains*. But the main point was that *vilania* was a useful way of reinforcing *cortesia*, for it offered a way of condemning the uncourtly. Another help in defining what was unacceptable conduct was the fact that there existed throughout the medieval period an undeniable social sump in society where the dregs collected. Outside the doors of the lord's hall and manor court lay the cottages and shacks of the

---

[1] *Omnia duplicia, unum contra unum*, Ecclus 42: 25a.
[2] *En una terr' estranha*, in Peire, 82 (ll. 50–56).
[3] *Villania in cui regna, cortesia lo disdegna*, Garzo, *Proverbi*, in *Poeti del Duecento*, 2: 311. A Provençal *sirventes* of the late twelfth century opposes *vilas* to being *gen noiritz* (well bred), Raimbaut, 274 (l. 47).

agricultural poor, whose standard of living, hygiene and education were a world away from his. He did not have to climb his castle keep to look down on people. Naturally some assumed that the conduct of the poor must therefore have been as fetid as their homes and clothing, or so it was convenient for anyone with social pretensions to believe. The morals of the poor had to be corrupt, which was one reason why the more perverted lords (and ladies) might expect them to cooperate readily in sexual acts.[4] It is irony of a high and tragic order that the usual Francien word for a peasant (*vilain*) was spelt the same as that for a corrupt and malignant rascal. Though the two words have entirely different roots, it was all too tempting for the medieval clerk and aristocrat to combine them in the social lexicon.[5]

Garin lo Brun conceived of a social world where his *cortesia* was mirrored (and so also defined in part) by a corresponding concept of 'low behaviour' or 'boorishness': *vilania*.[6] He was by no means unique in doing so. In the 1170s the troubadour Arnaut de Mareuil summed up the social usefulness of *vilania* by saying, 'A man will not ever be courtly (*cortez*), who does not recognize low behaviour (*vila*).'[7] At the other end of France in the same decade, Walter of Arras also contrasted *cortoisie* and *vilenie* and with even more effect than Arnaut, for he explained in dualist terms that Courtliness stemmed directly from God, while Villainy was spawned by the devil in hell. He made a neat wordplay on the word's origin: 'Villainy (*vilenie*) comes from a vile land (*vil lieu*).'[8] The term *vilania/ vileinie/vilonie* derives from the Latin adjective *vilis* (base, low, worthless, debased) and the related noun *vilitas* (baseness, corruption, low rank). Both words were frequently used in medieval Latin writings from the time of Gildas and Bede. *Vilitas* also produced the French and Occitan nouns *vilté/viltenénsa* (baseness) and *viltage* (shamefulness). Someone who wilfully embraced bad conduct was thus a *vilain*, an objectionable person who was, as Jean de Condé tells us around 1300, the very opposite of the *cortois*, the courtly man, and who was not fit to be in the company of the *preudomme*, the respectable public actor.[9] The opposition between the courtly man and the villain was being registered right at the beginning of the

---

[4] K. Gravdal, *Ravishing Maidens: Writing Rape in Medieval French Literature and Law* (Philadelphia, 1991), 105–21. It should be noted that Stephen de Fougères expected low-born male servants (*garcons*) readily to acquiesce when dissolute noblewomen recruited them for orgies; *Livre des Manières*, 86–8 (ll. 1077–82).

[5] For considerations of the polysemous nature of *vilain*, J. R. Crosland, *Medieval French Literature* (New York, 1965), 144–9; Freedman, *Images*, 133–5. A tendency for scholars nonetheless to assume a single sense of *vilain* as 'peasant' when it occurs in sources weakens scholarship on the subject. M-T. Lorcin, 'Du vilain au paysan sur la scène littéraire du xiiie siècle', *Médiévales*, 61 (2011), 163–86, argues a growing thirteenth-century resort in French literature to the word *paysan* when dealing with peasants, to avoid the equation with *vilain*. Wace of Bayeux was doing as much a century earlier, however.

[6] *E·l termini d'estiu*, 75 (ll. 119–22). An extensive and perpetually useful study of occurrences of the oppositional terms is S. L. Galpin, *Cortois and Vilain* (New Haven, 1905).

[7] *Rasos es e Mesura*, 18.

[8] *Ille et Galeron*, 54 (ll. 1617–20). The distinction was adopted by Jean de Meung a century later; Meung, *Rose*, 432 (ll. 7069–70): *Dieus li cortois sanz vilonie/de cui muet toute cortoisie*.

[9] This is the meaning behind William de Lorris's remark that 'A *vilains* who is *cortois* is out of his mind (*enrage*)'; Lorris, *Rose*, 242 (l. 3698). See also '*Vilain et cortois sont contraire*', 'Des Vilains et des Courtois', in *Condé*, 3: 189 (l. 1); '*Et hons de nation vilaine/Qui est vilains et qui vilaine/Cielz fait de tous à despiter/Ne entour prodome abiter/Ne doit…*', *Condé*, 3: 191 (ll. 53–57).

twelfth century, for in one of the poems of William IX of Aquitaine, the duke meditated on the power of his lady to raise up and dash down men: because of which she turned the most courtly man (*cortes*) into a villain and made every villain (*vilas*) courtly.[10]

When a medieval writer depicted a knight being abused for his bad faith and general wickedness, and he berated him as *vilain*, the knight was not being compared to a peasant (villein), or at least not directly (see below, Chapter 13). This is obvious when Wace of Bayeux writes in the late 1150s of knights who were rich and poor, *vilains* and *curteis*; the same passage mentions villeins as agricultural labourers, but uses the word *païssanz* to distinguish them.[11] A *chevalier vilain* was being called a low-born rascal, a villain and a reprobate, someone whose behaviour put him outside the pale of decent society and his own order, which was made up of people who liked to think of themselves as '*preudommes*' and '*preudefemmes*', people who were practitioners of Courtliness. The gravity of the insult could make people circumspect in using it. Gerald of Wales despised one of his cousins as an unpleasant, contemptuous and arrogant man, and since his name was Baskerville, he became *Bascrevillanus* in Gerald's writings, taunting him schoolboy-fashion in a tag which can be interpreted as 'low-born, black villain'.[12] Chrétien de Troyes in the 1170s makes a lot of use of the words *vilain* and *cortois*, *vilenie* and *cortoisie*, particularly in stigmatizing evil and corrupt knights as *vilain*. Since Chrétien's works occasionally have an overt teaching purpose—especially his *Conte de Graal*, which opens with depictions of the instruction of its hero—it is not surprising to find terms associated with desirable and undesirable conduct so prominent in them. Of course, one man's Villainy might well be another's courtesy. In his autobiography, King Jaume of Aragon (reigned 1213–76) expressed his disgust at the way his personal enemy Pero Aunès reviled men the king knew to be courtly as villains (*vilà*).[13] Villainy was what you projected on your enemies as a way of discrediting them, as Jean de Condé observed. It was not strictly speaking the opposite of Courtliness, but a tool to define closely what its components were, by highlighting what they weren't.

The sheer malevolent contrariness of practitioners of Villainy is assumed by some writers as enough of an explanation for what they did. The English author of the curious voyeuristic conduct tract *Le Donnei des Amanz*, which can plausibly be placed before 1200, complements well and in detail what we have already heard about the villain from contemporary Occitania and northern France.

But after that I ended by recalling that the low fellow (*vilein*) has a wicked heart (*fel quer*) and his life is blighted since he takes no pleasure in good cheer. His enjoyment

[10] *E·l plus cortes vilanejar/E totz vilas encortezir*, in 'Mout jauzens me prenc en amar', in *Les Chansons de Guillaume IX duc d'Aquitaine*, ed. A. Jeanroy (Paris, 1913), 23 (ll. 29–30).
[11] *Roman de Rou*, ed. A. J. Holden (3 vols, Société des anciens textes français, 1970–3) 1: pt 1, 110 (l. 2288); just to underline the difficulty, not much later in the same poem Wace denotes peasants as *villain* when he talks of King Louis summoning his host, calling up every knight and peasant, ibid., p. 111 (l. 2909).
[12] *Speculum Duorum*, ed. Y. Lefèvre and R. B. C. Huygens, trans. B. Dawson (Cardiff, 1974), 30.
[13] *Llibre dels Fets*, 67, *I aixo que no era ni vila ni descortes*.

is only in resentment, glowering, wrangling and quarrelling, in looking depressed all the time and in despising cheerfulness and song. Every part of his life is contrary to the harmony of Heaven and the angels of Paradise who sing anthems in God's presence. The mean fellow (*vilein*) who is God's enemy evidently has nothing to do with Heaven, nor does the ill-disposed oaf (*vilain grosus*) have anything to do with the rejoicing and happy angels. I believe the birds sing all the more sweetly when they sing louder at sunrise and sunset especially so as to annoy the wicked villain (*fel vilein*) and the contrary fellow (*gelus*), who utterly hate joy and song, for without a word of a lie our happiness is nothing but delusion and vanity to them. Our joy and delight is crabbiness to the ill-natured....A free spirit loves song and amusement. May God grant that the low-born rascal is deaf to it! Joy is as good as medicine to us but it rubs the villain the wrong way. For he has nothing whatever to do with open heartedness. If a villain cares nothing for good cheer how does he fall short of or contradict his own nature?...When the villain is speaking you fair, take care that he isn't stabbing you in the back. If the villain is being respectful it's not through good manners, but fear. You'll experience nothing from a villain of his free will other than his spite. Wherever a villain has power, as is well attested, he behaves without pity.[14]

The subject here is clearly not the agricultural peasant, but people who are contrary and ill-disposed by nature amongst those you have to deal with in leisured society: cheerless depressives, spoilsports, curmudgeons and backstabbers. Anything the courtly enjoy is anathema to the villain, such as music, high spirits, openheartedness, pastoral beauty, social harmony and true religious feeling. The author compares villains to snarling mastiffs who cannot do otherwise than bite because that is their nature.

For some writers, it followed from such meditations on social contrariness that if *cortesia* was a code of good conduct, then *vilania* must be a contrasting code of bad conduct. Twelfth- and thirteenth- century writers produced a number of odd mock *enseignements* which purported to teach not good conduct but bad. These are literary exercises designed to point out the shameless wickedness of a particular people or group of characters, so debased that they actually teach Villainy to their children and fellows. But they are by no means just whimsical literary conceits. They are further powerful evidence that in the twelfth century superior conduct was thought to be a code that could be acquired. For if bad conduct could be defined and taught, then good conduct has to have been thought to be a teachable set of skills too.

One of the earliest of these exercises is in Andrew de Coutances's *Roman des Franceis*, a work of the 1190s, an imagined final lecture delivered by the Arthurian character Frollo to his French subjects before he met Arthur in the single combat he did not survive. Frollo's mock *enseignement* was designed by a Norman writer as part of his project to ridicule and satirize the neighbouring French of the Parisis, whom he affected to despise. Andrew called it the 'commandments' or 'laws' that Frollo laid down for his people based on his own 'admirable manner of life'

---

[14] Translated from *Le Donei des Amanz*, ed. A. J. Holden (Anglo-Norman Text Society, Plain Text Series, 17, Oxford, 2013), 3–5 (ll. 25–80).

(*mes bones mors*). He enjoined the French to distance themselves from good Christians and trustworthy men; they were to embrace heedless cruelty; be capricious, faithless and perjured; be entirely selfish and appropriate everyone else's goods; gamble away their inheritances and take God's name in vain; in any courtly context they were to be arrogant, boastful and idle; and they were to be ungrateful, never keep their promises, and (in a parallel to *Le Donnei des Amanz*) 'live more vilely than a dog'.[15] Just to rub in the message, Andrew went on to depict the defeated French being reduced to the social level of serfs by King Arthur, subject to the payment of *chevage* (a poll tax demanded of bonded peasants).[16] Andrew's message is that if you act like villains you and your children deserve to be socially demoted to villeinage, and he was not alone amongst his French contemporaries in believing that to be right and proper. Peter of Beauvais's *L'Estoire Charlemeinne* (written before 1206) similarly has a king—in this case Charlemagne—sentencing those who failed to support his expedition to Constantinople to be disgraced by having to pay *chevage*, they and their descendants after them.[17]

THE ORIGINS OF *VILONIE*

The hereditary and genetically determined nature of Villainy was in fact implicit in medieval thinking and was a commonplace reflection deriving ultimately from, and supported by, the gospels.[18] The twelfth-century *Proverbe au Vilain* puts it unsurprisingly succinctly and in several ways: 'A rotten egg produces a wretched bird,' meaning that if a father is a felon, you can hardly expect good faith from his son. Likewise we find 'A sparrowhawk can't be bred from a buzzard,' explaining that a man is felonious and villainous from his birth, and you can't expect him to escape the disposition he was born with.[19] And if some people were doomed to Villainy because of their descent, others were stalked by it as if by a predatory nightwalker. William de Lorris, in his *Roman de la Rose,* imagined a spirit of Villainy which could consume a soul. He placed a sculpted female figure of *Vilonie* on the exterior of the wall of his Garden of Delight. It was skilfully carved so as to revolt those who viewed it, shamelessly exhibiting its innate wickedness, deceit, disrespect and slyness: 'it seemed undeniably a thing of villainy, full of malice.'[20]

---

[15] *Roman des Franceis*, 192 (ll. 135–55).

[16] *Roman des Franceis*, 194 (ll. 205–8), 195 (ll. 221–4).

[17] R. N. Walpole, 'Charlemagne's Journey to the East: the French Translation of the Legend by Pierre de Beauvais', in *Semitic and Oriental Studies: A Volume Presented to William Popper*, ed. W. J. Fischel (University of California Publications in Semitic Philology, 11, 1951), 446, for the significance of which see Freedman, *Images*, 111. Robert of Ho likewise notes that the inevitable and appropriate punishment for an unworthy nobleman is that he be placed in subjection to others 'as in bygone days'; *Enseignements Trebor*, 120 (ll. 2102–8).

[18] *Sic omnis arbor bona fructus bonos facit: mala autem arbor malos fructus facit. Non potest arbor bona malos fructus facere: neque arbor mala bonos fructus facere.* Matt. 7:17–18.

[19] *Proverbe au Vilain*, nos 6–7, 18–19.   [20] Lorris, *Rose*, 50 (ll. 156–72).

Not every medieval person was convinced by this sort of social determinism, of course. Philip de Novare, in his direct way, flatly contradicted the idea:

> There are some very silly people who quote a piece of foolishness masquerading as a proverb – although it is neither proverbial nor reasonable when it states: 'Saints and devils are made at birth'.[21]

He was considering the sincerity of religious feeling, which he regarded as behaviour acquired by constant practice. One can hardly expect consistency from proverbial collections either. They naturally contradict each other, for another says 'A black hen lays white eggs', meaning that 'often' a good heir has been born to a *mauvais lignage*.[22]

Talking of 'evil families', the proto-villain in medieval literature was Ganelon, the traitor to the French who betrayed Roland and Oliver to their death at the hands of the Saracens in the *Song of Roland*. By 1200, medieval writers took it as a matter of course that any of their villainous characters had to be descended from Ganelon, who tainted his entire line with his treason and even gave a name to his lineage—the House of Maience, from one of his supposed rebel descendants, Doon de Maience.[23] In the romance *Gaydon*, written during the 1230s, we find a creed of Villainy to which young members of the Maience lineage were obliged to swear when they were knighted, in what may have been a deliberate parody of the *Ordene de Chevalerie*. The aspiring villain-knight must swear never to be faithful and loyal to his lord and always to betray those who were; to promote wicked men and overthrow the good; to run down good men behind their backs while flattering them to their faces; to abuse and rob the poor; to make victims of widows and orphans; to retain murderers and thieves; to undermine the Church and not associate with clergy, especially the orders of friars; to rob monks; to murder and abuse children and the venerable; to burn down abbeys and seduce nuns; and to lie and cheat on all occasions and in all company.[24] To bring home the hypocrisy of the world, the writer depicted the new knight being pardoned for all the sins and wickedness he had already committed, by his uncle, a bishop before whom he was swearing to this code of Villainy, and pledging himself to its future pursuit. The knight in question was one Gui, and he was called in the text *lozengier*, one of those hypocritical plotters who make life at court dangerous, the archetypical rival to the *preudomme*, whom he always wishes to overthrow (see pp. 142–5).[25]

It occurred to medieval writers that people who deliberately committed evil acts and aggression were not necessarily people who were (or who at least did not consider themselves to be) immoral. For all that Villainy might be perceived as the antithesis to Courtliness and to be a negative image of its morality and goodness,

---

[21] *Quatre Tenz*, 34–5.   [22] *Proverbe au Vilain*, no. 51.
[23] M. Ailes, 'Traitors and Rebels: the *Geste de Maience*', in *Reading Round the Epic: A Festschrift in Honour of Professor Wolfgang von Emden*, ed. M. Ailes, P. E. Bennett, and K. Pratt (King's College London Medieval Studies, 14, 1998), 41–68.
[24] *Gaydon: chanson de geste du xiiiͤ siècle*, ed. A. Subrenat (Leuven, 2007), 410–12 (ll. 6445–78). See comments in Crouch, *Nobility*, 46–50.
[25] *Gaydon*, 370 (l. 5778).

those who did what others considered to be villainous deeds might very well consider themselves to be in fact virtuous, whatever the effects of their actions. The early thirteenth century had no difficulty in visualizing just this sort of hypocrisy. The Prose Lancelot (*c*.1215) has a scintillating study of just such a villain, King Claudas, who was the reverse image of King Arthur, his enemy. Claudas was convinced of his own righteousness and virtue as a king, and when he meditated on the virtues he prized he singled them out perfectly conventionally as *debonairetez* (civility), *largece* (generosity) and *fiertez* (boldness). But as Claudas explained what he meant by these, we find he meant *debonairetez* to be understood as affably patronizing people without discrimination, favouring good and bad people indifferently. 'Generosity' was about giving to people just enough to establish their dependency, but without any inconvenience to himself. For most courtly men it was generosity which was the prime virtue, but not for Claudas.[26] It was 'Boldness' which he preferred: it meant protecting friends but mercilessly persecuting people he singled out as enemies. Claudas thus perverted Courtliness to Villainy while thinking himself secure in his own righteousness, for he was at heart a villain. It is hard to escape the conclusion that the author was in this way morally satirizing the great of his own day for, as medieval people well knew, power makes self-righteous hypocrites.[27]

An example of a different sort of self-delusion involving *cortoisie* can be found in an early thirteenth-century moral drama based on the parable of the prodigal son, *Courtois d'Arras*. The younger son who, confident in his sense of his own superiority to his birth, quit the farm of his worthy and industrious father for the city, where he thought his talents would be recognized, is given the ironic name 'Courtois'. One of the ladies who will cheat him of his money and be his undoing rapidly assessed his degree of naivety and flattered his self-belief: 'There's nothing of the *vilains* about you! I have no doubts whatsoever that you're all that's *cortoisie* and intelligence.'[28] Yet behind his back she ridiculed Courtois as a strutting would-be Gawain, who was nothing but a *cortois vilain*, a deliberately ambiguous phrase.[29] The irony was completed when, after he had lost everything and was stumbling barefoot along the lanes of Artois, he encountered the very sort of man he imagined himself to be, 'Prodome'. Being the very soul of Courtliness and wisdom, Prodome stifled his amusement when Courtois introduced himself under that name, gave him charity, good advice and employment as a swineherd. Sitting hungry in a field amongst the pigs, Courtois eventually realized he must go home despite his sense of humiliation. And there he was welcomed by his father because he had come to a true realization of himself and repentance for his arrogance.

[26] Contrast the 'proper' view of generosity, according to Raoul de Houdenc, *Roman des Eles*, ll. 173–92.

[27] *Lancelot do Lac* 1: 71–2. The fact that power transcended morality is indeed the subject of the gloss on *Proverbe au Vilain*, no. 121 (*La force paist le pré*).

[28] *Courtois d'Arras: l'Enfant Prodigue*, ed. and trans. (Fr.) J. Dufournet (Paris, 1995), 50–2 (ll. 162–4): '*Vilains voir ne sanblez vous me/ dedenz mon cuer cuit je et pens/ qu'en vous ait cortoisie et sens.*'

[29] Ibid., 58–60 (ll. 246–8).

THE STINKING PEASANT

It was bad luck for the lower orders in early medieval society that one of the two principal words for 'agricultural worker' became *villanus* (Fr. *vilein, vilain*), a Latin term found universally with that meaning across western Europe from Carolingian times onwards and which spawned cognates in several vernaculars. The other was *rusticus*, which had its own well-embedded associations with rural awkwardness and ignorance.[30] Indeed, many of our words for social ineptitude come from the agricultural worker: English 'boorishness' derives from Low German *bur* (Ger. *Bauer*), meaning just that.[31] The medieval *villanus* got his name from his attachment to an agricultural estate (*villa*) and it had nothing to do with his innate vileness, but the association between the words became inevitable in view of the fact that the peasant was from the despised lower end of society. As we have seen, Garin lo Brun and his contemporary Marcabru had no problem in conceiving that people of low origins might actually be socially skilled and *cortois*, and their use of *vilania* did not of itself impute innate boorishness to the peasant, but others were quite happy to make the link. As we will see in Chapter 7, the courtly world in the twelfth century already defined socially inept outsiders as 'villeins' who could not be expected to know the refined manners of the hall. But to do so was not by any means to make a moral judgement on the 'villein' in question.

However, since *vilain, vilan,* or *vilein* in the various Romance languages and dialects would do for the senses of both 'villain' and 'peasant', it was just too obvious and too mischievous a wordplay for the ill-disposed to let pass. So the mid-thirteenth-century poem *Le Despit au Vilain* ('In Contempt of the Villein') ends: 'A villein is foolish, stupid and disgusting. Even if all the goods and wealth in the world were his, anyone called a villein (*vilains*) is by definition a villain (*vilains*).'[32] Thus also the thirteenth-century fable *Aloul*, where a cowherd is harangued by a maidservant : 'The one who invented the name *vilain* got it absolutely right, for you are properly called a *vilain*, as *vilain* comes from *vilonie*.'[33] In Lombardy at much the same time the poet Matazone de Calignano composed a work with the same intention of linking villeins to Villainy, which he does at great length. He was willing to confess to his audience that he was himself the son of a villein, and that he had gained an education to escape his birth defect, but that his innate villainous nature was as a result continually at war with his higher intellect.[34]

Since the 'peasant' and 'villain' were homonyms only in the Romance languages, it is perhaps not surprising that early German vernacular conduct works do not so

[30] Freedman, *Images*, 137–8. Ovid contrasted the *rusticus* with the *urbanus* (the cultivated man).

[31] Freedman, *Images*, 10, points out the relatively high status of the medieval *Bauer*. The social utility of the peasant and his acceptability as long as he toiled cheerfully for the common good surface in Germany in the fourteenth century, where Freedman points out a genre of praise literature for the Nobility of peasant labour (*Images*, 213–14).

[32] '*Vilains est fols, et sos et ors/Se toz li avoirs et li ors/De ceste monde estoit siens, par non/N'erts li vilains se vilains non*', 'Le Despit au Vilain', in *Jongleurs et Trouvères*, ed. A. Jubinal (Paris, 1835), 109.

[33] *Recueil général et complet des fabliaux des XIIIᵉ et XIVᵉ siècles imprimés ou inédits*, ed. A. de Montaiglon and G. Raynaud (Paris, 6 vols, 1872–90) 1: 268 (ll. 404–7).

[34] P. Meyer, 'Dit sur les vilains par Matazone de Calignano', *Romania*, 12 (1883), 20 (ll. 8–16).

loudly berate and characterize the peasant as generically corrupt, or even a boorish outsider to courtly life. Hartmann von Aue provided a memorable twelfth-century portrait of a virtuous and industrious free countryman (*frier buman*) who loyally supported and served in his terrible misfortunes the lord whose land he worked.[35] What the romance languages called a *vilain*, Middle High German called *ein bæsewiht*, which has the single sense of a corrupt, malign villain. The *Welsche Gast* (1216) of Thomasin of Zirclaria (whose first language was either Occitan or Italian) characterized peasants (*geburen*) as hard-working agriculturalists unburdened by the cares of the greater landlord, though Thomasin clearly thought of them as simple-minded and childlike. He reserved his moral opprobrium for the urban moneylender.[36]

Not everyone went along with the innate vileness of the peasant, even in the western lands. Philip de Novare offered a charitable and humane reflection on the heedless equation between villeinage and Villainy, though he assumed nonetheless that inborn shame goes along with peasant standing:

> Men are villains (*vilains*) who act dishonourably and in word and deed care to do nothing other than by means of domination or violence. All who act like this are truly as much villains (*vilain*) as those who are serfs or debtors of rich men: even if they are sprung from noble and distinguished fathers they shouldn't be called well-born and noble, for the nobility and valour of forbears only bring shame and pain to their wicked heirs. Such men incur as much shame (*honte*) when they go wrong as if they were born from peasants (*vilains*).[37]

Just after the end of the period of this book, the Hennuyer poet Jean de Condé roundly condemned ill-natured noblemen who freely berate anyone they dislike as 'villeins'.[38]

There is good evidence that the villein was thought of at least by some as a well-grounded character of insight and common sense in the matter of conduct in the twelfth century. One of Peter Alfonsi's early twelfth-century sermon examples poked fun at two merchants travelling with a peasant (*rusticus*), whom they assumed in their urban sophistication to be innately stupid, only to be comprehensively outfoxed when they tried to trick him out of the last of their joint food supplies.[39] This is the sort of peasant who became the hero of the later *fabliaux*. The social double vision of the High Middle Ages in the way it viewed the intelligence of the peasant is striking and has been extensively examined.[40] In the same generation as Peter Alfonsi praised the good sense of a peasant, Geoffrey of Monmouth came out with the view that, 'It is easier to turn a kite into a hawk than to make a peasant (*rusticus*) suddenly wise; to give him sound advice is just like

---

[35] *Der arme Heinrich*, ed. and trans. (Ger.) N. Busch and J. Wolf (Stuttgart, 2013), 24–6 (ll. 267–314).

[36] *Welsche Gast*, ll. 1097–99, 2639–40, 2667–8, 3107–15, 4281.   [37] *Quatre Tenz*, 112–13.

[38] '*Or m'enten, hons gentius ou frans/Qui es ireus et non souffrans/Qui despites les autres homes/Et par despit vilains les nomes/Rens moi raison de ta franchise/Dont vient et comment fu aquise?*', 'Des Vilains et des Courtois', 191 (ll. 69–74) : 'villein' is meant here rather than 'villain', as *vilains* is opposed to 'homs gentius ou frans'. See comment in Freedman, *Images*, 133–4.

[39] *Disciplina clericalis*, c. 19.   [40] Lorcin, 'Du vilain au paysan', 164–5.

casting pearls before swine.'[41] But popular French collections of vernacular wisdom, such as the *Proverbe au Vilain* (from the court of Flanders in the 1170s) and the *Proverbes au conte de Bretaigne* (from that of Peter Mauclerc before 1221), generally end each gem with the words '…so says the villein', originally meaning no more than '…as is commonly said'.[42] In the 1180s the English moralist Robert of Ho found nothing silly in the supposed origin of these proverbs, lauding on several occasions 'the saying of which the villein (*li vilain*) makes a proverb'.[43] But it is significant that an Anglo-Norman writer in the next century entitled his collection *Le Respit del Curteis et del Vilain* ('Sayings of the Courtly Man and the Villein'), and staged it as a dialogue in which a courtly man's wisdom is hailed as superior to that of the villein. He does, however, credit the villein as having some sense, for all his crude nature.[44] A later commentator on the *Proverbe au Vilain* felt called upon to defend the attribution of wisdom to a commoner by the aphorism 'Sensible men prefer mutton to venison'.[45]

Common sense and probity were increasingly difficult to credit to the peasant as social levels consolidated and were defined in the twelfth and thirteenth centuries, and defined in part by formal education and good manners. Paul Freedman points out that it was the easiest let-out for the educated to explain the sensible and honest peasant as possessed of a mixture of native shrewdness and wit, inferior to true wisdom.[46] The *Donnei des Amanz* tells the fable of the kindly peasant (*vilein*) who released a viper lashed to a thorn-bush by some shepherds. The viper naturally bit him and tried to evade guilt and further punishment by pleading before a fox as judge, but the peasant successfully outwitted the cunning serpent, who ended up back in the bush.[47] But there was a way to characterize such native wit as lazy slyness, such as Peter Alfonsi's idle servant Maimundus, who when asked by his lord if it was raining sent out his dog to see if it came back in with wet paws.[48] For all their objectionable 'common manners' referred to by an Oxford student of the 1240s, in a rhetorical exercise imagining the commiseration between two peasants on their lot, he still credits them with a 'rustic wisdom' (see below, pp. 107–8).

Some of the social demotion of the villein was undoubtedly due to legal changes in parts of Western society. But the *rusticus* in France was already regarded as a figure of social contempt by his betters in the first half of the eleventh century. The Count of Poitiers deliberately insulted his dependent castellan, Hugh de Lusignan, in the 1020s, as Hugh himself tells us, by observing to him that 'You are so

[41] *Historia regum Britanniae*, ed. M. Reeve and trans. N. Wright (Woodbridge, 2007), 112–13 (translation modified).

[42] E. Schulze-Busacker, 'Les "Proverbes au Vilain"', *Proverbium*, 6 (1989), 118. The practice of ending common proverbs with 'so says the villein' is found as early as the *Fecunda Ratis* of Ekkebert of Liège, which dates to the 1020s, whose proverbs end with phrases like *apud rusticos usitatem prouerbium*; Schulze-Busacker, *Didactique*, 74–5.

[43] *Enseignements Trebor*, 81 (ll. 1135–40), 134 (ll. 2464–7).

[44] E. Stengel, 'Handschriftliches aus Oxford', *Zeitschrift für französische Sprache und Literatur*, 14 (1892), 154–8.

[45] Schulze-Busacker, *Didactique*, 88; *Proverbe au Vilain*, 114.

[46] Freedman, *Images*, 205–8.   [47] *Le Donei des Amanz*, 22–7.

[48] *Disciplina Clericalis*, c. 27.

dependent on me that if I were to tell you to make a peasant (*rusticus*) your lord, you ought to do it!'[49] It is in the Empire that we first find an 'origin myth' of peasantry devised by intellectuals to justify their low status and servitude, drawing on the explanations of the Fathers as to why there were slaves in God's creation. Around 1100 Honorius Augustodunensis was willing to believe that serfs would be saved, because they supported the more worthy parts of society with their labour. On the other hand, he took on board the Fathers' theological explanation for their social debasement: peasants were descended from Ham, cursed by his father Noah to serve his more worthy brothers, Japhet, ancestor of knights, and Shem, ancestor of other free men.[50] The jurist Philip de Beaumanoir had a variety of historical explanations for why it was that people were born servile, and hardly any of them were creditable to the peasant.[51]

England has a lot to offer as a study of the deliberate and retrogressive abnegation of the villein within society. In the Domesday Survey of England in 1086 *villani* appear as a higher class of agricultural labourer distinct from lower groups—slaves, bordars and cottars—and generally they must have been a group of not inconsiderable 'free peasants' to be found across the kingdom, shading into the echelons of the freeholders or 'sokemen' of the north and east, local free landowners of some social weight, people Beaumanoir would characterize as *frans hommes de poosté* (free men of means, or freeholders). But by 1200 a person described as *villanus* or *rusticus* in England was more likely to be an unfree peasant bonded to the land, as English common-law justices developed procedures to define restrictively the burdens of villeinage, and rural peasant tenure developed in as constrained a way as in France. It has been pointed out that twelfth-century England developed its own characteristic word for serf, *nativus* (Fr. *neif*), which simply means 'someone born here', so the English peasant was subjected to ethnic in addition to legal subordination in the aftermath of his land's absorption into the francophone area.[52]

As with Honorius, it is not unusual to find a mixture of views about peasants in the same author's work, and for the same reason. Stephen de Fougères in the late 1150s is a good case in point. He was willing enough to concede that peasants were exploited, abused and ill-treated; they were denied the comforts that their betters enjoyed; they worked hard for little return; and yet, as Honorius also said, their labour supported the rest of society.[53] For all this, the best that Stephen could offer the peasant is the rewards of heaven if he took his privations in good part, which implied the peasant could live in a sort of austere and primitive dignity. But he was

---

[49] *Le Conventum (vers 1030): un précurseur aquitain des premières épopées*, ed. G. Beech, Y. Chauvin, and G. Pon (Geneva, 1995), 128.

[50] *De imagine mundi*, in *PL*, 172, col. 166, and see contextualization in Freedman, *Images*, 31–2, 92–100.

[51] *Coutumes de Beauvaisis*, 2: 235–6, c. 1453.

[52] R. V. Lennard, *Rural England, 1086–1135: A Study of Social and Agararian Conditions* (Oxford, 1959), 339ff; P. R. Hyams, *Kings, Lords and Peasants in Medieval England: the Common Law of Villeinage in the Twelfth and Thirteenth Centuries* (Oxford, 1980), 221ff; R. Faith, *The English Peasantry and the Growth of Lordship* (Leicester, 1997), 245ff.

[53] His contemporary Wace of Bayeux has been credited with similar mixed views; D. Buttry, 'Contempt or Empathy? Master Wace's depiction of a peasant revolt', *Romance Notes*, 37 (1996), 31–8.

still willing to scold the peasant for his impatience in his troubles, his greed and social ambition, and particularly the little deceits by which he tried to evade the burdens laid on him, especially his tithes.[54]

Sympathy for a peasant's life of deprivation can be found in unexpected places. Though the *Proverbe au Vilain* derived from the brilliant and noble court of the young Count Philip of Flanders (reigned 1157–91), it includes this solemn gloss on the proverb: 'A man digs his own grave' (*De meisme la terre fait l'on le fossé*).

> I know this all too well: a lord climbs in this life on the backs of his peasants. His ploughmen provide the money to marry off his daughters and make his sons knights.[55]

Then also there is this note of grim sympathy under the saying 'Straw tastes good when there's nothing else to eat' (*Mieuz vaut paille en dent que nïent*):

> Peasants have to eat bad bread more straw than wheat; they're so hungry they can't sleep but they still have to get up in the morning to manure the fields.[56]

These aperçus were intended to inform and provoke discussion in hall and chamber, so they indicate that a public stance of sympathy for the lot of the agricultural poor was not thought improper even in the highest circles of the twelfth century. The peasant and his way of life had open defenders and sympathizers amongst the educated elite. The early thirteenth-century Cambridgeshire grammarian Elias of Thriplow confessed himself to be from a family of free *ruricoli*, just as did his Italian contemporary Matazone de Calignano. Elias objected to those who would run down his people, especially when it came from 'the vaunting vanity of the puffed-up nobility'. He described the natural virtue, charity and piety, hard work, sobriety and industry of the peasant.[57] A rhetorical exercise in Oxford in the 1240s asked a student to imagine a conversation between peasants (*rustici*), and the results are not too distant from Stephen de Fougères's standpoint, bemoaning the peasant's hard lot and what he had to suffer. But it also noted the social contempt in which he was universally held. The scholastic nature of the prose in which the supposed peasant addresses his friend simply points up the enormous social gulf between the real-life peasant and the leisured classes:

> Most of the human race has degenerated to the point that, for its sins, it has caused slavery to emerge. For freedom is an inestimable thing; their slavery is burdensome to those who are property. You have seen well that we have a harsh lord, a sly serjeant, a wicked reeve, and almost barren land, and all these are adverse beyond measure. We almost entirely lack intervals of rest, and that which lacks daily rest cannot endure, just as a bow that you do not cease to bend will grow slack, nor is there on earth anything while we live that revives our spirits. I need advice with rustic wisdom from you; you must not fail me. And since men of free condition abhor both common manners and common people, were it not for our rational souls we would be held but as rabid dogs among them. In these things the ability to endure hardship is necessary

---

[54] *Livre des Manières*, 62–8.   [55] *Proverbe au Vilain*, no. 224.
[56] *Proverbe au Vilain*, no. 268.
[57] *Petronius Rediuiuus et Helias Tripolanensis*, ed. M. L. Colker (Leiden, 2007), 143–4. *Anecdota Literaria*, ed. T. Wright (London, 1844), 53–4.

for us because if, complaining, we resist, our misery will be cut short for us. We have but one solace: we shall die, and at our death our servitudes will end.[58]

Social awkwardness was to be expected of the agricultural poor in the sources, but so also were physical grossness and poor hygiene. It has been observed that when artists depicted the shepherds who came by night from the fields around Bethlehem to adore the newborn Jesus, they were increasingly caricatured towards the end of the twelfth century as gross and leering characters, with thick lips and matted hair.[59] At the end of the twelfth century we find two monks of Peterborough Abbey engaged in a literary duel, one berating the other as a man whose father was a peasant 'who slept in a dung-filled sty'.[60] Grossness and stink were the characteristics imputed by the leisured of the twelfth century to agricultural workers. Indeed, some thought them incapable of dealing with anything else. An early thirteenth-century joke had a peasant 'brought up in squalor and stench' fainting away when he caught the wholesome aromas emitting from an apothecary's shop, and having to be thrown on a dung heap to be brought round.[61]

Peasants were a social danger for several reasons in the twelfth and thirteenth century, and not because there was much chance of peasant insurrections, which are rare in the historical record of the period. Projecting animalistic characteristics and brute insensitivity on them was a strategy that intensified across Europe during the twelfth century. It was a way of marginalizing and diminishing the danger they represented. Peasants were a danger because in a society where social levels were being more closely defined, those who were already consigned to live outside the margins of *cortoisie* troubled their superiors when they tried to edge through their hall doors. There is a marked outbreak of resentment of the social-climbing peasant in Angevin England and Capetian France in particular in the last third of the twelfth century. Stephen de Fougères around 1160 was already criticizing the peasant who chafed under his lot. The next generation went a lot further. Writers of all sorts at the end of the century fulminated with abuse and warnings, especially about taking the peasant into a courtly environment. So the Anglo-French author of the *Song of Aspremont* around 1190 sternly warned: 'Do not make a lord of your serf, leave the peasant to do his proper work; a peasant has nothing to do with honour, at the end of the day he will return to his own nature.'[62] Alexander of Paris, in the early years of Philip Augustus, claimed the imaginary authority of Aristotle for the view that vile peasants (*sers de put aire*) ought never to be given a

---

[58] *Lost Letters*, no. 93. But for a vernacular thirteenth-century student poem, by contrast in contempt of the peasant, *Anecdota Literaria*, ed. T. Wright (London, 1844), 53–4.

[59] T. A. Heslop, 'Romanesque Painting and Social Distinction: the Magi and the Shepherds', in *England in the Twelfth Century*, ed. D. Williams (Woodbridge, 1990), 147–9.

[60] John of St Omer, *Norfolchiae descriptionis impugnatio*, in *Early Mysteries and other Latin Poems of the Twelfth and Thirteenth Centuries*, ed. T. Wright (London, 1838), 102.

[61] *A Selection of Latin Stories*, ed. T. Wright (Percy Society, 8, 1842), 84, which is paralleled by the vernacular tale *Du Vilain Asnier*; see *Cuckolds, Clerics and Countryman: Medieval French Fabliaux*, ed. R. Eichmann and trans. J. DuVal (Fayetteville, AR, 1982), 61–2, whose moral warned the low-born against aspiring beyond their sphere. For the widespread association of the peasant with stench and excrement, Freedman, *Images*, 133–56.

[62] *Aspremont*, 2 : ll. 19,214–26.

place at court: 'for many men have been as a result killed and tortured by their deceit, assassination and poisoning.'[63] In the schoolroom of the 1180s Daniel of Beccles set his students exercises which stated: 'Nothing is more harmful than a villainous pauper, should he rise in society he will repay your favour with evil.' Another of his aphorisms excluded them from the courtly hall: 'Servants shouldn't bring up a master in their own wretchedness: no shepherd or ploughman should sit at your table.'[64] In the same decade, the amiable Angevin courtier and cleric Walter Map was anything but affable at the thought of men of peasant origins rising through the Church hierarchy. He quoted the great justice Ranulf de Glanville on the subject: 'The serfs (*servi*), whom we also call peasants (*rustici*), vie with each other in bringing up their worthless and degenerate offspring to those arts which are forbidden to them; not that they may shed vices, but that they may gather riches; and the more they attain, the more ill they do.'[65]

Some writers had to admit that they knew perfectly decent and well-meaning peasants, such as the respectable peasants (*vilan proat*) the castellan Garin lo Brun acknowledged, men whose conduct he went so far as to say could be judged to be courtly. In England in the 1180s, Robert of Ho agreed with him in saying that the possession of qualities of a good heart might even justify calling a virtuous peasant noble (*gentiz*), though the man had to survive by begging on the streets.[66] An Occitan writer at the end of the thirteenth century came out with similar views: that the 'desperately poor' could be generous, cheerful and free-handed (*franx*) in what they did.[67] The thirteenth century may have elevated further the idea of Nobility, as it became the mainspring of social division and distinction, but still there were even then writers like Baldwin de Condé who could assert in his tract on Nobility that the nobleman with a wicked heart, however high his station, was worth less than a villein with a noble one. He rose to the polemical on the subject:

> Whoever may be noble of heart needs no other Nobility than that, even if he is son to the most lowborn (*vilain*) fellow in the empire of Rome, and for this he should not be despised for he is then as noble a man as he may be; the lowborn man (*hom vilains*) of noble heart should be rather more worthy of celebration than the nobleman with a wicked one.[68]

We might be justified in translating the villein here by the more modern term 'commoner', though that is a word opposed to 'noble' rather than 'courtly man'. Most revealingly, and almost shamefacedly, Ramon Vidal confessed that:

> When you're both young you can be close friends with a respectable peasant boy (*vilan cortes*), whose trivial accomplishment doesn't make him your equal and whose behaviour is awkward at the time; for it isn't likely that such a boy when he grows up will turn out to be a pauper or a criminal.[69]

[63] *Le Roman d'Alexandre*, ed. E. C. Armstrong and trans (Fr.) L. Harf-Lancner (Paris,1994), 92 (ll. 343–6).
[64] *Liber Urbani*, 29 (ll. 818–19), 76–7 (ll. 2323–4).
[65] *De Nugis Curialium*, 12 (translation modified as to social vocabulary).
[66] *Enseignements Trebor*, 116 (ll. 2013–18).   [67] *Enssenhamen de la Donzela*, 29–30.
[68] *Condé*, 1: 178–9 (ll. 85–93).   [69] *Abril issia*, 122 (ll. 1465–70).

It is the social embarrassment represented by peasants that most irks Ramon in the first decade of the thirteenth century. Such was the burden of the courtly, cultured and educated person in dealing with his well-meaning inferiors. But there was always this defensive position to fall back on: if peasants could not be faulted on their ambition, hygiene, honesty or goodwill, they were still uneducated and blind to the courtly habitus to which the educated were attuned by their apprenticeship of manners in the aristocratic hall. Robert de Blois a generation later summed up the fallback position in his instructions for lords: 'So far as the serf is the lowest of the low, he is the more ludicrous, arrogant, erratic, harmful and unbalanced when set on high.'[70] But, like Ramon Vidal, he is forced to admit that humble people should not be dismissed out of hand: 'The man who is upright and wise, and the son of a capable and civil peasant (*Fiz de vilain prouz et cortois*) is worth fifteen depraved king's sons.'[71]

THE TRANSGRESSIVE MERCHANT

It was the social danger that the rising peasant represented that brought the urban entrepreneur and merchant within range of the same stigmatization. Wealthy men of low or uncertain birth may not have had any connection with the agricultural *vilain*, but the fact that they had the resources to aspire to a noble lifestyle and appear at great courts was a challenge to the landed elite, to whom that environment was their birthright. This might particularly be the case where urban financiers achieved the dignity of knighthood, as members of several leading families did in London in the late twelfth and early thirteenth century. The Londoners had already trespassed on the goodwill of the elite by maintaining the use of the antiquated term 'barons' for themselves as citizens, even though the word was becoming restricted by the 1180s to the magnates of the realm. In the 1250s Matthew Paris put into the mouth of King Henry III the dismissive remark that 'those London peasants (*rustici*) who call themselves "barons" sicken me with their wealth'. He also recorded a riot breaking out in Westminster when a quintain contest between youths drawn from the City and from the court degenerated into a brawl when the aristocratic boys lost and abused their opponents as 'scabby peasants and soap-makers' (soap-making was a particularly noxious and smelly trade).[72]

A variant of this abuse from Capetian France is the popular and widespread tale of the comeuppance of Artaud de Nogent, which was circulating in the 1190s. The story may well have been a by-product of the powerful moral and intellectual movement against usurers and usury in that generation, which culminated in its prohibition in the Lateran Council of 1215. Artaud was a historical character of the 1170s and prominent at the court and in the council of Count Henry the

[70] *Enseignement des princes*, 113 (ll. 721–4).
[71] *Enseignement des princes*, 115 (ll. 792–4).
[72] *Chronica Majora*, ed. H. R. Luard (7 vols, Rolls Series, 1872–84) 5: 22, 367. For the changing term 'baron' in England, Crouch, *Aristocracy*, 111–14.

Liberal of Champagne (died 1181), whose chief financial officer he was for three decades. Through trade and finance Artaud acquired the wealth to build castles and live the noble lifestyle. But when in Jacques de Vitry's sermon tale he argued against the count's proposal to provide dowries for the two daughters of an impoverished knight, he was brutally put in his place. The count declared that since Artaud was his *villanus* and his to dispose of as he wished, he would grant him to the poor knight.[73] The literature of Capetian France crystallized the prejudice. The mid thirteenth-century *fabliau* known as *Bérenger au Long Cul* has as its anti-hero the son of a wealthy moneylender. The son was knighted and married to the noble daughter of a financially embarrassed father. The moneylender was called *vilain* and his son turned out to be a cowardly poseur as a knight, and so he was crudely humiliated by his disdainful and adulterous wife. The moral of the tale offered by Guérin, its author, is a social lesson along the lines of the story of Artaud: 'This is how good families are corrupted; castellans and counts brought to nothing and shamed: by marrying off their women for the sake of credit. But what they gain is only discredit and deep disgrace! You get just bad, corrupt and cowardly knights from such people, who are more interested in silver and gold than knightly deeds. So nobility declines and honour and achievement are debased.'[74]

The association between the social threat of the rising urban entrepreneur and the peasant, with all the taint of dung, low morals and debauchery that went with the equation, is very much something of the late twelfth century and the chivalric turn. Stephen de Fougères in the 1150s did not think much of *marchëant* or *borzeis*, especially those who were usurers. He credited them with social ambition and a willingness to pimp their own wives or daughters in pursuit of wealth and call it *courtoise*, but he did not demean them as peasants.[75] But Andrew the Chaplain's dialogues on seduction and social class a generation later in the 1180s adopted the same social rhetoric against the urban elites as we find in the tale of the socially transgressive Artaud. He talked of three social groups, the lowest of which is the *plebeius*, whom he intended to be taken as the wealthy merchant who had trespassed into high society. He attributed to them the same physical gracelessness as other writers did to the peasant: they were ignorant, credulous, physically awkward and unkempt. Andrew was aware of the agricultural labourer and he pondered whether it was possible that such a bestial creature might experience so exalted an emotion as love. He decided that love was beyond the peasant's capacity and that any urges he experienced should be sublimated in manual labour.[76]

These bourgeois traders or rising freeholders are the same characters who appear in the world of the romance from the 1180s onwards. The social comedy of the awkward 'villein' out of his proper place and the resentment that fuels it tells us well enough that the villein may not have been villainous, but his perceived conduct

---

[73] *Die exempla aus den Sermones feriales et communes des Jakob von Vitry*, ed. J. Greven (Heidelberg, 1914), 17; Jean de Joinville, *Vie de Saint Louis*, ed. J. Monfrin (Paris, 1995), 46. The actual relationship between Count Henry and Artaud was rather different; T. Evergates, *Henry the Liberal, Count of Champagne, 1127–1181* (Philadelphia, 2016), 82, 180–1.
[74] *Chevalerie et Grivoiserie*, 84 (ll. 24–35).   [75] *Livre des Manières*, 72–4 (ll. 837–52).
[76] *De Amore*, 222.

and appearance was still a tool of social formation and education. As well as the implied taint of filth and sweat he carried, his manners were not considered to come near the ideals of Courtliness. He was loud, ill-dressed, awkward and gullible, and his women were the same, though desirable enough as women to be sexually exploited. Yet this hostile construction of the villein as an 'anti-courtier' was only a generalized fiction, as medieval writers who were acquainted with wise, honest, decent and even courteous villeins knew well enough and who occasionally said so. It is perhaps most revealing that the final line of defence against a peasant, when all else was admitted, was his lack of liberal education, which, as Walter Map said, was the property of *liberi* (free men). The higher orders in society had the resources with which to employ tutors for their children and the contacts to send them either to the greater schools or the households of the great, where they might learn courtly conduct amongst their equals. These were sources of social capital none of the rural and urban poor and few of the middling order in town and village could hope to tap into.

7

The Courtly Habitus

THE LIMITS OF *CORTOISIE*

One of the more curious characters of the late twelfth-century romance epic is that of young Rigaud in the cycle of tales known as *Garin le Loherenc*. In this work, Rigaud was the result of the marriage between a granddaughter of a duke of Lorraine and a '*boen vilain*' called Hervey du Plessis. Rigaud, the duke's great-nephew by that unlikely union, was described by the author with evident relish as a mongrel. His father was a good fellow, as we are told, but he was nonetheless described as a 'villein'. It is more than a little bizarre then to find him married to a duke's niece, so the author took the trouble to sketch a tenuous court connection for Hervey. We are told his father was a soldier who joined a previous duke of Lorraine, his godfather, in battle against the Saracens. Hervey as a youth had himself also taken the field in the ducal army, and we are told his brother was a huntsman of the court who had acquired a noble fief.[1] Hervey was being portrayed as a man on the fringe of superior society, and his 'villein' label was not intended to portray him as a low-status serf but as an outsider uninterested in courtly society, a fellow of modest origins who had settled for life as a rustic backwoodsman on his estate at Le Plessis: his standing as a landowner earned him the description elsewhere in the work as 'the Lord Hervey'.[2]

Hervey's son Rigaud did not get the benefit of a courtly education in his father's rural retreat, which was hardly to his noble mother's credit. When he did appear at the ducal court, filthy and dishevelled, Rigaud's rusticity was even more noxious than that of Perceval at Arthur's court: 'he hadn't washed for over six months and had no acquaintance with any water apart from what fell from the sky.' His clothing was ragged and his hose out at heel.[3] But he was a strapping and forthright youth and his great-uncle, the duke, equipped him with horse and arms, for he was acknowledged as a 'noble squire'. When it came to the ritual of knighting Rigaud, however, the youth's lack of a courtly education was all too evident. He was disgruntled at the idea of a bath and baulked at putting on the long, furred robes, useless for his rural recreations of fishing and hunting: 'I'd rather the homespun my father Hervey has!' He promptly severed a good foot and a half of the train of his robe so he could get around with more ease. The emperor who was present was most amused, and even more so when Rigaud drew his new sword on the duke

---

[1] *Garin le Loherenc* 1: ll. 684–5, 1618.   [2] *Garin le Loherenc* 2: l. 8660.
[3] *Garin le Loherenc* 2: ll. 8272–6.

who had given him the ceremonial blow of the rite. When it was explained to Rigaud that it was just the custom, he burst out in rage: 'Then it's a stupid custom. A dire curse on him who thought it up!'[4]

Rigaud was a social caricature, but like all caricatures he made an exaggerated point, in this case that the courtly world had a way of defining itself by stigmatizing outsiders who did not share its accepted norms of behaviour, of which the definitive figure was the peasant. When new people came into a courtly environment, the less socially adroit and instructed among them stood out, becoming the subject of gossip and amusement, as they made their inevitable gaffes—unconscious trespasses against the habitus. Ramon Vidal provided for his fellow troubadours a patronizing sketch of just such people whom they might meet in the halls of Occitania:

> The fact of his birth forms the peasant in the same way as his learning forms the intellectual. They are what they are, as are those many others who are born wicked and stupid. But then there are the peasants you find at court (*vilan cortes*) who, for their lack of education, can't offer much in the way of conversation and when they see you've arrived in the company of ladies or among others, at that point their deficient education (*pecx ensenhamens*) is exposed to the assembled court.[5]

Here, as with the *Garin* cycle, intruders into the courtly world are being freely stigmatized as 'peasants', a social group who could not be expected to be sensitive to the society of the court and its customs—people like shepherds and ploughmen who, as Daniel of Beccles said, you would not want or expect to encounter in a hall at dinner.[6] Ramon described with a certain sarcastic relish an incident that had clearly riled him, where one of these outsiders, full of an insensitive self-consequence and obviously not suffering from 'imposter syndrome', attempted to badger and bully musicians and ladies into performing when they had no wish to. Ramon might at this point have been driven to reflect with humility that some inhabitants of the court would have classified troubadours of undistinguished birth (as he was) as being little more than domestic servants, for he added tolerantly:

> You mustn't use brusque and rude expressions to peasants just because they have the capacity to irritate you; they may very well wish to hear your song but are just brusque and impatient in their understanding of things. You should treat such people considerately for they aren't good for nothing; if you are antagonistic towards them they will be rude and sullen towards you.[7]

The courtly world, then, had its limits. It had insiders who were au fait with its norms and had the confidence that went with it—they were Bourdieu's 'fish in

---

[4] *Garin le Loherenc* 2: ll. 8880–914. On this incident see F. Lyons, 'Encore l'adoubement de Rigaut (Garin le Loherain)', in *Mélanges de littérature du Moyen Âge au XXᵉ offerts à Mademoiselle Jeanne Lods, professeur honoraire de littérature médiévale à l'École normal supérieure de jeunes filles, par ses collègues, ses élèves et ses amis* (2 vols, Collection de l'École normale supérieure de jeunes filles, 10, 1978), 1: 410–13; J-P. Martin, 'Garin, Begon, Rigaut: à propos de trois figures du guerrier dans Garin le Loherain', *Le monde des héros dans la culture médiévale*, ed. D. Buschinger and W. Spiewok (Greifswalder Beiträge zum Mittelalter, 35, 1994), 181–93.

[5] *Abril issia*, 96 (ll. 1020–9).

[6] *Liber Urbani*, 77 (l. 2324), *non famulans mense sit pastor siue bubulcus*.

[7] *Abril issia*, 96 (ll. 1040–7).

water' in the social field that formed within the environment of the hall and the court it housed. Medieval German courtly literature had the term *hoffähig* to express just this: a person 'fit for the court'. Insiders were also alert to those outsiders—fish out of water—who had flopped into the hall without the background and education to survive there, so could be stigmatized archetypically as 'peasants' who had no place within a hall. Courtly society was a habitus which could generate an idea of social exclusivity and in which cultural capital bought a place. I imagine that Rutebeuf was being at least half serious when he urged Jesus Christ to deny Paradise to villeins, because it would not be reasonable or right that people of that sort should be in such a berth (*herbergement*). He joked that Hell was too good for them.[8]

What then did it take to be such a self-assured insider—*curialis, li cortois or hovische man*, a courtly man? We can work out something of the size of this world, even in the twelfth century. It was by no means restricted to the royal and princely courts of Europe and its great lords and ladies, influential though they were. The rituals of the hall and conventions of the courtier were taught at much lower levels of landed society, anywhere indeed where there was a hall that needed to be appropriately serviced. It comprehended children and youths confided to a lord to be brought up in his household, whether they would go on to be lords of their own halls or not. It likewise included the knights, clerks, officials and servants who made the running of the hall possible and sustained its dignity. All of these needed to be fit for the courts in which they would live and make themselves pleasant and useful.

The courtly world needed many spear carriers: musicians, poets, cooks, ushers, butlers and stewards, and all sorts of minions who orchestrated and carried out its rituals and made its elaborate meals and festivals possible. Some of these more lowly inhabitants of the courtly world might be fiercer in the defence of its norms than were their employers, as we learn from contemporary opinion of the marshals, ushers and porters who literally kept its gate. But great and small alike were all tutored in the same social environment and the manners necessary to survive there, just like the Italian youth from Rome confided to the Angevin royal court in the 1150s, or the lads standing at the countess of Lincoln's table in Robert Grosseste's *Rules* in the later 1240s. They learned the culture of the hall among the tables where they genuflected and served, and between its aisles where they gossiped and connived, and not from any of the tracts we have looked at here, though those too were products of the same habitus.[9] They carried on their interaction with it as adults, training the next generation and travelling to new halls in different lands to learn that things were different there, or perhaps not so very different. And some of the more reflective of them picked up a pen to record what they had learned and what they thought was correct in conduct there, the standard of propriety which Germans called *Hofzuht*.

---

[8] *Le Pet au Villain*, in *Oeuvres Complètes de Rutebeuf*, ed. E. Faral and J. Bastin (2 vols, Paris, 1959–60) 2: 306 (ll. 10–22).

[9] Significantly, Brunetto Latini sent his ideal knight to the place where Cortesia resided, where he asked her to teach him *tutta la maestria de fina cortesia*; *Tesoretto*, 230–1 (ll. 1571–82).

THE COURTLY MARGINS

The argument of this book is that *cortoisie* was a supranational phenomenon and not specific to any linguistic group, though the Franciliens certainly already had the reputation in the later twelfth century of considering themselves to be its definitive practitioners. The scornful contemporary reaction to that claim even within France tells us something about how widespread then was the appreciation of *cortoisie* as the property of the social elite, not any particular nation. Attempts to hijack it to promote the self-image of a cultural and linguistic group around Paris and its royal court were resisted and ridiculed, most brutally by Andrew de Coutances, the satirical author of the *Roman des Franceis*, a Norman who had himself been educated in the Parisian schools (see pp. 176–7). Other foreigners however, such as Gerald of Wales, were happy to collude with the idea of a Parisian cultural predominance, in his case because his student experience there was the happiest time of his troubled emotional life, and ever thereafter he exalted his youthful Parisian residence in his mind as a background from which he could claim a certain social superiority. Late in life Gerald talked fondly of the manner of French of a young friend of his at Lincoln, who, though never having been in the Île-de-France, had taken pains to acquire its correct (*rectus*) manner of French, rather than the 'rough, corrupt French of the English people'.[10] But even Gerald's pretentious cultural one-upmanship was a testimony to the transnational nature of the culture we are examining here.

Gerald and his like took their understanding of *cortoisie* into every subsequent social environment where they found themselves, and these could be both rural and far-flung. At various times Gerald dined and interacted with his Welsh aristocratic relations, his relatives in the Irish province of Leinster, and at the humbler tables of the Anglo-Welsh clergy of his archdeaconry, who had to endure his inquisitorial visitations and entertain him suitably or be discredited, at the least in their own eyes. The trouble experienced by these local clergy in such circumstances can help us map out the margins of the courtly realm. Formulary letters in mid-thirteenth-century collections describe the problems caused when a bishop or archdeacon made a progress through a deanery and its local clergy had to sustain the burden of entertaining them and their retinues. In one collection you will find an archdeacon of the 1240s warning a local dean of the impending visitation of a bishop and the importance of finding all sorts of food for courses so he is 'suitably entertained' with a warning that failure could lose the goodwill of the offended prelate. A letter from a dean to a local rector 'writing as a friend' conveys the bad news down the hierarchy and urgently bids the unfortunate cleric to lay out wine and the sort of varied table the likes of a bishop would expect to sit at.[11] These letters were not just literary exercises. A missive from the 1190s miraculously survives which was written by a Yorkshire rector in a panic, begging provisions from a neighbouring

[10] *Speculum Duorum*, 56.   [11] *Lost Letters*, nos 17, 18.

abbot so he could appropriately entertain just a mere vice-archdeacon and his staff on a visitation.[12]

Every township and large village in twelfth-century western Europe was likely to have at least two households where the norms of courtly society were expected to be observed. The house of the incumbent of its church would, as we have seen, be expected to offer 'accommodation' (*hospitium*) to passing prelates, including fine dining.[13] So we find the situation we encounter in the *fabliau* 'The Knight and the Priest', where a knight on the road in northern France came to a village and needed to find suitable lodging, but the village population consisted of brute peasants living no better than animals, and the only accommodation he could possibly contemplate was that of the chief resident, its wealthy rector, who, though an unpleasant and avaricious personality, did at least have the skills and facilities to entertain appropriately a man of the knight's station. He could offer stabling, trained pages to serve, a staffed kitchen and a hall where the norms of civil dining were observed, and afterwards a bedchamber for the night. All that was lacking in the rector's case was a courtly demeanour.[14] Other occupants of a township might well come within the bounds of politesse: not just local knights, but members of an intermediate gentry (called variously in Latin *francolani* or *vavassores*, or, in French, *vavassors* or *li bon païsant*): men who had the resources to build a hall and chamber block, a neighbouring kitchen, even possibly an oratory, and who enclosed their residence with a bank and wall, which was more a symbol than a defence. Such halls had their small courtly households. The surviving will of just such a landowner, John de Charnelles of Muston in Leicestershire, which dates from 1301, lists legacies for his nurse, cook, groom and butler.[15] These local worthies had thus created and staffed what Late Latin called a *curtis*, the word which gives us the Old French *cort* and *cortois*.

Even unambitious timber provincial halls required numbers of servants to service and maintain them, and those underlings too came within the bounds of a courtly society, whose norms they had to understand or be a discredit to their master or mistress. It was common wisdom that: 'A youth must learn how to serve so that he best knows how to conduct himself well and courteously at a dinner in the presence of people.'[16] Daniel of Beccles observed, indeed, that 'no servant should be taken into employment unless he is aware of what it is to serve a person of consequence'.[17] The so-called 'Laws of Edward the Confessor', which in fact date from the later 1130s, tell us that at that time every touring Anglo-Norman noble household would be expected to feature numerous specialists—stewards, butlers,

[12] N. Vincent, 'William Marshal, King Henry II and the Honour of Châteauroux', *Archives*, 25 (2000), 2–3.
[13] See, for more on this, H. M. Thomas, *The Secular Clergy in England, 1066–1216* (Oxford, 2014), 196–9.
[14] *Chevalerie et Grivoiserie*, 10–26.
[15] *The MSS of His Grace the Duke of Rutland* (4 vols, London, 1905), 4: 14.
[16] *Urbain le Courtois*, ll. 48–51.
[17] *Liber Urbani*, 75 (ll. 2278–9): *Ullus seruorum non admittatur in usus/Cui non sit notum quid sit seruire potenti.*

chamberlains, cooks, bakers, squires and other lower servants—all of whom would come within the lord's '*fripborga*', his legal responsibility for his courtiers' actions.[18]

One class of lower servant which was by then already well in evidence in documents is criticized more than others. These were the servants stationed at the doors: the porters and ushers, whose duty it was to detain, interrogate, admit and announce visitors. This is a fact which may be a significant indicator of the inherent insecurity in the occupants of the courtly milieu and the reality of its margins. It was the unusual distinction of the early twelfth-century *preudomme*, Gilbert of Surrey, that when he attended the royal hall in the 1120s, such was his address and reputation that the smiling porters promptly threw back the doors for him, while keeping bishops and distinguished nobles cooling their heels outside.[19] It was thought a sign of exceeding virtue in a great lord, such as Boniface, marquis of Montferrat (died 1207), that he should have no porter at his door when he dined, as the troubadour Raimbaut de Vaqueiras observed in his eulogy of his patron in the 1190s. It demonstrated such a lord's confident liberality, and by one account it was King John of England's sole virtue.[20] At other times with such lords entry within their gates might not have been so easy.

Stories of the obstructiveness of porters are many, such as the one who prevented an entertainer from entering his master's hall on the grounds that he had refused to say who was his lord and,therefore, who was responsible for his behaviour. The defiant entertainer declared his only lord was God, but when the porter called out the steward of the hall because of the row the man was making, the entertainer claimed the devil for his master, at which the amused steward let him in.[21] In the Gascony of the 1170s, Arnaut-Guilhem de Marsan's *ensenhamen* advised lords not to employ ill-tempered porters who lash out with their staves at the squires, pages, entertainers and hangers-on 'who want to get inside the doors'.[22] In England at much the same time, Daniel of Beccles cautioned that 'An intimidating porter'—the word he used was Cerberus—'should not rule the roost in the outer court, rather it should be a kindly, freely spoken, discreet and respectful retainer. May the doorway collapse whose access is harshly ordered.'[23]

Ushers similarly had a duty to prohibit easy access to their master, notably his private chambers, and some were not above demanding fees for the privilege of their attention. Peter of Blois hated their sort: 'May the Almighty confound the ushers of the chamber! They have no shame in putting off an honest fellow with any old excuse. Beware their deadly staves! Give an usher nothing, and nothing

---

[18] B. O'Brien, *God's Peace and King's Peace: The Laws of Edward the Confessor* (Philadelphia, 1999), 273 (c. 21).

[19] M. L. Colker, 'Latin Texts concerning Gilbert, founder of Merton Priory', *Studia Monastica*, 12 (1970), 260–1.

[20] Raimbaut, 308 (l. 106). For John of England, see the comment: 'He was brimming over with bad qualities, but he did at least spend freely. He would keep a generous and open table, and indeed his gates and the door of his hall were never closed at meal times.' *Histoire*, 105.

[21] *A Selection of Latin Stories*, ed. T. Wright (Percy Society, 8, 1842), 129.

[22] *Qui comte vol apendre*, 85–6 (ll. 439–44).

[23] '*Cerberus in foribus non presideat dominator/ Immo cliens lepidus liber discretus honorus/ Ianua depereat, cui limen amare iubetur,*' *Liber Urbani*, 81 (ll. 2476–8).

gets done.'[24] The sensitivity of writers about the hall and its conduct on this particular subject is not surprising in an environment where acceptance was all. Here we see the actual force field which cut off and protected the margin of the courtly world from the outer social wilderness. For those low down in the courtly world, or those rising into it, even a temporary denial at the hall door was an acute humiliation; it implied they had been assessed as marginal to acceptable society, one with the peasants in their hovels down the road, and their standing took a brutal and very public blow. One can imagine that it was most likely to happen to up-and-coming youths, who might wince at the social trauma involved for many years thereafter.

In due course the courtly world was to produce specialists in social protocol and precedence—the heralds. Their very appearance would therefore be significant of the consolidation of the boundaries of that world, though dating it is difficult in view of the sparsity of early sources and the generally low status of early heralds. There is, however, evidence that heralds of some seniority occupied places and received robes at the Angevin royal court, where a king of arms (*rei d'armar*) is mentioned by Bertran de Born in 1184. This is the first appearance of that title, which in the thirteenth century would be applied to chief heralds who were acknowledged experts on the arms, nobility and precedence of the occupants of royal and princely courts, as well as organizing tournament fields. But since the court of Henry II of England and Eleanor in 1184 had little to do with the tournament, his 'king of arms' was doing something other than arrange and score sporting events.[25] When the profession of herald was first defined and described by Henry de Laon at some time in the decade or two before 1250, it was set up by Henry to be knocked down. The herald he described was a shiftless idler, good only at talking up his own importance and trading on the social insecurity and ignorance of his employer, who was being shaken down for the herald's exorbitant fees.[26] But that very criticism is some evidence that the herald had assumed an importance in the regulation of social life that many people resented, as gatekeepers very often are.

THE COURTLY CENTRE

If the courtly world had margins, then it must have had a social core of some sort. As has been explained, the generic aristocratic hall to some extent filled that function, in that no youth who aspired to *cortoisie* could get by without the training in acceptable manners and elite culture a hall and its household offered. But to regard

---

[24] '*Ostiarios camerae confundat Altissimus; faciem enim cuiuslibet boni viri confusione multiplici et rubore perfundere non verentur. Evasisti terribiles virgas! Si nihil dederis ostiario, nihil actum est.*' Peter also goes on to condemn the generically unpleasant porter as a 'Cerberus', *Petri Blesensis Epistolae* in, *PL* 207, col. 50.

[25] D. Crouch, 'The Court of Henry II of England in the 1180s, and the Office of King of Arms', *The Coat of Arms: the Journal of the Heraldry Society*, 3rd ser., 5 (2010), pt 2.

[26] A. Långfors, 'Le dit des hérauts par Henri de Laon', *Romania*, 43 (1914), 222–5, translated in D. Crouch, *Tournament* (London, 2005), 188–93.

a hall in that way was to award it no more than the sort of cultural centrality a school offers, as being a point of access for desirable and profitable knowledge. The social curriculum the generic hall taught itself responded to external forces. One such social force would be the courts, to which all naturally looked from considerations of wealth and patronage, to the courts of emperors and famous kings. As we have seen, the practice of hostage-taking and fostering means that royal courts can be demonstrated to have had a wide cultural influence, as the court of England did on youthful members of the Gaelic and Welsh aristocratic societies which also occupied the British Isles. The courtier-cleric Geoffrey of Monmouth experienced such a court in that of Henry I of England, and in 1136, when the glory of that court had already departed, he projected it on to the imaginary court of Arthur of Caerleon.

> Then he began to add to his household by inviting to join it the greatest of *preudommes* (*probissimi*) from distant realms, and in this he obtained so high a reputation for civility (*facetia*) in his hall that he inspired faraway peoples to imitate what he did. So even men of the most distinguished birth who came under his influence reckoned themselves as nobodies unless they dressed and equipped themselves the way Arthur's knights did.[27]

Aside from royal courts there were also the courts of particularly respected and influential princes, men who were acknowledged leaders in fashion, as Geoffrey put it. Such personalities might on occasion have sufficient weight to have a tidal effect on manners, one that might be noticeable to contemporaries. Robert de Beaumont (died 1118), count of Meulan in the Île-de-France (1080) and earl of Leicester in England (1107), was such a man. His great wealth was drawn not only from his many estates in three realms, but from the same economic windfall that enriched the counts of Champagne. He was well placed to benefit from the burgeoning wine trade between central France and the lands of the North Sea basin, which was channelled down the Seine past his castles and customs posts.[28] William of Malmesbury, a contemporary, said this of his effect on the society of their day:

> So great was his influence in England that his example could reverse traditional habits in dress or diet. For instance, the habit of dining once a day owes to him its universal adoption in the courts of the nobility. He himself had taken it over, for his health's sake, from Alexius emperor of Constantinople, by messengers (*nuntiis*), and passed it on to others, as I have said, by his example. He is blamed for having adopted and encouraged this practice more from reasons of economy than from fear of digestive disorders, but unfairly; for no one had a greater reputation for extravagant hospitality to others, combined with personal moderation.[29]

Not only was Robert a leader in fashion and as such a mediator of noble culture, he was also an intermediary in the practices of imperial and royal courts, which he apparently made himself acquainted with by third parties.

[27] *The Historia Regum Britannie of Geoffrey of Monmouth: Bern Burgerbibliothek, MS 568*, ed. N. Wright (Cambridge, 1985), 107.
[28] D. Crouch, *The Beaumont Twins: the Roots and Branches of Power in the Twelfth Century* (Cambridge, 1986) 185–7.
[29] Malmesbury, *GRA*, 1: 736.

In subsequent generations the personality and court of Count Philip of Flanders (reigned 1168–91) had a potent cultural effect on his contemporaries in France, England and the Empire. We have already seen (in Chapter 2) the attraction his household held for fathers who wanted to place their sons in a leading centre of courtly culture. But he was also a sponsor and propagator of another source of cultural formation, the great tournament circuit that had come into being in Picardy and the Low Countries by his day and which for several decades shaped and dominated western European aristocratic culture.[30] Count Philip's social ascendancy comes into view in the 1160s, though even then it did not come out of nowhere. His predecessor, Count Charles (1119–27), is known to have rejoiced in tourneying events in the 1120s and employed a large tourneying retinue, travelling on one known occasion into Hainaut for an event.[31] How much further back did this sort of event go in Flanders and its environs? Hermann of Tournai, writing in the 1140s, preserved a record of a count of Louvain who died in a jousting event within a tournament which supposedly occurred in 1095.[32] Lambert of Ardres, the chronicler of the counts of Guines, may not have much approved of tournaments, but he had a belief that the tourneying in which his patrons so rejoiced in his day went back in the family to the time of Count Manasses (died 1091).[33] Both Hermann and Lambert may of course be simply projecting the enthusiasms of the aristocracy of their own day on that of earlier times, but there is no reason to doubt that tourneying was already an obsession amongst the aristocracy of the generation of Count Philip's grandparents.

The generation of the 1160s and 1180s experienced a new intensity in the international culture of the tournament. There is no shortage of sources attesting to this, which is itself some witness to the cultural centrality of the phenomenon. Further testimony might be the stupendous expense and staging of the crown-wearing and military games that the Emperor Frederick Barbarossa held at Mainz in 1184 to celebrate the knighting of his sons. It has been seen as a twelfth-century high point of German imperial court culture, but in social terms it could equally be interpreted as an attempt by the Staufen to assert himself culturally against the social pull of the Low Countries and Picardy, where Philip of Flanders ruled and the emperor's western vassals tourneyed and competed. If Barbarossa was reacting to such attitudes, he certainly succeeded in capturing the attention and imagination of his own subjects by the sheer size and expense of the event.[34] But the Swabian poet Hartmann von Aue, writing in that same decade, nonetheless commented that though there were knights in Bavaria and Franconia, his aspirational young hero in *Gregorius* daydreamed rather about matching himself on the tourney field

---

[30] See, generally, Crouch, *Tournament*, 40–2.
[31] *Actes des comtes de Flandre (1071–1128)*, ed. F. Vercauteren (Publications de la commission royale d'histoire, Brussels, 1938), 249: *Attrebatum deinde veni rediens cum gloria militari de conflictu armorum habito inter me et Godefridum comitem Valentianensium.*
[32] *Liber de restauratione ecclesie sancti Martini Torniacensis*, ed. G. Waitz, *MGH Scriptores*, 14: 282.
[33] Lambert of Ardres, 579: *in nundinis etiam et bellicis illusionibus promptus.*
[34] Mons, *Chronique*, 155–60; Bumke, *Courtly Culture*, 203–6.

against those of Hainaut and Brabant.[35] It was to these lands and to Flanders and Picardy that the ambitious knight would go, not to Swabia, Saxony or Thuringia. The career of the English knight William Marshal is another case in point. It was built on his success on the tournament field, which he began to seek out in 1166. He first tourneyed as a retainer of the Norman baron William de Tancarville, in local tournaments on the frontiers of Brittany, Maine and Normandy, but he was looking to spread his wings, and so it seems he made his way into Flanders. His biographer tells us he harboured for years a grudge against Matthew de Walincourt, a knight attached to the retinue of Count Baldwin V of Hainaut, and later Count Philip, who captured, pauperized and humiliated Marshal as a tyro on some unnamed field.[36]

William Marshal was to return to Flanders a decade later but in very different circumstances, as the leader of the tourneying retinue of his master, the Young King Henry of England (died 1183). Young Henry escaped his father's supervision in 1176 and deliberately sought out Flanders and the court of his cousin Philip (they were both descendants of Fulk of Anjou, king of Jerusalem), looking for a new sort of eminence after his first political adventure in rebellion proved a disaster. The count, 'about whom many a fine story is heard', was happy to host Henry and his retinue for a season and according to the Marshal biography lavishly equipped them with horses and arms when the king first embarked on the circuit in a great event on the borders of Philip's principality.[37] In part Philip may have calculated that Young Henry, rich and personally attractive, would add a new glamour and indeed his own lavish sponsorship to the tournament circuit of the Low Countries and Picardy, on which he more or less lived until 1182. Buying the service of the best knights and bannerets, he and William Marshal carried all before them, winning fame and presiding over what became for a while the centre of elite culture in western Europe.[38]

The twelfth-century tournament event, usually two or three days of varied military games culminating in a grand charge of knights marshalled in two battalions, had its physical and competitive dimension. However, as important to its participants and the itinerant traders, prostitutes and craftsmen who serviced it was the social aspect. It was because of its support industry, clamour and itinerant nature that clerics from the early twelfth century onwards scoffed at the tournament as no

[35] *Gregorius*, ed. H. Paul (Tübingen, 1966), 41 (ll. 1573–8), referring to knights to be encountered in *Henegou* (Henegau, near Valenciennes), Brabant and *Haspengou* (Hesbaye, near Liège). Emperor Frederick II himself in 1241, in a letter addressed to the princes of Europe, was to allude to France as *strenuae militiae genetrix et alumpna*; Matthew Paris, *Chronica Majora*, ed. H. R. Luard (7 vols, Rolls Series, 1872–83) 4: 118.

[36] For the incident, *History of William Marshal*, 1: ll. 3337–52. For Matthew, Mons, *Chronique*, 111, 142. By 1189 Matthew had become a leading follower of Philip; *De Oorkonden der Graven van Vlaanderen*, ed. T. de Hemptinne, A. Verhulst, and L. De Mey, 3, *Filips van de Elzas* (Koninklijke Academie van Belgie and Koninklijke Commissie voor Geschiedenis, Verzameling van der Akten der Belgische Vorsten, Brussels, 2009) 3: 399.

[37] *History of William Marshal*, 1: ll. 2436–96; for quotation, l. 2466.

[38] For the association of William Marshal, the tournament world and Young King Henry, Crouch, *Marshal*, 31–59; M. Strickland, *Henry the Young King, 1155–1183* (New Haven, 2016), 241–53.

more than a fairground (*nundinae*).[39] The possibility for enrichment and pauperization amongst the knights who rode to it did not add to its respectability and certainly gave it the darker and desperate dimension of a casino. However, for the princes, barons and knights who thronged in their thousands to its greater events, these Flemish and Picard tournaments imparted a sense of being at the centre of their aristocratic world. The opening parade and review of the grand tournament (*li regars*), where heralds could be paid to shout out and praise the name of their employer as he rode unhelmeted on to the field amongst his squires, was designed to make that very point.[40] Princes offered lavish hospitality and networked; young knights found a forum in which to seek recognition, and (for those with the skills) employment, for the tournament was also a graduate job market. Nor was it an all-male event; aristocratic women were integral to its culture as patrons, judges and spectators as much as dance and bed partners (see Chapter 9). From the people Marshal and others met there, aristocrats were drawn to Flanders, Brabant and Picardy by the pull of the social gravity of its circuit from the Rhineland, Brittany, the Loire valley, Champagne, Burgundy and the British Isles. Apart from the season of Lent and times of crusade, the circuit (known as the *lonc sejour*) was continuous, and its Hellequin's Hunt of aficionados trekked from event to event, which generally happened every two or three weeks or so on customary sites over a broad geographical area. Each was publicized by its patron and sponsor, who financed the staging, the prizes, and the principal receptions and banquets.[41] As a result, the entertainments and rewards could be competitive in their sumptuousness and so shaped international aristocratic culture by setting new benchmarks for display (as we shall see in Chapter 10).

An instructive tournament career other than William Marshal's is that of young Arnold (II) of Guines, knighted at Pentecost 1181 along with four young companions; 'and so from that day for almost the next two years he travelled around many provinces and regions participating in tournaments – not entirely without his father's help and support.'[42] We are told Count Philip interested himself in the young knight's training as much as his proud father did. Just as the Young King Henry was supported by William Marshal as tutor and bodyguard in the field, young Arnold had his guide and protector in William de Cayeux, a man who, as it happens, had learned his own skills a few years earlier as a colleague of William Marshal in the tourneying retinue of the Young King Henry; the Marshal biographer preserved a high opinion of him.[43] So Arnold formed his own entourage of expert minders and like-minded youths from Guines and Ardres. He liberally rewarded them all, and Arnold and his friends lived expensively, delighting in the end for six years or so in physical and sexual adventuring, and excelling—to his homeland's

[39] *Les conciles œcumeniques: les decrets*, 2, pt 1, *Nicée à Latran V*, ed. A. Duval and others (Paris, 1994), 439.
[40] For the 'review' in tournament etiquette, Crouch, *Tournament*, 74–5.
[41] Crouch, *Tournament*, 19–38, 57–70, 105–9.   [42] Lambert of Ardres, 604.
[43] Lambert of Ardres notes William only as an unnamed nephew of Arnold de Cayeux, young Arnold's tutor, but his name is provided by the *History of William Marshal*, 1: ll. 4547–50, where he appears in the Young King's retinue at Lagny in 1179.

pride—in his martial and social exploits.[44] The cross-connections in his social world between Arnold's career and those of Count Philip, the Young King and William Marshal are very instructive. They lived within the same social nexus in both space and aspiration.

Twelfth- and thirteenth-century imaginative literature was drawn into that nexus, by frequently referring to its personalities and places and in placing its characters and adventures within it. John Baldwin has pointed out how a whole cohort of the leading writers of the late twelfth century and early thirteenth century, particularly Jean Renart and Gerbert de Montreuil, evoked in realistic detail this tourneying world, north of the Capetian demesne and in the west of the Empire.[45] But it was not just northern-French writers who sent their characters onto its tourney fields and into its entertainments. The Anglo-Norman romance of *Gui de Warewic*, commissioned by an earl of Warwick for performance at a family celebration in 1199, necessarily had its young English hero travelling to the Continent with a tutor and a retinue of his friends to establish his reputation on the foreign circuit, landing in Normandy and immediately seeking news from his host if any great tournament had been recently advertised, and then heading off into the western Empire.[46] Around 1240, Philip de Remy in his *Manekine* reversed the perspective; he himself actually lived on the site of one of the great tourneying grounds of Picardy. Philip had his hero, a king of Scotland, landing at Damme and, just like the Young King Henry, immediately seeking out the count of Flanders, to hear that he was at Ghent preparing for a great tournament. Philip then gave a literary sketch designed to establish the centrality and attractiveness of his native province of Picardy for international aristocratic culture, attractive even to distant northern kings:

> The count of Flanders had heard of the king of Scotland's arrival and hurried out to meet him, giving him greetings and a warm welcome. The count said: "My lord, I am delighted that you have chosen to come here. I and my people are entirely at your disposal, whatever you have in mind to do." The king replied: "Many thanks indeed". And so they came to Ghent, talking as they went, and spent the night with the count. The king asked him about the tournament and where it would take place. The count told him: "At Ressons".
>
> At this the king said: 'We will go there. We would ask one thing of you, that you will be willing to join my military household for the occasion.' The count happily consented. The Scots spent a very comfortable night, and nothing was lacking to put them at their ease. Very early the next morning they took to the road. They came that night to Lille. They spent a good night in the town, for it belonged to the count. The next day they again set off very early. They passed to the east of Artois and then entered Vermandois, taking the route through Roye and so they came to Ressons. The king dismounted in the town, and with him the Scots and the Flemings. People had begun to arrive and to arrange and occupy their lodgings, people from Boulogne, Artois, Brabant, Vermandois, Flanders, Normandy, Ponthieu, as well as Germans, Hennuyers and Bavarians.[47]

---

[44] Lambert of Ardres, 603–5.   [45] Baldwin, *Aristocratic Life*, 31–42.
[46] *Gui de Warewic* 1: ll. 705–96.
[47] Philip de Remy, *La Manekine*, ed. H. Suchier (Société des anciens textes français, 1884), 83–5. For Philip's career, L. Carolus-Barré, 'Origines, milieu familiale et carrière de Philippe de Beaumanoir', in *Actes du colloque international Philippe de Beaumanoir et les coutumes de Beauvaisis (1283–1983)*,

A complementary, pseudo-historical picture of the twelfth-century tourneying heartland emerges from the *Histoire de Gille de Chyn*, a work of the 1230s. The historical prototype of its hero lived in early twelfth-century Hainaut and, by one account, actually died at a tournament in 1137. However, so far as it goes, the *Histoire* is evidence only for the perception in the days of its author, Walter of Tournai, of what twelfth-century tourneying culture had been. Following his knighting, the fictional Gilles established his reputation and fame by embarking on the circuit across Artois, Hainaut and the Low Countries, 'from one end of the land to the other (*de marce en marce*)', meeting the same extraordinary and precocious success as had Guy of Warwick. He became an object of love to the women he encountered and of envy to other knights.[48] He distinguished himself in a particularly fine tournament (*bons tornois*) at Maastricht—'no man ever saw finer'—sponsored apparently by the duke of Limbourg, where the field was taken by nine counts against two dukes and two more counts. The celebrity of the field in which Gilles excelled was because the participants included all the princes of Lower Lorraine and the Rhineland.[49]

But these paeans to social exclusivity and ambition were for the most part retrospective. The great days of the tourneying heartland did not in fact long survive the deaths of its great patrons, Philip of Flanders, Baldwin V of Hainaut and Henry the Young King. The counter-attraction and many aristocratic fatalities of the Third and Fourth Crusades also played a part in the tournament's decline. To the biographer of William Marshal writing in the mid 1220s it was already a golden age long past. He expressed the wistful (and vain) hope that the new young king of England, Henry III, might restore what his late uncle had established and which collapsed on his death, and so *chevalerie* (meaning deeds of arms), *proëce*, *bonté de cuer* and *largesse* would be renewed.[50] By 1200 it already belonged (along with the Neverland of the Arthurian world) to the imaginary of what a great noble society should be, which is why Guy of Warwick and Gilles de Chin were sent there to triumph and assert their surpassing *cortoisie* and *chevalerie*. So in its day and after its decline it remained a high and definitive point of what a noble society should be, which, despite royal prohibitions and the hostility to tourneying in the expanding Capetian state, the thirteenth century was always trying to recapture.[51] Even in memory, that lost nexus exerted a huge influence.

AVATARS OF *CORTOISIE*

Count Philip of Flanders and the Young King Henry were in their day patterns for their social world of what a courtly prince should be and how his conduct would

---

ed. P. Bonnet-Labordière (Beauvais, 1983), 19–37; D. Crouch, 'La spiritualité de Philippe de Remy, bailli capétien, poète et seigneur de Beaumanoir', in *Chevalerie et christianisme aux xiie et xiiie siècles*, ed. M. Aurell and C. Girbea (Rennes, 2011), 123–35.

[48] *Gille de Chyn*, ll. 165–446.   [49] *Gille de Chyn*, ll. 855–1016.
[50] *History of William Marshal*, 1: ll. 2676–706, 4311–18.
[51] For the decline of the grand tournament, Crouch, *Tournament*, 125–31.

earn praise and admiration. *Cortoisie* as a habitus in fact depended on such characters to help establish and define desirable social traits. Philip and Henry demonstrated for the great of their day how such greatness should be acted out in society, and in their case it was in a new, expensive and attractive way. Because of them the Capetian kings of the thirteenth century came under a degree of criticism for their failure to engage with the tourneying world in the way their aristocracy wanted. *Cortoisie* could thus be taught by awarding celebrity to these heroes of Courtliness, both in their own day and in memory after they were gone. The use of such teaching avatars is a feature of twelfth-century Western literature, as much Celtic as French and Germanic.[52] But living heroes were also necessary for the purpose. It was not enough simply to have an idealized *preudomme* or *preudefemme* to teach courtly norms; ideals had to be seen in action by expert practitioners. It is common enough to find twelfth- and thirteenth-century historical characters, male and female, called *cortois* by contemporaries. Any successful medieval public person would need to be thought fit for the hall. But occasionally contemporaries focus on characters whose *cortoisie* was acknowledged to excel all others of their day, and whose personal qualities were thought definitive within their society.

I Thomas of London

Had not Thomas Becket's career ended with an assassin's blade and subsequent canonization, it is worth speculating how he would have been remembered, for his talents and career would have gained him historical notice even without his ecclesiastical struggle and martyrdom. He would have been remembered as a leading clerical courtier of the 1150s, certainly, for John of Salisbury dedicated his *Entheticus* and *Policraticus* to Becket while he was chancellor of England, the latter book being in part a critique of the life of the court. Becket's life became the subject of a frenzy of interest because of the manner of his death, and there is no escaping the retrospective hagiography that hijacked biography in his case. Nonetheless, the way writers deal with his early career, before his decision to accept the nomination to Canterbury, cannot disguise the secularity of his life and the grand style in which it was lived, because it was so notorious. His friend, adviser and employee while he was chancellor, Herbert of Bosham, regretfully listed the qualities that gained Becket credit with the world: his social ease, urbanity, friendliness, pleasantry and gregariousness, 'which made people apt to like him and which attracts the world's good opinion, but not so much God's'. Herbert, a man of some courtly gifts and pretensions himself, perhaps knew Becket best of all his circle.[53] Two of Becket's many biographers saw nothing wrong with the way he behaved in this part of his career, while for the others his subsequent dramatic and Damascene conversion

---

[52] H. Fulton, 'The *Mabinogi* and the Education of Princes in Medieval Wales', in *Medieval Celtic Literature and Society*, ed. H. Fulton (Dublin, 2005), 230–47.

[53] Herbert of Bosham, *Materials*, 3: 163: '... *et ad sui dilectionem invitans, qua homo plus placet seculo sed deo minus*'. See the study of Herbert by Martin Aurell, *L'Empire des Plantagenêt, 1154–1224* (Paris, 2003), 247–9; and for Herbert's opinion of Becket, Aurell, *Lettered Knight*, 286–8; Jaeger, *Envy of Angels*, 297–9.

towards ecclesiastical discipline helped the case for his sanctity. Becket's aspirations and pursuits between 1144 and 1162 were not, however, in any way spiritual, as Bosham freely admits. It was the lay ideal of the careerist *preudomme* he was pursuing, and in doing so he demonstrated courtly skills of a high order. This was the reason he was valued (and indeed envied) by some contemporaries before 1162, and criticized by others.

Becket may have been from a London patrician background, but his family's sources of wealth were not in land and could not be counted on to support him unassisted, so he was provided with an upbringing that would enable him to make his own way in the courts of the great. Thomas had natural advantages; his first social success was entirely down to his personality and address, and perhaps also the Frenchness of his upbringing, for his father and mother were Normans by birth.[54] His father customarily offered the young Anglo-Norman baron Richer de L'Aigle hospitality at his hall on Cheapside in the 1130s, and the lively, good-looking and intelligent child of the house caught Richer's interest; he would chat with the boy happily for hours and take him out on hunting excursions along the Thames valley, thus infecting Thomas with his long-standing love of dogs and hawks, as he later told his clerk, Guernes.[55] Since Becket's courtliness and social skills were so very notable to contemporaries, it became a matter of interest when and where he began practising them. It might have already been when he was just a young teenager. He gained the notice of the regular guests in his father's hall, who would go on to do him many favours, unasked, as did the marshal nicknamed Baillehache, who was credited with facilitating his entry into the household of Archbishop Theobald of Canterbury.[56] Guernes put Thomas's career-mindedness down to the difficult period in the young man's career in the early 1140s, after his mother's death, when he was a city clerk in the household of the wealthy financier and civic leader Osbert Huitdeniers.[57]

It was actually a sign of the Courtliness of a man that his precocity and ability to charm his betters inspired jealousy in others less well favoured, as we find in the comparable case of Thomas's younger contemporary, William Marshal. Since he was introduced into the archbishop's hall by one of his humbler officers, Becket was routinely mocked there as 'Baillehache's clerk', mockery he bore with the patient composure (*mansuetudo*) a courtly man should.[58] The rapid ascendancy and many favours Thomas acquired in the household of Archbishop Theobald earned him the undying enmity of some of his colleagues there, not least Roger de Pont L'Evêque, whom he succeeded as archdeacon of Canterbury when Roger was raised to the see of York in 1154.[59] Thomas may not have escaped scatheless from the relentless

[54] L. B. Radford, *Thomas of London before his Consecration* (Cambridge, 1894), 4–9.
[55] Guernes de Pont-Sainte-Maxence, *La vie de Saint Thomas Becket*, ed. E. Walberg (Classiques français du moyen âge, Paris, 1936), 7 (ll. 206–10).
[56] F. Barlow, *Thomas Becket* (London, 1986), 29.
[57] '*Dunc comença a estre e senes e curteis*', Guernes, *Vie de Saint Thomas*, 8 (ll. 241–5).
[58] Anonymous I, *Materials* 4: 10. For *mansuetudo*, Jaeger, *Courtliness*, 36–40, who observes the discussion of the word by John of Salisbury, in a work dedicated to Becket (36–7).
[59] Guernes, *Vie de Saint Thomas*, 8–9 (ll. 256–8); A. Saltman, *Theobald, Archbishop of Canterbury* (London, 1956), 166–8.

stress of the competitive and treacherous environment in which he found himself, as his sometime colleague John of Salisbury tells us.[60] But he rose above his enemies' barbs and confounded them all silently by the exercise of his talents, and was so close to the counsels of Archbishop Theobald that he was despatched to Rome to represent him before the pope, as part of the sensitive business after 1149 when King Stephen of England was attempting to get his son crowned associate king against the archbishop's wish.[61]

Thomas's leap into the office of chancellor of England at the beginning of 1155 at Archbishop Theobald's recommendation gave him even greater scope to acquire reward, friends and enemies. He had already gained a reputation as a man who worked hard for his employer, and otherwise played equally hard, for as Guernes says, he adored worldly pursuits (*dedut seculer*).[62] Thomas's delight in fine dining, clothing and all the symbols of wealth was hardly unusual in a young man who had risen rapidly in the world. But his Courtliness lay in the way he lavishly deployed his new riches and publicly made little of them. As Guernes and others of his biographers who knew him say several times, his disposition was self-effacing (*humles*), increasingly so when he had come to the point at which he was held by the world to be a very great man indeed.[63] But of course, if he was being put upon by rivals, he could be—and perhaps had to be—savage; it was the quality that ultimately got him killed. His household clerks at this time, however, tell us they themselves never had a single complaint about his treatment of them.[64] He used his wealth for a purpose, knowing how much the quality of largesse was valued in a courtly man, and he was in a position to be very generous. So his dinners were notoriously lavish and well populated, and the doors of his halls were left open during them.

As a man who wished to be noted as *preudomme*, Thomas embraced all the pursuits of the Anglo-French aristocracy of his day, which must necessarily include the military ones, embarrassing though that seems to have been to some of his hagiographers, who play this aspect down or even condemn it, as Edward Grim did. He had a large retinue of knights and led them into siege and battle while he was chancellor, being himself perfectly capable of unhorsing an opponent in action, as he did the French knight Enguerrand de Trie.[65] He equipped himself and them with the finest arms and horses, and it is something of a comment on Becket's ability to attach his military dependants that when these knights were obliged to quit his service before he went into exile in 1164 they were distraught at the necessity.[66] His grand embassy up the Seine to Paris in 1158 was a spectacle of wealth and secular grandeur, the like of which his world had never seen, and brought mobs of

[60] John of Salisbury, *Materials*, 2: 304–5.
[61] William fitz Stephen, *Materials*, 3: 16; Radford, *Thomas of London*, 45–52; D. Crouch, *The Reign of King Stephen, 1135–1154* (London, 2000), 245–7.
[62] Guernes, *Vie de Saint Thomas*, 9 (l. 276).
[63] Guernes, *Vie de Saint Thomas*, 9–11 (ll. 290–1, 331–2); Anonymous I, *Materials* 4: 11.
[64] Guernes, *Vie de Saint Thomas*, 11 (ll. 336–40).
[65] William fitz Stephen, *Materials*, 3: 34–5. For observations on this aspect of his life, J. Hosler, 'The Brief Military Career of Thomas Becket', *Haskins Society Journal*, 15 (2006), 88–100.
[66] Herbert of Bosham, *Materials*, 3: 323–5.

people to the roadsides to watch it pass by.[67] As chancellor he was asked by numerous aristocrats to foster their sons into his household, where he offered the boys a decent upbringing and courtly training. The seal was set on his reputation as the great courtier of his age when the king, his master, confided to Becket his heir, the Young Henry, at Easter 1162 for the boy to be given a suitable training in his household in the company of a number of other royal wards.[68] Becket's secular reputation by then reached well beyond his master's kingdom. As chancellor of England he was held in great respect in Flanders, and such was his courtly eminence that Thomas was asked by Count Arnold I of Guines to preside at the knighting of his eldest son and heir, Baldwin.[69] And in Capetian France, a well-informed theologian took Chancellor Becket as a notorious example of careerism and offensive secularity in a clerk, filling the margins of a manuscript with his disdain for what he had heard of Thomas's behaviour.[70]

One lesson the case of Thomas Becket illustrates is that some medieval boys had natural advantages of personal attractiveness and sociability that opened up for them greater opportunities than might be given to others, as is still the case in any human society. Much depended on the youth's native disposition, and Becket had confidence, charm and markedly good looks as a youth, as well as the real organizational ability and drive to succeed which made the most of the opportunities given him. Ramon Vidal, a man of low status who had to make his way among the great, knew what he was saying when he made the following recommendation: 'Affable conduct (*adzaut captenh*) provides a man of affairs with an immediate welcome in all his enterprises and allows him to employ his skills freely. It often happens that a polite fool gets more consideration than a man of ability who is disagreeable.'[71] The Milanese poet Buonvicino della Riva makes a similar observation at the other end of the thirteenth century: 'someone who is at ease (*asetilia*) excels in all courtliness.'[72] Society in the Middle Ages as much as today was geared to regard the affable, self-controlled extrovert as the normative human being, and a person like Thomas Becket who was exactly that had an immediate and innate advantage in all his social interactions, a little unfair though that was admitted to be, even in the thirteenth century.

II Gawain

It was acknowledged by some in medieval society that you could learn as much about good and superior conduct from characters you met between the covers of books as those you met in real life. An observation attributed to the courtly but

---

[67] Barlow, *Becket*, 55–7.

[68] William fitz Stephen, *Materials*, 3: 22; Strickland, *Henry the Young King*, 34–9.

[69] Lambert of Ardres, 596. It is unclear whether young Baldwin was knighted in Thomas's household in England or at home in Guines.

[70] B. Ross, 'Audi Thomas...Henriciani Nota: A French Scholar appeals to Thomas Becket?' *EHR*, 89 (1974), 333–8.

[71] *Abril issia*, 102 (ll. 1131–5).

[72] 'in tutę le cortesie ben fa ki se asetilia', *Poeti del Duecento*, i, 711.

low-born bishop Robert Grosseteste (died 1253), when challenged as to the source of his urbanity, was that he had learned it from the biblical characters he had read about, who were models of prudence, modesty, largesse and virtue.[73] When Arnaut-Guilhem de Marsan set about describing the defining characteristics of knight as lover for his young pupil, he selected Paris, Tristan and Aeneas to illustrate what a lover should be and Ignaura to illustrate the dangers a seducer might incur. Yvain was for him the figure who best illustrated male elegance and desirability, and it was Arthur who encapsulated honour in relations with ladies.[74] Characters from imaginative literature were not as solid as archetypes as those selected from scripture, which is doubtless why Thomasin of Zirclaria in 1216 believed that reading about superior characters in romances had a value, though a limited one and principally for the young:

> Adventure stories are good because they broaden a child's mind. Also, anyone incapable of learning in a better way should derive his examples from them.[75]

But as far as Thomasin was concerned, they should grow out of the practice of reading them as they grew older and less frivolous. He believed girls could look to patient dignity of characters like Andromache and Penelope from the classical world, or Enide (from the romances of Chrétien or Hartmann von Aue), 'from whom they can take their examples and good instruction'.[76] Boys, however, should look to the courtly warriors of the Arthurian world or the Carolingian epic, and he makes particular reference to one such character, Gawain, notable to Thomasin for his 'stainless virtue' (*reiner tugent*).[77] Literary characters could therefore be teaching devices: avatars of desirable conduct, and with the advantage of being malleable to the author's prejudices and intentions.

Gawain (*Gualguanus*), son of Duke Lot of Lothian and nephew of King Arthur, entered into the wider consciousness of medieval Europe when he rode as a redoubtable warrior on to the Arthurian stage of Geoffrey of Monmouth's *Historia Regum Britannie* in 1136.[78] As the Arthurian canon developed, so did the character of Gawain. Wace of Bayeux around 1155 represented him as a knight notable as much for his modesty and Courtliness as his courage. But it is in Chrétien's romances that he becomes fully developed as his uncle's principal support, chief courtier and heir presumptive, the knight against whom all others are measured:

---

[73] *The Lanercost Chronicle, 1201–1346*, ed. J. Stevenson (Edinburgh, 1839), 44–5. The young women counselled in godly living in the tract *Hali Meiðhad* (*c*.1224) were advised to meditate on the virgin saints in heaven (Catherine, Margaret, Agnes, Cecilia and so on); *Hali Meiðhad*, in *Medieval English Prose for Women: Selections from the Katherine Group and Ancrene Wisse*, ed. and trans. B. Millett and J. Wogan-Browne (Oxford, 1990), 40.

[74] *Qui comte vol apendre*, 73–8 (ll. 195–290).

[75] 'die aventiure die sint guot/ wan si bereitent kindes muot/ swer niht vurbaz kan vernemen/ der sol da bi ouch bilde nemen,' *Welsche Gast*, 30 (ll. 1089–92) trans. Gibbs and McConnell.

[76] 'da von si nemen/ mugen bilde und guote lere,' *Welsche Gast*, 29 (ll. 1030–1) trans. Gibbs and McConnell.

[77] *Welsche Gast*, 29 (l. 1044).

[78] For the antecedents of Gawain/Gauvain, see R. Bromwich, 'Gwalchmei m. Gwyar', in *Gawain: a Casebook*, ed. R. H. Thompson and K. Busby (Abingdon, 2006), 95–101.

'Gawain needs must be reckoned as the foremost of all fine knights.'[79] Though Chrétien's Gawain in the end is made by him to take some blame for the failure of knighthood at Arthur's court—which takes the edge off his courtly eminence—nonetheless, in the French, English, Dutch and German imaginary, he long remained the literary touchstone of Courtliness. In the *Lancelot* he is depicted as the definitive *preudomme*: loyal to his lord, incapable of slander or envy, unmatchable in his *cortoisie* and *chevalerie*, for which all women loved him. He never boasted of any of his great deeds and was wise, moderate, and in his speech incapable of *vilonie*.[80] So, in Huon de Méry's 'Tournament of the Antichrist', written in the same generation as Thomasin gave his shining verdict on Gawain, the character of *Courtoisie* wears a helmet on which the names of Roland and Gawain were incised.[81] Gawain was a fictional ideal, but nonetheless he formed men's minds, if not their sense of realism. So it was that the knight who was rather too full of himself might declare, as Raoul de Houdenc satirically commented: 'I am he who has conquered all, I am the best of my kind, I have surpassed Gauvain in arms!'[82] Just such a man was Peire Vidal, who, in the bombast he clearly thought was endearing to his day and age, declared he had experienced all the adventures of Gawain and more besides.[83]

Gawain was a character within the Arthurian canon attractive and intriguing enough to readers to inspire authors to compose romances in which he was the hero, not just a leading cast member of the Arthurian retinue. They were already doing so in Chrétien's generation, under his inspiration. As with other leading characters in this imaginary universe, such as Roland and Vivien, curiosity about the character of Gawain led to prequels, or origin stories, whose existence is known in Gawain's case, though they do not survive in full. These make Gawain less of a prince and more of an outsider in his world: he is Arthur's nephew from an illegitimate liaison, cast off by his mother and brought up in poor circumstances. As a youth, however, his virtue is recognized and he finds a place in the papal (or in another version, imperial) court, where he receives a noble education and is knighted. In the end it is his virtue, not kinship, that earns him a place at Arthur's court, as he defeats his uncle as an anonymous knight in a combat Arthur himself provoked.[84] It added to Gawain's profile as a courtly *preudomme* that he achieved recognition and his high place despite misfortune and rejection.

When he was himself in the limelight, as he was in the romances *Le Chevalier à l'Épée* and *La Mule sans Frein* (c.1200), Gawain shone as the sort of moral and

---

[79] '*Devant toz les buens chevaliers/ doit estre Gauvains le premier*,' *Eric et Enide*, ed. W. Förster (Halle, 1890), ll. 1691–2. For the literary development of Gawain, K. Busby, *Gauvain in Old French Literature* (Amsterdam, 1980), 30–82, 381–403; N. J. Lacy. 'Gauvain and the Crisis of Chivalry in the *Conte de Graal*', in *The Sower and his Seed: Essays on Chrétien de Troyes*, ed. R. T. Pickens (Lexington, KY, 1983), 155–64; 'Introduction', in *Gawain: a Casebook*, 1–9.

[80] *Le Livre de Lancelot de Lac*, in *The Vulgate Version of the Arthurian Romances*, ed. H. O. Summer (8 vols, Washington, 1909–16), 4: 358.

[81] *Li Torneiemenz Antecrit*, ed. G. Wimmer and trans. S. Orgeur (2nd edn, Paris, 1995), ll. 1840–1.

[82] *Roman des Eles*, 34 (ll. 132–4).   [83] Peire, 168 (ll. 49–50).

[84] For the *Enfances Gauvain*, R. H. Thompson, 'Gawain against Arthur', in *Gawain: a Casebook*, 210–12.

courtly *preudomme* who would indeed have appealed to Thomasin of Zirclaria, at least in his guise of moralist. Gawain was particularly attractive to writers of a moral turn, simply because he was a perfect foil to place in difficult courtly situations and try to extricate with some degree of credit.[85] In *Le Chevalier à l'Épée* Gawain has every natural advantage: the adventure was awarded to him as 'the good knight who upheld Loyalty, Prowess and Honour and who never for one moment valued a cowardly, false or villainous man'.[86] He was well brought up, talented as a soldier and it was impossible to number his good qualities. When Gawain appeared in his host's hall, his physical beauty was such that the man's daughter was stunned by his looks as much as impressed by his great civility (*grant afaitement*), and naturally she fell in love with him.[87] But the romance's main purpose is to illustrate Gawain's virtue when caught in an almost impossible moral dilemma. He cannot offend his host and refuse the offer of sharing a bed with his daughter, but when he does he learns that sex with her will lead to his death by sorcery. His somewhat involuntary virtue in going against his strong inclinations to take what was offered preserved his life and gained him the daughter. The story's subsequent turn to anti-feminism would have very much appealed to Thomasin's prejudices, as the woman proved worthless and abandoned Gawain at the first opportunity, while he vindicated his masculinity by violently despatching his rival and dumping the girl.[88] *Le Chevalier à l'Épée* could be taken as a lecture on the dilemma his powerful sexuality imposes on even the finest of *preudommes*, caught between desire and fear for his reputation, both for Courtliness and sexual potency. The author was sourly lecturing would-be *preudommes* that they had best embrace perpetual suspicion of women and assert their continence and self-control, even if through gritted teeth.

A few decades later the author of another Gawain romance, *L'Âtre Périlleux*, used Gawain with even more deliberation and some sophistication as a teaching aid in true *cortoisie* and its perils. The story is a curious fable in which a lady under Gawain's protection is kidnapped by the knight Escanor and Gawain pursues him for her sake, but does so anonymously, as he learns on the way that an unfortunate lookalike had been murdered and so it was generally now believed that Gawain himself was actually dead. In part, too, the death of his double was his fault, as if he had not felt bound by courtesy to stay at Arthur's table rather than depart promptly on his quest, he would have encountered the three murderers and dealt with them, so his unfortunate doppelgänger would have lived.[89] Therefore to some extent Gawain had to justify his own reputation to himself as he completed his quest to save the girl and put right the injustice of the murder. He was very much disturbed to encounter his supposed corpse and to be told that the Gawain lying dead in front of him had been the 'flower of knighthood' and that with him had

[85] K. Busby, 'Diverging Traditions of Gauvain', in *Gawain: a Casebook*, 140.

[86] '*Une aventure qui avint/ au bon chevalier qui maintint/ loiauté, proëce et anor/ et qui n'ama onques nule jor/ home coart, faus, ne vilain*', *Le Chevalier à l'Épée* in, *Two Old French Gauvain Romances*, ed. R. C. Johnston and D. D. R. Owen (Edinburgh, 1972), 30 (ll. 4–7).

[87] *Le Chevalier à l'Épée*, 36–7 (ll. 271–3).

[88] Busby, *Gauvain in Old French Literature*, 248–57.

[89] K. Busby, 'Diverging Traditions of Gauvain', in *Gawain: a Casebook*, 147–9.

died honour, civility, largesse and good lordship.[90] The logic of the romance is that Gawain has to rediscover himself and what he stands for in order to justify the world's faith in him and make good the tragedies he has inadvertently caused.[91] The situation Gawain encountered was further complicated when it turned out that the whole venture was a set-up devised by Escanor to ruin Gawain's reputation. The character of Escanor himself was deliberately fashioned to represent a negative and hostile image of Gawain, and the logic of the romance is that Gawain has therefore to destroy him to reassert true *cortoisie*.[92] It recalls Jacob's wrestling with an assailant at night at the Ford of Jabbok in the book of Genesis (32: 22–31), which may not be an entirely accidental hermeneutic. Escanor was an anti-Gawain, the way the *preudomme* was opposed to the *vilain* in what was the central dialectic of conduct literature.

ALIENATION FROM THE COURT

Gawain's literary life at court was depicted as one of relentless struggle with social expectations and the fragility of reputation, which was in itself a gloomy caution to any would-be *preudomme* about the trials he must face there. Gawain's ability to overcome these dangers was supposed to be encouraging to readers, but how many men were brought by reverses, humiliations and painful betrayals to the reluctant conclusion that the court was not a place where they would ever be successful, happy or fulfilled? This is not an easy question to answer in regard to laypeople. The difficulty is not because there were too few lay writers capable of criticizing the court in which they lived and worked. The twelfth and thirteenth centuries were anything but lacking in such writers, but in general they did not criticize the court, any more than Bourdieu's fish would criticize the water in which it swam. However, there are occasional exceptions which indicate both directly and indirectly that lay courtiers did pay a toll that public life was exacting from them, and experienced stress from the demands involved in asserting and maintaining a reputation for *cortoisie*.

One broad indicator that has been well explored is the pull of the cloister to the courtier and knight disenchanted with his secular world. The abbots Herluin of Bec-Hellouin and Ailred of Rievaulx are eleventh- and twelfth-century instances of men who could not resist the lure of the choir and cloister after markedly successful earlier secular careers at court as youths and mature men. Then there were eminent and capable princes like Theobald IV, count of Blois-Champagne (died 1152), 'a father to orphans, a husband to widows and a provider to the sick and poor', who felt the desire to renounce the world but were thwarted by the expectations the

---

[90] *L'Âtre Périlleux: roman de la table ronde*, ed. B. Woledge (Classiques français du moyen âge, Paris, 1935), 16 (ll. 493–504).

[91] E. Kinne, 'Waiting for Gauvain: Lessons on Courtesy in *L'Âtre Périlleux*', *Arthuriana*, 18 (2008), 55–68, esp. 60–2.

[92] For Gawain's 'doubles' in the romance, L. Morin, 'Le soi et le double dans *L'Âtre Périlleux*', *Etudes Françaises*, 32 (1996), 117–28.

world laid on them.[93] Theobald's disenchantment with the excess of contemporary courtly culture was recalled by his friend, Abbot Arnold of Bonneval:

> He put aside the indulgence of the court and the pride of rank in favour of humility and plain living. Nobody presumed to do or say anything crude in his presence. Those eager to earn his good opinion in this – either because they wanted to, or because of the appearance of the thing – increasingly did those things which they saw to be respectable in his domains.[94]

In this category might also be reckoned the attraction to such men of the crusade and crusading orders of knights. However, the decisions of these men to renounce the world are not usually explained by disenchantment with the court so much as fear for their chances of salvation, as with the sudden and startling conversion of mind of Margrave Wiprecht of Groitsch (died 1124) in 1090, after a remarkably prodigious career of warfare, brigandage and rapine across his native Nordmark and Lusatia, as well as Saxony, Bohemia, Lombardy and Latium.[95] In the conversion narratives of such men it was the attraction of sacrifice and the life of prayer that turned their minds outwards.

The vernacular romance was not unaware of such conversions, and can even offer some contemporary perspective on them. The late twelfth-century writer of the romance of *Gui de Warewic* depicted his hero renouncing his old life in several symbolic ways: giving up wife and lands to become a pilgrim and crusader, and on his return from the Holy Land coming back as an anonymous knight, which might be seen as a further deliberate renunciation of his fame, which he had found worthless. Finally, when he got home to Warwick he decided not to reveal himself to his wife and instead took the place of a dead hermit in the woods, spending the last nine months of his life in prayer and existing only on what the woodlands had to offer.[96] The author, however, does for once give us a view on why it was that Guy felt he had to give up all that life had given him after a hugely successful career in England and across the seas. His big decision was taken in a fit of introspection after a successful day's hunting, when Guy climbed to the top of the keep of his castle and looked out on his lands as the stars came out in the sky above him, 'and then he began to meditate'. He thought on his career and his knightly eminence but also the cities, churches, and lives he had laid waste for the sake of obtaining his true love, which was the cost others had to pay for his becoming *un home de grant affaire*. When he came down from the tower and announced his intention to give all up for the service of God, he rather harshly reproached his pregnant wife with the destruction wrought just so they could be together. He ignored her suggestion

---

[93] *Vita Norberti archiepiscopi Magdeburgensis*, in *MGH Scriptores*, 12: 689. For his reputation, J. W. Baldwin, *Masters, Princes and Merchants: the Social Views of Peter the Chanter and his Circle* (2 vols, Princeton, 1970), 2: 255–6.

[94] '… *luxum curiae et fastum altitudinis in humilitatem et honestatem convertit: nec erat qui in presentia eius auderet aliquid indecens vel agere vel loqui; sed in hoc etiam ei placere studentes sive ficto sive puro animo ea, in quibus dominium suum delectari videbant.*' *Sancti Bernardi Vita Prima* in *PL*, 185: 1, col. 299.

[95] *Noble Society: Five Lives from Twelfth-Century Germany*, trans. J. R. Lyon (Manchester, 2017), 55–60.

[96] *Gui de Warewic*, 2: 143 (ll. 11,417–46).

that the foundation of abbeys and the giving of alms would do quite as well as self-exile; it came down to the fact that his life had left him *las e chaitif*—depressed and disgusted with himself.[97]

Moral self-disgust amongst lay people might very well provoke extravagant renunciation of a hateful world, but would the routine tedium and everyday unpleasantness of the courtier's life be enough to bring on such a moral crisis? One can well imagine that courtier-knights of any introspective turn and piety might be uneasy with the excess and sinful violence of their lives when put under examination by confessors and moralists, and there is good literary and historical evidence that some were.[98] Generations of students of Arthurian literature have quirkily observed that whenever King Arthur appears in the romances his name inspired, he is as often as not in a state of depression with his court. But can we include the daily pettiness and stress of the life of the courtier-aristocrat as a motivation worthy of any dramatic act of renunciation? Probably not, but that it might irritate and disturb even a lay inhabitant of the courtly world is something that can be occasionally glimpsed. The poet-knight Raoul de Houdenc (*fl.* 1180–1230) was alluding to such discontent with the demands of the courtly life when he chose to depict Hell as an intolerably grotesque version of a noble banquet (see Chapter 9).

The views held by the knight Raoul and his clerical contemporaries on the courtly world they inhabited may not have been all that divergent. It has been suggested that Raoul, in his *Songe d'Enfer,* was adopting the jaded attitude towards contemporary society of his uncle, the famous academic theologian Peter the Chanter (died 1197), in his *Verbum abbreviatum*, who has much to say about wasteful banquets and the vain entertainments of the court.[99] However, there is a difference between lay and clerical courtiers in that the latter were much more forthright and circumstantial about their discontent with the public life of the court. This is perhaps hardly surprising in view of their vocation and its glaring mismatch with the aspirations of their lay colleagues. The twelfth century was in fact a great age of clerical literature against the court and the literature gives many particulars of precisely where the shoe pinched. A cautious attitude to courtly life was, of course, nothing new in the twelfth century; Peter of Blois quoted Horace approvingly when he said that intimacy with princes is a recommendation in a man, though hardly the greatest one. Peter Damian had inveighed against clerical courtiers in the 1060s, though when he did his rhetoric was energized by his antipathy to the anti-Gregorian court of the Emperor Henry IV as much as the generic court and its excesses.[100] The diatribes about the miseries inflicted on its inhabitants by the court a century later, in the tracts and letters of John of Salisbury, Gerald of Wales,

---

[97] *Gui de Warewic* 2: 26–9 (ll. 7563–676, esp. 7626). Kaeuper, *Holy Warriors*, 183–4, also considers Guy of Warwick as an example of renunciation, but uses the fourteenth-century Middle English text.

[98] Kaeuper, *Holy Warriors*, 131–7, 167–93.

[99] For the relationship between Raoul and Peter (de Houdenc) 'the Chanter', A. Fourrier, 'Raoul de Houdenc: est-ce-lieu?'. in *Mélanges de linguistique romane et de philologie médiévale offerts à M. Maurice Delbouille* (2 vols, Gembloux, 1964) 2: 165–93. For the literary kinship, ibid., 187–93, and see Peter the Chanter, *Verbum Abbreviatum*, in *PL* 205, cols 153–6.

[100] *Petri Blesensis Epistolae*, in *PL* 207, no. 150, col. 441. For Peter Damien and the court, Jaeger, *Courtliness*, 54–5, 66.

and particularly Peter of Blois, are different. They often protest deep respect for the king, while disdaining life at his court because of the moral dilemmas it posed and the stresses it imposed. As Stephen Jaeger points out, Thomas Becket may have been a giant of the courtly world, but even he was said by his colleague John of Salisbury to have been reduced to tears by the daily trials the court and its inhabitants put him through.[101]

In 1184, Peter of Blois (died 1212), archdeacon of Bath, in a trough in his career in the retinues of the archbishops of Canterbury, used his temporary unemployment to begin a bid for attention as a literary figure. One of the fruits of this period of contemplation in his life was a learned letter to the clerical courtiers of Henry II of England, which took issue with their way of life—the same way of life from which he was temporarily estranged. A version of the letter may actually have been sent, as it inspired an aggrieved corporate response from the chapel of royal clerks to whom it was addressed, and Peter had to write to them again to mend fences and clarify his objections. He had bewailed the 'grim struggle' (*militia*) of the court, he said, but he had not meant to imply it was 'a grimy one' (*malitia*); besides, he had been ill when he wrote it.[102] His principal objection to the life of the court as stated in his first letter was—naturally enough for such an audience—the obstacle it posed to salvation. However, he also meditated on what it was that caused him stress when he was at court. He had been led astray, he said, by a 'spirit of ambition' and a desire to accumulate wealth. Like his fellow archdeacon Walter Map, the management of the expensive household his position demanded caused him daily worry. Another cause of anxiety was the uncertain favour of the king on whom depended any hopes of fulfilling the fantasies of wealth, power and office into which 'Lady Ambition' deluded him. The incompetence and greed of some of his colleagues infuriated him, especially when they were more successful than he was. Peter was not above detailing the daily, petty annoyances of the itinerant Angevin court: the poor quality of the food and drink; the insanitary nature of the life there; and, in particular, the abuses and corruption of the marshal's and usher's departments, which had control over access to the king and the limited availability of lodgings in the king's vicinity. Peter used the same imagery as his lay contemporary Raoul de Houdenc, that the courtier was a vagrant and tormented knight of Hellequin and the court was the mouth of Hell.[103] His frustration is no more evident than in the wonderful creativity of the invective against the court it inspired:

> Men torment themselves by the graft of a wasted life, torture themselves with worry and rip out their own hearts with expense. Are they not spiders, who weave webs out of their own guts just to catch a filthy little fly? And what is the empty honour they pursue but a disgusting insect: buzzing, soiled and stinking?[104]

---

[101] For *miseriae curialium*, Jaeger, *Courtliness*, 58–60.

[102] *Petri Blesensis Epistolae*, in *PL* 207, col. 439.

[103] *Petri Blesensis Epistolae*, in *PL* 207, no. 14, cols 42–50.

[104] '*Perditae vitae homines se laboribus torquent, cruciant curis, expensis eviscerant; nonne figuram araneae gerunt, quae de suis visceris telam texit, ut capiat muscam vilissam? Quid est inanis gloria, quam venantur, nisi musca vilissima, murmurosa, sordida, pungitiva,*' *Petri Blesensis Epistolae*, in *PL* 207, col. 46.

Another indication of where Peter's stress lay can be found in his 1184 letter. Though he will colourfully curse the royal court and its inhabitants (and indeed his own weakness in seeking it out), he makes a particular point of absolving its central character from any criticism. Peter says he has nothing but veneration and gratitude for the king himself and for his generosity: 'if I was allowed a chance to talk to him, that day was to me as joyful as a wedding celebration.' Still, he nonetheless insisted that it was more appropriate for a clerk to serve the king in a church than in his palace—even though Henry was a kinder, wiser, more generous and vigorous prince than there had been since Charlemagne.[105] The caution he exhibited here might be to keep open an avenue for further promotion, should he ever come into favour with the king. But the true explanation is likely to be more sinister. He was trying to deny his enemies a chance to discredit him with a charge of *lèse majesté*, offending against the king's person and standing, a charge which was a swaying sword of Damocles above the head of every courtier. From his second letter to the royal chaplains, it seems that Peter might indeed have been threatened with it. He scrambled to protest to the royal clerks the holiness of their position, for since the king is Christ's anointed there can be nothing inappropriate in his service, and indeed clergy can do nothing more virtuous than to serve such a king. His point, he said, was that they must at the same time be allowed the privilege of a prophetic voice, to attest to God's purposes before the king's face.[106]

Two decades later Peter returned to the theme, when he wrote commending his friend and fellow archdeacon Geoffrey of Buckland in his decision to leave the court of King John. Clearly the old Adam was still lurking in Peter's soul even in his closing years. What irked him in 1203 were the unworthy careerists who were achieving promotion to bishoprics, a promotion that had eluded him, but which he most probably would not have turned down had it been offered. But in his frustration he passionately proved to his better self that such promotions were utterly worthless and no more than vanity; the truer servant of God was the one who resorted to study and to prayer, which perforce was the life that was now left to him.[107] Every now and then, lay writers can reveal something of that same stress to which Peter attested. When they do, they counter to some extent a problem identified with clerical witnesses to the court culture: that they were all too often stressed-out careerists whose view of the court was tainted with failure, who had retired to nurse their resentments and lick their wounds. They lacked the ability of the secular elite to ride above failure, and their negative view of the court was thus extreme.[108]

Surprisingly, considering how much in general his verse celebrates his way of life as baron, tourneyer and warrior, a lay critic of the court was Bertran de Born, viscount and magnate of the Limousin. In 1182, Bertran attended a court held by Henry II of England at Argentan in Normandy. In *Casutz sui de mal en pena*,

---

[105] *Petri Blesensis Epistolae*, in *PL* 207, cols 45–6.
[106] *Petri Blesensis Epistolae*, in *PL* 207, cols. 440–1.
[107] *The Later Letters of Peter of Blois*, ed. E. Revell (Auctores Britannici Medii Aevi, 13, Oxford, 1993), no. 5, 30–7.
[108] C. Uhlig, *Hofkritik im England des Mittelalters und der Renaissance* (Berlin, 1973), 175.

Bertran regretted the time he spent there. His complaints against that particular court was that it had been a humourless and joyless event, with nothing material to be gained by his attendance. It was tedious (*enois*), and he went so far as to denigrate it as an occasion of *vilania*, which is the very antithesis of *cortesia*. His time at court would have been entirely wasted had not Bertran consoled himself by conceiving an infatuation with the king's daughter, the duchess of Saxony.[109] Bertran's annoyance with that court may not have shared the depth of the angst of Peter of Blois, but if his time there brought no benefit in entertainment or political reward, then he found attendance irksome, to say the least.

Coincidentally, the next great Angevin court of 1182, held at Caen at Christmas, witnessed a very stressful episode in the egregiously courtly life of William Marshal. His relationship with his lord, the Young King Henry, had finally collapsed in bitter recriminations a few weeks earlier at a tournament in Picardy. So far as can be reconstructed, the principal charge against Marshal had been the same as Peter of Blois feared—*lèse majesté*. Marshal had insulted and endangered the king by placing his own profit and fame above the king's safety.[110] The king had been all too apt to resent this offence and was egged on in his animosity by Marshal's rivals in his household. Marshal as a result experienced a hurtful estrangement from his beloved lord, which made attendance at his court deeply uncomfortable to him:

> The king really showed him, not secretly, but for all to see, that he hated him with all his heart, and he was not in such great favour at court as he used to be, not so cherished by the king or in such a position of influence.[111]

In this difficult and unaccustomed place for him, Marshal withdrew from the court and distanced himself from the 'torment and pain' which he now experienced there, his biographer using the same image as had Peter of Blois. One reaction to his stress (according to his biographer) was to seek consolation in those courtly figures in the Bible who had fallen foul of kings through no fault of their own, notably Daniel at the court of Persia and the magi at the court of Herod. So miserable was he that Marshal made a pilgrimage to Cologne to seek their intercession at the grand new shrine of the Three Kings. He also looked for a more terrestrial intercessor in Count Philip of Flanders, the king's cousin. However, the count failed to move Henry and did more harm than good. As a final desperate throw, Marshal appealed to the elder king at Caen, where he found himself slighted and spurned by his former colleagues. He stood out before the kings, father and son, to protest his innocence, and challenged his accusers to meet him in judicial combat; this was a tactic he was to use more than once in his career when he was under great stress. It was refused him, and so he ceremoniously and publicly quit the Angevin court and left to take up service with the count of Flanders.[112]

---

[109] Bertran, no. 8, p. 165.   [110] For a discussion of the charges, Crouch, *Marshal*, 56–9.

[111] '*Quer le reis l'en fist bien semblant/ veiant toz, ne mie en emblant/ qu'il le haeit de tot son cuer/ ne qu'il n'ert pas de son cuer/ ne qu'il n'ert pas de si boen fuer/ a cort comme il i soleit estre/ ne si cher del rei ne si mestre*', History of William Marshal, 1: ll. 5429–35.

[112] *History of William Marshal*, 1: ll. 5452–832. For his move to Flanders, Crouch, *Marshal*, 61–2.

THE FAILURE OF COURTLINESS

The account of the downfall of William Marshal in 1182 is unique for a medieval source in its detailed reconstruction of the way the malice and manoeuvres of his rivals at court brought its hero down. They were men who had once been his equals but became envious when Marshal gained more regard and reward than they had from their lord, the Young King Henry. His Englishness also seems to have been an issue. So they formed a conspiracy, spread unfounded rumour behind his back, found the weak spot in their master's attitude to Marshal, and ultimately used it to lever the men apart. They were friendly enough to Marshal's face, and it was only when one of the courtiers whom they approached to join their cabal went straight instead to Marshal that he had any clue as to what was in the air.[113] The author calls these men, amongst other insults, *losengiers*—people who are by nature insincere.[114] They are malicious detractors who trade in *losanges* (sycophantic deceits). We have a very early and hostile definition of the concept. When in the 1120s Philip de Thaon discoursed on the way the stork cleaned its filthy backside with its beak, he remarked that it brought to mind the *losengier*, who was all sweetness to your face and spouted lies behind your back.[115] Stephen de Fougères already sees the *losengier* as a curse of the court and an enemy of the *preudomme* in the 1150s: 'No flatterer (*losengëor*) nor liar should expect anything from the king if he is trying to bring down a *prodome*, whatever grudge against him he may wish to pay off.'[116]

The term *losengier/lauzenjar* was well established in vernacular Francien and Occitan literature in the early twelfth century. By the end of the century it appears in Italian (*lusingare*) and in German (*losaer*). In the later twelfth-century romances and the poetry of Occitania the *losengier* is the stock character who is out to thwart lovers and run down the reputation of poets.[117] But the Marshal biography places him in a more political context. The weary fact of life for Marshal was that any fellow courtier might turn out to be a *losengier*, because every other courtier was a potential rival.[118] Medieval writers pinpoint *losengiers* as the main contaminant of courtly life. William de Lorris imagined the court of Lady Wealth populated with *losengiers*, who praised good men to their face but ran them down behind their backs, and who were the enemies of all *prodomes*.[119] Robert of Blois gives a striking rhetorical example of quite how much the two-faced conspirator was loathed and feared by courtiers:

So now I'll tell you that a *losenjors* should always be held to be little more than a piece of shit and a traitor; he is the most despicable vermin in the world. Such a one was the

[113] Crouch, *Marshal*, 56–9.

[114] *vos menzongiers, voz traîtres, vos losengiers...*, *History of William Marshal*, 1: ll. 6427–8.

[115] *Bestiaire*, in T. Wright, *Popular Treatises on Science written during the Middle Ages* (London, 1841), 122 (ll. 1347–8).

[116] *Livre des manières*, 24 (c. 21).

[117] E. Baumgartner, 'Trouvères et *Losengiers*', *CCM*, 25 (1982), 171–8.

[118] S. Kay, 'The Contradictions of Courtly Love and the Origins of Courtly Poetry: the evidence of the *Lauzengiers*', *Journal of Medieval and Early Modern Studies*, 26 (1996), 209–53.

[119] Lorris, *Rose*, 100 (ll. 1034–45).

serpent who brought mankind down. A prince who trusts such men cannot fail to fall into disgrace in the end. Such men carry honey on their tongues so as to attract flies; but below they have a fatal poison so as to deliver their sting. Never let them get near you. No crime is so damaging as treachery and nobody is more apt to be harmful to you as your secret enemies. One should always avoid employing such men whether for a salary or even for free. The closer these people are to you the more bitter will be the trials they put you to. A man who lives treacherously shames himself; a man capable of a crime such as no one could even contemplate cannot do the harm a traitor can![120]

But the problem was more complex than the dangers of resentfulness and rivalry in the emotional hothouse of the court. The fact was that success at court was founded on affable reticence in concealing one's true feelings. Hypocrisy of some degree is an inescapable trap for anyone who wishes to succeed socially, as medieval tracts on conduct have no choice but to admit. Jean de Meung long prefigured David Hume in his analysis of the daily hypocrisy of social interaction: 'One needs must kiss the hand one would wish burned.'[121] It was a fine line to trace between flattery, courtly reticence and hypocrisy, and many failed. The successful courtier and knight Sordello da Goito directed a neat little meditation at Ermengarde of Narbonne, telling her that her tendency to over-effusive praise (*trop lauzar*) made her opinions worthless.[122] Obscuring true feeling was the charge no courtly person could escape. To that extent every courtier had something of the *losengier* about him. The moral tipping point was that the hypocrite was plotting mischief behind an affable mask, while the courtly *preudomme* supposedly was not.

When medieval writers considered what was disrupting their courtly society, it was envy—which we might well translate as materialism—on which they fixed. Envy at others' success was the Marshal biographer's conclusion as to the motivation of those who brought his hero down in 1182. It was also William de Lorris's when he deplored the hateful *losengier* at court as 'brimming over with Envy'.[123] There were, however, other more heavyweight contemporary analyses on the same subject. The talented Picard knight Raoul de Houdenc had a jaundiced view of the courtly society of his own day, and in his way he saw himself as its reformer. His programme of reform was laid out in the *Roman des Eles*, but somewhat earlier he wrote verses where he attempted to pin down the materialistic forces destabilizing his society. The allegorical analysis he offered there is worth quoting at length:

Pride, which attacks Reason, has a saddle of Deceit, reins of Trickery, a martingale of Envy and stirrups of Shame. And what's the name of the horse Pride rides upon?

---

[120] *Enseignement des Princes*, 116–17 (ll. 803–24).

[121] Meung, *Rose*, 450 (ll. 7380–81). Jean later portrays Love reluctantly allowing Lady Restraint to bring False-Seeming into his garden, as Restraint claims that False-Seeming, her lover, had brought her many honours and comforts and without him she would have died of hunger, and so he should be recognized as *preudom*; Meung, *Rose*, 618–20 (ll. 10,479–96). On Hume's 'show of respect' in society, J. Q. Whitman, 'Enforcing Civility and Respect: Three Societies', *The Yale Law Journal*, 109 (2000), 1290–2.

[122] *Lai a·n Peire Guillem* in, *Le Poesie. Nuova edizione critica*, ed. and trans. (It.) M. Boni (Bologna, 1954), no. 39.

[123] *Li envois orent envie/del bien e de la bone vie/del Mareschal...*, *History of William Marshal*, 1: ll. 5127–9; *Icil losengier plain d'envie...*, Lorris, *Rose*, 100 (l. 1051).

It's called Betrayal, armoured with Cunning and Deceits (*losanges*). The baldric of his sword is gilded with Arrogance and Lies. Anyone wounded with such a sword cannot be cured: he's doomed – for Covetousness (*Covoitise*) is a poison by which many people are laid low. Pride's lance is Treachery and his banner is called Envy (*Envie*): Pride, Fraud and Bad-Living are reckoned as the greatest of vices. Covetousness is in front of the lists where the shamed and the treacherous are, and makes of the rich his fortress. Everything is falling apart; the rich have nothing whatsoever to do with honour, which they've never cared for. For corruption is such that the whole world is in collapse. All this wicked world has been seduced by Envy to turn to the Devil.[124]

Materialism was the disease at the heart of the courtly world as far as Raoul was concerned, and he went on to put his finger on the nub of the problem for us. In the *Roman des Eles* he argued *Envie* to be entirely incompatible with *Cortoisie*.[125] Anyone wishing to be seen to be truly *cortois* had to beware of resenting his lord's gift to another. The seneschals who routinely attempted to restrain their master's gifts on the grounds of economy ought to be ignored. Resentfulness created stress (*grieve*) when the envious saw others rewarded, which proved their unfitness for the court, for that stress is what made them act like *losengiers*.[126] Raoul's analysis matches what we have already seen about courtly behaviour in other sources. Notable here is a brief but telling satire, in which Sordello da Goito satirized the noble court of his day as a place where people went only to acquire gifts; otherwise it was just a meeting place of gangsters (*avols gentz*).[127] Those who entered public life to make their way in the world—as did William Marshal, Peter of Blois and so many other fellow courtiers, lay and cleric alike—were in competition for a limited number of favours. Their way of life was unstable and depended on pleasing greater men, who might well enjoy having power over others rather more than was good for them. Failure at court could have severe consequences, not just material ones but in the way it depressed a courtier's sense of self-worth. So greed for the good things on offer, envy of others' success, and desperation to achieve security might very well bring out the worst in career courtiers. Lies, conspiracy and betrayal were the resort of those who had less scruple, an unjustified high opinion of themselves, and a baffled realization that they were not doing as well as their sense of entitlement led them to believe.

Raoul de Houdenc did not just provide an analysis of what was wrong with courtly society; he offered a programme to put it right in his *Roman des Eles*. His simple and idealistic prescription was that Courtliness and generosity were complementary, and no man could be lifted out of himself without possessing both. Largesse for him cancelled out the materialism that destabilized the court. In his

---

[124] Bern, Burgerbibliothek MS 354, fo. 114v, printed as *Le Borjois Borjon,* in *Anecdota Literaria,* ed. T. Wright (London, 1844), 58–9. For its relationship to the genre of *similitudines,* see below, pp. 290–6.

[125] Raoul's view was close to the teaching Alan of Lille reportedly delivered to a party of knights at Montpellier in the 1180s, that *Liberalitas* was the 'summit of Courtliness' (*maxima curialitas*); *Anecdotes et apologues tirés du recueil inédit d'Etienne de Bourbon,* ed. A. Lecoy de la Marche (Paris, 1877), 246.

[126] *Roman des Eles,* 40 (ll. 337–45), 41–2 (ll. 390–8, 411–14).

[127] *Ben deu esser bagordada,* in *Le Poesie,* no. 35.

Roman, Courtliness and generosity were the 'wings' that together raised a knight to his true social eminence. The first great writer on Chivalry, Jean-Baptiste de la Curne de Sainte-Palaye, naturally enough saw the *Roman des Eles* as the earliest self-conscious statement of Chivalry as a social ideal. But in fact it is something quite different: a thoughtful critique of a centuries-old problem with the central institution of medieval society, the court. Since Raoul saw the ethical and unmaterialistic knight as an engine of reform in the courtly world, one can see why La Curne saw the *Roman* as the harbinger of a new world of *chevalerie*. But Raoul was actually looking backwards in attempting to address an age-old problem with dysfunctional *cortoisie*. Every social reformer had regret for a lost golden age as part of his armoury. Dante would do the same in his *Inferno*, lamenting his own times by projecting a golden age of *cortesia* on the period before 1216 and beginning of the Guelph and Ghibelline conflicts in his city. He too saw civil virtue as being eroded by materialism and the betrayal of old principles. And he too saw the only resolution as being to trust in the virtues now being represented by the knight.[128] In this way a weakened social body might be easy prey to the virus represented by Chivalry.

[128] K. M. Olson, *Courtesy Lost: Dante, Boccaccio and the Literature of History* (Toronto, 2014), 30–4.

PART III

STRESS IN COURTLY SOCIETY

8

The Insurgent Woman

A substantial proportion of the extant conduct literature of the Middle Ages relates to women, which might come as a surprise to those who may have considered medieval women to be more or less invisible. We can pursue the subject of female conduct from a large base of source material and from quite an early date. It is a point worth making again that the first vernacular conduct manual in Western society was Garin lo Brun's earlier twelfth-century *ensenhamen*, which was (according to the author) requested by a young aristocratic woman seeking his guidance on her proper behaviour in public. The problem in approaching medieval female conduct is not any scarcity of material. It lies in the difficult fact that hardly any of the literature tells us about the internal female world of desires and frustrations. Even where works by female authors survive (as they do in the case of Heloise and Marie de France), they adopt the dominant male-driven perspectives on their own sex. All literature about women in this period is framed by male expectations, and so medieval women have often been said with good reason to be 'caged by the words of men'.[1] The attitude towards women such a discourse projects is often consciously as well as unconsciously adversarial, and with clerical writers sometimes viciously so. The question is whether it is possible to get behind the rhetoric to some understanding of the place of women in medieval society or even to approach their own views. Georges Duby in his day thought not, but he may have been overly pessimistic.

The striking thing about the sources is that they cast women as insurgent, in conflict with social expectations, which were laid down by social necessity as much as by men. At the end of the period of this book, a thinker such as Jean de Meung could even theorize that insurgency was woman's natural state. The female, he said, like the male, was originally born into a state of freedom, but her freedom was constrained by law, marriage contract and custom, which 'wise men' formulated to avoid sexual and social anarchy. The necessity of rearing children put her under constraint to one man, when Nature urged her (as much as it urged men) to rebel and exert a choice society did not give her. From this internal conflict, said Jean, came many of society's troubles, and he translated for his bourgeois readers' benefit

---

[1] D. Régnier-Bohler, 'Voix littéraires, voix mystiques', in *Histoire des femmes en Occident 2, Le moyen âge*, ed. C. Klapisch-Zuber (Paris, 2002), 533–5. It was a view often repeated by Georges Duby, initially with pessimism, though with changing emphasis; see *Mâle moyen âge* (Paris, 1990), 119–21, and critique in A. Classen, *The Power of a Woman's Voice in Medieval and Early Modern Literatures* (Berlin, 2012), 233–8.

Horace's remark that wars were and continued to be fought for cunt.[2] In a striking parallel to the views of another Parisian public intellectual some seven centuries later, Jean de Meung engineered the image of a woman being like a songbird in a cage, apparently cheerful but longing for the free air and the greenwood; in other words, longing for complete sensual freedom and escape from her gendered prison.[3]

CONSTRAINT AND RESISTANCE

Women were thought (by men) to lack steady principles, to be wilful and more at the mercy of the impulses of their emotions and sexuality than were men. The dominant sex—whether as layman or clerk—had therefore to make an effort to guide and control them, though to expect resistance. The largest section of Stephen de Fougères's mid-twelfth-century *Livre des Manières* is directed at women and dwells obsessively on their weaknesses, their rampant and barely controllable sexuality, and the problems this causes both them and their families. Clerical writers on conduct were particularly given to harping on the frailty of the moral fabric of women, which was undermined by their uncontrollable lust. A seedy early thirteenth-century tale, attributed to the English teacher and grammarian Elias of Thriplow, is a vivid example. A knight and his lady on pilgrimage oppressed by the heat bathed in the River Jordan and lost their touring party, so they resorted to a cave, where they had sex while waiting for another party to pass by. The knight fell asleep well before his wife was satisfied, and when six virile and naked Saracens arrived in the cave she was dazzled by their endowments and betrayed her husband for sale into slavery while offering herself sexually to his captors. After an epic gang bang she wore down herself and them into sleep, during which the knight broke free. He killed the Saracens with their own weapons, but (being a knight) spared his treacherous wife, just beating her, never sleeping with her again, and abandoning her in Outremer.[4]

Patristic theology taught that 'woman is to man as matter is to spirit', meaning that men represented the superior spiritual and rational quality in humanity, whereas women represented the physical and material, and there is evidence in the writings of Hildegard of Bingen that even some contemporary women had internalized that understanding.[5] Medieval natural philosophy provided further intellectual justifications for this skewed balance between the sexes, drawing on the medical tracts of the ancients and more modern Arabic texts, the dominant influence from the mid twelfth century onwards being (even if by second hand) that of Aristotle, who regarded the female as a defective male.[6] The discourse on the

[2] Horace, *Satires* 1: 3.
[3] Meung, *Rose*, 812–16 (ll. 13,879–970). The reference is to Claude Lévi-Strauss, *Les structures élémentaires de la parenté* (2nd edn, Paris, 1979), 570.
[4] *Petronius Rediuiuus et Helias Tripolanensis*, ed. M. L. Colker (Leiden, 2007), 125–33.
[5] C. W. Bynum, *Holy Feast and Holy Fast: the Religious Significance of Food to Medieval Women* (Berkeley, 1987), 261–3.
[6] C. Thomasset, 'De la nature féminine', in *Histoire des femmes* 2, 65–98.

elements by William of Conches in his *De Philosophiae Mundi,* and expanded on in his *Dragmaticon* (likely composed while he was the tutor of the future Henry II of England at Bristol in the 1140s), is an example where the teaching of intellectuals could well have intersected with the minds of the lay elite.[7] If the subject had come up (and there is some evidence it might have), the boy Henry would have learned from his tutor that the elements of cold and moisture were particularly prevalent in women, and their pleasure in sex and susceptibility to lust was all the greater as a result, whereas men, governed by heat, were drier and therefore more controlled. One wonders what the infamously lascivious king he became would have made of that.[8]

For all the supposed dangers posed by the unfixed behaviour of women, it was not the practice in European society in the High Middle Ages to entirely enclose them for their own good.[9] No less a person than Cardinal James de Vitry, when bishop of Acre in the 1190s, expressed disgust at the practice he found in the Latin kingdom of Jerusalem of confining women to their quarters away from any men but their husbands and any social contact other than with women. It was a practice the nobility of the kingdom had acquired in the East, he said, and he found it degenerate. He expressed his disapproval in pastoral terms: women so cloistered could only hear Mass in private, if at all, and were closeted away from the wholesome discourse of clergy in confession and sermon, so their chances of salvation were compromised. But the roots of his profound disapproval were just as likely cultural, and he remarked that such a practice closed off such women even from contact with their brothers, which he found repugnant.[10] The author of the mid-twelfth-century *Roman de Thèbes* was much given to social commentary, and he remarked that it was *vilains* (uncourteous) in a father to forbid his daughters from freely associating with knights; one of his male characters, 'far from being distressed' at this freedom, was delighted by it.[11] It is sometimes asserted that men and women were segregated at medieval dinners, but there is very little evidence for this and an abundance of evidence that mixed dining was the norm (see Chapter 9). They may have regarded single-sex dining as a past feature of ancient societies. Women would thus be well in evidence at the central social ritual of the period and might very well preside over it.[12] Different reasons were given for this openness in contact between the sexes by a variety of writers. A well-known passage in his

[7] J. M. Ferrante, *Woman as Image in Medieval Literature* (New York, 1975), 6–8. It may account for the statement in a thirteenth-century legal text from Anjou that Nobility can only be reckoned from the male descent, *Établissements*, 2: 252–3 (c. 134).

[8] *Dragmaticon Philosophie*, ed. I. Ronca and trans. M. Curr (Notre Dame, IN, 1997), 135–8. The *Dragmaticon* was addressed to an unnamed *dux.* Henry was a duke after 1150, and indeed before if *dux* was interpreted in its literary sense as a 'count'.

[9] Karras, *Sexuality*, 90.

[10] *Historia orientalis*, ed. and trans. (Fr.) J. Donnadieu (Turnhout, 2008), 290–2 (c. 73).

[11] *Le Roman de Thèbes*, ed. F. Mora-Lebrun (Paris, 1999), ll. 1082–5.

[12] As in B. K. Wheaton, *Savoring the Past: the French Table from 1300 to 1789* (New York, 1983), 2, citing no evidence. Geoffrey of Monmouth in 1136 pictured the British males and females of Arthur's court dining separately at Caerleon 'in the manner of the Trojans', but he was not reflecting on contemporary practice; *Historia Regum Britanniae*, ed. N. Wright (Cambridge, 1984), 111. When Bartholomew of England made an extensive commentary on the biblical feast of Xerxes

Tristan by the vernacular poet Gottfried von Strassburg (died *c*.1210) registered the harsh controls (*huote*) imposed by some men on their female relatives. Just as did the author of the *Roman de Thèbes*, Gottfried condemned the practice as uncourtly and recommended that kindness and well-meant advice were better ways to control women.[13] The voice of a free-and-easy peasant girl (ventriloquized by Marcabru) laughed contemptuously at the aristocrats who kept their wives in strict isolation, insinuating that the guards the lord trusted with the task were actually impregnating his wife and that he was raising their bastards as his sons.[14]

The sexual career of Countess Ida of Boulogne, as reported by a misogynistic clerk, Lambert of Ardres, is characterized by exaggeration and was openly intended as a critique of women who had too much freedom. Nonetheless, his prejudices aside, Ida as a widow in her twenties between 1186 and 1191 certainly seems to have been able to place herself in adventurous and exposed situations as she flirted with several powerful men, setting one against another. Young Arnold of Guines was at the time living on the tournament circuit of northern France and caught her fancy, for she was herself an assiduous follower of the sport.[15] The way Lambert tells it, they entered into a life of mutual titillation, an extended foreplay of secret messages and assignations while she was simultaneously carrying on an affair with Reginald de Dammartin which did end up between the sheets, and indeed in her elopement with him. In all this, Lambert characterized her behaviour as 'female heedlessness and waywardness' (*feminea levitas et deceptio*) or 'a woman's thought-lessness' (*feminea imbecillitas*).[16] The conclusion that follows is that if you give women their freedom to act as they see fit, this is what happens.

Philip de Novare was a nobleman with an attitude as illiberal as Lambert's towards female independence, which may have had something to do with his social environment in Outremer. He was a strong advocate of the practice of keeping a woman under close supervision from her earliest age and cited the supposed authority of Christ on the matter: 'Men and women who bring girls up should strictly teach and press on them that they are under constraint and authority, and that they should not be crude and loose of speech nor get up to mischief. Girls should not walk streets and highways... this is why: Our Lord commands that women should be always in tutelage and under supervision.' His Gospel authority was shaky, though he could have found comparable views to his own in the Epistles of Paul.[17]

(Esther 1: 9–12) he made nothing of Queen Vashti's insistence on dining separately with her women (*De proprietatibus rerum*, Bk 6).

[13] O. V. Trokhimenko, 'On the Dignity of Women: the "Ethical Reading" of Winsbeckin in mgf 474 Staatsbibliothek zu Berlin-Preussischer Kulturbesitz', *Journal of English and German Philology*, 107 (2008), 490.

[14] *L'autrier, a l'issuda d'abriu*, in Marcabru, 370 (ll. 19–30).

[15] For Ida's prominent presence as a single woman on the tourney circuit after 1186, N. Ruffini-Ronzani 'The Knight, the Lady, and the Poet: Understanding Huon of Oisy's *Tournoiement des dames* (*ca.* 1185–1189)', in *Knighthood and Society in the High Middle Ages*, ed. D. Crouch and J. Deploige (Leuven, 2020), forthcoming.

[16] Lambert of Ardres, 605; E. Jordan, 'The "Abduction" of Ida of Boulogne: Assessing Women's Agency in Thirteenth-century France', *French Historical Studies*, 30 (2007), 1–20, argues against the assumption of a forced abduction of Ida by Reginald.

[17] *Quatre Tenz*, 14 (c. 21). For the Pauline view, see 1 Cor. 11: 3–10; Eph. 5: 22–4; 1 Tim. 2: 9–15.

However, he had travelled widely in his world, and knew that his views were more conservative than most would have accepted. But he put down many of the ills in his society to the opportunities men and women had to interact in public.

However, for all Philip's disgruntlement with what he saw as his own day's overliberal attitudes, and indeed despite some voices tolerating those attitudes, medieval Western society could hardly be characterized as generous in its attitudes to women. It believed that women at large in the community were at risk and were a danger to themselves and others, which was the source of the impulse towards their social control.[18] Such attitudes remain deeply embedded in the English language. If, for instance, I had taken as a title for this chapter 'The Public Woman' or 'Women on the Streets', the unpleasant and unintended double entendres would have been all too jarring. The streets and crowds are not even now in Western society always neutral or safe places for a woman. For a woman to go out in the world in the Middle Ages, other than in the relative security of her own local community and social métier, was to put herself at risk. Nonetheless, for a variety of reasons women did venture out into a censorious, risk-filled and male-dominated world, and when they did they were not entirely defenceless.

Tracts on proper conduct were consciously offered as a useful shield for women as much as a covert means of fixing what was thought by their authors to be acceptable female behaviour. Female sexuality could also be a defence of sorts, even a weapon (as a later part of this chapter will fully explore). There are early instances of women who resigned themselves to using their sexual desirability to try to influence their fates. The young Count Henry of the Cotentin, the brother of King William II Rufus (reigned 1087–1100) and soon to be King Henry I of England, was already noted for his taste for native-born English women in the 1090s. As he travelled in the Thames valley, a certain young and attractive English widow by the name of Ansfrida deliberately offered herself to gain influence at his royal brother's court and improve her and her children's difficult circumstances, caused by her late husband's political misjudgements. The result was at least one child by Count Henry; we never hear whether she reaped any other benefit.[19]

Garin lo Brun's Occitan world in the first half of the twelfth century was very different from the one Cardinal James deplored in late twelfth-century Latin Syria. However we interpret the poetic effusions of the troubadours of that age and place, there is no doubting it was a place where men and women associated frequently and interacted at a sophisticated level, for all the dangers such meetings might entail.[20] It was at such a social event that Garin tells us he was approached by an

---

[18] The *Miroir des Bonnes Femmes* comments with jaundiced disapproval on young women going out in the world that 'no merchant should advertise wares that he isn't going to sell'; J. L. Grigsby, 'Miroir des Bonnes Femmes', *Romania*, 83 (1962), 46. See in general for the containment strategy, Trokhimenko, 'On the Dignity of Women', 490–2, and for its theological justification, C. Casagrande, 'La femme gardée', in *Histoire des femmes*, 118–28.

[19] *Historia Ecclesiae Abbendonensis*, ed. and trans. J. G. Hudson (2 vols, Oxford, 2002–7) 2: 52–3, 180–1. For Henry's youthful sexual adventuring, D. Crouch, 'Robert of Gloucester's Mother and Sexual Politics in Norman Oxfordshire', *Historical Research*, 72 (1999), 323–33.

[20] A retrogressive model of female social standing in Occitania over three centuries is argued on the basis of marriage settlements: M. Aurell, 'La déterioration du statut de la femme aristocratique en

earnest young woman of his acquaintance who wanted his views on the right and proper way for her to behave: how she was to demonstrate Courtliness (*cortesia*) and avoid actions that would disgrace her (*vilania*). The advice he gave in response to the invitation (whether it was real or a poetic conceit) was entirely practical and geared to a world where a woman of good family was a public actor. To that extent the intended audience for Garin's work was rather more broad than a single gender, and he offered views on Courtliness and entertaining, for instance, which were intended to be read by both men and women, for there were areas of conduct which were not specific to either.

So far as women themselves were concerned, Garin believed they must be dressed elegantly but modestly, especially where a gown might cling too tight to those areas of the body which inflame men's sexual desire (an early secular instance of victim-blaming). A woman's retinue of maidens should be well disciplined and modest in their speech, ensuring they avoided crude language and innuendo which would reflect on her. He noted a woman's particular vulnerability when she was in the world's eye—as she passed down the street, when she attended church, and as hostess in her own hall.[21] But there were strategies she could employ, not least her projection of unassailable self-confidence. Under the gaze of the world she should walk confidently and sedately, or if on horseback manage her palfrey with skill and a tight rein, and thus project the social assurance and control which was her chief defence. In her own hall the ideal lady also had to be assured and alert. Garin's advice is worth repeating (and perhaps still relevant):

> Within her own home, a lady should be polite to every one of those who behave themselves well; she should be at ease with all men, bad or good; she should give no hint of irritation or resentment, unease or difficulty for any reason whatsoever. Whoever comes and goes should find in her a smile and a warm welcome, though not all men equally, the good along with the bad.[22]

The demands on a woman as a public actor were the same as those on any host: to offer courtly affability to all and sundry, but to cloak her true opinion of her guest. For a host, social tension should be avoided at all costs, even at the moral cost of hypocrisy. However, there were concerns particular to women who presided over the hall. They had social advantages in such circumstances, not least their natural

Provence (x^e–xiiie siècles)', *Le Moyen Age*, 91 (1985), 5–32; L. M. Paterson, 'L'epouse et la formation du lien conjugal selon la littérature occitane du xie au xiiie siècle: mutations d'une institution et condition féminine', in *Mélanges de langue et de littérature occitanes en hommage à Pierre Bec* (Poitiers, 1991), 425–42. For historians' tendency to construct progressive or retrogressive models of female golden ages, P. Stafford, 'Women and the Norman Conquest', *Transactions of the Royal Historical Society*, 6th ser., 4 (1994), 221–49. A thorough historical case study of a highly political and influential woman of that society is to be found in F. L. Cheyette, *Ermengard of Narbonne and the World of the Troubadours* (Ithaca, NY, 2001).

[21] C. Casagrande, 'La femme gardée', in *Histoire des femmes* 2: 131–2, traces a concern with modest demeanour to monastic sources.

[22] *E·l termini d'estiu*, 80–1 (ll. 257–72). The projection of an air of public confidence in a woman in the management of her palfrey is found elsewhere, as in the firm (*ferm*) but relaxed (*süef*) hold on her reins observed in a travelling lady in *Durmart le Galois: roman arthurien du treizième siècle*, ed. J. Gildea (2 vols, Villanova, PA, 1065) 1: 50 (l. 1892).

vivacity, gregariousness and attractiveness, as he says. But Garin was a man of the world and was well aware that in other ways things were harder for women in a public theatre. There were dangers in being too much at ease with the ill-disposed, delusional and possibly predatory male. So she should develop the intelligence and discrimination to identify who such men were likely to be.[23] Women who failed to appreciate this could make a misstep, and all too easily fall into sexual misconduct and promiscuity (*putage*). Besides, he knew his own gender was all too apt to misinterpret simple friendliness as sexual interest, and both obsessive stalking and harmful gossip would follow on inevitably. So this was his advice in how to avoid trouble from that sort of male: 'with a brisk greeting one can give them all they can expect; enough so that they feel treated graciously and that they've been given a civil welcome.' Garin was well aware that haughtiness is not a social virtue, but he said there were times when being stand-offish might well preserve a woman's reputation. His was a time when the indulgence in transgressive sex was so common a poetic theme that it must reflect a social reality where men and women crossed acceptable boundaries into adultery all too often, enough indeed for it to be a common resort for malicious gossip.[24]

The eight dialogues of Andrew the Chaplain on love and Nobility over a generation later than Garin's day portray just such a world in his own northern French milieu. Andrew happily cited examples gleaned from a wide reading in contemporary romance literature.[25] Since Ermengard of Narbonne (died 1196) is one of the pantheon of female oracles that Andrew cites in his advice on correct conduct between the sexes, it is evident his northern world was not socially disconnected from contemporary Occitania, for she was celebrated in the north as much as in the south, where she was a cultural icon. She was even talked of on the grey shores of the Scandinavian Orkney Islands.[26] For all their artificiality, Andrew's social discourses from the mouths of his imagined countesses, knight's and merchant's wives fit a secular world where men and women interacted in a variety of theatres and even between the social levels which came within the realm of *cortoisie*. They also echo the themes on intersexual relations Garin lo Brun explored. Andrew's 'judgements' on love likewise talk of women troubled by obsessional

---

[23] *E·l termini d'estiu*, 90 (ll. 511–16).
[24] *E·l termini d'estiu*, 81–2 (ll. 295–300), 85 (ll. 379–82). For a consideration of the social urgency of the theme of adultery, D. A. Monson, 'The Troubadour's Lady Reconsidered Again', *Speculum*, 70 (1995), 255–74, and for a mismatch with historical sources, W. Spiewok, 'L'adultère dans la réalité et dans la fiction', in *Les 'Realia' dans la littérature de fiction au Moyen Âge: Actes du colloque du Centre d'Etudes Medievales de l'Université de Picardie-Jules Verne, Chantilly, 1ᵉʳ-4 Avril 1993* (Greifswald, 1993), 169–76; Paterson, *Occitan Society*, 232–6. For a lucid overview of the problems, Karras, *Sexuality*, 90–6.
[25] For the influence of Ovid in the twelfth century, J. W. Baldwin, *The Language of Sex: Five Voices from Northern France around 1200* (Chicago, 1994), 20–3.
[26] Baldwin, *The Language of Sex*, 17–19. Paterson, *Occitan Society*, explores well the sense of difference which both Francien and Occitan speakers felt about the other's society, but I think overstates the cultural and social divergence between the two. The contemporary relationship between the French-speaking societies of England and northern France is an instructive and necessary comparison. For Ermengard's appearance in skaldic verse, F. L. Cheyette, 'Women, Poets and Politics in Occitania', in *Aristocratic Women in Medieval France*, ed. T. Evergates (Philadelphia, 1999), 150.

behaviour by delusional and threatening males; about the way reputation could be undermined by male gossip; and the necessity of a cautious and pragmatic assessment of male character before a woman committed herself to a relationship that could end up between the sheets. Andrew also admitted the possibility that a woman could be a skilled instructor in *curialitas,* and her guidance could be the best thing that could happen to a socially inept male.[27]

MALE SELF-DELUSION

Andrew the Chaplain's dialogues echo Garin's concerns about female vulnerability. They are all set at the same moment of social danger Garin illustrates, when a misguided male has decided a woman might possibly be persuaded to give in to his sexual advances. But even when an illustrious count is attempting to seduce a bourgeois woman, Andrew's ladies are as consistently resistant to male blandishments as the peasant girls of the early Occitan pastourelles.[28] They listen as politely as Garin would have them do; they smile but they are controlled and adroit enough to remain quite unswayed by flattery and specious reasoning. Andrew here may well be making another of his ironic comments, being aware that the society around him did not expect women to be so adamant or so untouchable, any more than Ovid said he did in his day. Indeed, one of the common high-school Latin texts of Andrew's day, the Facetus text *Moribus et Vita,* repeated Ovid's advice, telling adolescent boys that they should not be put off by female reluctance once foreplay had begun but should penetrate their victims by force.[29]

In reality, the more eminent and untouchable the man, the less compunction he might feel about the rape of the socially insignificant woman. Kings, of course, provide the most notorious examples of out-of-control predatory males, though even in this case there were limits. The predation of King John of England on teenage daughters of noble families was in the end one of the main items in the baronial justification for his deposition.[30] The entire poetic genre of the pastourelle, which appears in the work of Marcabru in the first half of the twelfth century, was based on the sexual power play between a higher-class male and a common woman he intended to seduce. Medieval societies did not in practice tolerate rape for a variety of reasons, but when records exist, it does appear that higher-status men brought to book for the rape of a lower-class woman were likely to escape with light penalties.[31] This was still the practice in the noble Augustan world of the much-admired socialite Charles-Joseph, Prince de Ligne and Field-Marshal-Lieutenant of the Empire (1735–1814), who pressed himself on vulnerable female servants with impunity and only a modicum of conscience.[32] It is perhaps not then

[27] *De Amore,* 250 (I), 256 (VI), 260 (XIII), 266 (XVIII).
[28] J. M. Ferrante, 'Male fantasy and female reality in courtly literature', *Women's Studies,* 11 (1984), 69–75.
[29] 'Facetus or the Art of Courtly Living', ed. and trans. A. Goddard Elliott, in *Allegorica,* 2 (1977), 44.
[30] See *Histoire,* 121.   [31] Karras, *Sexuality,* 126–7.
[32] P. Mansel, *Prince of Europe* (London, 2003), 233–4.

surprising that medieval female dress developed in ways that were intended to put a barrier between a woman and the would-be predator (for which, see pp. 170–2).

For all the dangers, women did enter into this risky world. The historical sources that conjure up northern tournament culture in the second half of the twelfth century, stretching as it did from Brittany to the Rhineland, show that Andrew the Chaplain's sexually charged world of social interaction between men and women was rather more than a prop for his pose as a modern Ovid. The many vivid descriptions of the lavish tournament events and festivals of the twelfth and thirteenth centuries make it perfectly clear that elite women and men and their respective followers frequented them in an atmosphere of remarkable freedom, for all the dangers and temptations this may have represented.[33] Though his biographer had a marked disinterest in the women in his life, William Marshal (died 1219) was portrayed frequently encountering ladies during his long career as a tourneyer across northern France and the western Empire from 1166 to 1183. He met them as patrons of major events, as spectators and enthusiasts from the stands, and in dance and song at the accompanying social events.[34] Marshal's contemporary, the poet-castellan Huon d'Oisy of Cambrai (died 1191), lists for us dozens of distinguished noblewomen who followed the tournament circuit in the 1180s, when it seems wives were happily included in their husbands' touring retinues during the season. In an ironic conceit, Huon composed an evening entertainment where he sang of the women on the circuit gearing up as knights to fight their own *Tournoiement des Dames*. Ironic it may have been, but it was a conceit which had a curious appeal across the European vernaculars in the generations on either side of 1200, when leading poets composed several similar exercises designed to exploit the gender divide for a variety of purposes—amusement, political commentary— and not simply as social critique of men or women, or both.[35]

In a different sort of conceit but in the same milieu, Ulrich von Liechtenstein donned a blonde wig and female dress over his armour when he travelled the Carinthian and Austrian circuit as the 'Lady Venus' in the 1220s. The many women he met were apparently most amused by it. Ulrich in his autobiography framed his entire tourneying career as 'the service of ladies' (*Frauendienst*), meaning that he

[33] For reconstructions of the twelfth-century tournament heyday, *Das ritterliche Turnier in Mittelalter: Beiträge zu einer vergleichenden Formen- und Verhaltensgeschichte des Rittertums*, ed. J. Fleckenstein (Göttingen, 1986), esp. M. Parisse, 'Le tournoi en France, des origines à la fin du xiiie siècle' (175–211); R. Barber and J. Barker, *Tournaments* (Woodbridge, 1989); Bumke, *Courtly Culture*, 247–73; Baldwin, *Aristocratic Life*, 77–90; D. Crouch, *Tournament* (London, 2005).

[34] Crouch, *Marshal*, 180–1.

[35] A. Jeanroy, 'Notes sur le tournoiement des dames', *Romania*, 28 (1899), 240–4. Huon's conceit was not unique, though it is the first known of a genre; see *Ludi e spettacoli nel Medioevo: I tornei di dame*, ed. and trans. (It.) A. Pulega, (Milan, 1970), and N. Ruffini-Ronzani, 'Understanding Huon d'Oisy's *Tournoiement des Dames*', in *Knighthood and Society in the High Middle Ages*, ed. D. Crouch and J. Deploige (Leuven, 2020), forthcoming. A similar *tournoiement des dames* was composed in 1214 by Guilhem de la Tor, *Pos n'Aimerics a fair far mesclança e batailla*, in *Le liriche del trovatore Guilhem de la Tor*, ed. and trans. (It.) A. Negri (Soveria Mannelli, 2006), 75–7. For its later manifestations, *Chevaleresses*, 81–5; A. Classen, 'Masculine Women and Female Men: The Gender Debate in Medieval Courtly Literature. With an Emphasis on the Middle High German Verse Narrative *Frauenturnier*', *Mittellateinisches Jahrbuch*, 43 (2008), 205–22.

paid court to those females who were to be encountered at such events, and one particular lady (not his wife) on whom he had stubbornly fixed his affections. He seems to have been at the time one of those very men Garin and Andrew warned women against: an obsessional with an invincible view of his own attractiveness. The older Ulrich in fact came to an embarrassed realization of the way his libido deluded him as a youth. As a mature man of affairs he pondered long and hard on the relationship between the sexes in an extended dialogue called the *Frauenbuch*. He came to similar conclusions Garin lo Brun had. He had a female character forensically dissect male self-delusion and how it deduced sexual desire from just a smile:

> You think to yourself: 'She fancies me! My lord! It's no less than I deserve that she looks so kindly on me, though I've not done her any service. So I reckon she's a frivolous woman. My looks please her very much, which is why she treats me so nicely and so it may be that she has a passion for me.'[36]

The younger Ulrich was probably already well on the way to working this out. His painful account of his first meeting with his unnamed lady around 1222 is particularly instructive as to interaction between the sexes at the time. She was itinerating with her household between her residences and took lodgings en route, into which the young Ulrich sneaked and watched her covertly as she heard dawn Mass said by her chaplain, offering her a shy greeting which she barely acknowledged. Her pages and squires were on the lookout to discourage men like him, and they shooed him out after the Mass. But he had an intermediary, his aunt, who conveyed what she claimed was the lady's willingness to have him approach her as she rode along her way that day; apparently it was an acceptable public occasion for casual chit-chat between the sexes. But Ulrich found she had allowed the same privilege to other knights, and was so daunted by both her and them that he was unable to put two words together, and he got no encouragement, even when they were otherwise alone. The ease with which older men talked to her humiliated him. Her dismounting as she came to her next night's lodging allowed Ulrich to seize the prize of her stirrup to assist her down, and he got the thrill of her touch as she grabbed his hair to steady herself as she dismounted, whispering in his ear, as he tells us, sardonically mocking his shyness, and then she escaped him again amongst her ladies and servants. His next meeting was as she rode past him while he stood bare-headed in the street, and he got a more forceful and indeed angry brush-off as he stood in her way, with a serious warning from the lady herself that people were watching them and that he was a pain in her neck.[37]

In other words, Ulrich's lady was an intelligent woman who knew very well how the social world worked. She got some amusement out of her situation but took care to erect barriers against the danger represented by besotted males like Ulrich and the malicious females who, for a variety of reasons, encouraged them in their

---

[36] *Ir daehtet also: 'Si ist mir holt!/Ja herre, wie han ich daz versolt,/Daz si mich als güetlich an siht,/Sit ich ir han gedienet niht?/Si mac wol sin ein gahez wip./Sit ir so wol behagt min lip/Und si so güetlich tuot gen mir/Si hat gen mir lihte minne gir.'* *Frauenbuch*, 62 (ll. 187–94).

[37] *The Service of Ladies*, trans. J. W. Thomas (Woodbridge, 2004), 21–6.

passions. Her servants were always alert to cover her retreat and she took care only to speak to males when in general company or out in the world. Women had to have social defences, the most effective of which was to meet men only in groups of their own sex, whether taking refuge amongst their maidens or amongst their friends and peers: the *Comtesse-zimmer* still important in nineteenth-century Habsburg high society. Descriptions of women at tournaments invariably place them gathered in chatting and commentating female groups; indeed, by the 1170s they were being offered roofed and seated enclosures erected just for this very purpose, though it seems that disengaged knights were also allowed within if they were not going on the field.[38] Amanieu de Sescás expected men and women in hall to engage in conversation but for a woman always to be alert as to where her friends were. A young woman bored with the advances of a man and unable to deflect the conversation without being thought rude had a way of escaping his attentions by retreating amongst the other girls.[39]

The short, popular and sexually charged tales called *fabliaux*, which first make their appearance in late twelfth-century France, were not intended primarily as social commentary or conduct literature—they might properly be called 'misconduct' literature. They were nonetheless intended to amuse their twelfth- and thirteenth-century audiences in part by depicting recognizable situations and then subverting them. Their vignettes of daily social life are therefore of some value in assessing what the *enseignements* of the day have to say about interaction between men and women. *Fabliaux* generated a good part of their humour out of the interplay, and indeed foreplay, between male and female characters in realistic situations. They did not stifle the dangers of sex by making it unmentionable, quite the opposite: the language and description is explicit, to make the message of the story all the more graphic.

Fabliaux in general adopted the common view of women as highly sexed. Consequently, they were inclined to cheat on their husbands and were easily corrupted by characters such as lecherous clerks or students.[40] So far as these tales had a general moral, it was 'distrust one's wife', in the words of Jean Bodel in his *Le Paysan de Bailleul*.[41] The variety of contexts the *fableors* imagine for these dubious meetings between the sexes (outside the family) are useful for our purposes. In poorer homes they happened when guests or lodgers were staying overnight or when the women were home alone at work about the house. Open, face-to-face encounters in the street were allowable at least between men and older women, who were generally less constrained in their conduct and movements than the younger, more nubile and desirable of their sex. Private meetings were always dangerous and illicit, though clerics had an advantage in arranging them, since they had a pastoral excuse. Sheltered interviews in enclosed gardens were a favourite resort in the writings of *fableors*, perhaps because of the metaphor of the breaching of female virginity that such a meeting might represent. The medieval male mind

---

[38] Crouch, *Tournament*, 81–3, 106–9.   [39] *Essenhamen de la Donzela*, 49.
[40] For their social value, Baldwin, *Language of Sex*, 36–42.
[41] *Fabliaux du Moyen Âge*, ed. and trans. (Fr.) J. Dufournet (Paris, 1998), 42 (ll. 114–16).

could therefore imagine many ways to get round the problems and barriers involved in being alone with the woman of its desire.

It was when a woman was alone with a man that social problems as much as sex were likely to happen, as is abundantly clear from what has already been said. An exploration of that very theme was undertaken by the poet Jakemes in *The Castellan of Coucy*, a work of the latter half of the thirteenth century but set in the times of the Third Crusade (1189–92). It was written for deliberate effect in a vein of social realism, employing the names and characters of genuine twelfth-century persons and real venues, events and locations. It initially follows the same script as Ulrich von Liechtenstein's shadow romance with his unnamed lady. Reginald the castellan was likewise obsessed from afar with his lady and tried to influence her in his favour by dedicating his tourneying deeds and poetry to her, as Ulrich did. The difference is that the fictional Lady of Fayel was ill-advised enough, when they met at a tournament social event, to entertain the possibility of inviting Reginald into her home in her husband's absence. A lamentable and stressful life of secret letters, intermediaries and dangerous liaisons then followed as their relationship became adulterous and very soon raised general suspicion.[42] The first to detect it was in fact a jealous woman from their social circle who confirmed her suspicions by setting a servant to spy on Reginald and then informed on the lovers to the husband. Though the pair evaded his vigilance and engineered other sexual encounters, eventually the husband worked out what was going on, and though he was unable himself to take personal vengeance on a knight as formidable as Reginald, he got even with his wife in a particularly vile, if poetic, way. He tricked her into eating the deceased Reginald's embalmed heart. Jakemes the poet tells us in conclusion that he was writing as a warning to people who were thinking of embarking on such a sexually heedless life, pointing out the danger in trusting to the professions of men who, when it comes down to it, may well not be as steady in love as Reginald the castellan, and will despise and shame the woman they so easily seduce. Though Jakemes did not condemn the illicit love he described for the entertainment of his own chosen lady, to whom he said his verses are dedicated, he made no bones that living such a double life would come to no good end, and the woman always carried the cost of it.[43]

INSURGENCY

In circumstances where a woman was so socially disadvantaged, the abuse of power held by the male might well justify and incite a degree of female resistance. This fear is in fact implicit in the tone of medieval social discourse. Much of it implies that women were out of control, and so were a social threat. Misogyny was one

---

[42] Andrew the Chaplain also assumed that his lovers would conduct a confidential correspondence, not employing their names or their seals, unless they had a *secretum* just for the purpose, *De Amore*, 270.

[43] *Le Roman du Castelain de Couci et de la Dame de Fayel*, ed. M. Delbouille (Paris, 1936), esp. 265–7 (ll. 8190–8265).

response. It is dominant in the moral commentaries of this period, particularly in clerical sources, where it is pervasive and indeed all but universal in Western Christendom from the eleventh century onwards. The clerical world was not detached from that of the laity, and it is generally assumed by modern academics that its influence and teaching made misogyny respectable in broader society. Open misogyny was indeed a feature of twelfth-century lay life and speech. The *Proverbe au Vilain* includes the casually shocking advice that: 'There's a proper limit to everything, apart from beating one's wife.' The medieval commentary on its meaning at least distanced itself from a literal interpretation, which showed some discomfort with the idea of unapologetic male violence against women.[44] The justification for misogynistic criticism at that time was that it was called for by the wilfulness of female carnality and the moral corruption and danger that followed on from it and which women inspired.[45] It drew on deep intellectual roots: the censoriousness of St Paul and the Fathers, the ambiguous sexual rhetoric of Ovid, and the speculations of ancient natural philosophy have all been mentioned. But its more acidic and urgent manifestation in the twelfth and thirteenth centuries was a new thing, and must have been energized by contemporary and pressing concerns, not least perhaps the increasing equivalency in the post-Gregorian age of celibacy with virtue. So, as the prime danger to celibacy, women were enemies to virtue and a pothole in the road to salvation. The physical allure of women became more than ever the chief danger to the ideal, celibate cleric.

Stephen Jaeger has drawn attention to the remarkably vituperative Latin poem of Marbod of Rennes (died 1123) against the evil a wicked woman can do.[46] But Marbod's fellow Breton Stephen de Fougères contributed something quite as vicious in French in his *Livre de Manières* (c.1160). In Stephen de Fougères's case the misogynistic sentiment clearly reached beyond the schools and cloisters, for his work was most probably intended to inform or record his preaching. Stephen did admit the possibility of there being exemplary women; indeed, his work is dedicated to such a one, the countess of Hereford. The problem with his rhetoric is that (unlike Marbod) he gave into the temptation to harp on the wiles and sins of the bad woman rather than temper it with the virtues of the good one, and so balance was lost; indeed, it was not even attempted. With Stephen de Fougères you can see a passive intellectual misogyny shifting into a more active anti-feminism. His views would have found a ready echo amongst the laity to whom he preached. His contemporary, the Occitan lay poet Marcabru, was no less misogynistic. When he warned young knights against treacherous whores (*falsas putas*), it is pretty clear he included all women within that description.[47]

---

[44] *Proverbe au Vilain*, no. 207, *De tout est mesure, fors de sa feme batre*.

[45] For the theology and construction of misogyny, M-T. d'Álverny, 'Comment les théologiens et les philosophes voient la femme', *CCM*, 20 (1977), 105–29; C. Casagrande, 'La femme gardée', in *Histoire des femmes* 2, 99–142; Bloch, *Medieval Misogyny*, 1–11; and see also Jaeger, *Ennobling Love*, 83–7; O. V. Trokhimenko, *Constructing Virtue and Vice: Femininity and Laughter in Courtly Society, ca.1150–1300* (Göttingen, 2014), 100–1.

[46] Ibid., 91–2.   [47] *Soudadier, per cui es jovens*, in Marcabru, 544 (ll. 1–4).

The popular books of Latin exercises for elementary and advanced pupils were rife with this sort of anti-feminism, and the basic texts called *Facetus* can be found across Europe, from the Pyrenees to Poland, and from Uppsala to Apulia. They were one route by which anti-feminism penetrated deep into superior lay society and crossed all frontiers of nation and even social level. The later twelfth-century English book of Latin exercises, the *Liber Urbani*, was not a strictly insular product; it had travelled to Dublin, Normandy and Paris by the 1220s. Its clerical author was particularly ferocious on the subject of the faults and wiles of women. His caustic sentiments were dripped into the uncritical ears of the male adolescents who encountered and translated his sophisticated Latin verses, who were not all (or perhaps not even most of them) intended for the Church. One can only hope they found him tiresome on the subject. Daniel (like Stephen de Fougères) made merely a tepid nod towards the idea of the virtuous woman; some, he assumed, were good people.

An analysis of the sentiments and language of such a writer poses the question as to what it was he thought he was reacting to. It was clearly more than a theological anxiety. In a society which professed that women needed to be constrained by those around them, the language indicates that such writers were expressing a basic fear that women had escaped or were escaping that control, that they were in fact insurgent and strove to be dominant. The Anglo-Norman *enseignement* of Chardri (who may or may not have been a cleric) called the *Petit Plet*, which was written around 1200, is remarkable for the open paranoia that is exhibited by one of his characters (an intellectually harsh male adolescent) that women were conspiring amongst each other against men and could not be trusted.[48] It was a view Ulrich von Liechtenstein had encountered, though in the serenity of his characteristic self-confidence, he discounted it.[49] Women's sexual voracity and power were thought by Daniel of Beccles to be beyond restraint and because of the weakness of men it was the female's ultimate weapon. Women made fools of their husbands and worked behind their backs. So a young male servant who found himself being stared at by his lord's wife was in the position of Joseph before Potiphar's wife. He was already doomed; his only option was to pretend a serious illness and hope that would put her off. If he gave in to her he was equally hapless; if ever rumour of his guilt got out, her husband would take a savage vengeance on him. A wife could defeat even the most determined husband, and she would turn to sorcery if all else failed: 'This is how the mistress of her own lord will tame her indomitable master, and the wretched fellow is made a stranger to all honour.'[50] Having failed in his duty of control, the man had no choice but to pretend to the world that everything was fine in their marriage, and his lady was a paragon. Meanwhile she had her lovers and denied him his rights; he got not even a handjob from her. So, said

---

[48] *Le Petit Plet*, ed. B. S. Merrilees (Anglo-Norman Text Society, 1970), 46 (ll. 1385–1414). See, for comment, N. Cartlidge, *Medieval Marriage: Literary Approaches, 1100–1300* (Cambridge, 1997), 169–73.

[49] *Frauenbuch*, 163 (ll. 1949–59).

[50] '*Sic domat indomitum dominum domini dominatrix/Sic miser exilium patitur totius honoris*', *Liber Urbani*, 66 (ll. 1969–70).

Daniel, women by their nature drew everyone into a web of deceit. The husband could say nothing even if he knew the worst. The cuckold lived a life haunted by the consequences for his reputation of exposure.[51]

Daniel was reflecting the sentiments on women found in earlier moral versification in the school and cloister, but his Latin verse was not detached from the prejudices of the vernacular world in which he and his pupils lived. As has been argued by Howard Bloch, the complaints of courtly poets, such as Daniel's contemporary Bernart de Ventadorn, that the women they love have rejected and destroyed them, are themselves tinged with anti-feminism, pullulating with suppressed anger, the ugly rhetoric found amongst contemporary 'involuntary celibates'. Men were the victims of their own narcissism.[52] Daniel's picture of intersexual relations in fact replicated exactly that of the vernacular writers of the contemporary *fabliaux* (see above, pp. 159–60). There too the burgeoning sexuality of a woman was treated as a danger and a destabilizing factor in society's expectations of individual behaviour. All Europe by 1200 knew the stories of Tristan and Iseut, and of Lancelot and Guinevere, and the unhappy moral to be drawn from them. The commentary in the *Proverbe au Vilain* explained the contemporary saying that 'the chance of a fuck has a bigger pull than a rope', by alleging that a woman will risk terror and dark of night for a lover, while she would protest her nervousness about going through the front door for her husband's sake.[53] Jakemes's Lady of Fayel, hapless though she was, constructed just such a web of deceit around her need for sex with the castellan of Coucy, entangling her lover, her servants and ultimately her husband in its net. Jean de Meung devoted hundreds of lines of verse offering ironic advice to stressed-out, cuckolded husbands and adulterous wives, whom he believed generally had the upper hand in the battle of the sexes.

The actual degree of adultery in medieval society outside its copious literature, as much as the contemporary attitudes behind that literature, cannot easily be assessed. Much of it was so obviously covert, and vernacular writers were often ambivalent about its immorality.[54] Sometimes even clerical writers were. Lambert of Ardres would not go so far as to condemn Count Baldwin of Guines outright for his sexual voracity outside marriage, and seems to marvel at the number of illegitimate children he fathered—so many that the count could never remember their names. Lambert tended to blame the women rather than Baldwin for sexual lapses.[55] The fact that married aristocrats frequently acknowledged bastard children in the post-Gregorian age, when such offspring sustained social stigma because of their birth, tells us, however, that adultery not infrequently happened at the top of society.[56] The *Usages of Barcelona* in the 1130s have a lot to say about adultery at all levels of society, from princes to peasants, and treat it as a breach of obligation

---

[51] *Liber Urbani*, 63–70.　　[52] Bloch, *Medieval Misogyny*, 143–6.
[53] *Proverbe au Vilain*, no. 217: *Plus tire cus que corde*. The saying was quoted around 1200 by Jean Renart, *Le Roman de la Rose ou de Guillaume de Dole*, ed. F. Lecoy and trans. (Fr.) J. Dufournet (Paris, 2008), 392 (l. 5300). My thanks to Keith Busby for a discussion on this.
[54] Karras, *Sexuality*, 88–96.　　[55] Lambert of Ardres, 603.
[56] See now, particularly, S. McDougall, *Royal Bastards: the Birth of Illegitimacy, 800–1230* (Oxford, 2017), 166–89.

on the lines of treason to a lord. The code only considered that women could be adulterous, not their husbands. But despite the severity of the language of the *Usages,* the penalties were confined to loss of material goods; clearance of guilt was allowed by communal oath and the code also allowed that husbands could be held to account for forcing wives into it, even to the extent of pimping them out. It may then be that the *Usages* reflect a Catalan society where frequent lapses had to be accommodated.[57]

Law codes are problematical guides to normative behaviour in a society. They have to accommodate all sorts of contingencies, and as a result they may give the false impression that what is exceptional was often to be encountered. The twelfth-century Welsh *Cyfraith y Gwragedd* (the 'law of women', in fact a codification of sexual offences) has a number of parallels with broader European practice. It too dealt at length with intersexual conflict: divorce, roadside rape, sexual exploitation of serving girls, adultery both covert and open, wife-beating, denial of sexual favours, sexual slandering and elopement all feature. All of these offences no doubt happened at some time in Welsh society, but that they were conceivable does not tell us how frequently they occurred. All we can conclude from the code is that such offences reflected as much on the authority of the king as the standing of the offender, who, if not cleared by communal oath, was brought to book and compensation imposed by kin and the neighbourhood, in a manner not that distant from the Barcelona code.[58]

There is indeed some further evidence of husbands' apparently indifferent complaisance to their wives having sex outside marriage other than the special case of kings and princes (whose sexual attentions to women who caught their fancy could not safely be resisted by any family). On rare occasions the mothers of bastards can be identified through the historical record, and when they are it raises interesting questions. Such women can be found to belong to the same social level as their lover—naturally so, or the sources would not register them—and are not inferiors or courtesans. So John Marshal of Hamstead (died 1194), marshal of England and sheriff of Sussex, had a son and possibly also a daughter by Alice de Colleville, the wife of a Sussex knight, with whom he apparently had a long-term extramarital relationship. Also in England, the remarkable record of the Anstey lawsuit of the mid twelfth century hinged on the fact that William de Sauqueville, an Essex knight, abandoned his uncongenial wife and instead lived openly with the daughter of the sheriff of the county, with whom he had several children.[59] We can then find some real justification for the twelfth-century idea that the relationship between the sexes was neither as stable nor under control as post-Gregorian conduct writers, moralists or law codes wished it to be, and that the intensity of their rhetoric was itself a symptom of that realization. It was more than a moral posture

---

[57] *Usatges,* 73 (c. 37), 86–7 (cc. 87–9).

[58] *The Welsh Law of Women,* ed. D. Jenkins and M. E. Owen (Cardiff, 1980), 132ff. for the laws. For a contextualization of Welsh marital rights with European mainstream practice, D. B. Walters, 'The European Context of the Welsh Law of Matrimonial Property', in ibid., 115–31.

[59] *English Lawsuits from William I to Richard I 2, Henry II and Richard I,* ed. R.C. van Caenegem, Selden Society, 107 (London, 1991), no. 408; and see, McDougall, *Royal Bastards,* 173–9.

when Alexander Neckam talked of the anxieties of parents that their beloved and unmarried daughter was sleeping around, and of a husband that his wife was in another man's bed. It was the same anxiety that also plagued that concerned parent and grandparent, Philip de Novare, six decades later.[60]

The medieval discourse on female conduct is not simply a literary manifestation of the legal concept of *couverture*: the male subjugation of the female. Sexual relationships are power relationships, a fact which would of itself concede a degree of power to the female—the power to refuse, ridicule and evade—and so put her in the dangerous role of insurgent. The twelfth-century drama *Le Jeu d'Adam* states what is obvious and universal about intersexual relations in a passage of breathtaking clarity: that the power of the male relies on the threat of violent anger, but the power of the female is in her ability to humiliate and intimidate the male.[61] The prologue to the 'Neutered Shrew', a thirteenth-century *fabliau*, hectors both men and women in terms we are already familiar with from a range of sources. It sarcastically addresses itself to men who have allowed themselves to be belittled, shamed and dishonoured by their dominant wives, and pretends to offer women encouragement in renouncing the disgrace of rising up against their husbands' control (*seignorie*). These were women who were indeed 'above themselves', or insurgent (*enorgelleuse*).[62] The *fableor* goes on to picture the sad life of a knight who had simply given up and resigned the direction of his life to his wife. His only tactic to counter her was to advocate the opposite of what he really wanted so she would wilfully do what he covertly wished. He even depicts the shrew offering a perverse *enseignement* to her daughter during her marriage festivities on how to diminish and humiliate her new husband if she wanted to achieve 'honour'. The *fableor*, like the common proverb, counsels extreme and sexually demeaning violence as a way of suppressing female rebellion.[63]

If this tension aligns the medieval social world described here with James Thurber's lugubrious, Martini-soaked and ironic picture of warfare between women and men in the constrained interwar society of suburban New York, it is not accidental. Philip de Novare repeated in 1260 a common joke that marriage was a battlefield from which only one side would emerge alive.[64] Power misused can generate insurgency in the powerless, and apprehension in the minds of the oppressors. The thirteenth century could employ military metaphors in describing relations between the sexes as much as did the twentieth century. The idealized model of the *preudefemme* is, then, very instructive. She stands at the heart of the reality, tensions and dangers of medieval society. The unapproachable ladies of the courtly-love

---

[60] *De naturis rerum libri duo*, ed. T. Wright (Rolls Series, 1863), 247.

[61] *Le Jeu d'Adam*, ed. W. von Emden (Société Rencesvals British Branch, British Rencesvals Publications, 1, 1996), p. 8: *Femme dë home n'i avra irur, ne home de femme verguine ne freür.* See the recent re-evaluation of its sources and provenance, which make it ultimately of Poitevin origin, *Le Jeu d'Adam*, ed. and trans. (Fr.) G. Hasenohr (Geneva, 2017), lxxi–xcvii.

[62] A point indeed made in her lectures in the 1930s by Eileen Power, *Medieval Women* (Cambridge, 1975), 11.

[63] *La Mégère Émasculée*, in *Chevalerie et Grivoiserie*, 106–40. *Frauenbuch*, 162 (l. 1958) uses the MHG word *übermuot* for female 'uppitiness' in a linguistic parallel to *enorgeller*.

[64] *Quatre Tenz*, 45 (c. 78).

tradition who enslave and diminish their suitors can be taken as some literary evidence of the subdued resentment of males towards the *preudefemmes* who could play them off the field in any social competition.

The *preudefemme* was devised by a male-dominated society to mark out for women elements of conduct which were acceptable and which not, and to that extent it was built on the ancient and long-standing literary dualism of comparing the 'good' and the 'wicked' woman as a way of establishing sexual roles.[65] But it was more than a crude social monitor and was not simply an instrument of male control. It arose out of a habitus which was negotiated on a daily basis between males and females, and its construction shows it. Its women were assumed to be social actors who could make choices and pursue ambitions within their admittedly small reserve of opportunity. They could verbally fence with men for their mutual amusement but might also be resorted to by men for counsel and consolation. Medieval women had a potential for eminence, however grey it might have been. Women's sexuality and wilfulness was believed to be a danger to themselves and their social world in general, and so the *preudefemme* must live constantly on edge if she were to retain her all-important reputation (*prez*). But likewise female attractiveness and capacity for social ease eroded the social edge that men might otherwise claim, as men had no choice but to seek out the *preudefemme* on her own terms and on her own turf, hoping eternally that her laces were not as straitened as the exemplars of conduct literature would have them be.

THE ARMOURY OF FEMALE RESISTANCE

Women had weapons, not least their tongue, a blade that could easily penetrate the chinks in the second-rate armour of the male ego. One such weakness was the relative status of the husband and wife. In *Berenger au Long Cul*, a castellan's daughter was disagreeably paired with a usurer's son. She soon became all too aware of the youth's idleness, cowardice, mendacity and greed. She could not deny his undeserved status as a knight but she had her noble descent as a retaliatory weapon: 'so she harped on her lineage in which there were many valiant knights, dauntless and brave in arms, men who despised idleness. Her husband was well aware that she was not going on about it so as to do *him* credit.'[66] The intersexual dialogues of Andrew the Chaplain in the 1180s likewise make strategic use of the concept of relative Nobility, while the men and women of various social levels verbally duel as attempts are made on the women's virtue. When a count attempted to seduce a knight's lady, she put him gently but firmly in his place, praising him as a great *preudomme* (*homo estis nimiae probitatis*) and a man of outstanding civility (*urbanitas*) and high birth (*generositas*). She then turned these virtues against him by observing

---

[65] Note that the oppositional poems, the *Bien des Fames* and the *Blasme des Femmes*, play on this strategy as late as the fourteenth century; *Three Medieval Views of Women*, ed. and trans. G. K. Fiero, W. Pfeffer, and M. Allain (New Haven, 1989).

[66] *Berenger au Long Cul*, in *Chevalerie et Grivoiserie*, 86 (ll. 58–63).

that any behaviour on his part that smacked of boorishness—such, we are to assume, as pressing himself on an unwilling woman—would be more demeaning in him than any other class of male.[67]

Ulrich von Liechtenstein's *Frauenbuch* is an extended and revealing dialogue between a knight and a lady which goes to town on intersexual tension and the frail realities of male domination. The spark that begins the interchange is that the knight bemoans that women of his day treat men with disdain. The lady bridled and stood up for her sex, going promptly on the attack. Men, she says, are a lost cause, too self-infatuated to give women the attention that is their right, whether socially or in bed. It was no wonder women despaired of them. Knights failed to assert their prowess in the field, which reflected poorly on their ladies. Instead they spent the day in field sports, came home tired and morose, took refuge in alcohol and ignored their wives' sexual needs. Men, she says, much prefer drinking and boasting in the company of other men, which is the only time they cheer up. Some of them openly preferred homosexual intercourse in any case. She particularly despised the arch, gossipy male (*der spottec man*), a cynical flamer who dealt in insinuation and innuendo, a man in other words who behaved as the worst of women was supposed to do. All her attacks are thus calculated to subvert a man's masculinity, and Ulrich did not defend his sex from the charges he put in her mouth. His knight back-pedalled furiously. He ostentatiously affirmed the norms in intersexual relations for which the woman was arguing, while offering a sympathetic take on the tragedy of a good and decent wife inescapably trapped in a relationship with a wretched and despicable man, a man who is thus 'fouler than any shit in the world'.[68]

Ulrich was registering more directly than Andrew the Chaplain the moral problem implicit in the fact that by his day European aristocracies had constructed social hegemony on an ideology of hypermorality we call Chivalry, which supposedly made the knight's Nobility and superiority inarguable. But Ulrich's *Frauenbuch* presents the argument that in failing to live up to the ideal, knights forfeited the respect they thought should be theirs automatically, and made themselves despicable. It was not just through irony that Ulrich used a female voice to point out the problem. Women were to him justified in becoming insurgent and challenging such males, in the same way that to the medieval mind a community of a realm was justified in taking arms against a king who failed to respect his coronation oath. There were other indications that the hypermoral stance of Chivalry provoked further strategies of resistance to those it repressed socially, not least in the frequent mocking in the *fabliaux* of hypocritical and deceitful knights, who were portrayed as far more interested in sexual satisfaction than truth and justice. No thirteenth-century woman could counter the male by embracing for herself knightly ideology, but there was another strategy she could use to sidestep his oppression other than by the use of her reproachful tongue. This was in embracing a claim that was open to all—hyper-religiosity.

---

[67] *De Amore*, 134.   [68] *Frauenbuch*, quote from pp. 105–6 (ll. 951–2).

There are indications that women were increasingly resorting to outward and ostentatious expressions of piety in the second half of the twelfth century. Aristocratic women naturally shared the general earnestness of the twelfth-century aristocracy in exploring and confessing their faith, such as those aristocratic women who were the correspondents of pastorally minded theologians like Bernard of Clairvaux (died 1152) or Bishop Gilbert Foliot (died 1187). The Anglo-Norman queens of the first half of the twelfth century led the way in establishing confessional piety in the royal household. Matilda II and Matilda III, as well as the Empress Matilda, were pious Catholic princesses who resided for extended periods in halls within or close to monastic precincts: Westminster, Holy Trinity Aldgate, St Augustine Canterbury and Notre-Dame-du-Pré near Rouen.[69] But besides this, the later twelfth century is characterized as a time when aristocratic and bourgeois women gravitated towards a variety of overt and often highly emotional expressions of religiosity without entering the cloister. This was particularly true of widows, who had some freedom of action in their society. Some became recluses under the guidance of confessors and followed the divine office within their household; others formed communities of prayer and lived in common, as with the beguines of the Low Countries and the English community which was given the famous *Ancrene Riwle*. In the cities of Italy and Flanders the new orders of friars encouraged women to act as tertiaries under their guidance, taking on the corporal works of mercy. It was a phenomenon observed with approval by James de Vitry as something which was characteristic of his own time.[70]

But in doing so, some women may well have discovered that a wholehearted embrace of religiosity gave them a social as much as a soteriological advantage, and an ability to deflect an increasingly assertive male moral hegemony. It is here we may find some evidence for what is signally lacking elsewhere in our sources, the medieval female voice, and it is an insurgent one. The early thirteenth-century English-language 'Letter on Virginity' (*Hali Meiðhad*) is a tract to persuade young women of the moral superiority of virginity as a female vocation. It may be English in language but it is not an entirely insular product, as its arguments are largely modelled on Pope Innocent III's *De miseria humanae conditionis*, published in 1195. The male clerical author (probably a regular canon of Wigmore in Herefordshire) set out the orthodox arguments for renunciation of the flesh and the embrace of a religious and contemplative life. However, his rhetoric against his society and the position of women within it led him further, into direct conflict with the habitus. *Contemptus mundi* was his guiding theology, the empty vanity of the world, and he argued that among its disappointments will be the man to whom the woman will be shackled: he will be 'worthless' (*an eðlich mon*) and her life with him will be entering into 'slavery to the male' (*into monnes þeowdom*), in which happiness was seldom experienced. Sex would not come up to the expectations of libido and will result in the humiliation, squalor and pain of childbirth and its consequences, which he graphically described. The author went so far as to blame married life for tempting weak women to resort to sorcery and even poison as a solution for

---

[69] Crouch, *Reign of Stephen*, 260–1.   [70] See Bynum, *Holy Feast and Holy Fast*, 13, 23–30.

their marital anguish, 'as many do'. The author's ferocious rhetoric is, however, double-edged. To argue the superiority of virginity, he not only had to demean the male and the normative heterosexual way of life, he also had to portray the celibate woman as sister to the angels and a truly superior and rational being, distanced from brute concerns.[71] It is not surprising to find a cleric adopting a stance counter to lay expectations so as to reform what he sees as objectionable in them. What is curious is that he has gauged his radical social critique in the assumption that aspirational women will sympathize with his views.

The author's picture of the trials a sensitive and intelligent woman will experience from her yoking to a brutish male cites female sensibilities, which it seems the author had absorbed from his pastoral experience. It matches closely the complaints of the wife which Ulrich von Liechtenstein sketches out in *Das Frauenbuch* a generation later, apart from Ulrich's insinuation that women are likely to be sexually disappointed by their husband's complete lack of interest in them. The canon of Wigmore said:

> For suppose now that you have wealth in abundance and your wide walls are proud and splendid, and you have many servants under you in hall, and your husband is angry with you or you have come to hate him, so that each of you is at odds with the other; what worldly wealth can give you pleasure? When he is out you are filled with anxiety and fear of his homecoming. While he is at home, all your wide halls seem to you too narrow. His attention makes you nervous; his detestable clamour and his ill-bred shouting frighten you. He rails at you and scolds you and abuses you shamefully, treats you disgracefully as a lecher does his whore, beats you and thrashes you like his bought slave and his born serf. Your bones ache and your flesh smarts, your heart within you swells with violent rage, and your outward countenance burns with anger.[72]

Men are perceived by women in this account as loud, angry, hateful, abusive, violent and lecherous, whose sexual attentions are as often as not unwanted and perverted. If this account (and indeed that of *Das Frauenbuch*) are echoes of thirteenth-century women's voices, then their frustrated rage (*sar grome*) might well push them towards insurgency, one avenue for which would be a resort to hyper-religiosity, a strategy that Ulrich von Liechtenstein observed and indeed resented, but which the canon of Wigmore recommends to oppressed women.

The hyper-religiosity of the sainted and holy woman of the thirteenth century is an extreme case which has been well explored by Joan Ferrante and Caroline Walker Bynum, but what is not so easy to penetrate is the degree to which the less spiritually ambitious daughters, wives and widows of the aristocracy and town—who were of no interest to hagiographers—embraced egregious religious practices.[73]

---

[71] *Hali Meiðhad*, in *Medieval English Prose for Women: Selections from the Katherine Group and Ancrene Wisse*, ed. and trans. B. Millett and J. Wogan-Browne (Oxford, 1990), 2–42, refs to pp. 4, 10, 20–2, 24, 28, 30–2. For some reflection on its date (favouring around 1224), see A. J. Fletcher, 'Black, White and Grey in HALI MEIÐHAD and ANCRENE WISSE', *Medium Aevum*, 62 (1993), 69–78.

[72] *Hali Meiðhad*, 28.

[73] C. W. Bynum, 'Women mystics and eucharistic devotion in the thirteenth century', *Women's Studies*, 11 (1984), 179–214; J. M. Ferrante, *To the Glory of Her Sex: Women's Roles in the Composition of Medieval Texts* (Bloomington, IN., 1997), 139–74.

However, hagiographers at least on occasion helpfully describe their holy women taking their own sex as subjects for domestic preaching within their own chambers, and finding there an audience. So we know something of what was urged on women in the refuge of the solar. Elizabeth of Hungary (died 1231), as a teenage mother and margravine of Thuringia, was apt to harangue 'worldly matrons' at her court about renouncing vanities such as dancing and ribbons, and to consider a future as a widow under vows of continence, the one she herself would embrace in 1225 at the age of 20.[74] Such a charismatic princess could have a wide secular influence within her class and heighten the spiritual enthusiasm in her chambers and hall. In her own case it led to hideous squalor, deprivation and self-abnegation in masochistic subjection to an abusive male confessor.

One approach to the theme of female resistance to male hegemony is to pursue male resentments at female behaviour, and one of them was the nature of female dress. The wimple (*guimple, guimpa, gimpel*, Lat. *peplum*) was a tight female head covering which swathed hair and head and is an item of dress found in England well before the Conquest; the word is attested in a Low German glossary of the eighth century.[75] It was not an item of dress definitively associated with nuns, but it formed part of their headdress, as we find from the rule of Robert of Arbrissel, which chided the nuns of Fontevraud around 1115 never to appear open-faced, without *vela* and *guimpa*.[76] Veiling was the distinctive sign of a professed nun by this date, and was the point of distinction from the garb of the lay woman. St Bernard's letter to an anonymous recreant nun in the 1130s says she was behaving more like a 'woman in a wimple' (*wimplata*) than 'a woman in a veil' (*velata*), meaning that unlike laywomen of the time nuns did not leave their faces open to the world, but wore both wimple *and* veil over their lower face.[77] The future Queen Matilda (II) of England seems to have seen the wimple-and-veil combination as a particular affliction on nuns. She was to testify that she had been sent to Romsey Abbey for her education as an adolescent girl early in the 1090s, where her aunt Christina had forced her unwillingly into the habit of a nun, whose black wrapping (*nigrum panniculum*) Matilda ripped off her head as soon as she could and which she trampled in her frustration.[78] Her resentment was ostensibly that she had no vocation to be a nun.

The current historiography of such female head coverings is dominated by later medieval evidence and has concluded from it that they were assumed by women

---

[74] *Dicta Quatuor Ancillarum*, in *The Life and Afterlife of St Elizabeth of Hungary: Testimony from her Canonization Hearings*, ed. K. B. Wolf (Oxford, 2010), 198.

[75] E. R. Goddard, *Women's Costume in French Texts of the Eleventh and Twelfth Centuries* (Johns Hopkins Studies in Romance Literatures and Languages, 7, 1927), 137–42. L. Sinisi, 'The Wandering Wimple', in *Medieval Clothing and Textiles*, 4, ed. R. Netherton and G. R. Owen-Crocker (Woodbridge, 2008), 39–54, esp. 46, argues an English origin for the wimple, but underplays Continental evidence. See also R. Boulengier-Sedyn, *Le vocabulaire de la coiffure en ancien français étudié dans les romans de 1150 à 1300* (Brussels, 1970), 147–55.

[76] *Regulae Sanctimonialium Fontis Ebraldi*, in *PL* 162: col. 1079 (c. 6).

[77] Epistola CXIV (c. 3), in *PL* 182: col. 260. See the observation in Goddard, *Women's Costume*, 221.

[78] Eadmer, *Historia Novorum in Anglia*, ed. M. Rule (Rolls Series, 1866), 122; see L. L. Huneycutt, *Matilda of Scotland: A Study in Medieval Queenship* (Woodbridge, 2003), 17–18.

on marriage.[79] However, the evidence does not support this assumption for the period before 1250.[80] The first appearance of the wimple in French literature is in Geoffrey Gaimar's *Estoire des Engleis*, where it is described as an obstacle to King Edgar's appreciation of the beauty of the young and unmarried Ælfthryth, so he simply removed it to get a better look at her.[81] The incident not only tells us that such headgear might be worn in the 1130s by any condition of woman, it also indicates that young women might take to it as a social defence in a society where creepy and powerful men had little compunction in harassing them. It was not imposed on them unwilling, as the Western liberal mind might these days assume.[82] Much of the earlier evidence in fact involves male resentment of such headgear. Chrétien de Troyes, in his *Eric et Enide*, has his knights riding into the lists exhibiting the wimples (*guimples*) and headscarves of their female admirers on their lances. If one interprets these as 'love tokens', then they are a symbolic male declaration of a preference that the female face and head should be uncovered. Likewise, when William de Lorris described the personified female virtues in the Garden of the Rose, all have their hair, brows and faces quite uncovered, for their physical and (hence) moral beauty must be seen by all. This is not in allusion to their youth. One only of his characters does wear a head covering 'just like a nun's', and she is Shame (*Honte*).[83] We find in the early thirteenth century that wimples might have been customary riding wear for women, but were still not thought appropriate indoors, and some men were not pleased to see them outdoors either.[84] Ulrich von Liechtenstein certainly took the fashion for the wimple in bad part and deplored its hideousness, especially when combined with a veil. The disgruntled male character in his *Frauenbuch* has this to say:

> Why should she want to be in a wimple wrapping you up to the eyes? Each wears a veil which so tightly constricts them the mouth and eyebrows are covered. You're left with no sight of either, your desire only satisfied by a glimpse of eyes.[85]

Was there a move amongst aristocratic ladies towards wearing the wimple more ostentatiously and indeed combining it with the veil at the end of the twelfth century, as if—like Lorris's 'Shame'—they were mimicking nuns? In the 1230s its use

---

[79] As summarized in R. Gilchrist, *Medieval Life: Archaeology and the Life Course* (Woodbridge, 2012), 85–6. A largely anachronic perspective dominates M. H. Caviness, 'Hats and Veils: there's no such thing as Freedom of Choice, and it's a good thing too', in *Founding Feminisms in Medieval Studies: Essays in Honor of E. Jane Burns*, ed. L. E. Doggett and D. E. O'Sullivan (Woodbridge, 2016), 73–94, esp. 93.

[80] Goddard, *Women's Costume*, 140.   [81] *Estoire*, 206 (ll. 3791–801).

[82] For a revealing analysis of the threatening male stare in the medieval context, where it perversely stoked misogyny, K. M. Krause, 'Gazing on Women in the *Miracles de Nostre Dame*', in *Gautier de Coinci: Miracles, Music and Manuscripts*, ed. K. M. Krause and A. Stones (Turnhout, 2006), 227–51, and for thoughtful comment see Caviness, 'Hats and Veils', 94–5.

[83] Lorris, *Rose*, 226 (ll. 3561–5).

[84] *Lancelot*, 1: 18: when the false Guinevere arrived at Camelot she appeared before Arthur straight from the road still *envolepée* by her wimple, which she hastily removed in his presence, and once *desvelopée*, the court marvelled at her beauty. *Lancelot*, 1: 319, has a lady wrapped up in a wimple out riding with Lancelot.

[85] *Frauenbuch*, 65 (ll. 232–8).

was certainly becoming widespread across Europe.[86] Elizabeth of Thuringia wore wimple and veil, though she accepted she had to lift the veil in hall and during the canon of the Mass, in the presence of Christ. In the next decade in France Robert de Blois regretted those women who chose to be covered up (*estoupée*), and those who did it in the hall and church were to him ill-bred (*maul endoctrinée*), though he mused theologically that it was a consequence of the shame of the sin of Eve.[87] Two generations earlier its use may not have been so general. The copious, later twelfth-century poetry of Peire Vidal describes what stirred him in the beauty of the women of Aragon, Toulouse, Provence, Liguria and Sardinia: their eyes, faces and smiles are frequently mentioned, and so he had clearly seen his ladies without veils. He also talks of the neck and hair of women he admired, so in his courtly circles in the time of Alfonso II of Aragon and Duke Richard of Aquitaine in the 1170s and 1180s wimples were not, it seems, generally worn by noblewomen, at least indoors.[88] The lavish description of the noble ladies of the court of Byzantium in the romance *Partonopeus of Blois,* written during that same period, rejoices in their long, golden hair and elegant necks, and it makes a point of saying they despised the wearing of a wimple, preferring instead to wear their hair loose, retained by a gold circlet.[89] Authors deliberately chose this mode of portrayal for ladies of high rank and unassailable self-confidence. Around 1200, the poet-knight Renaut de Beaujeu depicted a princess, 'the Maiden with the White Hands', out riding, wearing a cap against the weather but pointedly without wimple (*sans guinple*), her golden hair uncovered and flowing down her back.[90]

The sigillography of the time offers some support to a conclusion that there had indeed been a change around the end of the twelfth century. Seals of the earlier twelfth century show mature noblewomen with long hair falling free over their shoulders and with uncovered heads, as in the case of the fine seal of Constance, duchess of Brittany, which (since it alludes to none of her husbands) would have been sculpted for her on her accession to the duchy and to the earldom of Richmond in or soon after 1171; the seal was used throughout her reign.[91] The same applies to both faces of the seal of Constance of France, countess of Toulouse, sculpted before 1172, where she is both enthroned and on horseback uncovered,

[86] D. Koslin, 'The Robe of Simplicity: Initiation, Robing and Veiling of Nuns in the Middle Ages', in *Robes of Honor: the Medieval World of Investiture,* ed. S. Goron (Aldershot, 2001), 264–5, notes this and suggests it was the consequence of crusading exposure of women to oriental fashions.

[87] *Chastoiement des dames,* 143 (ll. 343–72); *Enseignement des princes,* 104 (ll. 449–54).

[88] Peire, 46 (l. 77), 173 (illus. 37).

[89] *Partonopeus de Blois,* ed. G.-A. Crapelet (2 vols, Paris, 1834) 1: 166–7 (ll. 4819–22).

[90] *Le Bel Inconnu,* ed. G. P. Williams (Paris, 1983), 121–2 (ll. 3965–82). The author of *Durmart* likewise describes a confident and beautiful maiden riding alone, without wimple and with her hair flowing free, though using as a riding scarf a sleeve of fine white linen; *Durmart le Galois: roman arthurien du treizième siècle,* ed. J. Gildea (2 vols, Villanova, PA, 1065), 1: 50 (ll. 1900–5).

[91] S. M. Johns, *Noblewomen, Aristocracy and Power in the Twelfth-century Anglo-Norman Realm* (Manchester, 2003), 66–7, 207; *The Charters of Duchess Constance of Brittany and her Family, 1171–1221,* ed. J. Everard and M. C. E. Jones (Woodbridge, 1999), 41–2. The earliest impression is dated to 1184 (c. 4). Queen Matilda II of England, for all her protestations against wimples as a girl, is depicted as wearing one on her seal.

with long hair flowing.[92] But when Margaret, daughter of Robert III, earl of Leicester, and wife since the 1180s of the Angevin bureaucrat Saher de Quincy, had a seal die sculpted on her husband's elevation to an earldom in 1206, the fine new obverse (perhaps one of the finest of its day) showed her head tightly swathed in a wimple and scarf covering the throat, the face visible, and topped with a hat in the fashion of a toque (an early example of the item called a *touret*).[93] To be sure, the result is elegant, but that was little compensation for the male who suspected the motivation for such headgear. There are a number of similar examples of such seal depictions of women from Margaret de Quincy's lifetime, enough to add evidence that the period around 1200 saw a move towards the more specific and general use of the wimple found in the later Middle Ages.

Another fashion Ulrich hated was the same one Ramon Vidal deplored: the female fashion of flaunting rosaries as jewellery across their breasts.

> But if one of you assumes a dress and costly robes, then the sable has to have a rosary for a clasp that lies on the bosom. This annoys us, of course. We're left with the conclusion that women hide themselves away in this way out of spiritual mortification. Your bosom needs a costly clasp rather more, believe me, than it does a rosary. Even if her disposition is spiritual a woman shouldn't tell anyone about it out loud; she should wear her rosary without ostentation.[94]

When men gazed at such objects of desire, the last thing they wanted was to be brought up short by a reminder of the demands of faith. Both Ulrich and Ramon interpreted this overt religiosity in female fashion as a claim to moral autonomy, an allusion to an authority beyond the control of the male. Ramon says it was a new practice when he wrote around 1210. In arguing against it, he harked back to the previous generation of great ladies, whose easy-going spirituality was to his mind not so threatening.

> They were such good and noble women...and caused God to be honoured and believed in. They endowed many priests and many churches for the service of God with no wish on their part to take oaths of profession, they simply desired to remain in the world without being such women as exchanged it for the cloister but rather to be together with people of all sorts. For this reason their deeds and their conduct have had a lasting impact down the years and ages.[95]

So when the hypermoral stance of male conduct we call Chivalry emerged in the generation at the end of the twelfth century, I would suggest that the increasing resort to a female mode of constricted dress in the same period can be seen as part of the reaction to it. There had always been a defensive element in the wimple which led women to assume it in circumstances where they might have felt vulnerable, as

[92] *The Charters of Duchess Constance of Brittany*, 545–6 (Fig. 8).
[93] For Margaret's seal, a reproduction is in Crouch, *English Aristocracy*, plate 3. The edifice the countess wears parallels the elaborate head wrappings Jean Renart described in significantly military terms (as if it were defensive armour) as being worn by his heroine Léonore in his early thirteenth-century *Roman de la Rose*: a *touaille* (or veil), a *hordaïs* (structure, or wrapping), a *ventaille* (or barbette) and a *heaume* (or hat) (356, ll. 4720–3).
[94] *Frauenbuch*, 65–6 (ll. 239–52).   [95] *Abril issia*, 90 (ll. 914–23).

is implied by Gaimar's account of the meeting of Edgar and Ælfthryth. Jean Renart for his part chose to describe female head wrappings as if they were defensive knightly armour (coif, ventaille and helm). A proverbial comment by Walter of Arras shows that men regarded the wimple as giving women a social advantage of sorts: 'a woman at first sight is polite, intelligent, demure and modest; and betrays nothing of what is under her wimple.'[96] Likewise, the long practice of nuns wearing head coverings associated the combined wimple and veil with a high idea of piety and renunciation of secular values, and so they could be used by women in general to identify and ally with another source of authority. Assuming the wimple and flaunting devotional objects could then in these circumstances become an act of insurgency and resistance to new claims of male hegemony, reinforcing with an additional buttress other traditional female defences: a screen of assiduous attendants; her reputation as *preudefemme* and the consequences of her disapproval and verbal rebuke; as well as the more double-edged and risky one of deploying her sexuality.

[96] *Eracle*, ed. and trans. K. Pratt (King's College London Medieval Studies, 21, London, 2007), 66 (ll. 2178–80), my translation (meaning that, as the editor nicely says, she keeps what she really is up her sleeve).

9

The Table

Medieval people might very well go to public dinners in a state of anxiety, though not necessarily so much about which utensil to use for which course since, apart from knives and the occasional spoon, cutlery was not much in evidence on the medieval table.[1] Table manners were certainly important and a diner would be judged on them, but it was the entirety of the experience which could be intimidating. The copious literature associated with the medieval hall is remarkably and significantly negative on the experience of dining out. There were a number of reasons for this—other than that some personality types would find any social gathering difficult. The principal cause of anxiety they advertise was that a person's social credit could be fatally damaged by a bad performance in the hall, where his rusticity or her lack of social grace might very well diminish their reputation and honour. So much for the guest, but the host too was warned of social danger. His accessibility, civility, generosity, quality of servants and organizational ability were all going to be judged, and such things counted in a society whose mainspring was the management of patronage. The verdict of his contemporaries on King John of England (reigned 1199–1216) was understandably hostile. But the considered view of one foreign guest in his realm was this: 'He was brimming over with bad qualities, but he did at least spend freely. He would keep a generous and open table, and indeed his gates and the door of his hall were never closed at meal times. Anyone could eat his fill at his court as he pleased.'[2]

DINING AND CIVILIZATION

Since it is a truism that sharing a meal is a way that as abstract a thing as society expresses and asserts itself, it is not surprising that its conduct became a measure of

---

[1] I talk here of 'dinners' as the routine and main daily meals of the hall, though much the same rituals were expected in the secondary medieval evening meals we call 'suppers'. I generally avoid here the words 'banquets' and 'feasts', which imply exceptionality, celebrating an occasion or a particular abundance (which is why Bartholomew the Englishman in the 1240s differentiated 'banquets' or *cenae* as being more ambitious and grander than 'dinners' or *prandia*). For the importance of the distinction and the bias in study away from routine dining, K. Twiss, 'The Archaeology of Food and Social Diversity', *Journal of Archaeological Research*, 20 (2012), 363–4. I must acknowledge the generosity of Martha Carlin in commenting on early drafts of this chapter.

[2] *Histoire*, 105. For the theological-literary motif of the open door, J. Kerr, 'The Open Door: Hospitality and Honour in Twelfth/Early Thirteenth-century England', *History*, 87 (2002), esp. 327–8. It also appears in Celtic cultures, Ll. Beverley Smith, 'On the Hospitality of the Welsh', in *Power and Identity in the Middle Ages: Essays in Memory of Rees Davies*, ed. H. Pryce and J. Watt (Oxford, 2007), 185–6.

civilization and a way of determining status in the Middle Ages.[3] Giving handsome dinners was recognized as the central ritual of courtly society around 1210 by that analytical knight, Raoul de Houdenc, and he went so far as to say that, for the lord, hosting a dinner was a matter of prowess.[4] In the classic essay on rites of passage by Van Gennep, commensality was the way society accommodated the social danger involved in changing status, but as we will see, the public meal might very well pose some dangers in its own right.[5] To begin with, to claim civility at table it was necessary not to be brutish. Master Reiner the German, in his thirteenth-century tract on dining, long pre-empted nineteenth-century anthropologists by saying food preparation and formal meals are part of what set humanity apart from the animals. The literature of dining is shot through with a revulsion at animalistic eating and appetites. Reiner's contemporary, the poet who called himself 'Der Tannhäuser', puts it succinctly: 'The fellow who hangs over his plate while he is eating, is like a hog.' Slobbering over food was to him an animalistic trait, the sort of thing peasants and Bavarians did. Civilized folk (*die hübschen*) did it very differently.[6] An unacceptable manner of dining was one way of identifying the unacceptable Other, as a medieval writer on ethnicity, such as Gerald of Wales, readily discovered. Unrestrained appetite at table was part of the discourse of what distinguished the barbarian kings from the admirable Romans they supplanted, which was for medieval historians the most notorious setback to their own civilization.[7] Looked at this way, medieval dining culture was a stage in the process which Bourdieu analysed at perhaps its chilly peak in *haut-bourgeois* Paris in the 1970s, where narrowly defined and acceptably cultured tastes in wine, food, and its presentation were a way of advertising the membership of a small, sophisticated social elite rich in cultural capital.[8]

When nearly eight centuries earlier a Norman writer wanted to diminish the civility of the neighbouring Parisians, it was through attacking their table manners that he did so. He provided a perfect study of how dining culture could be taken as a measure of civility. He depicted the Francilien at table violating every precept which features in early dining advice; his essay is in fact evidence that such rules were already well understood and widely circulated in European society. His Parisians were only willing to offer the coarsest of bread (rye), which in their miserliness they regarded as eating 'sumptuously' (*richement*). They fought over the breaking of the loaves and used their slices as sops to eat messily by dipping them

[3] For an exploration of the truism, M. Jones, *Feast: Why Humans Share Food* (Oxford, 2007).

[4] *Roman des Eles*, 38 (ll. 248–51).

[5] For a brief but telling sociological consideration of what danger lies behind hosting and commensality, J. M. Pitt-Rivers, 'The Law of Hospitality', in *The Fate of Shechem or the Politics of Sex* (Cambridge, 1977), esp. 107–12. For an analysis of the literature of commensality from Durkheim onwards, C. Fischler, 'Commensality, society and culture', *Social Science Information*, 50 (2011), 528–48.

[6] *Hofzucht*, 196–7 (ll. 41–48, 61–4).

[7] *Phagifacetus*, 13–14. See, on appetite, M. Montanari, *The Culture of Food*, trans. C. Ipsen (Oxford, 1994), 24–6.

[8] P. Bourdieu and J-C. Passeron, *The Inheritors, French Students and their Relation to Culture* (Chicago, 1979); P. Bourdieu, *Distinction: A Social Critique on the Judgement of Taste*, trans. R. Nice (London, 1986), 276–80.

in broth. They were so suspicious of each other's greed that they were satirized as tying a string to their bread slice when they dipped it in. They were equally as tenacious of the meat chunks in the broth. They paid no attention to the duty of the diner to leave food for the poor, and the dogs got little nourishment from the well-gnawed bones the French threw from their tables. Their greed meant that unless a guest fought for a share of his meal, all he would get was the garnish. 'That's the way they are in their own land, but when they're abroad they're even more greedy and shamefully gorge themselves at every table whenever they get near one.' To the French at table this is how you display good conduct (*bel contenir*), says our satirist: by greed, brawling, self-delusion and miserliness.[9] The blow was a low one. The French of Philip Augustus's day and domain flattered themselves that they had attained heights of civility unknown since the Roman Empire.

A contemporary variant on this strategy of using their alleged table manners to diminish a group is in Gerald of Wales's essay on the Welsh (written around 1194), amongst whom he lived for much of his career. He was himself descended from the native royal house of Deheubarth, and was fully conscious of it. He can there-fore be positive about the Welsh when it suited him, doing full credit to their ideals of generosity and hospitality, from which he himself often benefited. But he was also all too aware of the immoderate violence and instability of Welsh political culture, which he despised, so when he dealt with Welsh dining habits he was careful to distance them from the European mainstream where he did not feel they belonged. Unlike Anglo-French culture, he noted, the Welsh had only one large meal in a day, the evening dinner. There were understandably fewer courses than one would expect in a more prosperous land, and the flatbread was inferior. There were no long tables across which one would converse with one's dinner part-ner; no tablecloth or napkins; no procession of a variety of courses. For polemical purposes he chose to play down, ignore or make alien the congruences with the European mainstream, of which there were in fact many. From other sources we find the same importance was awarded in Welsh aristocratic halls as others to washing before dining (though foot-washing was also practised). There was the same favouring of guests with the sending of delicacies, wine or mead; the same care to seat guests according to status, with a cleric on the host's right hand to open the dinner with a benediction. The prosperous Welsh host served bread and wine with courses; he offered music in the hall; and employed the same household officers—doorkeeper, butler (*trulliad*) and steward (*distain*)—as would preside in any European hall.[10] For Gerald it was important to make the Welsh at table

[9] *Roman des Franceis*, 193–7. The author, Andrew de Coutances, thus prefigures by centuries the ironical genre gibbeting grotesquely comic ill manners at table which contradict accepted conduct precepts, for which see M. Visser, *The Rituals of Dinner: the Origins, Evolutions, Eccentricities and Meaning of Table Manners* (London, 1991), 64–6. For another contemporary example of this topos of gustatory trashing, Baldwin, *Aristocratic Life*, 175, citing Jean Renart's satirical take on the food at the Imperial court in his *Roman de la Rose*.
[10] *Descriptio Kambriae, in GCO* 6: 183–4. Gerald, however, elsewhere notes that the Welsh understood the idea of the lord of the hall honouring guests by passing them food from his plate; *Descriptio Kambriae, in GCO* 6: 144. For Welsh sources on the table and hall, T. M. Charles-Edwards, 'Food, Drink and Clothing in the Laws of the Court', in *The Welsh King and His Court*, ed.

strange, so as to exclude them from the civilized francophone world where he was most at home. He was by no means alone in his generation in deliberately marginalizing non-Romance cultures from the courtly world. Peire Vidal, a crusader, knight and poet of the Occitan world, had this to say of Germans around 1195:

> I find the Germans crude and vulgar,
> and if one of them should affect courtly behaviour (*d'esser cortes*),
> it is painfully embarrassing and annoying:
> their speech resembles the howling of dogs.[11]

EDUCATING THE DINER

Since dining was a measure of civility, most conduct tracts of the twelfth and thirteenth centuries have something to say about it, which is a textual confirmation of its social centrality.[12] These texts did not, of course, originate good practice in the hall; they simply drew on it for the benefit of instructing youths, who principally learned their manners in the hall itself as they attended on the tables. Nonetheless, the need to pin down good practice that these writers felt is significant of a growing awareness of the borders of the courtly world, where things had to be done the right way, so they played their part in homogenizing general practice. Part of the duty of teenage squires and valets was to attend their lord's guests, and it was in that environment, under the eye of their patron, the rods of marshals and the chastisement of seneschals, that they were drilled in social etiquette on the job. Herbert of Bosham discussed at great length the efforts Thomas Becket as chancellor of England put into the schooling of the noble youths confided in numbers to his care in the etiquette of the hall and its dinners.[13] We also see this process at work in the picture we will encounter below of the working household of Countess Margaret de Lacy of Lincoln and Pembroke in the late 1240s. Daniel of Beccles around 1180 intends his advice for youths whom he knew were in that position, reflecting for their benefit on their common experience of laying out tables; the correct posture in which to serve guests; collecting bread scraps for the poor; holding the towel when offering a basin for washing around the tables; and working out which guests should be offered water first.[14] He was using their daily experience as a teaching aid, as good teachers do.

The advice these tracts give is directed principally at guests, though hosts too are offered advice, recognizing that each has differing sources of anxiety with which to contend. Relatively few texts survive which are *exclusively* devoted to the subject of dining etiquette, however, and they mostly appear quite late. There are, however,

---

T. M. Charles-Edwards, M. E. Owen and P. Russell (Cardiff, 2000), 319–37; P. Russell, 'The Laws of the Court from Latin B', in ibid., 478–526; P. Russell, '*Canu i Swyddogion Llys y Brenin*', in ibid. 552–60.

[11] *Bon' aventura don Dieus als Pizas*, in Peire, 143 (ll. 9–12).

[12] M-G. Grossel, 'La table comme pierre de touche de la courtoisie: à propos de quelques *chastoiements, ensenhamen* et autres *contenances de table*', in *Banquets et manières*, 181–95.

[13] *Materials*, 3: 225–38.   [14] *Liber Urbani*, 83–4 (ll. 2559–62, 2578–90).

twelfth-century texts which have a lot to say on the subject and boil down table conduct into a series of pragmatic commandments for a youth to memorize, and which in turn influenced later work. Peter Alfonsi's *Disciplina Clericalis* was the first of them. It was written in the first decade of the twelfth century and was the work of a physician whose dining experience included the halls of Aragon as much as England. It contained a chapter headed *de modo comedendi*, which gives eight pragmatic pieces of advice to a youth concerned about the impression he might make in a hall. Its thirteenth-century translation reinforced its social message, for any transgression of its norms was stigmatized by the translator as *vilanie*, conduct that was the opposite of Courtliness. *De modo comedendi* became canonical: it was to provide much of the material for the essay on table manners required of royal children at the court of Alfonso X of Castile (reigned 1252–84).[15]

A similar sort of impact can be attributed to the most common and earliest Facetus text (*Cum nihil utilius*), which devotes around fifty scattered lines to varied practical advice for early twelfth-century schoolboys on table etiquette. Like other such tracts, it originated in the classroom and was intended to inform youth in correct Latin grammar and enlarged vocabulary rather than the way of the world they were entering. But as a result it was a text which came before the eyes of a large number of the literate of Europe while they were children, and it is not surprising that its recommendations were widely repeated in texts over the next two centuries. A less easily datable Latin text—brief but exclusively about dining—first appears in a copy of the later thirteenth century, though it is rather older than that and it may well also have arisen, as Haskins believed, from the twelfth-century school-room. Its opening line, *Quisquis es in mensa,* in fact paraphrases the Facetus text about keeping the poor in mind while dining. It also shows the influence of Alfonsi in two of its precepts, which is some argument for locating its origin where Haskins thought it belonged. The poem's circulation was (like the *Disciplina*) to span Christendom, but its earliest traces are to be found in northern Italy, where in 1216 it informed the work of Thomasin of Zirclaria.

The earliest substantial tracts which deal more or less exclusively with dining are to be found in England in the teaching exercises which Daniel of Beccles brought together as his *Liber Urbani*. The work itself is likely to have been compiled in its standard form around 1180, though it plainly was a compilation or recension of earlier materials. It had a circulation across England and northern France and its ideas travelled wider still. Daniel's passage on dining in the second book of his *Liber* takes its cue and some of its ideas from Facetus, whose miscellaneous nature might have spurred Daniel to pull its scattered observations together, expand on and satirize them, and make them his own. A later section of the book, under the incipit *Audi disce*, deals more with food and its preparation, and was in its way influential, though it has less to say on actual conduct at table.[16] The second book of the *Liber Urbani* had its influence too, however. There are sufficient close parallels with the strictures on dining by Tannhäuser to indicate that he used the second

---

[15] *Disciplina Clericalis*, c. 26; *Chastoiement d'un père* 155–6 (ll. 4031–86); *Siete Partidas* ii, tit. 7, ley 5.
[16] Whelan, *Making of Manners*, 1–25, 151–2.

book of *Liber Urbani* as a source for his *Hofzucht*. If so, he might well have consulted the copies that we know were to be found in Paris in the early thirteenth century.[17] *Liber Urbani* was to have a long afterlife in translation as the source for many of the pieces of advice in the popular fifteenth-century English language courtesy manual, *The Babees Book*.[18]

Approaching dining etiquette from Daniel of Beccles's texts as much as from Facetus is problematical, as the author's intention was clearly not just satirical but even deliberately contrary in places. What Daniel has to say needs to be tested against more straightforward authors. We have to wait till the thirteenth century for these. John of Garlande's Parisian teaching text, the *Morale Scolarium*, which dates to 1241, offered two brief Latin tracts on the subject of dining, *De curialitatibus in mensa conservandis* and *De ministratione decendis*. *De curialitatibus* is considerably more pragmatic in its teaching than Daniel's offerings.[19] The most extensive take on public dining in our period is offered in the mid-thirteenth-century literary effort composed by one Master Reiner of Germany, said to have been a clerk at the court of Thuringia. His *Phagifacetus* (the 'Civil Diner') is a weighty Latin verse work, as quirky in some ways as Daniel's, though more focused on solid and practical advice as to the table and its etiquette. Tannhäuser's *Hofzucht* is of much the same period and also exclusively concerned with dining. Though only half the length of Master Reiner's offering, it is in the vernacular and displays a more cosmopolitan understanding of the subject and (as suggested above) employed wider sources than were available in Germany. It was also directly aimed at the occupants of the hall. An Italian manual of the later thirteenth century is an equally serious attempt at teaching dining etiquette, and like *Hofzucht* is intended to be accessible, not just because it is written in a lively vernacular style, but because it was intended for the urban middle classes as much as the nobility. It was written by a man not dissimilar in background to Daniel of Beccles: Buonvicino (Bonvesin) della Riva, a citizen of Milan, teacher of Latin grammar, and lay member of the local Milanese order of the Humiliati.[20] The manual's Latin title is *De Quinquaginta Curialitatibus ad Mensam* ('On Fifty Courtly Precepts in Dining').[21] It offers an interesting mix of advice, whose basic inspiration is Facetus and *Quisquis es in mensa*: Buonvicino indeed borrows and translates the opening of Facetus and

---

[17] For Tannhäuser and what little can be established of his biography, see J. W. Thomas, *Tannhäuser: Poet and Legend* (Chapel Hill, 1974), 1–4, 14–17, which concludes he was under the patronage of the Duke of Austria (from whom he had an estate near Vienna), was active from the 1230s to the 1260s, was well-travelled, and was literate in French and Latin as well as German.

[18] *The Babees Book*, ed. F. J. Furnivall (London, Early English Text Society, 1868). Some of the direct borrowings from *Liber Urbani* are: advice on keeping hands still and avoiding scratching (ll. 292–3); not picking at teeth (l. 1017); sitting up straight (l. 1035); washing the lord's hands at the end of the meal (ll. 2582–90); and keeping to yourself (l. 919). *The Babees Book* also notices and takes issue with Daniel's ironic and contrary advice about sharing a cup with the lord of the hall (ll. 1066–9).

[19] *Morale Scolarium*, 202–6 (c. 9), 227–9 (c. 16).

[20] On his life, P. Pecchiai, 'I documenti sulla biografia di Bonvicino della Riva', *Giornale Storico della Letteratura Italiana*, 78 (1921), 96–127.

[21] *Poeti del Duecento*, i, 703–12. J. Lacroix, 'Un art des belles manières de table en Lombardie au xiiie siècle', in *Banquets et manières de table*, 71–91, interprets the work as primarily theological in form and function, privileging Buonvicino's membership of the Humiliati and their (supposed) communal life. The wider context of commensal literature with which to compare it indicates otherwise to me.

expands on several of the precepts of *Quisquis es in mensa*. But much of it is a distillation of a range of other advice drawn from Latin literature as well (apparently) as its author's own experience, and as such it can be taken as a good summation of idealized dining practice at the end of our period.

THE UNIVERSAL DINNER

A striking thing that emerges from dining literature from Aragon to Austria in the twelfth and thirteenth centuries is how the sequence of the dinner described is remarkably similar across the continent. This may be behind Peter Alfonsi's observation at the beginning of the twelfth century that dining is governed by the same courtesies whether at a royal court or anywhere else.[22] One of our earlier sources, the poem *Quisquis es in mensa*, was intended as a practical aide-memoire to contemporary custom at the table, and the ideal dinner it portrays is well structured and well understood by host and guest.[23] But the sequence of the dinner it describes is not just confined to northern Italy. It was also a sequence that was to be as long-lasting and standardized across Europe as that other universal banquet, the Mass. It was still the sequence expected of a public dinner in England at the end of the Middle Ages; and some aspects of it survive to this day in Oxbridge college halls.[24] In 1245 an English Franciscan academic called Bartholomew, who had already by then taught in the schools of Oxford and Paris, was presiding over the provincial school of his order in Magdeburg and there completed his great work, *De proprietatibus rerum*. Bartholomew offered within his encyclopedia a detailed definition of what he understood to be the dinner (*prandium*) of his day, for which he could by then draw on his experience in England, France and the Empire. It differed little from the sequence described in mid-thirteenth-century dining tracts from such diverse places as Paris, Burgos, Thuringia, Vienna and Milan: that is, John of Garlande's *De curialitatibus*, Alfonso X's *Siete Partidas*, Master Reiner's *Phagifacetus*, Tannhäuser's *Hofzucht* and Buonvicino della Riva's *Fifty Precepts*. This is Bartholomew's summary of the standard European public dinner, which is worth quoting in full:

> The food and drink for a dinner (*prandium*) and entertainment (*convivium*) have a sequence and proper order. In dinners the foodstuff should be first prepared as the guests are summoned. Seats and sittings should be set out in the hall. Tables and settings should be laid out and made neat. Guests should be placed with the lord on

---

[22] *Disciplina Clericalis*, c. 26.

[23] For a published text, S. Glixelli, 'Les Contenances de Table', *Romania*, 47 (1921), 1–40, esp. 31, and see C. H. Haskins, *Studies in Medieval Culture* (Oxford, 1929), 78–9; F. P. Donati, 'Les bonnes manières à table dans le discourse proverbial du moyen âge italien', in *Pratiques et discours alimentaires en Méditerranée de l'Antiquité à la Renaissance*, ed. J. Leclant, A. Vauchez, and M. Sartre (Paris, 2008), 378. It is noteworthy that most of its cautions turn up in the section on dining in Thomasin of Zirclaria's work, dated 1216 (*Welsche Gast*, 13–15), to the extent that *Quisquis es in mensa*, or a common twelfth-century source, might well be the source of Thomasin's reflections. Bumke, *Courtly Culture*, 197, notices the influence of Alfonsi on Thomasin, but if so it was filtered through *Quisquis es in mensa*.

[24] C. M. Woolgar, *The Great Household in Late Medieval England* (New Haven, 1999), 161, citing BL, ms Harley 6815, fos 29r-36r.

the high table but no one should take his seat at table before their hands are washed. The ladies and girls of the family should be seated among the others higher up the table with the household members further down. Spoons, knives and the salt cellars should first be placed on the table, and subsequently the bread and cups, and many and varied courses should follow on. Attendants and officers should serve each of them solicitously, and should talk cheerfully with the guests, who should be entertained with viol and harp as more wine and dishes are presented. The courses placed on the table should be cut up and arranged between the guests. At the end of the meal fruit and spices should be introduced, and the tables taken out from the centre of the hall. Once more hands should be washed and dried, and thanks offered to God and to the host. Grace cups should be circulated. At the end of the dinner the guests should be given a bed or allowed to depart to their own places.[25]

We can put this universality down more to the pan-European nature of courtly society than to the way early writers influenced a common dining tradition. The pattern is already evident at the beginning of the twelfth century, for Peter Alfonsi drew his experience from the halls of the king of Aragon as well as those of England. Twelfth-century tourneying culture had a homogenizing influence. Dinners and receptions were amongst its social rituals, and participants in the great tourneys of Picardy came from as far afield as Scotland, the Low Countries, the Rhineland and Brittany. A poet like Ramon Vidal dined in a world that included Lombardy, Provence, Auvergne, Barcelona and Aragon. English noble youths were educated at the courts of France, Flanders and Brabant, and one noble Italian boy is known to have been sent by the English-born pope, Adrian IV, to the court of Henry II of England to acquire courtly skills. This Italian *adolescens*, a relative of the future Pope Alexander III, was confided on his arrival to the seneschal of the hall for instruction in its customs and learned its conduct with some ease, as was reported back to Rome.[26] So such men would expect to find the same culture of dining wherever they went and would carry their experience with them into foreign halls.

The orchestrating and presiding presence was that of the host, on whom all depended for the success of the event. It was he or she whose appearance opened the occasion, sometimes in a procession headed by an officer, if the host was of great rank. A lord would take his place at the high (*grant*) table, and select who was to sit at his right hand (usually his wife), while he would seat the highest-ranking cleric or noble at his left; the rest would then take their places, presumably under guidance from a seneschal or other officer of the hall.[27] When the host sat, the rest of the hall did too. An appropriate benediction over the food from the host, or preferably from a visiting or resident cleric, was said before food appeared. The famous portrayal on the Bayeux Tapestry (*c.*1070) of a dinner held at the Norman court of Duke William depicts just this scene. Other sources, like Bartholomew the Englishman, give the cue for the beginning of the commensal ritual as the bringing in of ewers and basins for cleaning the hands, with the order to the

[25] Bartholomaeus Anglicus, *De proprietatibus rerum* (Nuremberg, 1492), Book 6 (*De Cibo*).

[26] For fostering, see above pp. 22–5. For the Italian youth sent from Rome to the Plantagenet court, *The Letters of Arnulf of Lisieux*, ed. F. Barlow (Camden Society, 3rd ser., 61, 1939), 18–21.

[27] As in the supper portrayed in *Ami et Amile*, ed. P. F. Dembowski (Paris, 1987), 37 (ll. 1138–54).

servants: 'Offer water for washing!'[28] According to *Phagifacetus*, after the water should come a procession bearing baskets of fragrant fresh bread, and then the wine was offered before the main courses were served.[29] At the other end of the meal, as the tables were cleared, the concluding ritual was the grace cup followed by the final washing of the hands (and the used drinking vessel) as servants went round at the lord's bidding with basin, towel and jug. Finally, the polite guest should take formal leave of the host, the act signified by the French word *congié*. To omit this was thought to be a serious discourtesy.[30]

We do not only find this universal sequence in encyclopedias and conduct tracts. It also appears in descriptions of meals in the varied twelfth- and thirteenth-century vernacular literature from across the wide spread of the francophone world as early as the supper in which Queen Dido entertained Aeneas at Carthage in the mid-twelfth-century *Eneas*. Then there are the lavish dinners and suppers in *Ami et Amile,* or in the Anglo-Scottish romance *Fergus* and the Franco-Scottish *La Manekine*, or the French *fabliau* 'the Knight and the Priest'. First was the setting of tables with cloths and salt cellars, the affable reception by the host, then the handwashing of the guests, succeeded by formal seating at tables, the bringing in of bread and wine, the courses marshalled by the seneschal and his many minions, served with more wine, with the servants offering water and drawing the cloths to mark the conclusion.[31] These were the essential civilities for the social elite in their central social ritual, and in following them a host would meet a standard of civilization which spanned political boundaries and cultures. The dining hall was the chief school and theatre of European Courtliness, and the consequences of bad performances and reviews troubled anyone who considered he had a place within that world. It was as much a generator of stress in that world as were inter-sexual relations.

THE ANXIOUS HOST

The stresses of dining within courtly society reached up to the top table. The giving of dinners was acknowledged to be central to noble life by Raoul de Houdenc, for whom it was a matter of *grant proece*, one of the feathers of the wing of largesse

---

[28] *Disciplina clericalis*, c. 26; *Liber Urbani*, 48 (l. 1393). This sequence is what Chrétien de Troyes portrays as happening in King Arthur's hall at Oxford, where towels and basins were presented to the guests before they took their seats; *Cligés*, ed. A. Micha (Paris, 1957), 151–2 (ll. 4970–7).

[29] *Phagifacetus*, 16 (ll. 76–91).

[30] S. D. B. Brown, 'Leavetaking: lordship and mobility in England and Normandy in the twelfth century', *History*, 79 (1994), 199–215, esp. 211–14; Kerr, 'Open Door', 335.

[31] *Eneas: roman du xiiᵉ siècle*, ed. J-J. Salverda de Grave (2 vols, Paris, 1964–8) 1: 26 (ll. 823–35), as noted in E. Esposito, 'Les formes d'hospitalité dans le roman courtois', *Romania*, 103 (1982), 201–3, who sees the sequence from welcome to *congié* already established as a central ritual of medieval civil society (*Romania*, 232). See also *Ami et Amile*, ed. P. F. Dembowski (Paris, 1987), 37–8 (ll. 1138–57), 104 (ll. 3242–62); *The Romance of Fergus*, ed. W. Frescoln (Philadelphia, 1983), ll. 1019–1104; Philip de Remy, *La Manekine*, ed. H. Suchier (Paris, 1884), ll. 2275–322; *Durmart le Galois: roman arthurien du treizième siècle*, ed. J. Gildea (2 vols, Villanova, PA, 1965), 1: 260–1 (ll. 9943–93); *Chevalerie et Grivoiserie*, 20–22 (ll. 289–337).

which lifted the reputation of a knight.[32] The English moralist Robert of Ho says much the same and at much the same time, though at greater length:

> My son, you should not be sparing nor miserly in giving dinners, for if you are too close-fisted to your household and to strangers, whatever other virtues you have, if you're reluctant to be generous for this alone you'll lose the credit you may gain for all the rest. But in doing it with all your energy you may achieve great credit for your dinners; you should be aware that when people are at table it is a feast of friendship![33]

Walter Map in the 1180s ironically bemoaned the necessity of offering dinners so as to establish advantageous social links, saying he was bullied into it against his inclinations by his household servants, who had their own agenda. The irony lay in the fact that he was one of the great raconteurs and *bons vivants* of his day (for which see pp. 197–8).[34] It is an unexceptional truism that giving dinners (hopefully) established social dependence or links of friendship.[35] Though we have nothing from the Welsh and Gaelic cultures of Britain in the period of this book to compare with the sources offered by Spain, England, France and the Empire, nonetheless the literature those societies generated describe the same social centrality of hosting (and associated discontents) that we find elsewhere in Europe.[36]

Vernacular sources from the 1150s onwards talk of the quality of food and the variety of courses being a feature of the successful dinner. From 1200 writers can go into exhaustive detail on the variety and expense of the foodstuffs served at the tables of the great: boar, pork, deer, cranes, geese, lamb, beef and gosling, some of them deliberately exotic, such as bear or roast peacock, each with the appropriate wine, and all manner of fish.[37] A host who wished to attain and maintain a high reputation must then give some thought and devote some expense to his entertainments. The great Christian prince Theobald IV of Blois-Champagne (died 1152) was particularly noted for the impressive banquets he offered, displaying plate of great value on his buffet, including two solid gold vessels encrusted with gems of wonderful workmanship and great weight which his uncle King Henry of England had previously used to elicit the admiration of his guests. But as a sincere follower of Christ, the good count also made a point of deploying almoners who would seek

---

[32] *Roman des Eles*, l. 1244.

[33] *Enseignements Trebor*, 124–5 (ll. 2215–27): *Fiz, de ta viande doner/Ne seiez eschars ne aver,/Car se tu trop ferm la retiens/Au[s] privez e as aliens,/Queus autre[s] bontez que tu as/Se tu de donner te feindras/ Per sol itant trestot perdras/Le los que d'autre part avras./Mes done lei a tun poeir/Par ce porras grant los aveir/Ker la viande, ce sachiez/Est aliance d'amistiez/Quant li uns o l'autre menjue.*

[34] *De Nugis Curialium*, 20–22.

[35] P. Freedman, 'Medieval and Modern Banquets: Commensality and Social Categorisation', in *Commensality: from everyday food to feast*, ed. S. Kerner, C. Chou, and M. Warmind (Bloomsbury, 2015), 99–108.

[36] K. Simms, 'Guesting and Feasting in Gaelic Ireland', *Journal of the Royal Society of Ireland*, 108 (1978), 67–100; Ll. Beverley Smith, 'On the Hospitality of the Welsh', 181–94.

[37] Baldwin, *Aristocratic Life*, 174–7. Surviving provisioning accounts from early thirteenth-century England confirm the wide variety of meat and fish routinely purchased for the elite table; *Household Accounts from Medieval England*, ed. C. M. Woolgar (2 vols, British Academy, Records of Social and Economic History, new series, 17–18, 1992–3) 1: 134 (for Eleanor of Brittany in 1225). See generally (though the bulk of the evidence is drawn from sources after 1300), C. Dyer, *Standards of Living in the Later Middle Ages: Social Change in England, c. 1200–1520* (Cambridge, 1989), 55–69; *Great Household*, 111–35.

out the sick beggars and lepers in the streets of the towns where he dined and feed them handsomely from his own heaped dish, a favour otherwise reserved for close friends and privileged courtiers.[38] His contemporary Thomas Becket, the low-born chancellor of Henry II of England, was able in the 1150s to make social capital out of his new wealth through his lavish entertainments. He invited earls and barons, who were all happy to honour his table, and he had his hall swept and decked with fresh rushes and cut flowers in season, so that the knights in the packed rooms could at least sit on clean and fragrant floors if they could not find benches. The buffet of his hall glittered with gold and silver plate, and the food and drink was the most expensive available.[39] It was an important part of Becket's campaign to acquire a high reputation for civility, which he might have regarded as achieved when his royal master confided his eldest son and heir to him to be instructed in Courtliness.

The great man could be an uncomfortable guest for a host who was not so elevated in society. The host was in a quandary; for his own social credit he had to offer as distinctive and handsome an entertainment as his limited resources allowed, not just for the great man but for the household that customarily rode with him. Daniel of Beccles's *Liber Urbani* offers straightforward advice to social aspirants for such occasions:

> Should a clergyman or knight arrive as a guest, you should come out to meet him and greet him warmly. If he is a good friend of yours embrace and kiss him. The best you have should be laid out on the table in a show of honour. All the household should be respectfully put at his disposal, with hay for his horses, and the occasion should call forth sufficient supplies. The guest should not encounter smoky and reeking fires; no hearth should be lighted in the hall if it is overheated. The abundance of the feast should make the diners cheerful; a freehanded generosity should add distinction to the food and drink. The offering of food and drink should satisfy the guests; cheerful stories should be kept back for the appropriate audience; the harmony of all sorts of song should follow on from the serving of wine; as you dine you should toast your guests....A free hand in throwing dinners bestows a reputation for generosity. Carousing attendants should down plenty of all sorts of drink so they don't speak ill of you.[40]

The advice is well and good (though the last remark may well be ironic), but the difficulties in which such a situation placed a man of limited means are graphically illustrated by a surviving letter from the 1190s sent by a Yorkshire parish priest facing an imminent visit from a vice-archdeacon on a Friday, a no-meat day. He had no resources to serve appropriate dishes to his superior, so wrote to a friendly neighbouring abbot begging him to favour him with suitable fish from the abbey pond, 'so that I do not lose my reputation for hospitality by lack of food'.[41]

---

[38] Arnold de Bonneval, *Sancti Bernardi Vita Prima*, in *PL*, 185, cols 300–2.
[39] William fitz Stephen, *Materials*, 3: 20–1. For the evolution of the buffet as display table, Woolgar, *Great Household*, 148–9.
[40] *Liber Urbani*, 77–8, (ll. 2344–56, 2359–61).
[41] N. Vincent 'William Marshal, King Henry II and the Honour of Châteauroux', *Archives*, 25 (2000), 15. See several formulary letters dating to before 1250 for more on this; *Lost Letters*, 79–83.

We occasionally hear of dinners in local society which fulfilled the host's intention and were remembered favourably for a generation and more. When Henry de Dive, a Shropshire knight, paid for an elaborate dinner to mark the birth of a male heir and the purification of his wife, to be held in the hall of the guest house of Wombridge Priory in June 1271, he invited local abbots, knights and worthies, and over twenty years later the servants and guests at the feast recalled its splendour. Not only was the feast remembered, but a written account of it was entered in the (now lost) chronicles of the priory where the dinner was held. However, one of the knights present particularly recalled the uncourtly bustle and noise of the servants of the hall on the occasion, which had echoed throughout the priory precinct. There were always people ready to criticize and cherish for decades memories of failures at table as much as splendid successes.[42]

When Bishop Robert Grosseteste (died 1253) composed a practical guide on household and estate management, and addressed a copy in French after 1245 to his dear friend Countess Margaret de Lacy of Lincoln and Pembroke (died 1266), the management of her hall was one of his main concerns, and it was at the time of the dinner that he thought her most exposed to comment.[43] Grosseteste's advice emphasized order, control and oversight. As a clergyman he was properly insistent that his countess make sure that the surplus food from her table went to the poor as alms, not as a perk to her manservants, whose behaviour always had to be reined in. The bishop made a point of the importance of welcome at the hall door by a courteous and well-spoken staff of doorkeepers, ushers and marshals, for her degree of hospitality would be judged by their words and demeanour. Such officers had been necessities in the noble households of France, the Empire, England and even Wales since before 1100, which is itself testimony to the long history of the formality of entertainment at the top of Western society.[44] The staff of the hall were to be in clean and new liveries, and when the principal guests and retainers were properly ordered and seated, the lesser household who were to eat should enter in an orderly fashion to take their seats respectfully lower down. The countess was to sit centrally on the high table on the dais of the hall so that she should be seen and could also herself monitor how well the dinner was being conducted. Valued guests to either side of her might be served from her own heaped plate as acts of favour. Two officers were delegated to orchestrate the meals and the standard of service, and maintain a decorous level of quiet in the hall; swearing and jostling amongst their underlings were to be firmly dealt with. Following the blessing the appropriate officers should introduce the courses, while three body squires (*vadlez*) circulated

---

[42] TNA: PRO, KB27/145, m. 29. For such celebratory dinners, J. Bedell, 'Memory and Proof of Age in England, 1272–1327', *Past & Present*, no. 162 (1999), 13–14.

[43] *Rules*, 388–406. Oschinsky dated the tract to the countess's first widowhood (1240–42) but failed to notice (p. 398) that one of her named estates was Caversham, Oxfordshire, which she had from her second marriage to Earl Walter Marshal of Pembroke (died 1245) whose death and her liberation into a second widowhood was maybe the reason for the bishop's offering her the copy.

[44] For the noble household in this period, which can be traced back to Carolingian models, Crouch, *Image*, 281–310. For the departmental breakdown of a late thirteenth-century household, Woolgar, *Great Household*, 19–20.

with wine and ale to the high table on the dais and the two side tables.[45] The marshal of the hall should designate servants in a rota so everyone knew his place and job. Confusion and bickering should be avoided at all costs, as smooth competence and calm in their hall reflected on the capacity of the lord or lady in whose presence all this was happening. The countess was warned that there was no escape from her social duty of entertainment. To eat in private was to harm one's reputation (*pru*) and honour.

The northern French 'social realist' novelists of the thirteenth century naturally make much of the dinner and associated entertainments in their evocations of high society and how it operated.[46] Their message, however, echoed a different concern: the more lavish and extraordinary the entertainment, the more honour there was due to the host; it was noble entertainment as an 'alms race'. There is an assumption in modern writings on medieval elite dining that it became increasingly formal and elaborate in the later Middle Ages, when tracts detailing formalized regulations for a highly structured meal begin to survive.[47] But though the limited survival of evidence from the earlier centuries makes it hard to differ with this assumption, taking a broad European perspective there is actually a fair amount of elaboration and formality in the dinners depicted in the sources available before 1300. The detailed description of the *après-tournoi* dining and entertainments offered by a countess of Champagne at Machault (Seine-et-Marne) in the mid thirteenth-century romance *Sone de Nansay* is a case in point, especially as it apparently recalled a historical event. Since it was high summer the countess arranged for two embanked enclosures to be raised, side by side, both entered by secure and well-staffed portals. One was surrounded by stands for viewing the jousting events held within, but the other was dedicated to entertainment, where there was to be dining, singing and partying. That the author was recalling or reporting a real event from the recent past is indicated by his comment that 'the lady who organised this was held in deep affection in her day' and was much regretted on her death as one who had upheld *gentilleche*. He meant her to be taken as the celebrated Countess Blanche, indomitable regent of Champagne from 1201 to 1222, who died in 1229.[48]

In the centre of the pavilion-filled entertainment enclosure was displayed the tourney prize, a magnificent example of the goldsmith's art—a hart fashioned in precious metal and gems—guarded by a detachment of men-at-arms in the livery of Champagne. A bell turret erected in the field gave the signals for the two main meals of dinner and supper, and hot water was at hand for the competitors to freshen up before putting on their party robes and beginning the two principal meals (approximating to lunch and supper). As the clear champion, the young knight Sone had the distinction of being handed to the table by the countess, who

---

[45] *Phagifacetus*, 23 (ll. 250–8), debates whether it is acceptable to let servants surreptitiously sip from the wine they are serving. As we have seen, Daniel of Beccles assumed they would.

[46] Baldwin, *Aristocratic Life*, 162–93.

[47] C. M. Woolgar, *The Culture of Food in England, 1200–1500* (New Haven, 2016), 172.

[48] *Sone de Nansay*, ed. C. Lachet (Paris, 2014), ll. 9789–804. For Countess Blanche, T. Evergates, *The Aristocracy in the County of Champagne, 1100–1300* (Philadelphia, 2007), 36–42.

placed him in the place of honour at her side on the high table, where men and women mingled, laughed and chatted (though not Sone so much, as he was depressed about his love life). The dinner ended with the folding of the countess's napkin and the entry of servants (as in *Quisquis es in mensa*), with basins and ewers for washing hands. All rose as the countess did, and she led them outside the dining marquee on to the lawn, where musicians waited to begin the singing and dancing (*esbanoie*). She sang a work of her own composition, and honoured Sone by asking him to sing the next piece. Supper followed, ending at the hour of vespers with the circulation once more of servants with water for ablutions. Wine, other drinks and fruit were served under the stars before all took themselves off to bed.[49]

We are meant to be impressed and even awed by the degree of organization and expense such a festivity involved. The elaborate nature of the event imagined at Machault does not seem to be fantasy, however. Not only was it likely to be drawn from memories of the past grandeur of the court of Champagne, the entertainment described prefigured a real-life jousting event held by the great tourneyer Edward I of England (reigned 1272–1307) in the open air at Nefyn in North Wales in the summer of 1284, when the collapse of the dance floor in the entertainment enclosure took some of the gloss off the event.[50] This brings us to the principal danger for the host. He may have got credit for the expense and originality of the event, but human nature meant that people tended to remember and even relish the entertainments which went spectacularly wrong, as with the modern equivalent extravaganzas of World Cups and Olympiads, where a personified Nation becomes the anxious host. So the degree of order and control urged on the host was almost obsessive. Failure in the performance of underlings or in the stage management of an ambitious spectacle reflected badly on the reputation of the lord or lady of the hall. Brunetto Latini spelled out the consequences for the host of his failure to plan and stage the event properly and for one who sat gloomily through the dinner he was offering; people would take him either for a grudging miser or a man without the resources to match his social ambitions.[51]

THE INSECURE GUEST

In the balance of power between host and guest, it was the guest who had the most to lose socially from a bad performance at table. A host could always recoup lost prestige by a better-organized subsequent event: unsatisfactory guests did not get invited back; such was common wisdom in the Middle Ages. The particular causes

[49] *Sone de Nansay*, ll. 10231–411, 10565–71, 10647–63, 10712–21. It might be observed that Countess Blanche's son, Count Theobald, was himself a noted singer and poet. The household accounts of Count Robert of Artois for Pentecost 1237 contain items for tables and decorations for an outside entertainment and dinner in the meadows of Compiègne; *Comptes des dépenses de la chevalerie de Robert comte d'Artois à Compiègne en juin 1237*, ed. M. Peigné-Delacourt (Amiens, 1857), 20.
[50] N. Denholm-Young, 'The Tournament in the Thirteenth Century', in *Collected Papers* (Cardiff, 1969), 118–19.
[51] *Tesoretto*, 182 (ll. 155–62), and see observations in Kerr, 'Open Door', 328.

of insecurity for the invited diner emerge as early as the tract *Quisquis es in mensa*. It reveals a nervous sensibility to the impression the guest was making on both his host and fellow diners. Between the opening blessing and the grace cup was the period when ill-instructed and poorly behaved guests could make fools of themselves in so many ways. To begin with, the state of the hands was a pressing concern, as people ate with them and used them to pass on the dishes. According to *Hofzucht*, people who eat without first washing are an utter disgrace (*übel*).[52] Master Reiner, Tannhäuser and Buonvicino della Riva in their day were insistent on clean hands and nails at dinner. A civil guest must come with fingernails pared and make his hands clean and presentable, and then be careful where he put them afterwards, an injunction which included refraining from patting or stroking animals in the hall.[53] The guest should not pick up food and put it back in dishes, finger the salt or sauces, nor idly pick his nose or teeth, nor excavate his ears with his fingers that will then pass around courses. These were transgressive acts which would turn people's stomachs, as would the greasy slick that soiled lips would leave on a common wine cup.[54]

Conversation was always a social danger, especially when combined with wine, and speech needed to be carefully constrained. The penalty for overfamiliarity and overconfidence at a strange table is illustrated by Roger of Howden's tale of an agent of Count John of Mortain in 1194, who carried messages for his lord into England and dined at the table of the archbishop of Canterbury in London. Full of himself and the prospects of his lord's planned seizure of the realm, he could not resist boasting of the coming plot and the count's friendship with the king of France. Though none of his astonished audience laid a hand on him because of their respect (*reverentia*) for the archbishop's table, he was arrested by the mayor of London's men on his way to his lodgings and his confidential papers seized.[55]

A truculent or boastful drunk could disrupt an entire event, but even a passing facetious remark could do as much damage. The way *Quisquis es in mensa* portrays it, a public dinner was a minefield of explosive gaffes for the guest. Fortunate was the one who through self-confidence was oblivious of the impact he had on others, or whose looks and social address allowed her to sail through it all perfectly untroubled. It is clear enough from the literature that behaviour in the hall was one of the most heavily structured areas in medieval social life. This can only be because it was recognized as a point of danger, and there were good reasons why this should be so. People of varying social levels interacted in the hall more freely than else-where in society and in an atmosphere where conversation was expected or at least allowed between them. There was a fine line between respect and familiarity, which was further obscured in practice by the fumes of alcohol. Heavily formalized behaviour was the only defence that could be offered the intelligent youth going out into society to become just such an uneasy guest.

---

[52] *Hofzucht*, 199 (ll. 141–3).
[53] *Phagifacetus*, 15 (ll. 47–60), 18 (ll. 126–8); *Poeti del Duecento* i, 709.
[54] See generally, Whelan, *Making of Manners*, 135–42.   [55] *Chronica*, 3: 236.

I Deference

We find a remarkable concentration in texts associated with dining on the deferential behaviour expected of inferiors towards their social superiors. Commensality in its way expressed and reinforced the social order, and this is frequently acknowledged in its rituals. So in 1194, at a banquet after a crown-wearing in the refectory of the cathedral priory of Winchester, the bishops, earls and barons were seated 'each in their own place according to their condition (*ordo*) and dignity'.[56] The host had a claim on a guest's deference, of course, but a high degree of social sensitivity was expected of a guest to those around him. When the newly knighted Perceval in the *Prose Lancelot* first sat at dinner in King Arthur's hall, he modestly took a place 'at the lower tables where the knights with less of a reputation for prowess might sit'. The Round Table knights sat closer to the king.[57] The dining advice in Facetus expected the youth to know who around his table was his 'greater' and who his 'equal', and behave accordingly. Politeness should comprehend both, but when it came to serving meat, the knife should be offered to the greater man to carve. Then there was the matter of conversation: 'If a great man is eating and drinking with you, don't trouble him until he has eaten his fill.'[58] Facetus inspired the thirteenth-century English author of the poem *Urbain le Cortois* to offer additional advice to the youth most in need of such advice—one who was serving at table—as to when and how to defer, with doffed hat and bent knee.

> Without being told you should take your hat off. As soon as you observe your lord, kneel straight away as of right and to your lady also, for in such a way you show your breeding. [A youth must learn how to serve] so that you best know how to conduct yourself well and courteously at a dinner in public. When the people of quality are seated and you have brought the bread, serve out cups of ale so as to put the guests at their ease and bring in the soup afterwards, following on from that with the other courses. With a polite, fine and affable air as is becoming to the occasion you should be busy about the hall as is appropriate to your work. You must be solicitous to the guests and make much of them. If the dinner is now done you must offer water for the baron and the knight and you should kneel to the chaplain and the rector, for that is what good breeding demands.[59]

Daniel of Beccles developed this theme extensively, if sometimes ironically. He commented that social consequence should be acknowledged from the beginning of the meal: 'You should take care to first offer water to a priest if he is among the guests, and when he is himself washing his hands you should pour out the water for him; afterwards you should offer water to the other guests as their condition (*ordo*) demands.'[60] The host automatically commanded respect, so no guest should turn his back on him; the host's reasonable requests should be honoured; the guest

---

[56] *Chronica*, 3: 248.   [57] *Lancelot*, 6: 191.   [58] *Facetus*, 290, 291.
[59] *Urbain le Courtois*, 399–401. Stephen de Fougères observes that lesser men should genuflect to the great on encountering them; *Livre des manières*, 96 (ll. 1233–4).
[60] *Liber Urbani*, 84 (ll. 2587–90). In a contemporary *fabliau* a priest with hopes of gaining advantage from a knightly guest 'as a great favour had the knight wash first, making him the lord of his hall!'; *Chevalerie et Grivoiserie*, 20 (ll. 296–7).

must beware of pointing at the host or his wife or being seen by them in the indelicate acts of clearing the nose or coughing up food. Other early sources make a point that when a great man is served, it should be on bended knee. That is the posture of the domestic servants depicted serving courses on the Bayeux Tapestry around 1070, and Daniel gave the same advice a century later.[61] Daniel advised that 'Precedence (*ordo*) should be observed in serving food and drink', and 'a course should first be offered to the most important person present'.[62] *Phagifacetus* warns a diner against starting a course before the lord of the hall had himself begun to eat it; not only was it discourteous, it exhibited greed.[63] The ill-bred guest was insensitive to this power play and grabbed at food, sometimes from another person's plate, thus nominating himself as the most important person present at the table and offending the rest. As Robert de Blois was to put it: 'Don't begin by selecting the biggest and finest dishes for your own benefit; it is simply not *cortoisie*.'[64]

Daniel echoed Facetus in saying that if there is a great personage at the table, the well-behaved guest should not commence a conversation with him unless first signalled that it is acceptable.[65] Master Reiner put it bluntly: 'If the host is a great and highly esteemed personage, he will speak if he wants to be spoken to and you shouldn't ever open your mouth to address him.' And if the host does want to be talked to, the guest must be sober and reasoned in what he says, 'like Cato'.[66] The poet Ramon Vidal, writing in the first decade of the thirteenth century, described the caution guests had to exercise in choosing to approach the great in such a venue. He reported a real-life encounter of his own with the great nobleman Robert IV 'le Dauphin' of Clermont-Auvergne (died 1234) in the course of a supper at the count's castle of Montferrand one Christmastide. Ramon was apparently at one point the count's tutor in composition, so had a claim on him.

> It was night, as I recall, a very dark one, after dinner and a fine entertainment next to a bright hearth, in a company of knights and entertainers who were witty, at ease, pleasant, worthy and most accommodating to courtly men, with not a lot of loud shouting or silliness going on there, at least at first. We had enjoyed there an entertainment more satisfying than I am able to describe. Without being asked, the knights made their way to bed, as the time was come for them to do that, for my lord wanted to linger at the hearthside with a friend. At which point, as I saw the time and opportunity to broach something that was causing me anxiety, I went up to him as he was seated on a bench covered with samite. And if ever I found the nerve (*bon cor*) to speak up for myself, I did it then.[67]

---

[61] *Liber Urbani*, 38 (l. 1078). It is worth noting that Abbot Hugh of Beaulieu (Hampshire) was deposed by the Cistercian General Chapter in 1216 for his extravagant lifestyle, including his lavish hospitality to earls and knights, and his employment of a lay household in his hall, where silver dishes were used at table and he was served on bended knee; *Statuta Capitulorum Generalium Ordinis Cisterciensis ab anno 1116 ad annum 1786*, 1, *1116–1220*, ed. J-M. Canivez (Leuven, 1933), 445, 460.

[62] *Liber Urbani*, 83 (ll. 2554, 2562).   [63] *Phagifacetus*, 16 (l. 74), 17 (ll. 111–21).

[64] *Chastoiement des dames*, 148.

[65] *Liber Urbani*, 35 (l. 996); 37 (ll. 1056–7); 38 (ll. 1064–5); 78 (ll. 2375–6).

[66] *Phagifacetus*, 17 (ll. 108–10).

[67] *Nouvelles occitanes*, 47–8 (ll. 158–77). Ramon in fact tells the encounter as happening to a third person, but it plainly was his own experience he relates.

Claim or no claim, Ramon had to choose his time with care: when the great man was relaxed after the sort of successful dinner that gave hosts credit, when everybody was leaving for bed and the count was chatting amiably with a friend on the warm benches ranged around the hearth of the hall. Ramon was in fact breaching etiquette in approaching a lord in his hall without first being invited to do so, hence his confession that he needed 'good heart' to do so. No wonder Master Reiner reflected fondly on the good luck that brought two close friends together at table so they could talk and laugh freely, exempt for once from the need to acknowledge the oppressive dignity of the great or the necessity of deference.[68]

II Bodily Processes

Peter Alfonsi's comments against indelicate eating were copied and repeated by several later writers. Eating should not be a matter of stuffing the face, spraying crumbs everywhere, and choking on food as it is crammed down one's throat; only a glutton behaved that way. Likewise, swilling down a mouthful of food with great gulps of wine would nauseate fellow diners and invite the criticism that a man was a compulsive drunk. Speaking with one's mouth full was not just disgusting but dangerous, as it might lead to choking. Alfonsi's thirteenth-century French translator condemned such behaviour as *vilenie*, the opposite of Courtliness. It was axiomatic that the villein ate in a gross and bestial fashion.[69] The well-instructed diner according to Alfonsi was a temperate and preferably sober person who ate moderately and carefully chewed his mouthfuls before swallowing. Moderation was self-control, and self-control was the essence of decorum in the hall.

Daniel of Beccles's work was even more urgent on the subject. He talked simultaneously about the ill-managed body and the ill-managed meal. Indeed, he related the two in a metaphorical way which would have impressed Claude Lévi-Strauss, to whom table manners were a semantic exercise as much as a category to be examined by cultural anthropology. Daniel was in fact deliberately offering an education in syntax in parallel with one on correct manners. So the grease-smeared hands and lips, phlegm, mucus and wind which revolted Daniel as natural processes were unwelcome metaphors of uncontrol in a formal, cultural syntax where dinners should ideally be as controlled as the diners' bodies. *Quisquis es in mensa* merely warned against picking the nose and belching at table. Daniel's cautions were more graphic:

> You shouldn't excavate at your teeth or gums with a pick. Clean them if you must by rubbing them with a rag. Things which are distasteful to see shouldn't be visible between your teeth. If it's permissible to drink, don't gulp it down.[70]

---

[68] *Phagifacetus*, 24 (ll. 288–95). A comment paralleled by Jean de Meung: 'Whatever a man chooses to think, he can mull it over with a friend as safely as turn it over in his own mind with no fear of persecution'; Meung, *Rose*, 302 (ll. 4693–6).

[69] As, for instance, *Liber Urbani*, 37: 'Don't be like a ploughman (*bubulcus*) and get your dinner all over your tunic' (l. 1034), and, 'if there is a blob of fat on a companion's dish don't point it out, or people will stigmatise you as a peasant (*rusticus*)' (ll. 1037–8).

[70] *Liber Urbani*, 36 (ll. 1017–20).

Then there is this:

> When dining, you shouldn't be like a peasant (*rusticus*) in clearing out your nostrils or coughing up phlegm. If you feel like coughing, keep it to yourself. If you have to belch, remember to look up and away. When clearing your nose in your hand take care to keep what you've blown into it hidden. Don't leave the table to cough up phlegm; if you can't turn around do it by means of a handkerchief.[71]

It is no surprise, then, that Daniel's marked anxiety about mouth, saliva, spillage and mucus was taken up by later writers. The *Hofzucht* ('Propriety in the Hall') of the mid-thirteenth-century Austrian courtier-poet who called himself Der Tannhäuser offered a parallel for the Empire. Tannhäuser intended to point out that lack of refinement at table is characteristic of the agricultural poor (*geburische*), who to him had no place at a civilized table and were antithetical to good manners (*hübsche*).[72] Daniel's expression of revulsion to bodily processes at table also had a purpose more direct than just social metaphor. It was part of his teaching strategy; he wanted his immature pupils to giggle as they unspooled the demanding syntax of his verse. He hoped to disconcert, and by shocking to educate them simultaneously in both acceptable grammar and acceptable behaviour. But his cautions were serious ones, and it is not then unsurprising to find them matched by other writers in different lands who owed nothing to his work. Master Reiner's *Phagifacetus* was a more sober and later attempt at a book reflecting on dining insecurities, and he too warned at length about hawking, choking and belching at table. He also condemned slurping at dishes noisily, poking one's nose into other people's dishes to get a scent of them, and gnawing and grumbling away at bones already stripped white of meat.[73] To these writers the diner's body and appetite can betray him socially into *vilenie*, and inevitable eructations must be concealed and contained so as to maintain social standing.

III Posture

One of the abiding (and still very much current) cautions about behaviour at table is to keep your elbows off the board. *Quisquis es in mensa* makes a point of it in the twelfth century. When Buonvicino della Riva picked up that very point and expanded on it in his fifth and sixth precepts, he cautioned: 'Sit at the table as you ought, courteously, politely, cheerfully and in good spirits; be neither argumentative, gloomy or awkward, and don't keep your legs crossed... if possible do not lean on the table cloth, because it is not polite to rest on your elbows or stretch out your arms.'[74] The instruction about elbows is one that has baffled centuries of childhood. But in part the rule is merely sensible in medieval terms when the guests take their places at benches in halls which might be so crowded (as in the case of Thomas Becket's dinners) that some diners are relegated to seats without access to the table

---

[71] *Liber Urbani*, 37 (ll. 1047–53).
[72] *Hofzucht*, 196 (ll. 47–8), as noted in N. Elias, 'On Medieval Manners', in *The Book of Touch*, ed. C. Classen (New York, 2005), 267.
[73] *Phagifacetus*, 20 (ll. 183–95), 21 (ll. 202–7, 214–17).   [74] *Poeti del Duecento*, 1: 704.

itself. It may be a natural response for a diner to hang over the plate and lean forward, but to do so would be to trespass aggressively on a neighbour's space at a packed board. It would be a use of the body which was counter to the accepted '*hexis*' in society, to use a sociological term. Medieval people tell us why it was so profoundly disturbing a social act and perhaps why it still lingers in current ideas about proper manners. The *Siete Partidas* says specifically that a diner shouldn't hang over food while eating as it gives the impression that he wanted all the food for himself and was warning off others, in other words acting bestially rather than as a civilized human.[75] The issue, however, was not just about personal space and animality. Diners sitting upright allowed servants easier access to the board, and so helped answer the host's concerns about order in the hall.[76] The other point is that an upright posture was a way of advertising to everyone around them the guest's own self-control, though perhaps at the cost of failing to project social ease; so Daniel of Beccles's caution was: 'Don't hang over your meal; you ought to sit silently with a straight back, not staring all around you.' He said gawping around themselves and reaching across the table were what peasants did.[77] Some versions of Facetus stressed this need to keep the body in check, instructing children not to fidget at the table or idly scratch themselves.[78]

IV Intoxication

Alcohol was the great enemy of the civil board and courtly guest, and all were forewarned against it, if the many cautions of Ecclesiasticus and St Paul on the subject were not enough.[79] Medieval sources do not in general praise alcohol for its usefulness in loosening inhibitions at social events; quite the opposite. Trouble was likely to begin once wine and ale were circulating. Peter Alfonsi warned his ideal guest to avoid the appearance of being a drunk (*vinosus*), and therefore out of control of both his limbs and appetite. Daniel of Beccles had much to say on the subject, and was perhaps the first writer to advise containing the risk of drunken argument across the table by keeping off the subjects of politics and money.[80] As much as other writers, he warned against 'Bacchus' and the effects unrestrained drinking can have on public behaviour. Medieval dining culture was as schizophrenic about alcohol as any other. Everyone knew the dangers of a weak head for drink, and of indulgence turning into overindulgence, but people did it all the same and often had to regret it afterwards. So Daniel curtly told his readers: 'Don't slurp down your drink like you're at a bacchanal. Cups should be emptied without

---

[75] *Siete Partidas*, pt 2, tit. 7, ley 5.

[76] Possibilities are listed, in Vasser, *Rituals of Dinner*, 330–2.

[77] *Liber Urbani*, 37 (ll. 1035–6).

[78] As, for instance, Trinity College Dublin, MS 97, fo. 254v.

[79] For the decidedly clerical aversion to excessive drink, J. D. Thibodeaux, *The Manly Priest: Clerical Celibacy, Masculinity and Reform in England and Normandy, 1066–1300* (Philadelphia, 2015), 142.

[80] *Liber Urbani*, 49 (ll. 1410–11). Buonvicino della Riva in his day also urged guests in conversation to keep off troubling issues and stick to uncontentious (*confortose*) subjects, *Poeti del Duecento*, 1: 710.

discredit to the drinker. You should not betray the symptoms of Bacchus in yourself. You shouldn't allow yourself to drink till you're senseless.'[81] Buonvicino della Riva put it succinctly in his fourteenth precept: 'When you're invited to a dinner try not to get drunk even if there is good wine on the table. Someone who gets out of his head offends in three ways: he harms body and soul, and he's wasted the wine he's drunk.'[82]

But as Buonvicino acknowledged in his thirteenth precept, the rituals of the table did not in fact allow any escape from alcohol. The well-ordered dinner began with the circulation of bread and pouring of wine, and it ended with a grace cup. In between these cues a host might well choose to honour a guest by sending a cup of fine wine to him with an invitation to drink from it. The caution to be taken by an inferior guest in such a situation is highlighted as early as Facetus: 'If anyone deigns to offer you a wine cup, take it cheerfully, drink sparingly and return it. Should you be a poor fellow and an inferior, drain the drink down and return the cup empty, but first rinse it thoroughly.'[83] Hosts were sometimes reluctant to let their guests escape intoxication: good and varied wines were a mark of a distinguished table, and it was the duty of a guest that they must be consumed with appreciation. So Lambert of Ardres describes a bumptious Count Baldwin of Guines hosting a dinner for the noble archbishop William of Reims in the 1170s. He honoured his chief guest with the most select wines in his cellar, as varied as the courses of the banquet. The generosity of his hospitality was demonstrated by circulating the flagons of fine wines not just in the hall but on the tables set up outdoors for the lesser guests. His visitors from the Rémois were, unsurprisingly, urgent that water should be served to temper the effects of the abundant strong drink. Count Baldwin took that as a reflection on his hospitality and not only ignored the request, but sent round white wine in small flasks in pretence that it was water, and since most of the visitors were far gone, no one noticed his little joke. When the rather more sober archbishop saw through this and was seething that the count's oppressive generosity had gone further than was acceptable, he insisted mildly but decidedly on having a flask of the supposed water to taste. The count in retaliation went out of the hall, smashed vessels, and kicked over every ewer in the buttery, pretending he was drunk. Lambert seems to imply this sort of behaviour was Count Baldwin's party piece.[84]

Louis IX of France (reigned 1226–70) for his part had different views on the situation alcohol put him in at dinners. His biographer remarked on his policy of adding water to his wine, despite the verdict of his doctors that he had a strong head for drink. He feared, he said, consequences for his health and his ability to

[81] *Liber Urbani*, 34 (ll. 949–52). But since Daniel was not composing a consistent essay on conduct he happily offered contradictory advice to those otherwise inclined: 'You should constantly urge a guest time and again to take a drink; drinkers like to party, and they should be urged to empty their cups, though an honest fellow should need no urging'; *Liber Urbani*, 78 (ll. 2371–4).

[82] *Poeti del Duecento* i, 705.

[83] *Facetus*, 289 (ll. 123–6). Daniel of Beccles gives advice in this social situation so contrary as to be intended to tease his pupils, *Liber Urbani*, 38 (ll. 1066–77).

[84] Lambert of Ardres, 601–2.

tolerate the effects of wine when he was older: 'and that is too dreadful a thing for a self-respecting man (*vaillant home*) to arrive at'.[85] At his table, diluted wine was the rule so far as his servants and the youth of his court were concerned. Mature knights at his dinners had two flasks placed in front of them, one of water and another of wine so they could suit their own taste, though the way it was served gave them a strong hint towards temperance. The contemporary court of Castile had a similar practice. Louis's second cousin Alfonso X of Castile, in his contemporary court regulations, also recommended temperance and diluted wine, especially for youths at dinner, for the benefit of their health as well as for their behaviour.[86] It would seem that the king's table, as the one to which all looked in imitation, might set a higher premium on temperance. One might conclude that the sobriety and good conduct of the king's hall was taken as a metaphor for his conduct of his realm.

V Performance

For all the constraints that writers want to urge on speech at dinner, to the extent that some recommend being more or less mute to avoid saying the wrong thing, there were expectations that a guest might by contrast seek credit through his words and music, if he had the nerve and the talent. Dinners were followed by all sorts of entertainments, of which communal singing, musical performance and dancing were the least challenging; competitive games and gambling were less innocent postprandial amusements.[87] Hosts generally hired entertainers to sing during the meal accompanied by viols, flutes or reed pipes, while others would be employed to entrance the sated diners as storytellers or to orchestrate word games (such as may be represented by the *Proverbe au Vilain*).[88] The *fabliau* 'The Buffet' lists many sorts of diversion professionals might offer in a great man's hall: play-acting as comical drunks or fools, singing, playing instruments, reciting debate poems, telling jokes, or indeed embarking on amusing *fabliaux*.[89] But, as we have seen, the guests at the Countess of Champagne's entertainment at Machault were expected themselves to sing for their supper. Robert de Blois regarded music-making for women as a duty both to society and to self:

[85] Jean de Joinville, *Vie de Saint Louis*, ed. J. Monfin (Paris, 1995), 10, 248.

[86] *Siete Partidas*, pt 2, tit. 7, ley 6.

[87] Such as Walter de Coinci's account of the *karoles* and *baleries* after the banquet following the marriage of a young clerk of Pisa; *Les miracles de la Sainte Vierge*, ed. l'Abbé Pocquet (repr. Geneva, 1972), col. 638 (ll. 340–3). The romance of Durmart says that, after the meal was cleared, 'many sang to viols, and others to harps, and as many played at dice, backgammon and chess, pursuing such amusements with enthusiasm'; *Durmart le Galois*, ed. J. Gildea (2 vols, Villanova, PA, 1965), 1: 10 (ll. 368–74).

[88] As in the dinner described in *Gille de Chyn*, 31 (ll. 784–7). By contrast, Thomas Becket as archbishop would not allow music at table, preferring learned discussions amongst the clergy; *Materials*, 3: 233.

[89] *The French Fabliau*, B.N. MS 837, ed. and trans. R. Eichmann and J. DuVal (2 vols, London, 1984) 2: 214.

If you are in the company of important people, and you are asked to play, you must in no way be reluctant. Nor should you resist the urge to play for your own amusement when you are in your chambers.[90]

The literature associated with the tourney culture of the twelfth and thirteenth centuries, not least the biography of William Marshal, makes it clear that the public meals he attended from the 1160s to the 1180s expected entertainments from the guest. The supper given to the successful defenders of Neufchâtel-en-Bray in 1166 was notable for loud reminiscence about the day's action and practical joking (of which the boy Marshal was the butt). Of course, it was the great men around the table who did the pranking, not their dependants. In due course, when in 1183 the Marshal was himself the host offering a generous table, he too played a joke on his guests, though being a courtly man the joke was not at the guests' expense but at his own.[91] Marshal's contemporary, Robert of Ho, put a pragmatic spin on this social duty, which no doubt the Marshal would have echoed. He urged a youth with any talent to volunteer promptly to tell tales and sing in hall, as that way he'd earn popularity and friends. He also warned against going on interminably and antagonizing the audience, something Jane Austen's depiction of her Regency society in *Pride and Prejudice* would in due course famously echo.[92]

One of the ways guests like Marshal might entertain was by the adroit telling of an anecdote, and there are signs from his biography that he was renowned in his day as a raconteur. Orderic Vitalis in the 1120s summons up a picture of the hall of the lady Isabel de Montfort, sitting around with young knights who were intriguing the company by recounting their dreams.[93] An accomplished diner who could tell a good tale or amuse the gathering gained popularity and notice, and was invited back. A fine example of such a raconteur at the Plantagenet court was the Ustinovian cleric, Walter Map. After Walter's death in 1208, his friend Gerald of Wales recalled for King John's benefit some advice Walter once gave him: '[He] used often to say whenever we met, in his usual witty and courteous way: "Master Gerald! You have written a good deal and have much yet to write, while I just talk a lot. You produce books and I produce words....I get some return from my conversational ability, but you are likely to get less feedback from your learned works, which are incomprehensible both to illiterate princes and the wider public".'[94] In fact, as Gerald knew, Walter wrote a considerable amount, and not least of his offerings was his *Courtier's Trifles*, which amounts to a large and miscellaneous book of anecdotes, many supernatural, some macabre, and some religious; some are tales of marvels and others historical reminiscences. Walter's mind was a warehouse of tales he had read or heard, and some he had himself coined, and he called them stories 'such as may serve either to excite merriment or edify morals'.[95]

[90] *Chastoiement des dames*, 147 (ll. 463–8).
[91] *History of William Marshal* 1: ll. 1107–60, 6817–52.
[92] *Enseignements Trebor*, 129 (ll. 2327–45).   [93] Orderic, 4: 216–18.
[94] *Expugnatio Hibernica*, ed. A. B. Scott and F. X. Martin (Dublin, 1978), 264–5.
[95] *De Nugis Curialium*, 210.

These were the sort of anecdote Walter purveyed at dinners, where his reputation as a raconteur brought him a 'return' and his *Courtier's Trifles* were an attempt to recycle them so as to bid for some literary reputation (though the book was not in the end published generally). His contemporary at the Angevin court, Gervase of Tilbury, produced what must have been another such, the *Liber Facietarum* ('Book of Courtly Matters') dedicated to the Young King Henry of England (reigned 1170–83). It does not survive, and though his subsequent and massive *Otia Imperialia* ('Tales for An Emperor's Leisure') does, it is a more encyclopedic and literary production. However, Gervase favours us in it with a description of a supper given one winter's night by a nobleman, after which the guests resorted to the warmth of the hearth 'and as is the custom among the nobility, turned their attention to recounting the deeds of people of old, or else settled down to listen'.[96] The compilers of the *Siete Partidas* of Alfonso the Wise's court of Castile describe the same culture, where guests and poets of the court were expected to tell and sing tales of deeds of wars and heroes of old in the course of dinner, or in the relaxation afterwards and so to amuse and inspire the gathering.[97] The various twelfth-century courts of the Angevin dynasty were famous for their entertainments in their day—a fact modestly conceded even by their rival Louis VII of France (reigned 1137–80), at least according to that modest man of the court, Walter Map.[98] We can see in the conversation pieces Walter and his colleague Gervase offered just such performative examples of Angevin dining culture.

THE LIVING HELL OF MEDIEVAL DINING

As with the writers on female conduct, we have to be cautious of the dominant voice of writers on dining etiquette. This is not so much because writers on dining derived their basic precepts from an international Latin schoolroom literature of the first half of the twelfth century meant to educate and socialize the child. The striking commonality is the way these writers talk of dining with what often amounts to trepidation, which had nothing to do with reception of others' views. Even when pragmatic thirteenth-century writers such as Master Reiner and Buonvicino della Riva offer more expansive and independent treatments which are based on their daily lives, they do not avoid the anxiety projected by the school-books, which are intended to alert the youth to sources of social danger he might not be aware of. The end result is to project an image of medieval dining culture as nervous and insipid, where its practitioners spend their time literally on the edge of their seats. We can imagine that the reality was not quite so edgy, though finding sources with which to contrast the handbooks is not easy. But it is striking that

---

[96] *Otia Imperialia*, ed. and trans. S. E. Banks and J. W. Binns (Oxford, 2002), 14, 670.
[97] J-L. Hague Roma and P. Zambrana Moral, 'Banquets et manières de la table du roi dans le droit des *Siete Partidas*', in *Banquets et manières*, 56–7.
[98] *De Nugis Curialium*, 451.

the dinners as depicted in literature associated with tourneying culture are rather more free and joyous events, if undeniably raucous. Laughter, friendship, singing, dancing and amusement are more prominent in these sources than anxiety.

It would not do to entirely discount the urgency of the strictures which dining literature broadcast, however. Its writers are focused on the sort of dinners where career and social contacts are at stake, not the sort of entertainment where everybody is blowing off steam after a hard day's sport, all knights together. To begin with, the handbooks are consistent across several European realms throughout the twelfth and thirteenth centuries. They offer answers to urgent social concerns that were common to any medieval court—the concerns of hosts and guests alike. Master Reiner, who seems otherwise a cheerful sort, explicitly tells us that joy at table is a rare event, and can only be experienced when the chances of seating place a diner next to a trusted friend, with whom one might get safely drunk and happily silly. Uncontained raucousness and drunkenness were in fact common at table, which was why the tracts are so urgent about self-control, the fruit no doubt of men waking up the next day wondering how in God's name they could have said and done anything so stupid. Other medieval diners were going to have a good time whatever the dangers. So cup after cup of wine was downed, laughter and practical jokes became loud and intrusive, and behaviour became transgressive, as in the dinners hosted by Count Baldwin of Guines. The fact that the social elite was warned in thirteenth-century French, Spanish, English and German sources alike about the necessity of dining in public, and not to take their meals in their private chambers, is enough to tell us that as many people found the demands of their dining culture difficult as found it enjoyable and hilarious.[99]

Perhaps the most telling witness to the diffidence—or even hostility—of some medieval people to the culture of the hall is Raoul de Houdenc's satirical choice to depict Hell as a princely dinner in his *Songe d'Enfer*, the host being, of course, Satan. Raoul was a poet-knight of the Beauvaisis, writing in the first years of the thirteenth century, so he was a man who must as often have been a host himself as he was a guest at the tables of the great. Like King John of England, Raoul's Prince of Darkness dined with the hall doors wide open so all could enter, though for different reasons. Water for washing and cleanliness was notably lacking in the description; all was stench and foulness. The cloths and napkins laid before the diners by his seneschal were made from the skins of whores and usurers; the fine meat dishes were cannibalized moneylenders, thieves, charlatans, prostitutes and heretics, well basted and oiled and in a suitably hot sauce. As a good host, Satan offered cuts around from his own plate. The second dish was the roasted tongues of fraudulent lawyers, followed by a pasty made of superannuated prostitutes, followed by an endless succession of imaginative confections of murdered children (instead of toasted cheese), bloody mercenaries, hypocrites, renegade clergy and sodomites. Since it was Hell, there was abundance of food, but little to drink. Raoul was, of course, satirizing the greed and competitive luxury of contemporary

---

[99] For literature in praise of excess in food and wine, Bumke, *Courtly Society*, 200–2.

fine dining. He was also satirizing the hypocrisy and hollowness of the courtly
entertainment, for despite the foulness of the banquet he was eagerly pressed by
Satan after the event for compliments on his entertainment, and, like such men
as Walter Map, was obliged to pay for it by performing verses to the postprandial
throng on the darkest depravities of humanity.[100]

---

[100] *The Songe d'Enfer of Raoul de Houdenc: an edition based on all the extant manuscripts*, ed.
M. T. Mihm (Tübingen, 1984), 76–88 (ll. 407–658). One might also compare the depiction of the
Antichrist presiding over a hellish tourney dinner in Huon de Méry, *Le Tournoi de l'Antéchrist*, ed.
G. Wimmer and trans. (Fr.) S. Orgeur (2nd edn, Medievalia, no. 13, Orléans, 1995), ll. 386–418.
For literature against gluttony, Y. Roguet, 'Gloutonnerie, Gourmandise et Caquets', in *Banquets
et Manières*, 257–77.

10

The Enemy

ONESELF

That you are your own worst enemy is a belief far older than Nietzsche, for it was implicit in most of the medieval conduct literature we have dealt with here. Occasionally, it is even explicit. Sordello da Goito ruefully began his *ensenhamen* with the sentiment, 'there is no opponent more fell than a man's own heart'.[1] The purpose of Sordello and his like was, after all, to signal points of social danger where you can let yourself down badly in your social performance. Usually it was the tongue which was portrayed as the likeliest traitor to the male social body (though the penis was a runner-up). Daniel of Beccles, who had a lot to say on the subject, put it graphically: 'A tongue may lack a bone but it can still cause bone to be crushed.'[2] So universal a source of advice as Facetus is full of warnings about incautious speech: 'Don't talk big about yourself in case you are taken for a fool'; 'Don't boast because praise of oneself sullies the mouth'; 'You should never talk dirty about women but respect those you meet as far as you can'; 'A man who speaks too much may be looked down upon, even though he be an honest fellow; uncontrolled, tiresome and insolent speech gets to be a total nuisance'.[3] These were sentiments that were drilled into the heads of medieval children from their time in the *parva schola* onwards, and they were recycled when the children became adults, as in Daniel's distichs in *Liber Urbani*:

> So my friend be very careful as to who, what, when and why you are talking; your speech should be good-natured as well as polite and cultured. No foul language should come out of your mouth, it has no place in the speech of a man of discretion. Filthy speech is to the detriment of the one who uses it, not the one who hears it, so take care you don't use bad language.[4]

Likewise, Robert of Ho had this to say, in a passage that also references the even more venerable cautions on speech provided by biblical wisdom literature:

> My son, running off at the mouth in company is not the best policy. A man who can't keep his opinion to himself can hardly avoid blurting out things better kept quiet and when he has finally spilled everything people say: 'It's that moron!' But if he'd kept himself to himself he would have been regarded as a man of some depth.[5]
>
> [cf. Prov. 10:9; Eccles. 5:2]

---

[1] *Ensenhamens d'Onor*, 202 (ll. 80–1): *Guerrier non a om ni plus mal de son cor.*
[2] *Liber Urbani*, 24 (l. 649): *Osse carens lingua quandoque teri facit ossa.*
[3] *Facetus*, 288, 290, 291, 292, 293.   [4] *Liber Urbani*, 24 (ll. 663–8).
[5] *Enseignements Trebor*, 34 (ll. 55–62).

We have already seen how foolish speech at dinner, where alcohol could let loose even the most guarded of tongues, was perceived as one of the prime dangers to reputation within courtly society. Some advised that saying nothing at all to a great man who was your neighbour at table was preferable to saying something that would reflect badly on you. In the proverbial words of Garin lo Brun, 'a reticent person is thought more of than someone who spouts drivel.'[6] At the end of the twelfth century Peter the Chanter deployed Scripture, the Fathers, and indeed Cato to demonstrate theologically and pragmatically that taciturnity was the wisest of courses in the world where loquacity and garrulousness spawned flattery, boasting, argumentativeness and social gaffes.[7] But taciturnity was only sidestepping the difficulty. Daniel of Beccles put the nature of the inevitable danger of sparking enmity by ill-chosen words rather well:

> If you want to give someone the rough edge of your tongue give some thought to who you are, who it is you're addressing and what sort of person he may be. You should beware of provoking someone to evil deeds by what you say, for it may be that one day you say such severe things that he will never again like you.[8]

Being argumentative was one danger, and being too clever by half and too effusive in praise were ones that Ramon Vidal warned courtly society about:

> Don't go over the top in praising honourable conduct. Don't attempt to be too clever or too simple-minded, nor choose to be downbeat, too withdrawn or too attentive and never choose to go overboard in anything for excess makes you as unpopular as easy-going moderation gains you respect.[9]

In languages where the second person singular denoted familiarity and the plural respect, as in German, there was also the minefield of deference to negotiate. The margravine and king's daughter, Elizabeth of Thuringia, wanted to advertise her humility by insisting her maidservants call her 'du', though the trespass against the habitus represented by that request caused the poor women some real discomfort.[10] Facetus had as much to say about gauging deference as it did about the dangers of speech: 'You should be humble enough, but not overly so, a man who is too subservient may be taken for a fool. Don't be too close up and friendly; you need to avoid anyone who wants to be too cosy.'[11] Because Facetus makes such a theme of it, twelfth-century writers who took it as their inspiration, such as Daniel of Beccles and Robert of Ho, also discoursed on the trials of deference at length. The *Liber Urbani* suggested one defence against gaffes was an embrace of highly formalized manners:

> Since you ought to stand while your lord is pleased to stand, when he decides to sit you can sit down without any instruction if you are a knight or a cleric, though the servants should stay on their feet. You should not take a seat next to your lord unless

6 *E·l termini d'estiu*, 64 (ll. 341–2).   7 *Verbum abbreviatum*, in *PL*, 205, cols 194–6.
8 *Liber Urbani*, 25 (ll. 695–701).   9 *Abril issia*, 136 (ll. 1724–30).
10 *Dicta Quatuor Ancillarum*, in *The Life and Afterlife of St Elizabeth of Hungary: Testimony from her Canonization Hearings*, ed. K. B. Wolf (Oxford, 2010), 213.
11 *Facetus*, 287 (ll. 27–30).

asked to do so. If you are sitting you should not stand for anyone unless instructed. Should the lord please to rise, you should get up promptly.'[12]

Enseignements do therefore try at least to alert the social actor to erect social defences against his own ineptitude or propensity to betray himself, which is some testimony to the extent of the danger. But there were, of course, other potent enemies against whom defence was difficult, for they were not open ones.

RESTRAINT

Self-control was at the core of success in a courtly world, if success is defined as evading conflict. It could be justified theologically and pragmatically. The godly evangelical Henry Venn (1725–97) summed up the theology of restraint in a later contentious age in his injunction never on any account to dispute: 'it is the work of the flesh'. It is, then, no great surprise to find that the ever-pragmatic William Marshal did not give in to his resentment and did not seek to punish actively those who worked behind his back against his interests at the Young King's court, though its abrupt dissolution with the young man's unexpected death in 1183 would have taken any point out of such an action in any case. The composers of texts which reflect on superior conduct would have approved of such forbearance, for that is the strategy they recommended. In the same tone of weariness as the biography adopted, Marshal's contemporary Daniel of Beccles recommended forbearance to his pupils: 'A tongue dripping with poison is to be expected of evil men. When the liar broadcasts his filthy rumours about you, carry on regardless, as the truth shames lies.' The author of *Winsbecke* was perfectly eirenic in his recommendation to young men who have been slighted: 'Bear hatred and vengeance toward no one. Be benevolent towards your enemies.'[13]

Behind this egregious forbearance lay the cautions of Solomon, the exhortations of the Sermon on the Mount and a consciousness that anger had been defined by the Church since the time of Gregory the Great as a mortal sin which imperilled salvation.[14] These were not minor considerations to the laity of the time, as several academic approaches have tended to confirm, whether from the viewpoint of the cloister or from medieval fictional literature. In a summative study drawn from both such sources, Stephen D. White offered an instructive listing of anger vocabulary and demonstrated its frequency in twelfth-century Latin and French literature, which would indicate that it was an emotion which very much troubled medieval minds in its deplorable consequences.[15] The discourse of Ramon Llull on anger as a mortal sin is as much pragmatic as theological: anger blinds understanding

---

[12] *Liber Urbani*, 42 (ll. 1200–5).　　[13] *Liber Urbani*, 15 (ll. 391–3); *Winsbecke*, 86, c. 39.

[14] For the ecclesiastical teaching on anger, urged on the faithful through church sculpture as much as texts, L. K. Little, 'Anger in Monastic Curses', in *Anger's Past: the Social Uses of an Emotion in the Middle Ages* (Ithaca, 1998), 14–27, and more broadly in A. Classen, 'Anger and Anger Management in the Middle Ages. Mental-Historical Perspectives', *Mediaevistik*, 19 (2006), 21–50.

[15] S. D. White, 'The Politics of Anger', in *Anger's Past*, 134–9.

and cripples speech; the angry man takes no heed of the consequences of his actions and once his emotion has ebbed he will be left with a mortifying burden of guilt. Since an angry man will say or do anything in his passion, the results will be evil, and everything done in anger tends to wickedness. One can guard against a liar, he said, but there is no defence against an angry man.[16] Clerical minds certainly expected little forbearance in their fellow men. In his *Dialogue*, Caesarius of Heisterbach reflected that annoyance and resentment may be natural enough, but sniffed: 'Amongst lay people getting angry and resentful is of no consequence, and a man who doesn't lose his temper is ridiculed by the rest.'[17]

Despite Caesarius's views, however, the independent lay viewpoints we can recover from non-theological medieval literature which is intended to form and reflect on lay conduct directly are actually not too different in their strictures on resentment from clerical sources. Around 1200 the literary knight William de Lorris reserved a niche in his allegorical wall of shame around the Garden of the Rose for the figure of *Haine* (Hatred, Malice). Just as in contemporary sculptural depictions of anger, its nature was reflected in its hideous appearance of choler and uncontrolled, bestial fury. William tells us that *Haine* was prone to quarrel and apt to the most shameful behaviour (*cuivertage*); it was tellingly set in the wall in a space between Felony and Baseness.[18] Twelfth-century vernacular proverbs have a perspective to offer on anger which aligns surprisingly well with that of the theologians, for the musings of John of Salisbury or Geoffrey of Vinsauf on the subject are not dissimilar to the concise wisdom of popular sayings. That may well be because the problem of anger and its disruptive consequences for society is one that was pretty much obvious to all classes and conditions of people. One proverb recorded in the 1170s had it that 'An angry man doesn't give a toss' (*Ireus n'a conseil*), and another, 'A festering hatred begets much evil' (*Veille haïne fait moult mal*), meaning that anger sets judgement to the winds and turns in on itself. In explaining the moral of the former example, the *Proverbe au Vilain* reflects that: 'an otherwise sensible man undoes any good he has done by losing his temper and he regrets it ever afterwards; if he had given it some thought he would have seen the stupidity, but anger knows no restraint.'[19] As another popular saying has it, 'It's a poor revenge that adds to the shame.'[20] Laymen understood that human (as opposed to divine) anger might recognize no limits to retaliation, and the actions inspired by resentment were not usually proportional to the offence. Anger was the enemy to justice and reason and disruptive to society. It was self-destructive, for it could turn in on itself and provoke despair and suicide, of which Judas Iscariot was the defining instance in popular theology.

---

[16] *Doctrine*, 141.

[17] *Dialogus Miraculorum*, ed. and trans. (Ger.) H. Schneider and N. Nösges (5 vols, Turnhout, 2009) 2: 716.

[18] Lorris, *Rose*, 54–6 (ll. 139–51).

[19] *Proverbes français*, nos 961, 2474; *Proverbe au Vilain*, no. 137. John of Salisbury in *Policraticus* likewise focuses on and deplores the irrationality of the angry man, as pointed out in Classen, 'Anger and Anger Management', 28.

[20] *Proverbes français*, nos 1185, 2351.

Courtly literature therefore has a good deal to say on the subject of not giving in to anger and hatred. The thirteenth-century conduct poem *Urbain le Cortois* urges the wise man to disengage quickly when he finds himself in a confrontation: 'If you have an enemy bear this in mind if he gives you abuse: I beg you for the love of God not to reply in kind but get quite away from the place.'[21] The same generation produced a very similar exhortation in the moral *enseignement* called the *Doctrinal de Courtoisie*:

> If you observe a fool in a grand passion you shouldn't in any way provoke him in company; for if he should attack or abuse you and commit some outrage because of you, you will indeed carry some share of the disgrace, and so you will get the more blame for his madness.[22]

Philip de Novare, as accomplished a courtier as William Marshal in his day, provided a good deal of pragmatic guidance to youth on the subject of anger, hatred and vengeance in his society, and his warning about unrestrained anger and its consequences is also framed in terms not dissimilar to those of the proverbial literature:

> An active man of affairs does not easily forget a grudge and his mind will dwell on vengeance. He who does wicked and sinful deeds and makes no amends for them is an object of distaste both to God and man, and so evil comes of it, and that very soon, and then there will be grief and woe.[23]

Philip urged the young and hopeful careerist to remember that the quality which most distinguished the successful magnate was restraint (*mesure*) under provocation, a sermon for which the career of William Marshal would indeed have been a powerful *exemplum*.[24] Robert de Blois provided a meditation on just that subject for the benefit of the young courtier in thirteenth-century Capetian France, echoing as he did the proverbial wisdom of the villein:

> Do not attempt retribution while you are enraged. Many a man has lost his reputation through his anger and ill temper. A man in a rage has no idea what he is doing. Deep-seated anger baffles perception, reason and restraint; when a man lacks judgement he is at the mercy of his rage and resentment, he very much worsens any situation and will regret it for a very long time.[25]

The pragmatic good sense in bridling anger is a theme in literature that has not perhaps had as much investigation as it should, as opposed to the theme of indulging it. But it is to be found, as in the *fabliau* 'The Priest and the Knight', where a young knight in embarrassed circumstances is gratuitously patronized and sneered at by an uncivil cleric. Despite being *plains d'ire*, the man contained his rage and responded mildly, persuading the cleric to give him hospitality, which he then thoroughly abused by playing on the priest's avarice to take his niece's virginity, humiliate him with his concubine, and walk off with a large part of his fortune.[26]

---

[21] *Urbain le Courtois*, ll. 160–5.   [22] *Doctrinal*, 66–7 (ll. 39–44).
[23] *Quatre Tenz*, 25.   [24] *Quatre Tenz*, 76–7.
[25] *Enseignement des Princes*, 128–9 (ll. 1251–61).
[26] *Chevalerie et Grivoiserie*, 4–78.

So he certainly wanted and indeed got his revenge, but in his own time and on his own conditions.

FAILURE OF CONTROL

The pragmatic idealization of *mesure* in the behaviour of the courtly *preudomme* by contemporaries is very much at odds with an old theme in scholarship on the Middle Ages, which stems from the works of historians of the art of the late Middle Ages and Renaissance, not least the nineteenth-century studies of Jacob Burckhardt. Johan Huizinga was the most influential of them, and he took to the limit Burckhardt's dismissive view that the people of the stage of civilization which preceded the supposedly humanistic and sophisticated one Burckhardt preferred were uncontained and childlike in their passions and unthinkingly violent and indeed sadistic in their conduct. For our purposes, it is this polemical observation of Huizinga's which long coloured the study of medieval social history: 'After the close of the Middle Ages the mortal sins of pride, anger and covetousness have never again shown the unabashed insolence with which they manifested themselves in the life of preceding centuries.'[27] As we have seen, such behaviour may well have been displayed, but it did not in fact gain anyone credit in the period of this book. In terms of pride and anger, more recent studies have found that males in a variety of medieval societies might very well compete and take offence at perceived slights, but that the social milieu in which they moved had ways of averting confrontation—such, for instance, as earnest warnings and measures against unmixed wine and resulting drunken argument—and that their society possessed ways and means to mitigate conflict once it had begun.

Medieval sources point the finger at one particular group in society most likely to offend in the matter of aggression and heedless conflict—the young. If (as is argued in Chapter 5) a defining quality of the mature *preudomme* was *mesure*, then a lack of it was to be expected in young male aspirants to that status. Since contemporary *enseignements* were directed at youth, they naturally contain an abundance of reflections on the inadequacy and instability of the young, and urgent advice as to how they should escape its consequences, which was by taking to heart the example their elders supposedly offered in self-control. Thomasin of Zirclaria compared the habitual behaviour of the young aristocrat to a drunkard: unrestrained, loud, boastful and intolerably boisterous.

> When young people leave the court they should be thinking quietly to themselves: 'That was how that good knight behaved at court today; I must try very hard to emulate him.' Anyone who does not take note of what he sees will not improve himself. He might just as well be in the woods as at court.[28]

---

[27] J. Huizinga, *The Waning of the Middle Ages: a Study of the Forms of Life, Thought and Art in France and the Netherlands in the XIVth and XVth Centuries* (London, 1924), 18. For this presupposition and its sources, S. D. White, 'The Politics of Anger', in *Anger's Past*, 128–31; B. H. Rosenwein, 'Worrying about Emotions in History', *American Historical Review*, 107 (2002), 821–45.

[28] *Welsche Gast*, 10 (quotation at ll. 343–54).

Both Garin lo Brun and Philip de Novare emphasized the danger to which his habitual rashness exposed the young male, not least sudden death (which in Philip's view was inevitably followed by damnation). Philip reflected on the innate tendency in the young to frustration and anger, the mortal sin to which they are particularly subject, and which threatened their salvation:

> Most jobs they have to do need skills and experience, so they just get annoyed. The anger of the young is too unrestrained, and bursts out without warning as a result of those two sources of irritation: the frustration itself, and their own youthful nature.[29]

Philip was in fact deterministic in his view of the behavioural problems of the young male: 'It is hardly avoidable for the young to misbehave; Nature pushes them into it. It has long been said that no one can avoid trouble when he is young.'[30] Like Thomasin, Philip urged that a young aristocrat should remain in tutelage to wiser and older heads, and be restrained from gathering around him a household of his own age, where he would encounter no restraint and much encouragement to dangerous behaviour. This indeed is what a thirteenth-century canon of Wigmore complained about in regard to the *losenger* associates of the young patron of his abbey, Roger de Mortemer, who did nothing but pander to his worst impulses.[31]

Another sort of behavioural determinism which has emerged in recent writing is the place of gender expectations in medieval behaviour and, beyond that, the way hormones can be said to act on the psyche of the male at any stage of life. The medieval framing of what was expected of the male leaves no doubt that they were expected to compete, and females to cheer them on. A succinct and proverbial comment, coined or repeated by Daniel of Beccles, rather gloomily sums up gender expectations in the twelfth century: 'Vengeance, like a whore, cheers on brawling men.'[32] The innate competitiveness of the male is registered in medieval literary sources by the centrality they award to the achieving of 'prowess' in a military career, which can only be done by competing against and defeating other males.[33] Indeed, it has been argued that medieval masculinity could only be established in the constant tussle for dominance with other males, whether in debate, extreme personal austerity or physical competition.[34] The modern take on the behavioural effects of male physiology is not, however, willing to believe uncritically that male behaviour is determined by endocrinal balance, only that it may be influenced by testosterone towards 'male-typical' emotions, meaning aggression and anger.[35] It is another moot point as to how this behavioural pattern which medieval writers

---

[29] *Quatre Tenz*, 22 (c. 35).   [30] *Quatre Tenz*, 36 (c. 61).

[31] *Historia fundationis prioratus de Wigmore*, in R. Dodsworth and W. Dugdale, *Monastici Anglicani* (2 vols, London, 1673) 2: 218.

[32] *Liber Urbani*, 25 (l. 687) *est meretricalis certantibus ultio talis*.

[33] A pioneering study here is R. W. Kaeuper, *Chivalry and Violence in Medieval Europe* (Oxford, 1999), 119–60, who identifies the search for *proesce* as a chivalric as much as a male characteristic.

[34] Karras, *Boys to Men*, 10–12, 47–53, is a statement of this position. See also, for competitiveness in willingly bearing suffering (*ascesis*) for the sake of salvation, Kaeuper, *Holy Warriors*, 116–30, though it might be argued that this was a virtue to which women could lay better claim.

[35] Without claiming anything more than surface knowledge of this subject, I cite here these current studies: J. Archer, 'The influence of testosterone on human aggression', *British Journal of Psychology*, 82 (1991), 1–28; D. B. O'Connor, J. Archer, and F. C. W. Wu, 'Effects of testosterone on mood, aggression

clearly had identified was related in the medieval mind to male physiology. There was certainly a contemporary belief that a castrated male's behaviour was milder than one who was in possession of his testicles. Jean de Meung commented at length on Abelard's notorious neutering, suggesting that castration robbed a male of his boldness (*hardemenz*) and the natural disposition of brave men: 'castrated men are perverse, malicious and cowardly because they possess the disposition of women; to be sure no eunuch has any bravery whatsoever in him.'[36] The best we can therefore say in this regard is the reductionist view that it was expected of medieval males to be aggressive, and of wiser men to curb the excesses of their natural disposition.

THE SECRET ENEMY: THE *LOSENGER*

A thirteenth-century canon of a small Herefordshire monastery, which suffered a good deal from the hostility of the son of its founder, reflected (in French) on this misfortune in a world-weary way: 'As one would expect from one of his age, the lad was cheery, immature and unfixed in his disposition but first and foremost he was wilful. His many intimates had little sense, and gave him only the sort of advice that would please but benefit him little; such is the way of those many *losengers* who make it their business to curry their lord's favour, which all too often ends up harming his interests.' Happily, this prodigal son of the Church in due course saw the error of his ways and became a good neighbour to the canons of Wigmore, 'at which all good folk rejoiced, but the ill-disposed were outraged'.[37] As we have seen (in Chapter 7), the *losenger* with his flattery and disguised but relentless malice was a stock character of twelfth- and thirteenth-century courtly literature, so it is no surprise to find him turning up in monastic histories: he and his deceit were just what you could expect to meet in the fallen world. The word itself was devised to tell us as much. A *losenger* principally operated through flattering praise (MFr. *los*, Occ. *laus*), which was a cloak for his malignity. It was a word that even migrated into the literature of the Empire as MHG *losaer*, directly absorbed into German from the Occitan culture of the south.[38]

Of course—as we have seen—any courtier or household servant was recommended to cloak his real feelings, so courtiers stigmatizing others as *losengers* might well be regarded as *losengers* themselves. Gerald of Wales, not a natural hypocrite,

and sexual behavior in young men', *Journal of Clinical Endocrinology and Metabolism*, 89 (2004), 2837–45.

[36] Meung, *Rose*, 1148 (ll. 20,055–66), as cited in L. Tracy, 'Introduction', in *Castration and Culture in the Middle Ages*, ed. eadem (Cambridge, 2013), 18. The same study comments that surveys of medieval eunuchism in general refer back to Byzantine and early Christian understanding before leaping on to the later Middle Ages, for which see K. M. Ringrose, 'Eunuchs in historical perspective', *History Compass*, 5 (2007), 495–506, esp. 497–8; M .S. Kuefler, 'Castration and Eunuchism in the Middle Ages', in *Handbook of Medieval Sexuality*, ed. V. L. Bullough and J. A. Brundage (New York, 1996), 279–306.

[37] *Historia fundationis prioratus de Wigmore*, in *Monastici Anglicani*, 2: 218.

[38] *Welsche Gast*, 99 (ll. 3637, 3643). *Winsbecke* warns youth against the *ungetriwen* as the enemy of Courtliness and honour, *Winsbecke*, 85 (c. 38).

in his old age tiredly recited the Latin tag that 'flattery makes friends and the truth enemies'.[39] William Marshal projected the same easy-going charm as his enemies affected, and like them he would keep his true feelings about his companions to himself. The difference we are invited to see between William and the *losengers* he often encountered is that he was not secretly undermining his rivals at court, while the *losengers* had no such scruples. As a true *preudomme* Marshal left it to his own talents to exalt him, and did not stoop to cunning. So in the happy aphorism which Sarah Kay crafted in her study of the *lauzengier* in Occitan love literature, 'they embody the real and ineradicable threat to courtly society: other courtiers'.[40] The *losenger* personified the fears of those for whom success at court was a matter of survival and often had to be earned at others' expense. The insecurity of medieval court life can be seen in the proverbial force given to the gospel saying that 'your enemies are to be found in your own household' (*inimici hominis domestici eius*).[41] Unsurprisingly then, the *losenger* is a character who featured prominently in the conduct literature of the twelfth and thirteenth centuries as much as in its fiction. He represents one level of the state of enmity into which medieval people might fall. Though covert and low-key, the malice of the smiling *losenger* was assumed to be pervasive within the culture of the court, and an inevitable obstacle to the success of the courtly medieval hero. As has been argued above, *losengers* were so pervasive and resented because they were a symptom of the stress point of a courtly society: the envy and materialism that was at its dark heart.

Some writers were willing to believe that there were people in whom contrariness and treachery were innate. The difficult history of the redhead in medieval popular culture is the defining instance of this. The Great and Excellent King who offered life lessons to Ruodlieb in the moral tale of the later eleventh century warned him never to take a redhead as a close friend, for once enraged such a man forgot any obligation and would stoop to any measure to get even. It was in his nature to pursue a grievance. And in due course Ruodlieb fell in with such a man who lived up to the king's warnings.[42] Gerald of Wales in the 1180s retold a family legend of an untrustworthy redheaded seneschal in the Pembrokeshire of days past whose malice was matched by supernatural powers, thus equating hair colour and character with diabolic influence, for under interrogation, once his pilfering and treachery were discovered, he admitted he had been fathered by a demon.[43] Naturally, any deceitful character might then be characterized as a redhead in medieval iconography, of which the definitive instance was Judas. Naturally also, his hair colour might be part of the critique of any tyrannical king, as happened with William II 'Rufus' of England (reigned 1087–1100).[44] It is not going too far to see in such

---

[39] *Speculum Duorum*, 140.
[40] S. Kay, 'The Contradictions of Courtly Love and the Origins of Courtly Poetry: the evidence of the *Lauzengiers*', *Journal of Medieval and Early Modern Studies*, 26 (1996), 227.
[41] Matt. 10:36, as employed by Gerald of Wales, *Speculum Duorum*, 78.
[42] '*sibi stat durabilis ira*', in *Ruodlieb*, 90–6.   [43] *Itinerarium Kambriae*, in *GCO*, 6: 96–7.
[44] J. C. Harvey, *Red: A History of the Redhead* (New York, 2015), 60–79. See the comments of Daniel of Beccles on the subject of the cunning and resentful redhead: unable to have any trusting human relationship, *Liber Urbani*, 57 (ll. 1676–80).

characterizations a rationalization of the pervasiveness of deceit and suspicion in any courtly environment.

Even the most gifted courtier might experience conspiracy and envy. Indeed, the more gifted a man was, the more he was likely to become a victim. Since men competed in the Middle Ages as a way of establishing their *proesce*, rivalry could be said to be the default mode of a medieval male, and with some people rivalry was powered by envy. Robert of Ho accepted envy of others' success as a logical reaction to the way his own society worked:

> Is there anyone who might be raised up high in the world who's going to be liked? In my view it certainly won't be by the person who loses his own position though the promotion, and is reduced to a dependent because of it, who'll often have cause to bemoan the fact.[45]

At the end of 1182, in the same decade in which Robert wrote, William Marshal experienced a major crisis of his career at the court of the Young King Henry. During the course of it he was brought down by a whispering campaign mounted by a coterie of Norman household knights jealous of his intimacy with the king and at his promotion over their heads to the status of banneret, and he an Englishman too. The conspirators were characterized by the author in a colourful lexicon of negativity: *envios, pautoniers, traïtres, menzongiers, felons* and, of course, *losengiers*. But what is equally interesting in this incident is the portrayal of the Marshal's reactions to the plot against him. He more or less shrugged his shoulders at the turn in Fortune's wheel and met his reverse as a *preudomme* should. Like Robert of Ho, he saw it as an inevitable consequence of his life, and took himself off to Cologne to the new shrine of the Three Holy Kings seeking their intercession, for they in their day had been played for fools at King Herod's court. But more pragmatically he left friends behind him at the Young King's court, who undertook a correspondence with him in exile so he could monitor any change in the winds of favour blowing from that direction.

The two friends named—Peter des Préaux and Baldwin de Béthune—were men he could sympathize with; they likewise rose high in the world from being unlanded knights. Baldwin is of some significance here, for he represented the one great defence of the courtly man against his detractors: a loyal, discreet, committed and capable friend, such a one as both *Winsbecke* and the *Roman de la Rose* advised all public actors to find—a fellow spirit who shares his joys and sorrows and in whom he can repose absolute confidence in his troubles. Sordello da Goito, a knight on the same career path as William Marshal, called such a man an *amic coral* (a 'bosom buddy'), a fellow spirit in alliance against the world, an essential ally in a public career.[46] Jean de Meung in fact portrayed his allegorical character Friendship as the natural enemy of Slander.[47] William and Baldwin were political allies for the rest

---

[45] *Enseignments Trebor*, 134 (ll. 2468–73): *Ki sei meëmes ne tient chier/Kil devreit donkes eshaucier?/ Nului, per certes, ce m'est vis,/Quant il de gré abat sun pris/E se de ce est costumier/Sovent en avra reprovier.*

[46] *Ensenhamens d'Onor*, 214 (ll. 527–42).

[47] *Winsbecke*, 82 (c. 29); Meung, *Rose*, 302–6 (ll. 4681–742), 448 (ll. 7335–43). Robert de Blois repeats the proverb ,'A friendless man is naked', *Enseignement des princes*, 120 (l. 962), in talking of the hostility to be experienced at courts.

of their careers: in due course Baldwin would take the Marshal's eldest son into his household for training as a squire, and would marry his daughter and heir to the boy.[48] One reaction we do not find on the Marshal's part in all this is physical retaliation or any attempt otherwise to punish the conspirators. Their names, however, were not forgotten. They passed into the family memory, and thence to the biographer. We can assume from this that the *losengers* of 1182 would find little favour thereafter from any of the Marshals when their paths crossed.

There is a tired assumption in the unique biographical passage cited above that backbiting and jealousy are to be expected within hall and household, for dispute is the way of the world. It should be noted that the *losenger* worked in the shadows and behind backs in part because he wished to avoid the appearance of animosity, which would not do him credit if he showed it openly. *Losengerie* was more likely to be a tactic pursued covertly by dependants with few sources of power. The behaviour of magnates at court might well be more confrontational, as they had less to lose and something to gain from open resentment. The great Norman magnate Robert de Breteuil (died 1204) had a European reputation as a hero of the Third Crusade and as a skilled captain and noble courtier. His indispensability gave him enormous influence with both King Richard and King John of England. He was thus able in the 1190s to pursue and harry those who stood in his way and offended him, not least Hugh of Avalon, bishop of Lincoln. Robert used his influence to resolve in his favour large local claims against the bishop in the English Midlands. The frustration and humiliation endured at his hands by Bishop Hugh at the Angevin court spills over into the hagiography written by his chaplain. After reciting the earl's persecution of his lord at court, the biographer falsely credited Robert's premature death to leprosy, an ugly end attributable to the great earl's wilful sinfulness in persecuting his bishop.[49]

THE MORTAL ENEMY

We need to beware of an intellectual trap at this point. Male competitiveness was certainly a manifestation of and stimulus towards rivalry, but it did not necessarily lead to enmity, though it might well do. Defeating another male in combat or game need not commence a state of animosity between the pair, and indeed taking defeat in good part was a characteristic that was praised in a *preudomme*. A male who could not stomach being bested by another and showed it was in general thought to be making a fool of himself. Roger of Howden's tale of King Richard of England's peevish and vengeful reaction to being defeated by the French paragon of knighthood William des Barres, on a ride through the Sicilian countryside, was not told to the king's credit. It occurred in what was meant to be a light-hearted and spontaneous roadside 'bohort' (a mounted competition) fought with canes rather than spears. Howden pointed out the triviality of it all by commenting that the king lost

---

[48] For the incident, *History of William Marshal* 1: ll. 5109–922; Crouch, *Marshal*, 56–9.
[49] *Magna Vita sancti Hugonis*, ed. D. L. Douie and H. Farmer (2 vols, Oxford, 1961–2) 2: 83–4.

his temper over having his hat torn by William's stick. The enraged Lionheart then swore mortal enmity against William, who took the threat seriously enough to quit Messina when it turned out that Philip of France would not support him in his difficulty.[50] Howden is a good source for the incident and its reception. He was in the king's household in Sicily at the time.

An aristocratic reflex to retaliate against perceived affronts has been identified as at the core of its male behaviour by several generations of historian, most recently repeated by Dominique Barthélemy, which he encapsulates in the phrase *la faide chevaleresque*.[51] It was perceived several generations ago by Marc Bloch as a characteristic of his 'first feudal age', and it is unnecessary to contest this consensus amongst historians or the reality of what they describe. However, it was not as deterministic a reflex as Bloch believed. A medieval awareness of the dangers of letting anger take control of your tongue and actions may not have been necessarily much of a restraint on it, especially amongst the young, but as a result there had to be ways to deal with the consequences. The best explanation of the mid-twelfth-century epic *Raoul de Cambrai*, which traced the blood-soaked relationship between the borderline psychopath, young Count Raoul, and his one-time friend, the admirable bastard and *preudomme* Bernier, is that it taught contemporary youth that unrestrained anger and feuding without restraint sucked in and destroyed guilty and innocent alike. Marc Bloch took it as his basic text in his reconstruction of medieval noble mores, but he would have better seen it as a medieval nightmare. The fact that *Raoul* was set back in the Carolingian era indicates that its twelfth-century author wanted to see such appalling deeds as a feature of a dark past his society had struggled out of. To admit the violence of the medieval aristocrat is not to say that these men were necessarily comfortable with their inconvenient habitus.

It was the medieval experience that a man who felt himself and his honour offended by the actions of another could still go against the Church's teaching and common wisdom, be borne away by the tide of anger, and take retaliatory action. It might even come to the point when it was expedient to do so. Living in a feud-ridden Tuscan society, Brunetto Latini nonetheless equated knightly prowess with the sort of behaviour which strenuously avoided giving or even taking offence. His ideal male aristocrat was to do his best to restrain himself if a confrontation broke out, though there was a limit. Restraint lasted till the point where he felt his honour was being compromised or if he was coming under murderous assault. At that point his reputation and prowess meant he had no choice but to draw on his enemy and strike hard, though with a cool head. He should not fear death if it came to violence, said Latini, as suffering shame (*vergogna*) was worse than going down under an

[50] *Gesta Henrici Secundi*, ed. W. Stubbs (2 vols, Rolls Series, 1867), 2: 155. This use of mortal enmity as threat by greater men against lesser was a commonplace. Marie de France's fable of the 'Lion's Share' appropriately had the lion threatening his companions on a hunt that they will be his *enemis mortels* if they dared claim a share of the deer he had caught; *The Fables of Marie de France*, ed. and trans. M. L. Martin (Birmingham, AL, 1984), 56, no. 11 (ll. 23–6).

[51] D. Barthélemy, *Chevaliers et miracles: la violence et le sacré dans la société féodale* (Paris, 2004), 11–17.

enemy's sword.[52] But to be prudent, he should avoid going out at night after declaring an enmity, and always have armed attendants at hand.

It is a little surprising to find not too dissimilar a view in common-law England, since murder and assassination were offences there against the royal majesty and prosecuted as a crown plea. At the end of the twelfth century Robert of Ho pointed out pragmatically what every parent and teacher knows: that threats against someone who has antagonized and threatened you which are not carried through are indeed worse than useless; they do more harm than good, so action must necessarily follow threats. He then went on to draw a very significant line in the sand:

> Your threats won't mean a thing to him if he is not your mortal enemy (*ennemi mortel*), for only in those circumstances can he be sure if he has the sense to see it that you will take vengeance on him when you see the right time and place.[53]

To Robert, there was a point when another man's hostility and behaviour had become so offensive and threatening that it could no longer be ignored and there had to be a response. But though there had to be action, the desired result was not necessarily going to be the bloodbath that Brunetto Latini feared or in which Raoul de Cambrai and his enemy Bernier drenched north-west France and met their respective ends.

Retaliation in medieval society might be structured. By the twelfth century it was framed as an open declaration of a state of mortal enmity, publicly proclaimed by word of mouth and sometimes even by letter, so that not just the participants but the community they belonged to would know of it and, one assumes, behave accordingly. In one Flemish instance the letter was posted up in a church. In 1224, the young King Jaume (James) of Aragon, aged then perhaps 16, came into the hands of a faction of his nobility by a deception, for which he blamed the magnate Pero (Peter) Aunès, one of his regency council. Baffled and chafing at the constraint he was under, Jaume in his autobiography recalls taking Peter to one side and deliberately swearing mortal enmity to his face (though with enough self-possession to retain the royal plural): 'From this time forth we abandon your friendship and as long as we live we shall not be friends with you.' When Peter asked why, the bristling adolescent curtly cited the dishonour he had placed him in, but the older man shrugged his protests off. He had better not have, for in due course Peter was to die at the king's side by a blow from one of the royal household knights after a troublesome career of opposition to his young lord, whom he had presumed to threaten with a knife on another occasion.[54]

An offender was left in no doubt that he would face the antagonism of his enemy till death, which is what the phrase 'mortal enmity' implied, not necessarily that he would be subject to assassination at the first opportunity (though that

---

[52] *Tesoretto*, 210–14 (ll. 2003–54).   [53] *Enseignements Trebor*, 94 (ll. 1475–80).
[54] *Llibre dels Fets*, 61. Note the formulaic similarity with the declaration of an offended duke in a romance of *c*.1200 that the protagonists were his *mortels enemis*, 'and we will never be reconciled'; *Gui de Warewic*, 1: ll. 3593–4. King Jaume had spent his early childhood in the household of Simon de Montfort the elder, count of Rochefort and Leicester, so his upbringing and experience spanned cultures as well as the Pyrenees.

might well be feared by the offender and it was what Peter Aunès in the end experienced).[55] In mid-thirteenth-century Tuscan society, though a man may have become a declared *nemico*, he was nonetheless to be treated with Courtliness (*cortesemente*) and with deference in any accidental meeting between the principals, even if the offender was less well born than the offended. Resort to knives or blows on the spur of the moment might not, as Latini observed, produce the result a man might wish.[56] A declaration of mortal enmity in Western society was, then, by this interpretation the entry point to a continuum of hostile behaviour which anthropologists have long characterized (a little unhelpfully) as feud, a construct which we will examine in detail later on. The social edginess and insecurity formal enmity inaugurated were always uncomfortable, might go further than the principals intended and might indeed become tiresome. Brunetto Latini expected enemies to brood on and pursue their grievances but was uneasy that in starting one off a man might commit his friends and kin to joining in an affair of honour that might never be settled.[57] Caesarius of Heisterbach offered a sermon *exemplum* to illustrate quite how disruptive and uncomfortable such a state might be. This concerned a state of *inimicitia mortalis* between two large peasant clans in the diocese of Cologne whose patriarchs were perpetually finding new reasons to quarrel and resisting efforts to resolve their differences. The men died on the same day and were laid to be buried in the same trench in the parish churchyard, but as soon as they were put together the corpses began to fight with ferocity. Their kinsfolk got the message and promptly settled their feuds, making sure to bury the corpses at a distance from each other in the cemetery.[58]

The medieval concept of mortal enmity has only recently been analysed as a contemporary category of behaviour in its own right. Robert Bartlett's investigation of peace legislation relating to twelfth- and thirteenth-century towns and provinces across Europe found that they accommodate the existence of such a state of open hostility between individuals in Spain, Normandy, Flanders, Holland, Denmark and Saxony. As well as their pan-European extent, the various codes anticipate a wide range of possible and permitted punitive actions within mortal enmity ranging from homicide to overcharging at a tollbooth.[59] The existence of an effective national common law, such as England possessed and enforced, did not mean that a state of extra-legal mortal enmity was unknown there. The existence of an effective legal process might even enhance the process of hostility and give an advantage

---

[55] A model letter including such a declaration (*me habebis inimicum quamdiu vixero*) can actually be found in a mid-thirteenth-century English formulary, British Library, MS Add. 8167, fo. 101r (*Lost Letters*, 161–4). The letter proclaiming mortal enmity was a common form in late medieval Flanders, Germany and Austria; see O. Brunner, *Land and Lordship: Structures of Governance in Medieval Austria*, trans. H. Kaminsky and J. van Horn Melton (Philadelphia, 1992), 63–7, and 64nn; H. Platelle, 'Vengeance privée et réconciliation dans l'oeuvre de Thomas de Chantimpré', *Tijdschrift voor Rechtsgeschiednis*, 42 (1974), 272n.

[56] *Tesoretto*, 216–18 (ll. 2082–120).   [57] *Tesoretto*, 218–20 (ll. 2135–42).
[58] *Dialogus Miraculorum*, 5: 2160.
[59] R. Bartlett, '"Mortal Enmities": the Legal Aspect of Hostility in the Middle Ages', in *Feud, Violence and Practice: Essays in Medieval Studies in Honor of Stephen D. White*, ed. B. S. Tuten and T. L. Billado (Aldershot, 2010), 197–212.

to one party against the other, because it offered (as indeed it still offers) another field in which personal enmity could be pursued.[60] When King Richard I gave in to the petition of his earls in 1194 to permit the mêlée tournament once again in England, he issued regulations which acknowledged that the personal resentments tourneyers brought with them to the field could pose a danger to public peace.

> If any tourneyer is at odds with another man, whether he is a servant or whoever he may be, he is to be under a binding truce with him during the tournament, and on the road there and back, and if he refuses to give truce then he should be forced to give a pledge to do it or not be allowed to tourney.[61]

We get some insight into the way that the tensions of mortal enmity might spread across society and prey on the mind of an individual in this account of the alarm of a Flemish knight, Walter Bertaut, when he was caught in a storm on the North Sea in 1215 and his vessel was driven eastward towards the coast of Holland: '. . . because of which Walter was very fearful, as Count William hated him to death for the sake of the count of Loos (whose first cousin Walter was) who had competed with Count William over the county of Holland by right of his wife.'[62] Mortal enmity sucked in the friends and kin of the parties. The group around the offended party is called the 'vengeance group' in anthropologically inclined writings, but there was also a corresponding defensive party which (like it or not) was assumed to support the offender.[63] So Walter Bertaut was also a mortal enemy of the count of Holland, by reason of being the cousin of his rival. A homicide was a more frequent trigger for such a state. At some time in the 1150s the Anglo-French knight Walter de St-Martin was killed by a young Norman magnate, William de Tancarville. Though the circumstances around the death are unknown, Walter was well connected enough to coalesce a dangerous vengeance group around his offended brother Geoffrey, including his lord and relative Count John of Eu and the magnate Reginald de St-Valèry. So despite his high status Tancarville was obliged to come

---

[60] As in 1217 when a physical assault which drew blood allowed one party to raise a 'hue and cry' against the other, as he had breached the king's peace and put himself at a disadvantage; P. R. Hyams, 'Feud in Medieval England', *Haskins Society Journal*, 3 (1993), 14–16. John Hudson argues an English exceptionalism within Europe in an absence not merely of feud there in the twelfth century but of any manifestation of mortal enmity (for which, however, see below pp. 216–17). His argument relies on law books, a narrow definition of blood feud and an optimistic idea of royal authority; J. G. Hudson, 'Faide, Vengeance et Violence en Angleterre', in *La Vengeance, 400–1200*, ed. D. Barthélemy, F. Bougard, and R. Le Jan (Rome, 2006), 375–82, translated as 'Feud, Vengeance and Violence in England from the Tenth to the Twelfth Centuries', in *Feud, Violence and Practice: Essays in Medieval Studies in Honor of Stephen D. White*, ed. B. S. Tuten and T.L. Billado (Aldershot, 2010), 29–54. Paul Hyams, by contrast, acknowledges the social context outside the law-books in his discussion of the pervasiveness of later medieval 'enmity culture', a culture which might itself motivate litigation; P. R. Hyams, *Rancor and Reconciliation in Medieval England* (Ithaca, 2003), 242–66.

[61] T. Rymer, *Foedera, Conventiones, Litterae et Acta Publica*, ed. A. Clarke and F. Holbrooke (7 vols, London, 1816–69) i, pt 1, 65.

[62] *Histoire*, 156.

[63] For a consideration of the influence of anthropological conceptualizations of conflict on historians of the Middle Ages, W. C. Brown and P. Górecki, 'What Conflict Means: the making of medieval conflict studies in the United States, 1970-2000', in *Conflict in Medieval Europe: Changing Perspectives on Society and Culture*, ed. W. C. Brown and P. Górecki (Aldershot, 2003), 1–36; and see also Hyams, *Rancor and Reconciliation*, 3–21.

to a settlement (*concordia*) by which he would endow a monk in the count of Eu's abbey of Le Tréport to say a perpetual Mass for Walter's soul.[64] At the level of nations, the vengeance group comprehended an entire realm. So Henry III of England in 1231 referred to Louis IX of France as his chief enemy (*capitalis inimicus*) because he had disinherited him of his ancestral lands, and he included all the sworn subjects of the Capetian king in his hostility.[65] Stephen D. White's noted study of feuding and settlement in eleventh-century Touraine uncovers how such groups might coalesce, and the occasional pragmatic unscrupulousness of an aggressor to maximize his chances of recovering face by declaring hostility against characters who were ill-provided with powerful kinsfolk and redoubtable neighbours to defend them.[66]

As in the eleventh-century Loire valley and twelfth-century Normandy, so too in thirteenth-century Britain. In the course of warfare between the rebel earl of Pembroke and a party of royalists in Leinster in 1234, the earl, Richard Marshal, was cut down while attempting to relieve a besieged castle, unnecessarily so as was claimed. His aggrieved brother and heir, a cleric as it happened, had a choice of parties to single out so as to hold them responsible and thus his mortal enemies. In the end he passed over the greater men present at the death: the regional magnates, Walter de Lacy, Earl Hugh de Lacy and Richard de Burgh, lords of whole provinces. Instead he pinned responsibility on the relatively insignificant baron Maurice fitz Gerald, who was the royal officer responsible for Dublin but also a Marshal tenant for some of his lands, and thus especially obnoxious. The vengeance group that rallied to the Marshals included their kin, who were some of the greatest earls in England, as well as their powerful political affinity. It was not then surprising that when Maurice sailed from Dublin to Bristol in a first attempt brokered by the king to settle the dispute, he would not leave the town, for 'he did not dare to go any further without a safe conduct, fearing for his life'.[67]

In England, as much as in Touraine and even in the feud-torn Empire portrayed so graphically by Otto Brunner, a formal arbitrated reconciliation (including the abject submission of the offender) was the desired aim of the process of feuding, rather than the spilling of blood. Though Brunner, developing a German legal-historical tradition, famously saw a feud mentality embedded in German medieval society at all levels and throughout the Middle Ages, he believed that its social effects were limited. He saw its elite moving away from the crude and unmitigated *Blutrache* of early times towards a moderated *Ritterfehde*, a condition whose meaning matches the milder aristocratic 'mortal enmity' as discussed and defined above.[68]

---

[64] The events can be reconstructed through these two principal sources: Archives départementales de la Seine-Maritime, 17 HP 1; Bibliothèque municipale de Rouen, Y 13, fo. 116v.

[65] *Patent Rolls of the Reign of Henry III* (6 vols, London, 1901–13) 2: *1225–32*, 435–6.

[66] S. D. White, 'Feuding and Peace-Making in the Touraine around the year 1100', *Traditio*, 42 (1986), 195–263, following on from his earlier path-breaking, ' "Pactum...Legem Vincit et Amor Judicium": The Settlement of Disputes by Compromise in Eleventh-Century Western France', *American Journal of Legal History*, 22 (1979), 291–309.

[67] *Annales de Oseneia*, in *Annales Monastici*, ed. H. R. Luard (5 vols, Rolls Series, 1864–9) 4: 81.

[68] H. Kamp, 'La vengeance, le roi et les compétitions faidales', in *La Vengeance, 400–1200*, 262–4, sees the search for compensation as the desired outcome even in the *Blutrache* of Ottonian Germany. See Brunner, *Land and Lordship*, 81–6, on the mitigation of aristocratic feuding.

In seeing the declaration of enmity as part of a process rather than the end of it, Brunner had in fact hit on one of those rare universals in medieval behaviour which span European cultures, though its intensity and mechanics varied from society to society. For instance, we might note a significant point about the thirteenth-century Marshal case which could not be found in many places in Europe. The king here was the third-party referee, while in Touraine and Flanders over a century earlier it had to be the neutral power of the local church.[69]

The articulation of state authority first in England and later in France changed the process of settlement somewhat, as the king's assertion of his right to take offence at a disturbance to the peace of his realm produced a formidable new forum for the settlement of differences. A formal declaration of reconciliation was indeed reached before King Henry III of England in August 1234, between the new Earl Gilbert and his brother's former adversaries, but it seems to have failed as far as Maurice was concerned, for one of his clerks was cornered and murdered at Westminster by members of the vengeance group the next year. It was not till 1240 that a second attempt was made, in which Maurice promised to expiate his offence by founding a monastery for the late Earl Richard's soul. Perhaps he failed to do so, as after Gilbert's death in 1241 his nephews, the earls of Norfolk and Gloucester, were still maintaining open hostilities with Maurice and his kinsfolk.[70] It is revealing of the all-consuming nature of such a conflict that Earl Gilbert's accidental death on a tourney field was put down by some to his reins having been cut through by an agent of his mortal enemies.[71]

BLOOD VENGEANCE AND CIVILIZATION

There have been a number of recent explorations of feud in medieval society which have challenged past assumptions and much enhanced our understanding of how such conflict within society came to be and how it might be concluded. Feud is a concept which was long ago drafted into the debate as to whether Europe became more civilized during the period of this study, with the assumption that, as men resorted less readily to violence to settle their disputes and looked more to ritualized behaviour and third parties to mitigate disputes, civilization was increasing and heading towards that halcyon state called 'the rule of law'. It is certainly possible to find wilful resort to violence and murder in the earlier period of the Middle Ages and on the wilder fringes of Europe, which do not look at first sight in the least civilized, though our judgement as to its unacceptability and exceptionalism might not have been shared by contemporaries.[72] Feuding was endemic in the war-torn

---

[69] It might be noticed that in an earlier England as much as in Hainaut ecclesiastical leaders might take up the role of peacemakers in a time of aristocratic feuds, as Bishop Wulfstan II of Worcester did with great energy after 1070; Hyams, 'Feud in Medieval England', 2–3.

[70] D. Crouch, 'Earl Gilbert Marshal and his Mortal Enemies', *Historical Research*, 87 (2014), 393–403.

[71] Matthew Paris, *Chronica Majora*, ed. H. R. Luard (7 vols, Rolls Series, 1884–7) 4: 135.

[72] G. Halsall, 'Introductory Survey', in *Violence and Society in the Early Medieval West*, ed. idem (Woodbridge, 1998), 1–37, is a magisterial survey of the subject, making much of the distinction between licit and illicit violence in assessing its objectionability in contemporary thought.

counties of Hainaut and Flanders in 1060, despite periodic attempts to broker the Peace of God in the previous generation. This was so much so that the monks of Lobbes took the opportunity to tour the region with the relics of their patron, who apparently had quite a gift for settling stubborn feuds which had defied the mediation and authority of bishops or counts. At Blaringhem near Saint-Omer they encountered a church harbouring a young knight who had just murdered another who had verbally demeaned him, despite a formal settlement pressed on him by his lord. One armed party was ready to kill the youth as he emerged, and another was ready to kill to prevent it. By an adroit use of relics, crowd management and liturgy they offered a way out of the impending bloodbath and reconciled the murderer and the lord he had offended. This was but one of several spectacular success stories in their tour of the troubled region, which at least had found the grace to tire of bloodletting and look for ways to mitigate it.[73]

Did things improve in later centuries as the theory of a rise of civilized values would have it? Not if we examine the action of William Marshal's contemporary, the Bavarian magnate Count Siboto IV of Hartmannsberg or Falkenstein (died *c.*1200) in procuring the murder of his enemy (*inimicus*), one Rudolf of Piesting, an associate of his bitter rivals in his long campaign to gain total control over the Falkenstein family lands. The fact that the count made the arrangements and promised a reward to his friend and retainer Ortwin of Merkenstein by means of the written word does not make his behaviour any more civilized. The fact that the letter urged secrecy, and visualized Ortwin having to do penance for the deed if it was done clumsily, are surer indications that Count Siboto knew he was transgressing acceptable conduct. The letter indeed may have been written to offer a security to the murderer that the count, not he, would be required to make the necessary financial compensation to Rudolf's kin that would follow the bloody deed.[74]

I will take here the term 'blood feud' to characterize the more extreme end of the continuum of hatred and vengeance in medieval society: vendetta, feud without restraint or even expectation of end.[75] To Brunner, *Blutrache* signified exactly that. This was apparently what the monks of Lobbes encountered all too often in Flanders in the 1050s. Even the gratuitously immoral action of Count Siboto's solicited assassination of his humble rival does not quite fit that description: he may have transgressed social norms but the count's deed, if on the windy side of what society found acceptable, held open the possibility of a financial settlement with Rudolf's kin. The Flemings of later centuries, despite continuing the practice of feud with

[73] *Miracula sancti Usmari*, in *MGH Scriptores*, 15, pt 2, 837–8, as analysed in G. Koziol. 'The Making of Peace in Eleventh-Century Flanders', in *The Peace of God: Social Violence and Religious Response in France around the year 1000*, ed. T. Head and R. Landes (Ithaca, 1992), 239–58. For the continuing presence of feud culture in Flanders in later centuries, Platelle, 'Vengeance privée et réconciliation', 269–81.

[74] P. J. Geary and J. B. Freed, 'Literacy and Violence in Twelfth-Century Bavaria: the "Murder Letter" of Count Siboto IV', *Viator*, 25 (1994), 115–29. See for comparison the list of political murders in Hohenstaufen Germany in Bumke, *Courtly Culture*, 2–3, and Brunner's discussion of the prevalence of murderous feud at all levels of society even in the fifteenth-century Empire; *Land and Lordship*, 9–22.

[75] F. Bougard, 'Les mots de vengeance', in *La vengeance, 400–1200*, 2.

some enthusiasm, at least developed the defensive belief that other peoples were more savage and ready to resort to homicidal violence than they were, as Thomas de Cantimpré believed of the marginal Frisians in the thirteenth century.[76] The same transference of one's own worst characteristics on to supposedly primitive neighbours is very much characteristic of the medieval British Isles. The English in the early twelfth century were already inclined to characterize other insular societies as feral, murderous and anarchic compared to the relative civil peace and commerce England enjoyed. So blood feud became explicitly identified with the moral bankruptcy of neighbouring societies which were undeveloped and barbarous in comparison with the dominant English polity. It did indeed continue in Celtic societies long enough for its practice to startle and shock their English neighbours, but these same English found the practice of mortal enmity acceptable in their own society nonetheless.[77]

For all the dismissiveness by their Anglo-French neighbours, however, Celtic British societies in 1100 were not divergent in their practice of feud from that of England or the Continent. They may not have been able to resort to a king as arbiter, but the Church and customary processes were available for the purpose. It is too easy to see the absence of central institutions as evidence of social anarchy in a society.[78] A common culture of feud management could be just as effective in limiting the damage, and something like it can be found across Europe. The part of the 'vengeance group' was as evident in non-English Britain as in contemporary Touraine; in Gaelic Ireland it was defined formally as the *gelfhine*, a defensive association of uncles, brothers and first cousins. Just as in Germanic societies, compensation from the offending party could settle the feud and was indeed the usual desired end of it. Irish society in particular had a well-structured approach to feud, which was for its members an institution governed by communal law rather than a state of uncontained hostility. The persistence of open extralegal feud in Ireland for centuries after 1100 may well be due not to Ireland's divergence from the civilized mainstream but to the fact that its own manner of conducting it worked very well as a means of containing the consequences of male aggression and territorial conflict.[79] We should beware a Whiggish assumption that medieval societies perceived a centrally regulated legal system as necessarily superior and indeed the natural ambition of every polity.

Irish society was, of course, violent: markedly and even unapologetically so, which provoked its incoming twelfth-century colonists and thirteenth-century visitors to a contempt barely mitigated by a reluctant admission that the Irish were nonetheless a Christian people. Echoing Gerald of Wales, an English Cistercian

[76] Platelle, 'Vengeance privée et réconciliation', 278 and n.

[77] J. A. Gillingham, 'The Beginnings of English Imperialism', *Journal of Historical Sociology*, 5 (1992), 392–409.

[78] For an analysis of the significance of threat, argument, ritual and reconciliation in a Provençal case of the 1060s, P. J. Geary, 'Vivre en conflit dans une France sans État', *Annales*, 41 (1986), 1118–25, rev. and trans. in idem, *Living with the Dead in the Middle Ages* (Ithaca, 1994), 130–60.

[79] N. McLeod, 'The Blood-feud in Medieval Ireland', in *Between Intrusions: Britain and Ireland between the Romans and Normans*, ed. P. O'Neill (Sydney Series in Celtic Studies, 7, 2004), 114–33, esp. 116–18.

abbot conducting a visitation of the Irish province in 1228 casually observed in a letter to the abbot of Clairvaux in Burgundy that he was dealing with a more or less 'bestial people'. Nor can one be entirely surprised at the abbot's verdict. The powerful king of Connacht, Cathal Crobderg Ua Conchobair, died four years before this visit and his (clerical) eulogist praised him for many things, including his lavish foundation of Cistercian houses. He also celebrated his king as the one who was 'fiercest and harshest towards his enemies that ever lived; the king who most blinded, killed and mutilated rebellious and disaffected subjects'.[80]

Sometimes these insular societies could themselves admit the charge of their egregious violence and even be ruefully self-critical, which in fact reveals amongst them a consciousness of wider and less violent European norms against which they felt themselves being measured. The contemporary Welsh national chronicle itself dryly comments on the murderous kin strife that broke out within the royal houses in the 1110s and 1120s as English power brutally subverted and compromised native power structures. We see here in early twelfth-century Wales the same relationship between burgeoning blood feud and the violent disruption of society by protracted war as the monks of Lobbes had encountered in Flanders of the mid eleventh century. The English justiciar of the March in 1111, when confronted with the request of the victor in a recent bloodbath over possession of the kingdom of Powys that he be recognized as ruler of the family lands, shrugged and complied. The Welsh writer then commented that the justiciar's action was 'not out of love for him but because he knew the ways of that land, that they were all of them slaying one another'.[81]

The fact that Welsh aristocrats acknowledged no limits to the bloodshed they might inflict on their enemies in pursuit of their ends raised the eyebrows of even the most hardened English marcher lord, as Walter Map observed in the 1180s.[82] Walter's English and French contemporaries were not, of course, strangers to the practice of feud, but they believed the Welsh acknowledged no such limiting structure to their aggression as the English and French possessed. In this they were, however, wrong. In fact instances of kin strife and murder receded in later twelfth-century Wales as the then resurgent Welsh lords reverted to more traditional and peaceful ways of handling competition for land. In the 1270s Welsh law, like Irish law, still accommodated the idea of vengeance killing with a compensation mechanism, which it called *galanas*. But naturally the common-law-trained English aristocrats and clerics would by then find such an institution barbaric and extra-legal, a relic of a time recalled by their society only in ancient and uncouth Anglo-Saxon texts. When a commission headed by the Archbishop of Canterbury encountered *galanas* in 1281, he rebuked the Prince of Wales in his astonishment. The archbishop—a natural Whig—found morally transgressive in every way the apparent fact that Welsh courts regarded murder and violent assault as acceptable, and he

---

[80] Stephen of Lexington, *Letters from Ireland, 1228–1229*, trans. B. O'Dwyer (Kalamazoo, 1982), no. 24; *Annals of Connacht*, ed. and trans. A. M. Freeman (Dublin, 1944), *s.a.* 1224; see commentary in K. Simms, *From Kings to Warlords: the Changing Political Structure of Gaelic Ireland in the Later Middle Ages* (Woodbridge, 1987), 25.

[81] *Brut, s.a.* 1111.   [82] *De Nugis Curialium*, 146.

took it as a sign of the depravity of the Welsh.[83] Once Wales was subjugated, its functional but objectionable native criminal law was promptly abolished on the grounds of its moral inferiority.

The study of anger-inspired violence in the medieval British Isles and on the Continent has, then, been locked into an unhelpful Enlightenment narrative of progress in civilization which has its roots in the later nineteenth century, going back beyond Guizot to Montesquieu. It saw medieval society emerging from the Teutonic forests in the baggage of warbands led by charismatic tribal kings to triumph over Roman civilization, to lay waste for a while the rule of law only in due course for an ideal of communal law to re-emerge and subjugate their worst impulses. This lies behind an understanding of social history articulated in Max Weber's *Wirtschaft und Gesellschaft* (1924), which suggested that the gradual transition of such heroic leaders into feudal landlords tamed their societies and ultimately made their leadership mundane, less violent and even bureaucratized as the idea of the State emerged. Otto Hintze and Norbert Elias in the interwar years endorsed this model, with Elias in particular pointing to the princely court as the engine for the transformation of the violent feudal castellan into the civilized and self-controlled courtier.[84] There is certainly something to this argument, for Western medieval societies after 1100 were increasingly apt to congratulate themselves on their recapture of the high ground of civilization lost by Rome, and—as we have seen with the English attitude to the Welsh and Irish—to distinguish themselves from the violent and primitive barbaric Other which occupied the same Atlantic archipelago they did.[85] Twelfth-century English writers, by then members of a vibrant francophone cultural community, also had by the 1120s cultivated very similar disparaging views of the insular pre-Conquest English, who were in fact for most of them their own grandparents.[86]

How much of this was simply a matter of self-presentation and indeed self-delusion? It hardly needs pointing out that the arc of civilized behaviour was not as uninterrupted as the theoretical literature of the nineteenth and twentieth centuries might assume. Unconstrained and systemic violent behaviour could in fact break out in any medieval society, even one with a strongly developed ideal of

---

[83] *Registrum Epistolarum fratris Johannis Pecham*, ed. C. T. Martin (3 vols, Cambridge, 1882–4) 1: 357, as analysed in R. R. Davies, 'The Survival of the Bloodfeud in Medieval Wales', *History*, 54 (1969), 338–40.

[84] See, for this model, Crouch, *Nobility*, 21–3, and for the place of feud in it, J-M. Moeglin, 'Le "droit de vengeance" chez les historiens du droit au moyen age', in *La Vengeance, 400–1200*, 101–58, esp. comments on p. 103.

[85] This is a theme of the work of John Gillingham, looking particularly at military customs in British societies; see 'From "Civilitas" to Civility: Codes of Manners in Medieval and Early Modern England', *Transactions of the Royal Historical Society*, 6th ser., 12 (2002), 267–91, and essays collected in *The English in the Twelfth Century: Imperialism, National Identity and Political Values* (Woodbridge, 2000).

[86] J. A. Gillingham, 'The Introduction of Chivalry into England', in *Law and Government in Medieval England and Normandy*, ed. G. Garnett and J. G. Hudson (Cambridge, 1994), 31–55, esp. 53. The famous Yorkshire feud which spanned several generations after the murder of Earl Uthred of Northumbria in 1016 is given a critical examination in R. Fletcher, *Bloodfeud* (Harmondsworth, 2002), and see Crouch, *Aristocracy*, 124–32.

law and an effective apparatus of criminal prosecution.[87] Late thirteenth-century England is a case in point. The tensions within the royal family in the 1260s led the Lord Edward, heir to the throne, to do much as Count Siboto had, if on a grander scale, and work not just to procure the death of his inconvenient uncle, Earl Simon de Montfort, on the field of Evesham in 1265, but deliberately to massacre his household around him and even to commission a gang of thugs to mutilate and desecrate his uncle's fallen corpse. Contemporary writers depicted this vengeful action as one that no true knight would have contemplated, and an outrage to the established habitus.[88] So in due course the atrocity was all too readily avenged on the body of Edward's unsuspecting first cousin, Henry of Germany, who was knifed to death in 1271 during a Mass in Italy by two of Montfort's refugee sons. It was a deed that shocked Europe, and the principal culprit, Guy de Montfort, was subsequently portrayed by Dante in the seventh circle of Hell, up to his neck in boiling blood.[89] It is perhaps the Dantean reaction to the deed that is the true evidence of the rise in ideals of restraint in medieval society, not any changes in behaviour itself. Dante's reaction may, however, have owed more to the social eminence of the victim than any discomfort with the idea of vendetta, which was endemic at all levels of his society.[90] Over the following half-century English political culture fell into a bloody pattern of politically inspired murder, retaliation and assassination, which included amongst its noble victims one of Edward's nephews, Thomas of Lancaster, and two of his own sons.[91] The more civilized moralists of the twelfth century would not have been surprised at this. They knew all too well that unrestrained violence did nothing but beget yet more violence.

[87] It hardly needs pointing out that it was early modern noble society which instituted and ritualized the duel across Europe, as a licensed form of homicide for a male who believed his honour had been challenged by another; M. Peltonen, *The Duel in Early Modern England: Civility, Politeness and Honour* (Cambridge, 2003).

[88] O. De Laborderie, J. R. Maddicott, and D. A. Carpenter, 'The Last Hours of Simon de Montfort: A New Account', *EHR*, 115 (2000), 378–412.

[89] J. R. Maddicott, *Simon de Montfort* (Cambridge, 1994), 370–1.

[90] A. Zorzi, 'I conflitti nell'Italia communale. Riflessioni sullo stato degli studi e sulle prospettive di ricerca', in *Conflitti, paci e vendetta nell'Italia communale*, ed. idem (Florence, 2009), 7–43.

[91] A thoughtful study in this regard is M. Strickland, 'Treason, Feud and the Growth of State Violence: Edward I and the "War of the Earl of Carrick"', in *War, Government and Aristocracy in the British Isles, c.1150–1500: Essays in Honour of Michael Prestwich*, ed. C. Given-Wilson, A. Kettle, and L. Scales (Woodbridge, 2008), 84–113. Strickland does not see any continuity between the events of 1265 and those of the later reign of Edward I and discounts the king's Welsh atrocities as visited on those outside the political community, inadmissible because of what he calls a 'species gap'.

PART IV

HEGEMONY

11

The Conspiracy of Deference

At the end of our period, at the close of the thirteenth century, William of Aragon, a physician and philosopher, published a tract on the subject of Nobility, specifically its ethical dimension. However, before he opened his argument, he made some observations about the difficulty in dealing with a term into which people read so many meanings. Indeed, his little work was intended to weigh in on one particular definition, that Nobility was a quality of character, superiority in virtue, which is why he called it *De nobilitate animi*, 'On Nobility of Mind'. But this was, as he said, only one definition of Nobility allowed in 'popular usage'. He identified two other common understandings. One was signified by the word *Generositas*, which he defined as the superior members of a particular superior family. Then there was *Altitudo Generis*, by which he meant the greatness of a family's power and its quality.[1] Power, riches, descent, family and superiority in conduct are all qualities we still associate with the word Nobility, but now as much as in 1290, the word is not easily pinned down, other than to the reductionist idea of 'superiority'. Nonetheless, William felt he had to try to pin down one dominant sense, which in itself is significant for the argument of this book.

Two centuries before William, another physician associated with the court of Aragon had also considered Nobility, though to considerably less effect in terms of any clear conclusion. When at the beginning of the twelfth century Peter Alfonsi pondered in one of his dialogues what true Nobility (*vera nobilitas*) was, he sidestepped the classical world in his answer and offered instead a dialogue based on the authority of the tenth-century Arabic text called the *Secretum Secretorum* and its compendium of fifteen virtues which its author, in the character of Aristotle, said ought to be found in the best of counsellors. This route offered Peter several ways in which Nobility could be defined by virtue and education: to him it was a combination of superior morality, superior learning and superior military skills. When the youth in his dialogue found this blizzard of virtues confusing in the light of the popular association of Nobility with wealth and birth, his wise old father did not disagree with the boy but still asserted that well-born men needed virtues to truly shine in the world as noble, and wealth was neither here nor there.[2] In his *Moralis Philosophia* Hildebert of Lavardin, in the same generation as Peter, pondered the

---

[1] Aragon, *De Nobilitate*, 60.
[2] *Disciplina clericalis*, c. 4. Alfonsi most likely used the Arabic text. The thirteenth-century French adaptation of this passage in *Chastoiement d'un Père*, 71–2 (ll. 835–86), chooses to recast it as a dialogue on clerical lack of virtue rather than on Nobility, perhaps because Peter's standpoint was by then far away from mainstream Western thinking on the subject.

polysemous nature of *nobilitas* from a different (but no more focused) angle. He saw it as being the fine physical qualities people desire, meaning Nobility of Form, but he also considered Nobility of Deeds and Nobility of Mind. He was the first medieval author to quote Juvenal directly on the subject, that true Nobility was virtue.[3] As well as these many perspectives, a well-established reductionist strand in thinking on Nobility was also to be found in the early twelfth century. Isidore of Seville in the seventh century had favoured the literate of Europe with a rather simpler definition of what the word *nobilis* was understood to be, which was to surface regularly in later periods. Isidore's conclusion matched the sense we would call 'notability': simply being 'known' (*notus*) to be good or respectable in name and family.[4]

Between 1100 and 1300 there was a rising and increasingly focused debate across Europe that developed by the end of the twelfth century into an attempt—which failed—to consolidate the understanding of Nobility on one dominant sense, to an extent that indicates that the literate, lay and cleric alike, realized that a lot was at stake.[5] If so, it was because one sense of the word had already been invested in heavily by the lay elites of 1100. The nobleman intended Nobility to be understood as an eminence he could claim through birth, and an eminence which commanded more than respect; he wanted his Nobility to command deference. Such an understanding may have suited the self-proclaimed nobleman, but not, of course, those of whom he demanded deference. It is not too difficult to find examples of medieval resistance to and resentment at this hegemonic understanding of Nobility as being genetic. Baldwin de Condé was amongst several writers who chafed against it, but he was more capable than most of getting to the heart of its irrationality and injustice:

> You, great man (*haus hom*), who prove yourself to be wicked and who put me down with your own eminence and who belittle me! My answer is ready for you: 'Great man, who calls *me* base-born (*vilain*)! Since there is no good deed or word of yours that would justify your airs, anyone who calls you eminent (*franc*) is lying. If you are exalted high on a throne and yet are devoid of any virtue, why is it you consider you are a noble man (*gentius hom*)?'.[6]

As far back as 1081 Pope Gregory VII had pointed out the same illogicality in linking together virtue, descent, Nobility and deference when he characterized kings and dukes as having founded their power on the theft, rape and murder carried out by their ancestors.[7] Those who most wanted this deference were most likely those

---

[3] *PL*, 171, col. 1043.

[4] *The Etymologies of Isidore of Seville*, ed. and trans. S. A. Barney and others (Cambridge, 2006), 224, and see M. Aurell, 'La noblesse au xiiie siècle: paraître, pouvoir et savoir', in *Discurso, Memoria y Representación: La nobleza peninsular en la Baja Edad Media* (Actas de la XLII Semana de Estudios Medievales de Estella-Lizarra, Pamplona, 2016), 12–13. This was in due course the basic philological understanding that informed William of Aragon, in *De Nobilitate*, 58, *nobilis enim nichil aliud est quam bene operans*.

[5] Bouchard, *Blood*, 30–6, observes the same but in the context of the French debate between old and new nobilities and a period of social mutation, rather than as related to the concept of Nobility itself.

[6] *Condé* 1: 179–80 (ll. 107–17).

[7] A. J. Duggan, 'Concepts, Origins, Transformations', in *Nobles and Nobility in Medieval Europe*, ed. eadem (Woodbridge, 2000), 9.

to whom fortune and descent had brought power by the chances of birth, not those whom William of Aragon, Baldwin de Condé and many other writers thought had earned it by their virtue and learning.[8] It must have frustrated William mightily that his own preferred interpretation, which was not the one the world followed, was readily justified by reason and by the views of the ancients, while the vernacular understanding he was arguing against was only justifiable by contorted theology and myths.

NOBILITY OF BLOOD

About six months before Duke Henry fitz Empress came to the throne of England in October 1154, his supporter Abbot Ailred of Rievaulx, himself a man with a long English descent, celebrated the royal Saxon lineage Henry had through his grandmother Matilda, the queen of Henry I. Ailred traced the West Saxon line back through names both historical and fanciful to Woden and thence through Noah to Seth, 'who was son of Adam, the father of all'. Ailred addressed his genealogy to Duke Henry, asking him to note the glory of its members and not to be surprised that it will be reflected in him:

> ...as it is the most pressing impulse towards acquiring the best conduct to know that one has achieved nobility of blood from the very best of people. It is ever a cause of shame in a high-minded man to be found to have fallen short of his glorious ancestry; it is against the nature of things for a good root (*radix*) to produce bad fruit.[9]

Explicit statements about the importance and significance of a good and ancient lineage are not that common in the earlier medieval period, but Ailred obliged us with both a rational and a theological explanation for its importance. A man's consciousness of the greatness and virtue of his ancestors was a spur to virtue in himself, for the shame of falling from their high standards would hurt him if he was of a moral turn of mind. If that were not enough, he said there was a shadowy impulse in a man's lineage that impelled him towards virtue—an impulse the modern mind would call 'genetic'. For this, Ailred has the weighty theological backup of the sayings of Jesus, as reported in St Matthew's gospel (7:17–19) and more briefly in Luke's (6:43). The context in Matthew's gospel is Christ's preaching against false prophets and how they should be seen for what they are: wolves in sheep's clothing.

---

[8] The intriguing lost work of the Cambridgeshire schoolmaster Elias of Thriplow, which he called *Contra Nobilitatem Inanem*, most likely belonging to the 1230s, apparently catalogued instances of public virtue by marginal characters, mostly from classical histories and principally from Valerius Maximus's first-century compendium *Facta et dicta memorabilia*, with the intention of demonstrating that true nobility was virtue; *Petronius Rediuiuus et Helias Tripolanensis*, ed. M. L. Colker (Leiden, 2007), 145–65.

[9] *Est enim ad optimos mores obtinendos maximum incentivum, scire se ab optimis quibusque nobilitatem sanguinis meruisse, cum ingenuum animum semper pudeat in gloriosa progenie degenerem inveniri, et contra rerum sit naturam de bona radice fructus malos pullulare*, Ailred of Rievaulx, *Genealogia Regum Anglorum*, in *PL*, 195: col. 716. Ailred particularly noted King Æthelwulf of Wessex as an outstanding source of his family's virtue, 'from which most precious root sprang most holy fruits'; ibid., col. 718.

The passage was in fact usually deployed against (and by) heretics, and in its gospel context was nothing to do with lineage, but it could easily be made out to be.[10] Ailred chose to interpret *radix* in the same way it was used to allude to Christ's genealogy, arising from the 'root of Jesse' (Isa. 11:1). He employed the passage to illustrate the effect on a man of *nobilitas sanguinis*, the 'nobility' (or rather, perhaps, 'excellence') of his blood filtered and purified through the many virtuous men, his ancestors. He went so far as to claim that among Duke Henry's was Melchizedek, the priest and king of Genesis, a theological archetype of Christ.

There were other contemporary genealogies offered to kings as a way of illustrating their long inheritance of virtue, and they relate it to the royal and holy blood that was said to pulse through their veins. They demonstrate how widespread were views of the hereditability of distinction, as they are found within one generation in all three of the major insular societies of Great Britain. A few years before Ailred wrote, a Welsh clerk praised the glory of the lineage of the long-lived ruler of the kingdom of Gwynedd, Gruffudd ap Cynan (died 1137). He preceded his account of Gruffudd's action-packed life by a lavish and wide-ranging recitation of Gruffudd's ancestry on the side of both parents, back indeed on his father's side to Seth, son of Adam, by way of the god Saturn. The Welsh writer hijacked as he went Geoffrey of Monmouth's imagined descent of the Trojan exiles Brutus and Aeneas. More pragmatically, in view of the political circumstances of the late 1140s, the author went out of his way to draw the link of cousinship between Gruffudd's mother and the royal Norman dynasty, ending with the contemporary King Stephen (reigned 1135–54), predecessor of Henry II.

In doing this, Gruffudd's biographer was doing no more than following the justification for kingship long paraded in insular societies—English, British and Gaelic—where massive genealogical tracts gave the material for poets to recite a king's lineage, which was no less than his title deed to royalty. The Welsh clerk wrote, he tells us, to establish the *nobilitas*, the excellence, of Gruffudd's family (*gens*): Gruffudd's was a 'celestial line' and a divine race, from which it naturally followed that Gruffudd must be expected to achieve fame and do great deeds, for the potential for his own excellence was embedded deep in his lineage.[11] Royal genealogy was a source of more than distinction and inspiration in insular societies; it was also a political asset. We find this as late as 1249 when the Gaelic court poet of Alexander III of Scotland had his time in the limelight at the royal inauguration at Scone, standing before the assembly to recite Alexander's full and very lengthy genealogy as his title to occupy his throne. It would be eighty years yet before a Scottish king would join the mainstream of European monarchy to be consecrated

---

[10] Andreas Florentinus, *Summa contra hereticos*, ed. G. Rottenwöhrer (MGH, Quellen zur Geistesgeschichte des Mittelalters, 23, Hanover, 2008), 19, 52, tussled with an imaginary Cathar heretic over the true significance of the passage.

[11] *Vita Griffini filii Conani*, ed. and trans. P. Russell (Cardiff, 2005), 52–8. A useful analysis of the structure of the genealogy is D. E. Thornton, 'The Genealogy of Gruffudd ap Cynan', in *Gruffudd ap Cynan: a collaborative biography*, ed. K. L. Maund (Woodbridge, 1996), 79–108, though it analyses the Welsh translations, not the subsequently found Latin original.

as king with holy oil, and crowned.[12] Ailred of Rievaulx had himself once been a court officer in the household of his friend King David I of Scotland, and had quite likely been a witness to David's own inauguration in 1124, when he would have heard the king's genealogy performed. So what he was doing in 1153 was expressing a deep sensibility of the place of descent in establishing the place of eminent people within society, a sensibility that was widespread across the British Isles in the mid twelfth century as sources right across the insular cultures—so very well populated by kings—tell us.

The same list-making sensibility can be found on the Continental mainland, though not always deployed for the same reason as in the insular societies. The long and formidable universal lists of kings and emperors compiled by the imperial chaplain Godfrey of Viterbo in Germany in the reigns of Frederick Barbarossa and Henry VI may have been designed in part to glorify the idea of empire and monarchy, but they had rather less to do with glorifying lineage.[13] But there is a more direct parallel in the determination of the adherents of the Capetian monarchy to work around its unfortunate lack of a direct descent from Charlemagne, the semi-legendary avatar of Frankish kingship, who was by the twelfth century seen in France as having decidedly been a Frenchman. The lack was seen as a problem from the beginning of the dynasty's tenure of the throne. It was especially uncomfortable for the Capetians in the 1180s when many of their vassals had the imperial bloodline they did not. Their vassals appear to have enjoyed their lord's discomfiture. Around 1180, in a particularly impish mood, the Angevin panegyrist Benoît de Sainte-Maure made an argument that the Capetians, for all their grandeur, were in fact ultimately descended from a count of Anjou.[14] As a result the fact that King Louis VII (reigned 1137–80) took as his second wife a lady with Carolingian blood was much trumpeted. The need amongst the Capetians' intellectual auxiliaries to bridge the yawning genealogical gap went on to spawn historical pamphlets, not least that of the canon lawyer Giles of Paris, whose *Karolinus* was begun in 1196. The finished work was presented in 1200 to the teenage Lord Louis of France, son of King Philip, and it demonstrated to the boy, with the help of diagrams, how the glories of the Merovingian and Carolingian past were the true property of the Capetians.

But unfortunately Giles could only do this for his patron by affirming the Capetian family's evident virtue and sanctity, not by any satisfactory genealogical descent. It had to be admitted by Giles that Hugh Capet had indeed usurped the throne of the Carolingians, so all he could do was draw a parallel between the similar transmission of royalty from the Merovingians to the usurping—but undeniably

[12] J. M. W. Bannerman, 'The king's poet and the inauguration of Alexander III', *Scottish Historical Review*, 69 (1989), 120–49.

[13] Godfrey of Viterbo, *Speculum Regum* and *Memoria Seculorum*, in *MGH Scriptores* 22: 21–106. Godfrey did, however, have the dynastic aim of proving that the separated lineages of Troy through Imperial Rome and the Franks were reunited in the Carolingians; ibid., 93. He also happily dismissed any concern for the genealogies of other lesser monarchies (such as the Danes, Scots and Welsh) as being merely incidental, excepting the English, whom he regarded as a tribe of Trojan Britons; ibid., 99, 102, 127.

[14] *Chronique des ducs de Normandie*, ed. F. Michel (3 vols, Paris, 1836–44), 3: 378–81 (ll. 41,837–928).

virtuous—Carolingians. Giles could not in his day offer a direct blood link that his contemporaries would expect to explain the succession of virtue. However, within a few years of his death a canon of Tours with a genealogical obsession at last turned up the missing link: Hawise, the mother of Hugh Capet, was in fact a granddaughter of Louis the German, himself a grandson of Charlemagne.[15] The intellectual contortions necessary to prove the golden line of descent from Clovis and Pepin to Philip Augustus is eloquent testimony to its importance. Virtue of itself was not enough; there had to be a genetic link to explain royalty, and at last for King Louis VIII of France, there was.

If royalty was a quality that descended by blood line, then so might other forms of superior standing, for royal blood was itself dispersed widely in European societies, far wider indeed than just among the claimants to thrones. The point has been made that the earliest non-royal potentates in Western society—such as the ealdormen of the English kingdoms—must have derived from a pool of families that originally had called themselves 'kings'.[16] So it is not unusual to find that a line of counts might be dignified by a friendly writer as having some alliance with or root in a royal line and thus a share in its distinction, even if it was not royal itself. Bishop Adalbero of Laon, in a praise poem of the late 1020s, imagined a conversation with King Robert II of France (reigned 996–1031). He put in the king's mouth the observation that 'the blood of kings is at the root of the descent of superior men (*stemmata nobilium*)', and went on to say that a 'noble birth' is an adornment to both kings and dukes alike.[17] So Godfrey II of Cappenberg (died 1126) was credited by his biographer with an entirely fictional descent from both the Carolingians and the ancient royal line of Saxony.[18] The monastic biographer of Count Ludwig III of Arnstein (died a monk in 1185) may have praised the count's indifference while a lay brother to his ancient and distinguished lineage, but nonetheless he assured us that it was distinguished and ancient and his relatives included the duke of Swabia, father of Emperor Frederick Barbarossa.[19] King Robert of

---

[15] K. F. Werner, 'Die Legitimität der Kapetinger und die Entstehung des *Reditus Regni Francorum ad stirpem Karoli*', *Die Welt als Geschichte*, 12 (1952), 203–25, repr., in *Structures politique du monde français (VIe-XIIe siècle)* (London, 1979), 203–25; C. Klapisch-Zuber, *L'Ombre des ancêtres: essai sur l'imaginaire médiéval de la parenté* (Paris, 2000), 163–6; J. Führer, 'Gegenwart der Vorgänger und genealogisches Bewusstsein bei den Kapetingern (987–1223)', in *Genealogisches Bewusstsein als Legitimation. Inter- und intragenerationelle Auseinandersetzungen sowie die Bedeutung von Verwandtschaft bei Amtswechseln*, ed. H. Brandt, K. Köhler, and U. Siewert (Bamberger historische Studien, 4, 2009), 145–66. The *Grands Chroniques* were later to make the point that Louis VIII's mother was herself of Carolingian descent; for this and the sources of Capetian anxiety, G. M. Spiegel, 'The *Reditus Regni ad Stirpem Karoli Magni*: A New Look', *French Historical Studies*, 7 (1971/2), 143–74.

[16] J. Campbell. 'Nobility and Mobility in Anglo-Saxon England', in *Soldiers, Noble and Gentlemen: Essays in Honour of Maurice Keen*, ed. P. Coss and C. Tyerman (Woodbridge, 2009), 20–1.

[17] Adalbero of Laon, *Poème au roi Robert*, ed. and trans. (Fr.) C. Carozzi (Paris, 1979), 2.

[18] *Die Viten Gottfrieds von Cappenburg*, ed. G. Niemeyer and I. Ehlers-Kisseler (MGH Scriptores, 74, Hanover, 2005), 29–38, 107, 153. Elsewhere (p. 139) Godfrey is called vaguely *cognatus* of Emperor Henry V. On the Cappenberg genealogy, G. Althoff, 'Genealogische Fiktionen und die historiographische Gattung der Genealogie im hohen Mittelalter', in *Staten-Wappen-Dynastien*, 18 (Veröffentlichungen des Innsbrucker Stadtarchivs, N.F. 18, 1988), 67–79, esp. 68–70.

[19] 'Die Lebensbeschreibung des Grafen Ludwig III von Arnstein', ed. S. Widmann, in *Annalen des Vereins für Nassauische Alterumskunde und Geschichtsforschung*, 18 (1883/4), 244–66: Ludwig III's father was described as *ab avorum suorum longa prosapia clarus* (p. 246) and his mother as *secundum*

France in his day had no choice but to acknowledge that noble blood was not just the possession of kings, for he too had to deal with the fact that he came rather inconveniently from the line of the Robertian/Capetian dukes of France, not that of Charlemagne. Ailred of Rievaulx's theological view of the 'good root' in fact could easily apply to more than the genetic superiority of kings, for a good root might produce other sorts of virtuous and eminent men, people you might call *nobiles*, that is (in Isidorian terms) 'notable people' or 'excellent people', which remained the general senses of the word *nobilis* into the twelfth century.[20]

So there was in the twelfth century a dominant group across the societies of Latin Europe which invested heavily in the rights its birth was said to give it. Such people were not shy of claiming Nobility, and the advantages in deference and prestige to which it was said to entitle them, even if they were not themselves at the head of the great lineage they shared. Only a couple of years after the publication of Ailred's tract, Peter of Celle wrote a letter of recommendation for a son of the count of Blois who was seeking a benefice. Peter commented on the young man's outstanding lineage and affirmed that 'this little branch does not fall short of the richness of the paternal root'.[21] The full virtue of that particular dynastic root was lovingly explored in the next decade by Guy de Bazoches for the benefit of Count Henry the Liberal of Champagne. Guy detailed the generations of the family of Blois-Champagne back through the Carolingians to its Merovingian roots and Clovis, first king of the Franks, a distinction the Capetian kings of his day could not, of course, then claim. As if to rub it in, he reflected grandiloquently to Count Henry that:

> There dwells in you a great Nobility of mind, whose blood originates in a deep well of royal and imperial majesty, a majesty which did not merely adorn in the distant past the ancient lineage of legendary Troy, but which through your eminent and thoroughly Christian forbears, men of outstanding works and virtues, elevates both God and the world rather more than would the wafting of the scent of incense in golden thuribles.[22]

Guy's endeavour had a personal motivation, for he too could claim the same lineage, and so it followed that he too must possess Nobility, even though (and this is significant) he was a poverty-stricken clerk and so could not claim any such Nobility through position and inherited property. The contrasting perspective of his contemporary Thomas Becket, who had wealth and position but no birth, is spelled out in a letter of 1164. Though he had no lineage of any distinction himself, Becket claimed the same *animi nobilitas* as Guy did, but flatly denied it came by descent.[23] We see here already the developing duel in the interpretations of Nobility in

---

seculum clari et alti sanguinis (p. 248), whereas Ludwig himself had no time for his own *nomen* and *genus* (p. 263). See translation and commentary in *Noble Society: Five Lives from Twelfth-Century Germany*, trans. J. R. Lyon (Manchester, 2017), 220–48.

[20] As analysed in Bloch, *Feudal Society*, 2: 283–6.

[21] *The Letters of Peter of Celle*, ed. and trans. J. Haseldine (Oxford, 2001), 10–12.

[22] *Liber Epistularum Guidonis de Basochis*, ed. H. Adolfsson (Acta Univeritatis Stockholmensis. Studia Latina Stockholmensia, 18, 1969), 59.

[23] *The Correspondence of Thomas Becket, Archbishop of Canterbury, 1162–1170*, ed. A. J. Duggan (2 vols, Oxford, 2000), 1: 402.

twelfth-century society. Becket's can serve as the archetypical reaction of a successful careerist of modest background to life in a society where social and moral eminence was generally believed to be hereditary. He was too dangerously honest to join the conspiracy of deference, an innate honesty that would eventually cost him his life.

There is a large array of twelfth-century sources in which is embedded the idea that personal qualities, good and bad, descend in families, parents' qualities being replicated in their children. It was not a view by any means unique to that time. Back in the tenth century Odo of Cluny observed that adolescence was a difficult time of transition for a boy, 'when a youth put off the voice and appearance of his mother and began to assume the voice and appearance of his father'.[24] At the most reductionist, it was always possible to excuse, or at least explain, the greed of humanity because all descended from Adam, whose desire for the fruit of knowledge was humanity's downfall.[25] There are many passages to confirm that what Ailred of Rievaulx and Guy de Bazoches said about the descent of noble qualities was a widely shared belief in their day. In Normandy, the elegaist of Waleran II of Meulan in 1166 talked of the count's heir as being the image (*species*) of his father and goes on to say: 'he is like him in mind, wealth, education and eagerness; in feelings, speech, generosity, understanding and enterprise.'[26] In Germany, Hartmann von Aue's aristocratic leper Heinrich was distinguished both by his high birth ('almost princely') and the moral excellence (*tugent*) associated with it.[27] When Ralph of Caen described Godfrey de Bouillon's excellences, he coined the aphorism 'On the battlefield you see his father; in his praise of God, you see his mother'.[28] A medieval metaphor for this was the way a matrix impressed a seal design on soft wax, the matrix being the parent and the wax the child. It was a metaphor Peter the Venerable used when he flattered his patron, the Empress Matilda (died 1164), the very image of the virtues of her great father, Henry I of England.[29]

Twelfth-century proverb collections assume that personal qualities derived from birth (see pp. 103–4), and a Breton chaplain in the young King Henry II's household quoted this vernacular tradition less than a decade after Ailred wrote:

> But if the heir is of bad blood, what can he do about it? What can a cat do but chase mice? What can a pig do but roll in muck? A man will only be good who is of good stock.[30]

[24] *Vita sancti Geraldi Auriliacensis comitis*, in *PL* 133, col. 652, trans. G. Sitwell, in *Soldiers of Christ: Saints and Saints' lives from Late Antiquity and the Early Middle Ages*, ed. T. F. X. Noble and T. Head (University Park, PA, 1995), 309.

[25] *Frequenter cogitans*, in *Poésies inédites du moyen âge*, ed. M. Edélstand du Méril (Paris, 1854), 316.

[26] Stephen de Rouen, *Carmen elegiacum de Waleranno comite Mellenti*, in *Chronicles of the Reigns of Stephen, Henry II and Richard*, ed. R. Howlett (4 vols, Rolls Series, 1886–9) 2: 767. This corrects my interpretation of the passage in Crouch, *Aristocracy*, 211 (with thanks to Liesbeth van Houts).

[27] Hartmann von Aue, *Der arme Heinrich*, ed. H. Paul, rev. K. Gärtner (Altdeutsche Textbibliothek, 3, 1996), ll. 2799–802.

[28] *Radulphi Cadomensis Tancredus*, ed. E. d'Angelo (Corpus Christianorum: Continuatio Mediaevalis, 231, Turnhout, 2011), 18.

[29] *Recueil des chartes de l'abbaye de Cluny*, ed. A. Bernard and A. Bruel (5 vols, Paris, 1876–1903) 5: no. 4183, pp. 532–3. See the exploration of such topoi in B. Bedos-Rezak, 'Le sceau et l'art de penser au xiie siècle', in *Pourquoi les sceaux? La sigillographie, nouvel enjeu de l'histoire de l'art*, ed. M. Gil and J-L. Chassel (Lille, 2011), 153–76.

[30] *Livre des Manières*, 88 (c. 273).

When he learned his letters as a boy, Ailred must have read in the *Cato Novus* this injunction: 'Have delightful offspring who are your equal in moral strength if you wish to lead an upright life in peace.'[31] The idea had some vernacular antiquity too. The hagiographer of St Alexis, writing in the final quarter of the eleventh century, marvelled that the holy man despised wealth despite his great *linage* and distinguished connections (*grant parage*). Lesser men would have luxuriated in and exploited them.[32] The twelfth-century mind would have absorbed from many directions, past and present, the idea that there was in especially favoured persons an inborn fount of virtue and social distinction which was their inheritance with their blood from their distinguished forebears and which demanded an entirely unearned deference.[33]

Therefore non-royal as much as royal houses across Europe might glorify and draw attention to their ancient genealogy, rich with saints and great warriors, in ways quite as obsessional as that pursued on the royal Capetians' behalf. It was not a new impulse in the twelfth century. The 'holy genealogy' of Count Arnulf of Flanders was itemized in a brief tract by a clerk of Compiègne in the 950s, in an evident attempt to prove his patron's hereditary moral excellence, an enterprise his contemporaries (especially his Norman neighbours, whose ruler he treacherously assassinated) may well have found unconvincing. It was one of several early genealogical works which made a point of tracing the lineages of Lotharingian dynasties (of Flanders, Brabant and Boulogne) back to Carolingian ancestors.[34] The most impressive example of this obsessional impulse was the detailed genealogy compiled in the 1170s for the Guelfs, a German family which traced back its line to the time of Charlemagne and then far back beyond that (as did the kings of Gwynedd and the counts of Blois-Champagne) to mythical Trojan refugees forging new realms in prehistoric northern Europe.[35] Its author was working for Count Welf VI of Altdorf (died 1191) and he took great pride in the direct line he could construct from the first Welf of those long-ago Carolingian days to his own patron; so much so that the various collaterals and cadets of his line were literally sidelined, even the distinguished Guelfs who had subsequently become dukes of Saxony and Bavaria and indeed been united in Welf VI's days with the family of King Henry II of England.[36] Antiquity always added flavour to social distinction, as it did with royal descents

---

[31] *Facetus*, 288.   [32] *La Vie de Saint Alexis*, ed. M. Perugi (Geneva, 2000), ll. 246–50.

[33] So it was that when the jurists who drew up the 'Usages' of the county of Barcelona in the 1130s pontificated on the compensation owed for the assault on or murder of a bailiff, they drew a distinction between the bailiff who was of good and noble birth, and the one who wasn't. The 'noble' bailiff was recognizable in part by his lifestyle (his horse and superior diet), but his nobility resided also elsewhere, and that can only have been in his descent. The compensation for an ignoble bailiff was half that of his superior; *Usatges*, 67.

[34] *Genealogia comitum Flandriae*, ed. L. C. Bethmann, *MGH Scriptores*, 9: 302–4. See further L. Genicot, 'Princes territoriaux et sang carolingien', in *Études sur les principautés lotharingiennes* (Louvain, 1975), 216–306.

[35] For the use of Trojan origins in exalting continental pedigrees (mostly royal), W. Brückle, 'Noblesse oblige. Trojasage und legitime Herrschaft in der französischen Staatstheorie des späten Mittelalters', in *Genealogie als Denkform in Mittelalter und Früher Neuzeit*, ed. K. Heck and B. Hahn (Tübingen, 2000), 39–67.

[36] O. G. Oexle, 'Die "sächsische Welfenquelle" als Zeugnis der welfischen Hausüberlieferung', *Deutsches Archiv*, 24 (1968), 435–97; Klapisch-Zuber, *L'ombre des ancêtres*, 112–17.

and of itself it created an *Adelshaus*, secure in its understanding of its greatness simply by pointing to its long lineage.

Can we define further the nature and consequences of the Nobility claimed in these works? The later twelfth century is happily forthcoming on this question, for in the same generation as the 'History of the Welfs' the nature of Nobility is a common theme in the burgeoning vernacular literature of the day, which is perhaps a truer indicator of common social attitudes than Latin tracts pondering questions which had been raised in the schools. Romance and epic writers were well aware that a long lineage and great connections distanced some men from others. The epic *Garin le Loherenc* (a work originating in the third quarter of the twelfth century) has many examples of this sort of thinking. When Duke Beugon had his enemy Bernard de Nesle at his mercy, he swore to Bernard he would hang him, 'Never mind your family and your distinguished friends!' Meanwhile Garin, the duke's brother, admired the powerful count of Lens for his many connections and his 'remarkable descent' (*mervilleus ling*). The King Pepin of the epic was not so easily impressed, however, even as he acknowledged the importance of descent. Confronted by an aristocratic brawl in his palace, he swore, 'I'll hang in the morning any baron I arrest this evening who I see up to no good with sword or other weapon in hand, whatever the distinction of his family!'[37] Counts and lords of old and distinguished families and wide connections in the mind of *Garin*'s author had claims to deference which was generally believed gave them the right to special treatment, a right not extended to lesser beings. To challenge that right, as the king did, ran counter to the habitus and was of itself thought shocking and troubling.

NOBILITY IN SOCIETY

Modern historians use the words 'noble' and 'nobility' freely in discussing the nature of medieval aristocracy. They are not wrong to do so, for medieval writers used the terms indiscriminately too, but the varied use of the words in medieval texts tells us they are words which need to be interpreted with care whenever they are met. Modern (and some medieval) commentators employ 'nobility' in the sense that the modern world has defined for it, the sense which we do in fact already see established in the twelfth-century *History of the Welfs* and in the epic *Garin*.[38] What men and women of the degree of Count Henry the Liberal and Count Welf of Altdorf had which set them apart from others was their distinguished descent and connections by blood, which Guy de Bazoches calls Nobility and locates in the mind and disposition of the recipient as much as his blood. It gave them an (unearned) right to consideration, respect and deference from their superiors, equals and subordinates alike. So a poet at the court of Philip of Flanders in 1176 came out with the view

---

[37] *Garin le Loherenc*, 1: ll. 4267–8, 11,254–5, 11,938–41.
[38] L. Genicot, 'The Growth of the Noble Class', in *Lordship and Community on Medieval Europe: Selected Readings*, ed. F. L. Cheyette (New York, 1968), 129–31, is of that persuasion. K. F. Werner, *Naissance de la noblesse* (Paris, 1998), 457–60, makes the link backwards from the modern idea of nobility to its medieval roots.

that a man of good birth (*gentis hon*) possessed innate honour (*enour*) which his behaviour and resources then needed to match, or he lost credit.[39] This is nobility as the twenty-first-century anglophone understands it, and it was acknowledged by a social deference in which all of society was or was supposed to be complicit. To do otherwise was to insult its supposed possessor.

But the primacy and privilege that supposedly came from noble birth had no legal or formal pronouncement to rely on in the earlier Middle Ages. That was not to come until the very end of the thirteenth century. Possession of Nobility was simply 'understood', and so was not defined in terms everyone would share and acknowledge. Nobility is not and never has been an easy quality to pin down and define at any period. But at the end of the twelfth century, as social levels began to be more closely defined, debates and resentments that congregated around the concept become much more visible, and the points at issue become clearer, even if they tell us that there was still no universally agreed definition. All the earlier sources agree on is the reductionist perspective that Nobility was a good thing to have. When sources talk of the 'noble man'—as Marc Bloch demonstrated—they may mean no more than that he was the opposite of the bonded serf, someone who was his own man, truly free (*ingenuus*). But this idea conflicted even then with the idea of a noble as a man set apart by superior descent, for it was obvious that not all free men were entitled to social deference.[40]

The Latin adjective *nobilis* (which was taken into French as *noble*) all too often means nothing more (or less) than the Isidorian sense of 'notable'. Horses, hawks, hounds, rivers and houses can be described as *nobilis* in sources of our period, and frequently were.[41] The application of the word to people could be as bland, indeed it was only one of a family of synonymous Latin adjectives descending from the late Empire, such as *praeclarus* and *illuster*, which were deployed before 1100 to indicate social distinction.[42] The lack of a specific sense of *nobilis* which this indicates tells us of a lack of contemporary debate about what it was that was being evoked. There are characters frequently found in the eleventh century described as *nobiles* and possessing *nobilitas*, and sometimes they are described as *nobilis miles* or *nobilis eques*. When they are so described the social superiority they are said to have had is bestowed often enough on them by a monastery they have patronized, or by a writer under a family's patronage.[43] So a person described as *nobilis, nobilis*

[39] *Proverbe au Vilain*, no. 24.

[40] As explored in D. Barthélemy, *La mutation de l'an mil, a-t-elle eu lieu? Servage et chevalerie dans la France des x*ᵉ *et xi*ᵉ *siècles* (Paris, 1997), 142–9, following on from Marc Bloch's essay on the subject. Peire Vidal in his literary duel with the impoverished Marquis of Sardinia baited him that he once was free (*francs*) and now was a serf (*sers*); Peire, 242 (l. 21).

[41] Aragon, *De Nobilitate*, 96–8, defined the 'nobility' and 'good breeding' of birds, horses and dogs as lying in the way they fulfilled their work, and also, of course, in the noble associations of the way they were employed by the elite. Silk too was called 'noble' by Roger of Howden because it was a fine fabric associated with superior people; *Du Yorkshire à l'Inde: une géographie urbaine et maritime de la fin du xii*ᵉ *siècle*, ed. P. G. Dalché (Geneva, 2005), 197.

[42] Bouchard, *Blood*, 13 ('the term *nobilis* may have been reserved for those whose status was not immediately evident from their titles').

[43] P. Van Luyn, 'Les milites dans la France du xi*ᵉ *siècle', *Le Moyen Age*, lxxvii (1971), 227–35, presents a perennially informative list of instances.

miles or noble vassal in these sources may well have been of good birth and notability, or it may be that the qualities reside only in the pen of the scribe, but whatever the case he should not be taken as a 'noble' in the sense as a member of a closed superior caste with an inborn and unearned right to social deference, as perhaps happens too often in past historiography. One man the *Song of Roland* called (ironically) *noble vassal* was in fact the traitor Ganelon, attacked later in the text as an evil man of 'vile background' (*de put aire*).[44]

The *nobiles* or *nobiliores* of an eleventh- or twelfth-century medieval realm are not necessarily intended as a caste of its 'nobles' as the modern meaning would have it, but its leading and wealthier inhabitants, and not every one of them was necessarily going to be particularly 'noble' in blood. You can only argue this if, like Karl-Ferdinand Werner, you argue that the medieval nobility can be defined functionally as the caste of those who inherited great honors and possessions from their forebears, that is, the magnates of a realm.[45] But to do so ignores the inconveniently untidy nature of medieval statements on the subject. Orderic Vitalis wrote around 1140 a well-known passage concerning the court of King Henry I of England (reigned 1100–35) and the way the king had rewarded his adherents, 'distinguishing' or 'ennobling' (*illustrare*) men who had proved themselves to be useful and loyal servants, though they were of 'insignificant descent' (*ignobile stirps*), and raising them above counts and noble (*illustres*) castellans. Orderic was not impressed by the king's indifference to the claims of lineage, and his raising of men without blood to public distinction.[46] The *Song of Aspremont*, a work of around 1190, has a less well-known but equally telling scene where Charlemagne rewards his followers, giving greater gifts to the 'well-born men who were of distinguished descent' (*gentilx homes qui sont de rice lin*) than to the men who were merely *gentilx*.[47] Nobility, like honour, was not then thought to be an absolute quality. Indeed, as Bloch said, the fact that the word frequently turns up in documents in the comparative form *nobilior*, tells us quite how uncertain a quality it was in the medieval mind, where one person's 'Nobility' was not the same or as admirable as someone else's.[48] It was a shifting scale: some people were nobler than others, just as some were more honourable than others. Walter of Arras took this idea of degrees of Nobility further when he suggested that the 'more noble' a person was, the more wise and accomplished (and thus in his tales would be more likely to get the girl).[49]

But a long lineage was nonetheless part of the understanding of Nobility and universally appreciated as being important, so much so that, as we have seen, Guy de Bazoches could claim Nobility through blood and its consequent distinction,

---

[44] *Song*,1: 24 (l. 352), 48 (l. 763).
[45] Werner, *Naissance de la noblesse*, 443–60, a perspective which relied on the older view of Georges Duby and Karl Schmid that the 'patrimonialization' of the aristocracy and the concentration of its inheritance in families were new phenomena in the eleventh century.
[46] Orderic, 6: 16.   [47] *Aspremont*, 1: ll. 132–9.
[48] Bloch, *Feudal Society* 2: 288. D. Barthélemy, *L'ordre seigneurial, xiᵉ-xiiᵉ siècle* (Paris, 1990), 129, elaborates on that point, noting that distinction of descent can be demonstrably greater in one person than another. Thomasin of Zirclaria also talks of one man thinking of himself as 'nobler' than others (*edeler danne ein ander*); *Welsche Gast*, 105 (l. 3857).
[49] *Ille et Galeron*, ll. 3603–6.

even though poor in material goods. In the later eleventh century the chronicler
Sigebert of Gembloux wrote in praise of Wicbert (died 962), the founder of his
abbey. Sigebert felt he had to say that it was reputed that Wicbert was derived
'from a long line of ancient nobility', though he could not actually give much in
the way of detail beyond Wicbert's grandparents. But, as he said, the way of the
world was that 'length of pedigree is an enhancement to power, and wealth comes
from wide lands, and this is the way the power of nobility as the world understands
it is established and advanced'.[50] In the French vernacular the adjective *noble* is
often linked with *gentil* in descriptions of particular individuals.[51] *Gentil* essentially
means 'well born' or 'high-born', and the pairing of the word with *noble* reinforces
the understanding that Nobility was inborn superiority. Indeed, the word *gentil*
is one that can itself readily be translated as 'noble' and was meant to be, as in
Gaimar's description of Count Alan of Brittany, 'a noble man (*gentilz hom*) of great
family (*grant parage*).'[52] That this was a common vernacular understanding of
Nobility even in 1100 is clear from the way it had spread across cultures. The idea
of 'innate nobility' was as widespread as were ideas about the source of royal blood.
Nobilis was being glossed in Old English as *æðela* perhaps as early as the eighth
century, and it can only be significant that the English language linked that status
with birth and family, for common signifiers for 'nobleman' from the ninth century
onwards are the compounds *æðelboren* or *æðelcund* ('noble-born' or 'noble-kin').[53]
A similar conjunction is to be found in the Middle High German *erkent* ('honour-
able-kin'), where the accent is likewise on superior descent. For the genealogically
obsessed Celtic cultures, Gerald of Wales offers a charming story of a Welsh lord of
impeccable descent whose *innata nobilitas* was acknowledged by the waterfowl of a
mystical Breconshire lake, who sang at his command as they only would for men
of his degree.[54]

The classic sense of 'Nobility' as being a quality of innate superiority demanding
deference was being established before 1100, the chief considerations being how
you defined what Nobility was and how much deference it entitled you to. Blood
and descent were the dominant sense, but even then not the only one. Sigebert
of Gembloux, who certainly believed in nobility of descent, can also talk of the
reforming abbey of Gorze as deserving respect from the humility and piety of its
monastic life and as that being the source of its *nobilitas*.[55] Likewise, the later
eleventh-century Latin moral treatise *Ruodlieb* introduced its knightly hero as 'a
man born of a noble family who enhanced his innate nobility with his conduct'.[56]
The Norman monastic poet Roger of Caen (died 1095) was just as well aware of
this and, as one of Christ's poor, he was not impressed overmuch by the claims of

[50] *Vita Wicberti*, in *MGH Scriptores*, 8: 507, 508, and see Bouchard, *Blood*, 27–8.
[51] Such as Buern Buccecarle, *ki mult ert nobles e gentilz, Estoire*, l. 2640.
[52] *Estoire*, l. 5322, my translation.
[53] J. Roberts, 'The Old English Vocabulary of Nobility', in *Nobles and Nobility in Medieval Europe*,
ed. A. J. Duggan (Woodbridge, 2000), 72 and n, 74.
[54] *Itinerarium Kambriae*, in *GCO*, 6: 34.   [55] *Vita Wicberti*, in *MGH Scriptores*, 8: 511.
[56] *Quidam prosapia uir progenitus generosa moribus ingenitam decorabat nobilitatem...*, *Ruodlieb*, 28.

those who boasted of royal ancestors and great kinsfolk—'the empty Nobility of the flesh':

> The court of heaven is impressed by one's conduct not one's kin; and it is the just man, not the nobleman (*generosus*), who will gain heaven. But neither the agent of Death or the demon of Hell will torment one of the damned any the less because of his innate superiority (*ingenium*). Nobody will honour him or defer to him nor is he any the better off for his nobility (*nobilitate sua*).[57]

THE GREAT DEBATE ON NOBILITY

As has been said, the final quarter of the twelfth century generated a considerable amount of new literature and speculation about the nature of Nobility, deriving from the pens of clerics and laity alike. The quantity is far too great simply to put it down to better survival of literary remains than those of previous generations. The paradoxes of Nobility were being addressed at this time with a new determination, which has to be because there was a live field of debate in which the writers were participating. This was the generation that was drawn to examine critically the assumptions we have just considered behind blood and Nobility, and define them more closely. It was this generation which, with the help of the Bible and Aristotelian ideas, first tried to give some intellectual integrity to the idea that blood was the repository of the soul and so transmitted a hereditary disposition from parent to child.[58] It was also this generation which kicked with more determination against the idea that Nobility arose simply from an ancient descent through many great men, however virtuous—a criticism which in turn inspired a counter-attack because it implicitly questioned the established social order.[59] It is a nice demonstration of this essentially Aristotelian turn in thinking that in Walter of Châtillon's popular Latin epic of the 1170s, the *Alexandreis*, it was Aristotle who himself lectured the young Alexander the Great at length on the meaning of *nobilitas*, which he says may even be possessed by the poor, concluding: 'True virtue's sought within: one who abounds in inner moral strength adorns his soul with true nobility.'[60]

Nobility as an innate quality demanding deference could be used in several negative ways. If you wished to insult a social group or people, there was no better

---

[57] Roger of Caen, *De contemptu mundi* (attrib. Alexander Neckam as *de vita monachorum*), in *The Anglo-Latin Satirical Poets and Epigrammatists of the Twelfth Century*, ed. T. Wright (2 vols, Rolls Series, 1872), 2: 185. For attribution, R. Sharpe, *A Handlist of Latin Writers of Great Britain and Ireland before 1540* (Turnhout, 2001), 584.

[58] M. van Proeyen, 'Sang et heredité: à la croisée des imaginaires médicaux et sociaux des xiiie et xive siècles', in *Le sang au moyen age*, ed. M. Faure (Montpellier, 1999), 69–75.

[59] So Eric Köhler saw its appearance as a symptom of a twelfth-century dissolution of the traditional bonds between upper and lower aristocracy, *Ideal und Wirklichkeit in der höfischen Epik* (Tübingen, 1956), 23–35.

[60] *Galteri de Castellione Alexandreis*, ed. M. L. Colker (Thesaurus Mundi, Bibliotheca Scriptorum Latinorum Mediæ et Recentioris Ætatis, 17, Padua, 1978), c. 1, ll. 103–4, *Non eget exterius qui moribus intus habundat/Nobilitas sola est animum que moribus ornat*. The translation is the elegant rendition, in *The Alexandreis: a twelfth-century epic*, trans. D. Townsend (Peterborough, ON, 2007), 36.

way than to declare, as James de Vitry did with the Eastern-born citizens of the Latin kingdom (the *Pollani*)—whom he despised—that they were the degenerate and effeminate offspring of the godly and manly generation of Western Crusaders who were their fathers. He implied that the *Pollani* took after their oriental mothers in their deceit, criminality and luxury.[61] Prejudice could thus easily trump theory. It operated on a personal level too. A great and noble king or lord might well have a dissolute and unworthy son who clearly could not be said to have inherited his virtue: sin was after all a matter of choice, not necessarily of disposition. To pursue virtue was certainly believed to be a moral choice, as in the miracle story of St Etheldreda which dealt with two adolescent novices at Ely cathedral priory who were sent off to London in King Stephen's reign. The younger of them, dazzled by the temptations of the big city, went completely off the rails. The other, however, kept to his vocation, and displayed *bone moralité*.[62]

The deference which noble descent demanded therefore needed a more logical justification for some scholars than birth, antiquity of blood, good luck or even military power and personal wealth. Alan of Lille in the early 1180s sardonically and cleverly commented on the fact that social distinction by descent was unearned when he portrayed *Nobilitas* as one of the daughters of Fortune (Ignobility was the other) and cousin of Chance, demonstrating humorously in this way that Nobility's own descent was, to say the least, compromised. For Alan, Nobility was the least of the virtues, who had few gifts to give his New Man, since she possessed nothing other than what her mother, Fortune, allowed her. So in the end, as the greater Virtues had endowed the New Man with all the moral qualities he needed, Nobility was only able to give him a famous and distinguished family and a free and noble birth.[63] Noble birth was a matter of luck and as far as Alan was concerned moral pre-eminence had nothing to do with real Nobility, which was ultimately moral superiority. The idea that there had to be more to Nobility than birth was widespread at the end of the twelfth century. So when Gerald of Wales praised the Emperor Augustus as the most glorious of rulers, he took the fashionable line of his day and praised him above all for his 'nobility of soul', quoting Juvenal for his authority. But he also, being a man of his time and with claims to the Nobility of royal blood himself, felt he had to mention in passing that 'Augustus not only possessed nobility of soul, but also the most noble of descents'.[64]

One of the poems within Boethius's much-studied *Consolatio* was particularly troubling to thinking men who contemplated the questions raised by such contingent

---

[61] James de Vitry, *Historia orientalis*, ed. and trans (Fr.) J. Donnadieu (Turnhout, 2008), 288–90.

[62] *The Life of Saint Audrey*, ed. and trans. J. H. McCash and J. C. Barban (Jefferson, NC, 2006), 216 (ll. 4024–30).

[63] *Anticlaudianus*, in *Satirical Poets of the Twelfth Century*, ed. T. Wright (2 vols, Rolls Series, 1872) 2: 396, 403; J. Simpson, *Sciences and Self in Medieval Poetry: Alan of Lille's* Anticlaudianus *and John Gower's* Confessio Amantis (Cambridge, 2005), 290.

[64] *De principis instructione liber*, in *GCO*, 8: 51–2. One could compare this with the praise Brunetto Latini heaped around 1270 on the *Franchezza* of the unnamed great personage who was the dedicatee of his *Tesoretto*, a man who was born of an *alto legnaggio* but was also characterized by virtuous acts, carelessness of the good things of life, and by learning and wisdom which made him a latter day Cato or Solomon; *Tesoretto*, 175–8 (ll. 1–69).

ideas of Nobility. It informed Roger of Caen's critique of Nobility in eleventh-century Normandy. It had some striking and disturbingly meritocratic arguments deriving from earlier classical moralists, and not least the ideas of Aristotle, of which Boethius was one of the conduits to the earlier medieval world, but it had more force in his case as it was from the pen of a man regarded as a Christian martyr.[65]

> Every sort of human on Earth arises from the same source, for One is Father of all and provides for all... God clothed in a body the soul issuing from its heavenly home. Every mortal can then claim the self-same noble origin (*nobile germen*). So why do you boast of family and ancestors?... None is debased unless he befouls his own origin through wilful sin.

Some liked this logical and theological argument, as clearly did Andrew the Chaplain in his essay on love. He used it as his reason for locating Nobility in character (*probitas morum*), not wealth, physical beauty or blood.[66] The vernacular moralist Robert of Ho was another commentator on the Boethian insight (see pp. 33, 242), so it seems there was a widespread debate about it in the later twelfth-century schools which spilled over into the lay world.[67]

Reactionaries were antagonized by it. In the same generation, Alexander Neckam, a theorist rather than a critic of Nobility as we understand the concept, growled out his disapproval when he came to defining *Nobilitas*. He recognized the argument that many were making, that there were people 'who want to include nobility of blood in being worthy of respect'.[68] He was reluctant to dismiss such a view. So his critical mind worried at the scholastic distinction between Nobility of blood and descent, which Boethius was discussing, and Nobility of mind, which Juvenal (and indeed many other classical authors) famously declared to lie in Virtue, an observation which Neckam knew ultimately derived from his much-admired 'Philosopher' (Aristotle), whose *Politics* urged that Virtue ennobled and Wickedness debased (a text whose full Latin translation finally exploded into the intellectual world of the 1240s).[69] Those who proved truly noble, Neckam concluded, were choosing to follow in their souls the noble path provided by their primary forebear, the Father of All, the Creator. Those, like Cain, who proved corrupt, were following their debased mother, the Earth. Nobility then was for Neckam a genetic predisposition

---

[65] For Boethius as a source of Aristotelian ideas, S. Ebbesen, 'Boethius as an Aristotelian Scholar', in *Aristoteles Werk und Wirkung. Paul Moraux gewidmet 2, Kommentierung, Überlieferung, Nachleben*, ed. J. Wiesner (Berlin, 1987), 286–311.

[66] *De Amore*, 44–5.   [67] *Enseignements Trebor*, 114 (ll. 1968–74).

[68] *Volet autem quis astruere nobilitatem generis dignam esse commendatione*, De nobilitate, in *De Naturis Rerum Libri Duo*, ed. T. Wright (Rolls Series, 1863), 244.

[69] Juvenal, *Satires*, 8: 20; see also Seneca, *De beneficiis*, 3: 28. Marvin Colker lists ten Greek and Roman *fontes* for the idea; 'De Nobilitate Animi', in *Mediaeval Studies*, 23 (1961), 47–8n. To date, these texts have tended to be discussed more by later medievalists; see P. and G. Contamine, 'Noblesse, vertu, lignage et "anciennes richesses": jalons pour l'histoire médiévale de deux citations: Juvenal, Satires 8.20 et Aristote *Politique* 5.1', in *La tradition vive. Mélanges d'histoire des textes en l'honneur de Louis Holtz*, ed. P. Lardet (Turnhout, 2003), 321–34; but see now the broader study in G. Castelnuovo, 'Juvénal et la noblesse au Moyen Âge ou les avatars d'une citation', in *Des plats pays aux cimes alpines. Hommages offerts à François Bertrandy*, ed. F. Delrieux and F. Kayser (2 vols, Chambéry, 2010), 2: 13–27. For the Aristotelian influence on Neckam's analyses, R. W. Hunt, *The Schools and the Cloister: the Life and Writings of Alexander Nequam (1157–1217)*, ed. M. Gibson (Oxford, 1984), 67–77.

to superiority, but it had to be fulfilled by a moral choice, as with the two clerks of Ely. 'Men of social distinction', he recommended, 'are urged to acquire the *further* distinction of noble conduct.'[70] So for Neckam distinguished descent was nearly but not quite enough to require social deference; a man's moral choices had to affirm his genetic inheritance of Nobility. How well you resisted the curse of original sin defined not just your chances of salvation but your worldly status.[71]

We have good evidence that it was not just scholastic thinkers who were worrying away at the meaning of Nobility in the generations around 1200. Indeed, the reason they turned to the concept may well be because it was a question all conditions of men and women of their own day and age were posing. Some later evidence for the urgent lay interest in the question in that generation can be found in William of Aragon's *De nobilitate animi*. Though his tract was composed as late as 1290, it was intended to sum up past arguments on the subject and settle them decisively in the intellectual direction the later twelfth century was moving a century earlier: that Nobility was acquired by virtue, and not by blood. William was energized by his grounding in Aristotelian thought, which had conquered the schools by the time he attended the university at Montpellier in perhaps the 1260s. Though he gave pride of place in his reasoning to the authority of Aristotle, William took care to build up an appendix of *pièces justificatives* to add broader authority to his case. One of his sources included a body of sentences translated into Latin from what are now mostly lost troubadour poems from the mid twelfth to the mid thirteenth century, citing verses from six different Occitan poets, all in support of the idea of Nobility of mind or beauty, but not of blood.[72] A casual look through the poetry of the same and similar authors would, of course, find in them differing and contradictory views on Nobility. So although William attributed to Arnaut de Mareuil the view that 'Beauty of body without beauty of heart and without nobility is ignobility and a flower passing away without fruit',[73] he might also have found Arnaut on another occasion saying something quite different:

> Be assured that people aren't born or grow up according to any other than the inborn qualities that are within their soul, which forms the child's disposition; would it not be strange if there should be a son of a good father, who is a byword amongst distinguished men, and has no mirror-image in his son.[74]

But William's florilegium goes to prove, if nothing else, that the nature of Nobility was quite as hot a topic of discussion amongst the laity of the second half of the twelfth century as in the schools.

Perhaps the most significant testimony to the state of the popular debate on Nobility in the late 1180s or 1190s was offered by Robert of Ho. In his *Enseignement* he provided us with a judicious and extended moral reflection on the subject of

---

[70] Neckam, *De nobilitate*, 243–4.

[71] M. A. Mayeski, '*Secundam Naturam*: the Inheritance of Virtue in Ailred's *Genealogy of the English Kings*', *Cistercian Studies Quarterly*, 37 (2002), 221–8, and eadem, *Women at the Table: Three Medieval Theologians* (Collegeville, MN, 2004), 36–9.

[72] Aragon, *De Nobilitate*, 100–4. [73] Aragon, *De Nobilitate*, 102.

[74] *Razos es e Mesura*, 20 (ll. 147–54).

Nobility (*Gentilesce*), which, from his choice to argue in vernacular French, was intended for a wider audience than the schoolroom, an audience he knew was eager for views on the subject. We know little about Robert and his background. There are many English settlements of the name of Ho, Hoo and Hoe, though none of any size, and several families take the toponym. That Robert was a literate member of a landed family and most likely a schoolmaster with modest literary ambitions seems an unexceptionable deduction.[75] His work had some circulation and copies survive in two late thirteenth-century manuscripts of English provenance, featuring alongside similar moral tracts. Robert's ideas were framed principally in the light of Scripture, and if there was any specific source which motivated him on the subject of Nobility it lay in the Boethian insight discussed above.

In his views on *Gentillece*, Robert warned his pupil that he shouldn't preen himself or be assertive about the fact of his high birth, and should not treat it as a thing which justified overweening pride (*grant orguel*). In doing this, Robert opened up a debate about why noble privilege (*franchise*) was the property of only a few when all are equal in God's eyes. His resolution was to look to a definition of *gentillece* as coming from the heart. He noted that many *preudommes* had sons who were immoral, who disgraced their father's name, and lost the paternal castles and inheritance. By contrast, men of no account had fathered children who were virtuous and accomplished and climbed high in the world. So high social eminence (*la grant franchise*) must arise from the heart. A man was proved noble (*gentil*) by his virtue, and was so 'even if he were the son of a peasant who went around begging his bread', and such a man's heirs might also be called noble. It necessarily followed, by contrast, that a man was a felon who gave way to his worst impulses, even if he were the son of a baron. His children too would be stained by his Villainy, 'for often they may betray their descent in deed, word and disposition', and they could only distance themselves from their birth by means of an innocent and wholesome upbringing. His argument did not rely on Juvenal or his like for authority, but referred to Boethius on the fate in Genesis of Cain or Ham, whose descendants were subject to hereditary subjection or marginalization.

> In my opinion it has always been a truism: anyone lazy and idle and careless of his reputation will soon enough be made subject to another, just as in days gone by.[76]

---

[75] For the date of his *Enseignements Trebor*, see below, p. 309. Since his work is saturated in Catonian references and sentences drawn from proverbs *au vilain*, he was likely enough a schoolmaster. A Robert of Ho appears as petitioner in a foot of fine relating to a place called Hoe in the Breckland of Norfolk in 1205 (though he is not called *clericus*); *Feet of Fines for the County of Norfolk, 1201–15; for the County of Suffolk for the Reign of King John, 1199–1214*, ed. B. Dodwell (Pipe Roll Society, 1958), no. 73, and a knightly family of that name can be found in the same county around 1200. A Master Henry of Ho was the tutor of the young Gilbert Marshal in the early 1220s; *Acts and Letters*, p. 27.

[76] *Enseignements Trebor*, 114–20 (ll. 1959–2108), quotation ll. 203–8: *Uncore, au mien escient,/ Est tenu cel ordenement/Ker qui est lache e pereçus/E de sun preu non curieus/Mout tost sereit au desouz mis/ Si comme il furent jadis*. A whimsically similar perspective is to be found rather later in the *Romance of Silence*, where the author credits the ineptitude of Nature in incorporating fine clay in the making of the low-born, 'and that is why lofty character may be found in many of low station', and vice versa, *Silence*, ed. and trans. S. Roche-Mahdi (East Lansing, 1992), 86 (ll. 1853–4).

Robert was the first vernacular writer to devote time to exploring Nobility in these binary terms: that it derived *either* from blood *or* from moral choices, a sign in itself that the concept was becoming better defined than it had been in the days of Hildebert of Lavardin and Peter Alfonsi at the beginning of the century. As with other writers of his day (and afterwards), he was unable fully to reconcile the two standpoints.[77] So his reasoning could not entirely argue away the fact that in his society *franchise* (by which he meant Nobility as social eminence or privilege) derived from descent (*lignage*) and was a quality which was both trumpeted by its owners and demanded acknowledgement. In the end, although it was intellectually and theologically more sustainable to define Nobility as the public acknowledgement of the achievement (*proece*) which came from a life well lived, Robert could not get away with the statement that 'a man's good deeds justify his title to be noble (*gentil*)'.[78] So he had to allow that if people in his society were not noble, it was because of the lack of virtue of themselves and their ancestors, which left them damned (*hostez*) to their low condition. It is possible here that, despite his appeal to biblical author-ity, these views could have made their way into Robert's head from ideas circulat-ing in the schools. Alan of Lille was said to have lectured a seminar of knights on just that subject in the schools of Montpellier in the 1180s, and a knight of the court of Provence, Sordello da Goito, came out in his old age in the 1230s with just such a view:

> So it is that the good a man does throughout his life – like it or not but it's the truth – depends on a noble disposition rather than whatever family he may be born to. Therefore it cannot be said that Nobility derives from noble birth alone as an aristocrat is often a villain and the common bourgeois worthy and reputable. So the noble and kindly disposition is the governor of all good deeds.[79]

A couple of generations later Jean de Meung, in his continuation of the *Roman de la Rose*, would come out with much the same view, in his case directly quoting Alan of Lille when he did: 'Nobody is so intrepid in his conduct that Nobility won't abandon him if he's given to low conduct. Nobility is superior in all things, and so is alien to any base disposition.'[80] We are evidently tapping here into a widespread and lively debate in later twelfth-century society, which had sprawled well outside the schools.

A similar binary perspective on Nobility is to be found in the *Liber Urbani* of Daniel of Beccles, writing perhaps within a decade of Robert of Ho. He provided his pupils with a number of Latin maxims to disentangle, and several of them concern Nobility. It was not his intention to express his own viewpoint on the subject, but his grammatical teaching exercises nonetheless attest to the binary view in circulation

[77] The same binary opposition is found in Peter the Chanter's *Verbum Abbreviatum*, where genetic Nobility is seen as the source of the sin of pride and contrasted with Juvenal's view; *PL*, 205, col. 47.

[78] *Enseignements Trebor*, 116 (ll. 2013–14): *Par ses biens fez a donc prové/Qu'il deit gentil estre apelé.*

[79] *Ensenhamens d'Onor*, 217 (ll. 631–40). *Per qu'es tot, qui que plaza o tire/En noble cor, qui·n vol ver dire/Lo be[s] que om fai tota vie/De qualque gen que mogutz sia./Donx non pot om dir que noblesa/Mova de sola gentillesa/Que·l gentilz es soven malvatz/E·l borges valenz e prezatz;/Pero nobles cors e gentils/Es de totz bos faiz segnorils.*

[80] Meung, *Rose*, 404–6 (quoted ll. 6572–6).

in the 1180s. So we find his approving comment on the innate nature of Nobility, which (in apparent contradiction on another occasion) he said demanded that the heir to a great lineage had to live up to the virtue of his forebears, or (presumably) he would lose his social eminence:

> It is a contradiction that a noble man can be born from ignoble blood: a noble man exudes and dispenses sweetness; the ignoble and debased man produces and spreads only poison. Good fruit are produced by their sort of tree. Should your father be excellent, wealthy, generous and upstanding you, noble heir, should take care you don't fall from his standards. Unworthiness is a disgrace to any man of good birth.[81]

The early thirteenth-century Picard author by the name of Renaut, who wrote the romance *Galeran de Bretagne,* began his work by posing the same paradox. He deliberately chose the ironic name of 'Gente' for his anti-heroine: a beautiful lady of exalted family descended from kings and counts, whose defining qualities were her lying and vicious tongue and her implacable anger against anyone who stirred her envy:

> So far as her person and what you could see of her outside was concerned she matched the name, but you had no idea what lay within. 'Noble' was a name that only fit her face, teeth and outer form. It may have fit her exterior, which was superior and fair in form, but her heart was without any nobility (*gentillise*) ... so for this she must be reckoned to be *villaine*.[82]

This was not by any means solely a western European debate. Thomasin of Zirclaria, a cleric of the romance world of Lombardy and Occitania, which he mediated for the elites of the Empire north of the Alps, wrote tellingly in 1216 of the central importance of instilling self-control and self-discipline (*zuht* or *meisterschaft*) in the upbringing of aristocratic youth. In his *Welsche Gast* Thomasin elevated mental training, discretion and studied poise to be the defining features of Nobility, entirely ignoring blood and its inheritance: 'their sense of honour should engender discipline in them ... they should keep this advice in their minds and spirits: he who does this is truly noble (*edel*).' He puts it pithily: 'If a man is well-born but lacks sense then his nobility (*edeltuom*) is entirely wasted.'[83] For Thomasin (as much as for the author of *Galeran*), Nobility was of the mind, and a healthy mind at that. He identified the core of the whole question for those who would question the idea of Nobility by descent:

> If a man is highborn (*wol geborn*) and yet has lost the nobility of his mind (*sins muotes adel*) I can tell you for a fact his birth actually brings shame upon him, for if someone is highborn his birth demands at all times that he behave well and do the right thing,

---

[81] *Liber Urbani,* 5–6 (ll. 104–10): *Dissonat ingenuo genitus de sanguine prauo:/Ingenuus mellita parit, mellita ministrat,/Prauus iners fellita pluit, fellita propinat./Arbore de qua sint se poma comesta figurant./Si pater egregius opulentus largus honestus/Sit tibi degenerare caue sis nobilis heres./Dedecus est cuiquam generoso degenerare.*

[82] Renaut, *Galeran de Bretagne,* ed. and trans. (Fr.) J. Dufournet (Paris, 2009), 62–4 (ll. 29–40).

[83] *Welsche Gast,* 16–17 (ll. 581–614), 24 (ll. 863–4).

but if he does not force himself to do this he will disgrace himself all the more: his birth will diminish his honour.[84]

The mid-thirteenth-century German *enseignement*, *Der Winsbecke*, a work of not dissimilar construction and intention to that of Robert of Ho, says bluntly that high birth (*wol geburt, hoh geburt*) without corresponding virtue (*tugend*) is worthless.[85]

So by the middle of the thirteenth century lines had been drawn. There was more or less a consensus amongst intellectuals and thoughtful laymen alike that true Nobility really was virtue, a position which Ramon Llull was to establish decisively in aristocratic lay consciousness with his influential moral tract the *Llibre de l'Orde de Cavalleria*. When his compatriot William of Aragon summed up his own thinking a decade after Llull in the 1280s, it was to say that though he could list several types of Nobility—of Form, Fortune, Power, Wealth and Fame—in the end he only admitted to serious consideration two definitions—Blood and Virtue—and since all forms of Nobility arose from the attainment of Virtue, he had no doubt that the first was just a common assumption, while the second was the true Nobility. But as much as such men proved their case to their own intellectual satisfaction, the world in which they lived had long decided it a different way, that Nobility, like royalty, came from a noble and distinguished descent. Since property and power also descended in families, it could hardly be otherwise, and there were intellectual models which could be made to prove it, at least to the satisfaction of the elites.

THE ORIGIN MYTH OF NOBILITY

There was a lot at stake in the later twelfth-century debate on the nature of Nobility, which is one reason so much material survives on the subject. Arguing Nobility of mind meant diminishing Nobility of blood, but the power of a great and noble lineage was by then universally recognized in its society, and was flaunted in the faces of all by (for instance) the symbology of heraldry, which had been adopted by every great lineage in Europe, including Norwegian kings and Welsh princes. Though the intellectual balance was tipping decisively against Nobility of lineage and towards Nobility of conduct as the defining meaning, those with great and heritable power in society found ways to rebalance the question to their own satisfaction and did so by endorsing a myth. At some time in the 1160s or 1170s, a prolific professional poet born in Périgord, Arnaut de Mareuil (whose theme was usually love and its trials), composed for the young Alfonso II of Aragon (reigned 1164–96) an uncharacteristic little social tract, *Razos es e Mesura*. He did not claim to be a man of learning, he said, though we do know he had attended a school as a child in hopes of a clerical career. He was a man like Thomasin of Zirclaria who moved between the clerical and aristocratic worlds and several cultures. He had

---

[84] *Welsche Gast*, 105 (ll. 3863–72), translation from Gibbs and McConnell, 101.
[85] *Winsbecke*, 81, 87.

travelled in Iberia, Occitania, and probably also the more northern Plantagenet domains. It seems he encountered there both of the current views about the origin of Nobility and was as diffident in deciding them as any of his contemporaries. 'There is', he said, 'no crest or heraldry better than high birth, but there is no power in gold or silver to buy you a good reputation if you lack greatness of heart; one should care for nothing other than a truly rational and distinguished spirit.'[86]

Arnaut recognized the brute facts of inherited wealth and high birth but, like others, realized that they were not in themselves quite enough in intellectual terms to command automatic respect from the world. They could be easily contested, as several widely read authors had already proved. The great needed that argument, however, for power demanded deference, which was perhaps more satisfactory to the recipients if it were unthinking. So Arnaut sidestepped both genetic tendency and moral education and found for King Alfonso a different answer in history. Towards the end of his poem he got on to the same territory as Boethius had long ago broached and made a similar response to Neckam's, but with this major difference. His answer was calculated not merely to question Boethian logic but to go further and provide a version of human history that would justify the privilege his patrons enjoyed and why they should be obeyed, other than that they had inherited the right.

> It's true, as I hear tell, that in the days of Adam and Eve when God created humanity leaders were selected for their excellent morals, because there resided in them peaceful-ness, rational behaviour, generosity and justice in greater measure than in others. Candidates would not be considered qualified if they were arrogant, corrupted by the world, complete strangers to intelligence and accomplishment and tainted by wickedness. In this way evil men would not destroy each and every one, and neighbours likewise turn on each other.[87]

In Occitania in the third quarter of the twelfth century we find a parallel theory to Neckam's idea of the two branches of human society defined by their choices, the moral and immoral. But in Arnaut's argument, those amongst the first humans who had made the choice to be moral, rational, just, and generous did not just preserve their souls by it; they were awarded a hereditary social distinction and leadership by the rest of human society in return for their protection against the wicked. And not just them, but also their offspring, for Arnaut was one of those who believed in the genetic inheritance of Nobility of soul.

> It's my belief that people aren't born or grow up according to any other than the inborn qualities that are within their soul, which forms the child's disposition. It would be strange indeed if there should be a son of a good, admired and highly respected father who isn't his mirror-image.[88]

For Arnaut there was a social contract at the root of society and it had been made in its first generations. It was from society's ancient post-lapsarian (or post-Fluvial) elected leadership that nobles were descended, and it was as much their moral

---

[86] *Razos es e Mesura*, 20, (ll. 162–6): *n'es caps e colors/paraje d'auta gen,/poders d'aur ni d'argen/no·us daran ja bon pretz/si ric cor non avetz,/ric cor sens desmezura,/que d'autre non ai cura.*
[87] *Razos es e Mesura*, 23 (ll. 307–24).   [88] *Razos es e Mesura*, 20 (ll. 147–54).

eminence as their blood that the latest generation of nobles inherited from their forebears. And that moral eminence and the history behind it demanded the deference of those who were not noble.

This is the first plain appearance in the record of the medieval origin myth of Nobility. It was to be repeated again and again throughout the Middle Ages. When Philip de Beaumanoir composed his tract on customary law in 1283, the origin myth was his explanation for the privileges of noblemen and (by contrast) the ignominy of serfdom.[89] It obviously cannot have been the invention of Arnaut de Mareuil himself. As he says, he merely repeated a current idea. We could find some inspiration for it in the Aesopian fables where a body of animals elect kings to rule over and preserve them (and usually suffer by their choice), of which Marie de France gives many examples. It is even possible that it filters the view of Cicero as to the choice of the first kings amongst the ancients as being on the grounds of their virtue, which fit them to be protectors of the weak.[90] We can also see in it some echo of the already ancient idea of the Three Orders as a way of explaining human society, with 'those who fight' demanding the support of 'those who work' in return for their protection.[91] Adalbero of Laon, in his exploration of the idea of the orders back in the 1020s, made the point that those who fought were therefore in a position of command: they were *nobiles* (men free of constraint), and those who worked were *servi* under their tutelage. The same law did not bind both in Adalbero's eyes, and the lesser must defer to the greater.[92] In the 1150s, Stephen de Fougères too played with the idea of the Three Orders and in doing so came to a position not unlike that of Adalbero over a century earlier and Arnaut a generation later. Warriors must use their arms to do justice and defend the powerless who were obliged to work cheerfully for the lords in return and accept their leadership. He too found a social contract in the model, but what he was most concerned about was that lords of his day were simply failing to maintain the high moral standard which was expected of them.[93]

But Stephen was a rational thinker, critical of his own day and age, and indeed possessing a theological outlook which was deeply pessimistic about human nature. So for him men of noble families might very well fall from the high moral standards which were expected of them, and it was implicit in his views that an origin myth which depended on innate virtue was a moral impossibility. Others of his contemporaries said as much explicitly. The grammar-school exercises of Daniel of Beccles deployed the same Gospel passage as Ailred of Rievaulx and Peter of Celle a generation earlier, but Daniel hesitated to be as deterministic in his interpretation as they were. Good fruit might be expected to come from a good tree, but heirs could make bad moral choices and so be unworthy of their birth. For Daniel it was just worse when the noble sinner was one who should know better and in sinning disgraced his progenitor—either his genetic father or God the Father of All. Like his contemporaries Alexander Neckam and Jacques de Vitry, Daniel was aware that

---

[89] *Coutumes de Beauvaisis* 2: 235–6 (c. 1453).   [90] *De Officiis*, 2: 12.
[91] Crouch, *Nobility*, 226–8.   [92] *Poème au roi Robert*, 20–2.
[93] *Livre des Manières*, 55, 61, cc. 139, 140, 159.

men sinned and when they did it was indeed a matter of their choice. Neckam was driven to ask sardonically, 'Why is it that the present generation of noblemen are asserted to be noble from their birth, when their predecessors were of the most debased life?'[94] Heredity and history were no preservative, though it might at least have provided for noblemen the shame at being caught out in wickedness that was otherwise a motivation toward good.

NOBILIZING THE KNIGHT

Arnaut de Mareuil's origin myth to explain innate Nobility was not his own idea, but one that he tells us was current in his mid-twelfth-century literary world, which was a world wider than Occitania. We can find allusion to it in the 1180s in northern France where, in Andrew the Chaplain's dialogues, a noble lady affronted by the approaches of a commoner reminded him curtly that social conditions (*ordines*) were established among men from the earliest times (*aevum primordium*) and from the time of that division the superior group had innate prerogatives and superiority.[95] By the first decade of the thirteenth century we find the origin myth to be a commonplace as much in Burgundy as in the south, and probably it had been a generation and more before. It was a view congenial to the aristocracy which patronized the poets, who responded accordingly by giving their patrons what they wanted to hear. However, writers of the early thirteenth century did not apply the myth just to *nobiles*, *ingenui* or *sires*, but to knights.[96]

It might have seemed natural that they should. In the last generation of the twelfth century, we find a mythical explanation of the foundation of his kingdom by Clovis in a pseudo-history of the Franks which commences the romance *Partenopeus de Blois*. It says that Clovis, their first Christian king, established his realm by attracting and enfeoffing capable knights and promoting thus the *cevalerie* the king prized. He suffered no son of a villein to be a knight in his realm, and therefore in this particular origin story the French nobility originated as knights from the word go.[97] So in the first decade of the new century Ramon Vidal could well comment in his great poem *Abril issia* that 'knights (*cavayer*) were selected as men chosen to protect weaker folk and to perform acts of bravery and generosity . . . All good, honest and distinguished qualities are more pronounced in them than in other people. Almighty God has no desire to make such qualities common to all.'[98] The inspiration of Arnaut is clear here, for Ramon both knew and quoted *Razos es e Mesura*. He went a step further than Arnaut, however, for he told his noble and knightly audience that God had ordained that Nobility of soul was theirs alone, as was the deference that went with it. Much the same view can be found in the same

---

[94] *De Nobilitate*, 244.   [95] *De Amore*, 62.
[96] M. Aurell, 'Rapport Introductif', in *Chevalerie et Christianisme aux xii᷎ et xiii᷎ siècles*, ed. M. Aurell and C. Girbea (Rennes, 2011), 14–15.
[97] *Partonopeus de Blois*, ed. G-A. Crapelet (2 vols, Paris, 1834) 1: 16–17 (ll. 445–72).
[98] *Abril issia*, 130.

decade at the other end of France, where Raoul de Houdenc wrote that knighthood was created for a moral reason and knighthood was the 'true name' of *Gentillece*.[99]

The talented Burgundian author who around 1215 composed the prose tale of Lancelot's birth and education did not cite the Occitan writers of the previous generation. But his version of the myth is not much different from theirs and must come from a set of social assumptions common by then to professional and amateur poets alike across Europe.

> So know this well, that knights were by no means created and exalted just for amusement's sake, nor because they were in origin more noble and exalted in birth than other people, for everyone descends from the same father and mother. When envy and greed began to increase and the brute force began to subvert justice all at that point were still equal in both descent and nobility. When the weak could no longer resist or stand up to the strong, knights were set up henceforth as protectors and defenders to safeguard the weak and the lovers of peace, to maintain justice, and to hurl down the powerful for the wickedness and crimes they committed.... From the start, when the order of knighthood began, it was laid on the one who wanted to be a knight and who secured a grant of it by right of election, that he should be courtly without any villainy, civil and free of wickedness, merciful to those in trouble, generous and ready to assist the needy, eager and able to frustrate robbers and killers; men of judgement without fear or favour, and with no desire to assist any crime and harm justice.[100]

The words were put in the mouth of the Lady of the Lake as she instructed the young Galaaz (Lancelot) in the 'big thing' (*grant fais*) that was *chevalerie*, and the assumption behind them is that knighthood and Nobility were synonymous. The very word 'knight' speaks of 'high standing' (*hautece*) and 'dignity' (*dignité*), said Raoul de Houdenc, at much the same time as his Burgundian colleague. Raoul too believed superiority was innate in the knight: 'knighthood', he says, 'is the fountain of *cortoisie*'; it came from God and knights possess it.[101]

The anonymous Burgundian went a step beyond the Occitans in his treatment of the origin myth, and it is a significant one. When he says that knights were to maintain justice and hurl down the wicked, he was including them within the duties long assigned to Western kings in their coronation oath. He was, of course, by no means the first to do so. But he makes it explicit that knights had as much right to be obeyed and respected as kings and greater nobles did. In this way the ideas behind genetic kingship and genetic Nobility were brought fully into alignment and made equivalent. In the great tract on law and governance issued around 1260 under his name and with his direct input, the learned King Alfonso X of Castile (reigned 1252–84) assumed that nobles *and* knights both drew their origins as social groups from an act of election in the far past, in which moral responsibility was one of the chief considerations.[102] So in this way, Nobility was folded into Chivalry and its implicit moral excellence was appropriated to its emerging rationale for the social hegemony of the male aristocracy. Ramon Llull puts things in just those terms in his *Doctrinal* when he deals with knighthood. Knights were

---

[99] *Roman des Eles*, 32 (ll. 35–9).   [100] *Lancelot do Lac*, 1: 142 (my translation).
[101] *Roman des Eles*, 31 (ll. 12–13, 15, 25–6).   [102] *Siete Partidas*, ii, tit. 21, leys 2–3.

to him men of *encien lignage*, but when it came to expressing their knighthood it was not so much their physical capacity and arms that defined them as their virtues: loyalty, truth, humility, intelligence, hardihood, propriety and Courtliness.[103] This was the understanding that also penetrated the dry world of Llull's contemporary, the Picard jurist and moralist Philip de Beaumanoir. In 1283, while discussing and affirming the idea of moral hegemony in the origin myth, Philip distinguished noble men (*gentius hommes*) from other free men as being 'those such as kings, dukes, counts *and knights*, who are born of an eminent lineage (*franche lignie*)'.[104]

So despite all the arguments of the schools and generations of debate and the disruptive authority of classical authors and mainstream theology, it is clear that by the mid thirteenth century the dominant idea of Nobility in general society was still not that it was earned by virtue, but that it came from descent and conferred an unearned right on its possessor to social eminence and deference, and indeed now comprehended the lower social group of knights. This accounts for the intolerant tone of the mid-thirteenth-century Angevin customary incorporated in the *Établissements de Saint Louis*, which on the subject of knighting says bluntly that only a *gentis hom de parage* (a noble man of good family) may be considered for knighthood, and (following to the extreme the idea that children drew their moral and physical qualities from their father) his noble connection could not be drawn even from his mother's side. The author goes as far as to say that a candidate for knighthood could achieve it even if his mother was a villein, providing the father was noble.[105] For all that Llull subscribed to the idea that knights drew Nobility from their moral excellence, in his tract on knighthood he commented that Noble Descent (*Paratje*) and Chivalry (*Cavaylaria*) cannot exist one without the other.[106]

When in that same generation Baldwin de Condé, a poet active in the western Empire and eastern France, constructed a brief but ambitious work on *Gentilleche*, he argued round and round the subject, attempting to reconcile Nobility of blood, which was undeniable in its social force, with Nobility of virtuous conduct, which was negotiable. The great men of his society drew their stature from a hereditary Nobility which made them privileged and powerful (*plus haus hom et plus poissans*), but he says they needs must possess great virtue to be recognized as deserving such social eminence (*hauteche*). It is a logical but uncomfortable consequence of his argument—as Thomasin of Zirclaria and others had already pointed out and which Baldwin was reluctant to fully follow through—that the son of such a man who embraced Villainy and every vice degraded himself from his Nobility (*forligner*), 'because the worth of a *preudomme* ought to be mirrored in his heir'.[107] In the

---

[103] *Doctrinal*, 176. Brunetto Latini at much the same time defined his knight by a comparable set of virtues: Courtliness, generosity, loyalty and prowess, all of which proceeded from his justice; *Tesoretto*, 166–8 (ll. 1335–62).

[104] *Coutumes de Beauvaisis*, 2: c. 1451, p. 234, as noted in M. Aurell, *La noblesse en Occident, v*-*xv*ᵉ *siècle* (Paris, 1996), 95.

[105] *Établissements*, 2: 252–3 (c. 134).   [106] *Llibre de l'Orde*, 191–2 (c. 8).

[107] *Condé*, 1: 177 (ll. 40–1).

end caught between the two poles of the debate, he had to conclude that public reputation had to be the ultimate judge of those with hereditary claims to possessing Nobility:

> The higher and nobler a man is, the more he must avoid scandal and is the more blackened by it; and, as is truly said, how can a man notorious for his wickedness be credited with Nobility (*gentius*)?[108]

By the mid thirteenth century the nobilizing impulse in society was reaching below the knight. Deferential styles (*dominus/sire/messire*) were not just being routinely applied in France to knights in formal legal instruments (which they had been fitfully since the 1170s) but to the next rank down in society, the squires, who were addressed as *domicellus* or *damoiseau*.[109] It was an institutionalization of the old idea that there were *nobiles* and *nobiliores* in society and Nobility might be a graduated property. The famous preacher Stephen de Bourbon (died 1261) provided a number of intellectual takedowns to those who argued that their birth demanded deference in society, but when he did so it is clear he was struggling against the social tide. He scoffed at those 'who puff up and pointlessly glorify the idea of Nobility of descent (*de carnis nobilitate*)', and in doing so Stephen used the arguments we have already encountered. However, the witty *exempla* he used tell us that his lay contemporaries were arguing their innate social superiority from whatever lines of descent they could usefully recruit, and covering up those that did them no credit. Stephen talked of the insignificant man of no personal gifts who looked down on others of more accomplishment if his family was the more distinguished. And most resentfully of all, he condemned the knights who aspired to the moral leadership of his society and yet who stripped the poor of their goods.[110] Not everyone was happy even then with the idea of the Noble Knight, who had been for centuries the butt of moral criticism.

---

[108] *Condé*, 1: 177 (ll. 51–6): *Que plus est haus et gentius hom,/Plus i a de honte fuison/Et plus l'en doit on ahonter;/Et, à droite raison conter,/Por coi seroit gentius clamés/Cius qui de mal ert diffamés?*

[109] Crouch, *Image*, 151–2, 169–70.

[110] *Anecdotes et apologues tirés du recueil inédit d'Etienne de Bourbon*, ed. A. Lecoy de la Marche (Paris, 1877), 242–6.

12

The Disruptive Knight

At the beginning of the thirteenth century knighthood was woven into the same origin myth that explained and justified noble status in society. This was part of what amounted to an apotheosis of knighthood and its formal assumption into the Olympian heights of European society. It has long been assumed by historians that the social elevation of the knight they have observed did not come out of the blue. Since the time of the Enlightenment the major national historiographies have assumed there was a relative rise in the status of the knight in the High Middle Ages, though each gives different reasons, some of which remain contested. Francophone historiography was tied as early as the eighteenth century into seeing the appearance of the knight in early medieval France as a symptom of the collapse of the Frankish empire into feudal anarchy. Until the 1990s the idea that knights were agents of anarchic violence who rose with the power of the lords they served was still the majority view. British historiography, dealing with a land where the knight appeared late, only in the 1060s, also believed knights rose socially, but used its wealth of social documentation to illustrate the complexity of the eleventh- and early twelfth-century concept of knight and the precise gradient of the rise in wealth, lifestyle and status the English knight experienced. German historiography developed a different scenario, however, for the historiography of the German knight is complicated by the existence into the thirteenth century in the Empire north and south of the Alps of the ministerial, the so-called 'peasant' knight bound to his lord from birth. Here the historiographical impulse is to see the rise of the knight as an enfranchisement rather than an ennoblement. It might be seen as theorizing a rise in knightly status, though it is not, of course, that simple a phenomenon. There is in sum a great weight of historiography as to what was going on with the medieval knight and his social impact before 1200, which it is not going too far to see as dragging down the present study, for all its importance in several areas of medieval social study. So we have a long journey ahead of us in mapping and assessing the ideas of historians before we can even begin to grapple with what actually happened at the end of the twelfth century.

THE RISE (OR NOT) OF THE KNIGHT

A baseline in the study of the knight's status can be found in the work of the prolific Jesuit antiquary Claude-François Menestrier (1631–1705), whose *Chevalerie ancienne et moderne* was published in 1683. In unpacking all its senses and in his discussion, Menestrier related *Chevalerie*—by which he meant 'knighthood', not the ideology we call Chivalry—to Nobility, and thus to superiority in society. Knights were to him noble because of the Nobility of their profession. Under the heading of the moral excellence of the knight, he was keen to emphasize the ideology to be found in the benediction of arms and the ceremony of inauguration of a medieval knight at the altar as it developed in the later Middle Ages. La Curne de Sainte-Palaye (1697–1781), who was happy enough to see himself as continuing Menestrier's work, produced a more familiar analysis of knighthood and Chivalry reconstructed laboriously and self-consciously from the analysis of literary remains as much as legal texts, which had been Menestrier's preferred source. Like Menestrier, La Curne recognized that the French word *chevalerie* can signify both the state of knighthood and the ideology that became attached to it. La Curne was a pioneering student of medieval French literature, and he encountered there model tracts, like the *Roman des Eles*, which described *chevalerie* in hypermoral terms. So he was well equipped to reconstruct from his reading an ideology of knighthood. La Curne located knighthood and its chivalric ideology entirely in the French Middle Ages, and since he saw the ceremony of the reception of arms as an indicator of *chevalerie* (in the sense of knighthood) and a statement of its ideals, he was happy to believe that it had been a reality as far back as the times of Charlemagne. But he made a distinction. The 'Golden Age of Chivalry' was for him in the later Middle Ages when there were romances and tracts to describe and exalt the virtues of the true *chevaler*. La Curne's assumptions about the superior status of medieval knights in society and their ideology of Chivalry are the ones that became embedded in European historiography, as we have seen in Chapter 1. Because of him the three principal traditions of European historiography were united in the early nineteenth century in seeing knights of the medieval centuries as noble or rising to Nobility. But that unanimity did not survive the twentieth century.

I The British Tradition

In the second half of the twentieth century there was a developing critical consciousness in Britain of the assumption made unthinkingly by Menestrier and his eighteenth- and nineteenth-century successors: that knights, by being knights, were noblemen. The idea that knights might not necessarily be regarded as 'noble' in any sense of the word before the thirteenth century emerged into conscious historiographical debate in Britain in the 1980s, though it was a view that can be found as early as the 1920s. In 1984, however, a senior British medievalist stigmatized the suggestion as unnecessary and unwelcome revisionism and so brought it into the realm of historical debate. In doing so he offered a useful study of the emergence of what to him was a heresy. It had arisen out of the potential in English historiography to use the exceptional survival of early national and regional surveys (including, but not only, the famous Domesday Book of 1086) to reach conclusions about the socio-economic standing of individual eleventh- and twelfth-century knights.

Sir Frank Stenton was in 1929 the first to observe from analysis of such sources that the Latin term *miles* was not used in England in any honorific sense before 1166, which he backed up by detailing the meagre resources commanded by many Anglo-Norman landowners called *milites*.[1] Stenton's pragmatic observation was to be pursued in some detail in 1970 by Sally Harvey, in her meticulous study of the *milites* who appear in Domesday Book and other contemporary and subsequent eleventh- and twelfth-century English land surveys. She arrived at the view that the *milites* of 1086 occupied a variety of economic levels, some eminent, some modest, and some lowly. Some were clearly landed vassals of good family, some men commanding only the resources comparable to a free peasant, and others no more than retained warriors, with the word *miles* intended in their case to evoke perhaps no more than the generalized sense of 'soldiers'.[2] That Anglo-Norman knights formed a continuum of wealth and status—from men of little standing other than what they drew from their profession, to well-born associates of princes—was an unexceptionable deduction from her mass of evidence. Harvey followed up her deduction, however, by pursuing Stenton's suggestion that what was true of the knight in 1100 was not necessarily true of the knight in 1200. Stenton had observed that ultimately 'the higher conception' of the knight prevailed in society. Harvey also thought the English sources allowed that between 1100 and 1200 the knight's status had risen. Over the century poorer men fell out of consideration as the dignity of knight was increasingly confined to the elite. She did not offer any extended explanation as to why this was so, speculating that it was due to the increase in the costs of knightly equipment and monetary inflation in twelfth-century society.[3] Nonetheless, her fine work and basic assumptions still inform the general understanding of the English knight in the Anglo-Norman period, that is up till 1154.

British historiography has adopted the idea of the rise in status and nobilization of the knight during the twelfth century, though without much real discussion of the social and ideological reasons why that should be: the arguments to support it have remained where Harvey left them, rooted in material economics and law codes. These are, however, strong arguments, so far as they go. In England, the survival of substantial record sources means it is possible to prove pragmatically and numerically that the knightly group across the kingdom shrank rather dramatically between 1180 and 1230, and that the remaining knights were largely those who could embrace and finance a noble material lifestyle from their own resources. It could be argued from this that the result was not so much that the status of knights rose in England, but that those who could not afford the noble

---

[1] R. A. Brown, 'The Status of the Norman Knight', in *War and Government in the Middle Ages: Essays in Honour of J. O. Prestwich*, ed. J. Gillingham and J. C. Holt (Woodbridge, 1984), 18–32; F. M. Stenton, *The First Century of English Feudalism, 1066–1166, being the Ford Lectures delivered in the University of Oxford in Hilary Term 1929* (2nd edn, Oxford, 1961), 142–5, notably p. 142, 'for although knighthood in the eleventh century implied military proficiency, it carried no social distinction'.

[2] S. Harvey, 'The Knight and Knight's Fee in England', *Past & Present*, no. 49 (1970), 3–43.

[3] Harvey, 'Knight and Knight's Fee', 39–42.

lifestyle it began to demand were squeezed out of the group in the generations on either side of 1200. The legalism of English medieval social history has also led to the conclusion that knights achieved a higher prestige in England during the twelfth century than the knights of other realms, due principally to their being conscripted by the king and his council in the 1160s as the recognized agents of local government and conceded formally a corporate controlling interest in their shires, which they continued to enjoy throughout the later medieval centuries.[4] County knights in England therefore had a direct connection with the royal court that was not to be found in Capetian France, where local power in his domain was conceded by the king to the powerful figure of the *bailli*, who may have been a knight but who accounted for his district as the single appointed representative of the king's interests and justice.

II The German Tradition

The German understanding of knights began with Büsching in the 1820s in much the same place as the French. The broad understanding of the Imperial knight as being more or less the same creature as the West Frankish one survived into the twentieth century, in part because of the way literary sources long remained the principal source for knightly life in German as much as in French historiography. The knight portrayed in late twelfth-century German romances owed a lot to those imagined by Chrétien de Troyes, which made it all the easier to assume, as Büsching had, that they were the same creature. So in 1906 Otto Hintze saw the knightly class, the *Ritterstand*, as a specialized mounted warrior class emerging in the Empire out of the collapse of the Carolingians, in much the same way as the French historian Paul Guilhiermoz had done four years earlier.[5] However, this was to change in the course of the century.

The implications of the existence of the *ministerialis*, the serf-knight, for the history of the German nobility was already disturbing historical debate in Hintze's time.[6] The consequences for Germany's place in the history of knighthood (as well as other matters) were to be spelled out with the publication of the extensive body of work by Karl Bosl on the *ministeriales* and free knights of the Empire, which began to appear at the end of the Second World War.[7] In fact the Franco-Germanic divergence had already been recognized in France before Bosl's work. A scholar of the stature of Marc Bloch could not miss the significance of ministerial knighthood, which he dealt with under the heading of 'servants' (*sergents*). Their servile birth, he concluded, compromised their status as knights and they were long 'un échelon

---

[4] Crouch, *Aristocracy*, 13–19, and references given on p. 225. For a study of the complex meaning and extent of local knighthood in England in this later period, P.R. Coss, *Lordship, Knighthood and Locality: a Study of English Society, c.1180–c.1280* (Cambridge, 1991), 210–63.

[5] O. Hintze, *Staat und Verfassung. Gesammelte Abhandlungen zur allgemeinen Verfassungsgeschichte* (3rd edn, Göttingen, 1970), 52–83.

[6] J. B. Freed, 'The Origins of the European Nobility: the Problem of the Ministerials', *Viator*, 7 (1976), 217–18.

[7] The definitive statement was K. Bosl, *Die Reichsministerialität der Salier und Staufer* (MGH Schriften, 10, Stuttgart, 1950–1).

à part' unique to the Imperial nobility—a useful but problematical lower level whose anomalies in the end broke it apart, some absorbed into the wealthier peasantry and the others into the lower nobility. This was for Bloch a social rise in German knighthood, but one which was consummated a century and a half later in the Empire than it had been in France.[8] The absence of ministerial knights in the development of French knighthood was taken by Bloch as a sign that France possessed a knighthood evolving at a different tempo from that of the Empire, even if their 'feudal' development moved in parallel. The fact that ministerial knighthood did not extend westward beyond the Empire was an evocative one for historians interested in the comparative development of aristocracies. It was to be found in the Imperial provinces of the Low Countries, even in French-speaking areas like Brabant and Limbourg, but not in neighbouring French-speaking Picardy, which was within the kingdom of France.[9] But all this should not necessarily suggest that German knighthood was insulated from the factors influencing and defining cultural knighthood elsewhere in Europe.

As it progressed, investigation has discovered that within the Empire there was to be found amongst the *ministeriales* or court officers of the ecclesiastical princes from the start of the eleventh century a form of *miles* who had the skills and equipment of the Western knight, but not the free status, for they were tied by birth to service to particular lords with no right to escape it. It followed from this scholarship that many German knights had low and unfree origins and could not in the Salian period be said to share standing with the free knights, or the lords who employed them. This changed of course. Bosl believed that ministerials already formed a self-aware class within the wider nobility in 1100, rising as they became useful governmental agents of the rulers of the emerging territorial principalities of the Empire, and ultimately of the emperor himself. With opportunities came social change as some ministerials acquired more land on different terms from their 'villein' tenements and followed a lifestyle no different from the wealthier free knights. The twelfth-century emperors enhanced the nature of the social division by creating a class of powerful Imperial ministerial knights who rose to the summit of Imperial society during the Investiture Dispute, and were to be indispensable to Frederick Barbarossa's rule of the Empire, particularly in Lombardy.

The *ministeriales* in present historiography are seen as the source of the knightly class in a good part of the Empire. As the 'free knights' still visible in the twelfth century declined as a group, the knights of ministerial origin intermarried with families of free knights and took their place. Indeed, in thirteenth-century Austria and southern Germany at least, ministerials might have been regarded as superior in standing to the poorer free knights. So there was in German scholarship an implicit 'rise' in knighthood from the eleventh century onward as the *Ritterstand* homogenized and nobilized in Germany by the thirteenth century and some of

---

[8] Bloch, *Feudal Society* (from French edn), 2: 96–8.
[9] See particularly J. M. van Winter, 'The Ministerial and Knightly Classes in Guelders and Zutphen', *Acta Historica Neerlandica* (Leiden, 1966), 171–87.

them were elevated further into the *Herrenstand*, the imperial landed nobility.[10] Unlike the rapid changes in the historiography of the knight since the 1980s found in France, and to a lesser extent in Britain, German scholarship seems to have stabilized in the course of the twentieth century, which may reflect on the quality of the work and debate of its later twentieth-century practitioners.[11] So, as in the current British tradition, knights in the Empire are to be seen in the way Josef Fleckenstein defined them in lapidary terms: an emerging eleventh-century social group whose status consolidated in the next century.[12] The difference from the West is that this knightly group was fractured by the divisiveness of free and unfree status within it, and so its consolidation was rather more fraught and extended than in England.

III The French Tradition

The French tradition has a right to claim priority in the argument over the status of the knight, in that the study of the knight has been for centuries principally conducted in that language. The idea of the social rise of the knight was integral to French historiography in the twentieth century, as in the other two traditions we have looked at. Marc Bloch had some influence on its articulation, when he restated the traditional French view—as old in fact as Montesquieu—that there was a social upheaval in ninth-century France in the late Carolingian period during which a new military aristocracy emerged and public authority collapsed. For Bloch the knights in this scenario emerged out of the warbands that had always been characteristic of Frankish society, but were different from their forebears in being tied by military service and homage to magnates rather than to the king, as well as being dependent on the new castles that were the local response to the time of invasions in which the Carolingian empire collapsed. Such knights were dependants of the magnates and princes who built their lordships out of the wreck of West Francia, and so were of less status than their lords, though it was relative, for some of these knights controlled fiefs of villages and peasants. To Bloch a change in the status of knights came when gifts of land to knightly vassals became

[10] For this standpoint, J. Fleckenstein, 'Die Entstehung des niederen Adels und das Rittertum', in *Herrschaft und Stand. Untersuchungen zur Sozialgeschichte im 13. Jahrhundert*, ed. idem (Göttingen, 1977), 17–39. The comparative anglophone historiographical work is useful on this, notably J. B. Freed, 'The Origins of the European Nobility', 211–41. See also idem, 'The formation of the Salzburg ministerialage in the tenth and the eleventh centuries', *Viator*, 9 (1978), 67–102; idem, 'The Ministerials and the Church in Twelfth-century Salzburg', *Medieval Prosopography*, 3 (1982), 1–20; idem, 'Nobles, ministerials, and knights in the archdiocese of Salzburg', *Speculum*, 62 (1987), 575–611. And see the extensive treatment in B. Arnold, *German Knighthood 1050–1300* (Oxford, 1985). Present German views are represented by T. Zotz, 'Die Formierung der Ministerialität', in *Die Salier und das Reich*, ed. S. Weinfurter (3 vols, Sigmaringen, 1991–2), 3: 3–50; J. U. Keupp, *Dienst und Verdienst. Die Ministerialen Friedrich Barbarossas und Heinrichs VI* (Stuttgart, 2002).

[11] See F-R. Erkens, 'Militia und Ritterschaft. Reflexionen über die Entstehung des Rittertums', *Historische Zeitschrift*, 258 (1994), 623–59, and the survey in W. Hechberger, *Adel, Ministerialität und Rittertum im Mittelalter* (Enzyklopädie deutscher Geschichte, 72, Munich, 2010), 27–37.

[12] J. Fleckenstein, 'Vom Rittertum der Stauferzeit am Oberrhein', *Alemannisches Jahrbuch* (1979/80), 21–42, at 39.

hereditary fiefs, an idea he acquired directly from Montesquieu, who saw military vassalization as one of the key shifts towards a post-Carolingian *gouvernement féodal*. By the eleventh century the undifferentiated free warrior of the Anglo-Saxon and Germanic societies, whom Bloch assumed to have been admitted into manly status by a delivery of arms, had disappeared and the rite of *adoubement* was restricted to the elite horseback warrior, the *chevaler*. But even within that elite he thought there was still a continuum of socio-economic standing: some were youths of good birth and wealth, others were 'fortunate upstarts' (*heureuses parvenus*) who had transcended their origins by favour from above. It was not till the middle of the twelfth century that knighthood became to him a fully nobilized and homogeneous order.[13]

As Montesquieu stood behind Bloch, so Bloch stood behind the developing and influential views of Léopold Genicot and Georges Duby in the 1950s and 1960s on knighthood as a social group and its impact on West Francia. Genicot's study of the region of francophone Namur, which was in the western Empire, naturally made much of the way the ministerial nature of its knighthood there severed *milites* from *nobiles*, as Bloch had suggested before him (though he and Duby alike believed that men called *nobiles* would not disdain the additional distinction of 'knight').[14] The key figure for the twentieth century proved to be Georges Duby. In his 1953 study on the society of the Mâconnais from the ninth to the thirteenth century, Duby did something similar to what Stenton had done before the Second World War on English earlier medieval society. They both constructed models of society using a dense charter-based empirical methodology, and it is perhaps not then accidental that they both came to see the knight as a more complicated social construct than the eighteenth century admitted, though for different reasons. For Stenton the wide variation in economic standing among men called *milites* made it self-evident they could not belong to a unified noble group, even as late as the mid twelfth century. Duby for his part, like Bloch, saw *milites* shifting in their social standing over the long period of his study as society changed. Duby's primary evidence was in the mutating treatment of the word *miles* in his chosen study of the Mâconnais in Burgundy from the 970s to the thirteenth century. Generation by generation till the 1030s the word became the term of choice for local lords. By 1100 *milites* were more clearly separated in his sources from lesser men and the word was being used as a title of honour, in which magnates of the region too were rejoicing. In the twelfth century knights formed a coherent body of local lords, with the title being the property of certain families. The reason for this rise in status was the same as Bloch's: the breakdown of old Carolingian social structures leading to the gradual usurpation by lower and lower groups in society of the 'ban' the right to do justice as lords. The violence implicit in this process brought military ideals to the fore as qualifications for local eminence.[15] Duby, rather unwisely, extended his model to the whole of France, making little allowance for regional

---

[13] Bloch, *Feudal Society*, (from French edn) esp. 1: 293–6; 2: 46–53.

[14] L. Genicot, *L'économie namuroise au bas moyen âge* (4 vols, Louvain, 1960–95), 2: 63–84.

[15] As summarized in 'Les origines de la chevalerie', in *Ordinamenti Militari in Occidente nell'alto medioevo, Spoleto 30 Marze—15 Aprile 1967* (Settimane di studio del Centro italiano di studi sull'alto medioevo, 15, 1968).

variation, and historians of Normandy and Picardy were naturally among the first to demonstrate its problems and inadequacies. But his ideas on the rise of the knight in this process—depending as it did on Bloch's authority—proved more resilient, since his colleagues shared it too.[16]

However, French historiography was about to diverge at this point from the other traditions. The doom of the Duby model of a mutating society—and along with it the idea of a rising knighthood—was sealed in his retention of the view that what sparked it off was a social breakdown accompanied by unrestrained violence as princes and magnates competed for power in the vacuum caused by the failure of monarchy in West Francia in or around the portentous year of 1000. It was this violence that opened the way for the social rise of a class defined by their warlike function, the *milites*. The 1970s produced a number of regional studies which to Duby fed back and confirmed his views of a social breakdown right across post-Carolingian Francia, not least the encyclopedic study of Pierre Bonnassie on Catalonia (which built on his earlier work on Provence).[17] This thesis of a feudal mutation in 1000 reached its most elaborate statement in Duby's *Les trois ordres* (1978), a rich and fascinating book but one whose master thesis proved to be flawed. In the third chapter of the section called *Circonstances*—a chapter called *La Révolution Féodale*—the thesis was set out starkly: the final failure of a monarchy which had for nearly two centuries pursued a 'vision of peace' removed the brakes on a medieval society already prone to violence. From 1000, bands of warriors and their captains began preying on and subjugating the unarmed peasantry, basing themselves in their bandit lairs, the castles, and existing on pillage. It was a new, violent age, in which the sword alone was respected, and in which power devolved to any unprincipled lord who commanded those swords. What was left of civil society was now centred on castellanries: it was seigneurial not civic.

Though Duby deliberately eschewed Montesquieu's characterization of what had happened as an anarchy followed by *un gouvernement féodal*, that was what he was in fact describing and closely locating the transformation on one narrow historical period. And like Montesquieu and Bloch before him, it was the violence of the knight which to him enabled this revolution. What was new, however, was Duby's use of the biography of Gerard, bishop of Cambrai (1012–51), to capture a moment in this process and analyse it. Its author, working around 1024, portrayed the aftermath of the supposed revolution of the 990s when Church authorities were despairing of the power of the king to prevent this anarchy and striving to curb by whatever means they could the violence of the knight through communal peacemaking, which of course itself demonstrated the bankruptcy of kingship in

---

[16] The regional studies of Lucien Musset for Normandy and Robert Fossier for Picardy implicitly rejected Duby's model of the collapse of authority down to village level. They still saw collapse in the tenth century, however, and both nonetheless saw a rise in knightly status during the eleventh and twelfth centuries. For Normandy, L. Musset, 'L'aristocratie normande au xie siècle', in *La noblesse au moyen âge (xie-xve siècles). Essais à la memoire de Robert Boutruche*, ed. P. Contamine (Paris, 1976), 71–96; D. R. Bates, *Normandy before 1066* (London, 1982), 109–11. For Picardy, R. Fossier, *La terre et les hommes en Picardie jusqu'à la fin de xiiie siècle* (2 vols, Paris, 1968).

[17] P. Bonnassie, *La Catalogne du milieu du xe siècle à la fin du xie siècle: croissance et mutations d'une société* (2 vols, Toulouse, 1975–6).

his day.[18] Gerard had lots of enemies, but notably the castellan of his city, the conscienceless employer of the *milites*, the 'soldiers' of his garrison, who can by this date be interpreted otherwise as horseback *caballarii*, or *chevalers*. The castellan himself was an adherent of the count of Flanders, an emerging princely power in the western Empire, who in extending that power was provoking regional violence and warfare. Bishop Gerard was portrayed by Duby as an enterprising and assiduous promoter of the peace in his diocese that neither the emperor nor the king could any longer guarantee. He manoeuvred deftly in his political world, promoting peace and undermining his enemy, the violent castellan, and the aggressive, power-grabbing Flemish prince who stood behind him. Mostly Gerard tried to get the king to assume responsibility for the situation and institute general peace by an oath binding all males to peace, and backing it up by the threat of excommunication. Duby thus portrayed this moment of social collapse in human history most compellingly and placed it within a frame of a general theory; and the enablers of the collapse were the knights.

However, the weaknesses of Duby's argument were too glaring for his gifts for exposition to obscure. It perpetuated the untested assumptions of Montesquieu and Bloch. Was the level of violence Cambrai was experiencing after 1000 really a new thing? Why do we assume that the count of Flanders, his puppet castellan and his knights were necessarily disruptors with an interest in continuing social disorder? Might they not rather have been the agents of a princely ideology of peace, which was all too competent for the Church's comfort in imposing on society? Duby's theories therefore did not long outlive him. In fact he already had critics in the 1970s, though principally among American historians of French society: British medieval historiography was slow to appreciate and assess Duby's work until the 1980s.[19] It was, however, a debate in the British historical journal *Past & Present* presented in 1996 and 1997, which contained a series of articles offering a criticism, reassessment and discussion, that has proved in the end to be fatal internationally to the Duby thesis.[20] The leading figure in the demolition of feudal mutationism has emerged as Dominique Barthélemy, whose counterarguments were appearing as early as 1990.[21] His logical and telling point was that the ecclesiastical rhetoric against the violence of the times can in fact be readily found at other periods, and any revolution we see is in fact an illusion encouraged by the expanding sources of the early eleventh century, *une mutation documentaire*, such

---

[18] *Les trois ordres ou l'imaginaire du féodalisme* (Paris, 1978), trans. A. Goldhammer as *The Three Orders: Feudal Society Imagined* (Chicago, 1980).

[19] Aspects of the feudal mutation model came first came under direct criticism by Constance Brittain Bouchard ('The Origins of the French Nobility: A Reassessment', *American Historical Review*, 86 (1981), 501–32) and Stephen D. White ('*Pactum legem vincit et amor judicium*. The Settlement of Disputes by Compromise in Eleventh-century France', *American Journal of Legal History*, 22 (1978), 281–308).

[20] *Past & Present*, nos 152: 1 (1996), 155: 1 (1997); the debate responded to a mutationist restatement by T. N. Bisson, 'The "Feudal Revolution"', *Past & Present*, no. 142 (1994), 6–42.

[21] D. Barthélemy, 'La mutation féodale a-t-elle eu lieu? Note critique', *Annales*, 47 (1992), 767–77, repr. with other studies in idem, *La mutation féodale a-t-elle eu lieu? Servage et chevalerie dans la France des x⁰ et xi⁰ siècles* (Paris, 1997).

as the new rhetoric in trying to justify and defend Bishop Gerard's own seizure of local power in the Cambrésis.

QUESTIONING KNIGHTS AS A SOCIAL GROUP

For our purposes here Dominique Barthélemy felt he necessarily had to eschew any 'rise of the knights' as had been entertained in the older French tradition. He directly engaged with the subject of knights in the Duby thesis in 1993 as a consequence of his own contrasting regional work on the Vendômois. By then he was abruptly dismissing past assumptions. He saw no reason to interpret the relationship between castellans and their knights in terms of the knights rising in the company of their betters. To him both made up one aristocratic class linked by their military ideals, and he shrugged at the fact that castellans are rarely called knights, since the social allusiveness of the documentation would hardly allow otherwise. Nor did he see 'knights' as a new phenomenon in society in the late tenth century; *miles* in Latin documents was simply a new word for the older *vassus*. So to him the 'knightly ethic' might be found as much in Carolingian capitularies as in the chivalric tracts of the thirteenth century and it was expected of all adult males who served their lord, as much as of the lord himself. His explanation of *chevalerie* was almost as globalizing as Père Honoré de Saint-Marie's back in the days of the Enlightenment: 'the *miles* was no more and no less than any mature and accepted member of feudal society: the knight was one who served and at one and the same time one who ruled. Knighthood was noble power and there was always something about it that had a hint of kingship.'[22] Within such a view there cannot therefore be any space for a rising class of knights, since there never was such a class; *chevalerie* was simply an aspect of the noble ethic—its honour-based violence and warrior solidarity—to be expected of the superior male in medieval society. He rather neatly summarized his case as regards a rising knightly class when he asked rhetorically how it could be that an inferior social group infected a superior one with its ideals? It is *une haute improbabilité sociologique.*[23]

The Barthélemy view on knighthood and *chevalerie* has been frequently restated and elaborated by its author.[24] It has not as yet been fully tested within French

[22] D. Barthélemy, *La société dans le comté de Vendômois de l'an mil au xive siècle* (Paris, 1993), 507–13, quotation translated from p. 511: 'le *miles* n'est rien d'autre que le membre à part entière, adulte et légitime, de la "société féodale": chevalier régnant et chevalier servant tout à la fois. La chevalerie, c'est le pouvoir noble, et en elle il y a toujours eu quelque chose de royal.' A summary is to be found in English in his 'Castles, Barons and Vavassors in the Vendômois and Neighboring Regions in the Eleventh and Twelfth Centuries', in *Cultures of Power: Lordship, Status and Process in Twelfth-Century Europe*, ed. T. N. Bisson (Philadelphia, 1995), 56–68. The most polemical restatement is in *La chevalerie: de la Germanie antique à la France du xiie siècle* (Paris, 2007), 168–78. See contextualization in M. Aurell 'Rapport Introductif', in *Chevalerie et Christianisme*, 12–13.

[23] Barthélemy, *La société dans le comté de Vendômois*, 513. Duby did, however, produce the instance that the urban-based religious enthusiasm of the early friars went on to infect the higher nobility in the thirteenth century.

[24] As, for instance, 'Le mot *Miles* et l'histoire de la chevalerie', in *La mutation féodale a-t-elle eu lieu?*, 173–8.

historiography, in perhaps what is a parallel to the dominance Duby's views enjoyed in his own lifetime.[25] There are some aspects of it which echo rather nicely other historiographies and which could be used to strengthen it, not least the British idea of a continuum of economic levels amongst those who called themselves *milites* in England between 1070 and 1166 in a country where such socio-economic judgements are possible. There are other areas where the Barthélemy view is weak. It assumes along with most earlier French historiography that the *milites* of eleventh-century sources have to belong to a landed class and share that character-istic with the magnates. Accept that there were knights who were unlanded, retained employees and the 'clivage' between knight and magnate he saw as illusory becomes rather more real. Another area that Barthélemy does not fully resolve is the association between knights and castles in the sources of the tenth and eleventh centuries, though he does not by any means ignore it.[26] His argument foregrounds the knight and it can be said to give too little attention to advances in the study of the second of those phenomena: those scientifically designed fortified residences we call 'castles', the larger of them garrisoned by full-time professional (and not necessarily landed) warriors in the employ of a lord, which begin to multiply across post-Carolingian Europe in the later tenth century and are everywhere to be found in the eleventh. Castles have been explained in a variety of ways in the twentieth century: a reaction to the migratory, marauding Hungarians and Vikings; a symptom of the collapse of public authority in a feudal mutation; or a principally socio-economic move towards localization of resources in a society which was growing in wealth and population, in an *incastellamento* that can be found across Italy, Catalonia, or indeed northern Europe as far east as the Slavic lands.[27]

The very lively area of current castle studies has reached a position where it does not see necessarily any specific point of origin for the castle, but a range of analogous fortifications out of which the seigneurial fortress emerged and increasingly proliferated in the tenth century, in (it is suggested) a slow wave moving from the south to the north of Latin Europe.[28] But however you explain the castle, archaeo-logical mapping and analysis indicate that it represents a progressive change in military technology which gathered momentum in the second half of the tenth century and rapidly proliferated across western and central Europe in the eleventh,

[25] For a brisk dismissal, however, Bouchard, *Blood*, 177.

[26] For Vendôme he addresses the problem directly, *La société dans le comté de Vendômois*, 581, taking on the argument as expressed by Jean Richard, 'Châteaux, châtelains et vassaux en Bourgogne aux xe et xiie siècles', *CCM*, 3 (1960), 433–47, and see further D. Barthélemy, 'Les comtes, les sires et les "nobles de châteaux" dans la Touraine du xie siècle', in *Campagnes médiévales: l'homme et son espace. Etudes offertes à Robert Fossier* (Paris, 1995), 439–53.

[27] For the basic theory, P. Toubert, *Les structures du Latium médiéval: le Latium méridional et la Sabine di ixe siècle à la fin du xiie siècle* (Rome, 1973).

[28] T. N. Bisson, *The Crisis of the Twelfth Century: Power, Lordship and the Origins of European Government* (Princeton, 2009), 41–2. The spread and elaboration of castles in Franco-Germanic Lotharingia during this period are evocatively mapped in G. Giuliato, 'Le château reflet de l'art defen-sif en Lorraine de xème au début de xiiième siècle', *Annales de l'Est*, 6th ser. 1 (2003), 55–76, though both studies are within the confines of Duby's mutationism.

and which had considerable consequences for the way wars were fought.[29] A question Barthélemy does not sufficiently consider is whether the warrior had to change to meet this new way of fighting. To be effective castles could not just be strongpoints to be occupied in times of instability; they had to have permanent garrisons. These need not be large, but they would need to be specialized, and, to fulfil the castle's potential, they would need to be mounted, for castles encouraged a small-scale warfare of raid and counter-raid, with an emphasis on the economic warfare of the *chevauchée*, a challenge to the effective lordship as much as to the military prowess of an opponent. Castles were most potent when combined in a strategic network with mounted field forces, and such an organization has been used to explain the survival against all the odds of the Latin kingdom of Jerusalem in the twelfth century.[30] Such mobile forces had to be permanently available to the castle lord, and it is a reasonable assumption—backed up indeed by some evidence—that the horse warriors would have embraced a corresponding ethos and identity. The sources at the end of the tenth and in the early eleventh century indicate no less, for we not infrequently hear of the *milites* of this or that castle as being important in local affairs and local hostilities. The mentality of Bloch would see such knights as the new vassals of a feudal age, landed warriors gathered into supporting their lord's castellanry. But they could easily be very different creatures: professional warriors of a new sort, a *mesnie castrale*.

In his *doctorat d'État* on the society of the great lordship of Coucy, between Laon and Soissons, Barthélemy was working with the notion that such *milites* might represent a lower level of knight based at a castle in garrison.[31] In 1990 he was still accepting of the idea that knights formed a rank of lesser nobility in eleventh-century society beneath the castle lords.[32] But by 1993 the rather more forthcoming early sources of the Vendômois and his anti-mutationist stance had convinced him otherwise. Barthélemy saw the phenomenon of the knight as capable of two interpretations: as the *mesnie castrale*, an elite garrison of mixed social origins, or as landowners tenurially bound to the castellan. His extended prosopographical analysis of these vassals over several centuries does not, however, offer much insight into the earlier period or establish anything other than that there was a community of several local landowners, as often as not called *barones*, focused on the castle, and in the case of eleventh-century Vendôme with an obligation to take command of

---

[29] On the origin of the castle as a distinct category of fortification, though written within the francocentric constraints of the Duby thesis, A. Debord, *Aristocratie et pouvoir: le rôle du château dans la France médiévale* (Paris, 2000), 27–48. For a much broader overview, O. Creighton, *Early European Castles: Aristocracy and Authority, AD 800–1200* (London, 2012), 36–84, 140–6, and for Germany, G. P. Fehring, *The Archaeology of Medieval Germany: An Introduction*, trans. R. Salmon (London, 1991), 108–18. For observations on the way that castles changed warfare, M. Strickland, 'Slaughter, slavery or ransom? The impact of the Conquest on conduct in warfare', in *England in the Eleventh Century*, ed. C. Hicks (Stamford, 1992), 41–59.

[30] J. France, *Western Warfare in the Age of the Crusades, 1000–1300* (Ithaca, NY, 1999), 102–6. Barthélemy seems, however, quite well aware of the nature of that warfare; see his 'Feudal Warfare in Tenth-Century France', in *Vengeance in the Middle Ages: Emotion, Religion and Feud*, ed. S. A. Throop and P. Hyams (Farnham, 2010), 105–13.

[31] D. Barthélemy, *Les deux âges de la seigneurie banale: Coucy, xi²-xiii² siècle* (Paris, 1984), 152–3.

[32] D. Barthélemy, *L'ordre seigneurial, xi²-xii² siècle* (Paris, 1990), 128–34.

the fortress on a monthly rota. He does not speculate about how its garrison of *milites* could have made the castle militarily effective, as the evidence is not there.[33] And so his position remains that the *chevaliers* of the eleventh-century Vendômois were part of the same group in society as their overlords.

There is, however, a source which has some vivid things to say about the standing of early knights and the relationships between the lords of castles and their dependants: the *Conventum* of the castellan Hugh of Lusignan and his lord, Count William V of Poitou, drawn up for Hugh as a statement of grievance (*querimonia*) around 1030 after a decade of frustration at the count's conduct towards him. Barthélemy has offered a perceptive reading of the document in his continuing campaign to undermine mutationism, but uses it to explore the relationships between a prince and his magnates, rather than what it reveals of the position of knights, which he perceives to be the way his own master theory requires—'sortis du rang'.[34] The document indicates otherwise, however. The Poitou of that decade was a land of castle lordships, which the count chose to treat as a chessboard in a game where the rules favoured him. What made the castles potent in the game were the horseback soldiers who garrisoned them. In one such gambit Count William engineered a war between Hugh and his neighbour, Geoffrey, viscount of Thouars. In the course of it the *caballarii* of Hugh's castle of Mouzeil were captured along with the castle by Geoffrey, who chose to sever their hands 'and did enough other things too'. As the war progressed, Hugh in his turn captured a company of forty-three of Geoffrey's *caballarii* of Thouars. He might have used them as leverage against Geoffrey, but the count tricked him out of them, to his loss of a possible 2000 *li.* in ransom, as he claimed.

These groups of *caballarii* are unmistakably *mesnies castrales*, and their status does not seem here to share much with their lord, for all their economic value to him. Hugh is defined in the document not as a fellow *caballarius* but as the 'chiliarch', their commander.[35] His subordinates can be mutilated or executed, or otherwise, if lucky, bought out of prison by the castellans who employ them, or traded between lords as commodities, as Count William did with Hugh's captives. The document mentions also the *homines* and *vassali* who held lands and fiefs (*feovi*) attached to castles, as in the case of Vivonne, but they cannot be automatically assumed to be the same as the *caballarii* of Mouzeil, though some may very well have been; they may have been like the *barones* of Vendôme, since when the *homines* and *vassali* appear it is not in the guise of combatants but in a civil context.[36] The gulf of subjection between a lord and his knights portrayed in this graphic and

---

[33] *La société dans le comté de Vendômois*, 581–622.

[34] D. Barthélemy, *L'an mil et la paix de Dieu: la France chrétienne et féodale, 980–1060* (Paris, 1999), 339–54, esp. 350.

[35] Barthélemy makes the somewhat illogical comment on Hugh's title of 'Chiliarch', designed to differentiate himself from his knights, that he was '...lui-même chevalier de tout premier ordre', in 'Note sur le "titre chevaleresque" en France au xiᵉ siècle', *Journal des Savants*, 1 (1994), 137n. For the Isidorian resonances of the title 'chiliarch' and its place in the evolution of the idea of the origin myth of Nobility, see p. 299 n100.

[36] *Le Conventum (vers 1030): un précurseur aquitain des premières épopées*, ed. G. Beech, Y. Chauvin, and G. Pon (Geneva, 1995), 123–47.

informative early source is too wide to allow us to include knights and lords within one undifferentiated noble group without qualification. Hugh did not deal with his *milites* in the way he dealt with his peers or with Count William. This was to change, but not till the twelfth century.

Another source reflecting on early eleventh-century knighthood is the hagiographical biography by Gilbert Crispin (*c.*1046–1117) of his former abbot, Herluin son of Ansgot of Bec-Hellouin (died 1078). Gilbert recalled Herluin's first vocation as a leading knight and vassal of the count of Brionne in the 1020s. Since he had been brought up as a boy amongst the *primates* of the court of Count Godfrey with Godfrey's son and heir, Gilbert, it would be a fair bet that Herluin was the sort of 'noble' landed knight that the French tradition expects to find. But other *milites* appear in this memoir. In the mid 1020s Count Gilbert recruited for a particularly difficult campaign 'a great band of knights (*multam militum manum contraxit*)', while Herluin, his vassal, gathered on his own account another company of twenty knights (*viginti secum delectos milites assumens*).[37] But these knights were not apparently tenants; their service was said to be for the campaign only. There is not just a gulf here between Count Gilbert and his retained knights, but a further remove between Gilbert and the retained knights of his vassal knight Herluin. All might be called *commilitones* on campaign, no doubt, but they were on several distinct and different social footings, distinct enough to justify the idea that they could not have seen themselves as within the same social group. Gilbert Crispin also has something to say about levels of prestige amongst land-holding knights. Herluin's brothers are mentioned in the source and, we are told, they also had a share of their paternal estate. As landowners all the brothers were by birth equal in *dignitas*, but Herluin was their superior in *vera nobilitas*, referring to the superiority of his conduct, not his descent.[38]

There is a lot to be said for and about the historiographical models analysed above, and to some extent they are complementary rather than contradictory. The British model is particularly useful in suggesting an economic continuum amongst people who took up knighthood, from aristocratic landed knights of a wealth not much inferior to the counts and barons who invited them into their courts, to the landless knights who lived off the salaries and board that lords would pay them, and counted on them for their arms and equipment. The knights of varying degree (and indeed their lords) had in common their skills, camaraderie and a liking for military games and rituals, but their individual material circumstances and relative prestige diverged. This view is not by any means incompatible with the radical French view espoused by Barthélemy, who also sees shared ideals between lords and followers in eleventh-century society. This was a society where the Breton cross-Channel lord Wihenoc could be unthinkingly described by a clerk of Saint-Florent de Saumur in 1081 as *miles*, and the many dependants who held land from him as also being *milites*.[39] Likewise, his hagiographer describes Herluin son of

---

[37] *Vita sancti Herluini*, in *PL* 150, cols 695–6.
[38] *Vita sancti Herluini*, in *PL* 150, col. 700.
[39] Archives départementales de Maine-et-Loire, H 3710, no. 1.

Ansgot as a *miles* and a vassal of the count of Brionne in the 1020s, and as he prospers in the count's service Herluin employs his own company of *milites*.

Dominique Barthélemy would not admit that dependent knights could in such circumstances be said to have formed a social group *an sich*, subordinate to a magnate class. The reasons for rejecting his radicalism are given above. It might be noted that at least one medieval mind would not have followed his logic. Ramon Llull's *Doctrina Pueril* observed the shared ground between magnate and knight without conceding any equality to the dependant: 'a knight is given a prince for his lord to organise and invest the knights by whom he is enabled to maintain and govern his realm and his lands. The prince himself needs to be a knight so there may be a better agreement and friendship between him and them.'[40] The emphasis on shared masculine ideals in Llull's thinking is no more than the concept I have demonstrated earlier of the *preudomme* being an expression of a common medieval idea of superior masculinity at all social levels (see above, pp. 78–82). Barthélemy does not fully account for the way that subjection can define a social group. Lords and men may have both aspired to *preudommie*, but in the hall the *dominus* sat on the great chair and his *milites* along benches or on the floor, whether they were retained soldiers or landed dependants. Knights within a household were defined as inferior by their subjection to and dependency on their lord and employer, a dependency which was affirmed by numerous social rituals. It is not out of place to compare the eleventh century with La Curne's eighteenth, where all educated men of means claimed the status of 'gentleman' but could not by that fact be regarded as forming a single class. They just embraced the same idea of male superiority. The German ministerial knight underlines this argument; his subjection was hereditary and inescapable, and what status he had depended absolutely on who owned him. We will now go on to analyse the complicated question of status and its variations amongst the men who called themselves knights before the end of the twelfth century.

KNIGHTS AND STATUS

Even the knight of a retinue with no other resources than his military skills might claim a certain status, not least as the rider of horses, long a measure of prestige as well as an expensive necessity: 'What fellow, however well fitted out, would get any respect without a horse?... A man on horseback is more looked up to than one on foot,' as Guiot de Provins summed up the distinction, in figurative fashion.[41] As the moral genre of *similitudines militis* evolved in the twelfth century, the horse was indeed taken by some writers as representing the moral capacity of mankind, as the pseudo-Anselm and Ralph Niger explained it. Being the riders of horses meant that even the least of knights had of necessity to afford—or more often find an employer who would pay for—decent mounts and attendants to groom and

---

[40] *Doctrine*, 176.   [41] *Armëure*, 110, ll. 521–2, 528–9.

feed them and maintain their equipment: the military underclass called broadly by 1100 'squires' (*scutiferi, armigeri*). So as early as 987 Richer of Reims could comment that Duke Charles of Lorraine had married beneath him to a woman 'of the condition of knight' (*militaris ordo*), who was thus not of his own 'condition'. His comment, however slighting, does imply that such knights had a status of their own, and it derived from their vocation.[42]

What was knightly status in the eleventh century? It was not necessarily a high one. The knights of Hugh the Chiliarch in the Poitou of the 1020s were pawns to their lord, to be sacrificed at need. In Germany in the later eleventh century, the hero of *Ruodlieb* was depicted as a well-born and worthy, if poor, *miles* whose natural sphere was the court of lords and princes and whose natural occupation was public duty. But its author tells us directly that it was from his service that Ruodlieb drew his status, and so he could not stand on the same level as his lords because he was defined by that subjection.[43] In England, Bishop Robert de Béthune was said to have been born at the end of the eleventh century to a family 'of a quite distinguished condition (*ordo*) of knight', which implies (as also does Gilbert Crispin and *Ruodlieb*) that the status knights enjoyed, along with that of the greater nobles, could be more or less distinguished depending on individual circumstances. There was no doubt already then a practice of sons of a knight following their father in his profession, as we find expected in an assize of 1140 for the kingdom of Sicily.[44] So in 1093 in England, a monk could write of a lady of his acquaintance of modest but not aristocratic claims, who had married a *miles*— 'a man of her sort of level (*parilitas*) in society'.[45] And it is the eleventh-century use of the language of subjection and words in reference to knights such as *ordo* and *parilitas* which betrays that they were seen as a social group, if broadly conceived, a 'condition' internally graduated by their resources, dependencies and connections. So far as they related to castle lords and magnates above them, it was in the way knights drew status from their service. Magnates and knights were not the same social group just from their riding their horses in armour.

THE PROBLEM OF *ADOUBEMENT*

Menestrier and La Curne de Sainte-Palaye in their day had little problem seeing knights as a social group, and their principal reason was because there was an act of knighting, an *adoubement*, where a senior figure admitted a tyro to the condition

[42] *Histories*, ed. and trans. J. Lake (2 vols, Cambridge, MA, 2011) 2: 220. Richer comments without apparent criticism that Eudes, elected king of France in 888, was the son of Robert *ex equestri ordine*; ibid. 1, 20. See J. M. van Winter, 'Uxorem de militari ordine sibi imponens', in *Miscellanea in memoriam J. F. Niermeyer* (Gröningen, 1961), 119–20.
[43] *Ruodlieb*, esp. 32 (ll. 65–6).
[44] M. Aurell, *La noblesse en Occident, v^e-xve siècle* (Paris, 1996), 100.
[45] William of Wycombe, *Speculum vitae viri venerabilis Rotberti episcopi Herefordiae*, in *Anglia Sacra*, ed. H. Wharton (2 vols, London, 1691), 2: 299; M. Winterbottom, 'An Edition of Faricius Vita S. Aldhelmi', *Journal of Medieval Latin*, 15 (2005), 127.

of knight by equipping him with arms and delivering a ceremonial blow.[46] Marc Bloch absorbed the views of these pioneers of the study of Chivalry, and for him the act of *adoubement* ('equipping') was characteristic of the knighthood of the post-Carolingian feudal age and defined it fully by the eleventh century as an *ordo*, a rising social group distinct from other laymen.[47] Where Bloch led, most subsequently followed until Dominique Barthélemy who, though with a better appreciation of the scarcity of descriptions of such acts in eleventh-century sources, is no less categorical about their meaning, but finds the meaning to be otherwise than Bloch: that it was a more generalized and less significant ceremony. His pithy view is that 'L'adoubement fait le chevalier, non la chevalerie au sens strict'. It follows that *adoubement* for him was as relevant to the magnate class as to its dependants and not in itself symbolic or definitive of any exclusive knightly class. There is something to recommend in this pragmatic view, at least as far as it concerns status. The developing consensus is indeed that the ceremony of *adoubement* only becomes of interest in terms of defining what *chevalerie* was said to be when it began to attract a self-conscious rationale, for which there is no evidence till the mid twelfth century.[48]

Eleventh-century instances of *adoubement* refer almost exclusively to royal and princely offspring, and some were clearly ceremonial events, such as the famous occasion in May 1098 when at Pentecost, a religious feast associated with courts and commencements, Guy count of Ponthieu at Abbeville was 'to equip and honour Louis the king's son [the future Louis VI] with the arms of a knight and advance and admit him to the condition of knight (*armis militaribus adornare et honorare et ad militiam promovere et ordinare)'*.[49] Nonetheless, a more general social significance to the ceremony of *adoubement* at this time can also be found in the act depicted on the Bayeux Tapestry, when in 1064 Harold Godwineson is shown being invested by Duke William with arms and a banner in an act intended to signify his submission, the banner being an item associated with counts and dukes, not knights.[50] How widespread this sort of ceremony may have been below the highest level of eleventh-century society is impossible to say, nor can we even be sure that any such ceremony was necessary at the time for the admission of a youth to the condition of knight, especially for those 'knights of middling rank and common origins' referred to in the 1070s as being in William the Conqueror's army.[51] For that we have to wait till the twelfth century.

The earliest comprehensive statement about the significance of admission to knighthood that can be made in any medieval European society concerns the

---

[46] For the varied terms for the act of knighting in several languages, whose variety he finds as of no broad significance, M. Lieberman, 'A New Approach to the Knighting Ritual', *Speculum*, 90 (2015), 399.
[47] *Société féodale*, 2: 49–50.
[48] Barthélemy, 'Note sur le "titre chevaleresque" en France', 103; Barthélemy, *Chevalerie*, 168–78, quotation p. 170. Lieberman, 'A New Approach to the Knighting Ritual', 391–423, covers the same ground.
[49] *Recueil des actes des comtes de Ponthieu, 1026–1279*, ed. C. Brunel (Paris, 1930), 9.
[50] Crouch, *Image*, 182–3, 183n; Lieberman, 'New Approach', 408–9.
[51] William of Poitiers, *Gesta Guillelmi*, ed. and trans. R. H. C. Davis and M. Chibnall (Oxford, 1998), 158: *milites mediae nobilitatis atque gregarios*.

England of the 1120s. Nothing as definitive can be said in terms of Capetian and Imperial society till the later twelfth century.[52] Anglo-Norman aristocratic society has advantages for the study, and needs to be carefully attended to, as it was not insular but closely interrelated with those of Brittany, northern France and Flanders, and in some respects is more thoroughly documented than they were. The surviving Exchequer pipe roll of 1129–30 makes it clear that, as far as the Exchequer of England was concerned, to 'become a knight' (*esse militem*) meant exactly what Barthélemy said it should: that an heir was admitted into adulthood and—in the case of the Exchequer references—possession of the parental lands, in which case he could be forced to argue in law for them. Two of the four cases noted on the roll refer to baronial successions, but one to a simple Lincolnshire manorial family.[53] However, the act could be one which had no other significance than to recognize adulthood. In 1128 a baron of the Welsh March made a grant noting that his son and heir had consented to it, he being *iam tunc miles*, which interprets the act as altering a boy's status to that of a legal adult on the basis of age, not succession to property.[54] A supposed act of King Henry makes a passing reference to a youth, Robert Ridel, who awaited his knighting and (presumably) his inheritance before he could make a marriage.[55] Again in the 1120s, the heir to the earldom of Northampton, Simon (II) de Senlis, was fostered by his stepfather, King David of Scotland, to his mother's uncle, Count Stephen of Aumale, until '... he assumed the equipment of a knight along with William, Count Stephen's son', in what was plainly a significant ceremony inaugurating the youth, with at least one other companion, into adulthood and in Simon's case (but not William's) control of the lands of his father, who had died a decade or so earlier. King Henry was apparently annoyed at the count for presiding over the ceremony without reference to him as overlord, which was very likely because land transfer had been involved.[56]

Writing largely in the decade of the 1120s, the Anglo-Norman historian Orderic Vitalis recorded acts of *adoubement* of his own lifetime in England, Normandy and elsewhere, almost always in terms of coming of age amongst the aristocracy. The most significant instance is when he recorded that King Henry 'gave arms to the twin adolescent sons of Count Robert of Meulan', an act we happen to know occurred in 1120 when the boys came to the age of sixteen and were delivered their

---

[52] For the Empire, E. Orth, 'Formen und Funktionen der höfischen Rittererhebung', in *Curialitas. Studien zu Grundfragen der höfisch-ritterlichen Kultur*, ed. J. Fleckenstein (Göttingen, 1990), 128–70.

[53] *Pipe Roll of 31 Henry I*, ed. and trans. J. A. Green (Pipe Roll Society, new ser. 37, 2012), 19, 74, 92, 94.

[54] TNA: PRO, C115/77, fo. 182r (Richard fitz Pons of Clifford). We might also note here the comments of Orderic Vitalis, who in the 1120s said that the premature death of Richard, son of the Conqueror, some four decades earlier happened 'before he had taken up the belt of knighthood'; Orderic, 3: 114.

[55] D. X. Carpenter, 'The marriage of Richard Basset: an undetected forgery in the name of Henry I', *Historical Research*, 91 (2018), 399–406. The act is probably a construct of the early 1140s, but the clause *donec Rob(ertus) Ridel possit esse miles et ducat in uxorem neptem Rad(ulfi) Basset* may nonetheless refer to an expectation of the 1120s.

[56] *Insignia militaria suscepit unacum Willelmo comite filio comitis Stephani, Vita et Passio Waldevi comitis*, in *Original Lives of Anglo-Saxons and others*, ed. J. Giles (Caxton Society, London, 1854), 20.

father's honors.[57] It was in 1128 that Count Geoffrey of Anjou was equipped with the arms of knight at Rouen by King Henry himself, in a lavish ceremony rather like that associated with Louis of France in 1098. Geoffrey shared the honour with many other aspirants, but unfortunately we only know of the event by the authority of John of Marmoutier, writing one or two generations later, and his account cannot be trusted as to the details of what may have occurred in 1128.[58] From these references we can be confident in stating that by the twelfth century in England and Normandy knighting was a routine but solemn ceremony at all levels of landed society which concluded a boy's tutelage and introduced him to adult society, sometimes in company with other tyros, and delivered him into possession of his lands, if he had any awaiting him. But even so there are hints at this time that more could be involved in the act of knighting than a family rite and that it might have a broader, political tinge. The Welsh annals record that King Henry made a particularly favoured Welsh lord, Owain ap Cadwgan of Powys, a knight when he entered into his military service, which recalls the delivery of arms by Duke William to Earl Harold in 1064.[59]

If, then, the act of *adoubement* is not much help in defining the condition and status of knighthood before the early twelfth century, what is? One answer that has long been discussed is an ideological one, a set of requirements laid on the knight to justify his status and distinguish him from his social inferiors. As we will go on to see in some detail in Chapter 13, the mid twelfth century did acknowledge an ideology to which the *chevalier* was supposed to adhere, which may not have exactly made him noble, but which did mark him as a figure with a social status which had to be justified morally. We have already seen some indication of this in the not infrequent reference in eleventh-century sources to people being from families which are categorized as 'knightly' (Lat. *militaris*) or to there being an *ordo* (a condition) of knighthood. Some significance has to be given also to the small body of evidence that eleventh-century knights can be shown to have followed a body of norms which amounted to a form of military code. John Gillingham has written at length on the fact that it had become the custom by the 1050s not to kill captured knights, but to ransom them, something we have observed as a possibility in Hugh of Lusignan's *Conventum* of 1028, though it was not in fact offered to the captured knights of Mouzeil, who were mutilated and rendered unfit for warfare instead. Gillingham tied this change into a narrative of the 'rise of chivalry', which he justified by defining Chivalry idiosyncratically as simply 'status-specific' warrior

[57] Orderic, 6: 42, 108, 134, 190, 328; Crouch, *Beaumont Twins*, 4–9. The several instances of equipping of youths with arms in the early and mid eleventh century at adulthood described by Orderic are taken by Dominique Barthélemy as reliable evidence of eleventh-century practice, rather than practice at the time Orderic wrote.

[58] *Chroniques des comtes d'Anjou*, ed. L. Halphen and R. Poupardin (Paris, 1913), 179–80.

[59] *Brut*, *s.a.* 1115. In 1210 King John did much the same to a king of Thomond he wanted to draw into a closer orbit to his court; *Miscellaneous Irish annals, AD 1114–1437*, ed. Séamus Ó Hinnse (Dublin, 1947), p. 86, *s.a.*1210 (Mac Carthaig's Book), a reference I owe to Colin Veach.

behaviour.[60] The point that can be taken away from his work is that what he described does betray fellow feeling amongst an eleventh-century group sharing a specialized military craft and a degree of status.[61] The *Song of Roland* preserves something of this secular bonding in depicting the French army at rest, the mature knights (*cevaler*) sitting around talking and enjoying board games, while the younger warriors (*bacheler leger*) took the opportunity to practise swordplay.[62] By the time the *Song* was committed to writing around 1100 knights had their own common resort and meeting place in the developing recreation called the mêlée tournament, where knights from a wide spread of kingdoms and regions associated, feasted and competed, in attendance on their lords and princes.[63]

Could not this sort of privileged solidarity and shared customs be interpreted as characteristic of knights as a social group, never mind that it included in its embrace the magnates who retained them, as Barthélemy would observe? It also closed the knight off from those perceived to be below him in society. The eleventh century offers nothing more than hints that this might have been so. It is not till the mid twelfth century that we find sure evidence of an ideology of knighthood that was developed, propagated and understood by knights and which distinguished them from society's other *preudommes*. It was not just to be found in a shared military culture of the camp amongst *commilitones*. Later twelfth-century writers give us the first evidence of a customary homily delivered to the tyro as part of the act of *adoubement* by the *preudomme* who was its president (see below, pp. 274–5), which included moral injunctions. We also glimpse from the writings of William of Malmesbury, John of Salisbury and Stephen de Fougères in the 1120s and 1150s the idea that a knight could theoretically be degraded from his condition for an act which dishonoured the status his order claimed.[64] So Malmesbury imagined a knight at Hastings degraded by Duke William for mutilating the body of the

[60] His first such statement was J. Gillingham, 'Kingship, Chivalry and Love: Political and Cultural Values in the Earliest History Written in France: Geoffrey Gaimar's *Estoire des Engleis*', *Anglo-Norman Political Culture and the 12th-Century Renaissance*, ed. C. W. Hollister (Woodbridge, 1997), 33–58, esp. 38–9. There have been a number of subsequent restatements, of which the more substantial include: '1066 and the Introduction of Chivalry into England', in *The English in the Twelfth Century: Imperialism, National Identity and Political Values* (Woodbridge, 2000), 209–31; 'Holding to the Rules of War (Bellica Jura Tenentes): right conduct before, during and after battle in North-western Europe', in *Anglo-Norman Studies*, 29 (2006), 1–15; 'Fontenoy and after: pursuing enemies to death in France between the ninth and eleventh centuries', in *Frankland: the Franks and the World of the Early Middle Ages*, ed. P. Fouracre and D. Ganz (Manchester, 2008), 242–65. It is a view also shared in M. Strickland, 'Killing or Clemency? Ransom, chivalry and changing attitudes to defeated opponents in Britain and Northern France, 7th-12th centuries', in *Krieg im Mittelalter*, ed. H-H. Kortüm (Berlin, 2001), 93–122. For a review, Kaeuper, *Chivalry*, 77–81.
[61] How to account for the appearance of this fellow feeling is probably a question without an answer, though Gillingham offers several lines of speculation; see 'Fontenoy and After', 242–65.
[62] *Song*, 1: 8 (ll. 110–13). [63] Crouch, *Tournament*, 2–9.
[64] Demotions of men unworthy by their conduct of the *cingulum militare* are entertained as possibilities in Carolingian ordinances; see K. Leyser, 'Early Canon Law and the Beginning of Knighthood', in *Communications and Power in Medieval Europe: the Carolingian and Ottonian Centuries*, ed. T. Reuter (London, 1994), 51–71. Kaeuper, *Chivalry*, 82–3, makes a comparison with the ecclesiastical condemnation of the notoriously violent Picard magnate Thomas de Marle, in 1114.

fallen Harold.[65] In the next generation Stephen urged this in the case of a reprobate and criminal knight:

> If he should wish to devote himself to treachery or to torture or assassination, then he ought to be deposed from his order, be deprived of his sword and be punished heavily, he should have his spurs lopped off and be excluded from the company of knights.[66]

There is even some evidence of this actually happening in practice in the mid twelfth century in the case of Henry of Essex, who was tried for abandoning the royal banner in Henry II's 1157 Welsh campaign, when he failed to exculpate himself in a trial by battle brought by his enemies several years later. Severely injured in the fight, his lands were confiscated and he was effectively un-knighted when he was obliged to make profession as a monk of Reading.[67] It was not these men's supposed noble status that was under question here, it was their fitness to be counted among the knights because of their actions. The subject of knighthood and Nobility, however, is a quite separate one. As long ago as the mid eighteenth century, La Curne de Sainte-Palaye detected a marked shift in expectations on the knight which he located in the latter part of the twelfth century, which was for him the beginning of the era of true Chivalry, its 'golden age' as he called it.[68] Being a literary scholar, La Curne was deriving his insight from the sort of knighthood he found portrayed in the romance literature of the time of Chrétien de Troyes. But a lot more can be said on the subject, and the next chapter will explore those avenues, which lead indeed by a number of routes to the hypermoral, elite stance we can properly call Chivalry, a word first defined in those terms by the knight and lay intellectual Ramon Llull in the mid 1270s, but implicit in sources since the end of the twelfth century.

---

[65] Malmesbury, *GRA*, 1: 456, *militia pulsus est*.

[66] *Livre des manières*, cc. 156–7 (ll. 623–8). See also John of Salisbury's comment in 1159 that unworthy knights ought to return the sword by which they were inaugurated to the altar they took it up from; see *Policraticus*, 1: 283, and comments in M. Aurell, 'L'épée, l'autel et le perron', in *Armes et jeux militaires (XIIe-XVe siècles)*, ed. C. Girbea (Paris, 2016), 55–6.

[67] William of Newburgh, *Historia Rerum Anglicarum* in, *Chronicles of the Reigns of Stephen etc*, ed. R. Howlett (4 vols, Rolls Series, 1884–9) 1: 108. It is worth noting that on the other side of the onto-logical divide, minor orders in the Church were held in the twelfth century to be cancelled by under-going knighthood; J. Dunbabin, 'From Clerk to Knight: Changing Orders', in *Medieval Knighthood*, 2, ed. C. Harper-Bill and R. Harvey (Woodbridge, 1988), 26–39.

[68] A modern historian of Chivalry who identifies it broadly with knightliness, as does Richard Kaeuper, is likely to acknowledge this cultural turn as 'a second chivalric phase'; Kaeuper, *Chivalry*, 104.

13

The Noble Knight

Knights were comprehended by 1210 within the same origin myth that explained the pre-eminence in society of people we can properly call, in the modern sense, nobles. If knights were being accepted as nobles, many, if not most, of them would have had some difficulty in demonstrating that they had Nobility of blood, so they must have argued for Nobility of mind, which was easier for most of them to demonstrate than Nobility of descent. This need might of itself account (at least in part) for the intensity of the late twelfth-century debate around the two Nobilities. After all, though knighthood and moral excellence may have been equated by 1210, we are hard put to find any coherent moral rationale underpinning the knighthood of most of the preceding twelfth century. At most it is implied there should be one in the negative portrayals of rapacious and corrupt knights of the Salomonic sermon literature of the early twelfth century. By implication these critiques claimed that knights should be better than they were, and there were moral standards they should embrace. Likewise, though there is no clear statement before the 1180s as to how knights should be better people, we do nonetheless know of some norms of moral conduct between knights that go back as far as the eleventh century—such as an expectation that knights will show mercy to their defeated fellows, if mercy is cried. But is there, then, any trace of an internal programme of moral teaching amongst knights that could provide a foundation for a claim to Nobility of mind among knights when the time came to accept knighthood as demanding social deference by its possession of Nobility?

KNIGHTS AND MORAL EMINENCE

The *Ordene de Chevalerie* preserves some indication that its author knew of a preceding set of moral expectations relevant to knights and even gives a clue as to where it was to be found. At the end of the work the author summarized four religious and moral obligations on a knight that he thought appropriate to his condition and readily achievable; rather more credible than the hypermoral aspirations attached to the items by which the young knight had just been inaugurated into his condition.

> Right from the start he mustn't be present at a corrupt trial nor witness any act of treason but distance himself from it at once; if he can't prevent evil he should promptly turn his back on it. The second thing is very pleasant, he must on no account forsake

a lady or young woman in trouble but if they need his abilities he must help them with all his power if he wishes to earn praise and reputation; for he needs must honour women and undertake great deeds on their behalf. The third thing in truth is that the young knight must needs be abstemious, and I tell you truly that he should fast on Friday in remembrance of Jesus who was pierced by a lance for our redemption but who pardoned Longinus. All his life long the knight must fast on this day for love of Him unless he leaves off because of illness or for the sake of his companions; and if he can't fast because of this he should make amends to God by giving alms or suchlike. The final thing is that he should hear mass daily to the end; if he has something he can share he should do so for the offertory placed on God's table is a very fine thing for it carries great virtue.[1]

Each of these aspirations was more 'knightly' than 'noble'. We can readily find traces of them in earlier twelfth-century literature directed explicitly at the knight. Stephen de Fougères late in the 1150s enjoined his model knight thus: 'A knight must draw his sword to do justice and to defend those who cannot implead others for themselves: he should suppress violence and theft.'[2] Stephen also expected the knight to be loyal, charitable, and temperate in his behaviour. He should pay his tithes and frequent his church, because he received his sword from the altar when he was knighted and so must support the institution which validated his status. Around 1141 William of Malmesbury commented in passing on 'the custom of honourable knights', who were expected to escort out of danger a defenceless (noble) woman, even if she were from amongst their bitterest enemies.[3] Most famously, Chrétien de Troyes around 1180 encapsulated similar cautions in his *Conte de Graal*, where the hero's mother and his mentor Gornemant instruct the boy Perceval at the outset of his career. His mother was very urgent on the subject of his behaviour and assistance towards women and maidens alike, as well as the necessity of his assiduous attendance at Mass and mattins. When the *prodom* Gornemant girded the young Perceval, he also enjoined him to assist women in distress and be regular in his church attendance. He had pragmatic advice about modesty and reticence in public, and the necessity of mercy to his defeated foes.[4]

From this we can suggest that the *Ordene* preserved in its concluding injunctions an earlier form of oral *enseignement* that had long been offered to the twelfth-century tyro at the conclusion of the ceremony by the *preudomme* who inaugurated him into his new condition of knight. The contemporary author of the early sections of the Prose Lancelot in fact refers to this as the usual practice.[5] The author of the *Ordene* clearly did not believe that repeating such traditional sentiments was sufficient as a moral foundation for the noble knight of his day, sufficient to maintain a claim to Nobility, but since the *enseignement* was an accepted part of

[1] *Ordene*, 112 (ll. 263–97).   [2] *Livre des Manières*, c. 135.
[3] Malmesbury, *HN*, 62. There are indeed other instances in the civil war of King Stephen's reign where contemporaries were reluctant to include women in hostilities; D. Crouch, *The Reign of King Stephen, 1135–1154* (Harlow, 2000), 80, 139–40.
[4] *Conte de Graal*, 21–3 (ll. 525–92), 54–5 (ll. 1637–68).
[5] *Lancelot do Lac*, 1: 144. *Lo jor qu'il reçoit l'ordre de chevalerie creante il a damedé qu'il sera tex com cil qui chevalier lo fait le di devise, qui miauz lo set deviser.*

the procedure, he included his own version of it. We can speculate that such a practice might very well have gone back to the eleventh century when we know that the practice of *adoubement* had a president, and saying a few suitable words to mark rites of passage is what their presidents often do. However, the earliest firm traces of the content of such a secular, ritual *enseignement* only date back to the fiction of the third quarter of the twelfth century. Elsewhere the *Chanson d'Aspremont* depicts Charlemagne delivering a brief homily to the young Roland when he girds him with Durendaal, enjoining him to be a man and to stand up for the Church against unbelievers.[6] The *adoubement* of Fromondin in the epic *Garin le Loherenc* was preceded by a bath, as was that administered to Saladin in the *Ordene*. The president of Fromondin's rite was his uncle, who delivered this little homily:

> I counsel you, fair dear nephew Fromondin, you are now more than just a lad or a lout! You will be a noble count should you live so long. So now be accomplished and victorious all your days; ruthless and fierce towards your enemies. Give fur robes to poor men, and in this way you'll gain reputation.[7]

The failure of the knight to live up even to these limited expectations into which they were inaugurated always provided ammunition to socially weaponize the rhetoric of clerks such as Stephen de Fougères. We find a number of instances of this. Well before 1180 we can find a tradition in clerical writing that obligations went with the status and public function of *chevalers*. Limited though they were, knights were falling short of them as far as clerics were concerned, as Stephen explained around 1160. John of Salisbury assumed much the same in the same decade, though his circle was not quite the same as the one in which Stephen moved. He talked in terms very close to Stephen's of the 'two swords', the military sword ordained to assist that of the Church in defending orthodoxy and the priesthood, and protecting the poor. Like Stephen, John deplored the fact that *milites* did not live up to this worthy ideal (see below for further on this).[8] These two writers of the 1150s indicate that there was already in England and northern France by 1160 a widespread view of the knight as possessing a duty to society. His disciplinary function imposed social obligations on him, and if these obligations were used to justify his status, then he had to live up to them. In Occitania in the 1170s the lay writers Arnaut-Guilhem de Marsan and Arnaut de Mareuil both conceded the knight's social status and assumed a *cavayer* was the occupant of an elite milieu. As far as Arnaut de Mareuil was concerned, the knight's claim to distinction that went with his name came from his possession of a variety of virtues, both civil and military:

> A knight obtains his fame in the ways you will now hear: some are fine warriors, others are excellent hosts, some gain merit from the service they offer, others for marshalling troops; some are fine horsemen and others are outstanding courtiers. These qualities

[6] *Aspremont*, 2: ll. 7485–90.

[7] *Garin le Loherenc*, 2: ll. 8450–60. The ritual bath is also mentioned in Chrétien's account of the *adoubement* of Alexander (who showed his hardiness by bathing in the sea); *Cligés*, ed. A. Micha (Paris, 1957), ll. 1134–8.

[8] *Livre de Manières*, cc. 135–68, pp. 54–62; *Policraticus*, 2: 22–3.

I've described to you are rarely to be found united in one man, but the more of them a man has the better claim he has to be reputable, and a man with none of them can hardly make a claim to the title of knight, and cannot be held to be righteous.[9]

Perhaps the most significant phrase in Arnaut's musings is that a knight who best fits the qualities he is sketching out has earned the right to be regarded as 'a righteous man' (*dreiturier*), a man of moral integrity. For Arnaut, superior moral standing was required in knighthood, and if it was not necessarily always to be found in knights, it was the basis of any claim they had to a status superior to other laymen, rather than the performance of any rite inaugurating them into their degree.[10]

I have argued in Chapter 12 that knights throughout the eleventh century had in fact already an acknowledged level of status within society, which went with their profession from as far back as we can detect it. Knights were perceived as a subordinate group to the magnates, and indeed gained some of their status from their employment by magnates and their presence in the castles and halls of the great. But I have also said that though they had status from their profession and were unified by a degree of common knightly culture, they could not be considered in the eleventh century to have been within the same group as the lords who employed them, simply by right of their knighthood. Some and perhaps most were anything but 'noble'. The materialist British historiographical tradition, which I follow, finds the late eleventh-century knight to have comprehended a variety of types, but most of them are best categorized as retained household soldiers. It is true, however, that the greater among them might be landed dependants of greater men, and they might very well see themselves as sharing some of the aspirations and trappings of their lords. Contemporaries noticed a materialistic self-elevation amongst the knights of their day. Writing probably in 1130, Bernard of Clairvaux gives us in his *De laude novae militiae* his take on the knights he encountered and from among whom he and his family derived, and he saw them as scrambling for the elite trappings of the aristocrat. Since Bernard's tract is a hermeneutic between 'worldly knighthood' and his idealized 'new knighthood', it was intended to define by contrast with the Templars the sort of knights he found most obnoxious. So Bernard's imperfect worldly knight respected birth rather than merit, which was quite otherwise than the Templar. The worldly knight rejoiced in elite pursuits such as field sports, gambling and the tourney, and he delighted in the diversions of the hall. He equipped himself with expensive gilded and bejewelled gear and silk clothing.[11]

---

[9] *Razos es e Mesura*, 21–2, ll. 231–46. The few twelfth-century Occitan epics assume the same stance on knighthood; L. M. Paterson, 'Knights and the Concept of Knighthood in the Twelfth-century Occitan epic', *Forum for Modern Language Studies*, 17 (1981), 117.

[10] Compare here the mid-thirteenth-century Orléannais custumary which opens with a poem in which 'Law' serenades the knight as righteous (*drois*) in counsel and judgement, and that his choice to do right in all circumstances makes him worthy to stand with all rulers (*princiers*); *Établissements*, 2: 329.

[11] Bernard of Clairvaux, *De laude novae militiae*, in *PL* 182, cols 921–40. For comments, see Barthélemy, *Chevalerie*, 275–7. A mid-twelfth-century *contemptus mundi* poem likewise excoriates the expensive lifestyle of the contemporary knight, and his taste for high living, which since he could not afford it, he financed by theft and extortion; *Poésies inédites du moyen âge*, ed. M. E. du Méril (Paris,

The sort of knights who could have embraced such a lifestyle on their own account would have been a very small minority even if they were a conspicuous one. Probably most knights of Bernard's day were soldiers seeking employment in the household of a lord, who would have provided them with the coveted equipment and horses they needed and possibly even a salary, as was certainly the case with the young and landless William Marshal in the 1160s. A few such men would, like Marshal, have been sons or brothers of magnates; more would have been men of a variety of landed backgrounds, some quite poor, poor enough to need to live by their swords in any way they could. Their fortunes would always have been precarious. Elements of this economic instability of unlanded *milites* persisted well beyond the end of the twelfth century. One of Ramon de Miraval's *sirventes* dating to around 1200 was addressed to a knight whose *senhal* was 'Bajona' (the man from Bayonne), whom Ramon said he found in a wretched state, unemployed and lacking a decent robe and horse. He advised him to take his song as a recommendation to Ramon's friends among the lords of the Carcassès, from whom Bajona would hopefully get horses, arms, a salary (*loguier*) and appropriately luxurious livery robes.[12] The fortunes of some knights remained frail even in the thirteenth century from this indication, and always depended on the resources of magnates, which is why a writer and career knight like Sordello da Goito urged on the society of the 1230s that poor knights were one of the groups most deserving of society's support (along with women and *trouvères*): 'How dare anyone humiliate a poor knight for any reason whatsoever, whom one should assist and promote, support and welcome nobly?'[13]

As late as the mid thirteenth century it is still possible to reconstruct the career of a man like Richard Siward (died 1248), whose origins lay in the free but low-born English peasantry and who owed his social climb entirely to the military skills which had impressed a succession of his employers: the count of Aumale, the earl of Pembroke, the king of England and finally the king of Scotland.[14] In Occitania, the career of Raimbaut de Vaqueiras (died 1207) offers a contemporary parallel to Siward's, though his gifts were principally poetic and musical. He too was low-born (though his later *vida* protests otherwise) and his early career included episodes of poverty and deprivation, but his considerable talents gained him employment first with the Prince of Orange and later with the Marquis of Montferrat. In 1194 his patron the marquis advanced Raimbaut in his mid to late thirties from body-squire (*escudiers*) to the rank of knight. The social elevation was not well received by some in the Montferrat circle, in much the same way as Richard Siward

1854), 316–17. For the rapacity of knights who aspire to be called noble, see also Bernard of Cluny, *De contemptu mundi*, ed. and trans. R. E. Pepin (East Lansing, 1991), 94.

[12] *Bajona, per sirventes*, in *Les poésies du troubadour Ramon de Miraval*, ed. and trans, (Fr.) L. T. Topsfield (Paris, 1971), no. 39. The editor's suggestion that 'Bajona' was a fellow poet makes no sense in light of his expectations of reward and suggested competition on the tourney field.

[13] *Ensenhamens d'Onor*, 215 (ll. 573–6), *Ni cavalier paubre con ausa/Destrigar nulz per nulla causa/ Qui om deu donnar e servir/Enanzar e gen acuillir?*

[14] D. Crouch, 'The Last Adventure of Richard Siward', *Morgannwg: Transactions of the Glamorgan History Society*, 35 (1991), 7–30.

was apparently slighted in English court circles for his lack of a liberal courtly education. In Raimbaut's case the criticism was based on his corpulence and his lack of a conventional knightly education, though he had in fact served with courage on earlier campaigns. A literary duel (*cobla*) in which he was gibbeted concluded: 'Sir Raimbaut, when he gallops in armour, looks far more like a *jocglars* than *cavalliers*.'[15] The fact that in the 1180s Walter Map could talk in one of his anecdotes of 'a worthless and insignificant knight' reflects the truth that still in his day many knighted men were of no great standing and to credit them with Nobility would have seemed absurd.[16] The reality was that knights at the end of the twelfth century were still in that economic and social continuum, uncomfortable though that might be when some and perhaps most knights considered they were entitled to the deference awarded to the noblemen who employed them, and they had adopted what they could of a noble lifestyle. Within a generation this would change, however.

Perhaps the most telling indication of the way that knighthood was being adjusted to meet the problems caused by the nobilizing impulse within it is the evolution in the later twelfth century of a superior rank of knight, the knight *portant banière*, the 'knight banneret' as he became known in Western societies (paralleling the Latinized title *banneretus* or *vexillifer*).[17] Already in the early twelfth century the magnate-knight was symbolically separated from his household knights by his carrying of a banner as a symbol of his command. It is to be seen in the Anglo-French seal designs of magnates as early as the 1140s, such as that of King Henry II's brother William fitz Empress, or that of Count Waleran II of Meulan and his nephew Earl Simon III of Northampton. The effigies are identified by armorial banners, shields and caparisoned horses. On every available surface was the symbolic sign of his genetic Nobility, his proto-heraldic device. This symbolic distinction might have been a product of the conditions of the mêlée tournament (rather than the battlefield), where the magnate needed to be clearly distinguished on the field from the common knights, so his household could rally to him and defend him from the knights who were trying to capture him for his ransom.[18] The retained knight followed a banner and did not possess one, as he had no need for it. Such a knight did not in any case have his own individual heraldic device but bore the colours and symbol of his lord's mesnie, or military household, as did William Marshal when he was within the Tancarville household in 1166.[19] A knight's individual heraldic device was not his routine prerogative till

[15] Raimbaut, 4–16, 139–41.   [16] *De Nugis Curialium*, 164.
[17] Crouch, *Image*, 114–19.
[18] Crouch, *Tournament*, 75–6, 139–41. For recent studies of the significance of the banner in military society, R. W. Jones, ' "What banner thine?" The banner as symbol of identification, status and authority on the medieval battlefield', *Haskins Society Journal*, 15 (2006), 101–9; idem, *Bloodied Banners: Martial Display on the Medieval Battlefield* (Woodbridge, 2010), 33–55; J-F. Nieus, 'L'invention des armoiries en contexte. Haute aristocratie, identités familiales et culture chevaleresque entre France et Angleterre, 1100–1160, *Journal des Savants* (2017), 124–5.
[19] *History of William Marshal*, 1: ll. 1470–8. The significance of such signs was registered by P. Adam, 'Les usages héraldiques au milieu du xiie siècle', *Archivum Heraldicum*, 7 (1963), 19; and see Crouch, *Aristocracy*, 228–35.

well into the thirteenth century, which is in itself evidence that the idea of inherited Nobility as applying automatically to the knight did not take hold till after 1200.[20]

The rank of banneret was first explicitly acknowledged by contemporary sources in a list of those who took the field in the great tournament of Lagny in 1179, the greatest such festival of its day; the list was partly preserved by extracts being copied into the biography of William Marshal, who was present and who raised his banner on the field that day, possibly for the first time.[21] Ralph Niger, William Marshal's clerical colleague in the household of the Young King Henry, explained the banner as symbolizing the right of command (*bannus*), which a lord's followers must acknowledge.[22] The identification of higher status with the banner was a solution to an old problem, which has already been considered in the previous chapter: that a magnate or great baron who was not a count would readily accept the designation of a *miles*, but that he then shared the title with the dependent *milites* of his household. Now with the banneret there was a generally accepted higher degree of knighthood which barons could formally embrace, and which enhanced their Nobility above whatever degree of noble status their knightly inferiors and employees were claiming. It maintained and indeed formalized the old separation of dependency between knight and his employer seen in eleventh-century sources. On the field of tourney or battle there would in practice have been no difficulty recognizing that the magnate's knightliness was not the same as the knightliness of his followers. William le Breton frames the status involved with economy when he talks of twenty-five *proceres* who were not counts taken captive at Bouvines in 1214 as being 'of such nobility that each of them might rejoice in the insignia of a banner (*qui tante erant nobilitatis ut eorum quilibet vexilli gauderet dignitatis*)'.[23] When he did, the *nobilitas* being evoked brings together lineage, resources and knightly leadership in a novel expression of superior rank that would penetrate and help define the Anglo-French and Imperial aristocracies for the next two centuries and more.[24]

This fissure opening within the late twelfth-century knightly continuum between magnate-knight and mesnie-knight can be taken as yet more evidence of a solidifying attitude towards the comparative Nobility of knighthood, which opened up definitive cracks between emerging social levels. The 'simple' *chevaler* was having his Nobility accepted but defined symbolically as a lesser quality than that of his lord. We have seen how the Nobility of knighthood was asserting itself

---

[20] Crouch, *Image*, 226–37.   [21] *History of William Marshal*, 1: ll. 4457–88; 3: pp. 33–4.
[22] *De re militari*, 130.
[23] *Gesta Philippi regis*, in *Œuvres de Rigord et de Guillaume le Breton*, ed. H. F. Delaborde (2 vols, Paris, 1882–5), 1: 290.
[24] The rank of banneret had certainly penetrated the western Empire before 1300, and the word was adopted as *baenrots* in Flemish, the etymology being suggested by recent writers to be from *baan* (command) and *rot* (troop); S. Boffa, 'Nobility and Chivalry in Brabant', in *Warfare in Medieval Brabant, 1356–1406* (Woodbridge, 2004), 127–9; M. Damen, 'Heren met banieren. De baanrotsen van Brabant in de vijftiende eeuw', in *Bourgondië voorbij. De Nederlanden 1250–1650*, ed. M. Damen and L. H. J. Sicking (Hilversum, 2010), 139–58. The banneret is found amongst all the late medieval nobilities of the Low Countries, and though infrequently encountered appears as the *baenritz* or *bannerheer* in fourteenth-century Middle High German sources; H. Denessen, 'De Gelderse bannerheren in de vijftiende eeuw', *Virtus*, 20 (2013), 11–37, esp. 13–16.

in the way that in the 1180s attitudes had formed which attempted to stigmatize knights who were regarded as unqualified to be considered noble; social friction we have seen in the contemporary reactions to the low-born knights Richard Siward and Raimbaut de Vaqueiras. There would only have been such friction if these two men were regarded as a mismatch to the rising status of the rank they had acquired. An easy target for stigmatization was the knight whose life and livelihood was centred entirely on his profession and who was in the market for his sword—the supposed symbol of Nobility of soul—to be hired out. These were mercenaries who fought for pay (*merces*) whom later twelfth-century sources tend to despise, knights or not.[25] In 1194 Bertran de Born came out with a frank view as to why mercenary knights should be despised, comparing mercenaries (*basclos*—literally, 'Basques') to greedy prostitutes (*putanas venaus*). A retained knight (*mainadier*) who showed himself eager for money ought, he said, to be executed by hanging.[26] Though Alfonso II of Aragon was generally regarded in his day by the southern troubadours as the pattern of a noble king, Bertran sneered at him around 1183 as a 'sword for hire' (*soudadiers logaditz*) when he sold his services for a campaign.[27]

The biographer of William Marshal, writing in a generation when knights were undoubtedly considered to be socially privileged by the fact of their knighthood, was harsh on the subject of those knights in earlier generations who were the short-term *routier* contractors of military companies whom Bertran de Born had despised: knights like Mercadier, Lupescar, Cadoc and Sancho de Savannac, so prominent in the armies of the Angevin kings of England and the Capetian kings of France during the 1180s and 1190s. This would be because, unlike Marshal, they stood outside the ethic of loyalty and self-sacrificing service which bound the retained knight of a *mesnie* to his lord, even if such a knight took money as a reward for that service. In the military circles of Angevin England there was a detectable move to exclude *routier* knights from the *ordo militum*.[28] King John of England's Norman and Tourangeau mercenary captains deeply antagonized the magnates of the England on which they were quartered between 1205 and 1224, to the extent that a clause of Magna Carta expelled many of them from the realm in 1215. The most powerful and despised of them was the Norman Faulkes de Bréauté (died 1226), who was of a knightly family, but contemporaries either sneered that he was the son of a knight born outside marriage or that his origins were rather in the servile peasantry. His military talents were what led the king to knight him around 1207, and his ruthless determination to use the circumstances of civil war to insert himself within the highest ranks of the English aristocracy led to his utter destruction when the earls turned on him in 1224.[29] His forced marriage to the noblewoman Margaret de Rivières was treated by Matthew Paris as an

[25] See comments in L. Napran, 'Mercenaries and Paid Men in Gilbert of Mons', in *Mercenaries and Paid Men: the Mercenary Identity in the Middle Ages*, ed. J. France (Leiden, 2008), 287–97, esp. 294–5.
[26] *Ar ven la coindeta sazos*, in Bertran, 433.   [27] *Pois lo gens terminis floritz*, in Bertran, 269.
[28] D. Crouch, 'William Marshal and the Mercenariat', in *Mercenaries and Paid Men*, 15–32.
[29] *Histoire des ducs de Normandie*, 173, and see D. J. Power, 'Sir Falkes de Bréauté', in *ODNB*.

example of foul miscegenation, the sort that the barons of 1215 in fact made unacceptable in Magna Carta as 'disparagement'.[30]

A knight who owed his elevation solely to his wealth attracted even more odium than did the mercenary and the low-born outsider, who might at least have military credibility. But since there was an identifiable noble lifestyle which involved the possession of a landed estate, hall, formal household and noble recreations (like hunting and hawking), it was possible for those with the wealth to buy the material trappings expected of a noble knight. When indeed in 1194 Pope Celestine III wrote of the offences alleged against Archbishop Geoffrey Plantagenet of York—among which was the objectionable secularity of his lifestyle including that, in contempt of his office, Geoffrey devoted himself to hawks and hounds 'and *other* knightly concerns (*et aliis curis militaribus*)'—the pope was explicitly conflating knights with the affectation of a noble way of life.[31] If wealthy men became invaluable to kings and princes and lived the same sort of high life, they might well receive the distinction of knighthood, a possibility to which Andrew the Chaplain refers in the 1180s.[32] Artaud of Nogent, the immensely wealthy financial agent of Count Henry the Liberal of Champagne, was the defining instance of such a man in late twelfth-century society, and apocryphal stories of the count's takedown of Artaud's arrogant pretensions to a noble life amused several generations thereafter. Significantly, it involved reducing the arrogant financier and parvenu to the status of serf and granting him to a simple and poor but deserving *chevaler*.[33]

Late twelfth- and thirteenth-century literature is shot through with negative portrayals of such offensively bourgeois characters and their disruptive effect on their society. Ramon Llull devoted his discourse on the mortal sin of pride to the example of men of low origins in trade aspiring to *noblesce*, and compared them to the rebel angels of Genesis. He particularly decried the unequal marriages that would result between bourgeois children and their betters.[34] This sort of social anxiety was increasingly widespread in writings of the thirteenth century. Sordello da Goito in the Provence of the 1230s wrote a powerful *sirventes* against a nobleman (*hom gentils*) so lost to shame that he bastardized his lineage by marrying beneath him for money.[35] The case was worse if the daughters of noble castellans married the sons of moneylenders; the theory of the descent of qualities through the male line meant that Nobility would itself then be contaminated. Such is the rationale behind the early thirteenth-century *fabliau* 'Berenger au Long Cul', whose author, Guérin, pontificated on that sort of miscegenation and the cowardice and imbecility of a youth who had come by a great estate and his knighthood in just that way. The young knight was son of a 'villein', a rich and well-provided-for moneylender, who

---

[30] As discussed in Aurell, *Lettered Knight*, 338–9.   [31] Howden, *Chronica*, 3: 279.

[32] *De Amore*, 78.

[33] T. Evergates, *Henry the Liberal, Count of Champagne, 1127–1182* (Philadelphia, 2016), 180–1. For the story of Artaud's humiliation, *Die exempla aus den Sermones feriales et communes des Jakob von Vitry*, ed. J. Greven (Heidelberg, 1914), 17, and see above, pp. 113–14.

[34] *Doctrina*, 137–8.

[35] *Qui be·is membra del segle*, in *Le Poesie. Nuova edizione critica*, ed. and trans. (It.) M. Boni (Bologna, 1954), no. 22 (ll. 22–4), *Ai com pot tan esser desvergoingnatz/nuls hom gentils qu·is vai enbastarden/so lignage per aur ni per argen?*

had plenty of wine and grain; he had cows and goats, cash, bushels of wheat and sesters of wine. The castellan owed him more than he could pay, so he gave his daughter to the usurer's son, and it is in this way, Guérin said, that good families were brought low and castellans and counts fell into contempt and shame; if people married beneath themselves for money, they could not but come to grief and lose their reputation. A villainous, low-born and cowardly knight was the result, the sort who was avid for gold and silver rather than the pursuit of arms (*chevalerie*), and this was how Nobility (*noblece*) collapsed.[36]

Guérin here defined *noblece* in relation to a knight, and when he did, the innate Nobility of a knight was being made apparent in the moral strength and physical dauntlessness (*chevalerie*) which he believed should properly be acquired through a distinguished ancestry. We have seen this anxiety earlier (see Chapter 6) in the way that any intruder into the world of Courtliness was defined as a 'villein', the classic outsider to courtly society. Such a man was the wealthy *vilain* who had usurped by purchase the noble and magnificent knightly estate at the centre of the mid-thirteenth-century *Lay of Oiselet*, an estate which he was incapable of maintaining as he did not have the superior education, aesthetic sense and intellectual aspirations to do so.[37] When in the 1180s Andrew the Chaplain's dialogues on love deal with the character of the 'commoner' (*plebeius*), who is to be taken as a wealthy bourgeois, it is this lack of sensibility which condemns him in his conversations with both the noble lady and the countess he presumed to address. The noble lady, who was of a knightly family, took considerable exception to the transgressive attentions of a man whose only business was trade. But she at least condescended to argue his case with him, which was based on his claim to possess Nobility of mind. When the same commoner went further and dared to address a countess, she coolly pointed out to him that he had none of the physical grace and fine proportions a knight should possess. She went on to criticize his lack of courtly virtues, not least the defining quality of largesse and failure to employ his wealth in a noble fashion, to the relief of the poor. She faulted him for the lack of courtly humility and reticence amongst his sort of inferior male, as well as for his poor social self-control and absence of education in the liberal arts. These things and others excluded the bourgeois from the 'court of love', in Andrew's opinion, but he might equally have said courtly society.[38]

THE SACRALIZATION OF ARMS

The materialist impulse in the social exaltation of knighthood is one thing; its exaltation by valorizing the tools of the knightly trade is another. A different concern in the literature on the question of military Nobility is the status which should be

[36] *Chevalerie et Grivoiserie*, 84 (ll. 14–34). Compare the verdict of Baldwin de Condé: 'I am quite right on this, as God is my help, for it is a tragedy and a source of grief when a great estate is enjoyed by a villain (*mauvais home*), a place where he can spawn others like him', Condé 1: 97–8 (ll. 49–52).
[37] *The Old French Lays of* Ignaure, Oiselet *and* Amours, ed. and trans. G. S. Burgess and L. C. Brook (Gallica, 18, Cambridge, 2010), 146–8.
[38] *De Amore*, 60–4, 78–84.

awarded to someone who wielded the sword. The sword was a symbol in its own right of public power and justice and thus of the high personal status of the great men who wielded such authority. Ralph Niger in the late 1180s traced the idea back to the Code of Justinian, which stated that in a troubled and violent world arms were a guarantee of peace and a hindrance to violence: an early instance of the facile argument that the best defence against a bad guy with a weapon is a good guy with one.[39] The sword was part of an image universally employed across eleventh- and twelfth-century Latin Europe, and indeed Outremer, in depictions of margraves, counts and occasionally lesser lords on seals, coins, and in other media. It does so as an allusion to the capacity to do public justice—the 'ban' in French terms—to which earls and counts had a historical right to aspire. The pose of this image is the same whether on the ivory seal matrices of the eleventh-century English ealdorman called Ælfric (c.1000) and a thegn called Godric (c.1050); the Bayeux Tapestry's image of Count Guy of Ponthieu in state in his hall (1070); the copper coinage of Count Baldwin II of Edessa (c.1110); the silver coinage of the margraves Jacza of Brandenburg and Albrecht of Anhalt (c.1150); the funerary enamel plaque of Count Geoffrey V of Anjou (c.1155); or the (now lost) ledger stone which was (c.1170) placed over the grave of Count William Clito of Flanders (died 1128).[40] The lord in these images features in bust or full figure, displaying an upright and (usually) unsheathed sword in his hand. Sometimes he is in armour, and quite often not, but the pose is the same. It is the reason why in Normandy and England criminal pleas which offended the dignity of earls (such as Chester), counts (such as Mortain) and the dukes of Normandy themselves were called 'pleas of the sword'.[41] In 1177, an arenga (or prologue) to an act of Count Philip of Vermandois and Flanders justified the symbol in high terms:

> Since we ought to protect the holy church of God and preserve each and every one of its privileges by the sword the All Highest has committed to us, it is proper that we should confirm for future ages the solemn agreements of ecclesiastical institutions made in our own days and with our consent, for the avoidance of any dispute.[42]

Count Philip's clerk was quoting here a theological commonplace about lay power that had been current for at least two generations in the schools, which had grown naturally out of the ancient Gelasian outlook on the balance (or imbalance) of lay and spiritual powers in Christendom. This commonplace statement envisioned the powers as two swords and first appears in the 1070s in the literary skirmishing of the rival thinkers Peter Damian and Gottschalk of Aachen during the Investiture Contest.[43] It quite likely informed the teaching at Paris of the English theologian Robert Pullen before 1144, which included the first instance of the observation

[39] *De re militari*, 98.
[40] A variant civilian image is that on the seal of Count Robert I of Meulan (cut c.1080), which has the count holding the sword point down; Crouch, *Aristocracy*, pl. 7.
[41] Crouch, *Image*, 190–8.
[42] *De Oorkunden der Graven van Vlaanderen, 2, Filips van de Elzas*, ed. T. de Hemptinne, A. Verhulst and L. de Mey (Brussels, 2001), 272.
[43] C. Erdmann and D. von Gladdiss, 'Gottschalk von Aachen im Dienste Heinrichs IV', *Deutsches Archiv*, 3 (1939), 115–74, and see the discussion in P. Healey, *The Chronicle of Hugh of Flavigny: Reform and Investiture Contest in the Eleventh Century* (Aldershot, 2006), 150–6.

that since the sword was in the shape of a cross, it should be properly used in the service of the Church.[44] Pullen's pupil John of Salisbury, and John's contemporary Stephen de Fougères, made play in the late 1150s with the idea of the 'two swords' in the particular context of knighthood. Stephen presented a somewhat contorted theological gloss on the Gospel passages concerning Jesus's arrest by soldiers of the High Priest (Matt. 26:51–2, Mark 14:47-8, Luke 22:38, 49–53). He invented a colourful sermon which he placed in the mouth of Jesus Christ as if He were commenting on the episode to those gathered around Him in Gethsemane. Stephen then presented Pullen's views in the vernacular when he concluded by chiding the knights who were listening to his exposition:

> One sword helps the other, the one to curse the other to slay. So if one sword mistreats or disputes with the other, farewell to all justice. God grant that they may continue in affection and one sword invoke the other, that both may be kindly to each other, and be merciless to such as are harsh to others.[45]

John of Salisbury's *Policraticus* described the same need for cooperation between regular knighthood (*militia ordinata*) and the Church for the good of broader society. His *milites* were bound to an ideology by their 'oath'. John's *sacramentum* is not to be taken literally, but as a vague expression with classical resonances, and in this case it meant no more than a conflation of a knight's fealty to his lord and the ideology of service behind it. His knight was bound to protect the Church and orthodoxy, assist the poor, maintain peace, and sacrifice himself for others if he must; so in this way knights shared the ideology of kingship, as far as they were the king's 'armed hand' in enforcing it.[46]

Jean Flori's two-volume publication in the 1980s on the evolution of the knightly ethic before 1200 has much to say on the sacralization of the sword that princes and their knights wielded, even outside its use in royal inaugurations: a sacralization whose moral and theological justification was eventually to feed into the first chivalric treatises. In a series of studies centred on the early rituals of the blessing of arms about to be conferred on princes, he identified an 'idéologie du glaive,' a moral-theological programme defining the rightful use of the secular power represented by the sword. It is one of his arguments that a well-defined set of biblical principles to be found in the Psalms and Books of Wisdom (a 'Davidic ethic' in my shorthand), which were marshalled into Carolingian expectations of righteous kingship, had travelled downward socially by the eleventh century to be employed in inauguration rituals of non-royal princes and lords. His belief was that it was applied exclusively to kings till at least 900 and not explicitly applied to knights as their own ethic before the 'classic age' of knighthood at the end of the

---

[44] *Sententiae*, in *PL*, 186, cols. 905–6; H. Hoffmann, 'Die beiden Schwerter im Hochmittelalter', *Deutsches Archiv*, 20 (1964), 93–4.

[45] *Livre des manières*, 62 (cc. 167–8).

[46] J. Flori, *Chevaliers et chevalerie au moyen âge* (Paris, 1998), 212–13. Flori's extensive study of the *miles* in John of Salisbury's thinking is stimulating and I do not differ from his conclusion that it contained nothing new, but he is not in my view cautious enough about its contemporary relevance; idem, *L'Essor de la chevalerie, xi⁰-xii⁰ siècles* (Geneva, 1986), 280–9.

twelfth century. Knights themselves, if they were discussed before then, were often enough framed morally in terms of the ancient Roman soldier, who was also called *miles* in Latin.[47] Flori saw the evolution of the concept of the Three Orders in the tenth century as one engine to transfer this ethic to all those who used armed force in society, of which the symbol was the sword. It was force that should be used righteously in defence of the Church, the faith, and the poor and defenceless.[48] He saw the act of the *remise d'armes* as central to instilling the ethic in knighthood, in which he may well be right, though few historians now would find any credible evidence of its application to such an act before the second half of the twelfth century (see pp. 267–70).[49] Flori subscribed to the idea that the preaching of the First Crusade was another engine which brought the Davidic ethic to bear on professional warriors as criticism of their conduct, and which if taken seriously by knights genuinely elevated and even sacralized their profession. This is a view which still commands general acceptance in the historiography of the knight.[50] To Flori the full ethicization of knighthood belonged to the later twelfth century, a conclusion few would dispute, and the Davidic ethic is to be found integrated into the first chivalric treatises directed at defining the status, condition, and power of the knight in society.

Though Flori's model has been attacked by Dominique Barthélemy on several grounds—as being too tied into Duby's now-discredited idea of a feudal mutation around 1000 and a 'rise of the knights', and as being too traditional in its interpretation of the sketchy material for the delivery of arms in the eleventh century—Flori's is an idea rather bigger than the narrow historiographical model its author tied it too. It is useful as a means of explaining the appearance of hypermoral Chivalry and its ethic, and its general outlines on that subject are accepted and followed in this chapter. One could argue as to what process is being actually described by the model. It might well be argued as to whether abstracting and valorizing Flori's instance of a Sombartian downward cultural diffusion of a noble ethic fully justifies in itself a conclusion that power diffused and knighthood rose in society in the eleventh and twelfth centuries. The diffusion might, for instance, be equally framed as a developing medieval debate on how to keep a moral and rational check on power within society by employing more widely well-established theological principles which had long applied to the king. In which case it is compatible with a century-old German historiographical tradition that the Imperial nobility was subject throughout the twelfth century to a defining *Tugendsystem*, derived from the schools, an idea which is still an ongoing and developing topic in German and American scholarship.[51]

---

[47] J. Flori, *L'Idéologie du glaive: préhistoire de la chevalerie* (Geneva, 1983), 61.
[48] *L'Idéologie du glaive*, 100–2. [49] *L'Essor de la chevalerie*, 78–80.
[50] Barthélemy, *Chevalerie*, 264–75.
[51] The idea can be traced to Gustav Ehrismann, 'Die Grundlagen des ritterlichen Tugendsystems', *Zeitschrift für deutsches Altertum und deutsche Literatur*, 56 (1919), 137–216, and see for an assessment *Ritterliches Tugendsystem*, ed. G. Eifler (Wege der Forschung, 56, Darmstadt, 1970). See also, for contextualization of virtue, love and nobility, Jaeger, *Ennobling Love*, 151–4.

Whatever might be said of the *status* of the eleventh-century knight, the conscious *ethicization* of his calling can be traced confidently only back to the first crusading generation, when we can for certain distinguish Flori's 'élévation idéologique de la *militia*'.[52] Bishop Bonizo of Sutri in the age of the First Crusade in the last quarter of the eleventh century sketched out in his vision of an ecclesiastical common-wealth, known as the *Liber de vita christiana*, what he believed his idealized knights ought to do: they ought to serve their lords loyally and protect them, if necessary, with their own lives. They should neither strive for booty nor commit perjury, but fight for the 'commonwealth' (*res publica*) and religious orthodoxy. Finally, they ought to defend the poor, widows and orphans.[53] The *milites* whom Bonizo was preaching at were the dependants of their lords, both of which groups were part of the *ordo pugnatorum*: those lay persons with authority and power to direct the secular world. The characteristic of the *miles* according to Bonizo is the same condition of obedience and dependency that defines the *miles* in the first half of the eleventh century in the *Conventum* of Hugh of Lusignan, but here it is framed in a duty to execute an ethical duty imposed on both the knight's lord and the knight himself, not simply as an obligation to work his lord's will, as the Lusignan knights did. In the next generation, in his brief notes for *sermones ad status*, Honorius Augustodunensis took the same stance as Bonizo. He addressed knights as members of a Christian commonwealth with a duty he described in the same terms as John of Salisbury would, as being the 'strong arm of the Church'—its defenders from its would-be oppressors.[54]

It was not just clergy with a utopian outlook who attributed the Davidic ethic to the knight at the turn of the twelfth century. The historian Orderic Vitalis is not necessarily a safe guide to eleventh-century Anglo-Norman aristocratic behaviour, for all that he writes on it extensively, but occasionally his sources are more direct than collected oral memories of earlier days. As a young monk in 1102 he com-posed an epitaph for the tomb of the leading knight of the earl of Chester, Robert of Rhuddlan, a formidable Marcher warrior of the post-Conquest generation, whose brother was Orderic's fellow monk and whom he had known personally. It praised Robert not just for his military prowess but because 'all priests, monks, orphans and homeless men, held in honour by him, received his gifts.'[55] It is not relevant here whether Orderic's praise was merited or rooted in any more than pious hope for salvation. What is relevant is the moral expectations it laid on an eleventh-century flesh-and-blood warrior. They were also the virtues which—in the opinion of his former employers and lords—distinguished Robert of Rhuddlan's

[52] *L'Essor de la chevalerie*, 290. Studies of the ideological consequences for knighthood of the cru-sading movement begin with C. Erdmann, *The Origin of the Idea of Crusade* (Princeton, 1977), and see H .E. J. Cowdrey, 'Pope Gregory VII and the Bearing of Arms', in *Montjoie: Studies in Crusade History in Honour of Hans Eberhard Mayer*, ed. B. Z. Kedar, J. Riley-Smith, and R. Hiestand (Aldershot, 1997), 21–35.

[53] *Liber de vita christiana*, ed. E. Perels (Texte zur Geschichte des römischen und kanonischen Rechts im Mittelalter, 1, Berlin, 1930), 248–9; see G. Althoff, 'Nunc fiant Christi milites, qui dudum extiterunt raptores. Zur Entstehung von Rittertum und Ritterethos', *Saeculum*, 32 (1981), 317–33; Aurell, *Lettered Knight*, 259–60.

[54] *Speculum Ecclesiae*, in *PL* 172, col. 865.   [55] Orderic, 4: 142.

German literary contemporary, the retained free knight Ruodlieb. He was sound in advice and judgement, and the author (who may or may not have been a cleric) remarked that he defended 'the widow and orphan when they are hurt by cruel greed and who weep bitterly when they are oppressed'.[56] It is on the development of that ethic that knights would come to justify their social eminence and indeed their Nobility by the end of the coming century. It provided the foundation of hypermoral Chivalry.

By the mid twelfth century the ethical obligations laid upon knights to safeguard the Church, the poor and the defenceless had become a commonplace expectation as much as a rebuke to those that fell short in their duty. We have already seen above (p. 274) the comment of William of Malmesbury in the 1140s that disinterested and protective behaviour was expected of knights towards noblewomen at least. In 1146 a solemn diploma issued by the distinguished Capetian prince Count Ralph of Vermandois contained an arenga which lectured its auditors that those in the condition of knight (*in ordine... militari*) should be respectful to written grants to the Church, as it was by their swords that peace and peaceful possession of goods were maintained.[57] So the rhetoric of Stephen de Fougères directed late in the 1150s at knights would have found an audience familiar with this idea of moral obligation symbolized by their sword: 'A knight must draw his sword to do justice and to defend those who cannot implead others for themselves: he should suppress violence and theft.'[58] The knight would also have been familiar with the material in Stephen's accompanying bitter homily on his shortcomings in living up to this expectation, since it drew on the homily he had been lectured with at his inauguration into his degree (see above, pp. 273–4):

> Knighthood was once a high order,
> but it is now no more than debauchery.
> Knights love dancing and diversions rather too much
> and know nothing of responsibility.
>
> Born of a free (*franc*) father and a free mother,
> a man is invested as a knight
> to pursue a strenuous life, so he should be sensible,
> and should not be corrupt and full of vice.
>
> He should be sensibly prudent and tough
> and of honest conduct.
> He should bear himself courteously
> towards the Church and all folk.
>
> The knight should keep frequently in mind,
> that he should spend his days of vigour in loyal service
> more so than any monk in his community.
> He takes up the sword in such a spirit

---

[56] *Ruodlieb*, 78. c. 5 (ll. 238–42).

[57] *The Cartulary and Charters of Notre Dame of Homblières*, ed. W. M. Newman, T. Evergates, and G. Constable (Cambridge, MA, 1990), 120–1.

[58] *Livre des manières*, 54 (c. 135).

> That he should neither commit a crime nor lie,
> nor either should he contemplate deceit;
> He should assist Holy Church and should attend it
> and live only on what is his rightful estate.[59]

Stephen's reflections are a summative critique of knights as social actors. The mismatch between the secular way of life of the knight with the symbolism represented by his sword is at the heart of it. It registered the pull of the noble lifestyle and the luxury it involved, whose frivolity was so much at odds with the ethos of loyal service, self-discipline and hardihood expected of the retained or enfeoffed knight, and already drummed into him during the *adoubement* which made him a knight. Stephen's was a critique of the knight for his lack of serious engagement with the Davidic ethic which was the only moral justification for his privilege. It shows, however, little trace as yet of any idea that a knight was a person of superior moral authority, just by virtue of his knighthood. The knight's self-professed superiority which Stephen criticized here rests only on his aspiration to the same material lifestyle as his lord.

This interpretation in fact chimes quite well with the literature of conduct generated within the aristocracy itself in the generation of Stephen de Fougères. The *ensenhamen* of the noble Gascon lord Arnaut-Guilhem de Marsan (*Qui comte vol apendre*), which derives from the 1170s—by which time Stephen was bishop of Rennes—takes a precisely opposite outlook on the knightly life to that of the good bishop, whom he might possibly have encountered in person at one of the Angevin courts. Nowhere in its 628 lines does Marsan reflect on the ethics or morality expected of his ideal *chivayer*, beyond the good service, skills and hardihood that his occupation demanded. Nor is there very much religious feeling other than an expectation that he would attend dawn Mass. We meet in Marsan's *ensenhamen* several knightly characters, not least a dozen retained knights of his *mesnie* who were attending him as he visited his mews. The tyro knight whom Marsan encountered there, as he inspected his falcons and talked shop to the squires in charge of them, had no moral concerns at all. All his visitor wanted to discuss in his depressed state was how to be the sort of superior knight who was worthy of the love of a lady. Marsan in reply scorned the suggestion that knighthood could be understood as superior intellectual understanding (*grans sens*), for which he said he himself couldn't care a fig.[60] He does not seem to be exercising irony in this instance. So far as Marsan was concerned, knights founded their superiority on commanding the resources of an aristocrat and pursuing aspirations to a noble life, which was for him a facility with courtly conduct and adopting elegant dress, as typified by several avatars he named. If a knight dressed as well as he could afford, took care of his physical appearance, behaved with due caution in the public assembly, employed sensible squires, was a good host to his guests, bought the best of equipment and horses for the tourney, and was forward in combat, then that should be the summit

---

[59] *Livre des manières*, 56–8 (cc. 147–51).
[60] '*D'aver ni de gran sen/no·us parlarai nien,/Car so son doas res/De qu'ieu gaire non pes*', *Qui comte vel apendre*, 72 (ll. 171–4).

of his aspirations and any expectations on him. So in this way the noble lord of Marsan sketched out with evident self-satisfaction just those same limited moral horizons for knights that Stephen had despised and had warned them that they must surmount.

If we are looking for a point where the hypermoral and ethical understanding of *chevalerie* penetrated and took possession of lay consciousness, we will not find it in scholastic writers, for though Alan of Lille and Ralph Niger in the 1180s continue to preach the Davidic ethic at the knights of their day, they were critics and not analysts. One could indeed make the same objection also to that chivalric ur-text, the anonymous *Ordene de Chevalerie*, whose clerical author was certainly engaging with the aristocratic world of his day but was not part of it. Nonetheless, as I have said above, an idea that the knight was noble by virtue of his knighthood was a commonplace by the decade in which the *Ordene de Chevalerie* was written. And if he were noble, so must be his conduct. It is in the genre of the *ensenhamen* that the closest approach to this chivalric moment can be made. When in the early thirteenth century the Occitan *ensenhamen* loses the sort of pragmatic secularity Marsan exhibited and adopts the same moral-theological outlook as the *Ordene* and the *Roman des Eles,* that moment had arrived. It had already done so by 1210 and when it did the genre can be seen to have been changing in the face of a newly dominant ideology. So when between 1200 and 1210 Ramon Vidal de Besalú in his *Abril issia* wrote that *cavayer* drew their social eminence from their moral excellence and the protection they offered lesser folk, then we clearly are dealing with knightliness as more than just knightly skills and lifestyle; it is being perceived by an intelligent and perceptive lay person as bound up with a moral ideology—'All good, honest and distinguished qualities are more pronounced in [knights] than in other people,' as Ramon blithely proclaims.[61] Instead of virtue being urged on imperfect and corrupt knights, as the twelfth-century preaching tradition had done, exceptional virtue by 1200 is itself the qualification and badge of the order of knighthood, 'which must be untainted by base conduct'.[62] These last are the words Chrétien de Troyes around 1180 put in the mouth of the *prodome* Gornemant as he girded the sword on Perceval, and then offered the youth an *enseignement* as to how such a knight should properly conduct himself.[63] By 1210 European society had been convinced of this, and the knight was understood by virtue of his condition to be a nobleman, to whom social deference was properly due as much as to his lord.

THE FIRST CHIVALRIC TRACTS

Another symptom of the chivalric turn also relates to literary genre. There were tracts which can readily be called 'chivalric', though defining what made a tract chivalric is rather more difficult than some studies might have assumed or suggested. Later

---

[61] '*E tug bon aip adreg onrat/ son mielhs en lor qu'en autra gen*', *Abril issia*, 130 (ll. 1635–6).
[62] '*qui doit estre sanz vilenie*', *Conte du Graal*, 1: 54 (l. 1636).
[63] *Conte du Graal*, 1: 54–5 (ll. 1631–68).

medieval studies tend to assume, as Léon Gautier had in the nineteenth century, that chivalric literature emerged from the courtly romance of the twelfth century, like a fully formed Athene from the head of Zeus with a war cry and the brandishing of a lance.[64] Germanists, long influenced by the idea of a knightly *Tugendsystem*, see chivalric literature by contrast as an outgrowth of a preceding literature of moral education.[65] The argument I present here is more along these lines: that the chivalric tract was not so much a genre in its own right, but a subgenre which developed over generations in the twelfth century out of an intersection between several influences within the much older forms of conduct tract—the Catonian (grammatical), Salomonic (preaching) and Instructional (the *Enseignement*). In terms of current literary theory, it could be seen as a classic instance of 'hypo-textuality', the way genres are not hard and fast categories, but mutate as they are exploited and referenced by later writers.[66] So identifying the beginnings of the chivalric tract may not be an easy exercise, and rather more taxing than simply pointing to the influence of Chrétien de Troyes or Raoul de Houdenc, but its appearance does tend to fit into the way texts are known to arise within a literate society, as the medieval courtly habitus was.

For my purposes here I will point to a writer associated with the circle of St Anselm of Canterbury (archbishop 1093–1109) a decade and more before Bernard of Clairvaux wrote in the 1120s in praise of the 'new *militia*' by which the Templar knights would redeem the violence and vices of the all-too-secular knights of the camp and court. This anonymous writer expounded a very elevated ideal of human nature, taking the military equipment of the knight as his metaphorical material. His *Similitudo militis* was not a tract on knighthood as such. The *militia* with which it concerned itself was the struggle of the inner man to live according to the Gospels, as it also was in its inspiration, St Paul's adoption in his epistles of Isaiah's theological imagery of military equipment (Eph. 6:10–18, 1 Thess. 5:8, Heb. 4:12).[67] Though this anonymous early twelfth-century author (sometimes called the Pseudo-Anselm) directly quoted the epistles to the Ephesians and Thessalonians on the *lorica*, *scutum*, *galea* and *gladius*, his imagery extended rather wider than the apostle's. His conceit was to extend Paul's analogy to the panoply of the twelfth-century knight: the horse, its bridle, reins and saddle, and the knight's spurs and lance. At the very least, we can conclude from the fact that the writer took the 'worldly' knight's equipment as his sermon material that he was willing to confer some sort of moral expectation or potential on a knight as distinct from the rest of the population.[68]

---

[64] N. Saul, *For Honour and Fame: Chivalry in England, 1066–1500* (London, 2011), 37–45.

[65] Jaeger, *Courtliness* (esp. 221–6), is the most influential recent example of this tradition.

[66] The idea begins with the semiotician Gérard Genette, *Palimpsestes: la littérature au second degré* (Paris, 1982), 7–16.

[67] K. A. Smith, 'Saints in Shining Armor: martial asceticism and masculine models of sanctity, *ca.*1050-1250', *Speculum*, 83 (2008), 577–9.

[68] *Similitudo militis*, in *Memorials of St Anselm*, ed. R. W. Southern and F. S. Schmitt (British Academy, 1969), 13, 97–102. Bernard of Clairvaux himself made a Pauline analogy between the *lorica* of iron that protected the knight and its counterpart of faith that protected his soul; *De laude novae militiae*, in *PL* 182, col. 922. Alan of Lille's sermon *ad milites* also includes a Pauline *similitudo*, though he adds to Paul's list the lance, representing charity, an analogy which seems unique to Alan; *PL* 210, col. 187.

At the other end of the century St Paul, 'who was the greatest of clerks', also provided the supposed inspiration for the trouvère Guiot de Provins's vernacular work *L'Armëure de Chevalier,* which also addressed the subject of the daily Christian struggle through the allegorical weaponry and equipment with which his Christian was invested against the snares of the Enemy of Mankind, though he did it at greater length than had the Pseudo-Anselm.[69] For all that Guiot frequently trumpeted that he was quoting the wisdom of 'St Paul', none of his armorial analogies matched those of the epistles (or those of the Pseudo-Anselm), and it is probable that his tract was mining an earlier *similitudo* which he had decided to invest with biblical authority.[70] Neither the Pseudo-Anselm nor Guiot can be categorized as offering works which were properly 'chivalric', even though the *miles/chevaler* is the central character, since neither author directly addressed the moral expectations on the knight as a knight. All that could be made of them in chivalric terms is that the knight was—as with Alan of Lille's *Anticlaudianus* and in his sermon *ad milites*—thought to be a fitting archetype for an idealized Christian in his struggle with the demands of faith.

It was, however, this minor devotional genre which produced a work which was chivalric in its assumptions, the one I would categorize as the first of its sort. This was a *similitudo* tract of the historian and theologian Ralph Niger (died *c.*1199), sometime chaplain of the knightly icon Young King Henry of England (died 1183). Ralph's views on knights and knightliness are significant for the courtly *habitus* of his day, not least from the fact that till 1183 he was a cleric attached to the household of the Young King Henry, the tourneying paragon of the 1170s. After the king's death, Ralph seems to have found patronage, as did other of the Young King's followers, with his youngest brother, Count John of Mortain. Whatever his origins, which remain stubbornly obscure, Ralph Niger undeniably spent many years in contact with the courts of the younger royal Angevins, in whose very noble households knightly pursuits, festivals and amusements attained a height they previously never had, nor ever were to again according to writers of the next generation. That in itself may account for what we find in Ralph's use of the genre of the *similitudo militis*.

Ralph's essay on 'the military art', written several years after the death of his former lord, also relates *militia* to the daily struggle of man towards his Creator and, as many before him, he took secular arms as a metaphor for spiritual struggle, 'as without it no knightly service is pleasing to God'.[71] At the beginning of the tract's first book Ralph also quoted rather ambiguously from the Code of Justinian

---

[69] *Armëure,* 94–113. The date of the work might be at any time in the last quarter of the twelfth century till as late as 1206, a period which also produced Raoul de Houdenc's *Borjois Borjon,* which includes a briefer *similitudo* passage; *Anecdota Literaria,* ed. T. Wright (London, 1844), 57–9 (for a translation, see above, p. 144).

[70] For instance: 'St Paul, who was so great a clerk, explained the meaning of the lance, so that St Paul by his incomparable words is our authority for all this'; *Armëure,* 108 (ll. 464–7). St Paul did not, of course, mention any lance, though a *similitudo* passage in an anonymous early twelfth-century sermon uses it (for instance) as an analogy for the New Law of Christ; *PL,* 171, col. 867. The modifying of Paul's list by authors to suit their point has a history going back to the Fathers; M. Evans, 'An Illustrated Fragment of Peraldus's *Summa* of Vice: Harleian MS 3244', *Journal of the Warburg and Courtauld Institute,* 45 (1982), 17–19.

[71] *De re militari,* 93.

that arms suppress violence and assist the maintenance of peace. In doing so he was in this case going beyond allegory and being complicit in the moral justification of military aristocracy long deployed in the Davidic ethic.[72] It is very revealing of the status of knighthood in the Young King's household—where it was believed by contemporaries that knightliness reached unprecedented levels of distinction and celebrity—that such intellectual resources and such talent might be available to be conscripted to debate its principal calling if and where it fell short of the ideal.[73] *De re militari* is equally revealing that what particularly irked Ralph about the knights of his day (apart from their sexual and dietary excesses) was the way clergy and commoners alike looked up to them and imitated their vain and wasteful fashions. If society was looking to knights for moral leadership, knightly vices were not only diminishing their own chances of salvation, but those of their inferiors.[74]

One of the delights of Ralph Niger's work is its almost obsessive endeavour to find moral messages in the full range of knightly equipment of his day. He made a point of pride in his prologue that he had made a particular study of knighthood over the years and deployed in his *De re militari* things he had learned 'on the tourney field and at various sieges'.[75] So we not only get disquisitions on the horse and the major items of arms; Ralph also discoursed to an even greater degree than Guiot de Provins on such items as chausses, ventailles, laces, visor-plate, cuisses (*genicularia*), mail and leather horse armour and tack, not to mention the linen padding beneath the hauberk and the efficacy of boiled-leather plate armour. We see here a result of Ralph's long exposure to knightly shop talk in the Angevin royal households and reflection on what he had watched from the stands of the tournament circuit. His work may possibly preserve a trace of word games once played in the hall of the Young King. Though generally true to his Pauline inspiration (and indeed the pseudo-Anselm, whom he had read)[76], Ralph did not always confine himself to theological allegory; sometimes he directly addressed the worldly knight. So he compared the soiling and ripping that might happen to the proud ensigns of the knightly company to the failure of knights to live up to the worthy deeds expected of them, and their embrace instead of empty entertainments, jokes and banter. He particularly blamed the tournament circuit (on which his late master had rejoiced for years and which he tells us he had himself frequented) as the source of the debasement of knightly life. Knights wasted their substance, energy and their chances of salvation on following the circuit in hopes of popular fame for their exploits, but all they achieved in the end was vanity, greed and foolery.[77] There might perhaps be more here, however, than simple moral scolding. The shock that Angevin courtly society experienced at the sudden death of the Young King is well attested, and Ralph's marked aversion to the tournament circuit over

---

[72] *De re militari*, 98.
[73] See, for the ethos of his court, M. Strickland, *Henry the Young King, 1155–83* (New Haven, 2016), 239–58.
[74] *De vitiis militaris conditionis*, in *De re militari*, 222 (IV, 49).   [75] *De re militari*, 92–3.
[76] Ralph copies the Pseudo-Anselm in his interpretation of *calcaria* as representing *timor* and *amor*.
[77] *De re militari*, 114 (I 36).

which his one-time, beloved young lord reigned from 1176 to 1182 is arguably rooted in that same trauma.

Ralph Niger was willing to take time between discoursing on items of horse armour and battle cries to offer asides as to the life knights should be leading. He scorned his own generation as lacking martial toughness and self-discipline:

> Not much can be said nowadays about the exploits of knights, due to the excess of their equipment; rather we can talk of their stumblings, because when one is thrown from his horse he cannot get back up off the ground without help. Furthermore their limbs are heavily padded, so their skin is not chafed by their armour. For this reason the knightly way of life is fallen into decadence, and needs more pampering than the delicacy of women demands.[78]

The multiplication and elaboration of equipment and the new demands in the luxury of dress were such that a knight's baggage needed rather more than a single packhorse to carry it, according to Ralph. We can see in this a recognition that the material goods expected of a knight were by the 1180s nearly as elaborate as those of his lord. Curiously, the biography of William Marshal preserves a similar comment made by Ralph's one-time colleague in the Young King's household. The old Marshal in his later days commented on the 1150s as a time when a youth would ride out with no more than a servant and groom: 'For in those days the world was not so proud as nowadays, and a prince, dispensing with all pomp and ceremony, would ride with just a cloak in his pack; now there is scarcely a squire who does not require a packhorse.'[79]

Well before 1200 the *similitudo* genre was thus turning to the moral and spiritual conduct expected of knights as much as to that of generalized Christians. By the 1180s the *similitudo* was mutating into a chivalric genre, as also was its sister genre, the *enseignement*. Chivalric literature approached its moment of maturity when motifs of both these genres were combined in the second decade of the thirteenth century by an anonymous Picard cleric into the work entitled the *Ordene de Chevalerie*.[80] From Menestrier in the seventeenth century to Maurice Keen in the twentieth, this hybrid work has been taken as an identifiable point which marked the chivalric turn in medieval society, and I see no reason to differ from this conclusion. The elegant literary conceit behind the *Ordene* is that King Saladin satisfied his curiosity about Western knighthood by intimidating his noble captive, Hugh de Tabarie, into putting him through the rite of knighting and explaining its symbolism as he led him through it and invested him with each of the necessary attributes. A case can be made that this hybrid work also borrowed from a third source of inspiration: the ordinal by which the Church invested its major orders, which also made symbolic use of objects. In the *Ordene* it is, of course, the knight,

---

[78] *De re militari*, 222–3 (IV, 50).   [79] *History of William Marhal*, 1: ll. 763–8.

[80] Keith Busby (*Ordene*, 92) makes a case for the date based on its crusading fixation and its placing of the Albigensians among the enemies of Christianity, a view which became current in the first decade of the thirteenth century. Clerical authorship is indicated in lines 433–5, where the author defines himself as one among those whom knights protect, and also at lines 478–80, where he enjoins all to respect the knights above others, apart from priests.

not the nobleman, who was being regarded as one who should be the summit of lay virtue, and of whom there were those hypermoral expectations which for Maurice Keen was summed up by the term 'chivalry'.

The *Ordene* is thus a teaching tract for superior moral conduct, an allegory for the Christian life, and an explanation for a ritual induction into the *sainte ordre de chevalerie* (line 83); it inaugurated a new form of literature. Its allegories of the virtues embraced only the spurs and sword amongst the knightly arms which usually feature in the *similitudo*. Neither are explained as earlier *similitudines* did. The spurs of the *Ordene* represented eagerness to serve God, and by its two edges the sword represented justice and loyalty, where the earlier *similitudines* usually treat it in its theological sense of the Word of God. However, it is in the passage about the sword that the *Ordene* unites itself with the sentiments of the twelfth-century origin myth of Nobility, by discoursing on the knightly sword as the symbol for its wielder, '... that he must protect the poor man so that the rich man cannot oppress him, and he must uphold the weak man so more powerful men cannot demean him. Such is a work of charity' (lines 215–19). This expressly burdens the knight with the expectation previously laid on the king, prince and noble that he should shoulder the moral expectation framed by the Davidic ethic. The contemporary Burgundian *enseignement* placed in the mouth of the Lady of the Lake says exactly the same (see p. 249). If knighthood claimed Nobility, it must exhibit the Nobility of mind that justified the deference that went along with it, and which was increasingly being equated in the generations on either side of 1200, as indeed the *fableor* Guérin did, with the word *chevalerie*.[81]

There was a burst of fully chivalric tracts, which cluster in the first two decades of the thirteenth century. The poet-knight Raoul de Houdenc contributed his *Roman des Eles*, an elevated allegory of the virtues which defined Nobility on the representative figure of the knight: for the name the knight bears, he says, is the 'proper name of *Gentillece*'. So formidable are Raoul's claims for the moral stature of the knight, that he says he finds himself unable to entertain the notion of a *chevalier vilain*, a base knight. But he may have had his tongue in his cheek when he wrote that, for he does admit that some knights are better men than others.[82] Just as much to the point is the *enseignement* of the Lady of the Lake on knighthood directed at her ward Galaaz, which is embedded in the non-cyclic Prose Lancelot, which derives from Burgundy. It was one of the first works explicitly to include knights within the origin myth of Nobility, allowing in this way an assumption that the knight could claim the same genetic Nobility as his lord. But that was not enough for its author. The young Galaaz had already concluded for himself that knights must also have Nobility of mind, which the Lady Vivien confirms for him, and she details the virtues demanded of the knight in much the same way as does the *Ordene*, by providing a *similitudo militis* of her own, focusing her teaching on shield, hauberk, helm, lance, sword and horse, which all symbolize in some way

---

[81] This is the explicit position on knighthood and nobility of Alfonso the Wise and his advisers around 1260; *Siete Partidas*, pt 2, tit. 21, leys 5–7.

[82] *Roman des Eles*, 32 (ll. 37–9), 34 (ll. 116–19).

the knight's duty to the Church, rather than each representing a virtue. The exception is the sword, which features here in its two sharp edges as to be used both against unbelievers and those who undermine human society (*l'umane compaigne*), who murder and assault their fellows. The sword point, on the other hand, represented the obedience which the knight could demand of others in society. The homily on the sword in fact treats the knight as one who is entitled to the deference of the lesser folk in society, as being indeed thus a nobleman. The point is further illustrated in Vivien's lecture on the horse:

> The knight must be placed above the people, for just as the rider spurs and directs the horse as he wishes, so must the knight direct the people according to his will through their lawful subjection to him, because he is their superior and so he should be.[83]

Naturally and not unexpectedly, her firm injunction that the knight is bound by the Davidic ethic follows on from this social elevation.

The formidable moral eminence demanded of the knight in Vivien's teaching is indeed such that he puts his soul at risk who takes it up:

> A man who wishes to be knight must be of the purest and simplest disposition; and if he has no wish to be knight, a man must take care to keep clear of such an exalted state, for it is better for a squire to live his life and not take up knighthood than be disgraced in this world and lost to God in the next, knighthood being so serious a matter.[84]

Here in this hypermoral stance is at last brute Chivalry: a claim to social hegemony by a small male cadre which brooks no argument, and is intended as a challenge to those who would have things otherwise. We may find some echo of this world-embracing power in the emerging theological image of the Christ-knight which is first found in the *Ancrene Riwle*, where the Church is his lady.[85] The Burgundian *enseignement* of the Lady of the Lake was paralleled not long afterwards in an even more challenging *similitudo* essay by Robert de Blois in the mid 1230s, which again uses knightly equipment to morally and socially exalt knights, '...who are to be valued more than anyone, for all men cherish the name of knight'. The pommel of the sword, for instance, is to be understood as the whole world, which is obliged to honour the knight, which is why the knight must not fail to give the world an example to respect (which his brightly painted shield symbolizes). The power and deference which are the knight's due are all related by Robert to true religion and moral eminence, for 'it is wrong to call a man who finds Villainy attractive a knight'.[86] By his combined use of the theory of the two swords, the Davidic ethic and the device of the *similitudo*, Robert in the 1230s presents the most fully articulated and radical chivalric treatise to appear before the generation of Ramon Llull.

The spread of such ideas beyond the Romance world can be fortuitously mapped with the help of *Der Welsche Gast*, a moral tract written in 1216 by Thomasin of

---

[83] *Lancelot do Lac*, 1: 144.   [84] *Lancelot do Lac*, 1: 145.

[85] Evans, 'An Illustrated Fragment of Peraldus's *Summa* of Vice', 20–1.

[86] *Enseignement des Princes*, 94–101, esp. ll. 72–84, 111–16, 155–8. For the date of the work, see p. 310.

Zirclaria, a north Italian cleric, to instruct the German public on ideas current in the Occitan south. It is a long and miscellaneous work but has in its Sixth Book extended reflections on the knight and the moral expectations on him. It includes yet another *similitudo militis* passage of a conventional sort, though the moral analogies for the equipment are more or less unique to Thomasin.[87] In most respects Thomasin repeats vernacular and Latin themes and motifs that we can find elsewhere and earlier. The idea he sketches in his Sixth Book of a battle between knights armed by the Virtues engaged in a battle with personified Vices—in this case led by Arrogance (*Übermuot*)—is one Raoul de Houdenc explored in *Li Borjois Borjon* maybe a decade before Thomasin and by Alan of Lille in the generation before Raoul.[88] It would be brought to its fullest development in Huon de Méry's *Tournament of the Antichrist* a decade and more later.

The most important observation in *Der Welsche Gast* is to be found in Thomasin's comments about 'true' *Ritterschaft* being a moral struggle against a man's inner demons. It aligned Thomasin with the chivalric turn in literature, for he was not here just equating *militia* with the Christian life but specifically defining knightly conduct as moral eminence and speaking to knights directly. He enjoined them in their actions always to recall their *Orden* and what it meant.[89] His analysis of the moral failings of knights, which get in the way of justifying the office (*Ambet*) from which they derive their high standing, broached themes familiar since the time of Bernard of Clairvaux. The weaknesses of knights, he says, lie in overindulgence in fine food, luxurious clothing and equipment, and empty social graces.[90] Some consequently found it necessary to argue that if the justification for the Nobility of knighthood was the exalted morality of those who claimed it, then it lay in civil conduct and elevated manners, framing the ideal knight around the unexceptionable, older male avatar of the *preudomme*. So by this argument military expertise and the practice of arms could not be central to it. This would be why the earlier thirteenth-century lay author of the *Doctrinal de Courtoisie* came out with this disconcerting view:

> If a man is a knight he ought not so much to be tough and aggressive, travelling in search of tournaments and wars, as to be noble, civil and distinguished, a polite guest and cheerful in the hall, generous to the poor and dutiful to God; for a *preudomme* is respected for his discriminating intelligence.[91]

The Picard author of the *Doctrinal* sketches by contrast the objectionable tournament addict who lacks any moral virtue and is tainted by every vice, who will be 'more

---

[87] *Welsche Gast*, ll. 7471–500. Thomasin's sword is given to his knight by Justice (*Reht*), which alone matches the sense given it by an earlier author, Guiot de Provins, though the symbolic sense of the sword (see pp. 282–5) makes the coincidence explicable.

[88] *Welsche Gast*, ll. 7385–418.

[89] *Welsche Gast*, ll. 7769–70: *Gedenket ritr an iuwern orden/zwiu sit ir ze riter worden?*

[90] *Welsche Gast*, ll. 7771–96. There are many parallels with these views in the later tract *De Militibus* by Thomasin's contemporary Elias of Thriplow, *Petronius Rediuiuus et Helias Tripolanensis*, ed. M. L. Colker (Leiden, 2007), 136–9.

[91] *Doctrinal*, 78–9 (ll. 149–54).

despised for his great vices than he may be praised for his knightliness, because deep villainy can cancel out any good reputation'.[92]

The chivalric ideas that Thomasin was propagating are to be found in the Empire in his lifetime, whether or not he was himself responsible for them. The Franconian *enseignement* called *Der Winsbecke* is difficult to date, but is generally believed to derive from sometime in the first half of the thirteenth century. It is advice given by a noble father on a whole range of social subjects to his noble son, who was not yet a knight. Knighthood is one of the subjects he touched on. When he did, he discoursed on the subject through the representative analogy of the shield, though not by any other item of arms. The author of *Der Winsbecke* talked of knighthood as an elevated moral calling which had to be lived up to by anyone who took it up. The knight must demonstrate loyalty, Courtliness, generosity and boldness, but above all outstanding virtue (*tugend*). He assumed that knights—or at least the particular young man he was addressing—would be men of birth and wealth. But he did not go so far as to say that knights were intrinsically men of high moral authority, and indeed the failure of a man to live up to his calling as a knight was to him a possibility, and such a man had better have left the shield hanging on the wall.[93]

CHIVALRY AND SOCIAL HEGEMONY

A lull followed this first early thirteenth-century propagation of chivalric texts and ideas. It is not till the 1260s that we find a return to these first thoughts on noble knighthood and its ethical justification. Such a generational gap may not, of course, have any particular significance, but it is arguable that it was more than coincidence. The 1260s and 1270s did, in my opinion, experience a second burst of reflection on what we can now call Chivalry, this time from vernacular authors well outside the francophone core area: principally Ramon Llull in Majorca, Brunetto Latini in Florence and Philip de Novare in Cyprus. It is worth pointing out in this regard that all three directly refer back to the first chivalric generation, citing and copying ideas from earlier French tracts. We can regard this new wave of writers as being representative of a generation of translators and transmitters of the new chivalric social dogma, though Novare (in origin a Lombard) at least lived within a francophone culture, even if in Outremer. So we can see the new wave as symptomatic of social ideas slowly embedding themselves within the European consciousness. Novare's *Quatre Tenz* is an extended example of the *enseignement* genre, which included ideas he tells us he had picked up from the Prose Lancelot. His long disquisition on the qualities of the mature knight and man of affairs draws on the earlier paired lists of vices and virtues we find in the *similitudines*: good sense against foolishness, hardiness against cowardice, generosity against

---

[92] *Doctrinal*, 80 (ll. 164–6).

[93] *Winsbecke*, 76–8 (cc. 17–20). The selection of a shield as representative of virtue and struggle, in this case the Passion of Christ, is also encountered in the *Ancrene Riwle*; see *The English Text of the Ancrene Riwle*, ed. M. Day (London, 1952), 132.

avarice, trustworthiness against treachery and so on. It makes particular cases to the great of his world for civility, humility, largesse, hardihood and peaceability, but as with earlier moralists he praised *Mesure* above all other virtues.[94]

The *Tesoretto* of Latini, composed around 1270, is a pocket version of his French *Le Livre du Trésor*, a book which Maurice Keen called Latini's 'gentleman's encyclopedia'. The *Tesoretto* is, however, a didactic text in Italian, designed for the education of his own Tuscan society.[95] It presented his compatriots with a succinct and current compendium of theology and the liberal arts, drawing heavily on French vernacular sources, particularly the *Roman de la Rose*, for many of its ideas. When he turned to moral instruction, which made up the largest part of the *Tesoretto*, Latini adopted and improved the by-now established imaginative device of describing a knight as a representative human being seeking the means to superior conduct, in this case by having him travel from castle to castle to be schooled by the four principal social virtues, which Latini defined as Largesse, Courtliness, Loyalty and Prowess. In this can be seen an extension of the literary conceit first adopted in the vernacular by William de Lorris over half a century before.[96] Latini regarded Largesse as the principal virtue that the knight should seek, providing it was not perverted though gambling and gluttony. Courtliness indeed confessed to the knight that all her teaching (*maestria*) was founded on Largesse.[97]

It was Ramon Llull whose contribution was to prove to be the most weighty of his generation, and indeed it brings this book to its conclusion. His *Llibre qui és de l'Orde de Cavalleria* (in the original Catalan) belongs to the mid 1270s. It was framed by the now-venerable device in Occitania of presenting an *ensenhamen*, with a squire on his way to his *adoubement* at a royal court encountering deep in a forest his teacher—an aged hermit who had turned from knighthood to a life of prayer. However, what followed was not an exercise in pedagogy as, rather than explaining things to the youth in person, the hermit gave him a book on the subject to read it up at his leisure and to share with those he encountered. The teaching offered was a skilful reworking of many of the themes and social ideas we have already encountered in looking at the first phase of chivalric literature. The *Llibre*'s fourth book is a return to the moral exploration of knighthood through the *adoubement* ceremony we find in the *Ordene de Chevalerie*. The fifth book is a *similitudo militis* exercise fully as comprehensive as Ralph Niger's nearly a century earlier, though its moral analogies are entirely idiosyncratic to Llull.[98] Right from

---

[94] *Quatre Tenz*, 23 (c. 37), 71–7 (cc. 126–38).

[95] For Latini as intermediary for French ideas during his period of French exile in the 1260s, K. Brownlee, 'The Practice of Cultural Authority: Italian Responses to French Cultural Dominance in *Il Tesoretto, Il Fiore* and the *Commedia*', *Forum for Modern Language Studies*, 33 (1997), 258–61. For its overt intention to reform Florentine elite conduct, P. W. Sposato, 'Reforming the Chivalric Elite in Thirteenth-century Florence: the evidence of Brunetto Latini's *Il Tesoretto*', *Viator*, 46 (2015), 203–28.

[96] E. Costa, 'Il Tesoretto de Brunetto Latini e la tradizione allegorica medievale', in *Dante e la forme dell'allegoresi*, ed. M. Picone (Ravenna, 1987), 43–58.

[97] *Tesoretto*, 230–1 (ll. 1571–82).

[98] See generally M. Aurell, 'Chevaliers et chevalerie chez Raymond Llulle', in *Raymond Llulle et le Pays d'Oc* (Cahiers de Fanjeaux, 22, 1987), 141–68, esp. 146 on his treatment of *chevalerie* as an ethic, not a way of life.

the beginning the tract was designed to justify the social hegemony of male Nobility in the person of the knight: Llull in fact went out of his way on more than one occasion to explain that female Nobility was inferior to that of the male.[99] In explaining the source of Chivalry, we find the origin myth of Nobility we first encountered in the 1170s being applied here to knights, in the same way as had the Prose Lancelot's *enseignement* two generations earlier.[100] Quirkily, Llull did this by having the principle of moral election producing the horse as the noblest of beasts, and it being awarded to the noblest of men, who is thus the *cavaller*. The assumption Llull made was that the moral eminence of a knight made it inevitable that he would be a lord of lesser men—the possessor of a castle and town, and a workforce of artisans and peasants.[101]

Llull was out to reinforce as far as he could the status and social hegemony of knighthood, declaring that Noble Descent (*Paratje*) and Chivalry (*Cavaylaria*) could not exist one without the other.[102] For him the knight, by virtue of his condition, must be morally superior to his inferiors and that was the basis of his right to command. It is no surprise to find Lull deploying in full the Davidic ethic to justify this pre-eminence theologically.[103] He made explicit what the *Ordene de Chevalerie* implied: that knighthood should be seen as an order much like those of the Church, and, like deacons and priests, knights should be trained for their role and ordained into it. Their offices (*offici*) were for him entirely comparable.[104] He suggested, indeed, that the training of a knight should be entrusted to a seminary for squires and that an aspirant should be examined in his understanding of (and suitability for) his order before being judged suitable to take it up.[105] He mused that simony was an offence that could disqualify a knight as much as a cleric.[106] He later told us that this strand was so prominent in his thinking because he intended to go on and write a book about the nature of the clergy as soon as he had finished writing about knights.[107] Llull's conclusion is a startling social polemic making explicit what earlier writers had only implied or suggested. Knighthood existed to support the common good of human society (*communitat de gens*), and so the knight deserved the best the world could offer in repayment, providing he himself respected the moral eminence his office and order necessitated.[108] The partnership of kings and princes with their knights in the governance of their realm was inextricable, and as they respected their own knighthood, princes must ensure that of knights was also honoured.[109] To Llull, knighthood and social privilege (*Franquesa*)

---

[99] *Llibre de l'Orde*, 168 (c. 7), 191 (c. 7).

[100] Llull enhances the myth (*Llibre de l'Orde*, 167, cc. 2–3) in an Isidorian philological exercise by having the initial election by groups of 1000 (Lat. *mille*) whose chosen one was the knight (Lat. *miles*); see L. Badia, J. Santanach, and A. Soler 'Ramon Llull as a Vernacular Writer', in *Style and Genre in the Writings of Ramon Llull* (Woodbridge, 2016), 98.

[101] *Llibre de l'Orde*, 182–3 (c. 22).　　[102] *Llibre de l'Orde*, 191–2 (c. 8).

[103] *Llibre de l'Orde*, 181 (c. 19).　　[104] *Llibre de l'Orde*, 201 (c. 1).

[105] *Llibre de l'Orde*, 170 (c. 14), 189–90 (cc. 1–2).　　[106] *Llibre de l'Orde*, 193–4 (c. 13).

[107] *Llibre de l'Orde*, 221 (c. 9).　　[108] *Llibre de l'Orde*, 216–17 (c. 21).

[109] *Llibre de l'Orde*, 219 (c. 2).

were indeed linked, and the obligation on lesser folk in society was simply to accept their hegemony, for their own good.[110]

So at last here in a Catalan book of the 1270s we find stated in clear terms a conjunction of hypermoral excellence and social hegemony situated in the knight, which is what the eighteenth century understood Chivalry to be. The rapid spread across Europe of Llull's *Llibre* after 1300 in a French translation (which failed to attribute its authorship to him) propagated his ideas on Chivalry like a virus in an all-too receptive body, and made it the intellectual justification for noble privilege and predominance long after the end of what we call the Middle Ages. Llull's tract indicates that Europe's phase of social hysteresis was over, and a new habitus had formed, one that had a particular resilience as it accommodated and flattered so well the ancient justification of aristocracy as lying in the licensed violence of the prince and magnate, the leaders of European society. Its own moment of crisis lay far in the future when Ramon Llull lay down his pen.

---

[110] *Llibre de l'Orde*, 219–20 (c. 3).

14

The Chivalric Virus

At the end of a book which has tested out centuries of historiography on a variety of themes in social history, it is a bit of a relief to conclude that generations of historians have not wasted their time. The assumption that our Enlightenment forebears made was not mistaken: there was an idea they called Chivalry—a shared explanation of superior behaviour which emerged into the full consciousness of medieval people around the beginning of the thirteenth century. Not only that, but medieval people were calling it by that name within a generation or two, and meaning by it what we mean. The chivalric turn of the end of the twelfth century can be established as a historical phenomenon and to some extent its appearance can be mapped and explained. Perhaps most importantly, an analysis of the century of conduct literature which preceded it reveals the seedbed of social ideas from which it grew and allows us fully to comprehend not just Chivalry but what had been regarded as superior conduct in the pre-chivalric centuries.

Chivalry was by this explanation a mutation within a pre-existing social field whose parameters had been well appreciated by medieval Europeans. This field was the culture and society of the aristocratic hall, and its practitioners called it Courtliness, for its ideals were formed and taught within the precincts and under the rafters of early medieval halls. Courtliness was not just to be found in the palaces of kings, princes and great prelates, as nineteenth-century writers tended to assume, since they explored it through the romances written for princely courts. Courtliness spread much deeper into society, as it had to be acquired by all who had ambitions to flourish within public life as much as elite society, whether as lords, dependants or servants, a need whose urgency accounts for the extensive twelfth-century literature on how to make friends and influence people. The audience for that literature was a broad one. Its authors expected their works to inform the minds of any youth with expectations of a public career, even at the level of local county society or the ecclesiastical deanery or archdeaconry. Courtliness was, however, more than just a social tool for careerism; it also included normative expectations of public conduct and gender roles across society.

Courtliness did not disappear as Chivalry emerged, and the *preudomme* and *preudefemme* who were its ideal types of superior male and female remained as models of proper behaviour in society, with the qualification that, though respectable enough as human beings, they were not necessarily Noble and thus entitled to the social deference that the embrace of Chivalry demanded for its possessor. They represented only the better ideals of public life, not the summit of human virtue, who was now the knight. The *preudomme* and *preudefemme* had to be content with the lesser reward of the social respect which was awarded to those who could conduct themselves with credit as public persons—being *de bon aire,* as twelfth-century French expressed it—which was a fine enough thing to have, of course. Respect also was given to those *preudommes* and *preudefemmes* who maintained religious orthodoxy and expressed its ideals in their lives. *Preudommes* were men who were efficient, honest and effective in their daily business with their neighbours. All these qualities raised men and women in the eyes of their neighbours; they earned respect.[1] But earning respect was one thing and demanding deference was quite another.

The distinction between Courtliness as a mode of behaviour and Chivalry is that Courtliness asked only for public respect for its accomplished practitioner, male or female. Chivalry was a claim to unique prestige by a small group within courtly society, indeed a small male elite. It claimed a hegemony expressed through a claim to moral superiority over all others in society (courtly or not) and the possession of a Nobility that demanded social deference, on pain of physical as much as social punishment. Non-nobles who laid violent hands on noble knights in Louis IX's France risked having their hands severed.[2] It was possible for women, clerics, bourgeois and even servants to claim a degree of respect in their area of public life through their mastery and display of courtly ease and their social leadership, as much as knights could. But after Chivalry had formed as the ultimate ideal of conduct, only men admitted to the noble condition of knight could aspire to occupy the apex of social distinction it represented. So the courtly *preudomme* who was not a knight was diminished in his possession of cultural capital within European society and lost ascendancy, since he was not distinguished by the hypermoral behaviour a knight must display to be worthy of his order and thus Noble. We see in chivalric literature how the worthy and wealthy bourgeois (such as Artaud de Nogent) and the accomplished and dependable mercenary captain (such as Mercadier) were ruthlessly diminished in the last quarter of the twelfth century against the knight of mesnie and hall.

For a historian, it is tempting to look for a nexus point where the beginnings of the turn can be found. But to do that begs questions: do we look for its origins in the way knights were slowly conceded a public authority, or in the way the justifications for public authority, which were first framed for kings and princes (called here the Davidic ethic), were applied to members of their military households? Did it begin with the way the papacy at the end of the eleventh century (fearing the collapse of the Eastern Empire) modified its opinion of the violence of the Western warrior? Did it begin even earlier with the emergence of a fellowship of arms amongst the professional horseback warriors in the mesnies of eleventh-century lords in France and the western Empire? Arguments have been made for prioritizing each of these in a narrative of origins, and most, I think, can be proved to have had

---

[1] In social-science thinking relating to modern periods 'respect', which is awarded to individuals for their personal qualities, stands apart from social prestige, which can derive from other sources. See M. Lamont and A. Lareau, 'Cultural Capital: Allusions, Gaps and Glissandos in Recent Theoretical Developments', *Sociological Theory,* 6 (1988), 153–68, esp. 157.

[2] Jean de Joinville, *Vie de Saint Louis,* ed. J. Monfrin (Paris, 1995), 252.

a part to play. But were I to worship before the idol of origins, as historians do, I would take a more limited view.

A study of genre, which has been much of the business of this book, brings us to one particular social nexus, the dazzling court society of northern France in the 1170s and 1180s. By this I do not mean the court of the Capetian kings, but the rival courts of the younger Angevin princes and their friend and cousin of Flanders, Philip of Alsace. I am not brought to this conclusion so much by the fortuitous survival of a biography of one of its leading characters, though that helps, as by the literature those courts generated and encouraged. The first tract that can be characterized as chivalric is by one of the Young King Henry's clerks, the *De re militari* of Ralph Niger, written in the later 1180s several years after the traumatic end to the king's career. Ralph took the older devotional genre of the *similitudo militis* and modified it to explicitly award the knight the moral leadership of his society, and warn him against his fallibility under the burden of such an eminence. We find traces in the Marshal biography of other lost chivalric works exalting the knight and knightliness originating in the same court of the Young King, which survived long enough in the old Marshal's record chest to be consulted by his biographer: a vernacular tourney roll celebrating the hundreds of knights who participated in the state tournament of Lagny in 1179, and a chronological history of the triumphs of the king's tourneying *mesnie* across France and the Empire in its heyday between 1176 and 1182.[3]

My argument here is that since the only business in the court of the Young King Henry in those years was the pursuit of knightly excellence and of social eminence within the Anglo-French aristocracies, expressed through phenomenal expense and ambitious entertainment, then it was a reflexive response to the lifestyle involved—which was readily criticized as wasteful—to exalt the knighthood that the court favoured in high moral terms, and so put it beyond criticism—the criticism indeed that Ralph Niger, one of the disillusioned inhabitants of that court, actually formulated for us. The cross-connections and interplay between Young Henry's court and those of Flanders, Guines and Hainaut are readily demonstrated, and these would easily have been infected by the moral virus the king's insecurity and grandiose social ambitions created. It is argued here that the social gravity well this particular courtly society formed was so potent it had a detectable influence even on the court culture of the Emperor Frederick Barbarossa, for all its great wealth and power. It is not, then, surprising that the earliest statement expressing openly this idea of knightly moral eminence is to be found in a work dedicated around 1180 to the man who, we are told, had commissioned it—Philip of Flanders, 'the greatest *prodome* in the Empire', as Chrétien de Troyes flattered him in the introduction to his *Conte de Graal*. Count Philip is depicted there as a paragon of Courtliness: he respected the Davidic ethic, exercised moderation in his speech, was generous to a fault, pursued justice, and was opposed to all *vilenie*. He was by this description a prince who was a *preudomme* in the grand old style. But the knighthood Chrétien described in the *enseignement* he put in the mouth of Gornemant when

---

[3] *History of William Marshal*, 3: 33–7.

he knighted Perceval in the *Conte* is not the old style, for it was described as the moral pinnacle of society, sanctioned by God himself: 'the highest order God has created and instituted, which must be free of all *vilenie*.'[4]

But a virus can only get a grip on a body which is weakened, and the earlier society of Courtliness was already compromised when the idea of chivalric hegemony was unleashed. I explored in Chapter 7 the twelfth-century perception that the courtly world was dysfunctional, the court corrupted by a spirit of materialism which the *preudomme* was unable to overcome, all too easily falling prey to his envious and unscrupulous rivals. My analysis of Raoul de Houdenc's treatise, the *Roman des Eles*, is that it was in fact the poet-knight's programme for the reform of Courtliness, which looked to the ethical and unmaterialistic knight who had an unwavering allegiance to the moral quality of Largesse to assert social leadership and bring balance back to courtly society. But how to relate moral eminence and leadership in a society where power actually lay with the magnates, whose military predominance and inherited resources gave them weight, influence and powers of patronage? The only answer was for the reforming knight to be awarded the quality of Nobility on which magnates had long relied to affirm their eminence. But if so, the knight was left in a questionable social space, because his state of dependence did not allow him to stand on the same level as his master. So two things happened. An intense debate in both school and hall was joined across Europe during the last third of the twelfth century as to how Nobility might be defined, whether it could be done by blood or by virtue, with the latter explanation the one that would assist the rising knight and which earned academic (though not general) approval. A second development was to get round the problem by arguing for graduated degrees of Nobility, with that of the knight judged to be noble but less so than the count or baron, which is also paralleled in a bid to make the knightliness of the magnate superior to that of his dependent knight, for the magnate to become the banneret-knight, a figure who appears in the sources of the 1180s. This allowed a hierarchy of noble ranks to evolve step by step, with the lesser nobility of the squire being acknowledged in France and Castile by the 1250s. The sumptuary regulations of Alfonso X of Castile in 1258 strictly demarcate the relative privileges and standing of royal siblings and magnates (*ric omme*), knight (*cavallero*) and squire (*escudero*), even prohibiting them from occupying the same tables at dinner.[5] In England the formal nobilization of the squire came a generation later: but across thirteenth-century Europe we find a cascade effect as the noble habitus adjusted to new tensions.[6]

So in the last quarter of the twelfth century courtly society was experiencing a generation unbalanced by a form of hysteresis, an internal stress which had to be accommodated and was resolved by shifts in its habitus. This dramatically narrowed social hegemony on a small, male elite, by virtue of its innate Nobility founded on blood and hypermoral aspirations. This can be seen happening in several ways.

---

[4] *Conte de Graal*, ll. 7–32, 1630–6.
[5] *Cortes de los antiguos reinos de Leon y de Castilla*, ed. anon. (5 vols, Madrid, 1861–3), 1: 58–9.
[6] For the idea of a 'cascade' of social definition between 1100 and 1300, Crouch, *Nobility*, 243–52.

Most obviously, it is in the infection of conduct tracts by chivalric principles in the first decade of the thirteenth century, where the old pragmatic principles of Courtliness were no longer enough to establish social eminence: the virtuous *chevaler* not the *preudomme* was now the social leader. Most evocatively, it can be seen in the shifting position of women in society, for the chivalric virus was more deadly to the female of the species. Under this new pressure women reacted to the intensified principle of male moral and social pre-eminence, and some found a defence in inoculating themselves against male hypermoral authority with the claim to a hyper-religiosity which was open to both sexes. Others, such as Ulrich von Liechtenstein's insurgent lady, scornfully argued that in failing to live up to their chivalric ideal, knights forfeited the respect and deference they thought should be theirs and made themselves despicable. Elsewhere the way the genre of the *fabliau* joyously picked on the social hypocrisy and sexual fallibility of the knights it described is yet more evidence of awareness of the closing-in of a new social hegemony.

There remain several questions, not least as to why it was felt so pressing at the end of the twelfth century to define Nobility in terms of the male figure of the knight and to narrow social hegemony so drastically that some were even prepared to diminish the noble status of the highest-born of women. The intense debate in the sources amongst lay and clerical thinkers alike may be a cause as much as a symptom of change. The rise of talented but low-born outsiders into the courts of the great was resented well before the chivalric turn, and such men would have been the ones who argued that they possessed their own sort of Nobility, that of mind and virtue. The loud vituperation against low-born outsiders in the courtly world we find across Latin Europe in its literature in the last third of the twelfth century cannot be coincidental and justifies, in my view, the idea of a social hysteresis in its courtly habitus. It would have been triggered by the sort of social rise represented by the (relatively) low-born servants who gained such power at the courts of Henry I of England and Louis VI of France that they drew outspoken criticism. That and the other reasons we have explored would have brought about a crisis in the idea of Nobility we have observed at the end of the twelfth century and brought out vociferous defenders of the idea of Nobility of blood. There are other possible factors, notably the one already explored in Chapter 11, that the newly wealthy always had the means to affect the material lifestyle expected of the magnate and noble knight, and the resentment at this would have increased at a time when the rank of knight was defined as Noble but had become achievable simply by the grace of a prince's favour. But such men were unable to argue their Nobility of blood, which was always a put-down available to curb their social ambition.

Another possible avenue not explored here directly is the way that emerging bureaucracies, particularly the specialists in civil law they employed, might question in their masters' interest the unwritten privilege that magnates had long claimed as their right and which was universally and anciently signified by the swords of justice they posed with when they occupied the judgement seat and which figured on the seals they commissioned, the coins they issued, and tombs they occupied. There is evidence in the most bureaucratized part of twelfth-century Europe—the Angevin realms—that noblemen at the end of the century felt that their natural privileges were being encroached upon by an aggressive monarchy and that they were obliged to defend them.[7] The best-documented instance is the way that from the 1180s King John, as lord of Ireland, worked persistently to undermine and diminish the huge privileges his marcher aristocracy had assumed to themselves in the previous Conquest generation. By 1210 John had succeeded in intimidating the lords of the great Irish liberties into renouncing any more privileges than a baron might have across the Irish Sea in England, and had substituted a pale facsimile in Ireland of the common law and mechanisms of the English state. Meanwhile, in England lords were facing inexorable pressure on their prescriptive rights. They pushed back, finding a means of resistance when their privileges to do justice on their estates were questioned by royal officers.[8] Lords took an ancient phrase from the Anglo-Saxon past, the right of 'sake and soke and tol and team', and used it as their justification to exclude royal officers from exercising direct jurisdiction on their estates. By the mid thirteenth century the weak and incompetent kingship of Henry III had been intimidated into ceding the right of justice on their estates to lords as their 'liberty'.[9]

Was bureaucratization and an activist royal government sufficient to destabilize the habitus when the autonomy and ancient privileges of the old aristocracy came under challenge? It would account for the late twelfth-century attempt to reinforce and define the possession of Nobility as an exalted social condition; another form of defence of a threatened social group. That royal aggression introduced social stress into some polities of medieval Europe can be convincingly argued, and has been for quite some while, as it was a component of the old idea of a French feudal mutation which supposedly ended in a Capetian reassertion of royal power over its barons. But the chivalric turn happened across Europe and in a variety of polities, some of which possessed nothing which looked like a princely administration of any threatening capacity. So in my view royal aggression against noble privilege could at most be argued to be a catalyst rather than a cause of hysteresis, though one which certainly affected the core area of social change. And this is as far as this study in genre and society can take us, with the raising of further questions that need more detailed consideration through rather different historical sources.

---

[7] For the intrusive assize triggering this (called *quo warranto*), D. W. Sutherland, *Quo Warranto Proceedings in the Reign of Edward I, 1278–94* (Oxford, 1963), 1–6.

[8] M. T. Flanagan, 'Defining lordships in Angevin Ireland: William Marshal and the King's justiciar', in *Seigneuries dans l'espace Plantagenêt: actes du colloque de Bordeaux-Saint-Emilion (3–5 mai 2007)*, ed. F. Boutoulle (Ausonius, 2009), 41–9; C. Veach, 'King John and Royal Control in Ireland: why William de Briouze had to be destroyed', *English Historical Review*, 129 (2014), 1051–78.

[9] Crouch, *Aristocracy*, 178–89.

Analytical Index of Sources
on Conduct before 1300

ABRIL ISSI' E MAYS INTRAVA

Provenance: Girona, Spain. Date: 1200 × 1210. Authorship: Raimon Vidal of Besalú, lay poet. Occitan *ensenhamen* of 1,767 lines, much influenced by earlier vernacular writers. Talks of the three elder sons of Henry II of England and Mercadier (died 1200) as being of the past generation (lines 272–81, 576–81, 678–80). Written within the reign of Peter II of Aragon (lines 734–5) and probably before the Albigensian wars.

EDITION: Raimon Vidal, *Abril issi' e Mays intrava*, in, *Nouvelles occitanes du moyen age*, ed. J-Ch. Huchet (Paris, 1992).

L'ARMËURE DU CHEVALIER

Provenance: Champagne, France. Date: 1180 × 1206. Authorship: Guiot de Provins, lay poet, turned Cluniac (*c*.1200). Francien *similitudo* tract of 612 verses in fullest version. Could date to any period of Guiot's literary activity, both outside and within the cloister, but precedes his *Bible* (1206).

EDITION: *Les œuvres de Guiot de Provins, poète lyrique et satirique*, ed. J. Orr (Publications of the University of Manchester, French Series, 1, 1915), 94–113.

CHASTOIEMENT DES DAMES

Provenance: Eastern France. Date: 1230 × 1240. Authorship: Robert de Blois, lay poet. A general guide (*commun ensoignemant*) of 757 lines addressed solely to women. Not as closely datable as Robert's *Enseignment des Princes* (1234 × 1238), but as a paired work may be contemporary with it.

EDITION: J. H. Fox, *Robert de Blois, son oeuvre didactique et narrative* (Paris, 1950), 133–55.

LE CHASTOIEMENT D'UN PÈRE À SON FILS

Provenance: Northern France. Date: mid thirteenth century. Authorship: Anonymous translator and embellisher of *Disciplina Clericalis* (below).

EDITION: *Le Chastoiement d'un Père à son Fils: a critical edition*, ed. E. D. Montgomery (Chapel Hill, 1971).

LI CONTES DE GENTILLECHE

Provenance: Western Empire. Date: mid thirteenth century. Authorship: Baldwin de Condé, lay poet. Francien poem of 140 lines on nobility and inherited virtue. Undatable other than a likely *floreat* of the mid to later thirteenth century.

EDITION: *Dits et contes de Baudouin de Condé et de son fils Jean de Condé*, ed. A. Scheler (3 vols, Brussels, 1866–7) 1: 175–80.

LI CONTES DOU PREUDOME

Provenance: Western Empire. Date: mid thirteenth century. Authorship: Baldwin de Condé, lay poet. Francien poem of 201 lines on *preudommie* and *vilonie*. Undatable other than a likely *floreat* of the mid to later thirteenth century.

EDITION: *Dits et contes de Baudouin de Condé et de son fils Jean de Condé*, ed. A. Scheler (3 vols, Brussels, 1866–7) 1: 95–105.

DE RE MILITARI

Provenance: Lincoln, England. Date: 1187 × 1188. Authorship: Ralph Niger, canon of Lincoln. Latin moral tract and polemic of four books.

EDITION: *De re militari et triplici via peregrinationis Ierosolomitane*, ed. L. Schmugge (Beiträge zur Geschichte und Quellenkunde des Mittelalters, 6, Berlin, 1977).

DISCIPLINA CLERICALIS

Provenance: Aragon. Date: *c.*1106. Author: Peter Alfonsi (Moses Sefardi), physician and teacher. Latin moral tract in 34 chapters. Written subsequent to his conversion in 1106.

EDITION: *Disciplina clericalis*, ed. F. W. V. Schmidt (Berlin, 1827), trans. as *The* Disciplina Clericalis *of Petrus Alfonsi*, trans. E. Hermes and P. R. Quarrie (London, 1977).

DOCTRINAL DE COURTOISIE (ALIAS DOCTRINAL SAUVAGE)

Provenance: Artois, France. Date: *c.*1220 × 1240. Authorship: attrib. Sauvage d'Arras, lay poet. Francien moral *enseignement* of 317 lines addressed to the aristocracy, whose purpose is given as follows: *Courtois enseignemens fait vivre sagement/Et sage vie doune hounour er sauvement* (lines 7–8). It talks of the Franciscans as a leading spiritual force and is uncomfortable that the order was attracting too many aristocratic adherents as brothers (line 288), which matches the circumstances of the 1220s and 1230s. Five MS copies of the second half of the thirteenth century indicate an early propagation.

EDITION: *Doctrinal Sauvage: publié d'après tous les manuscrits*, ed. A. Sakari (Jyväskylä, 1967).

DOCTRINA PUERIL

Provenance: Majorca. Date: 1274 × 1276. Authorship: Ramon Llull, moral theologian and knight. Catalan *enseignement* addressed to the knowledge essential for an aristocratic youth.

EDITION: *Doctrina pueril,* ed. G. Schib (Barcelona, 1972).

LE DONEI DES AMANTS

Provenance: England. Date: 1180 × 1200. Authorship: Anonymous lay poet. Anglo-Norman *enseignement* of 1,244 verses addressed to a young magnate. For date, Gaston Paris, 'Le donnei des amants', *Romania,* 25 (1896), 497–541.

EDITION: *Le Donei des Amanz,* ed. A.J. Holden (Anglo-Norman Text Society, Plain Text Series, 17, Oxford, 2013), from Cologny-Genève, Fondation Martin Bodmer, Cod. Bodmer 82, fos 17ra–24vb.

E·L TERMINI D'ESTIU

Provenance: Auvergne, France. Date: 1130 × 1160. Authorship: Garin lo Brun, castellan of Veillac. Occitan *ensenhamen* of 649 lines addressed principally to female aristocrats. Garin died in 1162, and his literary career can be projected back to at least the 1140s.

EDITION: *L'Enseignamen alla dama,* ed. and trans. (It.) L. R. Bruno (Filologia occitanica Studi e testi, 1, Rome, 1996).

ENSEIGNEMENTS TREBOR

Provenance: Southern England. Date: 1187 × 1216. Authorship: M. Robert of Ho. Anglo-Norman moral *enseignement* of 2,636 verses largely based on Catonian commonplaces. The poem refers (lines 1741ff.) to the need to recover the Latin kingdom of Jerusalem indicating a date after 1187, and it is quoted by Chardry's *Petit Plet* (*c.*1216) so must precede it.

EDITION: *Les Enseignements de Robert de Ho: dits Enseignements Trebor,* ed. M. V. Young (Paris, 1901) from Paris, BnF, ms français 25408 (formerly library of Notre Dame de Paris), fos 1r–24v.

ENSENHAMENS D'ONOR

Provenance: Provence. Date: 1246 × 1257. Authorship: Sordello da Goito (Mantua), knight and poet. Occitan moral *enseignement* of 1,327 verses addressed to the male and female lay elites. Dated to his time in the entourage of Charles of Anjou in Provence.

EDITION: *Le Poesie. Nuova edizione critica,* ed. and trans. (It.) M. Boni (Bologna, 1954), no. 43, pp. 200–73.

ENSOIGNEMENT DES PRINCES

Provenance: Eastern France. Date: 1234 × 1238. Authorship: Robert de Blois, lay poet. Francien moral *enseignement* of 1,414 verses addressed principally to knights. The poem refers in an extended passage to Louis IX as having recently come to full power and facing challenge from his aristocracy (lines 1057–78) and not as being a crusader, so a date during the period of aristocratic discontent after the end of the regency (1234–8) is credible.

EDITION: J. H. Fox, *Robert de Blois, son oeuvre didactique et narrative* (Paris, 1950), 93–132.

HISTORY OF WILLIAM MARSHAL

Provenance: England. Date: 1224 × 1226. Authorship: John, a lay poet (probably of Tourangeau origin). Francien biography of Earl William Marshal (died 1219) in 19,214 lines, intended in part to teach the ideal life of a *preudomme*.

EDITION: *History of William Marshal*, ed. A. Holden and D. Crouch, trans. S. Gregory (3 vols, Anglo-Norman Text Society, Occasional Publications Series, 4–6, 2002–7).

HOFZUCHT

Provenance: Austria. Date: 1230 × 1266. Authorship: Der Tannhäuser, lay poet. MHG tract of 266 verses concerning conduct in the hall. Can only be dated to the broad period of Tannhäuser's known literary activity.

EDITION: *Der Dichter Tannhäuser*, ed. J. Siebert (Halle, 1834), 195–203.

DIE KLAGE

Provenance: Swabia. Date: *c.*1180. Authorship. Hartmann von Aue, lay poet. MHG debate poem of 1914 lines between mind and body, principally on self-control in love and virtue.

EDITION: *Die Klage*, ed. K. Gärtner (Berlin, 2015).

LIBER URBANI (ALIAS URBANUS MAGNUS)

Provenance: Suffolk, England. Date: 1177 × 1183. Authorship: Daniel, secular clerk of Beccles (died *c.*1205). Latin advanced grammatical exercise collection of 2,840 lines. Introduction alludes to an intended audience of youths of the *magna schola* (lines 1–11). The work refers to a time when there were two kings in England, so probably before the death of the Young King (1183). It also seems to allude to the repeated failures of Henry II to fulfil his crusading oaths, the latest instance being 1177 (lines 830–2, 2836–7). For authorship, Whelan, *The Making of Manners*, 16–18.

EDITION: *Urbanus Magnus Danielis Becclesiensis*, ed. J. G. Smyly (Dublin, 1939), from Trinity College Dublin, MS 97, fos 253–75.

LIVRE DES MANIÈRES

Provenance: Southern England. Date: *c.*1159 × 1163. Authorship: M. Stephen de Fougères, chaplain of King Henry II of England. Francien moral treatise of 1344 lines drawn from or compiled for a collection of *ad status* sermons. The author describes himself in a colophon as *Mestre*, thus predating his election as bishop of Rennes (1168). The dedication to the widowed Countess Cecilia of Hereford (lines 1205–24) indicates a composition during the long period of the residence of the Angevin court in England (1155–63) apparent quotation of *Policraticus* would indicate a date after 1159 (lines 637–52).

EDITION: *Le Livre des Manières*, ed. and trans. (Fr.) J. T. E. Thomas (Leuven, 2013), from Angers, Bibliothèque municipale, MS 295, pp. 141–50.

LLIBRE DE L'ORDE DE CAVALLERIA

Provenance: Majorca. Date 1274 × 1276. Authorship: Ramon Llull, moral theologian and knight. Catalan tract on the origins and meaning of knighthood.

EDITION: *Llibre de l'Orde de Cavalleria*, ed. A. Soler i Llopart (Barcelona, 1988); trans. as *The Book of the Order of Chivalry*, trans. N. Fallows (Woodbridge, 2013).

ORDENE DE CHEVALERIE

Provenance: Picardy, France. Date: 1200 × 1210. Authorship: Anonymous cleric. Francien *enseignement* of 502 lines addressed to young knights. The arguments for the date depend on its author's fixations with the crisis in crusading and the danger of the Albigensian movement.

EDITION: *The Anonymous Ordene de Chevalerie*, ed. and trans. K. Busby (Utrecht Publications in General and Comparative Literature, Amsterdam, 17, 1983).

LE PETIT PLET

Provenance: West of England. Date: end of twelfth century. Authorship. Chardri. Anglo-Norman *enseignement* of 1,780 lines, in which a *prudum* (or *veillard*) discourses with a *vaslet* (or *enfant*) on a variety of moral issues the boy raises, notably focused on mortality and the life cycle. Shows inspiration of Seneca's *De remediis fortuitorum*.

EDITION: *Le Petit Plet*, ed. B. S. Merrilees (Anglo-Norman Text Society, 1970).

PHAGIFACETUS

Provenance: Thuringia. Date: mid thirteenth century. Authorship: M. Reiner the German, secular cleric. Latin tract on civil dining. Undatable other than the known *floreat* of M. Reiner at the court of Thuringia.

EDITION: *M. Reineri Alemanici Phagifacetus*, ed. F. Jacob (Lübeck, 1838).

LI PROVERBE AU VILAIN

Provenance: Flanders. Date: 1176. Authorship: Anonymous court poet. A glossed Francien collection of 280–300 common proverbs (depending on the reconstruction of the MS) intended for a courtly entertainment, most probably a guessing game, with several amusing asides directed at Count Philip of Flanders. No. 91 ('Far-fetched tales from faraway places') talks of the death of Nur-ad-Din and the succession of Saladin to Syria (Babylon), which had been achieved by 1175. Since Count Philip was preparing for a pilgrimage to Outremer in 1176, this consciousness of events in the Holy Land also indicates that year.

EDITION: *Li Proverbe au Vilain: die Sprichtwörter des gemeinen Mannes: altfranzösisiche Dichtung*, ed. A. Tobler (Leipzig, 1895).

LES QUATRE TENZ (ALIAS LES QUATRE ÂGES DE L'HOMME)

Provenance: Cyprus. Date: *c*.1265. Authorship: Philip de Novare, poet, bailli and knight. Francien moral *enseignement* of 236 chapters entitled by the author *Des.iiii. Tenz d'Aage d'Ome*, addressed to male and female of the conditions of childhood, youth, maturity and old age.

EDITION: *Les quatre âges de l'homme, traité moral de Philippe de Navarre publié pour la première fois d'après les manuscrits de Paris, de Londres et de Metz,* ed. M. de Fréville (Paris: Société des anciens textes français, 1888).

QUI COMTE VOL APENDRE

Provenance: Gascony, France. Date: 1170 × 1180. Authorship: Arnaut-Guilhem de Marsan, lord of Rocquefort and Cauna. Occitan *ensenhamen* of 628 lines with Arnaut-Guilhem posing as mentor to an unnamed young knight. The author was dead by 1185 at the latest; see, for the date, R. Lejeune, 'La date de l'Ensenhamen d'Arnaut-Guilhem de Marsan', *Studi Medievali* (new ser. 12, 1939), 160–71.

EDITION: *Testi Didattico-Cortesi de Provenza*, ed. G. E. Sansone (Bari, 1977), 119–80; trans. (Fr.) G. Gouiran. in *L'Ensenhamen ou code du parfait chevalier* (Mounenh en Biarn, 2007), 64–95.

DE QUINQUAGINTA CURIALITATIBUS AD MENSAM

Provenance: Milan, Italy. Date: later thirteenth century. Authorship: Buonvicino (Bonvesin) della Riva, teacher of grammar. Italian tract offering fifty precepts for civil dining.

EDITION: *Poeti del Duecento*, ed. G. Contini (2 vols, Milan, 1960) 1: 703–12.

QUISQUIS ES IN MENSA

Provenance: Northern Italy. Date: 1160 × 1200. Authorship: Anonymous. Latin *aide-mémoire* of twenty-three verses on dining etiquette. Quotes *Facetus* and *Disciplina Clericalis*, and appears to have influenced *Der Welsche Gast*, which locates it as product of the later twelfth-century schools, as Charles Homer Haskins believed.

EDITION: S. Glixelli, 'Les Contenances de Table', *Romania*, 47 (1921), 28–9.

RASOS ES E MESURA

Provenance: Périgord, France. Date: 1164 × 1180. Authorship: Arnaut de Mareuil, lay poet. Occitan moral *ensenhamen* of 345 lines. Its internal mention (line 45) of Alfonso II of Aragon (reigned 1164–96)—*li rey cuy es Lerida*—gives a broad indication of the date of composition and since Arnaut says that the king is still young at the time he is writing the 1160s or 1170s seem the most likely decades.

EDITION: M. Eusebi, 'L'ensenhamen di Arnaut de Mareuil', *Romania*, 90 (1969), 14–30 (with Italian trans.).

ROMAN DES ELES

Provenance: Picardy, France. Date: 1200 × 1215. Authorship: Raoul de Houdenc, poet and knight. Francien reformist tract of 660 lines on *cortoisie*. Argued by Busby and others to be one of Raoul's earlier works, certainly earlier than his *Songe d'Enfer* (*c.*1215).

EDITION: *Le Roman des Eles*, ed. and trans. K. Busby (Utrecht Publications in General and Comparative Literature, Amsterdam, 17, 1983).

LE ROMAN DES FRANCEIS

Provenance: Western Normandy. Date: 1180 × 1194. Authorship: Andrew de Coutances, secular cleric. Anglo-Norman satire of 396 lines on the social vices of the English and Capetian French, particularly at the table. The date is suggested on the basis of the author's Arthurian and Waldensian references.

EDITION: D. Crouch. 'The *Roman des Franceis* of Andrew de Coutances : Text, Translation and Significance', in *Normandy and its Neighbours, 900-1250: Essays for David Bates*, ed. D. Crouch and K. Thompson (Turnhout, 2011), 175–98.

RUODLIEB

Provenance: Bavaria. Date: later eleventh century. Authorship: Anonymous. Incomplete Latin moral fable on the subject of service and lordship. Includes an *enseignement* passage.

EDITION: *The Ruodlieb*, ed. and trans. C. W. Grocock (Warminster, 1985).

IL TESORETTO

Provenance: Florence. Date: *c.*1270. Authorship: Brunetto Latini, diplomat, statesman and lay poet. Italian moral compendium of 2,944 lines condensed from his earlier Francien, *Livres dou Tresor* (written in exile in France).

EDITION: *Poeti del Duocento*, 2: 175–277. Trans (Fr.) as *Le Petit Trésor*, ed. and trans. (Fr). B. Levergois (Aubenas, 1997).

URBAIN LE CORTOIS

Provenance: England. Date: mid thirteenth century. Authorship: Anonymous. Anglo-Norman *enseignement* addressed to male youth, in two versions around 250 verses in fullest text. Can only be broadly dated.

EDITION: H. Rosamond Parsons, 'Anglo-Norman books of courtesy and nurture', *PMLA*, 44 (1929), 383–455.

DER WELSCHE GAST

Provenance: Aquileia, Italy. Date: 1216. Authorship: Thomasin of Zirclaria, secular canon of Aquileia. MHG extended moral treatise in ten books, totalling 14,742 lines, addressed to various conditions, notably knights (Book 6) and women (Book 1). Large parts of Book 1 may be an MHG translation of a lost, earlier Occitan or Italian *enseignement* Thomasin says he had addressed to women. He declares he was writing twenty-eight years after the fall of Jerusalem to the Muslims (lines 11,717–22).

EDITION: *Der Wälsche Gast*, ed. H. Rückert (Quedlingen, 1852), trans. as *Der Welsche Gast*, trans. M. Gibbs and W. McConnell (Kalamazoo, 2009).

WINSBECKE

Provenance: Franconia. Date: First half of thirteenth century. Authorship. Anonymous. MHG *enseignement* addressed to male youth. Probably responds to the late twelfth-century and early thirteenth-century French models, hence the broad dating. Shows influence of MHG romances of *c.*1200.

EDITION: *Der Winsbecke*, ed. and trans. A. M. Rasmussen and O. Trokhimenko, in *Medieval Conduct Literature: An Anthology of Vernacular Guides to Behaviour for Youths*, ed. M .D. Johnston (Toronto, 2009).

WINSBECKIN

Provenance: Empire. Date: First half of thirteenth century. Authorship: Anonymous. MHG *enseignement* addressed to female youth. Clearly inspired by Winsbecke, but by a different author.

EDITION: *Die Winsbeckin*, ed. and trans. A. M. Rasmussen and O. Trokhimenko, in *Medieval Conduct Literature: An Anthology of Vernacular Guides to Behaviour for Youths*, ed. M. D. Johnston (Toronto, 2009).

Bibliography

MANUSCRIPT SOURCES

Angers, Archives départementales de Maine-et-Loire, H 3710.
Bern, Burgerbibliothek, MS 354.
Cambridge, Gonville & Caius College, MS 385.
Douai, Bibliothèque municipale, MS 751.
Dublin, Trinity College MS 97.
Kew, National Archives, C115/77; KB27/145.
Leeds University, Brotherton Library, Yorkshire Archaeological Society Collection, DD5/3/1.
London, British Library, Additional MS 8167.
Oxford, Bodleian Library, MS Rawlinson C 552.
Paris, Bibliothèque nationale de France, MS latin 6765.
University of Pennsylvania Library, Special Collections MS 659.
Rouen, Archives départementales de la Seine-Maritime, 13 H 15, 17 HP 1.
Rouen, Bibliothèque municipale, Y 13.

PRINTED PRIMARY SOURCES

Actes des comtes de Flandre (1071–1128), ed. F. Vercauteren (Publications de la commission royale d'histoire, Brussels, 1938).
Acts and Letters of the Marshal Family, Marshals of England and Earls of Pembroke, 1145–1248, ed. D. Crouch (Camden Society, 5th ser., 47, 2015).
Adalbero of Laon, *Poème au roi Robert*, ed. and trans. (Fr.) C. Carozzi (Classiques de l'histoire de France au moyen age, 32, 1979).
Ailred of Rievaulx, *Genealogia Regum Anglorum*, in *PL* 195.
Alan of Lille, *Anticlaudianus*, in *Satirical Poets of the Twelfth Century*, ed. T. Wright (2 vols, Rolls Series, 1872), 2.
Alexander Neckam, *De naturis rerum libri duo*, ed. T. Wright (Rolls Series, 1863).
Alexander of Paris, *Le Roman d'Alexandre*, ed. E. C. Armstrong and trans (Fr.) L. Harf-Lancner (Paris, 1994).
Amanieu de Sescás, *Essenhamen de la Donzela*, ed. and trans. M. D. Johnston, in 'The Occitan *Enssenhamen de l'Escudier* and *Essenhamen de la Donzela*', in *Medieval Conduct Literature: an Anthology of Vernacular Guides to Behaviour for Youths*, ed. M. D. Johnston (Toronto, 2009).
Ami et Amile, ed. P. F. Dembowski (Paris, 1987).
Andreas Capellanus on Love, ed. and trans. P. G. Walsh (London, 1982).
Andreas Florentinus, *Summa contra hereticos*, ed. G. Rottenwöhrer (MGH, Quellen zur Geistesgeschichte des Mittelalters, 23, Hanover, 2008).
Anecdotes et apologues tirés du recueil inédit d'Etienne de Bourbon, ed. A. Lecoy de la Marche (Paris, 1877).
Annales Monastici, ed. H. R. Luard (5 vols, Rolls Series, 1864–9).
Annals of Connacht, ed. and trans. A. M. Freeman (Dublin, 1944).
Arnaut de Mareuil, *Rasos es e Mesura*, in M. Eusebi, 'L'ensenhamen di Arnaut de Mareuil', *Romania*, 90 (1969), 14–30 (with Italian trans.).

Arnaut Guilhem de Marsan, *Qui comte vol apendre*, in *Testi Didattico-Cortesi de Provenza*, ed. G. E. Sansone (Bari, 1977), 119–80; trans. (Fr.) G. Gouiran, in *L'Ensenhamen ou code du parfait chevalier* (Mounenh en Biarn, 2007), 64–95.

Arnold de Bonneval, *Sancti Bernardi Vita Prima*, in *PL*, 185.

A Selection of Latin Stories, ed. T. Wright (Percy Society, 8, 1842).

Bartholomaeus Anglicus, *De propietatibus rerum* (Nuremberg, 1492).

Baudrey de Bourgueil, *Carmina Historica*, in *PL* 166.

Benoît de Sainte-Maure, *Chronique des ducs de Normandie*, ed. F. Michel (3 vols, Paris, 1836–44).

Bernard of Clairvaux, *De laude novae militiae*, in *PL* 182.

Biaudouz, ed. J-Ch. Lemaire (Liège, 2008).

Bonizo of Sutri, *Liber de vita christiana*, ed. E. Perels (Texte zur Geschichte des römischen und kanonischen Rechts im Mittelalter, 1, Berlin, 1930).

Brunetto Latini, *Il Tesoretto*, in *Poeti del Duocento*, 2: 175–277. Translated as *Il Tesoretto (The Little Treasure)*, ed. and trans. J. Bolton Holloway (New York, 1981); *Le Petit Trésor*, ed. and trans. (Fr). B. Levergois (Aubenas, 1997).

Bruno of Querfurt, *Epistola ad Henricum regem*, ed. J. Karwasinska, in *Monumenta Poloniae Historica* (new ser., 4: 3, Warsaw 1973), 97–106.

Brut y Tywysogyon: the Red Book of Hergest Version, ed. T. Jones (Cardiff, 1955).

Caesarius of Heisterbach, *Dialogus Miraculorum*, ed. and trans. (Ger.) H. Schneider and N. Nösges (5 vols, Turnhout, 2009).

Calendar of Patent Rolls preserved in the Public Record Office (6 vols, HMSO, 1901–13).

Cato a Facetus, ed. L. Zatočil, (Spisy Masarykovy University v Brně, Filosofická Fakulta/ Opera Universitatis Masarykianae Brunensis, Facultas Philosophica, 48, 1952).

Chanson d'Aspremont, ed. L. Brandin (2 vols, Paris, 1923–4).

Chanson de Walther: Waltharii Poesis, ed. and trans. (Fr.). S. Albert, S. Menegaldo, and F. Mora (Grenoble, 2008).

Chastoiement d'un père à son fils, ed. E. D. Montgomery Jr (Chapel Hill, 2017).

Chevalerie et Grivoiserie: Fabliaux de Chevalerie, ed. and trans. J-L. Leclanche (Paris, 2003).

Chrétien de Troyes, *Cligés*, ed. A. Micha (Paris, 1957).

Chrétien de Troyes, *Eric et Enide*, ed. W. Förster (Halle, 1890).

Chrétien de Troyes, *Le Conte de Graal*, ed. F. Lecoy (Paris, 1984).

Chronica magistri Rogeri de Houedene, ed. W. Stubbs (4 vols, Rolls Series, 1868–71).

Chronique de Gislebert de Mons, ed. L. Vanderkindere (Recueil de textes pour servir à l'étude de l'histoire de Belgique, 1904).

Chroniques des comtes d'Anjou, ed. L. Halphen and R. Poupardin (Paris, 1913).

Colker, M. L. 'Latin Texts concerning Gilbert, founder of Merton Priory', *Studia Monastica*, 12 (1970).

Comptes des dépenses de la chevalerie de Robert comte d'Artois à Compiègne en juin 1237, ed. M. Peigné-Delacourt (Amiens, 1857).

Cortes de los antiguos reinos de Leon y de Castilla, ed. anon. (5 vols, Madrid, 1861–3).

Couronnement de Louis: chanson de geste du xii˚ siècle, ed. E. Langlois (Paris, 1984).

Courtois d'Arras: l'Enfant Prodigue, ed. and trans. (Fr.) J. Dufournet (Paris, 1995).

Coutumes de Beauvaisis, ed. A. Salmon (2 vols, Paris, 1899–1900), trans. as, *The Coutumes de Beauvaisis of Philippe de Beaumanoir*, trans. F. R. P. Akehurst (Philadelphia, 1992).

Crouch, D. 'The *Roman des Franceis* of Andrew de Coutances: Significance, Text and Translation', in *Normandy and its Neighbours, c. 900–1250: Essays for David Bates*, ed. D. Crouch and K. Thompson (Turnhout, 2011).

Cuckolds, Clerics and Countrymen: Medieval French Fabliaux, ed. R. Eichmann and trans. J. Duval (Fayetteville, AR, 1982).

De Laborderie, O. Maddicott, J. R., and Carpenter, D. A. 'The Last Hours of Simon de Montfort: A New Account', *EHR*, 115 (2000), 378412.

De Oorkonden der Graven van Vlaanderen, ed. T. de Hemptinne, A. Verhulst, and L. De Mey, (3 vols, Koninklijke Academie van Belgie and Koninklijke Commissie voor Geschiedenis, Verzameling van der Akten der Belgische Vorsten, Brussels, 2009).

Der altprovenzalische 'Boeci', ed. C. Schwarze (Forschungen zur romanischen Philologie, 12, Münster, 1963).

Der Dichter Tannhäuser, ed. J. Siebert (Halle, 1834), 195–203.

Dhuoda, *Handbook for her Warrior Son: Liber Manualis*, ed. and trans. M. Thiebaux (Cambridge Medieval Classics, 8, 1998).

Dicta Quatuor Ancillarum, in *The Life and Afterlife of St Elizabeth of Hungary: Testimony from her Canonization Hearings*, ed. K. B. Wolf (Oxford, 2010).

Die exempla aus den Sermones feriales et communes des Jakob von Vitry, ed. J. Greven (Heidelberg, 1914).

Die Klage, ed. C. Kiening (Altdeutsche Textbibliothek, no. 123, Berlin, 2015).

'Die Lebensbeschreibung des Grafen Ludwig III von Arnstein', ed. S. Widmann, in *Annalen des Vereins für Nassauische Alterumskunde und Geschichtsforschung*, 18 (1883/4), 244–66.

Die Viten Gottfrieds von Cappenburg, ed. G. Niemeyer and I. Ehlers-Kisseler (MGH Scriptores, 74, Hanover, 2005).

Dits et contes de Baudouin de Condé et de son fils Jean de Condé, ed. A. Scheler (3 vols, Brussels, 1866–7).

Doctrinal Sauvage: publié d'après tous les manuscrits, ed. A. Sakari (Jyväskylä, 1967).

Donei des Amanz, ed. A. J. Holden (Anglo-Norman Text Society, Plain Text Series, 17, Oxford, 2013).

Donizo, *Vita Mathildis*, in *MGH Scriptores* 12.

Durmart le Galois: roman arthurien du treizième siècle, ed. J. Gildea (2 vols, Villanova PA, 1965).

Du Yorkshire à l'Inde: une géographie urbaine et maritime de la fin du xii* siècle, ed. P. G. Dalché (Geneva, 2005).

Eadmer, *Historia Novorum in Anglia*, ed. M. Rule (Rolls Series, 1866).

Elias of Thriplow, *Petronius Rediuiuus et Helias Tripolanensis*, ed. M. L. Colker (Leiden, 2007).

Eneas: roman du xii* siècle, ed. J-J. Salverda de Grave (2 vols, Paris, 1964–8).

English Lawsuits from William I to Richard I, 2, *Henry II and Richard I*, ed. R. C. van Caenegem, Selden Society, 107 (London, 1991).

Établissements de Saint Louis, ed. P. Viollet (4 vols, Paris, 1881–6).

Fables d'Eude de Cheriton, ed. P. Ruelle (Recueil Général des Isopets, 4, Paris, 1999).

Fabliaux du Moyen Âge, ed. and trans. (Fr.) J. Dufournet (Paris, 1998).

Facetus or the Art of Courtly Living, ed. and trans. A. Goddard Elliott, in *Allegorica*, 2 (1977).

Foedera, Conventiones, Litterae et Acta Publica, ed. A. Clarke and F. Holbrooke (7 vols, London, 1816–69).

Frequenter cogitans, in *Poésies inédites du moyen âge*, ed. M. Edélstand du Méril (Paris, 1854).

Friend, A. C. 'The Proverbs of Serlo of Wilton', *Mediaeval Studies*, 16 (1954).

Galteri de Castellione Alexandreis, ed. M. L. Colker (Thesaurus Mundi, Bibliotheca Scriptorum Latinorum Mediæ et Recentioris Ætatis, 17, Padua, 1978), trans. as *The Alexandreis: a twelfth-century epic*, trans. D. Townsend (Peterborough, ON, 2007).

Garin le Loherenc, ed. A. Iker-Gittleman (3 vols, Paris, 1996–7).

Garin lo Brun, *Ensegnamen alla Dama*, ed. and trans. (It.) L. R. Bruno (Filologia Occitanica Studi e Testi, 1, Rome, 1996).

Gaydon: chanson de geste du xiiiᵉ siècle, ed. A. Subrenat (Leuven, 2007).

Genealogia comitum Flandriae, ed. L. C. Bethmann, *MGH Scriptores*, 9.

Geoffrey Gaimar, *Estoire des Engleis*, ed. and trans. I. Short (Oxford, 2009).

Geoffrey of Monmouth, *Historia regum Britanniae*, ed. M. Reeve and trans. N. Wright (Woodbridge, 2007).

Gerald of Wales, *Expugnatio Hibernica*, ed. and trans. A. B. Scott and F. X. Martin (Dublin, 1978).

Gerald of Wales, *Speculum Duorum*, ed. Y. Lefèvre and R. B. C. Huygens, and trans. B. Dawson (Cardiff, 1974).

Gervase of Tilbury, *Otia Imperialia*, ed. and trans. S. E. Banks and J. W. Binns (Oxford, 2002).

Gilbert Crispin, *Vita sancti Herluini*, in *PL* 150.

Giles of Paris, 'The "Karolinus" of Egidius Parisiensis', ed. M. L. Colker, in *Traditio*, 29 (1973), 303.

Giraldi Cambrensis Opera, ed. J. S. Brewer, J. F. Dimock, and G. F. Warner (8 vols, Rolls Series, 1861–91).

Glixelli, S. 'Les Contenances de Table', *Romania*, 47 (1921), 1–40.

Godfrey of Viterbo, *Opera*, in *MGH Scriptores* 22.

Guernes de Pont-Sainte-Maxence, *La vie de Saint Thomas Becket*, ed. E. Walberg (Classiques français du moyen âge, Paris, 1936).

Gui de Warewic: roman du xiiiᵉ siècle, ed. A. Ewert (2 vols, Paris, 1933).

Guiot de Provins, *Armëure de Chevalier*, in *Les Oeuvres de Guiot de Provins*, ed. J. Orr (Manchester, 1915).

Guiot de Provins, *La Bible*, in *Les Oeuvres de Guiot de Provins*, ed. J. Orr (Manchester, 1915).

Hartmann von Aue, *Der arme Heinrich*, ed. H. Paul, rev. K. Gärtner (Altdeutsche Textbibliothek, 3, 1996).

Hartmann von Aue *Gregorius*, ed. H. Paul (Tübingen, 1966).

Hermann of Tournai, *Liber de restauratione ecclesie sancti Martini Torniacensis*, ed. G. Waitz, *MGH Scriptores*, 14.

Hildebert of Lavardin, *Moralis Philosophia*, in *PL* 171.

Histoire des ducs de Normandie et des rois d'Angleterre, ed. F. Michel (Paris, 1840).

Historia Ecclesiae Abbendonensis, ed. and trans. J. G. Hudson (2 vols, Oxford, 2002–7).

Historia fundationis prioratus de Wigmore, in R. Dodsworth and W. Dugdale, *Monastici Anglicani* (2 vols, London, 1673).

Historia Regum Britannie of Geoffrey of Monmouth, ed. and trans. N. Wright (Cambridge, 1991).

History of William Marshal, ed. A. J. Holden and D. Crouch, trans. S. Gregory (3 vols, Anglo-Norman Text Society, Occasional Publications Series, 4–6, 2002–7).

Honorius Augustodunensis, *De imagine mundi*, in *PL*, 172.

Honorius Augustodunensis, *Speculum Ecclesiae*, in *PL* 172.

Household Accounts from Medieval England, ed. C. M. Woolgar (2 vols, British Academy, Records of Social and Economic History, new series, 17–18, 1992–3).

Huon de Méry, *Le Tournoi de l'Antéchrist*, ed. G. Wimmer and trans. (Fr.) S. Orgeur (2nd edn, Medievalia, no. 13, Orléans, 1995).

Isidore of Seville, *The Etymologies*, ed. and trans. S. A. Barney et al. (Cambridge, 2006).

James I, king of Aragon, *Llibre dels Fets*, ed. J. M. Pujol (Barcelona, 1991); trans. as *The Book of Deeds of James I of Aragon*, trans. D. J. Smith and H. Buffery (Farnham, 2003).

James de Vitry, *Historia orientalis*, ed. and trans (Fr.) J. Donnadieu (Turnhout, 2008).

Jean de Joinville, *Vie de Saint Louis*, ed. J. Monfrin (Paris, 1995).

Jean de Meung, *Roman de la Rose*, ed. and trans. (Fr.) A. Strubel (Paris, 1992).

Jean Renart, *Le Roman de la Rose ou de Guillaume de Dole*, ed. F. Lecoy and trans (Fr.) J. Dufournet (Paris, 2008).

John of Saint Omer, *Norfolchiae descriptionis impugnatio*, in *Early Mysteries and other Latin Poems of the Twelfth and Thirteenth Centuries*, ed. T. Wright (London, 1838).

John of Salisbury, *Entheticus Maior and Minor*, ed. and trans. J. van Laarhoven (Studien und Texte zur Geistesgeschichte des Mittelalters, 17, 1987).

John of Salisbury, *Policraticus*, ed. C. C. I. Webb (2 vols, Oxford, 1909).

Jongleurs et Trouvères, ed. A. Jubinal (Paris, 1835).

Lai de Conseil, ed. and trans. B. E. Grigoriu, C. Peersman, and J. Rider (Liverpool Online Series, Critical Editions of French Texts, 18, 2013).

Lamberti Ardensis historia comitum Ghisnensium, ed. J. Heller, in *MGH Scriptores*, xxiv, trans. as *The History of the Counts of Guines and Lords of Ardres*, trans. L. Shopkow (Philadelphia, 2001).

Lamentationes Matheoluli, ed. T. Klein (Quellen und Untersuchungen zur lateinischen Philologie des Mittelalters, 17, Stuttgart, 2014).

Lancelot do Lac: the Non-Cyclic Old French Prose Romance, ed. E. Kennedy (2 vols, Oxford, 1980).

Lancelot: roman en prose du xiiiᵉ siècle, ed. A. Micha (9 vols, Geneva, 1978–83).

Långfors, A. 'Le dit des hérauts par Henri de Laon', *Romania*, xliii (1914), 222–5.

L'Âtre Périlleux: roman de la table ronde, ed. B. Woledge (Classiques français du moyen âge, Paris, 1935).

Le Bel Inconnu, ed. G. P. Williams (Paris, 1983).

Le Chevalier à l'Épée, in *Two Old French Gauvain Romances*, ed. R. C. Johnston and D. D. R. Owen (Edinburgh, 1972).

Le Conventum (vers 1030): un précurseur aquitain des premières épopées, ed. G. Beech, Y. Chauvin, and G. Pon (Geneva, 1995).

Le Jeu d'Adam, ed. W. von Emden (Société Rencesvals British Branch, British Rencesvals Publications, 1, 1996).

Le liriche del trovatore Guilhem de la Tor, ed. and trans. (It.) A. Negri (Soveria Mannelli, 2006).

Le Livre de Lancelot de Lac, in *The Vulgate Version of the Arthurian Romances*, ed. H. O. Summer (8 vols, Washington, 1909–16).

Le Petit Plet, ed. B. S. Merrilees (Oxford, 1970).

Le Respit del Curteis et del Vilain, in E. Stengel, 'Handschriftliches aus Oxford', *Zeitschrift für französische Sprache und Literatur*, 14 (1892), 154–8.

Le Roman du Castelain de Couci et de la Dame de Fayel, ed. M. Delbouille (Paris, 1936).

Les conciles œcumeniques: les decrets, ii pt 1, *Nicée à Latran V*, ed. A. Duval et al. (Paris, 1994).

Les poésies du troubadour Ramon de Miraval, ed. and trans, (Fr.) L. T. Topsfield (Paris, 1971).

Liber Epistularum Guidonis de Basochis, ed. H. Adolfsson (Acta Univeritatis Stockholmensis. Studia Latina Stockholmensia, 18, 1969).

Life of Saint Audrey, ed. and trans. J. H. McCash and J. C. Barban (Jefferson, NC, 2006).

Li Torneiemenz Antecrit, ed. G. Wimmer and trans. S. Orgeur (2nd edn, Paris, 1995).

Lost Letters of Medieval Life: English Society, 1200–1250, ed. and trans. M. Carlin and D. Crouch (Philadelphia, 2013).

Ludi e spettacoli nel Medioevo: I tornei di dame, ed. and trans. (It.) A. Pulega, (Milan, 1970).

Magistri Reineri Alemanici Phagifacetus, ed. F. Jacob (Lübeck, 1838).

Magna Vita sancti Hugonis, ed. D. L. Douie and H. Farmer (2 vols, Oxford, 1961–2).

Marcabru: a critical edition, ed. S. Gaunt, R. Harvey, and L. Paterson (Cambridge, 2000).

Marie de France, *Les Fables*, ed. and trans. (Fr.) C. Brucker (Paris, 1998).

Martin, J. *'Die Proverbes au Conte de Bretaigne': nebst Belegen aus germanischen und romanischen Sprachen* (Erlangen, 1892).

Materials for the History of Thomas Becket, Archbishop of Canterbury, ed. J. C. Robertson and J. B. Sheppard (Rolls Series, 1875–85).

Matthew Paris, *Chronica Majora*, ed. H. R. Luard (7 vols, Rolls Series, 1872–84).

Medieval Conduct Literature: an Anthology of Vernacular Guides to Behaviour for Youths, ed. M. D. Johnston (Toronto, 2009).

Medieval English Prose for Women: Selections from the Katherine Group and Ancrene Wisse, ed. and trans. B. Millett and J. Wogan-Browne (Oxford, 1990).

Meyer, P. 'Dit sur les vilains par Matazone de Calignano', *Romania*, 12 (1883).

Miracles de la Sainte Vierge, ed. l'Abbé Pocquet (repr. Geneva, 1972).

Miracula sancti Usmari,, in *MGH Scriptores* 15, pt 2.

Miscellaneous Irish annals, AD 1114–1437, ed. Séamus Ó Hinnse (Dublin, 1947).

Morale Scolarium of John of Garland, ed. and trans. L. J. Paetow (Memoirs of the University of California, 1, no. 2, Berkeley, 1927).

Morel-Fatio, A. 'Mélanges de littérature catalane', *Romania*, 15 (1886), 224–35.

Noble Society: Five Lives from Twelfth-Century Germany, trans. J. R. Lyon (Manchester, 2017).

Nouvelles occitanes du moyen age, ed. J-Ch. Huchet (Paris, 1992).

O'Brien, B. *God's Peace and King's Peace: The Laws of Edward the Confessor* (Philadelphia, 1999).

Oeuvres Complètes de Rutebeuf, ed. E. Faral and J. Bastin (2 vols, Paris, 1959–60).

Orderic Vitalis, *The Ecclesiastical History*, ed. and trans. M. Chibnall (6 vols, Oxford, 1969–81).

Ordines Coronationis Franciae, ed. R. A. Jackson (Philadelphia, 1995).

Partonopeus de Blois, ed. G.-A. Crapelet (2 vols, Paris, 1834).

Patent Rolls of the Reign of Henry III (6 vols, London, 1901–13).

Peter Alfonsi, *Disciplina clericalis*, ed. A. Hilka and W. Söderheljm (Heidelberg, 1911), trans. as *The Disciplina Clericalis of Peter Alfonsi*, trans. P. R. Quarrie (Berkeley, 1977).

Peter the Chanter, *Verbum Abbreviatum*, in *PL*, 205.

Petri Blesensis Epistolae, in *PL*, 207.

Philip de Novare, *Les quatre âges de l'homme, traité moral de Philippe de Navarre publié pour la première fois d'après les manuscrits de Paris, de Londres et de Metz*, ed. M. de Fréville (Paris, Société des anciens textes français, 1888).

Philip de Remy, *Jehan et Blonde*, ed. S. Lécuyer (Paris, 1984).

Philip de Remy, *La Manekine*, ed. H. Suchier (Paris, 1884).

Philip de Thaon, *Bestiaire*, in T. Wright, *Popular Treatises on Science written during the Middle Ages* (London, 1841).

Philip de Thaon, *Comput*, ed. I. Short (London, 1984).

Philip of Harvengt, *De institutione clericorum*, in *PL* 203.

Philip of Harvengt, *Epistolae*, in *PL* 203.

Pipe Roll of 31 Henry I, ed. and trans. J. A. Green (Pipe Roll Society, new ser. 37, 2012).

Poésies inédites du moyen âge, ed. M. Édélestand du Méril (Paris, 1854).

Poeti del Duecento, ed. G. Contini (2 vols, Milan, 1960).

Proverbe au Vilain: die Sprichwörter des gemeinen Mannes: altfranzösische Dichtung, ed. A. Tobler (Leipzig, 1895).

Proverbes de Salemon, ed. C. C. Isoz (3 vols, Anglo-Norman Text Society, 44, 45, 50, 1988–94).

Proverbes français antérieurs au xvᵉ siècle, ed. J. Morawski (Paris, 1925).

Radulphi Cadomensis Tancredus, ed. E. d'Angelo (Corpus Christianorum: Continuatio Mediaevalis, 231, Turnhout, 2011).

Ralph Niger, *De re militari et triplici via peregrinationis Ierosolomitane*, ed. L. Schmugge (Beiträge zur Geschichte und Quellenkunde des Mittelalters, 6, Berlin, 1977).

Ramon Llull, *Doctrina pueril*, ed. G. Schib (Barcelona, 1972).

Ramon Llull, *Llibre de l'Orde de Cavalleria*, ed. A. Soler i Llopart (Barcelona, 1988), trans. as *The Book of the Order of Chivalry*, trans. N. Fallows (Woodbridge, 2013).

Ramon Vidal, *Abril issi' e Mays intrava,*, in *Nouvelles occitanes du moyen age*, ed. J-Ch. Huchet (Paris, 1992).

Raoul de Cambrai, ed. and trans. (Fr.) W. W. Kibler (Paris, 1996).

Raoul de Hodenc, Le Roman des Eles. The Anonymous Ordene de Chevalerie, ed. and trans. K. Busby (Utrecht Publications in General and Comparative Literature, Amsterdam, 17, 1983).

Raoul de Houdenc, *Le Borjois Borjon*, in *Anecdota Literaria*, ed. T. Wright (London, 1844).

Recueil des actes des comtes de Ponthieu, 1026–1279, ed. C. Brunel (Paris, 1930).

Recueil des chartes de l'abbaye de Cluny, ed. A. Bernard and A. Bruel (5 vols, Paris, 1876–1903).

Recueil général et complet des fabliaux des XIIIᵉ et XIVᵉ siècles imprimés ou inédits, ed. A. de Montaiglon and G. Raynaud (Paris, 6 vols, 1872–90).

Registrum Epistolarum fratris Johannis Pecham, ed. C. T. Martin (3 vols, Cambridge, 1882–4).

Regulae Sanctimonialium Fontis Ebraldi, in *PL* 162.

Renaut, *Galeran de Bretagne*, ed. and trans. (Fr.) J. Dufournet (Paris, 2009).

Richer of Reims, *Histories*, ed. and trans. J. Lake (2 vols, Cambridge, MA, 2011).

Robert de Blois, son oeuvre didactique et narrative. Étude linguistique et littéraire suivie d'une édition critique avec commentaire et glossaire de l''Enseignement des princes' *et du* 'Chastoiement des dames' ed. J. H. Fox, (Paris, 1950).

Robert de Boron, *Merlin: roman du xiiiᵉ siècle*, ed. A. Micha (Geneva, 2000).

Robert of Ho, *Les Enseignements de Robert de Ho: dits Enseignements Trebor*, ed. M. V. Young (Paris, 1901).

Roger of Caen, *De contemptu mundi* (attrib. Alexander Neckam as *de vita monachorum*), in *The Anglo-Latin Satirical Poets and Epigrammatists of the Twelfth Century*, ed. T. Wright (2 vols, Rolls Series, 1872), 2.

Roger of Howden, *Gesta Henrici Secundi*, ed. W. Stubbs (2 vols, Rolls Series, 1867).

Roman de la Rose, ed. and trans. (Fr.) A. Strubel (Paris, 1992).

Roman de Thèbes, ed. F. Mora-Lebrun (Paris, 1999).

Rosamond Parsons, H. 'Anglo-Norman books of courtesy and nurture', *PMLA*, 44 (1929), 383–455.

Rotuli Litterarum Patentium in Turri Londinensi asservati, ed. T. Duffus Hardy (Record Commission, 1835).

Ruodlieb, ed. and trans. C. W. Grocock (Warminster, 1985).

Siete Partidas del Rey Don Alfonso el Sabio, ed. anon. (3 vols, Madrid, 1807), trans. as *Las Siete Partidas* 2, *Medieval Government*, trans. S. P. Scott and ed. R. I. Burns (Philadelphia, 1996).

Sigebert of Gembloux, *Vita Wicberti*, in *MGH Scriptores*, 8.

Silence, ed. and trans. S. Roche-Mahdi (East Lansing, 1992).

Similitudo militis, in *Memorials of St Anselm*, ed. R. W. Southern and F. S. Schmitt (British Academy, 1969).

Sone de Nansay, ed. C. Lachet (Paris, 2014).

Song of Roland: An Analytical Edition: Introduction and Commentary, ed. and trans. G. J. Brault (2 vols, University Park, PA, 1978).

Sordello da Goito, *Le Poesie. Nuova edizione critica*, ed. and trans. (It.) M. Boni (Bologna, 1954).

Spitzer, L. 'Remarks on the "Sirventese Lombardo"', in *Italica*, 28 (1951).

Statuta Capitulorum Generalium Ordinis Cisterciensis ab anno 1116 ad annum 1786, 1, *1116–1220*, ed. J-M. Canivez (Leuven, 1933).

Stephen de Fougères, *Le Livre des Manières*, ed. and trans. (Fr.) J. T. E. Thomas (Leuven, 2013).

Stephen de Rouen, *Carmen elegiacum de Waleranno comite Mellenti*, in *Chronicles of the Reigns of Stephen, Henry II and Richard*, ed. R. Howlett (4 vols, Rolls Series, 1886–9), 2.

Stephen of Lexington, *Letters from Ireland, 1228–1229*, trans. B. O'Dwyer (Kalamazoo, 1982).

The Babees Book, ed. F. J. Furnivall (London, Early English Text Society, 1868).

The Book of the Foundation of Walden Monastery, ed. and trans. D. Greenway and L. Watkiss (Oxford, 1999).

The Cartulary and Charters of Notre Dame of Homblières, ed. W. M. Newman, T. Evergates, and G. Constable (Cambridge, MA, 1990).

The Charters of Duchess Constance of Brittany and her Family, 1171–1221, ed. J. Everard and M. C. E. Jones (Woodbridge, 1999).

The Chronicle of John of Worcester 3, ed. P. McGurk (Oxford, 1998).

The Correspondence of Thomas Becket, Archbishop of Canterbury, 1162–1170, ed. A. J. Duggan (2 vols, Oxford, 2000).

The Disciplina clericalis of Petrus Alfonsi, ed. E. Hermes and trans. P. R. Quarrie (Berkeley, CA, 1977).

The English Text of the Ancrene Riwle, ed. M. Day (London, 1952).

The Fables of Marie de France, ed. and trans. M. L. Martin (Birmingham, AL, 1984).

The French Fabliau, B.N. MS 837, ed. and trans. R. Eichmann and J. DuVal (2 vols, London, 1984).

The Lanercost Chronicle, 1201–1346, ed. J. Stevenson (Edinburgh, 1839).

The Langley Cartulary, ed. P. R. Coss (Dugdale Society, 32, 199, 1980).

The Later Letters of Peter of Blois, ed. E. Revell (Auctores Britannici Medii Aevi, 13, Oxford, 1993).

The Letter Collection of Peter Abelard and Heloise, ed. D. Luscombe and trans. B. Radice (Oxford, 2013).

The Letters of Arnulf of Lisieux, ed. F. Barlow (Camden Society, 3rd ser., 61, 1939).

The Letters of Peter of Celle, ed. and trans. J. Haseldine (Oxford, 2001).

The Old English 'Boethius': an Edition of the Old English Versions of Boethius's 'De Consolatione Philosophiae', ed. and trans. M. Godden and S. Irvine (2 vols, Oxford, 2009).

The Old French Lays of Ignaure, Oiselet *and* Amours, ed. and trans. G. S. Burgess and L. C. Brook (Gallica, 18, Cambridge, 2010).

The Poems of the Troubadour Bertran de Born, ed. and trans. W. D. Paden Jr, T. Sankovich, and P. H. Stäblein (Berkeley, 1986).

The Poems of the Troubadour Raimbaut de Vaqueiras, ed. J. Linskill (The Hague, 1964).

The Romance of Fergus, ed. W. Frescoln (Philadelphia, 1983).

The Rules of Robert Grosseste, in *Walter of Henley and other Treatises on Estate Management and Acccounting*, ed. and trans. D. Oschinsky (Oxford, 1971).

The Songe d'Enfer of Raoul de Houdenc: an edition based on all the extant manuscripts, ed. M. T. Mihm (Tübingen, 1984).

The Songs of Peire Vidal, ed. and trans. V. M. Fraser (New York, 2006).

The Usatges of Barcelona: Fundamental Law of Catalonia, trans. D. J. Kagay (Philadelphia, 1994).

The Welsh Law of Women, ed. D. Jenkins and M. E. Owen (Cardiff, 1980).

Thomasin of Zirclaria, *Der Wälsche Gast*, ed. H. Rückert (Quedlingen, 1852), trans. as *Der Welsche Gast*, trans. M. Gibbs and W. McConnell (Kalamazoo, 2009).

Thomas of Kent, *Le Roman de Toute Chevalerie*, ed. B. Foster (2 vols, London, 1976–7).

Three Medieval Views of Women, ed. and trans. G. K. Fiero, W. Pfeffer, and M. Allain (New Haven, 1989).

Ulrich von Liechtenstein, *Das Frauenbuch*, ed. and trans. (Ger.) C. Young (Stuttgart, 2003).

Ulrich von Liechtenstein, *The Service of Ladies*, trans. J. W. Thomas (Woodbridge, 2004).

Urbanus Magnus Danielis Becclesiensis, ed. J. G. Smyly (Dublin, 1939).

Vie de Saint Alexis, ed. M. Perugi (Geneva, 2000).

Vincent of Beauvais, *De eruditione filiorum nobilium*, ed. A. Steiner (MAA Publication, 32, 1938).

Visio Tnugaldi Lateinisch und Altdeutsch, ed. A. Wagner (Erlangen, 1882).

Vita et Passio Waldevi comitis, in *Original Lives of Anglo-Saxons and others*, ed. J. Giles (Caxton Society, London, 1854).

Vita Griffini filii Conani, ed. and trans. P. Russell (Cardiff, 2005).

Vita Norberti archiepiscopi Magdeburgensis, in *MGH Scriptores* 12.

Vita sancti Geraldi Auriliacensis comitis, in *PL* 133, trans. G. Sitwell, in *Soldiers of Christ: Saints and Saints' lives from Late Antiquity and the Early Middle Ages*, ed. T. F. X. Noble and T. Head (University Park, PA, 1995).

Wace of Bayeux *Le Roman de Brut*, ed. I. Arnold (2 vols, Paris, 1938–40).

Wace of Bayeux, *Roman de Rou*, ed. A. J. Holden (3 vols, Société des anciens textes français, 1970–3).

Walpole, R. N. 'Charlemagne's Journey to the East: the French Translation of the Legend by Pierre de Beauvais', in *Semitic and Oriental Studies: A Volume Presented to William Popper*, ed. W. J. Fischel (University of California Publications in Semitic Philology, 11, 1951).

Walter Map, *De Nugis Curialium or Courtiers' Trifles*, ed. and trans. M. R. James, rev. C. N. L. Brooke and R. A. B. Mynors (Oxford, 1983).

Walter de Tournai, *L'Histoire de Gille de Chyn*, ed. E. B. Place (New York, 1941).

Walter of Arras, *Eracle*, ed. and trans. K. Pratt (King's College London, Medieval Studies, 21, London, 2007).

Walter of Arras, *Ille et Galeron*, ed. and trans. P. Eley (King's College London, Medieval Studies, 13, 1996).

William le Breton, *Gesta Philippi regis*, in *Œuvres de Rigord et de Guillaume le Breton*, ed. H. F. Delaborde (2 vols, Paris, 1882–5), 1.

William of Aragon, *De Nobilitate Animi*, ed. and trans. W. D. Paden Jr and M. Trovato (Harvard Studies in Medieval Latin, 2, Cambridge, MA, 2012).

William of Conches, *Dragmaticon Philosophie*, ed. I. Ronca and trans. M. Curr (Notre Dame, IN, 1997).

William of Malmesbury, *Gesta Regum Anglorum*, ed. R. A. B. Mynors, R. M. Thomson, and M. Winterbottom (2 vols, Oxford, 1998–9).

William of Malmesbury, *Historia Novella*, ed. E. King and trans. K. R. Potter (Oxford, 1998).

William of Newburgh, *Historia Rerum Anglicarum*, in *Chronicles of the Reigns of Stephen etc*, ed. R. Howlett (4 vols, Rolls Series, 1884–9), 1.

William of Poitiers, *Gesta Guillelmi*, ed. and trans. R. H. C. Davis and M. Chibnall (Oxford, 1998).

William of Wycombe, *Speculum vitae viri venerabilis Rotberti episcopi Herefordiae*, in *Anglia Sacra*, ed. H. Wharton (2 vols, London, 1691) 2.

Winsbecke and *Winsbeckin*, ed. and trans. A. M. Rasmussen and O. Trokhimenko, in *Medieval Conduct Literature : An Anthology of Vernacular Guides to Behaviour for Youths*, ed. M. D. Johnston (Toronto, 2009).

Winterbottom, M. 'An Edition of Faricius *Vita S. Aldhelmi*', *Journal of Medieval Latin*, 15 (2005).

SECONDARY WORKS

Adam, P. 'Les usages héraldiques au milieu du xiie siècle', *Archivum Heraldicum*, 7 (1963), 18–29.

Ailes, M. 'Traitors and Rebels: the *Geste de Maience*', in *Reading Round the Epic: A Festschrift in Honour of Professor Wolfgang von Emden*, ed. M. Ailes, P. E. Bennett, and K. Pratt (King's College London, Medieval Studies, 14, 1998), 41–68.

Allan, D. '"An Institution Quite Misunderstood": Chivalry and Sentimentalism in the Late Scottish Enlightenment', in *Chivalry and the Medieval Past*, ed. K. Stevenson and B. Gribling (Woodbridge, 2016), 15–34.

Althoff, G. '*Nunc fiant Christi milites, qui dudum extiterunt raptores.* Zur Entstehung von Rittertum und Ritterethos', *Saeculum*, 32 (1981), 317–33.

Althoff, G. 'Genealogische Fiktionen und die historiographische Gattung der Genealogie im hohen Mittelalter', in *Staten-Wappen-Dynastien*, 18 (Veröffentlichungen des Innsbrucker Stadtarchivs, N.F. 18, 1988), 67–79.

Anger's Past: the Social Uses of an Emotion in the Middle Ages, ed. B. H. Rosenwein (Ithaca, 1998).

Archibald, E. 'Ruodlieb and Romance in Latin: Audience and Authorship', in *Telling the Story in the Middle Ages: Essays in Honour of Evelyn Birge Vitz* (Cambridge, 2015), 171–86.

Aristocratic Women in Medieval France, ed. T. Evergates (Philadelphia, 1999).

Arnold, B. *German Knighthood 1050–1300* (Oxford, 1985).

Ashley, K. 'The *Miroir des Bonnes Femmes*: Not for Women only?', in *Medieval Conduct*, ed. K. Ashley and R. L. A. Clark (Minneapolis, 2001), 86–105.

Aurell, M. 'La déterioration du statut de la femme aristocratique en Provence (x^e–xiiie siècles)', *Le Moyen Age*, 91 (1985), 5–32.

Aurell, M. 'Chevaliers et chevalerie chez Raymond Llulle', in *Raymond Llulle et le Pays d'Oc* (Cahiers de Fanjeaux, 22, 1987), 141–68.

Aurell, M. *La noblesse en Occident, v^e–xve siècle* (Paris, 1996).

Aurell, M. *L'Empire des Plantagenêt, 1154–1224* (Paris, 2003).

Aurell, M. *Le chevalier lettré: savoir et conduite de l'aristocratie aux xiie et xiiie siècles* (Paris, 2006), trans. as *The Lettered Knight: Knowledge and aristocratic behaviour in the twelfth and thirteenth centuries*, trans. J. C. Khalifa and J. Price (Budapest, 2017).

Aurell, M. 'La noblesse au xiiie siècle: paraître, pouvoir et savoir', in *Discurso, Memoria y Representación: La nobleza peninsular en la Baja Edad Media* (Actas de la XLII Semana de Estudios Medievales de Estella-Lizarra, Pamplona, 2016).

Aurell, M. 'L'épée, l'autel et le perron', in *Armes et jeux militaires (XIIe–XVe siècles)*, ed. C. Girbea (Paris, 2016).

Badia L., Santanach J., and Soler A. 'Ramon Llull as a Vernacular Writer', in *Style and Genre in the Writings of Ramon Llull* (Woodbridge, 2016).

Baldwin, J. W. *Masters, Princes and Merchants: the Social Views of Peter the Chanter and his Circle* (2 vols, Princeton, 1970).

Baldwin, J. W. *The Language of Sex: Five Voices from Northern France around 1200* (Chicago, 1994).

Baldwin, J. W. *Aristocratic Life in Medieval France. The Romances of Jean Renart and Gerbert de Montreuil, 1190–1230* (Baltimore, 2000).

Bannerman, J. M. W. 'The king's poet and the inauguration of Alexander III', *Scottish Historical Review*, 69 (1989), 120–49.

Banquets et manières de table au moyen âge, ed. M. Bertrand and C. Hory (Provence, 1996).

Barlow, F. *Thomas Becket* (London, 1986).

Barthélemy, D. *Les deux âges de la seigneurie banale: Coucy, xie–xiiie siècle* (Paris, 1984).

Barthélemy, D. *L'ordre seigneurial, xie–xiie siècle* (Paris, 1990).

Barthélemy, D. *La société dans le comté de Vendômois de l'an mil au xive siècle* (Paris, 1993).

Barthélemy, D. 'Note sur le "titre chevaleresque" en France au xie siècle', *Journal des Savants*, 1 (1994).

Barthélemy, D. 'Castles, Barons and Vavassors in the Vendômois and Neighboring Regions in the Eleventh and Twelfth Centuries', in *Cultures of Power: Lordship, Status and Process in Twelfth-Century Europe*, ed. T. N. Bisson (Philadelphia, 1995), 56–68.

Barthélemy, D. 'Les comtes, les sires et les "nobles de châteaux" dans la Touraine du xie siècle', in *Campagnes médiévales: l'homme et son espace. Etudes offertes à Robert Fossier* (Paris, 1995), 439–53.

Barthélemy, D. *La mutation de l'an mil, a-t-elle eu lieu? Servage et chevalerie dans la France des xe et xie siècles* (Paris, 1997).

Barthélemy, D. *L'an mil et la paix de Dieu: la France chrétienne et féodale, 980–1060* (Paris, 1999).

Barthélemy, D. *Chevaliers et miracles: la violence et le sacré dans la société féodale* (Paris, 2004).

Barthélemy, D. *La chevalerie: de la Germanie antique à la France du xiie siècle* (Paris, 2007).

Barthélemy, D. 'Feudal Warfare in Tenth-Century France', in *Vengeance in the Middle Ages: Emotion, Religion and Feud*, ed. S. A. Throop and P. Hyams (Farnham, 2010), 105–13.

Bartlett, R. *The Making of Europe: Conquest, Colonization and Cultural Change, 950–1350* (London, 1993).

Bartlett, R. '"Mortal Enmities": the Legal Aspect of Hostility in the Middle Ages', in *Feud, Violence and Practice: Essays in Medieval Studies in Honor of Stephen D. White*, ed. B. S. Tuten and T. L. Billado (Aldershot, 2010), 197–212.

Bates, D. R. *Normandy before 1066* (London, 1982).

Baumgartner, E. 'Trouvères et *Losengiers*', *CCM*, 25 (1982), 171–8.

Bedell, J. 'Memory and Proof of Age in England, 1272–1327', *Past & Present*, no. 162 (1999), 3–27.

Bennewitz, I. 'Der Körper der Dame. Zur Konstruktion von "Weiblichkeit" in der deutschen Literatur des Mittelalters', in *'Aufführung' und 'Schrift' im Mittelalter und Früher Neuzeit*, ed. J-D. Müller (Stuttgart, 1996), 222–38.

Bisson, T. N. 'The "Feudal Revolution"', *Past & Present*, no. 142 (1994), 6–42.

Bisson, T. N. *The Crisis of the Twelfth Century: Power, Lordship and the Origins of European Government* (Princeton, 2009).

Bloch, M. *La société féodale* (2 vols, Paris, 1949), trans. as *Feudal Society*, trans. L. Manyon (2nd edn, 2 vols, London, 1962).

Bloch, R. H. *Medieval Misogyny and the Invention of Western Romantic Love* (Chicago, 1991).

Boethius in the Middle Ages, ed. M. J. F. M. Hoenen and L. Nauta (Leiden, 1997).

Bonnassie, P. *La Catalogne du milieu du xe siècle à la fin du xie siècle: croissance et mutations d'une société* (2 vols, Toulouse, 1975–6).

Bosl, K. *Die Reichsministerialität der Salier und Staufer* (MGH Schriften, 10, Stuttgart, 1950–1).

Bouchard, C. B. 'The Origins of the French Nobility: A Reassessment', *American Historical Review*, 86 (1981), 501–32.

Bouchard, C. B. *Those of my Blood: Constructing Noble Families in Medeval Francia* (Philadelphia, 2001).

Boulengier-Sedyn, R. *Le vocabulaire de la coiffure en ancien français étudié dans les romans de 1150 à 1300* (Brussels, 1970).

Bourdieu, P. *Esquisse d'une théorie de la pratique: précédé de trois études de ethnologie kabyle* (Paris, 1972), trans. as *Outline of a Theory of Practice*, trans. R. Nice (Cambridge, 1977).

Bourdieu, P. *La distinction: critique sociale du jugement* (Paris, 1979), trans. as *Distinction: A Social Critique on the Judgement of Taste*, trans. R. Nice (London, 1986).

Bourdieu, P. *Le sens pratique* (Paris, 1980), trans. as *The Logic of Practice*, trans. R. Nice (Stanford, CA, 1990).

Bourdieu, P. *La Noblesse d'état: grandes écoles et esprit de corps* (Paris, 1989), trans. as *The State Nobility: Elite Schools in the Field of Power*, trans. R. Nice (Stanford, CA, 1996).

Bourdieu, P. *Raisons pratiques: sur la théorie de l'action* (Paris, 1994).

Bourdieu P. and J-C. Passeron, *Les hériteurs: les étudiants et la culture* (Paris, 1964) trans. as *The Inheritors, French Students and their Relation to Culture*, trans. R. Nice (Chicago, 1979).

Bozoky, E. 'L'épée d'Attila', in *Armes et jeux militaires dans l'imaginaire, xiie–xve siècles*, ed. C. Girbea (Bibliothèque d'histoire médiévale, 15, Paris, 2016), 357–68.

Brown, R. A. 'The Status of the Norman Knight', in *War and Government in the Middle Ages: Essays in Honour of J.O. Prestwich*, ed. J. Gillingham and J. C. Holt (Woodbridge, 1984), 18–32.

Brown, S. D. B. 'Leavetaking: lordship and mobility in England and Normandy in the twelfth century', *History*, 79 (1994), 199–215.

Brown, W. C. and P. Górecki, 'What Conflict Means: the making of medieval conflict studies in the United States, 1970–2000', in *Conflict in Medieval Europe: Changing Perspectives on Society and Culture*, ed. W. C. Brown and P. Górecki (Aldershot, 2003), 1–36.

Brückle, W. 'Noblesse oblige. Trojasage und legitime Herrschaft in der französischen Staatstheorie des späten Mittelalters', in *Genealogie als Denkform in Mittelalter und Früher Neuzeit*, ed. K. Heck and B. Hahn (Tübingen, 2000), 39–67.

Brunner, O. *Land and Lordship: Structures of Governance in Medieval Austria*, trans. H. Kaminsky and J. van Horn Melton (Philadelphia, 1992).

Buc, P. *The Dangers of Ritual: Between Early Medieval Texts and Social Scientific Theory* (Princeton, 2001).

Bumke, J. *Höfische Kultur: Literatur und Gesellschaft im hohen Mittelalter* (Munich, 1986), trans. as *Courtly Culture: Literature and Society in the High Middle Ages*, trans. T. Dunlap (Berkeley, CA, 1991).

Busby, K. 'Plus ça change…A case of medieval interlanguage', *Interlanguage Studies Bulletin*, 3 (1978), 118–26.

Busby, K. *Gauvain in Old French Literature* (Amsterdam, 1980).

Büsching, J. G. G. *Ritterzeit und Ritterwesen* (2 vols, Leipzig, 1823).

Buttry, D. 'Contempt or Empathy? Master Wace's depiction of a peasant revolt', *Romance Notes*, 37 (1996), 31–8.

Bynum, C. W. 'Women mystics and eucharistic devotion in the thirteenth century', *Women's Studies*, 11 (1984), 179–214.

Bynum, C. W. *Holy Feast and Holy Fast: the Religious Significance of Food to Medieval Women* (Berkeley, 1987).

Carl, G. W. ' "Tu cuides que nos seions taus come autres femes comunaus": the sexually confident woman in the *Roman de Troie*', in *Gender Transgressions: Crossing the Normative Barrier in Old French Literature*, ed. K. J. Taylor (New York, 1998), 107–27.

Cassagnes-Brouquet, S. *Chevaleresses: une chevalerie au féminin* (Paris, 2013).

Castelnuovo, G. 'Juvénal et la noblesse au Moyen Âge ou les avatars d'une citation', in *Des plats pays aux cimes alpines. Hommages offerts à François Bertrandy*, ed. F. Delrieux and F. Kayser (2 vols, Chambéry, 2010), 2: 13–27.

Castration and Culture in the Middle Ages, ed. L. Tracy (Cambridge, 2013).

Chadwick, H. *Boethius* (Oxford, 1981).

Chevalerie et christianisme aux xii et xiii* siècles*, ed. M. Aurell and C. Girbea (Rennes, 2011).

Cheyette, F. L. 'Women, Poets and Politics in Occitania', in *Aristocratic Women in Medieval France*, ed. T. Evergates (Philadelphia, 1999).

Cheyette, F. L. *Ermengard of Narbonne and the World of the Troubadours* (Ithaca, NY, 2001).

Chibnall, M. *The Empress Matilda* (Oxford, 1991).

Classen, A. 'Anger and Anger Management in the Middle Ages. Mental-Historical Perspectives', *Mediaevistik*, 19 (2006), 21–50.

Classen, A. 'Masculine Women and Female Men: The Gender Debate in Medieval Courtly Literature. With an Emphasis on the Middle High German Verse Narrative *Frauenturnier*', *Mittellateinisches Jahrbuch*, 43 (2008), 205–22.

Classen, A. *The Power of a Woman's Voice in Medieval and Early Modern Literatures* (Berlin, 2012).

Claussen, M. A. 'Fathers of Power and Women of Authority, Dhuoda and the *Liber Manualis*', *French Historical Studies*, 19 (1996), 785–809.

Cohen, R. 'Genre Theory and Historical Change', in *Theoretical Essays of Ralph Cohen*, ed. J. L. Rowlett (Charlottesville, VA, 2017), 145–69.

Colker, M. '*De Nobilitate Animi*', in *Mediaeval Studies*, 23 (1961), 47–79.

Communities of Learning. Networks and the Shaping of Intellectual Identity in Europe, 1100–1500, ed. C. Mews and J. Crossley (Turnhout, 2011).

Coss, P. R. *Lordship, Knighthood and Locality: a Study of English Society, c.1180–c.1280* (Cambridge, 1991).

Cowdrey, H. E. J. 'Pope Gregory VII and the Bearing of Arms', in *Montjoie: Studies in Crusade History in Honour of Hans Eberhard Mayer*, ed. B. Z. Kedar, J. Riley-Smith, and R. Hiestand (Aldershot, 1997), 21–35.

Creighton, O. *Early European Castles: Aristocracy and Authority, AD 800–1200* (London, 2012).

Cropp, G. M. 'The Medieval French Tradition', in *Boethius in the Middle Ages*, ed. M. J. F. M. Hoenen and L. Nauta (Leiden, 1997), 243–65.

Crosland, J. R. *Medieval French Literature* (New York, 1965).

Crouch, D. *The Beaumont Twins: the Roots and Branches of Power in the Twelfth Century* (Cambridge, 1986).

Crouch, D. *The Image of Aristocracy in Britain, 1000–1300* (London, 1992).

Crouch, D. *The Reign of King Stephen, 1135–1154* (Harlow, 2000).

Crouch, D. *The Birth of Nobility: Constructing Aristocracy in England and France, 900–1300* (Harlow, 2005).

Crouch, D. *Tournament* (London, 2005).

Crouch, D. 'William Marshal and the Mercenariat', in *Mercenaries and Paid Men: the Mercenary Identity in the Middle Ages*, ed. J. France (Leiden, 2008), 15–32.

Crouch, D. *The English Aristocracy, 1070–1272. A Social Transformation* (New Haven, 2011).

Crouch, D. 'Earl Gilbert Marshal and his Mortal Enemies', *Historical Research*, 87 (2014), 393–403.

Crouch, D. *William Marshal* (3rd edn, London, 2016).

Crouch, D. 'The Violence of the *Preudomme*', in *Prowess, Piety, and Public Order in Medieval Society: Studies in Honor of Richard W. Kaeuper*, ed. C. M. Nakashian and D. P. Franke (Turnhout, 2017), 87–101.

Cullum, P. H. 'Clergy, Masculinity and Transgression in Late Medieval England', in *Masculinity in Medieval Europe*, ed. D. M. Hadley (Harlow, 1999), 178–96.

Curialitas. Studien zu Grundfragen der höfisch-ritterlichen Kultur, ed. J. Fleckenstein (Göttingen, 1990).

d'Alverny, M-T. 'Comment les théologiens et les philosophes voient la femme', *CCM*, 20 (1977), 105–29.

Damen, M. 'Heren met banieren. De baanrotsen van Brabant in de vijftiende eeuw', in *Bourgondië voorbij. De Nederlanden 1250–1650*, ed. M. Damen and L. H. J. Sicking (Hilversum, 2010), 139–58.

Das ritterliche Turnier im Mittelalter: Beiträge zu einer vergleichenden Formen- und Verhaltensgeschichte des Rittertums, ed. J. Fleckenstein (Göttingen, 1986).

Davies, R. R. 'The Survival of the Bloodfeud in Medieval Wales', *History*, 54 (1969), 338–57.

Debord, A. *Aristocratie et pouvoir: le rôle du château dans la France médiévale* (Paris, 2000), 27–48.

de la Curne de Sainte-Palaye, J-B. *Mémoires de l'ancienne chevalerie considérée comme un établissement politique et militaire* (2 vols, 2nd edn, Paris, 1826).

Delhaye, P. *Enseignement et morale au xiiᵉ siècle* (Paris, 1988).

Denholm-Young, N. *Collected Papers* (Cardiff, 1969).

Dette, C. 'Kinder und Jugendliche in der Adelsgesellschaft des frühen Mittelalters', *Archiv für Kulturgeschichte*, 76 (1994), 1–34.

Dictionnaire des lettres françaises: le Moyen Âge, ed. G. Hasenohr and M. Zink (Paris, 1992).

Die Deutsche Literatur des Mittelalters: Verfasserlexikon, ed. W. Stammler and K. Langosch (2nd edn, 14 vols, Berlin, 1977–2008).

Donati, F. P. 'Les bonnes manières à table dans le discourse proverbial du moyen âge italien', in *Pratiques et discours alimentaires en Méditerranée de l'Antiquité à la Renaissance*, ed. J. Leclant, A. Vauchez, and M. Sartre (Paris, 2008).

Dronke, P. 'Ruodlieb: The Emergence of Romance', in *Poetic Individuality in the Middle Ages* (Oxford, 1970), 33–65.

Dronke, P. *Women Writers of the Middle Ages: A Critical Study of Texts from Perpetua to Marguerite Porete* (Cambridge, 1984).

Duby, G. 'Les origines de la chevalerie', in *Ordinamenti Militari in Occidente nell'alto medieoevo, Spoleto 30 Marze–15 Aprile 1967* (Settimane di studio del Centro italiano di studi sull'alto medieoevo, 15, 1968), 739–61.

Duby, G. *Les trois ordres ou l'imaginaire du féodalisme* (Paris, 1978), trans. A. Goldhammer as *The Three Orders: Feudal Society Imagined* (Chicago, 1980).

Duby, G. *Mâle moyen âge* (Paris, 1990).

Duggan, A. J. 'Concepts, Origins, Transformations', in *Nobles and Nobility in Medieval Europe*, ed. eadem (Woodbridge, 2000), 1–16.

Dunbabin, J. 'From Clerk to Knight: Changing Orders', in *Medieval Knighthood 2*, ed. C. Harper-Bill and R. Harvey (Woodbridge, 1988), 26–39.

Duncan, A. A. M. 'Yes, the earliest Scottish charters', *Scottish Historical Review*, 78 (1999), 2–13.

Dyer, C. *Standards of Living in the Later Middle Ages: Social Change in England, c. 1200–1520* (Cambridge, 1989).

Ehrismann, G. 'Die Grundlagen des ritterlichen Tugendsystems', *Zeitschrift für deutsches Altertum und deutsche Literatur*, 56 (1919), 137–216.

Elias, N. *Über den Prozess der Zivilisation* (2 vols, Basel, 1939), trans. as *The Civilizing Process*, trans. E. Jephcott (2 vols, Oxford, 1994).

Elias, N. *Die höfische Gesellschaft: Untersuchungen zur Soziologie des Königtums und der höfischen Aristokratie* (Soziologische Texte, 54, Berlin, 1969), trans. as *The Court Society*, trans. E. Jephcott (Oxford, 1983).

Elias, N. 'On Medieval Manners', in *The Book of Touch*, ed. C. Classen (New York, 2005), 266–72.

Erdmann, C. *The Origin of the Idea of Crusade*, trans. M. W. Baldwin and W. Goffart (Princeton, 1977).

Erdmann, C. and von Gladdiss, D. 'Gottschalk von Aachen im Dienste Heinrichs IV', *Deutsches Archiv*, 3 (1939), 115–74.

Erkens, F-R. 'Militia und Ritterschaft. Reflexionen über die Entstehung des Rittertums', *Historische Zeitschrift*, 258 (1994), 623–59.

Esposito, E. 'Les formes d'hospitalité dans le roman courtois', *Romania*, 103 (1982).

Evans, M. 'An Illustrated Fragment of Peraldus's *Summa* of Vice: Harleian MS 3244', *Journal of the Warburg and Courtauld Institute*, 45 (1982).

Evergates, T. *The Aristocracy in the County of Champagne, 1100–1300* (Philadelphia, 2007).

Evergates, T. *Henry the Liberal, Count of Champagne, 1127–1181* (Philadelphia, 2016).

Fehring, G. P. *The Archaeology of Medieval Germany: An Introduction*, trans. R. Salmon (London, 1991), 108–18.

Ferrante, J. M. *Woman as Image in Medieval Literature* (New York, 1975).

Ferrante, J. M. 'Male fantasy and female reality in courtly literature', *Women's Studies*, 11 (1984), 69–75.

Ferrante, J. M. *To the Glory of Her Sex: Women's Roles in the Composition of Medieval Texts* (Bloomington, IN., 1997).

Feud, Violence and Practice: Essays in Medieval Studies in Honor of Stephen D. White, ed. B. S. Tuten and T. L. Billado (Aldershot, 2010).

Fischler, C. 'Commensality, society and culture', *Social Science Information*, 50 (2011), 528–48.

Fleckenstein, J. 'Die Entstehung des niederen Adels und das Rittertum', in *Herrschaft und Stand. Untersuchungen zur Sozialgeschichte im 13. Jahrhundert*, ed. idem (Göttingen, 1977), 17–39.

Fleckenstein, J. 'Vom Rittertum der Stauferzeit am Oberrhein', *Alemannisches Jahrbuch* (1979/80), 21–42.

Fletcher, R. *Bloodfeud* (Harmondsworth, 2002).

Flori, J. *L'Idéologie du glaive: préhistoire de la chevalerie* (Geneva, 1983).

Flori, J. *L'Essor de la chevalerie, xie–xiie siècles* (Geneva, 1986).

Flori, J. *Chevaliers et chevalerie au moyen âge* (Paris, 1998).

Fossier, R. *La terre et les hommes en Picardie jusqu'à la fin de xiiie siècle* (2 vols, Paris, 1968).

Fourrier, A. 'Raoul de Houdenc: est-ce-lieu?', in *Mélanges de linguistique romane et de philologie médiévale offerts à M. Maurice Delbouille* (2 vols, Gembloux, 1964), 2: 165–93.

France, J. *Western Warfare in the Age of the Crusades, 1000–1300* (Ithaca, NY, 1999).

Freed, J. B. 'The Origins of the European Nobility: the Problem of the Ministerials', *Viator*, 7 (1976), 211–41.

Freedman, P. *Images of the Medieval Peasant* (Stanford, CA, 1999).

Freedman, P. 'Medieval and Modern Banquets: Commensality and Social Categorisation', in *Commensality: from everyday food to feast*, ed. S. Kerner, C. Chou, and M. Warmind (London, 2015), 99–108.

Friend, A. C. 'Master Odo of Cheriton', *Speculum*, 23 (1948), 641–58.

Führer, J. 'Gegenwart der Vorgänger und genealogisches Bewusstsein bei den Kapetingern (987–1223)', in *Genealogisches Bewusstsein als Legitimation. Inter- und intragenerationelle Auseinandersetzungen sowie die Bedeutung von Verwandtschaft bei Amtswechseln*, ed. H. Brandt, K. Köhler, and U. Siewert (Bamberger historische Studien, 4, 2009), 145–66.

Fulton, H. 'The *Mabinogi* and the Education of Princes in Medieval Wales', in *Medieval Celtic Literature and Society*, ed. H. Fulton (Dublin, 2005), 230–47.

Galpin, S. L. *Cortois and Vilain* (New Haven, 1905).

Garver, V. L. *Women and Aristocratic Culture in the Carolingian World* (Ithaca, NY, 2009).

Gawain: a Casebook, ed. R. H. Thompson and K. Busby (Abingdon, 2006).

Geary, P. J. 'Vivre en conflit dans une France sans État', *Annales*, 41 (1986), 1118–25, rev. and trans. in idem, *Living with the Dead in the Middle Ages* (Ithaca, 1994), 130–60.

Geary, P. J. and J. B. Freed, 'Literacy and Violence in Twelfth-Century Bavaria: the "Murder Letter" of Count Siboto IV', *Viator*, 25 (1994), 115–29.

Genicot, L. 'The Growth of the Noble Class', in *Lordship and Community on Medieval Europe: Selected Readings*, ed. F. L. Cheyette (New York, 1968), 128–36.

Genicot, L. *Études sur les principautés lotharingiennes* (Louvain, 1975).

Gilchrist, R. *Medieval Life: Archaeology and the Life Course* (Woodbridge, 2012).

Gillingham, J. 'The Beginnings of English Imperialism', *Journal of Historical Sociology*, 5 (1992), 392–409.

Gillingham, J. 'The Introduction of Chivalry into England', in *Law and Government in Medieval England and Normandy*, ed. G. Garnett and J. G. Hudson (Cambridge, 1994), 31–55.

Gillingham, J. 'Kingship, Chivalry and Love. Political and Cultural Values in the Earliest History Written in French: Geoffrey Gaimar's *Estoire des Engleis*', in *Anglo-Norman Political Culture and the 12th-Century Renaissance*, ed. C. W. Hollister (Woodbridge, 1997), 33–58.

Gillingham, J. *The English in the Twelfth Century: Imperialism, National Identity and Political Values* (Woodbridge, 2000).

Gillingham, J. 'Fontenoy and after: pursuing enemies to death in France between the ninth and eleventh centuries', in *Frankland: the Franks and the World of the Early Middle Ages*, ed. P. Fouracre and D. Ganz (Manchester, 2008), 242–65.

Giuliato, G. 'Le château reflet de l'art defensif en Lorraine de xème au début de xiiième siècle', *Annales de l'Est*, 6th ser. 1 (2003), 55–76.

Goddard, E. R. *Women's Costume in French Texts of the Eleventh and Twelfth Centuries* (*Johns Hopkins Studies in Romance Literatures and Languages*, 7, 1927).

Gossman, L. *Medievalism and the Ideologies of the Enlightenment: the World and Work of La Curne de Sainte-Palaye* (Baltimore, 1968).

Grant, L. *Blanche of Castile Queen of France* (New Haven, 2016).

Grigsby, J. L. 'Miroir des Bonnes Femmes', *Romania*, 83 (1962), 30–51.

Grossel, M-G. 'La table comme pierre de touche de la courtoisie: à propos de quelques *chastoiements, ensenhamen* et autres *contenances de table*', in *Banquets et manières de table au moyen âge*, ed. M. Bertrand and C. Hory (Provence, 1996), 181–95.

Halsall, G. 'Introductory Survey', in *Violence and Society in the Early Medieval West*, ed. idem (Woodbridge, 1998), 1–37.

Harvey, J. C. *Red: A History of the Redhead* (New York, 2015).

Harvey, R. 'Languages, Lyrics and the Knightly Classes', in *Medieval Knighthood*, 5, ed. S. Church and R. Harvey (Woodbridge, 1995), 197–220.

Harvey, S. 'The Knight and Knight's Fee in England', *Past & Present*, no. 49 (1970), 3–43.

Haskins, C. H. *Studies in Medieval Culture* (Oxford, 1929).

Hauck, K. 'Heinrich III und der Ruodlieb', *Beiträge zur Geschichte der deutschen Sprache und Literatur*, 70 (1948), 372–419.

Hay, D. J. *The Military Leadership of Matilda of Canossa, 1046–1115* (Manchester, 2008).

Healey, P. *The Chronicle of Hugh of Flavigny: Reform and Investiture Contest in the Eleventh Century* (Aldershot, 2006).

Hechberger, W. *Adel, Ministerialität und Rittertum im Mittelalter* (Enzyclopädie deutscher Geschichte, 72, Munich, 2010).

Hemptinne, T. de 'Les épouses des croisés et pèlerins flamands aux xie et xiie siècles: l'exemple des comtesses de Flandre Clémence et Sibylle', in *Autour de la Première Croisade: actes du colloque de la 'Society for the Study of the Crusades and the Latin East'*, ed. M. Balard (Paris, 1996), 89–92.

Hentsch, A. A. *La littérature didactique du moyen âge* (Cahors, 1903).

Heslop, T. A. 'Romanesque Painting and Social Distinction: the Magi and the Shepherds', in *England in the Twelfth Century*, ed. D. Williams (Woodbridge, 1990), 137–52.

Hexter, R. J. *Ovid and Medieval Schooling* (Münchener Beiträge zur Mediävistik- und Renaissance-Forschung, 38, Munich, 1986).

Hintze, O. *Staat und Verfassung. Gesammelte Abhandlungen zur allgemeinen Verfassungsgeschichte* (3rd edn, Göttingen, 1970).

Histoire des femmes en Occident 2, Le moyen âge, ed. C. Klapisch-Zuber (Paris, 2002).

History of Twelfth-Century Western Philosophy, ed. P. Dronke (Cambridge, 1998).

Hohler, C. 'A Note on Jacobus', *Journal of the Warburg and Courtauld Institutes*, 35 (1972), 33–48.

Hosler, J. 'The Brief Military Career of Thomas Becket', *Haskins Society Journal*, 15 (2006), 88–100.

Hudson, J. G. 'Faide, Vengeance et Violence en Angleterre', in *La Vengeance, 400–1200*, ed. D. Barthélemy, F. Bougard, and R. Le Jan (Rome, 2006), 375–82, trans. as 'Feud, Vengeance and Violence in England from the Tenth to the Twelfth Centuries', in *Feud, Violence and Practice: Essays in Medieval Studies in Honor of Stephen D. White*, ed. B.S. Tuten and T. L. Billado (Aldershot, 2010), 29–54.

Huizinga, J. *The Waning of the Middle Ages: a Study of the Forms of Life, Thought and Art in France and the Netherlands in the XIVth and XVth Centuries* (London, 1924).

Huneycutt, L. L. *Matilda of Scotland: A Study in Medieval Queenship* (Woodbridge, 2003).

Hunt, R. W. *The Schools and the Cloister: the Life and Writings of Alexander Nequam (1157–1217)*, ed. M. Gibson (Oxford, 1984).

Hunt, T. *Teaching and Learning Latin in Thirteenth-Century England* (3 vols, Cambridge, 1991).

Hyams, P. R. 'Feud in Medieval England', *Haskins Society Journal*, 3 (1993), 1–21.

Hyams, P. R. *Rancor and Reconciliation in Medieval England* (Ithaca, 2003).

Innes, M. '"A Place of Discipline": Carolingian Courts and Aristocratic Youth', in *Court Culture in the Early Middle Ages. The Proceedings of the first Alcuin Conference*, ed. C. Cubitt (Turnhout, 2003), 59–76.

Jaeger, C. S. *The Origins of Courtliness: Civilising Trends and the Formation of Courtly Ideals, 939–1210* (Philadelphia, 1985).

Jaeger, C. S. *The Envy of Angels: Cathedral Schools and Social Ideals in Medieval Europe, 950–1200* (Philadelphia, 1994).

Jaeger, C. S. *Ennobling Love: In Search of a Lost Sensibility* (Philadelphia, 1999).

Jaeger, C. S. 'The Origins of Courtliness after 25 Years', in *Haskins Society Journal*, 11 (2009), 187–216.

Jeanroy, A. 'Notes sur le tournoiement des dames', *Romania*, 28 (1899), 240–4.

Johns, S. M. *Noblewomen, Aristocracy and Power in the Twelfth-Century Anglo-Norman Realm* (Manchester, 2003).

Jones, M. *Feast: Why Humans Share Food* (Oxford, 2007).

Jordan, E. 'The "Abduction" of Ida of Boulogne: Assessing Women's Agency in Thirteenth-century France', *French Historical Studies*, 30 (2007), 1–20.

Kaeuper, R. W. *Chivalry and Violence in Medieval Europe* (Oxford, 1999).

Kaeuper, R. W. *Holy Warriors: the Religious Ideology of Chivalry* (Philadelphia, 2009).

Kaeuper, R. W. *Medieval Chivalry* (Cambridge, 2016).

Kamp, H. 'La vengeance, le roi et les compétitions faidales', in *La Vengeance, 400–1200*, ed. D. Barthélemy, F. Bougard, and R. Le Jan (Rome, 2006), 259–80.

Karras, R. M. *From Boys to Men: Formations of Masculinity in Late Medieval Europe* (Philadelphia, 2003).

Karras, R. M. *Sexuality in Medieval Europe: Doing unto Others* (London, 2005).

Kay, S. 'The Contradictions of Courtly Love and the Origins of Courtly Poetry: the evidence of the *Lauzengiers*', *Journal of Medieval and Early Modern Studies*, 26 (1996), 209–53.

Keen, M. *Chivalry* (New Haven, 1984).

Kerr, J. 'The Open Door: Hospitality and Honour in Twelfth/Early Thirteenth-century England', *History*, 87 (2002), 322–35.

Keupp, J. U. *Dienst und Verdienst. Die Ministerialen Friedrich Barbarossas und Heinrichs VI* (Stuttgart, 2002).

Kinne, E. 'Waiting for Gauvain: Lessons on Courtesy in *L'Âtre Périlleux*', *Arthuriana*, 18 (2008), 55–68.

Klapisch-Zuber, C. *L'ombre des ancêtres: essai sur l'imaginaire médiéval de la parenté* (Paris, 2000).

Köhler, E. *Ideal und Wirklichkeit in der höfischen Epik* (Tübingen, 1956).

Köhler, E. *L'aventure chevaleresque* trans. E. Kaufholz (Paris, 1974).

Koslin, D. 'The Robe of Simplicity: Initiation, Robing and Veiling of Nuns in the Middle Ages', in *Robes of Honor: the Medieval World of Investiture*, ed. S. Goron (Aldershot, 2001), 255–74.

Kosto, A. J. *Hostages in the Middle Ages* (Oxford, 2012).

Koziol, G. 'The Making of Peace in Eleventh-Century Flanders', in *The Peace of God: Social Violence and Religious Response in France around the year 1000*, ed. T. Head and R. Landes (Ithaca, 1992), 239–58.

Krause, K. M. 'Gazing on Women in the *Miracles de Nostre Dame*', in *Gautier de Coinci: Miracles, Music and Manuscripts*, ed. K. M. Krause and A. Stones (Turnhout, 2006), 227–51.

Kuefler, M. S. 'Castration and Eunuchism in the Middle Ages', in *Handbook of Medieval Sexuality*, ed. V. L. Bullough and J. A. Brundage (New York, 1996), 279–306.

Lachaud, F. 'L'Enseignement des bonnes manières en milieu de cour en Angleterre d'après l'Urbanus magnus attribué à Daniel de Beccles', in *Erziehung und Bildung bei Hofe*, ed. W. Paravicini and J. Wettlaufer (Stuttgart, 2002), 43–53.

Lachaud, F. 'Ethics and Office in England in the Thirteenth Century', in *Thirteenth-Century England*, 11 (2005), 16–30.

Lacroix, J. 'Un art des belles manières de table en Lombardie au xiiie siècle', in *Banquets et manières de table au moyen âge*, ed. M. Bertrand and C. Hory (Provence, 1996), 71–91.

Lacy, N. J. 'Gauvain and the Crisis of Chivalry in the *Conte de Graal*', in *The Sower and his Seed: Essays on Chrétien de Troyes*, ed. R.T. Pickens (Lexington, KY, 1983), 155–64.

Lamont, M. and Lareau, A. 'Cultural Capital: Allusions, Gaps and Glissandos in Recent Theoretical Developments', *Sociological Theory*, 6 (1988), 153–68.

Le Goff, J. *L'Europe, est-elle né au moyen age?* (Paris, 2003).

Lett, D. *Hommes et femmes au moyen âge: histoire du genre, xiie-xve siècle* (Paris, 2013).

Leyser, K. 'Early Canon Law and the Beginning of Knighthood', in *Communications and Power in Medieval Europe: the Carolingian and Ottonian Centuries*, ed. T. Reuter (London, 1994), 51–71.

Lieberman, M. 'A New Approach to the Knighting Ritual', *Speculum*, 90 (2015), 391–423.

Little, L. K. 'Anger in Monastic Curses', in *Anger's Past: the Social Uses of an Emotion in the Middle Ages*, ed. B. H. Rosenwein (Ithaca, 1998), 14–27.

LoPrete, K. A. *Adela of Blois, Countess and Lord* (Dublin, 2007).

Lorcin, M-T. 'Du vilain au paysan sur la scène littéraire du xiiie siècle', *Médiévales*, 61 (2011), 163–86.

Lyons, F. 'Encore l'adoubement de Rigaut (Garin le Loherain)', in *Mélanges de littérature du Moyen Âge au XXe offerts à Mademoiselle Jeanne Lods, professeur honoraire de littérature médiévale à l'École normal supérieure de jeunes filles, par ses collègues, ses élèves et ses amis* (2 vols, Collection de l'École normale supérieure de jeunes filles, 10, 1978), 1: 410–13.

McDougall, S. *Royal Bastards: the Birth of Illegitimacy, 800–1230* (Oxford, 2017).

McLeod, N. 'The Blood-feud in Medieval Ireland', in *Between Intrusions: Britain and Ireland between the Romans and Normans*, ed. P. O'Neill (Sydney Series in Celtic Studies, 7, 2004), 114–33.

McLoughlin, N. *Jean Gerson and Gender: Rhetoric and Politics in Fifteenth-century France* (Basingstoke, 2015).

McNamara, J. A. 'The *Herrenfrage*: the restructuring of the Gender System, 1050–1150', in *Medieval Masculinities: Regarding Men in the Middle Ages*, ed. C. A. Lees (Minneapolis, 1994), 3–29.

Maddicott, J. R. *Simon de Montfort* (Cambridge, 1994).

Martin, J-P. 'Garin, Begon, Rigaut: à propos de trois figures du guerrier dans Garin le Loherain', *Le monde des héros dans la culture médiévale*, ed. D. Buschinger and W. Spiewok (Greifswalder Beiträge zum Mittelalter, 35, 1994), 181–93.

Medieval Conduct, ed. K. Ashley and R. L. A. Clark (Minneapolis, 2001).

Medieval Conduct Literature, ed. M. D. Johnston (Medieval Academy Books, no. 111, Toronto, 2009).

Medieval Masculinities: Regarding Men in the Middle Ages, ed. C. A. Lees (Minneapolis, 1994).

Menestrier, C-F. *Chevalerie ancienne et moderne* (Paris, 1683).

Mills, C. *The History of Chivalry or Knighthood and its Times* (2 vols, London, 1825).

Moeglin, J-M. 'Le "droit de vengeance" chez les historiens du droit au moyen age', in *La Vengeance, 400–1200*, ed. D. Barthélemy, F. Bougard and R. Le Jan (Rome, 2006), 101–58.

Monson, D. A. *Les ensenhamens occitans: essai de définition et délimitation du genre* (Paris, 1981).

Monson, D. A. 'The Troubadour's Lady Reconsidered Again', *Speculum*, 70 (1995), 255–74.

Montanari, M. *The Culture of Food*, trans. C. Ipsen (Oxford, 1994).

Montesquieu (Charles-Louis de Secondat), *De l'esprit des lois* (5 vols, Paris, 1824).

Montoya, A. C. 'Bourgeois versus Aristocratic Models of Scholarship: Medieval Studies at the Académie des Inscriptions, 1701–1751', in *The Making of the Humanities 2, From Early Modern to Modern Disciplines*, ed. R. Bod, J. Maat, and T. Weststeijn (Amsterdam, 2012), 303–20.

Morin, L. 'Le soi et le double dans *L'Âtre Périlleux*', *Etudes Françaises*, 32 (1996), 117–28.

Musset, L. 'L'aristocratie normande au xie siècle', in *La noblesse au moyen âge (xie–xve siècles). Essais à la memoire de Robert Boutruche*, ed. P. Contamine (Paris, 1976), 71–96.

Napran, L. 'Mercenaries and Paid Men in Gilbert of Mons', in *Mercenaries and Paid Men: the Mercenary Identity in the Middle Ages*, ed. J. France (Leiden, 2008), 287–97.

Neal, D. *The Masculine Self in Late Medieval England* (Chicago, 2008).

Nederman, C. J. 'Nature, Ethics, and the Doctrine of "Habitus": Aristotelian Moral Psychology in the Twelfth Century', *Traditio*, 45 (1989–90), 87–110.

Nelson, J. L. 'Monks, Secular Men and Masculinity, c.900', in *Masculinity in Medieval Europe*, ed. D. M. Hadley (Harlow, 1999), 121–42.

New Cambridge Medieval History, 4, pt. 1, *c.1024–c.1198*, ed. D. Luscombe and J. Riley-Smith (Cambridge, 2004).

Nicholas, K. S. 'Countesses as Rulers in Flanders', in *Aristocratic Women in Medieval France*, ed. T. Evergates (Philadelphia, 1999), 111–37.

Nicholls, J. W. *The Matter of Courtesy: Medieval Courtesy Books and the Gawain-Poet* (Woodbridge, 1985).

Nieus, J-F. 'Early Aristocratic Seals: an Anglo-Norman Success Story', in *Anglo-Norman Studies*, 38, ed. E. van Houts (Woodbridge, 2016), 97–123.

Oexle, O. G. 'Die "sächsische Welfenquelle" als Zeugnis der welfischen Hausüberlieferung', *Deutsches Archiv*, 24 (1968), 435–97.

Olson, K. M. *Courtesy Lost: Dante, Boccaccio and the Literature of History* (Toronto, 2014).

Parisse, M. 'Le tournoi en France, des origines à la fin du xiiie siècle', in *Das ritterliche Turnier im Mittelalter: Beiträge zu einer vergleichenden Formen- und Verhaltensgeschichte des Rittertums*, ed. J. Fleckenstein (Göttingen, 1986) 175–211.

Paterson, L. M. 'Knights and the Concept of Knighthood in the Twelfth-century Occitan epic', *Forum for Modern Language Studies*, 17 (1981), 117–30.

Paterson, L. M. 'L'epouse et la formation du lien conjugal selon la littérature occitane du xie au xiiie siècle: mutations d'une institution et condition féminine', in *Mélanges de langue et de littérature occitanes en hommage à Pierre Bec* (Poitiers, 1991), 425–42.

Paterson, L. M. *The World of the Troubadours: Medieval Occitan Society, c.1100–c.1300* (Cambridge, 1993).

Paul, N. L. *To Follow in their Footsteps: the Crusades and Family Memory in the High Middle Ages* (Ithaca, NY, 2012).

Pecchiai, P. 'I documenti sulla biografia di Bonvicino della Riva', *Giornale Storico della Letteratura Italiana*, 78 (1921), 96–127.

Peters, U. and Köhn, R. 'Höfisches Liebeswerben oder politisches Heiratsangebot? Zum Brief der Konstanze von Bretagne an Ludwig VII von Frankreich', *Beiträge zur Geschichte der deutschen Sprache und Literatur*, 111 (1989), 179–95.

Petrus Alfonsi and his Dialogus: *Background, Context, Reception*, ed. C. Cardelle de Hartmann and P. Roelli (Florence, 2014).

Pierre Bourdieu: Key Concepts, ed. M. Grenfell (2nd edn, Abingdon, 2012).

Pitt-Rivers, J. M. 'The Law of Hospitality', in *The Fate of Shechem or the Politics of Sex* (Cambridge, 1977).

Platelle, H. 'Vengeance privée et réconciliation dans l'oeuvre de Thomas de Chantimpré', *Tijdschrift voor Rechtsgeschiednis*, 42 (1974), 269–81.

de Pontfarcy, Y. 'Si Marie de France était Marie de Meulan', *CCM*, 38 (1995), 353–61.

Poos, L. R. 'Sex, Lies, and the Church Courts of Pre-Reformation England', *Journal of Interdisciplinary History*, 25 (1995), 585–607.

Por le soie amisté. Essays in Honor of Norris J. Lacy, ed. K. Busby and C. M. Jones (Amsterdam, 2000).

Pour une histoire des traités de savoir-vivre en Europe, ed. A. Montandon (Clermont-Ferrand, 1994).

Radford, L. B. *Thomas of London before his Consecration* (Cambridge, 1894).

Rattunde, E. *Li Proverbes au vilain. Untersuchungen zur romanischen Spruchdichtung des Mittelalters* (Heidelberg, 1966).

Régnier-Bohler, D. 'Voix littéraires, voix mystiques', in *Histoire des femmes en Occident 2, Le moyen âge*, ed. C. Klapisch-Zuber (Paris, 2002).

Religious Men and Masculine Identity in the Middle Ages, ed. P. H. Cullum and K. J. Lewis (Woodbridge, 2013).

Richard, J. 'Châteaux, châtelains et vassaux en Bourgogne aux xe et xiie siècles' *CCM*, 3 (1960), 433–47.

Ringrose, K. M. 'Eunuchs in historical perspective', *History Compass*, 5 (2007), 495–506.

Ritterliches Tugendsystem, ed. G. Eifler (Wege der Forschung, 56, Darmstadt, 1970).

Roberts, J. 'The Old English Vocabulary of Nobility', in *Nobles and Nobility in Medieval Europe*, ed. A. J. Duggan (Woodbridge, 2000), 69–84.

Rocher, D. 'Tradition latine et morale chevaleresque (à propos du *Ritterliches Tugendsystem*)', *Études germaniques*, 19 (1964), 127–41.

Rosenwein, B. H. 'Worrying about Emotions in History', *American Historical Review*, 107 (2002), 821–45.

Ross, B. '*Audi Thomas…Henriciani Nota*: A French Scholar appeals to Thomas Becket?' *EHR*, 89 (1974), 333–8.

Roussel, C. 'Le Legs de la Rose: Modèles et préceptes de la sociabilité médiévale', in *Pour une histoire des traités de savoir-vivre en Europe*, ed. A. Montandon (Clermont-Ferrand, 1994), 1–90.

Rudin, J. 'Between Concealment and Eloquence: the Idea of the Ideal Woman in Medieval Provençal Literature', in *The Inner Life of Women in Medieval Romance Literature*, ed. J. Rider and J. Friedman (Basingstoke, 2011), 146–58.

Sainte-Marie, Père Honoré de (Blaise Vauzel), *Dissertations historiques et critiques sur la chevalerie, ancienne et moderne seculière et regulière* (Paris, 1718).

Santenelli, E. *Des femmes éplorées? Les veuves dans la société aristocratiques du haut moyen âge* (Lille, 2003).

Saul, N. *For Honour and Fame: Chivalry in England, 1066–1500* (London, 2011).

Schulze-Busacker, E. 'Les "Proverbes au Vilain"', *Proverbium*, 6 (1989), 113–27.

Schulze-Busacker, E. *La didactique profane au moyen âge* (Paris, 2012).

Sharpe, R. *A Handlist of Latin Writers of Great Britain and Ireland before 1540* (Turnhout, 2001).

Short, I. 'On Bilingualism in Anglo-Norman England', *Revue Philologique*, 33 (1979–80), 467–79.

Simms, K. 'Guesting and Feasting in Gaelic Ireland', *Journal of the Royal Society of Ireland*, 108 (1978), 67–100.

Simms, K. *From Kings to Warlords: the Changing Political Structure of Gaelic Ireland in the Later Middle Ages* (Woodbridge, 1987).

Sinisi, L. 'The Wandering Wimple', in *Medieval Clothing and Textiles*, 4, ed. R. Netherton and G. R. Owen-Crocker (Woodbridge, 2008), 39–54.

Smith, K. A. 'Saints in Shining Armor: martial asceticism and masculine models of sanctity, *ca.*1050-1250', *Speculum*, 83 (2008), 572–602.

Smith, Ll. Beverley 'Fosterage, Adoption and God-Parenthood: Ritual and Fictive Kinship in Medieval Wales', *Welsh History Review*, 16 (1992), 1–35.

Smith, Ll. Beverley 'On the Hospitality of the Welsh', in *Power and Identity in the Middle Ages: Essays in Memory of Rees Davies*, ed. H. Pryce and J. Watt (Oxford, 2007).

Solterer, H. 'Figures of female Militancy in Medieval France', *Signs* 16 (1990), 522–49.

Spiegel, G. M. 'The *Reditus Regni ad Stirpem Karoli Magni*: A New Look', *French Historical Studies*, 7 (1971/2), 143–74.

Spiewok, W. 'L'adultère dans la réalité et dans la fiction', in *Les 'Realia' dans la littérature de fiction au Moyen Âge: Actes du colloque du Centre d'Etudes Medievales de l'Universite de Picardie-Jules Verne, Chantilly, 1ᵉʳ-4 Avril 1993* (Griefswald, 1993), 169–76.

Stenton, F. M. *The First Century of English Feudalism, 1066–1166, being the Ford Lectures delivered in the University of Oxford in Hilary Term 1929* (2nd edn, Oxford, 1961).

Strickland, M. 'Slaughter, slavery or ransom? The impact of the Conquest on conduct in warfare', in *England in the Eleventh Century*, ed. C. Hicks (Stamford, 1992), 41–59.

Strickland, M. 'Killing or Clemency? Ransom, chivalry and changing attitudes to defeated opponents in Britain and Northern France, 7th-12th centuries', in *Krieg im Mittelalter*, ed. H-H. Kortüm (Berlin, 2001), 93–122.

Strickland, M. 'Treason, Feud and the Growth of State Violence: Edward I and the "War of the Earl of Carrick"', in *War, Government and Aristocracy in the British Isles, c.1150–1500: Essays in Honour of Michael Prestwich*, ed. C. Given-Wilson, A. Kettle, and L. Scales (Woodbridge, 2008), 84–113.

Strickland, M. *Henry the Young King, 1155–1183* (New Haven, 2016).

Stuard, S. Mosher 'Fashion's Captives: Medieval Women in French Historiography', in *Women in Medieval History and Historiography*, ed. eadem (Philadelphia, 1987), 59–80.

Stuart, G. *A View of Society in Europe, in its progress from rudeness to refinement: or, Inquiries concerning the history of law, government, and manners* (Edinburgh, 1778).

Subrenart, J. 'e Oliver est proz', in *Études de philologie romane et d'histoire littéraire à Jules Hovrent*, ed. J-M. d'Heur and N. Cherubini (Liège, 1980), 461–7.

Taylor, C. *Chivalry and the Ideals of Knighthood in France during the Hundred Years War* (Cambridge, 2013).

The Inner Life of Women in Medieval Romance Literature, ed. J. Rider and J. Friedman (Basingstoke, 2011).

The Sermon, ed. B. M. Kienzle (*Typologie des sources du moyen âge occidental*, fascs 81–83, 2000).

The Study of Chivalry: Resources and Approaches, ed. H. Chickering and T. H. Seiler (Kalamazoo, MI, 1988).

The Welsh King and His Court, ed. T. M. Charles-Edwards, M. E. Owen, and P. Russell (Cardiff, 2000).

Thibodeaux, J. D. *The Manly Priest: Clerical Celibacy, Masculinity and Reform in England and Normandy, 1066–1300* (Philadelphia, 2015).

Thomas, H. M. *The Secular Clergy in England, 1066–1216* (Oxford, 2014).

Thomas, J. W. *Tannhäuser: Poet and Legend* (Chapel Hill, 1974).

Thornton, D. E. 'The Genealogy of Gruffudd ap Cynan', in *Gruffudd ap Cynan: a collaborative biography*, ed. K. L. Maund (Woodbridge, 1996), 79–108.

Toubert, P. *Les structures du Latium médiéval: le Latium méridional et la Sabine di ixe siécle à la fin du xiie siècle* (Rome, 1973).

Trokhimenko, O. V. 'On the Dignity of Women: the "Ethical Reading" of Winsbeckin in mgf 474 Staatsbibliothek zu Berlin-Preussischer Kulturbesitz', *Journal of English and German Philology*, 107 (2008), 490–505.

Trokhimenko, O. V. *Constructing Virtue and Vice: Femininity and Laughter in Courtly Society,* ca.*1150–1300* (Göttingen, 2014).

Uhlig, C. *Hofkritik im England des Mittelalters und der Renaissance* (Berlin, 1973).

Van Luyn, P. 'Les milites dans la France du xie siècle', *Le Moyen Age*, lxxvii (1971), 227–35.

Van Proeyen, M. 'Sang et heredité: à la croisée des imaginaires médicaux et sociaux des xiiie et xive siècles', in *Le sang au moyen age*, ed. M. Faure (Montpellier, 1999), 69–75.

Van Winter, J. M. 'Uxorem de militari ordine sibi imponens', in *Miscellanea in memoriam J.F. Niermeyer* (Gröningen, 1961).

Van Winter, J. M. 'The Ministerial and Knightly Classes in Guelders and Zutphen', *Acta Historica Neerlandica* (Leiden, 1966), 171–87.

Veach, C. *Lordship in Four Realms, the Lacy Family, 1166–1241* (Manchester, 2014).

Vincent, N. 'William Marshal, King Henry II and the Honour of Châteauroux', *Archives*, 25 (2000), 1–15.

Visser, M. *The Rituals of Dinner: the Origins, Evolutions, Eccentricities and Meaning of Table Manners* (London, 1991).

Wei, I. 'Scholars and Travel in the Twelfth and Thirteenth Centuries', in *Freedom of Movement in the Middle Ages*, ed. P. Horden (Harlaxton Medieval Studies, 15, Donington, 2007), 73–85.

Welti, M. '*Vir Bonus, Homo Bonus, Preudome*: Kleine Geschichte dreier nahe verwandter Begriffe', *Archiv für Begriffsgeschichte*, 38 (1998), 48–65.

Werner, K. F. 'Die Legitimität der Kapetinger und die Entstehung des *Reditus Regni Francorum ad stirpem Karoli*', *Die Welt als Geschichte*, 12 (1952), 203–25, repr. in *Structures politique du monde français (VIe-XIIe siècle)* (London, 1979), 203–25.

Werner, K. F. 'Les femmes, le pouvoir et la transmission du pouvoir', in *La femme au moyen âge* (Maubeuge, 1990).

Werner, K. F. *Naissance de la noblesse* (Paris, 1998).

Whelan, F. *The Making of Manners and Morals in Twelfth-Century England: the Book of the Civilised Man* (Abingdon, 2017).

White, S. D. '"Pactum…Legem Vincit et Amor Judicium": The Settlement of Disputes by Compromise in Eleventh-Century Western France', *American Journal of Legal History*, 22 (1979), 291–309.

White, S. D. 'Feuding and Peace-Making in the Touraine around the year 1100', *Traditio*, 42 (1986), 195–263.

White, S. D. 'The Politics of Anger', in *Anger's Past: the Social Uses of an Emotion in the Middle Ages*, ed. B. H. Rosenwein (Ithaca, 1998), 134–9.

Whitman, J. Q. 'Enforcing Civility and Respect: Three Societies', *The Yale Law Journal*, 109 (2000), 1279–398.

Wickham, C. *The Inheritance of Rome: a History of Europe from 400 to 1000* (London, 2009).

Willard, C. C. 'Gilles de Chin in History, Literature and Folklore', in *The Medieval Opus: Imitation, Rewriting and Transmission in the French Tradition* (Amsterdam, 1999), 357–66.

Woolgar, C. M. *The Great Household in Late Medieval England* (New Haven, 1999).

Woolgar, C. M. *The Culture of Food in England, 1200–1500* (New Haven, 2016).

Ziino, F. 'Alcune osservazioni sul *Facet* catalano', in *La narrativa in Proenza e Catalogna nel XIII e XIV secolo* (Rome, 1994), 185–215.

Zorzi, A. 'I conflitti nell'Italia comunale. Riflessioni sullo stato degli studi e sulle prospettive di ricerca', in *Conflitti, paci e vendetta nell'Italia communale*, ed. idem (Florence, 2009), 7–43.

Zotz, T. 'Die Formierung der Ministerialität', in *Die Salier und das Reich*, ed. S. Weinfurter (3 vols, Sigmaringen, 1991–2), 3: 3–50.

Index

accomplishment, achievement (*proesce*) 64–5, 75–6, 85–6, 183–4, 207–8, 210, 243
Adalbero bishop of Laon 230–1, 247
Adam, patriarch of humanity 227–8, 232, 246
Adela countess of Blois 95
Adeliza queen of England 44–5
adoubement, see knights, inauguration of
Adrian IV pope 182
adultery 151–2, 154–5, 160, 163–4
affability, social ease 42–4, 49, 65–6, 132
Ailred abbot of Rievaulx 136–7, 227–9
Alan of Lille 67–8, 144n.125, 239, 243, 290n.68, 291, 295–6
Alexander I king of Scots 24
Alexander III king of Scots 228–9
Alexander Neckam 164–5, 240–1, 246–8
Alexander of Paris 111–12
Alexis, saint 233
Alfonso II king of Aragon 245–6, 279–80
Alfonso X king of Castile 178–9, 195–6, 249–50, 304
alienation, self doubt 61–2, 75, 80n.99, 136–41
alms 184–7
alterity 75, 220–1
Amanieu de Sescás 90–2, 158–9
Amaury de Montfort 12–13
amour cortois 54, 54n.46
Ancrene Riwle 168, 295
Andrew de Coutances 102–3, 119, 176–7, 313
Andrew the Chaplain 26, 92n.40, 93n.41, 114, 155–6, 166–7, 240, 248, 281–2
anecdotalism 197–9
anger 203–6
Ansfrida, mistress of Henry I of England 153
anti-feminism 134–5, 161–3
Aristotelianism 3–4, 241
Aristotle 111–12, 150–1, 225–6, 238, 240–1
Arnaut de Mareuil 7, 64–5, 85–6, 97–8, 100–1, 241, 245–9, 275–6, 313
Arnaut-Guilhem de Marsan 63, 76–7, 121, 132–3, 288–9, 312
Arnold abbot of Bonneval 136–7
Arnold I count of Guines 131–2
Arnold II count of Guines 23–4, 126–7, 152
Arnulf bishop of Lisieux 22–3
Arnulf count of Flanders 233–4
Artaud de Nogent 113–14, 281
Arthur of Caerleon, king of the Britons 99, 122–3
Arthurian literature 20–1, 33, 69, 102–3, 132–6, 138, 163, 190
avatars of conduct 128–9, 132–3
Azelinus, bishop of Hildesheim 50

Baldwin count of Guines 131–2, 163–4, 195, 199
Baldwin de Béthune count of Aumale 210–11
Baldwin de Condé 62–3, 65–6, 70, 72–4, 77, 112, 226, 250–1, 282n.36, 308
Baldwin, John 127
banner, as symbol 268, 278–9
banquet, definition of 175n.1
Barthélemy, Dominique 260–4
Bartholomew the Englishman 175n.1, 181–2
bastards 163–5
Baudrey de Bourgeuil 95
Benoît de St-Maure 229
Bernard of Clairvaux 170, 276, 290n.68
Bernier, epic character 69–70
Bertran de Born 5, 92–3, 140–1, 279–80
Biaudouz, romance 73–4
biography 58–9
Blanche countess of Champagne 187–8
Bloch, Howard 163
Bloch, Marc 212, 235–6, 255–9, 262–3, 267–8
bodily processes, as social danger 192–3
body theory 80–1, 97
Boethius 46–7, 239–42, 246 and see *Consolatio philosophiae*
Boniface marquis of Montferrat 22, 63–4, 121, 277–8
Bonizo bishop of Sutri 286
Bosl, Karl 255–6
Bourdieu, Pierre 3–5, 41–2, 117–18, 175–6
Brun, archbishop of Cologne 49
Brunetto Latini 77, 188, 212–14, 298, 313
Brunner, Otto 216–17
Bumke, Joachim 46n.23
Buonvicino della Riva 132, 180–1, 193–5, 198–9, 312
bureaucracy, social effects of 305–6
Büsching, Johann 10–12
Bynum, Caroline Walker 169

Caesarius of Heisterbach 201, 203–4
Capetian dynasty 229–31
careerism 53–5
Carolingian dynasty 229–31, 284–5
castles 259, 261–5
castration 207–8
Cathal Crobderg Ua Conchobair, king of Connacht 219–20
Catonian moral tradition, see *Disticha Catonis*
Cecilia countess of Hereford 95, 161
celibacy 80–1, 160–1, 168–9
Chardri 162–3, 311